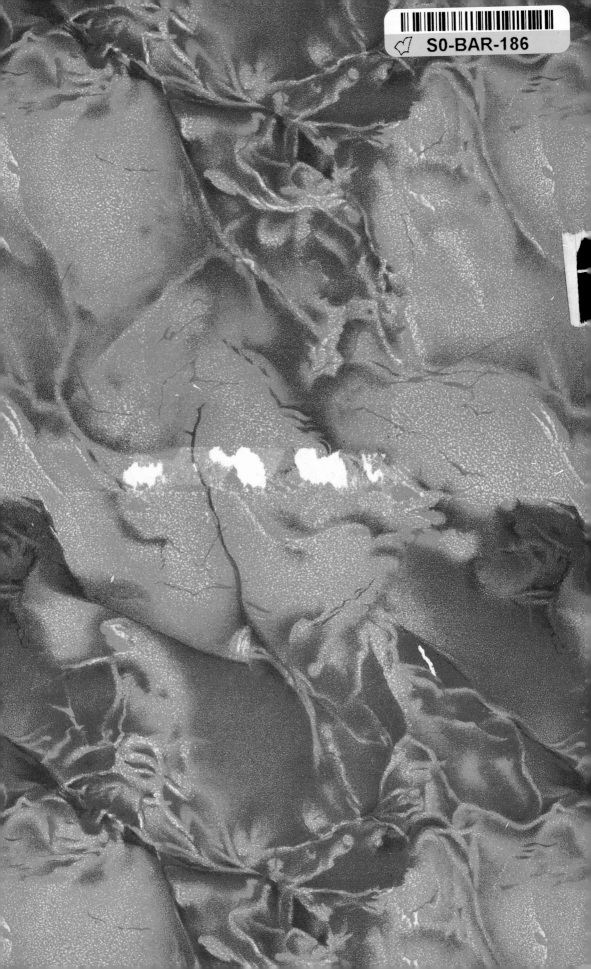

VIRGINIA

REBIRTH OF THE OLD DOMINION

Virginia Biography
By Special Staff of Writers

Issued in Five Volumes

VOLUME III

ILLUSTRATED

THE LEWIS PUBLISHING COMPANY
CHICAGO AND NEW YORK

1929

HISTORY *of* VIRGINIA

HARRY FLOOD BYRD was barely forty years old when elected governor of Virginia, being one of the youngest in the long list of executives of the state during one and a half centuries. As governor he at once instituted a large number of constitutional reforms, which were confirmed by popular vote in June, 1927. Some account of these reforms is given in Volume II of the present history of Virginia.

It is doubtful if any family of Colonial Virginians has been more persistently productive of men talented for professional, business and public life. Governor Byrd is the seventh generation from the first William Byrd of Westover, whose son, William Byrd II, has been called the founder of Richmond.

Governor Byrd was born in Berkeley County, Virginia, June 10, 1887. His father, Richard Evelyn Byrd, was born in Texas, August 13, 1860. His birth in Texas was due to the fact that his father, Col. William Byrd, had moved to Texas a short time before the outbreak of the war between the states, and became a colonel in the Confederate army. After the war he returned to Virginia and practiced law at Winchester. Richard Evelyn Byrd, Sr., was reared at Winchester, attended the University of Virginia and the University of Maryland, was admitted to the bar in 1884, and for over forty years practiced law at Winchester and Richmond. He was speaker of the House of Delegates from 1908 to 1914, served as United States district attorney of the Western District of Virginia from 1914 to 1920, and for some months following that was special assistant to the attorney general of the United States. He also served as a member of the State Tax Commission and as a member of the Educational Commission of Virginia from 1908 to 1912, was a member of the State Commission on Efficiency and Economy from 1916 to 1918, was chairman of the State Industrial Council of Safety in 1917.

Richard Evelyn Byrd, Sr., married, September 15, 1886, Miss Elinor Bolling Flood, daughter of Maj. Joel W. and Ella (Faulkner) Flood. They had three sons, all of whom have become prominent, Harry Flood, Richard Evelyn, Jr., and Capt. Thomas Bolling Byrd. All the world knows of the great exploits of Richard Evelyn Byrd, Jr., who by special act of Congress in January, 1927, was promoted from lieutenant commander of the United States Navy retired to the grade of commander on the retired list, and was also presented with a medal of honor for his achievement in making a successful flight across the North Polar regions.

Governor Byrd was reared in Winchester, attended the Shenandoah Valley Academy, and chose a business rather than a professional career. At the age of sixteen he was manager of the *Winchester Evening Star,* subsequently was superintendent of the Southern Bell Telephone & Telegraph Company, and in 1907, at the age of twenty, started the *Martinsburg Journal.* He turned from the newspaper business to become one of the outstanding fruit growers and orchardists of the Shenandoah Valley, acquiring by planting and purchase 1,500 acres containing 65,000 trees, one of the largest individually owned apple orchards east of the Mississippi. He became president of the Winchester Cold Storage Company and was identified with a number of other business organizations at Winchester.

It was his qualifications as an unusually successful business executive that gave him such a notable influence with the people of Virginia in general. For a number of years he has been a leader in politics in his section. In 1917 he was elected a member of the State Senate and was reelected without opposition in 1921. He was a leader in good roads legislation, becoming chairman of the Senate Committee on roads. In 1922 he became chairman of the State Democratic Central Committee, and in that year for the first time in twenty years Virginia sent a solid Democratic delegation to Congress.

Governor Byrd married, October 7, 1913, Miss Annie Douglas Beverly, daughter of J. B. Beverly, of Winchester. Their children are: H. F. Byrd, Jr., Beverly Byrd, Miss Westwood Byrd and Richard Evelyn Byrd.

EDWIN ANDERSON ALDERMAN is a native of North Carolina, and that state recognizes a lasting debt of gratitude to him for his pioneer work as an educational statesman. From North Carolina his work extended to other states, and since 1904 he has been president of the University of Virginia and has long been regarded as the strongest single constructive influence in the educational progress of the entire South.

He was born at Wilmington, North Carolina, May 15, 1861, son of James and Susan J. Alderman, and member of a family that has been in North Caroline since Colonial times, one of his forefathers having been a soldier of the Revolution. He attended Bethel Military Academy of Virginia, in 1878 entered the University of North Carolina, and graduated in 1882 with the Bachelor of Philosophy degree and the Mangum Medal in oratory. His first intention was to practice law, but a year of teaching gave him a stronger interest in education. In 1885 he became superintendent of the city schools of Goldsboro. In 1889 he and Charles Duncan McIver took upon themselves the heavy and unpopular responsibilities of leading a crusade throughout North Carolina in behalf of educational reform, involving primarily the fundamentals of popular education supported by general taxation. In 1892, when Doctor McIver founded and became president of the Normal and Industrial College for Women at Greensboro, Mr. Alderman accepted the chair of history, but in 1893 took the chair of education in the University of North Carolina, and in 1896 was elected president of that institution. In April, 1900, he became president of Tulane University at New Orleans. In 1897 Armistead Gordon had as a member of the Board of Visitors started an inquiry into the expediency of creating the office of president for the University of Virginia, and after some years such an office was created and Edwin A. Alderman was invited to become the first incumbent. Doctor Alderman was installed as head of this old and famous institution of learning in the South in 1904. During the past quarter of a century the university has been thoroughly reorganized, and without the loss of any of its splendid traditions and atmosphere of quiet culture the various schools and departments of the university proper have been so strength-

Edwin A. Alderman

ened and improved as to conform to the highest standards of later day educational classification, and the opportunities of some of the departments are not excelled by any university in the country.

In his native state, at Tulane, at the University of Virginia, over a period of forty years, the labors of Doctor Alderman have been directed to the fulfillment of a great ideal, and the measure of that fulfillment is the real basis of Doctor Alderman's greatness as an educational leader and builder. The definition of his ideal of education he gave in an address many years ago in the following words: "Humanism produce the man of culture, and his peril was self-sufficiency and a conception of culture as ornament. Applied science and the interior demands of commerce have produced the man of efficiency, and his peril is personal barrenness and instinctive greed. Our country needs the idealism of the one and the lordship over things of the other, and such a blend will be the great citizen whose advent industrial democracy has so long foreshadowed. The kind of work he shall do in the world is immaterial. He shall be an upward striving man who wants the truth and dares to utter it, who knows his own need and the need of his age, who counts adaptability and toleration among his virtues, who insists on a little leisure for his soul's sake, and who has a care, whether amid the warfare of trade or in the quiet and still air of study, for the building of things ever better and better about him."

Doctor Alderman has not neglected the manifold agencies and organizations outside of his immediate sphere of duties in order to give full expression to his influence and usefulness. He is a member of the General Educational Board, the Board of Trustees of the Woodrow Wilson Foundation, member of the Board of Governors of the Institute of Economics, the Thomas Jefferson Memorial Foundation, the Board of Advisors of the Institute of Politics, member of the American Academy of Social Sciences and a member of the American Academy of Arts and Letters. His chief writings comprise *A Brief History of North Carolina, Life of William Hooper, Life of J. L. M. Curry, Obligations and Opportunities of Citizenship, Southern Idealism, The Spirit of the South, Sectionalism and Nationality, The Growing South, Can Democracy be Organized? Causes of European War, Some Tests of an Educated Man, Function and Needs of Schools of Education in Universities and Colleges, Memorial Address on Woodrow Wilson, The Nation Exalts Jefferson.* He was editor in chief of the Library of Southern Literature.

The degree Doctor of Civil Law was conferred on him by the University of the South in 1896, and that of Doctor of Laws by Tulane, Johns Hopkins, Columbia, Yale, University of North Carolina, Williams College, Harvard, University of Pennsylvania and the College of William and Mary.

Doctor Alderman married, in 1886, Miss Emma Graves, whose brother, Ralph Graves, was a professor in the University of North Carolina. She died in 1896, and in 1904 he married Bessie Green Hearn, of New Orleans. He has one son, Edwin Anderson, Jr., born in 1905.

CARTER GLASS has given a consecutive service to the Nation of such value as to make him one of the most distinguished men at Washington. That service began more than a quarter of a century ago when he went to Congress. He resigned his seat in the House of Representatives to become secretary of the treasury, and that cabinet post was relinquished to become United States senator from Virginia. Senator Glass' home community is Lynchburg, where he was born January 4, 1858. His father, Major Robert Henry Glass, was born in Amherst County, Virginia, in 1822, son of Thomas and Lavinia (Cauthorne) Glass. Major Glass was one of the great newspaper men of Virginia, a vigorous, fearless writer, possessed of physical and moral courage to perform his duties as he saw them, but never intentionally or carelessly wounding the feelings of an honest man. He was for many years editor and proprietor of the *Daily Republican* at Lynchburg, and in his advanced years still kept in touch with newspaper work in the editorial office of the *Lynchburg Advance*. He died May 6, 1896. For many years he was also postmaster of Lynchburg, and at the close of the Civil war was offered reappointment by President Lincoln. For a portion of the war he served with the rank of major on General Floyd's staff. Major Glass married Elizabeth Augusta Christian, daughter of Judge Samuel Christian and granddaughter of Capt. Henry Christian, a Revolutionary officer. She was born in 1826 and died January 15, 1860, Carter Glass being one of her five children.

Carter Glass was educated in public and private schools in Lynchburg, and at the age of fourteen went to work in his father's printing office. He served in the mechanical department of a printing office for eight years, that experience being the foundation of his profession as a newspaper man. He was with the *Lynchburg Republican* and also with the *Petersburg News* while his father was editor of that paper. For several years he had some experience as clerk in the auditor's office of what is now the Norfolk and Western Railway.

In 1880 he became local reporter on the staff of the *Lynchburg News*, was promoted to editor, and in 1888 acquired the plant of the *News*, and has owned that influential morning newspaper of Southwest Virginia for forty years. In 1895 he bought the *Lynchburg Virginian* and the *Evening Advance*, merging the *Virginian* with the *News*, and has continued the publication of the *Advance* as an evening daily.

Carter Glass was one of the first Virginia newspaper men to achieve some of the highest honors of leadership in the Democratic party of the state and nation. His first important political service was in making the nominating speech for J. Hoge Tyler for governor in 1897. In 1899 he was elected a member of the State Senate, served as a member of the Virginia Constitutional Convention of 1902-03, and wrote the suffrage article in the new constitution. He resigned from the State Senate in 1902, when elected to the Fifty-seventh Congress as successor to Peter J. Otey, deceased, and by reelections continued to represent this district through the Fifty-eighth and Sixty-fifth Congresses. He resigned his seat in 1918 to accept the invitation of President Wilson to become secretary of the treasury in the Wilson cabinet. While in Congress Mr. Glass had gained great distinction by his service in connection with the passage of the Federal Reserve Act, and his close study of banking and financial questions made him an authority on those subjects, and this was the basis of his appointment to the cabinet. Mr. Glass in February, 1920, resigned to accept the appointment of

United States senator for the unexpired term of Thomas S. Martin. He was subsequently elected for the remainder of the unexpired term, and in 1924 was elected for the full term expiring in 1931.

Senator Glass married, in 1886, Aurelia Caldwell, of Lynchburg. He is the father of four children.

HARRIS HART, state superintendent of public instruction at Richmond, has held that office since 1918.

He was formerly a member of the State Board of Examiners of Teachers, and has given nearly thirty years to the responsibilities of teaching and school administration. Mr. Hart was teacher and principal of the Roanoke High School from 1900 to 1909, and superintendent of Roanoke schools until he became state superintendent. He is a graduate of Richmond College and has been a graduate student at the University of Chicago and Harvard University.

Mr. Hart was born in Richmond, Virginia, February 24, 1878, son of John and Sallie L. (Coleman) Hart, the father a native of Louisa County and the mother of Spotsylvania County, Virginia. The father served in an engineers corps in the Confederate army. He then became an educator and was president of Richmond Female Institute and later of Albemarle Female Institute and co-principal in several academies for boys. He died in March, 1897, and the mother died in October, 1914.

Harris Hart was educated in Bowling Green Academy, Caroline County, Virginia, and in high school in Bowling Green, Virginia. He married Miss Mayola Gillespie, of Tazewell, Virginia, in June, 1922. She is a daughter of A. P. and Mary (Higginbotham) Gillespie, natives of Virginia. The parents are deceased. The father was a member of the State Constitutional Convention in 1901. He was a very distinguished attorney and resided at Tazewell, Virginia. He died in 1913 and the mother died in 1914.

Mr. and Mrs. Hart have three children, namely: Olivia Johnston, born in June, 1923; Helen Lewis, born in October, 1925; and Harris II, born in April, 1928.

From 1905 to 1909 Mr. Hart served as district school supervisor in charge of Southwest Virginia. He is a director of the Richmond Trust Company, a member of the Westmoreland Club, Hermitage Club, Richmond Country Club and is a teacher of the Young Men's Business Class in the Second Baptist Church of Richmond. Politically he is a Democrat and is a member of the Sons of Confederate Veterans.

LEROY HODGES, managing director of the Virginia State Chamber of Commerce, is both a scholar and a practical expert in the field of economics and commercial administration.

He was born at Tarboro, North Carolina, July 12, 1888, son of Eli Blucher and Rosa Hammond (Warrington) Hodges. During 1905-06, before he was eighteen years of age, he had experience in railroad and topographical surveying which took him over the Southern and Southwestern states and Mexico. During 1906-08 he was a student in the School of Commerce of Washington and Lee University, and subsequently was a student in the department of political economy at the University of Chicago and in the Law School of Washington and Lee University. Mr. Hodges was a special agent of the United States Immigration Commission, 1908-1910, was commercial geographer of the United States Tariff Board, 1910-11, commissioner of immigration for the Southern Commercial Congress in 1911, field secretary of the National Citizen's League for Promotion of a Sound Banking System in 1912. He served as secretary of the Winston-Salem Board of Trade in 1912-13, and in 1913 was chosen Virginia's representative on the American Commission for the investigation in Europe of coöperative agricultural finance and other subjects. He was also assistant to the United States commission on rural credits. During 1915-16 he was director of the Department of Municipal Efficiency and Administration in the Bureau of Applied Economics at Washington, served as associate editor of the *Petersburg Daily Index-Appeal,* and during 1916-17 as a member and secretary of the Virginia Commission on Economy and Efficiency.

Mr. Hodges in 1917 was appointed a special field representative of the United States Food Administration, and was director of the Petersburg Bureau of Governmental Research. He also engaged in private practice as a consulting economist. Mr. Hodges had charge of the preparation of the Virginia State budget from 1918 to 1924, was president of the Virginia Prison Board from 1920 to 1926, was a director of the National Budget Committee, 1922-24, and the first director of the Budget of the Commonwealth of Virginia, 1922-24. He has been managing director of the Virginia State Chamber of Commerce since February 1, 1924.

He served as secretary and personal military aide to the governor of Virginia with the rank of colonel, February 1, 1918-1922. He was commissioned major, Ordnance Department, Virginia National Guard, September 11, 1920, and assigned to duty as state ordnance officer and on September 29, 1921, was commissioned major, Ordnance Officers' Reserve Corps, United States Army.

Among the many responsible duties with which he has been charged he acted as technical advisor to the Virginia Commission on Simplification of State Government, as chairman of the Committee in Allocation of Prison Industries, and as a director of the National Committee on Prisons and Prison Labor, and national treasurer of the Lower Taxes—Less Legislation League.

Major Hodges is a Phi Beta Kappa, a Democrat and an Episcopalian. He is an officer of the Order of the Crown of Italy, and an officer of the Order of the White Lion of Czecho-Slovakia; and a member of the Country Club of Virginia and Westmoreland Club at Richmond, the country clubs at Petersburg and Fredericksburg, and of the National Press Club of Washington. He married, January 18, 1911, Almeria Orr Hill, of Petersburg, Virginia. They had three children, LeRoy, Rosa Batte, and Almeria Hill (deceased). In connection with his work Major Hodges has prepared for the press a great many bulletins and other articles, and some of the formal publications which attest his scholarship and experience include: *Agricultural Credit Systems Abroad,* published in 1913; *Petersburg, Virginia—Economic and Municipal,* published in 1917; *Post-War Ordnance,* published in 1923. He was editor of *The South's Physical Recovery,* published in 1911, and *Agricultural Coöperation and Rural Credit in Europe,* published in 1913.

F. H. McGurn

FRANCIS HOWE MCGUIRE, who was called the father of the Virginia Bar Association, achieved an eminence in his profession that cannot be measured by the comparatively brief period of years allotted him by the destiny of life.

He was born in Mecklenburg County, Virginia, June 4, 1850, and died October 30, 1894, at the age of forty-four. The name McGuire brings up a host of distinguished associations in Virginia. The Virginia McGuires were descended from the Chiefs of Fermanagh, one branch of which was established in County Kerry, Ireland, in 1641. The founder of the Virginia family was Edward McGuire, a native of County Fermanagh, who came to this country in 1754, settling at Winchester in Frederick County. Some of his descendants have gained great distinction in the field of medicine and surgery, others in the law, and still others in the educational field and in the clergy. One of the ancestors of the late Francis Howe McGuire was Col. William McGuire, of Winchester, who enlisted at the age of thirteen for service in the War of the Revolution and became a lieutenant of artillery. At the battle of Eutaw Springs he was permanently disabled. After the war he studied law, and became the first chief justice of the Territory of Mississippi, but because of ill health left that territory and removed to land he owned on the Ohio River near Wheeling, where he died November 20, 1820. He was at one time paymaster at Harpers Ferry and was a member of the Society of the Cincinnati. Col. William McGuire married Mary Little, daughter of William Little. She died in April, 1821. Colonel McGuire was a member of the Virginia Legislature during 1796-1799. Part of his education was acquired in William and Mary College. One of his grandsons was the noted Richmond educator, John P. McGuire.

A son of Col. William McGuire was at one time mayor of Winchester and county magistrate for many years. This McGuire was the father of Rev. Francis H. McGuire and grandfather of the Richmond attorney of the same name. Rev. Francis H. McGuire was born in Virginia, in 1809, was educated at Kenyon College in Ohio and in the Episcopal Theological Seminary of Virginia. He was ordained in the Episcopal Church in 1836, preached at Christs Church at Lancaster, Virginia, and subsequently went to the Mecklenburg parish, where he remained until a few years before his death on April 22, 1865. Rev. Francis H. McGuire married Mary Willing Harrison, of the distinguished Harrison family of Virginia.

Francis Howe McGuire was educated in private schools, in Randolph-Macon College and the University of Virginia, entering the latter institution in 1871. He also taught school at Huntsville, Alabama, and in Col. Thomas Carter's School in King William County, Virginia. He completed his law studies under John P. Minor at the University of Virginia, was admitted to the bar in 1874, and by his industry and good character soon established the reputation his abilities so justly merited. In 1878 he formed a partnership with Col. Tazewell Ellett, and they were together for twelve years. Mr. McGuire was a student of the law, and always regarded it as a profession rather than a vocation. Even after he had made a reputation as a lawyer he continued to take summer courses at the university. He was a charter member of the Richmond Bar Association, of which he was at one time president, and was chairman of the executive committee of the Virginia State Bar Association from its inception until one year before his death. Another fact that should be mentioned to his credit was his work in bringing about the establishment of the Court of Law and Equity at Richmond. A great part of his extensive law practice was in chancery and common law cases. He was noted for his thoroughness, energy and tenacity. One of his best known cases was that of Bosher versus the Harrisburg Land Company, and in winning this case before the Supreme Court of Appeals the decision of the court established a new principle of law in Virginia. Mr. McGuire was counsel for Colonel Spottswood in the contested primary election case of Spottswood versus Smith.

He was always a loyal friend of the University of Virginia. He was for a number of years a member of the Howitzer Battery at Richmond and at one time lieutenant in command. He was a member of the committee on statistics of the Chamber of Commerce, member of the Society of Alumni of the University of Virginia, was director of the Male Orphan Asylum, and the Board of Incorporators of the Protestant Episcopal Church Home, a director of the Peterkin Memorial Association, treasurer of the church fund of the diocese, member of the Virginia Historical Society, and was on the board of the Virginia State Insurance Company. He was a member of the vestry of St. James Episcopal Church and prominent in the Brotherhood of St. James, which he founded.

Mr. McGuire married a daughter of Emile Otto Knolting, who was Belgian consul at Richmond during the Civil war and became president of the National Bank of Virginia. After his death two brothers of Mrs. McGuire served successively as Belgian consul. Mrs. McGuire is a member of the Richmond Woman's Club. She has been deeply interested for a number of years in mountain mission work, and she donated the cost of a house at Schiflets Hollow, made as a memorial to Francis Howe McGuire, though the title she chose for the building was simply the Mission Home.

The only child of the late Francis Howe McGuire is Susie, now Mrs. Tazewell Ellett, Jr. Mr. and Mrs. Ellett were married December 14, 1917, and have three children, Helen McGuire, Tazewell III and Josephine Scott. Mr. Ellett was formerly an official of the Chesapeake & Ohio Railway and is now a member of the State Highway Commission of Virginia. Mrs. Susie Ellett is a member of the Richmond Woman's Club.

ANDREW JACKSON MONTAGUE is a lawyer and scholar whose services have done much to enrich Virginia's distinctions abroad, and he has earned notable dignities and positions in his own state and nation.

He was born in Campbell County, Virginia, October 3, 1862, son of Robert Latané and Gay (Eubank) Montague. Graduating from Richmond College in 1882, he took his law degree at the University of Virginia in 1885, and so far as the cares and responsibilities of public life would permit has practiced law steadily since that year. Brown University and the University of Pennsylvania have honored him with the degree Doctor of Laws.

He was United States district attorney for the Western District of Virginia from 1894 to 1898, was attorney general of Virginia, 1898-1902, and came to the office of governor in 1902, serving four years and one month. When he retired from this office in 1906 he accepted the position of dean of the Law School of Richmond College. Governor Montague in 1909 resumed his private law practice at Richmond, but in 1912 again accepted an opportunity to serve his state when he was chosen from the Third Virginia District a member of the Sixty-third Congress. That district has continued his representation at Washington and in 1928 he was elected a member of the Seventieth Congress. He is now the senior member of the Virginia delegation.

Governor Montague was a United States delegate to the Pan-American Conference at Rio de Janiero in 1906, to the Third International Conference on Maritime Law at Brussels in 1909-10, in 1917 was president of the American Society for the Judicial Settlement of International Disputes, and from 1920 to 1924 was president of the American Peace Society. In 1910 he became a trustee for the Carnegie Institution of Washington and the Carnegie Endowment for International Peace. William and Mary College elected him a member of the Phi Beta Kappa fraternity in 1908. Author, *Life of John Marshall, Secretary of State* (in *American Secretary of State and Their Diplomacy*), Volume II.

Governor Montague married, December 11, 1889, Elizabeth Lyne Hoskins.

HENRY G. SHIRLEY, chairman of the State Highway Commission of Virginia, has had a successful career as an engineer, in railroad and general engineering as well as highway building.

He is a native of West Virginia, born at Locust Grove, Shenandoah Valley, Jefferson County, son of Robert Vincent and Julia (Baylor) Shirley. His maternal grandfather was Col. R. W. Baylor, a Confederate officer of the Twelfth Virginia Cavalry.

Henry G. Shirley was educated by a private governess, also in public schools, preparing for college at the Charles Town Male Academy and graduating with the degree Civil Engineer from the Virginia Military Institute. Then followed several years of practical experience, after which he submitted a thesis and received a formal degree of Civil Engineer. Since then two institutions of learning have seen fit to recognize his service and attainments, Maryland University and Hampden-Sidney College having conferred upon him the honorary degree Doctor of Science. For a time Mr. Shirley was commandant of Cadets at Horner Military School in North Carolina. His professional experience includes service in the engineering departments of the District of Columbia, New York Central Railroad, West Virginia Central Railroad and Baltimore & Ohio systems. He was formerly road engineer of Baltimore County and chief engineer of the State Roads Commission of Maryland. During the World war he was a member of the Highway Transport Committee of the Council of National Defense and secretary of the Federal Highway Council. He was then called to his work as state highway commissioner of the Virginia Highway Department.

Mr. Shirley is a member of the American Society of Civil Engineers, is a past president and member of the Board of Directors of the American Road Builders Association, and had the honor of being elected the first president of the American State Highway Officials Association. His home is in Richmond. Mr. Shirley married Miss Alice Graham, member of one of the most distinguished families of North Carolina, daughter of Judge A. W. Graham, of Oxford. They have five children.

ROBERT RIDDICK PRENTIS, chief justice of the Supreme Court of Appeals of Virginia, has a distinguished ancestry, and his own career has been animated by the spirit of service which seems inherent in the name and lineage.

Judge Prentis was born at University, in Albemarle County, May 24, 1855, and is in the fifth generation from William Prentis, who was born in Norfolk County, England, in 1701, and as a young man came to America, settling in York County, Virginia. He was a merchant of the firm Blair & Prentis at Williamsburg, where he died August 4, 1765. William Prentis married Mary Brooke, who was born in 1710 and died April 9, 1768, daughter of John and Ann Brooke, of York County, Virginia.

Their son, Joseph Prentis, of Williamsburg, born January 24, 1754, was a member of the Virginia Convention which met in December, 1775, was appointed a commissioner in admiralty in 1776, was a member of the first House of Delegates in 1777 from Williamsburg, subsequently serving as a member from York, and was speaker of the House in 1788. He was a member of Governor Patrick Henry's Privy Council in 1779, and was judge of the General Court from 1789 until his death June 18, 1809. He was also credited with an important share in the negotiations and propositions on the part of Virginia which led to the convention for the drawing up of the Federal Constitution. He married, December 16, 1778, Margaret Bowdoin, who was born November 27, 1758, and died August 27, 1801. She was a daughter of John Bowdoin and also a descendant of Sir George Yeardley, colonial governor of Virginia.

Their son, Joseph Prentis, Jr., of Suffolk, was born at Williamsburg January 24, 1783, and died at Suffolk April 29, 1851. He was a lawyer, was a member of the convention of 1829-30, and for many years clerk of Nansemond County. He married, January 10, 1810, Susan Caroline Riddick, who was born in Nansemond County and died October 19, 1862, being a daughter of Col. Robert Moore and Elizabeth Riddick, she being a daughter of Col. Willis and Mary (Foulke) Riddick.

Robert Riddick Prentis, Sr., representing the fourth generation of the family, was born at Suffolk April 11, 1818, and died at Charlottesville November 23, 1871. He was educated for the bar, but spent most of his life in the University community at Charlottesville, serving as proctor of the University for some years, as clerk of Albemarle County, and during the Civil war as collector of internal revenue. He married Margaret Ann Whitehead, who was born August 8, 1826, and died February 16, 1910, daughter of Elliott and Catherine Flynn Whitehead.

Judge Robert Riddick Prentis was sixteen years old when his father died. He had attended the Oak Grove Academy at Charlottesville, but after the death of his father had to make his own way and also contribute to the support of his widowed mother and younger children. In 1874 he graduated from the Eastman Business College at Poughkeepsie, New York, and after one session at the University of Virginia was given the Bachelor of Laws degree in 1876. He at once engaged in practice at Charlottesville, remaining there until 1879, during that year was at Norfolk, and in 1879 established his home and law business at Suffolk. He served as mayor of Suffolk in 1883-85, and gave his time to a growing law practice until 1895. During the past thirty years his attention has been fully taken up by judicial and other official duties. He was judge of the Virginia

John A. Oke

Circuit Court in the Norfolk Circuit from 1895 until he resigned in 1907 to become chairman of the State Corporation Commission. Judge Prentis left the chairmanship of the Corporation Commission in 1916 to become associate justice of the Supreme Court of Appeals. Since March 10, 1925, he has been president or chief justice of the Supreme Court. His offices are at Richmond and he still retains his residence at Suffolk.

Judge Prentis was a member of the Democratic State Committee from 1887 to 1892, was a presidential elector in 1892, a member of the Virginia State Tax Commission in 1910, member of the State Advisory Board on Taxation in 1916, and during 1915-16 was president of the National Association of Railway Commissioners. He also served for some years as director of the Lee Camp Soldiers Home, the state institution for disabled Confederate veterans. He is a member of the Virginia State and American Bar Associations, Virginia Historical Society, Virginia Society of Colonial Wars, Sons of the Revolution. He is a Phi Beta Kappa, member of the Episcopal Church, and is a member of a number of clubs at Richmond, Norfolk and other communities. In 1919 he became a member of the Virginia War History Commission. He was given the LL. D. degree from the College of William and Mary in 1925. He was chairman of the Judicial Section, American Bar Association, 1926; chairman of the Commission on Revision and Amendment of the Virginia Constitution, 1927; chairman of the Judicial Council in Virginia in 1928.

Judge Prentis married, January 6, 1888, Mary Allen Darden. She died in 1904.

JOHN ARCHER COKE. It is well that this publication enter a memoir to the late Capt. John Archer Coke, who was long one of the leading members of the Virginia bar, who stood exponent of the patrician regime of the fine old Southern school of culture and refinement, and who was a representative of a Virginia family whose name has been one of prominence and influence in the history of the Old Dominion since the early Colonial period. Captain Coke was long engaged in the practice of law in the City of Richmond, and was here the senior member of the representative law firm of Coke & Pickrell at the time of his death, which occurred on the 27th of January, 1920.

In the historic old city of Williamsburg, Virginia, the birth of Captain Coke occurred July 14, 1842, he having been a direct descendant of John Coke, who was born in England, in 1704, of patrician ancestry, and who thence came, from Derbyshire, to America in the year 1724 to become a member of the original English colony founded at Williamsburg, Virginia. Representatives of the Coke family were patriot soldiers in the War of the Revolution, as well as in subsequent wars in which the nation was involved. Captain Coke of this memoir and his seven brothers all volunteered for service in defence of the cause of the Confederate States when the Civil war was precipitated on a divided nation, and each of the brothers gained in this service the rank of captain. One of the number was Capt. Octavious Coke, who later served as secretary of state in North Carolina, and another of the brothers was Capt. Richard Coke, who went to Texas after the close of the war and who there had a long and distinguished career in public life, he having served as governor of Texas and having long represented the Lone Star State in the United States Senate. Of this remarkable group of brothers the subject of this memoir was the last survivor.

Capt. John A. Coke was a student in historic old William and Mary College at the inception of the Civil war, and he forthwith subordinated all other interests to volunteer for service in the Confederate army. In April, 1861, he initiated his service as lieutenant in a battery of artillery that became a part of the forces under the command of Gen. Robert E. Lee. In the reorganization of his battery in 1862 he was made its captain, and he continued in service in the Army of Northern Virginia until, in 1864, he was assigned to special recruiting service at Richmond, where he was thus stationed until the close of the war. While in active field service he was slightly wounded in connection with the Dahlgreen raids about Richmond.

After the close of the war Captain Coke turned his attention to the study of law, and upon gaining admission to the bar he engaged in the practice of his profession in the City of Richmond in 1866. Here he continued in individual practice until 1883, when he formed a partnership with John Pickrell, under the firm name of Coke & Pickrell. His firm gained precedence as one of the strongest and most influential of the Virginia bar, gave special attention to corporation law, and was retained as counsel for the Life Insurance Company of Virginia, the Virginia-Carolina Chemical Company, the Imperial Tobacco Company and numerous other corporations of major importance. Captain Coke continued as senior member of the firm of Coke & Pickrell until his death, and as lawyer, citizen and man of exalted integrity he ever commanded inviolable place in popular confidence and esteem. In his bearing he exemplified the best in the typifying of a Southern gentleman of the old school, as he was courtly and dignified, affable and considerate, striking in appearance by reason of his superior height, his patrician face and commanding presence, and was known for his high intellectual and professional attainments, as well as for his abiding human sympathy and tolerance.

April 17, 1867, recorded the marriage of Captain Coke and Miss Emma Overby, likewise a representative of an old and distinguished Virginia family, she having been a daughter of Robert Y. and Mary (Pool) Overby, both natives of Mecklenburg County, Virginia. Mrs. Coke preceded her husband to the life eternal, as her death occurred October 5, 1917, and of their children one son and one daughter are living. The historic old capital city of Richmond long claimed Captain and Mrs. Coke as leaders in its social and cultural life, and here they shall long be retained in gracious memory by those who came within the sphere of their benignant influence.

JOHN ARCHER COKE, JR., is well upholding in his native city of Richmond the high civic and professional honors of the family name. He is one of the representative members of the bar of Virginia's fair old capital city and is here attorney for the Life Insurance Company of Virginia. Mr. Coke is a scion of one of the old and distinguished families of Virginia, and adequate data concerning the family history are given in the preceding sketch, in the memoir dedicated to his father, the late Capt. John Archer Coke.

John A. Coke, Jr., was born in Richmond on the 15th of January, 1877, and after his course in Richmond College he continued his studies in the historic old University of Virginia, in the law department of which he was graduated as a member of the class of 1898. After thus receiving his degree of Bachelor of Laws he became associated with his father's law firm, that of Coke & Pickrell, of which he was made a constituent member and with which he continued his alliance until the firm was dissolved by the death of his father in 1920. Since that year Mr. Coke has given much of his professional attention to his service as counsel for the Life Insurance Company of Virginia, with headquarters in the company's fine building in Richmond.

Mr. Coke has continued unreservedly in the ancestral political faith, that of the Democratic party, and his patriotic antecedents are shown in his affiliation with the Society of the Sons of the American Revolution and also the Society of the Cincinnati, his eligibility for the latter being through his ancestor in the maternal line, Capt. Robert Yancey of the First Continental Dragoons. In the suburban district of Westhampton Mr. and Mrs. Coke have their beautiful home, named "Trusley," after the title of the Coke ancestral estate in England.

Mr. Coke wedded Miss Anne Elizabeth Harrison, representative of the historic old Virginia family of that name, and the two children of this union are daughters—Elizabeth H. and Archer.

SIMON H. ROSENTHAL, M. D. With the exception of a short period of army service during the World war and the time spent in taking post-graduate work, the entire career of Dr. Simon H. Rosenthal has been passed at Lynchburg, where through industry, close application and natural and acquired talent he has risen to a recognized position among the leaders of his profession. During recent years Doctor Rosenthal has found his greatest field of usefulness in the special field of urology, a department in which he has gained a widespread reputation and which he follows as a member of the staffs of all the Lynchburg hospitals.

Doctor Rosenthal was born at Lynchburg, December 16, 1890, and is a son of M. and Rebecca (Tobac) Rosenthal. M. Rosenthal was born in Russian Poland and was a man of splendid education, being a master of seven languages. This knowledge led him to become an interpreter, which vocation he followed in Russia until 1880, in which year he immigrated to the United States, feeling that here he could find better opportunities for the achievement of success. He gathered together his somewhat meager capital and started on his journey, but while on shipboard fell in with bad companions and was robbed of all his means. Thus he arrived at Danville, Virginia, in a strange country, without means or friends, and the next eight years of his life were ones of stern struggle. Eventually he became the proprietor of a small furniture store, made possible by his work as an interpreter. This was the first furniture store of Lynchburg and was built up to important proportions by Mr. Rosenthal, who conducted the business until his death in 1919. He was a man of excellent ability, great industry and fine judgment and won his own way to success and preferment. Of his five children four are living: Louis E., who has conducted the furniture business since the death of his father; Simon H., of this review; Mrs. J. Klots, a resident of Staunton; and Mrs. Maurice Klots, also of Staunton. Mrs. Rosenthal was born in Russia, and she and her husband were orthodox Jews. He was a member of the

Independent Order of Odd Fellows and the Knights of Pythias, and in his political allegiance was a stalwart Democrat.

Simon H. Rosenthal attended the public schools of Lynchburg, including high school, and then entered Jefferson Medical College, from which institution he was graduated as a member of the class of 1913, receiving the degree Doctor of Medicine. He then spent eighteen months as an interne in the Philadelphia General Hospital, but at the end of that period returned to Lynchburg, where he engaged in the general practice of his professsion. He was called into the army in February, 1918, and as a member of the Medical Corps served at the Base Hospital at Camp Lee until receiving his honorable discharge in April, 1919. He then returned to Lynchburg, but in 1920 went to New York, where he did post-graduate work in urology at the New York Post-Graduate College and Hospital. Upon his return to his home city he became a specialist in urology and has practically confined himself to this department ever since. In addition to a large private practice Doctor Rosenthal is a member of the staffs of all of the hospitals at Lynchburg, and is held in the highest esteem by his fellow practitioners, who have realized his worth and accorded him that respect due those who have achieved distinction in any line. He maintains well appointed and perfectly equipped offices at 1112 Church Street, and is a member of the Campbell County Medical Society, Virginia State Medical Society, South Piedmont Medical Society and American Medical Association. He is a Mason and a member of the Phi Delta Epsilon fraternity, and holds membership in the Jewish Synagogue. He has never been sufficiently interested in politics to seek preferment at the hands of any party, but is a good citizen of public spirit.

On June 5, 1920, Doctor Rosenthal was united in marriage with Miss Bettye Greenberg, of Danville, Virginia, who was educated at the public schools of Danville and at Randolph-Macon Institute at Danville, Virginia. To this union there have been born two children: Macey Herschel, born in December, 1921; and Ceevah Miriam, born in September, 1924.

EDGAR L. SUTHERLAND, M. D. The broad field of medical endeavor offers much to the conscientious man in the way of public service, research, teaching, surgery, public health, general practice, or in following, perhaps, some particular path, and through some combination of methods and manners which are individual and distinctive, prove natural ability and careful training. The physician of today must possess a wide range of general culture, must be an observant clinician and well read neurologist. The stamp of an original mind is never more to be observed than in the case of the hard worked medical man whose soul has often fainted within him when studying the mysteries of his calling. Among the many skilled and distinguished medical men of Virginia, one who has gained special notice through his steady nerve, patience, technical manual skill and the courage which are distinctive of his profession is Dr. Edgar L. Sutherland, physician and surgeon of Lynchburg. He was born in Hillsville, Virginia, December 5, 1875, a son of William Hamilton and Rhoda J. (Cassell) Sutherland, he born in Rockingham, North Carolina, and she in Wythe County, Virginia, and both are deceased. They had five children, four of whom survive: Doctor Sutherland, who is the eldest; Alice, who married Robert M. Black, cashier of the Hillsville Bank; Walter, who is deceased;

Mrs. C. E. Lundy, who resides in Raleigh, North Carolina, where her husband is a realtor; and Mrs. J. C. Rutrough, who resides in Willis, Virginia, where her husband is engaged in the practice of medicine. The mother was a devout member of the Lutheran Church, and active in church and charitable work. An active Democrat, the father held the office of county clerk for forty-two years, from 1865 until 1907, a record of faithful service not often found. During the war between the states, which brought out all of the valor and courage in human nature, he served as captain of a local company, and was wounded in the battle of Gettysburg, but recovered, rejoined his regiment and was present at the surrender at Appomattox when a great cause was relinquished at the word of the immortal leader Gen. Robert E. Lee. A few days prior to the surrender he had been elected county clerk, so upon his return home from the army he had definite work to do, and discharged his duties so admirably that his fellow citizens kept him in office for the longest consecutive period in the history of this part of Virginia, and he was still in office when claimed by death. He was a son of John L. Sutherland, a native of North Carolina, but for many years a resident of Saint Joseph, Missouri, where he was first engaged in the practice of law, and later served on the bench, in which capacity he was rendering a valuable service when he died. The maternal grandfather, J. F. Cassell, was a farmer of Carroll County, Virginia.

Doctor Sutherland grew up in his native place, attended its schools, and early decided upon a professional career. He therefore entered Roanoke College, where he was prepared for the University of Virginia, and was graduated from the latter in 1898, with the degree of Doctor of Medicine, and the youngest man in his class. While at college he was a member of the Phi Delta Theta. For several years thereafter he was engaged in a general practice in Pulaski County, Virginia, but then took post graduate work in the New York Post-Graduate School and Hospital, New York City, studying diseases of the eye, ear, nose and throat. With this country's entry into the World war he offered his services through enlistment, but was rejected, and he then made himself useful by serving in the examining of the recruits on the draft board in Pulaski County. After the close of the war he was engaged with a partner in practice at Roanoke for a short time, going from there to Charlottesville, and finally coming to Lynchburg in May, 1927. While he was engaged in a general practice he was also surgeon for the Norfolk & Western Railroad, the Virginia Iron, Coal and Coke Company and the Pulaski Iron Company. He belongs to the Virginia Society of Opthalmology and Oto-laryngectomy, the Campbell County Medical Society, the Virginia State Medical Society, the Southern Medical Association and the American Medical Association. His fraternal affiliations are those which he mantains with the Masonic Order and the Elks. While a resident of Charlottesville he belonged to the Kiwanis Club. He is a member of the Presbyterian Church.

In October, 1898, Doctor Sutherland married Miss Vera Robinson, born in Fluvanna County, Virginia, and educated in the Woman's College, Richmond, Virginia. She is a consistent member of the Presbyterian Church, and continues as active in its good work as she has always been, and she is also prominent in social life, so that she is a valuable addition to Lynchburg.

CHARLES W. BROOK is one of the active business men of Lynchburg, owner and active head of the Harris Carriage Company, manufacturers of bodies for automobiles.

Mr. Brook was born in Amherst County, Virginia, July 9, 1881, son of George H. and Mary Elizabeth (Jones) Brook and grandson of William Nickolas Brook and Thomas Jones. William Nickolas Brook brought his family from England and became a farmer in Amherst County, Virginia. Thomas Jones was born in Amherst County and was a great plantation owner before the Civil war, using the labor of forty slaves. Two of his sons were Confederate soldiers. George H. Brook was born in England, while his wife was a natve of Amherst County. He was for many years identified with merchandising. They were members of the Methodist Episcopal Church, South. They had six children: William N., a jeweler in Georgia; Annie L., wife of Edward M. Wright, superintendent of the Lynchburg Foundry Company; Miss Ola, of Amherst; Mary and Dora, twins, the former the wife of Charles E. Bell, manager of the R. C. Dunn & Company of Lynchburg, while Dora is the wife of Norvell N. Holt, a Lynchburg insurance man; and Charles W.

Charles W. Brook was educated in a private school conducted by an aunt, a very brilliant woman, well known in educational circles. He also attended the Lynchburg High School, and for fifteen years was identified with the tobacco business of that city. On February 1, 1919, he acquired the plant and business of the Harris Carriage Company and has greatly extended the facilities and service of this organization in the manufacture of bodies and tops for automobiles. He is a director of Lynchburg Finance Company.

Mr. Brook married in June, 1920, Miss Emma Berford, a native of Marshall, Texas, who was educated in that state and in Tennessee and Virginia. Mr. and Mrs. Brook are members of the Methodist Episcopal Church and he is a steward of the Rivermont Church at Lynchburg. He is a member of the Lions Club and a Democrat in politics.

WALTER FREDERICK WHATELY is secretary and treasurer of the Lynchburg Lumber Company. Mr. Whately has had a widely extended experience in commercial affairs, and is one of the prominent business men of Lynchburg, where he has lived most of his life.

He was born in Campbell County, Virginia, in 1876, son of W. E. and Rosa L. (Fore) Whately. His mother was born in Campbell County, Virginia, where her father was a well-to-do farmer. W. E. Whately was born in England, son of George Frederick Whately, a prominent surgeon who spent all his life in England. W. E. Whately on coming to America located in Campbell County, Virginia, and engaged in farming. He was a Democrat in politics, and served as vestryman of the Episcopal Church. He and his wife had five children, four of whom are living: Walter Frederick; Lena, wife of C. A. Tanner, of Gladys, Virginia; William E., connected with the C. & P. Telephone Company at Roanoke; and C. F. Whately, a farmer in Campbell County.

Walter F. Whately attended school in Lynchburg, graduating from high school, and has made an intensive application of his energies to business ever since leaving school. For several years he was employed by a tobacco company, spent four or five years with R. C. Scott & Company, flour millers, and for three years

was with the Alkali Works at Saltville, Virginia. Having thus acquired a good general training in business, he became identified with the lumber industry with C. I. Johnson at Wingina in Nelson County. He was located there for eleven years and since then has made his headquarters at Lynchburg as secretary and treasurer of the Lynchburg Lumber Company, one of the very prosperous and successful organizations in the city.

Mr. Whately is a vestryman in Grace Memorial Episcopal Church at Lynchburg. He is a past high priest of the Royal Arch Chapter of Masonry and a member of the Lions Club. He married, in 1907, Miss Bessie Rosen, a native of Buckingham County, Virginia, daughter of Charles R. Rosen. They have two children, Mable Elizabeth and Walter Roy. The daughter Mable has completed a high school education.

JAMES TAYLOR ELLYSON, who was lieutenant governor of Virginia from 1905 to 1917, was well worthy of all the official distinctions conferred upon him, but the real value of his life could not be measured by offices and titles. He was a man of unusual breadth of interest and varied gifts, and his activities and positions he held represented a steady force and influence for uplift and advancement exerted over a long period of years and characterized by a completeness of devotion and a fidelity to high ideals unusual even in the great commonwealth of Virginia.

James Taylor Ellyson was born at Richmond May 20, 1847, and died in that city March 18, 1919, at the age of seventy-two. He represented the seventh generation of the Ellyson family in America, which was founded by Capt. and Dr. Robert Ellyson, who first came to Maryland and afterwards to Virginia, where in 1656-1672 he served as justice, high sheriff and burgess of James City County. He was the father of Gerard Ellyson, grandfather of Robert Ellyson, who lived in Henrico County. William Ellyson, of Chesterfield County, was a son of Robert Ellyson and was the father of Onan Ellyson, who married Mary Huot, of French Canadian ancestry. They were the parents of Henry Keeling Ellyson, who was born in Richmond in 1823 and died in 1890. Henry Keeling Ellyson married, in 1843, Elizabeth Pinkney Barnes, and they reared four children: Theodore Ellyson, who married Elizabeth Walker; James Taylor Ellyson, who married Lora Effie Hotchkiss; William Ellyson, who married Mary Morris Johnson; Miss Bettie, who died in 1922, the last of her family; and three, Luther Barnes, who was born September 30, 1849, and died November 7, 1864; Nannie, who was born December 6, 1857, and died February 28, 1864; and Sally, who was born February 13, 1853, and died July 15, 1853.

James Taylor Ellyson was educated in Columbia College, and in Richmond College, and graduated from the University of Virginia in 1869. At the age of sixteen, in 1862, he became a member of the Second Company of the Richmond Howitzers. He surrendered with that company at Appomattox. Mr. Ellyson had many years of successful activities as a business man at Richmond, but the greater part of his time was devoted to civic and religious service, and most of the positions he held were without remuneration. He was a member of the Common Council of Richmond from 1881 to 1887, being president of that body in 1884, and in 1888 was elected mayor, serving three terms. He was a member of the Virginia Senate in 1885-87, and was lieutenant-governor three terms, a period of twelve years. For more than a quarter of a century he was chairman of the Democratic State Committee of Virginia, and was also national committeeman of his party. He was for sixteen years president of the Richmond School Board, for more than twenty years represented the state as director of the Richmond, Fredericksburg and Potomac Railroad, and was a member of the Richmond Chamber of Commerce. He was lieutenant governor when the Jamestown Exposition was held in 1907, and besides being a member of the Board of Governors of the exposition he acted as governor of history and education and social economy.

Governor Ellyson was a member of Lee Camp and Pickett Camp of Confederate Veterans, member of the Richmond Howitzer Association, member of the Jefferson Davis Monument Association and president of the Confederate Memorial Association which erected the Confederate Memorial Institute. This remarkably beautiful building and institution, one of the finest in the South, will always recall to those who know of its inception and progress the important services rendered by the late Mr. Ellyson. He was also a life member of the Confederate Memorial Literary Society, was a memer of the Virginia Historical Society, life members of the Association for the Preservation of Virginia Antiquities, member of the National Geographic Society, and on the executive committee of the American National Red Cross. He was affiliated with Richmond Lodge No. 10, Ancient Free and Accepted Masons, Washington Chapter No. 9, Royal Arch Masons, Commandery of St. Andrew, Knights of Malta No. 13, member of the Grand Council of the Royal Arcanum, and Richmond Lodge, Independent Order of Odd Fellows.

Governor Ellyson for over thirty years was a deacon of the Second Baptist Church of Richmond, was a member of the Board of Trustees of the Virginia Baptist Orphanage, in 1908 became president of the Board of Trustees of Richmond College, served three terms as president of the Virginia Baptist General Association, was vice president of the Southern Baptist Convention in 1895, and for forty-six years corresponding secretary of the Virginia Baptist Education Board. Perhaps no better estimate of the qualities of his character can be found than the following sentences taken from a memorial adopted by the deacons of the Second Baptist Church: "A noble spirit has gone from us, and we do well today not only to honor his memory but to catch inspiration from his life. He was not given to thinking too highly of himself. There was a modesty about him, almost a shyness at times, which strangers or casual acquaintances may have mistaken for coldness or indifference, but those who knew him intimately need no assurance of the wealth of his nature, the strength of his friendship or the genuineness of his heart. The nobility and fineness of his spirit was exhibited in many ways, but in no way more strikingly than in his attitude toward those who were unfriendly to him. How freely he forgave them and how unwillingly he was to cherish in his heart anything akin to hatred. He had a host of friends who loved to come to him for counsel and who never came to him in vain.

Lora Hotchkiss Ellyson.

bell County Bar Association, the Virginia State Bar Association
and the American Bar Association. For a time after his arrival
Mr. Smith was engaged in practice with Alfred B. Perry, but
since the latter's death, October 19, 1927, has practiced alone.

Mr. Smith married Miss Gladys Millar Reams, daughter of
Mr. and Mrs. G. L. Reams, of Lynchburg. He belongs to the
Baptist Church and the Kappa Sigma and Delta Theta Phi
fraternities, and in his political views is a Democrat.

GREENWOOD H. NOWLIN, JR., of Lynchburg, is a prominent
coal operator of Southern West Virginia, and his talents have
been employed in the exploitation of the Pocahontas and other
smokeless coal areas of West Virginia for many years.

He was born at Lynchburg, August 30, 1878, son of G. H.
and Lelia (Pendleton) Nowlin, and grandson of Peyton Wade
Nowlin and James Shepherd Pendleton, the former a native of
Virginia, also the latter, born at Clifford in Amherst County.
James S. Pendleton was a doctor and farmer, having attended
the Virginia Military Institute about 1836, and afterwards
graduated from the Jefferson Medical College of Philadelphia.
Peyton Wade Nowlin lived near Brookneal, Virginia, and his
ancestors came to Virginia from County Carlow, Ireland. G. H.
Nowlin, Sr., was born in Osage County, Missouri, but spent most
of his life in Virginia and died in 1914. He was on detached
duty for the Confederate government during the Civil war, and
at the end of the war had only fifteen cents in money. He cut
wood and hauled it to town as a means of supporting himself
and getting a start, and for several years was in the leaf tobacco
business. He became associated with the coal industry on the
opening up of the Pocahontas fields in West Virginia, and became
one of the large operators. Through all the years he retained
some connection with the tobacco business and was a director
of the Lynchburg and Durham Railway Company. He was a
member of the vestry of St. Paul's Episcopal Church of Lynchburg, was a Mason and a Democrat. His wife died in 1899, and
of their five children four are living: Greenwood H., Jr.; R. P.
Nowlin, in the tobacco industry, Lynchburg, Virginia; R. A.
Nowlin, associated with the Crozer Land Association and the
Crozer Coal & Coke Company at Elkhorn, West Virginia; and
James Pendleton, in the coal business at Beckley, West Virginia.

Greenwood H. Nowlin, Jr., attended school at Lynchburg,
continuing his education in the Virginia Polytechnic Institute
and the University of Virginia, and took a special course in
steel analyses and metallography under Dr. Albert Saveur at
Boston in 1903. He was an assistant metallurgist for the United
States Steel Corporation, assigned to duty at the Illinois Steel
Works at Chicago, and later with the Tennessee Coal, Iron &
Railway Company at Ensley, Alabama. He was taken ill at
Ensley, and after recuperating he engaged in the coal business,
becoming secretary of the Killarney Smokeless Company. He
is now president of that company and is also president of the
Lynchburg Coal & Coke Company, president of the Eureka Coal
& Coke Company, president of the Lynchburg Colliery Company.
The source of production of coal by all these organizations is in
West Virginia, and Lynchburg is the headquarters of the busi-
ness management and sales agencies.

Mr. Nowlin married, in 1917, Beulah Terrell, who was born
in Bedford County, Virginia, but has spent all her life in Lynchburg, attending public schools there. Her father, Charles H.

Terrell, was a farmer in Bedford County. Mr. and Mrs. Nowlin are members of St. Paul's Episcopal Church and he has been a member of the church choir for over thirty years. He is a York Rite Mason and Shriner, member of the B. P. O. Elks, the Piedmont Club, and has membership in the American Institute of Mining and Metallurgical Engineers, the American Chemical Society, and not only enjoys prominence among the coal operators and executives of the industry, but also with the technical and engineering side of the industry.

JAMES A. FIX. Among the building contractors who have contributed by their expert labors to the development, upbuilding and architectural beauty of Lynchburg, none are more worthy of mention than James A. Fix, head of the old established firm of J. A. Fix & Sons. Starting to learn the trade of carpenter when a lad of but fifteen years, by industry, honest workmanship and close application to his calling he has worked his way to a leading position among the contractors of Campbell County, where numerous commodious and attractive structures of various kinds stand as monuments to his ability.

Mr. Fix was born at Staunton, Virginia, December 30, 1865, and is a son of Joseph H. and Barbara (Snapp) Fix. His father, a native of Pennsylvania, came to Virginia in his youth and learned carpentry, a vocation which he followed until the outbreak of the war between the states, when he enlisted in the Confederate army and saw active service until the close of hostilities. He then returned to Staunton and continued to follow his trade until his death, at which time he was also the owner of a valuable farm. He was a man of integrity and one who was held in high esteem in his community, was active in the Methodist Church, and a Democrat in his political allegiance. He married Barbara Snapp, also a native of Pennsylvania, and a member of the Methodist Church, in the faith of which she died. They were married in Virginia and became the parents of eleven children, of whom nine are living.

The second in order of birth of his parents' children, James A. Fix received only a common school education, as his assistance was needed to help support the family, and when he was only fifteen years of age he began to learn the carpenter trade under the preceptorship of his father. While his schooling was not extensive in his youth, in later years he has attained a good practical education through reading, observation and constant contact with his fellow men. For a number of years he worked as a journeyman, but finally embarked in business on his own account at Charlottesville and later at Staunton, and finally, in 1894, settled at Lynchburg, where he has since been known as one of the city's leading contractors. His sons are now associates in the firm of J. A. Fix & Sons, and this concern has erected many of the substantial and attractive residences, business structures and public buildings of this and adjacent communities. Mr. Fix is a member of the Rivermont Presbyterian Church, and as a fraternalist belongs to the Woodmen of the World. He is a Democrat in politics, but has found little time to devote to public affairs aside from those which affect the immediate welfare of his community, when he can be relied upon to support measures for the general progress and advancement of Lynchburg.

In 1898 Mr. Fix married Miss Fannie Dooms, who was born and educated in Nelson County, Virginia, and is a daughter of

Henry Dooms, who was a life long farmer in that county. To this union there were born six children: Henry S., who is associated with his father in business; Gussie Elizabeth, who resides at home; George W., who is associated with his father in business; Anna Belle, the wife of Dr. W. C. Adkinson, a practicing physician of Lynchburg; Gladys, the wife of Lloyd Rickets, identified with a mercantile establishment at Lynchburg; and Mary Frances, attending a school at Farmville, where she is preparing for a career as an educator. Mr. Fix's offices are located in the Lynch Building.

LAWRENCE H. McWANE. Among the former business men of Lynchburg who have now completed their labors and passed to the Great Beyond, one who left the impress of his personality upon his community and generation was the late Lawrence H. McWane. At the time of his death, in 1925, he was still a young man, being but forty-two years of age, but already had accomplished much in the way of advancing himself in public confidence and esteem and was the capable and energetic president of the Lynchburg Foundry Company, one of the city's principal manufacturing industries. Without any time for the activities which bring men before the public as molders of thought and opinion, he nevertheless was accounted a good and public-spirited citizen who discharged his duties and responsibilities in a commendable manner.

Mr. McWane was born at Wytheville, Wythe County, Virginia, in 1883, and received a public school education at Lynchburg. A complete report of the life of his father will be found on another page of this work, included in the sketch of F. W. McWane. After leaving public school Mr. McWane entered Milligan College, Tennessee, where he completed a full course, and then enrolled as an employe of the McWane Pipe Works, at Lynchburg, of which his father had been the founder. He was content to begin his work in a humble capacity and to learn the business thoroughly, with the result that at the time of his father's demise he was ready to step into the elder man's place as president at the time of his death and to hold this position until his own demise. As before noted, Mr. McWane was a man of energy and sound ability and one who was achieving an enviable success when called in death. He had won the respect and esteem of his associates and of the employes of the plant, who found him a man who was fair-minded and possessed of a sense of justice. The business profited materially under his administration of its affairs, and is still operated as the Lynchburg Foundry Company.

In 1904 Mr. McWane was united in marriage with Miss Carrie Witt, daughter of J. F. and Dora (Hurst) Witt, natives of Virginia, both of whom survive as residents of the southwestern part of the state. For many years Mr. Witt was a merchant at Pennington Gap, Virginia, but is now retired from business affairs. To Mr. and Mrs. Witt there were born seven children, Mrs. McWane, of this review, being the eldest. Mr. and Mrs. Witt are active members of the Christian Church, and Mr. Witt is a Democrat in his political allegiance.

To Mr. and Mrs. McWane there was born one daughter, Maurine, who attended the public schools of Lynchburg and the Holton-Arms School, Washington, D. C., and now resides with her mother in their home on Lee Circle, Lynchburg. On April 7, 1928, she was united in marriage with Garnett Sowder, of

Radford, Virginia. Mrs. McWane and her daughter are members of the Christian Church, to which Mr. McWane belonged. He was appreciative of the society of his fellows and was a member of the Benevolent and Protective Order of Elks and at one time president of the local Lions Club. He was always interested in civic affairs, to which he gave of his time, ability and means.

RICHARD A. CARRINGTON, the chief expression of whose commercial energies has been a large and successful wholesale shoe business at Lynchburg, is a member of the distinguished Carrington family of Virginia which has given men of leadership in the professions, business and military affairs for generations.

He was born at Rustburg in Campbell County, Virginia, August 17, 1869, son of Dr. George W. and Mary A. (Alexander) Carrington, and his grandfather was Dr. Richard Carrington, a Virginian, who for many years practiced medicine at Richmond, where he owned a beautiful home, burned during the Civil war. The maternal grandfather was John D. Alexander, a native of Campbell County, who was clerk of courts in that county for many years. One of the Alexander family was the first clerk of courts in the county. Dr. George W. Carrington was born at Richmond, was educated in the University of Virginia, had hospital training in New York and practiced in Richmond and Ashland, and in his later years lived at Rustburg. He finally gave up his professional practice to serve as grand secretary of the Grand Lodge of Masons of Virginia. He was a Democrat in politics, had served as a surgeon in the Confederate army during the Civil war, and was a vestryman of the Episcopal Church. He and his wife had five children, the three now living being Richard A.; Mary, wife of L. T. Stanard, connected with the Chesapeake & Ohio Railway at Richmond; and Louise, wife of P. C. Hubard.

Richard A. Carrington was educated in common schools and began work at an early age. He was first employed in a tobacco factory, for five years was with the Virginia Nail and Iron Company, and his first connections with the shoe business were as a traveling salesman. He was on the road ten years and in 1905 became one of the organizers of the Lynchburg Shoe Company, Incorporated. He was president of this company for some years, and the active officers today are: R. A. Carrington, Jr., president, and E. L. Carrington, vice president, with Mr. Carrington still on the Board of Directors. This is one of the large wholesale shoe houses of the Southeast, and maintains a staff of twenty-six traveling salesmen covering territory in West Virginia, Kentucky, Ohio, Virginia and all the other Southern states.

Mr. Carrington began work at the age of sixteen and his well directed energies brought him a competence at a comparatively early age. Among other property he owns the old estate of the late John W. Daniel. Mr. Carrington attends St. Paul's Episcopal Church at Lynchburg and is affiliated with the Masonic fraternity and B. P. O. Elks.

He married, November 8, 1893, Miss Katherine Page Langhorne, a native of Lynchburg, daughter of Charles S. and Katherine Page (Haller) Langhorne, the former of whom was in the milling business. Mr. and Mrs. Carrington have two sons. Edward Langhorne Carrington, the older, vice president of the Lynchburg Shoe Company, was educated at Bellevue, Virginia,

and the Episcopal High School at Alexandria. He married
Nannie O. Pettyjohn. Richard Alexander Carrington, Jr., was
educated in the Episcopal High School at Alexandria and the
University of Virginia. He married Miss Harold James, who
was born at Danville. Her father, Dr. Bruce James, is a professor in the Virginia Military Institute. Richard A. Carrington, Jr., and wife have one daughter, Kate Langhorne Carrington.

JOHN EARLY JACKSON. With the ever-expanding need for
electricity has come technical training for the various phases
of the industries thus created, and then men thus prepared are
able to assume vast responsibilities and to render valuable service, not only to the companies employing them, but to their
communities as well. One of these thoroughly trained and
responsible men above referred to is John Early Jackson, manager of the Appalacian Electric Power Company of Lynchburg,
whose ability is unquestioned and whose citizenship is productive of great constructive results. Mr. Jackson was born
in Nashville, Tennessee, January 29, 1902, a son of Granbery
and Margaret (Early) Jackson, he born in Mount Pleasant
and she in Nashville, Tennessee, and they are still residing in
Nashville. Although a civil engineer the father is not now
practicing his profession but is engaged in the phosphate business, in which he was a pioneer in his part of Tennessee. He
owns considerable phosphate land that is operated by different
big corporations. Vanderbilt University, Nashville, educated
him, and he is a worthy product of that great instittuion. Two
children were born to him and his wife, of whom Mr. Jackson of
this review is the elder, the other being Granbery, Junior, who
is studying architecture in the University of Pennsylvania. The
father is a Presbyterian and the mother a Methodist, and both
are devoted church workers. The Democratic party has his
staunch support. His father, paternal grandfather of John
Early Jackson, was a native of Virginia. The maternal grandfather, John F. Early, was a son of Right Reverend John Early,
the Methodist Bishop so long a resident of Lynchburg.

Growing up in his native city, John Early Jackson attended
its public schools and Vanderbilt University, and later was a
student of Massachusetts Institute of Technology, from which
he was graduated in 1924. For a year thereafter he was in
the employ of the General Electric Company, Schenectady, New
York, and then, in 1925, he came to Lynchburg to become manager of his present company, in which connection he is giving
unqualified satisfaction.

In June, 1926, Mr. Jackson married Miss Elinor Jones, who
was born in Saint Louis, Missouri, and was educated in Farm-
ington College and the Choate School, Brookline, Massachusetts.
Mr. and Mrs. Jackson have one daughter, Margaret Early Jackson. They are members of the different social organizations of
their neighborhood, and have a delightful home life. She is an
Episcopalian and he a Methodist. While in Vanderbilt University Mr. Jackson made Kappa Alpha, and he is a member of the
Lynchburg Rotary Club. All of his time is taken up with his
responsibilities as manager of his company so he has no other
business connections. Mrs. Jackson is a daughter of George R.
Jones, a native of Nashville, and a shoe merchant of that city.
At one time he had a shoe factory in Saint Louis, and it was
while living there that Mrs. Jackson was born. The Jones

family originated in Virginia, and it is claimed that Petersburg, this state, was named in honor of Peter Jones, a pioneer of the region, from whom Mrs. Jackson is directly descended.

HOWELL C. FEATHERSTON. In almost every case those who have reached high position in public confidence and esteem and who are accounted among the most influential in business and professional lines are those whose lives have been devoted without cessation to deep study and close application. It is probable that the law has been the main highway by which more men of merit have advanced to prominence and position in this country than any other road, and it is not unusual to find among the leading citizens of a community a legal practitioner. To respond to the call of the law, to devote every energy in this direction, to broaden and deepen every possible channel of knowledge and to finally enter upon his chosen career and find its rewards worth while—such has been the happy experience of Howell C. Featherston, one of the leading legalists practicing at the bar of Lynchburg. Mr. Featherston has gained honor and prestige in his profession through the application of honesty, energy, perseverance, conscientiousness and self-reliance, and has kept abreast of his calling in its advancement; but it is not alone as a lawyer that he is known to the people of Lynchburg, for he has a recognized standing as one who understands sound investments, and is the owner of large real estate holdings.

Howell C. Featherston was born in Campbell County, April 27, 1871, a son of John C. and Letitia Preston (Floyd) Featherston, he born in Limestone County, Alabama, and she in Campbell County, Virginia, and both are now deceased. The father was a farmer for many years, and for a long period he served as chief of the business bureau of the State Grange. Active in politics, he was sent to represent Campbell County in the Virginia General Assembly, and he held minor local offices as well. Two children were born to him and his wife, namely: N. F. Featherston, who is connected with the United States Treasury Department, Washington City and Mr. Featherston of this review. Both of the parents were active workers, he as a Methodist and she as an Episcopalian. In fraternal affairs he was a Mason and was advanced to the Chapter in his order. During the war between the states he served as a first lieutenant and later as captain, remaining in the service until peace was declared, although he was shot through the body in the battle of Gettysburg. After the close of the war he wrote a description of the battle of the "Crater" at Petersburg which Senator Daniel declared was the best ever written. Captain Featherston delivered it before a meeting of the Grand Camp of Confederate Veterans at Petersburg, and later delivered it before a meeting of the Pottsville Camp of the Grand Army of the Republic at the organization's annual meeting in Pennsylvania, and among his audience were veterans who had blown up the crater July 31, 1864, leaving a hole 170 feet long, sixty feet wide and thirty feet deep, into which the Union forces poured before they could be stopped, and were engulfed and smothered. It was generally conceded by both sides as being the most horrible of any of the engagements of the war. A fine portrait of Captain Featherston hangs in the Confederate Battle Abbey at Richmond, Virginia. The paternal grandfather of Attorney Featherston was Maj. Howell C. Featherston, a native of South Carolina, who moved to Alabama, and there became an extensive cotton planter. The maternal grandfather was Nathaniel Wilson Floyd, born in Kentucky, but a resident of Virginia for the greater part of his life, and a very large cotton planter, not only of Virginia but of Texas as well. His brother, Charles Floyd, was a sergeant on the Lewis and Clark Expedition into what became the Northwest Territory.

Howell C. Featherston of this review first attended the schools of Lynchburg, New London Academy, and finally the University of Virginia, and was graduated from the latter in 1893, with the degree Bachelor of Laws. Immediately thereafter he began the practice of his profession in Lynchburg, and here he has since remained, having built up a very large and valuable connection, and handling a general line of cases. Like his father he is deeply interested in politics, and served in the Lower House in 1908, and in the Senate in 1912, and he is accepted as one of the leaders of the Democratic party in his part of the state.

In 1909 Mr. Featherston married Miss Virginia Carroll Kelly, who was born in Frankfort, Kentucky, a daughter of Rev. Gilby C. Kelly, a minister of the Methodist Episcopal Church, South. Mrs. Featherston was educated in Louisville, Kentucky, Nashville, Tennessee, and Birmingham, Alabama, and in Randolph-Macon College. Reverend Kelly is now retired and is residing in Norfolk, Virginia, after a long and useful ministerial career. Mr. and Mrs. Featherston have one child, Virginia Kelly Featherston, who is attending school. Both Mr. Featherston and his wife are Methodists, and he is a steward of the Court Street Methodist Episcopal Church, South. Fraternally he is a Mason; and he belongs to the Piedmont Country Club, the Campbell County Bar Association, the Virginia State Bar Association and the American Bar Association. Mr. Featherston is a man who has ever lived up to high ideals in his profession, and is now reaping the rewards of his years of faithful service. Standing high among his associates, he earnestly strives to prove worthy of his responsibilities, and the success which attends him proves that his skill is unquestioned and the confidence he inspires well merited. Broad in his sympathies, he has always given liberally to aid worthy charities, and his support can be depended upon in the furtherance of measures he believes will work for the advancement of the majority.

MARTIN L. BROWN. Printing, the art of producing impressions from characters or figures on paper or any other substance, is of comparatively modern origin, only about four and a quarter centuries having passed since the first book was issued from the press, yet there is to be found proof that the principles on which it was ultimately developed existed among the ancient Assyrian nations. Printing from movable types was practiced in China as early as the twelfth or thirteenth century, as there are Korean books printed from movable clay or wooden types in 1317. The great discovery was that of forming every letter or character of the alphabet separately, and the credit of inventing this simple yet marvelous art is contested by the Dutch and Germans. Among the men of Virginia who have made the art of printing their life work, and who have won success and position in this line of endeavor, one of the best known is Martin L. Brown, who in 1909 founded at Lynchburg the present firm of Brown-Morrison Company, printers and engravers.

Mr. Brown was born on a farm in Amherst County, Virginia, August 13, 1877, and is a son of Martin L. and Flora

(Higginbotham) Brown, natives of Amherst County, both of whom are now deceased. Mr. Brown traces his ancestry on the paternal side directly to another Martin L. Brown, who was a soldier of the Continental forces during the winning of American independence. The paternal grandfather of Mr. Brown was Joseph M. Brown, a pioneer of Amherst County, who passed his life there in agricultural pursuits. Martin L. Brown, the elder, father of Martin L. of this review, grew up in a tobacco country and as a young man engaged in business as a tobacconist, which vocation he followed for some years. During the war between the states he enlisted in the Confederate army, with which he served until the close of the struggle. During his service he contracted consumption, but managed to keep the dreaded disease at bay for many years. On leaving Amherst County he took up his residence at Lynchburg, where he engaged in the grocery business, and this home continued to be his place of residence until his death in 1893. He and his wife were the parents of ten children, of whom seven are living: James R., a traveling salesman of Benefield, West Virginia; William T., a woodworker of Washington, D. C.; Martin L., of this review; Mrs. J. W. Coleman, of Lynchburg; Miss Lottie K., secretary to the pastor of the First Baptist Church of Lynchburg; Walter W., who is engaged in business with his brother, Martin L.; and Mrs. James T. Spracher, the wife of a department store proprietor of Bluefield, Virginia. The parents of the foregoing children were honorable God-fearing people and active members of the Baptist Church. He was a Mason fraternally and a Democrat in his political views, and for some years served in the capacity of justice of the peace. The maternal grandfather of Martin L. Brown was James A. Higginbotham, a pioneer farmer and sheriff of Amherst County, where he, his father and his grandfather all were born. This was one of the old and honored families of the Old Dominion, and its members were highly respected and esteemed people of high character.

Martin L. Brown received only a public school education, following which he applied himself, when only a youth, to the mastery of the printer's art, in which he has been engaged throughout a long, active, varied and ultimately successful career. For an extended period he was employed by others in various places, and for three years he was the manager of a printing business at Canton, China, but eventually returned to the city of his youth and in 1909 founded the present business of Brown-Morrison Company, which has been developed into one of the best in the state. The large, modern plant, located at 718 Main Street, in the heart of the business district, is equipped with the latest improved machinery of every character, so that the company is capable of turning out all kinds of work in printing, engraving and lithographing. Approximately fifty-five skilled printers are given employment in the various departments of this concern, in the operation of which the skilled, guiding hand of Mr. Brown can everywhere be seen. He bears an excellent reputation in business circles as a man of integrity and a master of his trade, and also has the respect, esteem and loyalty of his employes. While he is a very busy man with extensive interests, Mr. Brown has been active in civic and other affairs. He is a member of the College Hill Baptist Church, in which he has held numerous offices, and has been a member of the Board of Directors of the local Young

Men's Christian Association. He is a Scottish Rite Mason and divan of the Mystic Shrine, and also belongs to the Benevolent and Protective Order of Elks.

On May 24, 1900, Mr. Brown married Miss Annie Yoder, who was born at Lynchburg, a daughter of Jacob E. Yoder, who came to Lynchburg with the Freedman's Bureau following the close of the war between the states. Her father married Anna Frances Whittaker, who came to Lynchburg with the North Baptist Missionary Society, and was a descendant of Roger Williams, the founder of the State of Rhode Island, and nobly distinguished as the first asserter in modern Christendom of the sanctity and perfect freedom of conscience. To Mr. and Mrs. Brown there were born five children: Wayland Y., of Hopewell, Virginia, who is identified with the silk company there and is the father of one daughter, Corinne Wayland, born in 1923; Calvin C., who is superintendent of his father's printing plant and a young man of much ability; Mary E., a student at Randolph-Macon Woman's College; Martin L., who is attending high school at Lynchburg; and Annie Yoder, a pupil in the public school.

WILLIAM D. MOUNT, M. E. One of the outstanding figures of Lynchburg, William D. Mount, with offices in the Peoples Bank Building, has steadily advanced in his profession of engineering until today he is one of the leading consulting engineers of Virginia, and a man who has been connected with some of the most important construction operations not only of private corporations, but of the Government. He was born at Groton, Tompkins County, New York, July 13, 1867, a son of William and Lucretia (Giles) Mount, both of whom were natives of New York State, and are now deceased. He was a carpenter by trade, but became a school teacher and served as local magistrate. Two children were born to him and his wife, Mr. Mount of this review and his younger brother, Joseph Mount, of Tonawanda, New York, where he is superintendent of a pulp mill. The father belonged to the Congregational Church. In politics a Prohibitionist and Republican, he lived up to his convictions, and being a well educated man, could always give cogent reasons for his actions. During the war between the states he served as captain of Company F, One Hundred and Ninth New York Volunteer Infantry. His father, William D. Mount, was born in New Jersey, but moved to New York at the time of his marriage, settled in a wilderness, and became a tanner, and later was made a magistrate. The maternal grandfather was James Giles, a native of New York, who pioneered into its sparsely settled regions and became a very successful farmer. He was a contemporary and personal friend of Ezra Cornell, whose donations of $750,000 made possible the founding of Cornell University at Ithaca, New York, named in his honor.

William D. Mount attended public schools and Sibley College, Cornell University, and was graduated from the latter with the degree of Mechanical Engineer in 1890. From 1890 to 1894 he was a member of the faculty of Brown University, for three years being an instructor in physics and for one year, assistant professor of mechanical engineering.

In July, 1894, Mr. Mount began work as an electrical engineer for the Mathieson Alkali Works, Saltville, Virginia. During 1895 and 1896 he was in charge of the development work of the Castner Process for electrolytic production of caustic soda and bleaching powder, which work afterward developed into the Castner Electrolytic Alkali Company, Niagara Falls, New York. In August, 1898, he was made general superintendent of the Mathieson Company, in entire charge of all operations as well as all engineering work. Later he was made general manager and a director of the company, which positions were held until November, 1918, since which date he has been in business for himself as consulting mechanical and electrical engineer, giving special attention to development of continuous gas fired vertical lime kilns, continuous causticizing and lime recovery; filtration problems and chemical plant design. During the period of his connection with the Mathieson Company very extensive changes and improvements in the plant and processes were planned and carried through under his supervision. He also had charge of the commercialization of the Bucher Process for the fixation of nitrogen, which process was taken over by the Government, and he served in a consulting capacity during the construction of Government Chemical Plant Number 4.

Since 1897 Mr. Mount has been a full member of the American Society of Mechanical Engineers, and he is also a member of the American Chemical Society and an honorary member of the Alpha Chapter of Sigma Xi. In addition he is a member of the American Institute of Chemical Engineers and the Technical Association of the Pulp & Paper Industry.

The following is a list of foreign patents which have been issued in the name of William D. Mount: *Canadian Patents*—Methods and Apparatus for Handling Foaming and Frothing Liquids, Pat. No. 246859, February 17, 1925; Causticizing Units, Pat. No. 249783, May 19, 1925; Continuous Filters, Pat. No. 257166, January 12, 1926. *French Patents*—Improvement in Kilns, Pat. No. 602729, dated August 28, 1925; Continuous Filters, Pat. No. 610898, dated August 28, 1925; Causticizing Unit, Pat. No. 608190, dated September 15, 1925; Process and Apparatus for Wood Pulp Production, Pat. No. 607726, dated October 15, 1925. *Norway Patents*—Causticizing Unit, Pat. No. 43059, dated September 2, 1925; Continuous Filters, Pat. No. 43784, September 11, 1925. *Sweden Patents*—Causticizing Units, Pat. No. 62972, dated August 22, 1925. *Belgian Patents* —Continuous Filters, Pat. No. 328924, dated August 29, 1925; Causticizing Units, Pat. No. 328686, dated August 29, 1925; Kilns, Pat. No. 328652, dated August 29, 1925; Process and Apparatus for Wood Pulp Production, Pat. No. 329414, dated October 17, 1925. *Finland Patents*—Causticizing Units, Pat. No. 11287, dated September 2, 1926; Continuous Filters, Pat. No. 11454, dated September 7, 1925; Method and Apparatus for Handling Foaming and Frothing Liquids, Pat. No. 11526, dated September 3, 1925; Process and Apparatus for Wood Pulp Production, Pat. No. 11527, dated November 3, 1925. *English Patents*—Continuous Filters, Pat. No. 265679, dated August 12, 1925; Causticizing Units, Pat. No. 265669, dated August 12, 1925; Kilns, Pat. No. 265654, dated August 12, 1926; Process and Apparatus for Wood Pulp Production, Pat. No. 269256, dated August 12, 1925. United States—Flakers, No. 1340732, Patented May 18, 1920; Filters, No. 1348036, Patented July 27, 1920; Power-Transmission Devices, No. 1392348, Patented October 4, 1921; Storage Devices, No. 1526171, Patented February 10, 1925; Filters (Washers), No. 1558038, Patented October 20, 1925; Methods and Apparatus for Handling Foaming and Frothing Liquids, No. 1560286, November 3, 1925.

PHILIP W. PAYNE. Those who daily see the thousands of automobiles which crowd every street and highway, passing and repassing in countless numbers, find it hard to reconcile themselves to the fact that in point of years this is still really an infant industry, the extent of whose growth in the future cannot be even approximated. Yet the fact remains that the automobile still is to be considered as only in its first growth of maturity. In 1902, which is but a quarter of a century ago, one of the most authentic encyclopedias gave the following somewhat quaint description: "Automobiles, a term under which are comprised horseless carriages, motor vans, motor omnibus, and all other motor traction vehicles adapted for use on ordinary roads unprovided with rails." The same work is authority for the fact that in the summer of 1898 there were not thirty automobiles in use in the United States, but by August, 1899, at least eighty companies had been organized for the manufacture of motor cars. By 1926, according to the number of cars registered, there were 19,237,171 passenger cars and 2,784,222 trucks in use in this country.

One of the men who had the vision to note the great opportunities which the future held out in this business was Philip W. Payne, who first became identified with the industry in 1910, and since 1919 has been the head of the Phil Payne Motor Company of Lynchburg, dealers in Nash and Marmon automobiles. Mr. Payne was born at Lynchburg, October 27, 1889, and is a son of Elias and Belle Stuart (Walker) Payne. His paternal grandfather, Philip W. Payne, was born in Campbell County, Virginia, and at the outbreak of the war between the states enlisted in the Confederate army, with which he served until the close of hostilities. He then located at Lynchburg, where for many years he was engaged in the dry goods business, and where he was known as a substantial business man of high character and personal probity.

Elias Payne was born at Lynchburg, where he secured a public school education, and was in the coal, lumber, wood and general supplies business in association with the firm of Adams & Brothers & Company, being with that concern at the time of his death in 1916. He was an active member of the Westminster Presbyterian Church, was affiliated with the Masonic Order, and his political convictions made him a Democrat. He married Miss Belle Stuart Walker, who was born at Richmond, and died in 1919 at Lynchburg, and they became the parents of thirteen children, of whom three survive: Isabelle, the wife of J. R. Wheeler, a druggist of Lynchburg; H. A., who is connected with the Southern Railway at Lynchburg; and Philip W., of this review. The maternal grandfather of Philip W. Payne was Lindsey Walker, a native of Richmond, who was a noted civil engineer of his day and assisted in the building of the Chesapeake & Ohio Railroad from Richmond to Lynchburg.

The public schools of Lynchburg furnished Philip W. Payne with his educational training, and following his high school training he secured a position as clerk and bookkeeper in a retail shoe store. From this position he advanced to that of bookkeeper for an insurance company, but in 1910 resigned his position to enter the employ of the Apperson-Lee Motor Company. Mr. Payne knew immediately that he had found the business for which he was best equipped, and set about learning its every detail. In the meantime he conserved his financial resources, and in 1919 found himself in a position to establish

an automobile agency under the style of the Payne and Dillon
Company, at first handling the Chandler car. Later he took
over the Nash and Marmon agencies, for which he is the authorized agent in six counties surrounding Lynchburg. He has
built up a large and successful enterprise and maintains a commodious and modern salesroom and service and filling station at
815 Fifth Street, where he also handles all kinds of automobile parts and accessories. The firm is now known as the Phil
Payne Motor Company.

Mr. Payne is unmarried. He is a Scottish Rite Mason and
Shriner, and belongs to the Benevolent and Protective Order of
Elks, the United Commercial Travelers and the Travelers Protective Association. As a citizen he has always been public
spirited and a supporter of the causes of education, religion and
higher morality.

EDGAR PATTON MILLER, president of the First National Bank
of Lynchburg, was born in that city December 12, 1861, son of
John M. and Mary E. (Norvell) Miller. His great-grandfather
was a teacher at Richmond, and the grandfather, Samuel T.
Miller, who was born at Richmond November 22, 1789, gave
practically his entire life to educational work, and for many
years conducted a noted boys school at Cedar Forest on the
Staunton River. He died at Lynchburg March 30, 1870. By
his marriage to Frances Fitzpatrick he was the father of eight
sons and six daughters, all of whom were educated and in one
way or another continued the educational tradition and interest
of the family.

John M. Miller, one of the sons, was born October 5, 1827,
left school at the age of sixteen to take up a commercial career,
soon located at Lynchburg, and was teller and subsequently
cashier of the Exchange Bank of Virginia before and during the
Civil war. When the First National Bank of Lynchburg was
organized in 1865 he was offered but declined the office of cashier.
Subsequently he became associated with James Franklin in the
private banking firm of Miller & Franklin, and was active in this
banking house until his death on January 25, 1881: After his
death the interests of the firm were taken over by the newly
organized National Exchange Bank, which subsequently became
the Lynchburg National Bank.

John M. Miller was for many years a prominent official in
St. Paul's Episcopal Church of Lynchburg. His wife, Mary E.
Norvell, was a daughter of Lorenzo and Lucy (Harrison) Norvell, and her maternal grandfather located at Lynchburg about
1785 and was a member of the first town council when Lynchburg was incorporated in 1805.

Edgar Patton Miller was educated in private schools, in
Doctor Abbott's Bellevue School in Bedford County, and in 1878
became a junior clerk in the banking firm of Miller and Franklin.
After his father's death he continued with the National Exchange Bank as junior clerk, and later was made teller. In
September, 1890, he became the first cashier of the Lynchburg
Trust & Savings Bank, and in June, 1895, became cashier of the
First National Bank of Lynchburg, an institution with which he
has been identified for over thirty years. Mr. Miller has been
continuously in the banking business at Lynchburg for just half
a century. He has been president of the First National Bank
since December 2, 1909. He is a former president of the Virginia
State Bankers Association, and was one of the organizers of

the Cooperative Building and Loan Association and one of the founders of the Lynchburg Chamber of Commerce. He attends the Episcopal Church and has served as a trustee of the Lynchburg Orphan Asylum, and has also been on the City Council.

He married, October 15, 1903, Eleanor Selden Lucke. They had three daughters: Eleanor Selden and Lucy Harrison, and Norvell Harrison, who died at the age of two years.

JAMES W. WALTERS, a specialist in eye, ear, nose and throat, is a native of Virginia and since establishing himself at Lynchburg has gained a reputation that has extended all over Central Virginia as a man of acknowledged skill and resourcefulness.

Doctor Walters was born in Madison County, Virginia, in 1880, son of John P. and Anna J. (Walker) Walters, and a grandson of Isaac H. Walters and Col. James W. Walker, all residents of Madison County. His maternal grandfather was a colonel of militia before the Civil war. Isaac H. Walters spent his life as a farmer. John P. Walters, who died in 1895, was educated in the University of Virginia, was a civil engineer by profession, but devoted most of his active years to farming in Madison County. His widow died June 19, 1928, at Orange. Both were active members of the Methodist Episcopal Church, South, and John P. Walters was a Confederate soldier. There were four children and the three now living are Dr. James W., Annie E., wife of E. B. Grimes, of Orange, and Charles, a resident of Orange, who is interested in the lumber business at Charlottesville.

Dr. James W. Walters was educated in the public schools of Madison County, in the Woodbury Forest School, Randolph-Macon College at Ashland, and in 1901 entered the Medical College of Virginia at Richmond, graduating in 1905. He was a member of the Pi Mu medical fraternity at Richmond. Doctor Walters distinguished himself for his scholarship and all round ability, and after taking his medical degree he spent eighteen months as an interne in the Memorial Hospital at Richmond, and for three years was on the adjunct teaching staff of Cornell University of New York, and was resident physician at the New York Eye and Ear Infirmary in New York City. With this exceptional training and experience he located at Lynchburg in 1911, and has since limited his work to eye, ear, nose and throat. He is a member of the Lynchburg and Campbell County and South Piedmont Medical Societies, the Medical Society of Virginia, and the American Medical Association. Doctor Walters is a Methodist, a Scottish Rite Mason and Shriner, and member of the Kiwanis Club. He was a captain in the Medical Corps during the World war.

He married, in 1914, Miss Kate E. Edmunds, of Lynchburg, who was educated in Randolph-Macon Woman's College. He is a member of the Episcopal Church. They have one daughter, Harriett Prescott Walters, born in 1919.

BENJAMIN ALLEN RUFFIN was born in Richmond, Virginia, May 9, 1879. He is a son of George Edwin and Ada Cora (Harden) Ruffin and a grandson of George Edmund Ruffin, a relative of Judge Thomas Ruffin of North Carolina.

Mr. Ruffin was educated in the public schools of Chesterfield County, Virginia, the Chester Academy and Randolph-Macon College. His business career begun in Richmond as an insurance agent. After twenty-five years in business in Richmond and New York City Mr. Ruffin is today president and principal owner of B. A. Ruffin & Company, general insurance agents, is a partner of Charles M. Robinson, architects, and vice president of W. C. Hill Printing Company.

From 1914 to 1918 Mr. Ruffin served on the Insurance Committee of the American Bankers Association and is the author of various copyright insurance policies and bonds adopted and used by member banks of the association. He is a past grand chancellor of the order of Knights of Pythias and at this writing is president of Lions International.

He is also lecturer for the Greater Men's Bible Class of Monument M. E. Church at Richmond. In these various activities he is widely known as a speaker and author.

CHARLES S. ADAMS, president of the Adams Brothers-Paynes Company of Lynchburg, is with the lumber organization of which his father was one of the founders, and has had a very successful experience of nearly thirty years in the lumber business in Virginia.

Mr. Adams was born at Lynchburg, Virginia, November 28, 1873, son of Richard H. T. and Susan (Scott) Adams. His grandfather, Isaac Adams, was a farm owner in Appomattox County, Virginia. The maternal grandfather, Charles Scott, was a railroad contractor of Lynchburg and also owned a large farm in Bedford County. Richard H. T. Adams grew up on a farm, and as a young man was in the grocery business at Richmond until the war broke out. He then joined the Home Guard at Lynchburg and served throughout the war under the command of Gen. A. P. Hill. He rose to the rank of captain. After the war he removed to Lynchburg, where he joined an older brother, I. H. Adams, who had started a coal, lumber and building supply business. Still another brother, W. D. Adams, came into the partnership and finally J. G. Payne entered the business. In 1898 the Adams Brothers-Paynes Company was incorporated, and that name has been retained for thirty years. It is one of the oldest incorporated lumber firms in Southwest Virginia. The original officers of the corporation were: I. H. Adams, president; C. I. Johnson, vice president; J. G. Payne, secretary and treasurer. The officers of the company today are: Charles S. Adams, president; J. C. Dabney, vice president; J. G. Payne, secretary and treasurer. Richard H. T. Adams continued active in this organization until his death in 1901, but for some years had also given much of his attention to the export tobacco trade. His widow is still living in Lynchburg. Both were active members of the Court Street Methodist Episcopal Church and Richard H. T. Adams was a Mason and a Democrat in politics. There were nine children, eight of whom are living: Mrs. H. H. Harris; R. H. T. Adams, Junior, a Lynchburg attorney; Charles S.; Jack Adams, connected with the George W. Helme Snuff Company; James D. Adams, secretary-treasurer of Harris Woodson Company; Susan Scott Adams, who lives with her mother; Mrs. D. D. Hull, of Roanoke; and H. C. Adams, proprietor of the White Star Laundry.

Charles S. Adams attended school at Lynchburg and was a boy of seventeen when he first became an employe of the Adams Brothers-Paynes Company in 1890. However, in 1896 he left the firm to become associated with his father in the tobacco business. In 1903 he returned to the lumber business and for a quarter of a century has had a prominent part in its growth and development as one of the largest wholesale lumber and building supply firms of the state. Mr. Adams is also a director in the Peoples National Bank of Lynchburg.

He married, in 1905, Miss Lottie Griffin, who was born in Bedford County and was educated in the Girls' Seminary at Bedford. Her father, Samuel Griffin, was a lawyer at Bedford and Roanoke. Mr. and Mrs. Adams have three children. Charlotte Russell is a graduate of the Cathedral School for girls at Washington. Nancy Scott Adams is a student in the Gardner School at New York. Charles S. Adams, Junior, was born in 1914 and is attending the Lynchburg High School. The family are members of the Saint Johns Episcopal Church. Mr. Adams is a York Rite Mason and Shriner, member of the B. P. O. Elks, the Piedmont Club, the Oak Wood Country Club and is a charter member of the Rotary Club.

ROBERT S. BURRUSS. The successful man in any line is the one who first determines his natural abilities and the occupation in which they will have free play, and then operates so as to provide something for which there is a demand, or goes about creating such a demand. In spite of all of the inventions of substitutes, and the discoveries of other substances to take the place, lumber remains the basic need for countless industries, and its production is of vast importance, especially in those sections adjacent to the timberlands. Virginia still has large stores of timber upon which, even in strict compliance with conservation laws and principles, its operators in the industry may still draw, and so has its sister state of North Carolina, and one of the men who is doing a very large business in manufacturing lumber and wholesaling it is Robert S. Burruss, of Lynchburg, one of the city's substantial business men.

Robert S. Burruss was born in Campbell County, Virginia, August 6, 1884, a son of James M. and Ida F. Pringle Burruss, the latter of whom, a native of Halifax County, Virginia, is still living on the home farm, but the former, born in Campbell County, died in September, 1904. He was a farmer and lumberman. The parents had six children, two of whom survive, Mr. Burruss of this review, and W. H. Burruss, the two being in partnership in their lumber business. W. H. Burruss was also born in Campbell County. He married Miss Helen Currell, and they have three children: Sarah, Helen and William H., Junior. The parents belonged from youth up to the Methodist Episcopal Church, South, in which he was a leader, and she continues to be active in it. He was a Mason and a Democrat, and zealous in behalf of fraternity and party. His father was Thomas Burruss, a native of Virginia, and with five brothers served in the Confederate army. The paternal great-grandfather was an Englishman who settled in Virginia at an early day. The maternal grandfather, Richard Pringle, was a native of Halifax County, Virginia, and a physician, and he, too, was a veteran of the Confederate army.

Robert S. Burruss attended public school until he was sixteen years old, at which time he began working in his father's lumber business, remaining with him until his death. In 1905 he and his brother came to Lynchburg and established themselves in the lumber business here, and have built up very wide connections, having mills in Virginia and North Carolina, and selling their product at wholesale. Theirs is one of the largest concerns of its kind in this part of the state.

In 1913 Mr. Burruss married Miss Ada Moorman, who was born in Campbell County, Virginia, and here educated. Mr. and Mrs. Burruss have one child, Robert S., Junior, a schoolboy. Mrs. Burruss belongs to the Methodist Episcopal Church, South. As a York Rite and Shriner Mason, an Odd Fellow and Elk, and as a member of the Hoo Hoos, Mr. Burruss lives up to high ideals, and he has served the last named order as vice president since moving to Lynchburg. It is his honest belief that what he has accomplished any industrious young man can do, especially when so many advantages are now offered that never came his way. He is never satisfied to rest upon what he has done, but is ever working for something just beyond, and as he has great ability he never fails to grasp firmly what he undertakes. Having worked his way up from the bottom of his business, he knows what to expect of his men, how to make due allowance for them, and is greatly respected by them and by his whole community, in his neighborhood and in his fraternities.

JAMES MORRISON, M. D. Medical science has so progressed that advances are made in it almost hourly. Specializing observations on disease have worked marvelous changes in methods of treatment; tireless theoretic experiments have proven the truth of contentions, and only after results have been demonstrated beyond any reasonable doubt are discoveries given to the public. In the work of the past quarter of the century are to be noticed such practical advances as the development of bacteriology, the partially successful effort to wipe out tuberculosis, bubonic plague, cholera, diphtheria, typhoid, spinal meningitis and similar maladies. This marvelous progress has not come naturally, but is the outcome of the tireless, aggressive and self-sacrificing work of the men who have devoted themselves to the profession of medicine. One of the men whose name is connected with some excellent work in his large practice at Lynchburg is Dr. James Morrison, a physician who has risen through his own efforts to a high position. Having the misfortune to lose his parents while still small, he was early thrown upon his own resources, and must be regarded as self-made in the highest conception of the term.

Doctor Morrison was born in Lexington, Rockbridge County, Virginia, November 2, 1871, a son of Dr. Robert Hall and Margaret (White) Morrison, the former of whom was born in Rockbridge County and the latter in Lexington. The father was a physician, educated in the University of Virginia and Jefferson Medical College, and when he had received his degree he engaged in the practice of his profession in Lexington. With the outbreak of war between the states he offered his services to the Confederacy, and served under Gen. Fitzhugh Lee. He and his wife had three children born to them, but Doctor Morrison is the only survivor. Both were active members of the Presbyterian Church and very fine people, and their son inherits many of their admirable characteristics.

From childhood he resolved upon a medical career, Doctor Morrison struggled to secure the necessary education, first along academic lines, and later in medicine, studying the latter in the medical department of the University of Virginia, from which he was graduated in 1898, with the degree of Doctor of Medicine. Later he took work in the New York Polyclinic, and had an interneship in New York City. After several years devoted to a country practice he did post-graduate work in diseases of the eye, ear, nose and throat, and in 1901 came to Lynchburg, where he has since been specializing in this branch of the domain of medicine.

In 1901 Doctor Morrison married Miss Elizabeth McCulloch, a daughter of Fred McCulloch, he born in Fort Wayne, Indiana, a son of Hugh McCulloch, who served in the cabinet under President Lincoln. Doctor and Mrs. Morrison have had two children born to them: Fred McCulloch, who is studying medicine in the University of Virginia, and a prominent member of Phi Kappa Psi, and Margaret Carolyn. Robert Dabney is an adopted son, is also attending the University of Virginia. Mrs. Morrison is an Episcopalian, and he is a Presbyterian. His fraternal affiliations are with the Masonic Order and the Elks. He belongs to the Oakwood Country Club, the Campbell County Medical Society, the Virginia State Medical Society, the Southern Medical Association, the American Medical Association, the State Eye, Ear, Nose and Throat Association, and he is a Fellow of the American College of Surgeons. His entire time is devoted to his practice so that he has no business connections, but he is interested in the progress and continued prosperity of Lynchburg and its vicinity, and willing to give liberally of his means to forward and maintain these conditions.

RICHARD E. WHITE, of Bedford, is a banker, president of the Citizens National Bank, one of the strongest financial institutions in that section of the state. Its officers and directors include some of the outstanding citizens of Bedford County. The Citizens National Bank has capital and surplus of $200,000, and it is one of the banks whose steady growth has brought its resources above a million dollars. At the close of business in 1927 the resources stood at the figure of over one million six hundred thousand dollars.

Mr. White was born on a farm in Bedford County, March 10, 1870, son of Henry Milton and Louise (Majors) White and grandson of Jacob S. White. The White family for several generations have been identified with farming and planting in Bedford County. His maternal grandfather, Howard Majors, was also a Bedford County farmer. Henry Milton White was reared on a farm and at the age of twenty-two engaged in merchandising at Big Island, and died at the comparatively early age of thirty-one. His widow, who was educated at Hollins College, died in 1897, having married a Mr. Smith. By the first marriage there were two children, Richard E. and Samuel, the latter of whom died at the age of eight years. The three children from the second marriage were: Robert Fullerton Smith, with the National Stock Yards at Saint Louis; Duncan Smith, an architect at Saint Louis; and Harry Pritchard Smith, also with the National Stock Yards at Saint Louis. Henry Milton White was a member of the Masonic fraternity.

Richard E. White received his early education in country schools and the New London Academy, and had his first business training in a store at Bedford. From there he went with the Lynchburg Trust & Savings Bank, and was with that institution nine years, gaining a thorough knowledge of banking. He started as bookkeeper and was assistant cashier when he left. Returning to Bedford, he was made cashier of the Citizens National Bank in 1914, and has been president of the institution since 1921. He has concentrated his business energies fully on the bank and personally deserves a large amount of credit for its steady growth and prosperity.

Mr. White married, in 1898, Magnolia Pendleton Wright, who was born in Nelson County, Virginia, daughter of William H. Wright, who moved to Bedford County about 1888 and lived the rest of his life on the Colonel Davis farm. Mrs. White was educated at Bedford and in the Belmont Seminary there. They have two children, Marion Louise and Isabelle, the former a student in Hollins College. Mr. and Mrs. White are active members of the Methodist Episcopal Church at Bedford. He has been on the Board of Stewards of the church for twenty-seven years, chairman of the financial committee, and for seventeen years has taught a Bible class of young men. He is affiliated with the Masonic fraternity.

E. CRAIGE PELOUZE, manager of Pelouze Printers Supply Company, is a prominent citizen of Richmond, and a member of a family of famous typefounders, of whom the best known, perhaps, was the late Henry L. Pelouze, father of E. Craige Pelouze, and he was a son of Edward Pelouze, the first of the name to engage in typefounding. Edward Pelouze was born in West Windsor, Connecticut, March 22, 1799, of French parents. His father, who was an officer in the French army, was imprisoned at the time of the French Revolution, but made his escape and came to America.

In 1801 Edward Pelouze was taken by his parents, Dr. Edmond Pelouze and Sarah de'Jean Pelouze, to Charlestown, New Hampshire, where the Pelouze home remains to this day in an excellent state of preservation. In 1794 Doctor Pelouze was employed in a French printing office in Philadelphia as translator. During the interruption of his practice in medicine Edward was reared and educated in Charlestown.

From boyhood he exhibited a taste for mechanics, and in 1818, leaving his old home, went to Boston, Massachusetts, seeking an opportunity to develop that taste. There he entered the only type foundry in the city, that had just been opened by Bedlington & Ewer, and in it he soon proved his ability. One of his associates was Michael Dalton, and these two formed a warm friendship. Mr. Dalton married the sister of Mr. Pelouze. The latter learned typemaking in all of its branches, as was the custom in those days, but became especially skillful in mold-making and matrix fitting. He also learned punch-cutting, and was one of the few cutters at that time.

Not long after he came to Boston Mr. Pelouze married Harriet Maria Thompson, of New York, and he continued to make that city his home until 1829, when he went to New York City and was employed in White's foundry as punch-cutter and matrix fitter, but did not remain there long, for in June, 1830, he embarked in his own business, corner of Fulton and Nassau streets. While there his three sons, Edward, William and Henry, took their first lessons in typefounding, each starting as a breaker boy, and working up through the various branches as they grew older.

In 1849, like so many others, he decided to go to California on the quest for gold, and therefore sold his business, but did not succeed, as he had expected, so returned to New York in 1850 and took a position in the foundry of James Conner, with whom

he continued for about three years, going then to Boston once more, and with John K. Rogers and David Watson purchased the Boston Typefoundry, operating it under the name of John K. Rogers & Company. His health failing, in 1864 he sold his interests in Boston and went to Camden, New Jersey, where he continued to reside at the home of a daughter until his death, June 4, 1876.

The life of Edward Pelouze was too active to allow him to remain idle, and much of his time in his later years was spent with his brother Lewis in Philadelphia, where he continued to assist by his advice and experience in the foundry of the latter. During the many years he was connected with typefounding he made numerous inventions and added largely to the improvements of the tools of his trade. He was the inventor of a type-casting machine which was used for some time, until superseded by the more perfect one of David Bruce, Jr., which was so long in use, and continues as the only practical machine for hand casting. He is also given credit for the invention of the electro-typed matrix, which permitted a rapid duplication of type faces. As a moldmaker he had no superior in his day, and but few equals. While not ranking high as a punch-cutter, he produced several faces which were used extensively. Belonging to a period in typefounding when rapid changes were taking place, he had an opportunity of observing and aiding in the wonderful advances. He was contemporary with Bruce, White, Conner, Hager, Smith and Cortelyou, and shared with them the honors of typefounding.

While Edward Pelouze was making a name for himself in New York City in connection with the typefounding industry, his younger brother, Lewis Pelouze, was gaining a strong foot-hold in Philadelphia. He was born in North Charlestown, New Hampshire, March 25, 1808, and he too learned typefounding, passing through all the different branches and became proficient in all to a degree seldom attained by the workmen of today. For fifteen years he was with Binny & Ronaldson, later the Ronald-son Type Foundry, and then, in 1841, he established himself in business as a typefounder, corner of Third and Chestnut streets, Philadelphia, and there he continued actively in business until his death, March 5, 1876, the original sign bearing the name "Lewis Pelouze" being a landmark to the printing fraternity of that city long after he was no more. He soon built up a lucrative business, having among his life long patrons such news-papers as the *Public Ledger*, the *Philadelphia North American*, the *Baltimore Sun* and the *Washington Evening Star*. His foundry was among the first to introduce typecasting machines, and at one time the Lewis Pelouze Type Foundry gave every indication of becoming one of the leading concerns of the country. Ill health and the preference of the two sons for other pursuits, the elder entering West Point Military Academy, and afterwards achieving success as an officer in the Regular Army, caused his foundry to fall behind in the race, although he continued to retain the good will and patronage of his friends and early customers as long as he lived.

After the death of Louis Pelouze the business descended to relatives, and was conducted under the old name until 1892, when it was sold to the American Type Founders Company, and by them closed out. Thus passed out of existence one of the landmarks of Philadelphia, and a business which had been hon-

orably conducted and enjoyed the patronage and good will of
so many.

Henry L. Pelouze, son of Edward Pelouze and nephew of
Lewis, was born at the time that his father was carrying on the
business of typefounding in New York City and his uncle was
engaged in the same business in Philadelphia, and he grew up
in the business and mastered all of its branches under his
father's supervision. When he was eighteen years old he became
foreman of his uncle's foundry in Philadelphia, then one of the
leading foundries of the country. In 1854 he made a trip to
Chicago, where he was convinced there was an opening for a
typefoundry, and he received so much encouragement from
printers and publishers that he decided to locate there, and
returned to Philadelphia to complete his arrangements. His
wife, Eliza Jane Tuthill, was so opposed to the idea of leaving
her friends and old associations for what was then the "far
West" that he was forced to abandon the project. Soon thereafter he as offered an opportunity to locate in New York City,
and he and S. R. Walker founded the firm of Walker & Pelouze,
and their foundry was located corner of Fulton and Dutch
streets, then in the heart of the printing district. The new firm
secured the business of the *New York Tribune,* and among the
warm personal friends of Mr. Pelouze at that time was Thomas
Rocker, so long foreman of that newspaper, and Robert Bonner,
a compositor on the same paper, and they greatly aided the
new firm.

In 1859, in order to enlarge the business, a branch was
opened in Richmond, Virginia, by Mr. Pelouze, Mr. Walker remaining in charge of the New York business. Before his plans
were completed, however, war was declared, and Mr. Pelouze
was not able to get through the lines until 1862, when, receiving
permission, he returned to New York to learn that because of
the illness of his partner the business had become demoralized,
and a fresh start had to be made. While he was in Richmond
he was imprisoned for some time in Libby Prison as a Northern
sympathizer, but later, through the intercession of the proprietors of the *Richmond Whig* and influence of Gen. Harry
Pelouze, adjutant under General Grant, he was paroled and
engaged in typefounding, as the whole Confederacy was suffering for type. Many were the straits he experienced to get the
raw material. It was impossible to secure antimony and tin,
so the principal ingredients of his type-metal were lead and
what little old type could be secured. One dress of the *Richmond
Dispatch* lasted just six weeks as it was almost entirely of lead.

At the close of the Civil war Mr. Pelouze returned to Richmond and found his machinery in working order. With the
assistance of his cousin, Charles E. Pelouze, and his nephew,
H. L. Hartshorn, he began to rebuild his fortunes under the
style of H. L. Pelouze & Company. In spite of adverse circumstances the firm prospered fairly well and in 1869 the idea was
conceived of starting a branch at Washington to be near the
Governmental printing office, and this was placed under the
charge of the nephew, H. L. Hartshorn. The venture was successful until 1875, when the nephew retired from the firm to go
to Philadephia, and he was succeeded by Frank Pelouze, and the
style was changed to H. L. Pelouze & Son.

The new firm purchased the old Baltimore Type Foundry in
1879, thus establishing a chain that embraced Baltimore, Rich-

mond and Washington, the head of the firm giving the most of his attention to the Richmond house, while Washington and Baltimore branches were managed by the son. The Baltimore branch was sold to Charles J. Cary about 1883, and the firm concentrated on the Richmond and Washington branches. In 1895 Henry L. Pelouze made over his interests to his youngest son, E. Craige Pelouze, who reorganized under the name of the Pelouze Paper and Type Company.

In the meanwhile Mr. Pelouze had become interested in politics, and was nominated for Congress from the Richmond district in the campaign which elected Garfield to the Presidency. The situation in Virginia was very much mixed up, and in the interests of harmony he was induced to withdraw in favor of John S. Wise, the representative of what is known as the Mahone wing. Later he was asked to accept the position of postmaster at Richmond, but again declined in the interest of harmony in his party. Dropping politics, he gave more of his time to social and other duties, and served for two terms as worshipful master of Lodge Francais, A. F. and A. M. He also served Richmond Commandery as its eminent commander, and was a member of the Ancient Arabic Order Nobles of the Mystic Shrine.

It was the ambition of Henry L. Pelouze to see opened at Richmond a successful hotel, and this idea became so absorbing that after he had disposed of his business he purchased the Law Building and began to remodel it for a hotel. This occupied his time and energies until the time of his death. During the winter of 1895-96 he was attacked with Bright's disease, and this malady increased until August 11, 1896, when death relieved his sufferings.

Henry J. Pelouze was a very active man, one of untiring energy, but of a nervous temperament, but, while at times his manner was brusque, those who knew him admired him for his many excellent qualties of mind and heart. He was well known to the old school of typefounders—Dalton, Bruce, James, William Connor, Hager, MacKellar, grandfather of Joseph Hergesheimer, the writer, and in fact all of those engaged in the industry during the last half of the nineteenth century. That he was popular in the city of his adoption is shown by his election and appointment for several years to the City Council of Richmond, where he ever labored for the development and improvement of its material affairs. He also served as director in several state institutions in Virginia, giving his time and talents to their cause. While always an avowed Union man, he was none the less popular with his neighbors, who were almost unanimous in their allegiance to the cause of the Confederacy, and numbered many of them among his most intimate friends.

E. Craige Pelouze attended Claverack College, New York, from which he was graduated in 1887. He had grown up in the typefounding business, as had his father before him, and has always been identified with it. As above stated, in 1895, his father made over the business to him, and he reorganized as the Pelouze Paper and Type Company, continuing to operate it until it was absorbed by the American Typefounders Company, he continuing as manager of the Richmond branch until February, 1928, when he severed his connections to establish the Pelouze Printers Supply Company, in the same building his father started the type founders business in 1859.

Although he has never cared to enter politics, E. Craige
Pelouze has always been active in civic affairs, and he accomplished especially effective work, covering a period of four years,
in bringing about the construction of the Washington-Richmond
Highway, which was completed in June, 1927. Among other
interesting events of his career may be mentioned that he was
the owner and driver of the first automobile in Virginia.

For many years Mr. Pelouze has been prominent in Masonry,
and belongs to Joppa Lodge No. 40, A. F. and A. M.; Washington
Chapter No. 9, R. A. M.; Richmond Commandery No. 2, K. T.;
and Ancient Arabic Order Nobles of the Mystic Shrine. He was
the originator of Samis Grotto of the Mystic Order Veiled
Prophets of the Enchanted Realm in Richmond, and is a past
grand monarch of this order in the United States and Canada.
At the annual convention of the order in Cleveland, Ohio, in
June, 1927, he was instrumental in having Richmond designated
as the place for the annual gathering in 1928.

Mr. Pelouze married Miss Nannie J. Tillyer, of Philadelphia,
Pennsylvania, a descendant of one of the prominent American
families of Colonial and Revolutionary history through inter-
marriage of the Rapaley family, of French origin, and Hogeland
family of Holland, who were among the original settlers of New
Amsterdam, New York City. Mrs. Pelouze is active in the
affairs of the local chapters of both the Daughters of the American Revolution and the Colonial Dames. Mr. and Mrs. Pelouze
have two children: Henry L., who is a graduate of the Virginia
Polytechnic Institute; and Lucile Tillyer Pelouze.

HOWELL A. ROBINSON is a prominent Lynchburg citizen and
business man. He has lived in that locality practically all his
life, started his career without financial resources, and has been
instrumental in giving widespread distribution to one of the
most important of Virginia's agricultural products, the peanut.
Mr. Robinson is head of H. A. Robinson & Company, Incorporated, manufacturers and distributors of peanut products.

He was born at Lynchburg, July 19, 1857, son of James A.
and Mary V. (Love) Robinson, his father a native of Lynchburg, while his mother was born in Bedford County, Virginia.
His grandfather, Howell Robinson, was born in Bedford County,
and when he died in 1855 was the first person buried in the
Spring Hill Cemetery at Lynchburg and was accorded the
honors of a military funeral. The maternal grandfather,
Charles Love, was born at Lynchburg and through his life was
connected with the tobacco business. James A. Robinson was
also a tobacconist. He was in the provost marshal's office during the Civil war. He began voting as a Whig and later became
a Democrat, and both he and his wife were active members of
the Baptist Church. Of their seven children Howell A. is the
only one now living.

Howell A. Robinson had his educational advantages in
Lynchburg and Petersburg, and he came to manhood about the
close of the reconstruction era. On leaving school he clerked
in a tobacco house, and it was in 1895 that he engaged in the
peanut business. The firm of H. A. Robinson & Company, Incorporated, has developed an extensive business in the roasting
of peanuts, the making and packing of peanut butter and other
peanut products. These products are widely distributed under
the brand Robinson Crusoe Salted Peanuts and Glove Kid Peanut Butter. The output is sold chiefly through brokers and job-

bers over twelve states of the Union, and the firm also keeps several traveling representatives on the road.

Mr. Robinson married, in 1883, Miss Nanie Gresham, who was born in Chesterfield County, Virginia, and was reared and educated at Richmond. Her father, Edwin A. Gresham, was born in King and Queen County, was a lumberman, and in his later years lived at Washington and was in the insurance business. Mr. and Mrs. Robinson had a family of four sons and one daughter: James Edward, who was educated at Lynchburg and is now a traveling representative for his father's firm; Mary, wife of S. B. Fishel, of Lynchburg; Charles Eaton, who attended school at Lynchburg and the University of Virginia, is associated with his father's business; William G. and Joseph A., both of whom are in business with their father. The mother of these children died in May, 1925. Mr. Robinson is a member of the First Baptist Church, is a Scottish Rite Mason, a past grand of the Independent Order of Odd Fellows, and for a number of years was treasurer and director of the Odd Fellows Home at Lynchburg.

JESSE L. DAVIDSON, co-publisher of the *Bedford Bulletin,* has been interested in the publishing and printing business since early manhood and has also been an important citizen in the affairs of his home locality.

He was born at Bedford, August 22, 1876, son of Arch V. and Amanda F. (Sublett) Davidson, both natives of Charlotte County, and grandson of Allen Davidson and Benjamin F. Sublett, also of Charlotte County, farmers of that locality. Arch V. Davidson followed the trade of blacksmith at Bedford for a great many years, and died in 1903, at the age of seventy-nine. His widow is now ninety-one years of age, living at Bedford. Both were active members of the Baptist Church and Arch Davidson was a Confederate soldier in the Civil war. Of his seven children four are living.

Jesse L. Davidson, who has never married, was educated in public schools and as a boy learned the printing trade. That trade has given him his chief occupation and his main business for over thirty years, and he has made the *Bulletin* a very strong and influential newspaper. Mr. Davidson served some time as president of the Rotary Club, is active in Democratic politics and is supervisor of game wardens in the Lynchburg District. He holds stock in several banks and has employed his personal influences as well as the power of his newspaper to promote better schools and other organizations connected with community welfare.

DICE ROBINS ANDERSON since April, 1920, has been president of Randolph-Macon Woman's College at Lynchburg. As an institution for the higher education of young women Randolph-Macon has had a splendid history, and fortunately its modern equipment, facilities and personnel enable it to take advantage of its traditions. According to the exacting standards of present day classification it ranks as one of the leading colleges for women in the United States.

Dice Robins Anderson is a native Virginian, born at Charlottesville April 18, 1880, son of Rev. James Madison and Margaret Olivia (Robins) Anderson. His father was born in Amelia County, Virginia, in 1837, received part of his education in Randolph-Macon College, then located at Boydton, Virginia, was ordained in the Methodist ministry at the age of nineteen, and labored in the Virginia Conference until his death in 1906. He was chaplain of a Virginia regiment during the Civil war. Among other pastorates he was located at Norfolk in the Cumberland Street Church, at Hertford, North Carolina, Blackstone, Virginia, and for four years each was presiding elder of the Danville and Charlottesville districts. His second wife, Margaret Olivia Robins, was born in Accomac County in 1842, of a family that has lived on the eastern shore of Virginia for many generations. They had two sons, Dice R. and Joseph E., the latter a Methodist minister and business man.

Dice Robins Anderson was educated in the Hoge Military Academy, subsequently known as the Blackstone Military Academy, took his A. B. degree at Randolph-Macon College for Men, at Ashland, in 1900, his Master of Arts degree there in 1901, and the Doctor of Philosophy degree at the University of Chicago in 1912. William and Mary College in 1924 bestowed upon him the Doctor of Laws degree. His early service as an educator was spent with a number of institutions. He was professor of mathematics at the Central Female College of Lexington, Missouri, in 1901-02, instructor in history at Randolph-Macon Academy at Bedford City, Virginia, in 1902-03, principal of the Chesapeake Academy at Irvington, Virginia, from 1903 to 1906, and president of the Willie Halsell College at Vinita, Oklahoma, in 1906-07. During 1907-08 he was fellow in history at the University of Chicago, and instructor in history there in 1908-09.

Doctor Anderson in 1909 took the chair of history and political science at Richmond College, and for ten years was a resident of the capital city. During 1919-20 he was professor of economics and political science, and director of the School of Business Administration. From 1915 to 1920, in addition to his work at the college, he was executive secretary of the Richmond Civic Association. In December, 1919, he was elected president of Randolph-Macon Woman's College and took up his administrative duties there in April of the following year. He was a lecturer at the Richmond School of Social Economy in 1917, at the Virginia Mechanics Institute in 1919, was president of the Department of Colleges of the Virginia Educational Conference in 1922-23, president of the Virginia Association of Colleges in 1923, was editor of the Richmond College Historical Papers for 1915, 1916 and 1917, and has prepared and delivered and also published many articles on historical and political subjects. He is author of *William Branch Giles: A Study in the Politics of Virginia and the Nation, 1790-1815*, published in 1914, and Edmund Randolph, second Secretary of State, is in the Secretaries of State Series.

Doctor Anderson is a Phi Beta Kappa, also a Tau Kappa Alpha and Phi Kappa Sigma, member of the American Historical Association, and has been a member of the Virginia Annual Conference of the Methodist Episcopal Church, South, for a number of sessions. He was a member of the General Conference of the church at Hot Springs, Arkansas, and was recently elected Lay Leader for the Virginia Conference of the Methodist Church, South. He is a Democrat.

Doctor Anderson married, June 24, 1903, Miss Ada James Ash, who was born at Somerset, Perry County, Ohio, daughter of James Ash. She graduated from high school at Kansas City, Missouri, also attended Vassar College, and is a graduate in

Jefferson Hughes M.D.

music from Oberlin College, continuing her musical studies in Saint Louis and Chicago. Mr. and Mrs. Anderson have two children, Dice R., Jr., and William Dodd. The older son graduated from Randolph-Macon College at Ashland in 1925.

THOMAS JEFFERSON HUGHES, M. D. Success in life along any path of endeavor demands honesty, energy, proper preparation, conscientiousness and self-reliance. Genius may also be present, but for permanency, practical qualities and the homely virtues are necessary. To the undoubted possession of these may we, in part, attribute the success that has crowned the efforts of Dr. Thomas Jefferson Hughes, who has figured prominently in the medical profession of Roanoke for a number of years, and has maintained throughout his entire career a high standard of professional ethics and scientific principles.

Doctor Hughes was born in Smyth County, Virginia, November 27, 1876. He was the second son of William Hector Hughes, who was the fifth son of Jesse Hughes. Jesse Hughes was in the fourth generation of descent from Robert Hughes, who immigrated to Virginia from Toffe, near Cardiff in Wales, England, and who was a direct descendant of the King of Gwent, Prince of Cardigan. The Hughes family belonged to the Welsh nobility and had their coat-of-arms and motto. Robert Hughes on coming to Virginia settled in Powhatan and Cumberland counties, reared a large family, members of which intermarried with the well known Colonial families of Randolph, Jefferson, Woodson and Flemings.

Through his father's mother Doctor Hughes is descended from William Randolph of Yorkshire, England, who settled at Turkey Island on the James River in Virginia, and afterwards acquired Curles Neck just across the river. William Randolph married Mary Isham, of Gloucester County, and one of their children was Isham Randolph, who settled at Dungeness, a splendid estate on the Upper James River in what is now Goochland County. His eldest daughter, Jane, married Peter Jefferson, from which union sprang the immortal Thomas Jefferson, third President of the United States. A sister of Mrs. Peter Jefferson was Dorothes Randolph, who married Col. John Woodson. Col. John Woodson was a son of Dr. John Woodson, who came over with Sir George Yeardly. Mary Royal, daughter of Col. John and Dorothes (Randolph) Woodson, married Thomas Cheadle, of Cheadletown, England. Their son, John Cheadle, married Judith Clarke, of Albemarle County, Virginia, and their daughter, Mary Woodson Cheadle, became the wife of Jesse Hughes. They were the grandparents of Dr. Thomas Jefferson Hughes. Thus Doctor Hughes is descended from families whose names and deeds have gone into the making of history across the seas and have been foremost in the upbuilding of and making famous the Old Dominion of Virginia.

William Hector Hughes, father of Doctor Hughes, was born in Prince Edward County, Virginia, and married Mary Davis, who was born in Smyth County. For years William H. Hughes was secretary of what is now the Norfolk & Western Railroad Company, holding that office for the fourteen years immediately preceding the war period of the '60s. He entered the army, but was sent back to the railroad, where the authorities felt he was more urgently needed. Four sons were born to his wife and himself: Jesse Martin Hughes, who lives near Washington City, being connected with the Farm Loan Bank there; Doctor Hughes; William Hector, Jr., a farmer in Smyth County; and Dr. Robert E. Hughes, who practices medicine at North Holston, Smyth County. Both parents were active members of the Methodist Episcopal Church, South. His father was a York Rite Mason, being a past master of the lodge.

The early educational training of Doctor Hughes was secured in the public schools of his native county, and he later entered Sharron College, Bland County, Virginia, and he took his professional work in the Virginia College of Medicine, Richmond, and was graduated therefrom in 1898, with the degree Doctor of Medicine. Later he did post-graduate work in the New York Polyclinic. After ten years practice in Smyth County he spent eighteen months in Europe studying surgery. Upon his return home he began the practice of his profession at Roanoke, in 1910, and since then has remained in this city. For some years he was a general practitioner, but is now specializing in surgery, in which he is a recognized expert, and he is serving as president of Shenandoah Hospital.

In 1910 Doctor Hughes married Florence Preston Starritt, born in Albemarle County, Virginia, and educated in Roanoke. Doctor and Mrs. Hughes have one child, Thomas J., Jr., who was born December 12, 1911, and is a student of the Augusta Military Academy. Doctor Hughes belongs to the Presbyterian Church, and for several years was deacon of the West End Church of that denomination. He is a York Rite and Shriner Mason, being a past master of the Blue Lodge; and belongs to the Knights of Pythias, the Benevolent and Protective Order of Elks and the University Club. Dr. Hughes is a Democrat. In addition to his practice he has other interests and is president of the Graham-White Sander Corporation, and a director of the American National Bank, the Shenandoah Life Insurance Company and General Finance Corporation. Although he began life with very little he has now an extensive and lucrative connection and is justly numbered among the leading professional men of his city, which is distinguished for high rank in the medical profession. The spirit of progress which has been the dominant factor of the first quarter of the new century has been manifest in no connection more strongly than in the science of medicine. Investigation and research have brought forth many scientific facts and established principles, and Doctor Hughes has kept pace with the advance. His professional service has ever been discharged with a keen sense of conscientious obligation and his skill has brought him to a prominent position. He is intelligently interested in all that pertains to modern progress and improvement, not only along professional but material and moral lines, and he always finds time to study great public questions and is ever ready to lend his influence for the betterment of humanity.

DAVID A. CHRISTIAN, M. D., descended from some of the first families to settle in Appomattox County, is a highly educated physician and surgeon, a man of leadership in his profession and has also been a positive factor in the good citizenship of his locality.

Doctor Christian was born in Appomattox County, May 20, 1880, son of David A. and Mary A. (Thornhill) Christian. His mother was a daughter of Albert T. Thornhill, a native of Appo-

mattox County, son of Thomas G. Thornhill, who secured a deed
to attractive land in that county from King George of England.
Doctor Christian is a grandson of William Diuguid Christian, a
pioneer physician, who graduated in medicine from the University of Pennsylvania and practiced his profession in Appomattox
County from 1832 until his death in 1880. Doctor Christian's
father continued the tradition of the family for important service in the office of judge of the County Court for fifteen years.
He graduated in law from the University of Virginia and since
1906 has been a resident of Richmond, where for a number of
years he was a clerk in the department of public instruction.
He is now eighty-two years of age. For two years he was a
Confederate soldier, joining the army at the age of fifteen, and
was in the Signal Corps. He has been a life long Baptist.

Dr. David A. Christian was the oldest in a family of eight
children, six of whom are living. He was educated at the South
Side Academy at Chase City, and while getting his higher education and preparing himself for a professional career he did
farm work, for two years was a mail carrier and was also census
enumerator. Doctor Christian graduated from the Richmond
Medical College in May, 1908, and has given twenty years of
service in his profession in his home county. He is a member
of the Medical Society of Virginia and since 1909 has been physician to the Woodmen of the World. He is on the medical staff
of the Southside Community Hospital at Farmville, Virginia.
During the World war he was a member of Medical Advisory
Board No. 36. He was a delegate to the conference on higher
education at Richmond in February, 1927, this conference having been called by Governor Byrd. Doctor Christian is a member of the Baptist Church and the Masonic fraternity.

He married, in 1916, Miss Bessie S. Stratton, who was born
in Appomattox County, and taught school there two years before her marriage. Her father, Chesley Stratton, is a farmer
in the Stonewall Community. Doctor and Mrs. Christian have
six children: Agnes Virginia, born in 1918, Bessie, born in 1920,
Mildred, born in 1922, David A. III, born in 1924, Catherine
Thornhill, born in 1926, and Chesley Stratton Christian, born in
1928.

WILLIAM LYLE OULD, physician and surgeon, now established
in his professional work at Appomattox, was a brilliant student
when in school and college, and graduated with a diploma and
other qualifications for the practice of medicine when he was
only nineteen and one-half years old.

Doctor Ould was born in Bedford Springs, Campbell County,
Virginia, November 3, 1874, son of William and Ellen (O'Drain)
Ould. His father was a native of Halifax County, was a lawyer
with an extensive practice in that and adjoining counties and
held the office of commonwealth attorney. He was very active
in politics. He served as a captain of militia before the war and
during the war between the states, but most of his time was
given up to recruiting duty. He was a member of the Presbyterian Church. By his first marriage he had three children, and
Ellen O'Drain was his second wife. She was born in Canada
and now lives at Lynchburg, being the mother of three children.
One son, Eugene, now deceased, served several terms in the
Legislature.

Dr. William Lyle Ould was educated in the New London
Academy and in the University of Virginia attended four ses-

sions of medical lectures, 1891-93. On March 13, 1894, he graduated M. D. from the University of Louisville. Doctor Ould practiced for over thirty years at Concord in Campbell County. In 1925 he removed to Appomattox, where he has found important responsibilities of a professional nature. He is also interested in local real estate, in a hardware store, and has been prominent in Masonry, being a past district deputy and now conducts a class in lodge work at Appomattox. He is a Royal Arch Mason and a member of the Methodist Episcopal Church.

Doctor Ould married in 1895 Florence Ballou, granddaughter of General Ballou, of a prominent family of Halifax County, where she was reared and educated. Doctor and Mrs. Ould have three children. The son William Carroll is a salesman at Roanoke and the second son, L. Herman, is in the automobile business at Appomattox.

The daughter, Ruth Ould, has had a distinguished career as a scholar and teacher and is the wife of Robert W. Manton, who is head of the department of music in the University at New Hampshire. Mrs. Manton graduated from Randolph-Macon Woman's College at Lynchburg, obtaining an A. M. degree, also studied at Columbia University, where she received her B. A. degree, and in other institutions, including Yale, and for some time held the chair of English at the University of New Hampshire, being the youngest woman head of a department in any university in the country. She was the assistant in the Department of Corrective Work. She has always been interested in athletics, and has spent much time in encouraging physical training and athletic work among women in different schools. Robert W. Manton, her husband, served with the United States Marine Corps during the World war. He is a graduate of Harvard University, and while overseas with the Fifth Regiment of the Marines and after the armistice he continued his musical studies in Paris. He was a volunteer, and was at the front when the armistice was signed and was one of the first Americans to land in France. He has held the chair of music at the University of New Hampshire since June, 1903. Mr. and Mrs. Manton have one son, Robert W., Junior, born October 15, 1927.

EDWARD C. GLASS. Some superintendents of schools, old in their ways, combat the application of modern standards to escape disturbance by new conditions. They do not wish to bear the responsibility, and so they retard progress in their systems and have no place as leaders any longer. However, when one is found who is both able and willing to take up everything calculated to advance his schools, then additional power should be accorded him. To such a man all the phases of administration should be left, for he understands the needs of the pupils and how to meet them. Such a man in addition to being a good educator would be one who would not bend to the pressure of political or other vicious influences, whether exerted by school boards or others. The superintendent, with the cooperation of the teachers, should develop an educational policy to fit the local conditions, which would include the curriculum, textbooks, promotions, salaries and similar matters. The developing of policies with the cooperation of the teachers is necessary because the joint wisdom of all is better than the wisdom of one individual or of one working with a hand-picked group of friends. No one is an educational automaton and no one superintendent without the cooperation of the teaching force can accomplish what should be accomplished in the system. The policy of cooperation is for growth. One of the very able men who fully measures up to the above standards, and who is securing in a marked degree the cooperation of all with whom he is associated, is Edward C. Glass, superintendent of the schools of Lynchburg.

Superintendent Glass was born in Lynchburg, September 7, 1852, and he has the distinction of being the oldest, in point of service, of the school superintendents in the United States. He is a son of Robert Henry and Betta Augusta (Christian) Glass, she born in Appomattox, Virginia, and he in Amherst County, Virginia. A very prominent citizen of Lynchburg, Robert Henry Glass left his impress upon the history of his own times. For many years he was editor of the *Lynchburg Republican*, and served as postmaster of the city from 1852 until the outbreak of the war between the states, and throughout that great conflict he remained in office in spite of the difficulty in getting the mails through the lines. A strong Democrat and a sesessionist, he served for six months on the staff of John B. Floyd, and participated in the battle of Winchester. For years he took a leading part in the work of the Court Street Methodist Church, South. Of the twelve children born to him and his wife nine are now living, and of them all Superintendent Glass is the third in order of birth. The paternal grandfather of Superintendent Glass was Thomas Glass, a native of Virginia. The family was established in Virginia at a very early day, in the beginning of the seventeenth century, by John Glass.

Superintendent Glass remembers distinctly the troubled period immediately preceding the outbreak of war, although then but a mere child. His father was a spirited defender of State's Rights, and bitterly opposed to the newly organized Republican party, fighting it by the spoken and written word. Because of a trenchant editorial voicing a bitter denunciation, true in every contention, of the dishonesty of certain office holders of the new political faith, he was shot and lost an eye in the affray. After the close of the war his friends nominated him for Congress, desiring to have him represent their district in the National Assembly, but his name was withdrawn.

During his boyhood Superintendent Glass attended a private school, and later took his high school work at Norwood, Nelson County, Virginia. He began his educational work in Lynchburg April 5, 1871, the first day the public-school system began to function in Lynchburg. For the succeeding five years he continued teaching, for one of those years being principal of the grammar school, and on January 9, 1879, he was appointed superintendent of schools, and has continued to hold that position ever since with distinguished capability.

On November 4, 1879, Superintendent Glass married Miss Susie G. Carter, who was born in Appomattox County, Virginia, and educated in the preparatory seminary of Lynchburg, being a member of its first graduating class. Ten children were born of this marriage, seven of whom are living: E. C., Junior, who is in the Lynchburg street car service; Mary C., who married W. P. Tyree, a tobacconist of Lynchburg; Robert, who was educated in Lynchburg and at Washington and Lee University, where he obtained his A. B. degree and who is now the editor of the *Lynchburg Morning News*; Nannie G., who married Edward Mayfield, and is now a widow residing in Lynchburg; Henry B., who is an attorney, but has been in the insurance business at

Lynchburg since his return from the World war, in which he
served overseas, was gassed, and had conferred upon him for
valor the Distinguished Service Medal; Elizabeth C., who was
graduated from Randolph-Macon College, is a teacher of Latin
in the Lynchburg High School; Susie Sanford, who was graduated from the Lynchburg High School and the Washington Normal Training School, married Richard Henry Lee, an Episcopal
clergyman, now stationed near Norfolk, Virginia. The children
have all done well, and are a great credit to their parents, who
have reared them with loving watchfulness. All the children
and their parents belong to the Court Street Methodist Church,
South, which he has served as steward. In addition to his long
and valued service to Lynchburg Superintendent Glass was for
sixteen years the conductor of the Virginia Summer School of
Methods, was a member of the first board of William and Mary
College, and of the first State Board of Education. He is a member of the present state board of education from Lynchburg. A
close student, he has not only perfected himself in the classics,
but kept abreast of modern thought and progress, and has inaugurated many innovations and carried them out most successfully
in the Lynchburg schools. During his entire term of service as
superintendent of the Lynchburg schools he has been a member
of the National Education Association.

GEORGE JOHNSON TOMPKINS, physician and surgeon, was one
of the first members of his profession at Lynchburg to limit his
practice to a special field. In eye, ear, nose and throat he is
not only one of the oldest in point of service in that city but one
of the doctors of generally recognized ability and standing in
Central Virginia.

Doctor Tompkins was born in Lexington, Virginia, March
27, 1873, son of J. Fulton and Sallie D. (Pendleton) Tompkins.
His grandfather, Edmund Giles Tompkins, was a commission
merchant at Richmond and one of the founders of Saint James
Episcopal Church in that city, where he died. He married a
sister of the mother of Senator Thomas Staples, who after his
death moved to Lexington. Both are buried in the Hollywood
Cemetery at Richmond. Doctor Tompkin's maternal grandfather was Dr. Micajah Pendleton, a physician who practiced at
Buchanan, Virginia, and was a splendid type of the old time
country doctor, riding horseback over a great extensive country
in his own and adjacent counties. He had been educated for his
profession in the University of New York. Doctor Pendleton
married Louisa Jane Davis, a native of Amherst County, Virginia and a member of the old family of that name there.

J. Fulton Tompkins, father of Doctor Tompkins, was born in
Albemarle County, Virginia, attended common schools, and as
a young man entered the employ of Percell Ladd & Company, a
drug house at Richmond. He left that city in 1851 and moved
to Buchanan, where he was in the drug business. For a short
period he was engaged in the drug business at Columbus, Mississippi. Then returning to Buchanan he reentered the drug
business. Later he moved to Lexington, Virginia, and engaged
in business until the outbreak of the war, when he volunteered
with the Richbridge Artillery and fought in several battles, including the first battle of Manassas. At the close of the war he
returned to Lexington and in 1867 married Sallie D. Pendleton,
widow of George W. Johnson. For many years he lived at
Lexington, where he served as apothecary to the Virginia Mili-

tary Institute. He became a member of the Grace Memorial
(Episcopal) Church at Lexington. He finally located on a farm
near Natural Bridge, Virginia, where he lived out his life. He
was a member of the Episcopal Church there, which he helped
build, and served as vestryman and warden. He was a member
of the Masonic fraternity and for a number of years held the office of justice of the peace in Rockbridge County. He was the
father of four children: Dr. E. Pendleton Tompkins, of Lexington; Sallie Louise, wife of W. M. McNutt, of Rockbridge County;
Dr. George Johnson, and Bertie Lee.

George Johnson Tompkins attended public and private
schools, the Fishburne Military Academy and was graduated
from the Medical College of Virginia in 1894. He had hospital
experience at Washington, D. C., and for several years was engaged in general practice at Roanoke. He spent some time in
New York City in eye, ear, nose and throat work, and after this
special preparation located at Lynchburg in 1899. Doctor
Tompkins is a member of the staff of all three hospitals at
Lynchburg and has charge of the eye, ear, nose and throat clinic
for the city. He is a member of the Virginia State Society of
Oto-Laryngology and Ophthalmology, is a member of the South
Piedmont Medical Society, the Medical Society of Virginia, the
Lynchburg and Campbell County Medical Society, and Ameri-
can Medical Associations.

Doctor Tompkins married in December, 1904, Miss Elizabeth
Haskins Dillard, who was born at Lynchburg, daughter of James
P. and Ellen N. (Woodroof) Dillard. They have a family of
five children: Ella Pendleton, wife of John M. Robeson, Jr., who
with her husband is a student in the University of Virginia;
Miss Margaret Louise, attending the Woman's College at Farmville; Elizabeth Dillard, wife of William J. Paxton, a commercial artist at Roanoke; Sallie Dudley, member of the class of
1928 in Lynchburg High School; and George Johnson Junior,
born October 6, 1922.

Doctor Tompkins has given many years of faithful service
to the Episcopal Church in Lynchburg, having served as vestryman and warden in Saint Paul's Church and in 1928 helped reorganize and build the new Grace Memorial Church, of which he
is vestryman and warden. He is a member of the Masonic fraternity.

WADE HILL ADAMS, vice president and general manager of
the Southern Biscuit Company, although comparatively a new-
comer in Richmond, has been signally honored in this city by
various civic, business and social organizations. He is president
of the Sphinx Club, a member of the Rotary Club, active in the
affairs of the Chamber of Commerce and a director thereof, a
member of the Country Club of Virginia and the Commonwealth
Club, and he is a thirty-second degree Mason and a Shriner. He
is a communicant of the Presbyterian Church.

Born in Mooresville, Iredell County, North Carolina, November 2, 1876, he is a son of James Pinckney and Julia (Proctor)
Adams, the latter being a daughter of Richard and Elizabeth
(King) Proctor, of Lincoln County, North Carolina. His
branch of the Adams family originated in South Carolina, and
its members were among the very prominent people of its earlier
history.

In spite of the fact that he had to work his way through
Trinity College, now Duke University, Durham, North Caro-

lina, Wade Hill Adams had the highest standing in his class when he was graduated with the degree of A. B. in 1899. In the following year he took his A. M. degree. Having in view a scholastic career, it was his ambition that he might return to Trinity College in the department of English. He attended the Graduate School of English at Harvard University in 1901-02. With the completion of his education, however, he decided to enter a business career instead of taking up educational work.

In 1902 Mr. Adams entered the service of the American Tobacco Company in New York. There he gained experience in the various departments of this great corporation, becoming acquainted with accounting, financing, production, marketing and sales methods; in fact every activity of a modern industrial corporation. After being with the American Tobacco Company for about eight years he became affiliated with the Durham Duplex Razor Company, whose plant is at Jersey City, New Jersey. He started in with that company as secretary and later became vice president in charge of sales and advertising. While with the Durham Duplex Razor Company he went to Paris, France, where he established and put in operation the Paris plant of this company, and remained in France for a year. At the beginning of 1918 he was commissioned captain in the United States Army and assigned to the Ordnance Department, Washington, D. C., where he remained until after the Armistice.

In 1925 Mr. Adams came to Richmond and took over the active management, as vice president, of the Southern Biscuit Company. It is needless to say that with his wide and varied experience with two great industrial concerns Mr. Adams at once inaugurated modern methods in every department of the local plant and began to build up an organization of note. In 1927 he began the preliminary work for the erection of a $500,000 plant on Terminal Place in the West End of Richmond. In addition to a completely modern building, the plant has the latest types of ovens and baking equipment.

The new building conforms to the classic style of architecture, and is somewhat patterned after Battle Abbey in its facade. This type of architecture was more expensive, but the Board of Directors and stockholders preferred to invest a little more money in order to erect a plant that would serve as a monument to the industry of the company which originated in Richmond, and whose stock is owned by local people. At the same time it was their intention to produce an artistic building for Richmond and depart somewhat from the old-time conception of an industrial plant.

Seven stories in height, this building is constructed of white concrete; is 100 x 140 feet, thus giving a floor space of 100,000 square feet. The same architects, Francisco and Jacobus, who built many of the plants for the American Tobacco Company and those for many other tobacco and bread-baking corporations throughout the country, designed the new building for the Richmond people.

This plant is not only a beautiful example of industrial architecture, but it is also the exemplification of labor-saving devices and modern conceptions of efficiency. All flour, sugar and other raw materials used in the work of the company are conveyed to the top floor by elevators, and from there are distributed through gravity conveyers to the shipping floor, thus saving much operating cost. All of the manufacturing equipment is motor-driven, and the greater part of the baking is done with gas.

Refrigerating and humidifying plants, designed by the most up-to-date engineers in the country, have been installed at a cost of about $30,000.

The company was established in 1899 in Richmond, and was from the start a successful venture, but as its volume increased those in charge saw that a large expansion was necessary, and therefore looked about to find the man best fitted for the work of carrying on these improvements, and in Mr. Adams found the ideal man. Since the completion of the new building there has been a large increase in the output as compared to the previous year. The company manufactures more than a hundred varieties of soda crackers, saltines, oyster crackers, cookies, plain and fancy cakes. Sales in Richmond have increased more than 600 per cent under Mr. Adams' management, and in outside territory more than 300 per cent.

In the erection of this handsome building the company has shown to the world its faith in the South, and followed out the suggestions made along this line by the state and city Chambers of Commerce. Associated with Mr. Adams in this work are B. M. Gwathmey, president; W. E. Albus, treasurer; Harry L. Stone, secretary; and Ernest G. Gustafson, superintendent of the plant.

Mr. Adams married Miss Jane Douglass Cockrell, a daughter of the late Judge Joseph E. Crockrell, an eminent lawyer and jurist, and one of the most distinguished citizens of Dallas, whose death April 7, 1927, removed one of the leading men of Texas, who at the time of his death was president of the Board of Trustees of the Southern Methodist University, and president of the Dallas National Bank. Mr. and Mrs. Adams have four children, namely: Wade Hill Adams, Jr., who was born July 24, 1911; Joseph Cockrell Adams, who was born January 23, 1915; Mary Jane Adams, who was born July 6, 1919; and Julia Proctor Adams, who was born June 19, 1925.

Wade Hill Adams is a man who carries great responsibilities and is deeply engrossed in business, but not so much so that he cannot find time for civic betterment work. He is a great captain of industry, all who know him readily admit this, and many men earn their living because of his enterprise, ability and command of resources. Whatever success he has accomplished is largely due to himself, and one of his most marked characteristics is his bravery of belief in himself. He adheres in action to whatever his reason brings forth. Under the strain of great business operations he has never faltered in confronting risks. His whole business life has been a campaign of pluck, perseverance and principle. To extol his benevolence, his sympathy for the suffering of others, his never-sleeping generosity, his hand ever open to patriotic causes and to charity, is but to repeat a well-known tale. That the people of Richmond know all this, and appreciate the man and his character, is shown by the local honors which have been bestowed upon him from the beginning of his residence here. His genial manner, magnetic personality and dynamic force make him a leader, and those following him in different lines of work know that they will reach the goal of their endeavor, for he has never learned the meaning of failure.

DUNCAN DRYSDALE, Lynchburg attorney, is a native of Scotland, though his father was a naturalized American citizen.

He was born at Stirling, Scotland, January 13, 1861, son of Alexander and Janet (Smart) Drysdale, both natives of Scotland. His father came to the United States when a young man, and while here took out naturalization papers. He went back to Scotland to visit, married while there and never carried out his intentions of returning to America. He was a member of the Presbyterian Church, and of his ten children Duncan was the oldest. The Drysdale family were originally members of the Douglas family or clan. The tradition is that members of the family became engaged in a feud with their neighbors, the Johnstones, over water rights and after a number on both sides had been killed this branch of the Douglas clan left the country, moving many miles distant, and in their new home took the name of a Parish known as Drysdale in their old locality.

Duncan Drysdale was reared and educated in Scotland, attending common schools there. In 1899 he came to Virginia, locating at Norfolk, and for three years was in the confectionery business there. While in business he studied law, took his law degree at Richmond College in 1903 and began practice at Rustburg. In 1906 he located at Lynchburg, and has had a very large practice in that city and section of the state.

Mr. Drysdale married in June, 1918, Margaret Pollock, who was born in Scotland. Her family came to the United States in 1915 and two of her brothers were soldiers in the World war, John Pollock going with the One Hundred Sixteenth Regiment from Lynchburg while George Pollock enlisted from Philadelphia. Mr. and Mrs. Drysdale have two children: Jean, now in school, and Douglas, born in 1925. They are members of the Unitarian Church at Lynchburg and Mr. Drysdale is chairman of the Church Board.

He is affiliated with the Masonic fraternity, is a member of the City, Virginia and American Bar Associations and has been admitted to practice before the United States Supreme Court. He handles a general law practice, and at one time probably no other Lynchburg attorney had so large a practice in the criminal branch of the law.

HON. WALLER J. HENSON, former judge of the Circuit Court, and one of the ablest lawyers practicing at the bar of Roanoke, has been general counsel for the Shenandoah Life Insurance Company since 1914, and is a recognized authority in all matters pertaining to corporation law. He exemplified at the bar before his elevation to the bench a quiet exactness, a profound knowledge of the law, and a clear, impartial judgment, which characteristics are invaluable to both a lawyer and judge. When he retired from the bench he came to Roanoke, and here he has found the environment for which his abilities fit him, and is here accorded an appreciation to which he is justly entitled.

Judge Henson was born in Buckingham, Virginia, November 18, 1864, a son of John Waller and Martha A. (Chambers) Henson, both natives of Virginia, the latter born in Buckingham. The former was a clergyman of the Baptist faith, having been prepared for his work in Richmond College, but his life was terminated by death in 1873, when he was only thirty-five years old. She survived him many years, passing away in 1920. Of the four children born to them, three are now living, and of them all Judge Henson was the first born. The father served all through the war between the states, and, being captured, was confined in a Federal prison. He was a zealous Mason, and lived up to the highest ideals of church and fraternity. The Henson family was founded in Virginia by John Henson, an extensive planter, and a member of the Legislature. When the capitol building collapsed he was in it, and only saved his life by his quickness in clutching a window sill, to which he held until rescued. The maternal grandfather, William A. Chambers, was a native of Virginia.

Judge Henson attended private schools, in which he was prepared for high school, and he took his high school work in the night sessions in Lynchburg, and at the same time worked as telegrapher and train dispatcher. From 1883 to 1888 he continued in that work, and also studied law. In July, 1888, he resigned his position, took a course in the summer school of the University of Virginia, took the state bar examinations, and was admitted to the bar in September, 1888. He began his practice in Giles County, Virginia, and became so prominent and generally esteemed as an able lawyer that February 1, 1904, he was elected Circuit Court judge, and so served until 1909. With the expiration of his term of office he came to Roanoke, where he has since been engaged in private practice, as already noted. All his life he has been very active in Democratic politics, and served as commonwealth attorney in Giles County, but has not been willing to accept nomination since coming to Roanoke. The Baptist Church holds his membership. He is a York Rite and Shriner Mason, and takes great interest in his fraternal work.

On July 4, 1887, Judge Henson married Cornelia Dulaney, who was born in Giles County, Virginia. They have had three children born to their marriage: William E., who was educated in Washington and Lee University, and is an attorney engaged in the practice of law with his father; Mary E., who is a resident of Washington, District of Columbia; and Poindexter S., who was educated in the University of Virginia, and died February 28, 1928.

WILLIAM S. MEGGINSON. There is no work which makes such incessant demand upon the sympathies of those engaged in it than as of caring for the children orphaned and left to the mercy of an unkind world. Parents sheltering their own loved ones, tenderly watching over them with brooding thoughtfulness, seldom spare the time to reflect that there are little ones lacking the actual necessities of life, to say nothing of the attention to their needs from a moral and spiritual standpoint. Fortunately there are those whose minds and hearts are open to the appeals of these unfortunates and some noble characters who are devoting themselves, their lives and their talents to substituting for the parents many of these children have never known. Of a verity such work is divine in its scope and effects.

One of the men whose broad sympathies and Christian character, as well as his ministerial training, fit him for work among the orphans, Rev. William S. Megginson is now rendering a wonderful service as superintendent of the Presbyterian Orphans'

Home at Lynchburg, one of the splendidly managed institutions of the Presbyterian Church in Virginia.

William S. Megginson was born in Greenville, Tennessee, July 30, 1869, a son of John Thomas and Sarah Emily (Smith) Megginson, natives of Virginia and Tennessee, respectfully, both of whom are now deceased. A college man, John Thomas Megginson took up engineering, and followed that profession for many years, but, retiring, spent the remainder of his life in the enjoyment of the comforts his former activities had provided. During the war between the states he raised a company and served under the command of Gen. John Mosby. Owing to the hardships he suffered in the war his health was never very good thereafter, and this in part led to his retirement. His death occurred in 1897, but his wife survived him until 1921, she passing away at the age of eighty-one years. There were three children: Rev. William Megginson, who was the first born; Edward T., who lives in Northern Georgia; and Henry E., who is a merchant of El Paso, Texas. The parents were both members of the Presbyterian Church, and very active in all of its work. The paternal grandfather, William Cabell Megginson, married Miss Amanda Bocock, of Buckingham County, Virginia, and through her Rev. Mr. Megginson is connected with another very prominent family of Virginia, in addition to the Cabell family. The maternal grandfather, Jordan Smith, was a cattle raiser of East Tennessee, and owned a large plantation, well-stocked with cattle and horses, and he was also an extensive slave owner. During the war between the states he suffered heavy losses in addition to that incurred by the freeing of the negroes.

Rev. Mr. Megginson first attended several excellent private schools, but at the same time had to work, as his father was ill, and he was the eldest child. Later he secured a secretaryship with the Atlanta, Georgia, Young Men's Christian Association, and while discharging its duties he secured further educational training. Subsequently, he attended the Louisville, Kentucky, Seminary, and was licensed to preach in 1897, and continued his ministerial work until 1900, when he took post-graduate work in the same seminary, paying his own way through at the time he was studying. In the meanwhile, in 1897, he had gone to San Antonio, Texas, as pastor of Utica Presbyterian Church, returning to Kentucky to carry on his further studies, and when that course was completed he went to Elizabethtown, Kentucky, and was engaged there in ministerial work for three and one-half years, and when he left it was to spend four years in the General Sunday School work of the Presbyterian Church. From that work he accepted a call to the church in Biloxi, Mississippi, for six years, and at the expiration of that period he went to Richmond as Dean of the Assembly Training School, which he organized, and placed the institution upon a solid basis. In that work he displayed executive ability of such a high order that he was transferred to the Presbyterian Orphanage.

The Presbyterian Orphanage of Lynchburg has 165 children, and conducts a school in connection with it that employs nine teachers and carries the pupils from the first grade through the high school work. The moving spirit in the Home, in work and play is Superintendent Megginson, and that he encourages wholesome activities and sports may be gleaned from the following excerpt from the *Bulletin* of the Presbyterian Orphans' Home:

"Our Football Team: Our team is still the 'Shoeless Wonders,' although four of the original team left us during the sum-

mer and some lighter boys had to be substituted. They hold the title for three reasons: First, because they play barefooted, second, because they really are the most agile, smoothest piece of machinery about here, and third, because so far this year they have maintained the record of the last two years, having not allowed an opposing team to score."

In 1895 Reverend Megginson married Miss Amanda Leonard Allen, born in Louisville, Kentucky, and there educated a daughter of David H. and Mary (Waters) Allen, and a direct descendant of Barthomew Dupuy. Mr. Allen was a manufacturer and merchant, but is now deceased. There are no children in the Megginson family, and therefore Reverend and Mrs. Megginson lavish upon their little charges the tender parental affection and care they would have given their own had they been sent into their home. He is a Knight Templar Mason and belongs to the Kiwanis Club, and both are members of the Presbyterian Church. Reverend Megginson is admirably fitted for his present labor of love, for he has known poverty and hardships and has been given a wide and broadening experience since he entered the ministry. The children are devoted to him and his wife, and they are making splendid progress in their school work.

THOMAS BURTON SNEAD of Richmond, descends from a very old family in England, and is a lineal descendant of Robert Sneade, one of the pioneer settlers of Virginia, who settled in Elizabeth City County in 1654. The name Snead is very ancient in England and signifies the handle of a scythe. It has taken many forms, such as Sned, Sneyd, Sneed, but the most usual form in modern times is Snead, as adopted by this family. William Snead, great-grandfather of the subject of this sketch, served in the Revolutionary war as a non-commissioned officer, having volunteered for service at the age of eighteen, and his grandfather, whose name was also William, served in the Confederate army throughout the entire period of the Civil war.

William Snead II, who was born in 1811 in Nelson County, afterwards moved to Albemarle County, and there married Sarah Elizabeth Clark. They were the parents of Chapman Price Snead, born July 25, 1850, in Albemarle, died October 7, 1907. His wife, Frances Elizabeth (Hutchinson) Snead, was a daughter of Warner Winston and Mary Ella (Harris) Hutchinson. Chapman Price Snead was a farmer in King William County, and in political alliance a Republican.

Thomas Burton Snead, a son of Chapman Price Snead, was born March 10, 1878, at Etna Mills, King William County, Virginia, and received his early education under the direction of private tutors in his father's home. He later attended the College of William and Mary, and was a student there in 1895-98. In the fall of 1900 he entered the law department of the University of Virginia, from which he received the degree Bachelor of Laws in the class of 1902. He was immediately admitted to the bar and begun the practice of law at Richmond. On January 16, 1905, he was appointed referee in bankruptcy by the District Court of the United States, Eastern District of Virginia, for the district composed of the City of Richmond and the counties of Henrico, Chesterfield, Powhatan and Goochland, which position he has held continuously since.

In his position as referee in bankruptcy during the past twenty-three years Mr. Snead has rendered decisions in hun-

dreds of cases, some of them involving nice questions of law and
important interests. Considering these facts his record as
referee in bankruptcy has been quite unusual. Only fourteen
of his many decisions have reached the Circuit Court of Appeals
for review, and in only three of these was he reversed. Only two
of the cases decided by him have reached the Supreme Court
of the United States for review and in both of these his decisions
were sustained. Though he attends to the bankruptcy business
for a population of some 300,000, Mr. Snead also practices law,
and one-third of his professional work consists of his private
practice.

Of modest and retiring nature, Mr. Snead has never sought
to mingle in the conduct of public affairs, and devotes most of
his spare time to his family and home. He is a friend of education, and is ever ready to lend his time, influence and support
to those higher social movements which are calculated to develop
the best in man and promote the progress and welfare of the
community. He is a Republican in politics and a communicant
of the Episcopal Church. He served his enlistment as a member
of Company C, Richmond Blues, one of the finest and oldest military organizations in the United States. He is a member of the
Richmond Bar Association, the Virginia State Bar Association,
the American Bar Association, the Commonwealth Club, University Club, Country Club of Virginia and Sons of the American
Revolution.

Mr. Snead has been twice married. His first wife, whom he
married April 19, 1911, was Miss Mary Cooke Branch, the only
daughter of Col. James Ransom and Lilian (Hubball) Branch,
and a lineal descendant of Christian Branch of "Arrowhattocks"
and "Kingsland," who came from England in 1620. She died
December 31, 1921. On April 18, 1927, he married Miss Mary
Ragan Macgill Bertrand, daughter of Frederick Olia and Minnie
(Drewry) Bertrand, a granddaughter of Dr. Samuel Davies
Drewry, and a lineal descendant of the great Presbyterian divine,
Samuel Davies, first president of Princeton University.

COL. WILLIAM RICHARD PHELPS is principal of the Randolph-
Macon Academy of Bedford, a boys' preparatory school, one of
the fine institutions comprised in what is known as the Randolph-
Macon System, including several academies for boys and girls
and culminating in the Randolph-Macon College for men at
Ashland and Randolph-Macon Woman's College at Lynchburg.

Colonel Phelps is a cultured Virginia gentleman, and has
a thorough understanding of the spirit and traditions of the
educational institutions with which he has been identified. He
was born at Keyton Plantation, in Bedford County, August 2,
1886, and is a descendant of the Key family which founded
Keyton Plantation. His people have been in Bedford County
since early Colonial times. One of his ancestors, John Phelps,
Sr., was a member of the House of Burgesses and served as
lieutenant-colonel of militia in Bedford County. His son, John
Phelps, Jr., was the father of Thomas Phelps and grandfather
of Thomas J. Phelps, who married Malinda Perkins Key. These
latter were the grandparents of Colonel Phelps. The father of
Colonel Phelps was Thomas Key Phelps, who was born September 21, 1847, and married Sarah Elizabeth Moulton, who was
born in Bedford County May 8, 1849, and died in 1914. Her
father, Dr. Benjamin H. Moulton, practiced medicine for many

years at Davis Mills and served as a member of the Virginia Senate. Thomas Key Phelps was one of the cadets called out from the Virginia Military Institute to take part in the battle of New Market. His father, Thomas J. Phelps, was also a soldier of the Confederacy.

William Richard Phelps was one of a large family of eleven children. These children were educated at home under instructors employed by their father, and later the older sons and daughters took charge of the instruction of the younger members of the household. Education has been an essential tradition of the Phelps family.

Colonel Phelps completed the four-year course at Randolph-Macon College at Ashland in three years, graduating second honor man of his class in 1908. Since graduating he has been connected with the Randolph-Macon System, for the first three years as instructor of mathematics in the academy at Bedford, seven years as assistant principal of Randolph-Macon Institute at Danville, and in 1918 returned to the academy at Bedford as associate principal, and since June, 1922, as principal. Colonel Phelps has the degree Master of Arts, given him by Columbia University of New York, where he spent four summers in residence as a graduate student. He is a member of the Virginia Association of Preparatory Schools and in 1925 was made its president. He is also a member of the Virginia Commission of Southern Association of Schools and Colleges.

Colonel Phelps was chairman of the Red Cross Chapter at Danville and member of the Legal Advisory Board during the World war. He has been a steward in the Methodist Episcopal Church, South, is a member of the Sons of Confederate Veterans, the Phi Delta Theta college fraternity, and Pi Gamma Mu social fraternity. He married, August 9, 1911, Miss Mildred May Davis of Dinwiddie County, Virginia. She is a graduate of the State Teachers College of Farmville and taught school several years before her marriage. Their children are: Rosa King, William Richard, Jr., and Moulton Davis.

GORDON B. PACE, president of the Pace Construction Company, Incorporated, is connected through the operations of his corporation with some of the most extensive construction projects, bridge building, the installation of sewers, waterworks and similar important contracts, in this part of the country, and has built up a reputation that is second to none for carrying out the spirit as well as the letter of his agreements. He was born in Roanoke, July 18, 1895, a son of Sidney B. and Carrie (Backus) Pace, natives of Virginia and West Virginia, respectively. Coming to Roanoke when it was still a village, Sidney B. Pace began operating in real estate, in which line he has been engaged all his life, and subsequently he was engaged in organizing the Mountain Trust Bank, was its first president, and is now its vice president. Four children have been born to him and his wife: Gordon B., who is the eldest; Lloyd, who is in the real estate business with his father; Madeline, who married C. R. Wentworth, of Roanoke, engineer with the Virginia Bridge & Iron Company; and Dorothy, who married Everett Richardson, a manufacturer of the State of Massachusetts. Mr. Pace is a member of the Baptist Church, and his wife of the Presbyterian Church, and both are active in church work. He is a Mason, a Shriner and an Elk, and is active in

the Rotary Club. In political faith he is a Democrat. The
paternal grandfather, Sidney W. Pace, also a native of Virginia,
served in the Confederate army during the war between the
states. The maternal grandfather was a native of Pennsylvania, but was living in Virginia at the time of his death, and
was connected with the Norfolk & Western Railroad.

Growing to manhood in Roanoke, Gordon B. Pace was given
the advantage of attending its excellent schools and a military
institute, and was graduated from the latter in 1915, after
which he took two years in the University of Virginia, but his
studies were interrupted in 1917 by this country's entry into
the World war, and he entered the service and was trained in
Camp Lee, Virginia; Camp Taylor, Kentucky, and Camp Lewis,
Washington, near Tacoma. He served as first lieutenant of the
Thirty-eighth Field Artillery. In January, 1919, he was honorably discharged, and returned to Roanoke. Here he organized
the Pace Construction Company, of which he is president, and
his father vice president. The company is incorporated and is
a close corporation. In addition to private contracts, the company is doing a large amount of work for the Norfolk & Western
Railroad, the Virginia Highway Commission and the Tennessee
Highway Commission, and has numerous contracts for cities,
towns, counties and private industrial works.

On June 18, 1918, Mr. Pace married Miss Louise Vaughan,
who was born in Roanoke, where she attended school, later
going to National Park Seminary, Forest Glen, Maryland. She
is a daughter of L. H. Vaughan, retired railroad contractor and
capitalist. Mr. and Mrs. Pace have one son, Gordon Vaughan
Pace. Mrs. Pace belongs to the Christian Church, while Mr.
Pace belongs to the Presbyterian Church. While in college he
made Delta Tau Delta, and he belongs to the Shenandoah Club
and the Roanoke Country Club, but aside from these has but
little contact with anything but his business affairs, to which
he is devoting himself with wholehearted absorption.

WILLIAM THOMAS MCNAMARA, JUNIOR. Within the memory
of those now only middle aged has come what amounts to a revolution in household furnishings and methods of housekeeping.
So many and varied are the inventions to make easy the life of
the homemaker, and assist her in solving the many times bewil-
dering problems of securing adequate assistance in her household tasks, that those who learned to keep house in the days
when servants were plentiful and could be secured for a mere
pittance feel that an era of great ease has dawned, and many
whose means would justify their living in complete idleness have
resumed, of their own free will, the conduct of their homes to
enjoy the many comforts and conveniences now on the market.
Perhaps none of them afford such comfort, and at the same time
gratify the inherent love of the beautiful, as the floor coverings
now manufactured and distributed that require no dusty sweep-
ing, but can be easily cleaned with a damp mop, and in this way
the problem that could formerly only be solved by hours of back-
breaking labor has practically disappeared. Another feature
that attracts many women is the fact that they can secure comfortable sleeping accommodations, at a reasonable price, without
extra floor space, and consequent additional rent. While the
manufacturers of these different aids to the housekeeper, to say
nothing of the inventors of them, deserve great credit, those who
distribute them play an important part in the business life of

every community and render a much appreciated service to its people. One of these men, alert and progressive, is William T. McNamara, Jr., president of the American Beauty Mattress Company of Lynchburg.

William T. McNamara, Jr., was born in Lynchburg, February 3, 1874, a son of W. T. and Johanna (Martin) McNamara, both of whom were born in Ireland, from whence they came to the United States in childhood. For years the father was a contracting plumber and steamfitter, and had charge of the steamfitting on the Norfolk & Western Railroad from Lynchburg to Bristol. During the early days of its existence he was a captain of the Lynchburg Fire Department, and he also owned and conducted a heater and range establishment. He put in the city water works at Dublin, Virginia, and had other important contracts, and evinced a strong interest in public affairs. After other contractors had declared it impossible to fix the water works in the Blue Ridge Springs Hotel he took the contract and carried it out in a very satisfactory manner. In spite of all he accomplished he was only twenty-nine years old when he died in 1877, and his prosperity was the result of his own, unaided efforts, for he began life with absolutely nothing. A zealous Catholic, he was very active in the church and various Catholic societies. He and his wife had two children: William T. and Alice J., the latter being the wife of Thomas F. Driscoll, of Chicago, who has charge of all of the advertising for Armour & Company all over the United States. At the time of her marriage to Mr. McNamara, Mrs. McNamara was the widow of James Byrne, to whom she had borne three children, one of whom survives, Mary T. Byrne, a Sister of Charity in Washington City. The paternal grandfather was William McNamara, a native of Ireland, who settled in Lynchburg upon coming to this country, and became an officer of the Lynchburg Gas Company. The maternal grandfather was also a native of Ireland, and settled in Richmond, Virginia.

William T. McNamara was educated in the parochial schools of Lynchburg, in Rock Hill College, Maryland, and Eastman's Business College, Poughkeepsie, New York. From 1893 to 1900 he was engaged in work as a bookkeeper in Roanoke, Virginia, but in the latter year he returned to Lynchburg and for a short time continued work as a bookkeeper, but in 1901 became secretary and treasurer of the Lynchburg Lounge Company, manufacturers of lounges, couches and parlor furniture. After about eight years' connection with this company he left it, in 1909, to engage with the National Manufacturing Company, manufacturers of mattresses, which he served as president and general manager until 1911, when the plant was destroyed by fire. The following year he organized the National Mattress Company, which was operated under that name until the spring of 1926, when it was reorganized as the American Beauty Mattress Company, of which Mr. McNamara has since continued president. The company employs one regular mattress man and two commission men, and covers Virginia, parts of North Carolina and West Virginia, and sells mattresses to the trade in other places. The principal brand is the American Beauty, a very fine mattress made from the best material. The business has been greatly increased, and the sales in 1927 were greatly in excess of those of previous years. The company manufacture mattresses, pillows and awnings, and distributes the Simmons beds and springs, and Gold Seal Congoleum and Linoleum.

In 1901 Mr. McNamara married Miss Norah Regina Wholey, who was born in Staunton, Virginia, where she attended the Mary Baldwin School. She is a daughter of William Wholey, who for the last twenty years of his life lived retired. During the war between the states he had the honor to serve as Ordinance Sergeant under Gen. "Stonewall" Jackson. Mrs. McNamara is active in the United Daughters of the Confederacy, Old Dominion Chapter of Lynchburg, having served as secretary and treasurer, and organized its Junior Chapter. She is an active member of the Carrie Harper Club of Lynchburg and is an active member of the Travelers' Aid Society. Four sons have been born to Mr. and Mrs. McNamara, namely: William Francis, who was educated in the Virginia Military Institute, is in his father's office and is a reserve officer in the United States army; Maurice, who was also educated in the Virginia Military Institute, is in the employ of the Chesapeake Telephone Company as office manager and assistant to the company manager at Lynchburg; Charles Edwin, who is a medical student in the Georgetown University, Washington City; and Richard, who is attending the high school at Lynchburg. The family all belong to the Holy Cross Catholic Church, and Mr. McNamara is a member of the Knights of Columbus, and is a life member of the Benevolent and Protective Order of Elks. While he devotes himself to his business he is deeply interested in civic affairs, and has always been an active participant in them. He served as secretary of the Lynchburg Woodrow Wilson Club.

THOMAS X. PARSONS. One of the brilliant young attorneys practicing at the bar of Roanoke, Thomas X. Parsons has attained to an enviable prestige through his undoubted talents, both natural and acquired, and he is regarded as one of the most desirable of the city's citizens. He was born in Independence, Virginia, September 3, 1896, a son of John M. and Mary Belle (Bryant) Parsons, both of whom were born in Virginia, he at Potato Creek and she at Fox. Her death occurred in 1907, but he survives and is living in Independence, where he is engaged in the practice of the law, and he is representing his district in the Virginia State Senate. A strong Republican, at present he is the only Republican from his part of the state in the Senate. Several years ago he served as commonwealth attorney of Grayson County, and at one time he was his party's candidate for Congress. Although defeated, his opponent won by only sixty-two votes, so personally popular is he. Of the five children born to the parents, Thomas X. Parsons is the second in order of birth.

Growing up in Independence, Thomas X. Parsons attended the Virginia Military Institute, from which he was graduated in 1915, and took his law training in Washington and Lee University, from which he was graduated in 1921. After leaving the university he taught law for one year as associate professor of law. Coming to Roanoke in 1923, he formed a partnership with Judge Clifton A. Woodrum and John W. McCauley, and they enjoy a large patronage and are connected on one side or the other with much of the important jurisprudence of this section. Mr. Parsons is unmarried. Like his father, he is an ardent Republican, and was appointed in 1927 assistant district attorney, in which office he is making an admirable record. At the university he made Phi Delta Phi, the honorary law fraternity, and Phi Kappa Psi. He is a Blue Lodge Mason, and

B. Morgan Shepherd

he is a member of the Shenandoah Club, the University Club, the Country Club, the Roanoke German Club, and the Lions Club. During the World war he served as captain of infantry and was stationed at Fort Myer until his honorable discharge September 8, 1919.

B. MORGAN SHEPHERD. The evolution of a newspaper is a difficult problem, for in addition to the physical property there is that something which is of much greater value, the vital spark of the personality of those who have established and developed it. This, of course, applies in some degree to other great enterprises. It may be said of a bank or railway or shop, but conducting a newspaper is more than management, it is an entirely different thing in essence from the providing of public transport, the handling of moneys or the sale of merchandise.

When this country was ninety years younger than it is today *The Southern Planter*, the oldest agricultural paper in the United States, came into being. It was founded in 1840 by Charles Tyler Botts, and has been published regularly during the many years which have passed. At the evacuation of Richmond publication was immediately resumed, and not an issue was missed. It is the recognized authority on agriculture throughout the South, and a most helpful journal in bringing about efficient organization for farmers, constructive legislation for the agricultural interests. B. Morgan Shepherd, mayor of Ashland, and one of the outstanding figures in this part of Virginia, is the secretary of the company and managing editor.

The birth of Mayor Shepherd occurred at Berryville, Clarke County, Virginia, in 1878, and he is a son of J. H. and Martha Elizabeth (Morgan) Shepherd, and grandson of Champe Shepherd, the latter of whom was one of the prominent old-time citizens of Clarke County. The maternal grandfather of Mayor Shepherd was Col. Benjamin Morgan, belonged to the historic Morgan family of Virginia, whose valorous leadership in the American Revolution gives all bearing the name a distinguished place in the history of the Old Dominion.

Mayor Shepherd was educated in the public schools of Berryville and by private tutors. When only sixteen years old he began working for himself, and came to Richmond, the mecca for so many ambitious youths of Virginia, and became connected as an employe with *The Southern Planter*. From then on he has continued with this famous publication, and gradually bought stock in it until he acquired a substantial interest in the business. For many years he has been vice president of the publishing company issuing the paper and executive manager of it. His home is at Ashland, the historic town of Hanover County, a few miles north of Richmond. For a number of years he has served as mayor of Ashland and as judge of the Juvenile Court of Hanover County, striving to express in his newspaper and his life a courageous condemnation of what he believes to be wrong, and an encouragement of what is proper and right, and to get others to join and sympathize in his work, so that the tide will gather volume till the whole of public opinion is affected. It is his contention that there is as much good in men's hearts as there is evil, but selfishness so controls the majority that it is difficult to awaken public condemnation and arouse a better spirit and an ambition toward nobler aims. Experience has taught him that these things cannot be accom-

plished by standing remote, but only by active personal labor.
For twenty-two years he has been secretary of the Virginia State
Farmers Institute, and needless to say he is vitally interested
in everything pertaining to the agricultural situation.

Mr. Shepherd is the oldest active worker in agriculture in
the state in point of service. He was president of various farm
organizations and a director in a number of others, and is a
member of practically all farm organizations in the state.

JOHN BROCKENBROUGH NEWTON, president of the Virginia
Iron, Coal & Coke Company of Roanoke, bears the name of his
father, who was a bishop of the Episcopal Church in Virginia,
and represents the ninth generation of the family which has
given many distinguished men to Virginia's annals.

Mr. Newton was born in Westmoreland County, Virginia,
son of Rt. Rev. John Brockenbrough and Roberta Page (Williamson) Newton, grandson of Willoughby Newton, who was in
the seventh generation of descent from Thomas Newton, a resident of Yorkshire, England. Capt. John Newton, son of Thomas,
came to Virginia about 1666, establishing his home in Westmoreland County, where the Newtons have lived for nearly three
centuries. The Newtons intermarried with some of the other
distinguished families of old Virginia.

Willoughby Newton, grandfather of the Roanoke business
man, was born in 1802 and died in 1875. He owned the "Linden"
estate in Westmoreland County. He was a member of Congress
and at one time president of the Virginia State Agricultural
Society. His wife, whom he married in 1829, was Mary Stevenson Brockenbrough, whose father, Judge William Brockenbrough, was a judge of the Virginia Court of Appeals.

Bishop John Brockenbrough Newton was born February 7,
1840. Before the war he had graduated from the Virginia Medical College and served with the rank of major and surgeon in the
Confederate army. Later he attended the Episcopal Theological
Seminary, was ordained in 1871, served several prominent
churches in Norfolk and Richmond, and on May 16, 1894, was
consecrated Bishop Coadjutor of the Diocese of Virginia. He
had filled that office about three years before his death, which
occurred in 1897. His wife, Roberta Page Williamson, was a
daughter of Joseph A. and Mary Mann (Page) Williamson, her
mother being a daughter of Robert Page, who served with the
rank of captain in the Revolutionary army and was a member
of the First Congress. Among other noted names in her ancestry was that of Col. William Byrd, founder of Richmond.

John Brockenbrough Newton, Jr., was one of a large family
of eleven children. He was educated in the Norfolk Male Academy, the Episcopal High School at Alexandria, and had the
training of a civil engineer. As a civil engineer he became interested in railroading, particularly construction of lines for the
development and proper utilization of the rich mineral resources
of the West, and finally became identified with and active head of
that great group of financial and industrial interests comprised
under the corporate title of Virginia Iron, Coal & Coke Company.
He was vice president and general manager until 1907, and since
that date has been president of the corporation. Since 1914 his
home and the home offices of the company have been at Roanoke.
This company controls and directs operations covering half a

dozen states, including the ownership of great tracts of mineral lands, coal mines, iron mines, furnaces and factories.

Mr. Newton has served as senior warden of St. John's Episcopal Church at Roanoke. He is a member of the Shenandoah and Country Clubs. He married, in 1890, Laura Neal, a native of Marion, North Carolina, daughter of J. G. and Rowena Neal. They have a son, John Brockenbrough Newton III, who on April 29, 1915, married Dorothy Ball Judkins, of Virginia, she being a direct descendant of Mary Ball, mother of George Washington.

GARNETT OWEN LEE. Among the far-sighted business men who have taken advantage of the opportunities offered by the wonderful growth and development of the automobile industry is Garnett O. Lee, who conducts the agency for Ford automobiles at Lynchburg. He has been identified with his present business since 1910, and it now bears the name of the Apperson-Lee Motor Company, of which he is president, and which is one of the most successful concerns of its kind in the city. During his career he has won a reputation for business ability and judgment, as well as for public-spirited cooperation in all movements pertaining to the welfare and progress of the city.

Mr. Lee was born March 14, 1881, at Lynchburg, and is a son of James I. and Nannie B. (Anthony) Lee, natives of Virginia, who are both deceased. This branch of the Lee family traces its ancestry back to France, whence the original American ancestor came to Colonial Virginia long prior to the war of the Revolution. The Town of Leesville, in Campbell County, was named in honor of the great-grandfather of Mr. Lee, and there was born his grandfather, John Lee. James I. Lee, father of Garnett O., was for many years a wholesale grocer at Lynchburg, where he was the owner of a prosperous business and the possessor of a splendid reputation for business integrity and straightforward dealing. He and his worthy wife were members of the Methodist Church, in the work of which both were active, and Mr. Lee was also a leading public figure, serving for many years as a member of the City Council of Lynchburg, to which he was elected on the Democratic ticket. Fraternally he was a Mason. During the war between the states he enlisted in the Confederate army under Gen. J. E. B. Stuart, and saw four years of service as a member of Company F, Second Regiment, Virginia Volunteer Infantry, during which time he sustained three wounds. At the close of the struggle he returned to Lynchburg to resume his business activities, in which he continued until the close of his life. He and his wife became the parents of four children: James I., Jr., who is identified with the Southern Railway of Washington, D. C.; Garnett O., of this review; Alice Anthony, the wife of Mr. Van Swearingen, who is connected with the Republic Rubber Company of Boston, Massachusetts; and Mary Gill, the wife of Alfred Farrar, of Saint Louis, connected with the International Shoe Company of Saint Louis, of which he is one of the three principal owners, and a man who has been very successful in his business career.

Garnett O. Lee acquired his education in the public schools of Lynchburg, and after graduating from high school his first work was with the Oglesby DeWitt Company, a wholesale dry goods concern, with which he remained for five years. When he started he was first employed in the house, but later was advanced to traveling salesman and thus gained much valuable experience and a wide acquaintance. Later he went to Boston, where he was associated with the Interstate Chemical Company for one year, at the end of which time the plant of the company was destroyed by fire and Mr. Lee returned to Lynchburg, where he acquired a position as teller in the American National Bank. Mr. Lee remained in this bank until 1910, when he saw an opportunity to embark in the automobile business as representative of the Palmer-Singer car. Four years later he took over the agency for the Hudson and Haines cars, but at the end of four years' time disposed of his holdings and took over the Ford, which he has handled ever since as president of the Apperson-Lee Motor Company, P. D. Winston being vice president. This company does a large and profitable business and maintains a salesroom, office and service station at 516 Main Street, Lynchburg, as well as branches at Rustburg, Amherst and Farmville. Mr. Lee is widely and favorably known in business circles and has numerous friends.

In 1910 Mr. Lee was united in marriage with Miss Jessie Apperson, who was born at Little Rock, Arkansas, and educated at Mary Baldwin's School at Staunton. Four children have been born to this union: Jacqueline Apperson, born in 1912; Geraldine Anthony, born in 1914; Garnett Owen, Jr., born in 1916; and Richard Adams, born in 1918. Mr. and Mrs. Lee are consistent members of St. John's Episcopal Church, and Mrs. Lee has been particularly active in religious and charitable work. Mr. Lee is an ardent fisherman and hunter, and possesses many trophies of these sports. His hobby is research work and investigation along the lines of agricultural activities, and he is a close student of the problems of the soil.

BLAIR J. FISHBURN in his individual career has been closely identified with the rise of a most important city of Southwest Virginia, Roanoke. He was born at what was known in local geography as the village of Big Lick, the site of which long since has been taken into the City of Roanoke, and he was a boy during the '80s when Roanoke acquired its first city charter.

The Fishburns have been a family of pioneers in Virginia and many of the names have reached positions of distinction and success. His father, Reuben Harvey Fishburn, was born in Franklin County, Virginia, February 27, 1835, son of Samuel Washington and Frances (Tyree) Tinsley Fishburn. As a youth he learned the business of farming and tanning. He volunteered at the outbreak of the Civil war, joining Company A, Thirty-seventh Battalion, Virginia Cavalry, participated in some of the early campaigns in Southwestern Virginia and West Virginia, and then fought up and down the Valley of Virginia until the end of the war. Afterwards he became a merchant, and in 1873 moved to the village of Big Lick, where he and his brothers, Tipton T. and John Robert Fishburn, engaged in tobacco manufacture. They gave early Roanoke one of its largest commercial and industrial establishments. Reuben Fishburn retired from business in 1905. He married, April 27, 1873, Emma Virginia Phillips, daughter of Joshua and Sallie (Hughes) Phillips, of Campbell County, Virginia. Of their five children the only son is Blair J.

Blair J. Fishburn was educated in public schools at Roanoke, in Randolph-Macon Academy at Front Royal, and also had the

benefit of travel and study abroad in Europe and the Holy Land.
For several years he was associated with R. H. Fishburn & Company, manufacturers of smoking tobacco, who sold out their
business in 1905, but the business which has absorbed most of
his energies has been the S. P. Hite Company, manufacturers of
drugs and flavoring extracts. He acquired a financial interest
in this in 1905, and is now its president and manager. Mr.
Fishburn is a director of the First National Exchange Bank of
Roanoke, Virginia Bridge & Iron Company, Roanoke Securities
Corporation and Shenandoah Life Insurance Company, and,
like his late father, his financial connections would comprise
almost a directory of the leading commercial and industrial
affairs of Roanoke.

He has been none the less helpful and public-spirited in his
citizenship. He was a member of the City Council of Roanoke
from 1907 until 1918, his last term closing at the time Roanoke
adopted a new city charter, providing for a city manager. In
1922 he was elected one of the five councilmen of the city, and
was president of the council and mayor of the city from then
until September 1, 1926. He is now president of the Playgrounds and Recreation Association of Roanoke, so that the city
is not without his wise participation in its continued growth and
development.

He is a steward of the Greene Memorial Methodist Episcopal
Church, of which both his parents were members. He is a
thirty-second degree Scottish Rite Mason, member of Kazim
Temple of the Mystic Shrine, belongs to the Knights of Pythias,
B. P. O. Elks, Rotary Club and for many years was a prominent
official in the United Commercial Travelers. He is a member
of the Roanoke Gun Club, Shenandoah Club, Roanoke Country
Club, United States, State of Virginia and City of Roanoke
Chambers of Commerce.

HON. JOSEPH CROCKETT SHAFFER, United States District attorney, with headquarters in Roanoke, is one of the ablest lawyers in this part of the Old Dominion, and a man whose knowledge of the law and brilliant attainments are recognized by the
profession and public as well. He possesses a vigorous mind that
seems never to need rest or to become dull. His memory is
phenomenal. He knows not dimly or hazily, but with substantial
accuracy, the law and how to interpret it. In his office he is
utterly indifferent to the applause of the multitude, the blandishment of power, as well as the bitterness of those who take offense
at his conduct, and with these characteristics he is invaluable
to the Government, and at the same time he is safeguarding the
rights of the citizens by refraining from the arbitrary exercise
of the powers invested in him. He was born in Wythe County,
Virginia, January 19, 1880, a son of Joseph B. and Elizabeth
(Crockett) Shaffer, both of whom were also born in Wythe
County. She is deceased, but he is living, and, after a lifetime
of farming, is residing in Wytheville. There were two children
born to the parents: Edith, who married J. P. Hert, of Wytheville, employed by a West Virginia coal company; and Attorney
Shaffer. Both parents early united with the Presbyterian
Church, and they reared their children in that faith, to which
she adhered until her death, and to which he still subscribes.
Fraternally he belongs to the Independent Order of Odd Fellows.
A strong Republican, he has held several county offices, and has

always been interested in party affairs. The paternal grandfather of Attorney Shaffer was Joseph Shaffer, born in Virginia,
but the great-grandfather was a Pennsylvanian, and came to
Virginia many years ago, and here he lived and died, as did the
grandfather. The maternal grandfather was Montgomery
Crockett, a native of Wythe County, Virginia, and a member of
one of the very old families of Virginia. In fact on both sides
of the house Attorney Shaffer comes of fine old Virginian stock,
of which he may well be proud.

After the usual preliminary schooling Joseph Crockett Shaffer entered the University of Virginia, and was graduated therefrom in 1904 with the degree of Bachelor of Laws, and he
entered at once upon the practice of his profession in Wytheville,
where he remained until he was appointed United States district
attorney January 13, 1924, and took charge of his office with
characteristic energy and efficiency. Prior to his appointment
he had already demonstrated his fitness for the office he now
holds by serving for four years as commonwealth attorney of
Wytheville, and he was also attorney for the prohibition administrator for a short period, so that his appointment caused no
surprise. Since he cast his first vote he has been a Republican,
and he is active in his party.

On May 15, 1912, Attorney Shaffer married Miss Ada Honaker, born in Bland County, Virginia, and educated in Sullivan's
College, Bristol, Virginia. Five children have been born to
them, namely: Joseph C., Junior, John Scott, Mary Elizabeth,
Edwin Gray and Edwina Gay, the last two being twins. The
three elder children are attending school in Roanoke. Mr.
Shaffer is a Presbyterian, while Mrs. Shaffer is a Methodist,
and both are active in church work. Fraternally he has been
advanced in the Scottish Rite in Masonry, and he also belongs
to the Mystic Shrine. It would be difficult to find a man more
generally representative of the best ideals of his learned profession and of good citizenship than he, and further advancement is looked for him by his many friends.

ISAAC ELDRIDGE HUFF, physician and surgeon at Roanoke,
graduated from the University of Maryland in 1892, and for
many years has been recognized as a man of real distinction in
his profession, with a wide scope of service for his talents.

He was born in Floyd County, Virginia, May 26, 1866, and
his people have lived in that section of Virginia for several generations. His parents, Isaac and Adeline (Kitterman) Huff,
were born in Floyd County. His father was a Confederate
soldier, a farmer, and died in November, 1895.

Doctor Huff finished his medical education in what was then
known as the College of Physicians and Surgeons of Baltimore,
now the Medical Department of the University of Maryland.
He was an interne in Mercy Hospital of Baltimore, and for
twelve years practiced in Floyd, his home county. His home has
been at Roanoke since 1904. Doctor Huff has offices in the
Shenandoah Life Building, and for a number of years has been
president of the Shenandoah Hospital. He has conducted a
general practice, and has a high reputation as an obstetrician.
He has been president of the Roanoke Academy of Medicine, an
active member of the Medical Society of Virginia, the Southwest Virginia Medical Society, Southern and American Medical
Associations. He became a member of the Roanoke Board of

Health upon its organization. Doctor Huff has been active in
the First Baptist Church of Roanoke, serving as a deacon of
the church and a teacher in the Sunday School. He is a member of the University Club and Kiwanis Club.

He married at Roanoke Miss Flora McIvor Francis, daughter
of Capt. W. H. and Eliza A. (Shelor) Francis, of Floyd County.
Her father commanded a company in the Confederate army. Of
the three children of Doctor and Mrs. Huff, William Banks is an
A. B. graduate of Roanoke College, took his medical degree in
1922 at the University of Maryland, was connected with the
Walter Reed Hospital at Washington during the World war, and
began practice with his father. The daughter, Doris, graduated
with the A. B. degree from Hollins College, and married D. R.
Hunt. Francis Eldridge, the second son, was educated in Richmond College and Washington and Lee University, and took up
a business career.

CHARLES G. LINDSEY. Among the men who have worked
their way to prominence and affluence solely through the medium
of their own efforts, one of the foremost at Roanoke is Charles
G. Lindsey, president of Lindsey, Robinson & Company, wholesale distributors; president of the Victory Specialty Company;
president of Maddox & Jennings Bakery and a stockholder or
director in various other enterprises. The business qualities
that are essential for the management of so vast and intricate
operations are obvious. To breadth and comprehensiveness of
mind, quickness to perceive opportunities and readiness to grasp
them, energy and push, there must be added a capacity for organization, as well as an attention to detail, that every part of
the complicated machinery move harmoniously. The difference
between profit and loss in a great industry often turns on nice
calculations of cost of production and small economies. He who
neglects little things often fails in great ones. In all these
qualities Mr. Lindsey excels. Under his quiet but efficient control the diversified operations move with the regularity and
power of one of his great machines, he himself being the balance
wheel that controls and steadies the action of all the parts.

Mr. Lindsey was born in Carroll County, Virginia, February
6, 1879, and is a son of Charles Wesley and Margaret Louise
(Quesenberry) Lindsey, and a grandson of Henry K. Lindsey,
also a native of that county, where he passed his entire career in
agricultural pursuits. Charles Wesley Lindsey was born in
Carroll County, Virginia, and during his young manhood taught
school in the rural districts. Later he turned his attention to
farming, which he followed for many years, but at present is
engaged in general merchandising in Pulaski County, this state.
He married Margaret Louise Quesenberry, daughter of Crockett
Quesenberry, who was born in Pulaski County, where he spent
his entire life in farming with the exception of the duration of
the war between the states, in which, as a soldier of the Confederacy, he saw much hard fighting, and suffered both wounds and
capture. Mrs. Lindsey was reared in the faith of the Methodist Church, in the work of which she always has been active.
She and her husband have had eight children, of whom seven
survive, Charles G. being the fifth in order of birth.

Charles G. Lindsey received his education in Carroll County,
where he taught school for two years, and then came to Roanoke,
a poor but ambitious youth, to seek his fortune. He subsequently became cashier of the Virginia Iron and Coal Company

at Crosier Furnace, Roanoke, and remained with that concern
for four years, resigning to accept a position as a traveling salesman for a flour milling concern.   During the next four years he
traveled through Virginia, West Virginia, North Carolina and
South Carolina, learning every detail of the business, and in
1911 returned to Roanoke to join the firm of Davis, Robinson &
Company.   Later Mr. Davis sold his interest and the firm became
Lindsey, Robinson & Company, under which style it was incorporated in July, 1918.   This has grown to large proportions and
Mr. Lindsey is now president and manager, George C. Huff, vice
president, J. E. Robinson, secretary, and J. M. McGee, treasurer.   This concern makes certain kinds of feeds, including
poultry feed and meal, and does a general jobbing business in
flour and groceries.   In addition to a large force at the headquarters, 365 Salem Avenue, Roanoke, the concern keeps six
traveling salesmen on the road, covering Virginia, West Virginia and North Carolina.   Mr. Lindsey naturally centers his
interests in this enterprise, but also has other important connections.   He is president of the Victory Specialty Company,
manufacturers and distributors of candies, cigars, cigarettes and
tobacco; and president of the Maddox & Jennings Bakery, Inc.,
and is importantly interested in the Roanoke Ice and Cold Storage Company and in the Griggs Packing Company.   He has
been very active in civic affairs, and is an enthusiastic member
of the Chamber of Commerce and the Booster Club.   He is a
Democrat in his political views, but not a seeker for public
office, and is a consistent member of the First Presbyterian
Church, in which he is an elder.   He likewise belongs to the
Benevolent and Protective Order of Elks, the Lions Club, the
Country Club and the Shenandoah Club, in all of which he is
very popular and has numerous warm friends.

In 1909 Mr. Lindsey was united in marriage with Miss Annie
Snyder Huff, who was born at Roanoke, daughter of George C.
Huff and Blanche Vinyard Huff, now residents of Washington
County, Virginia.   To this union there have been born two children: Blanche Vinyard, born in 1912, who is in third year of
high school; and Charles Grattan, Jr., born in 1916, who is
attending public school.   Mr. Lindsey had been previously married, in 1904, to Miss Lula Belle Smith, of Pulaski County, Virginia, who died in 1905 without issue.

ROBERT L. McGUIRE.   For a number of years Robert L. Mc-
Guire has been engaged in the real estate business in Richmond,
and it is partially due to his efforts that Bellevue Court, Sum-
merfield, Wildwood, Westover Gardens and other choice residential developments have been successfully carried on, both in
Virginia and other Southern States.   In his operations he has
developed into a financier with extensive interests in the states
of Florida, Georgia, Kentucky, Missouri, South Dakota and Tennessee.   He is now president of the National Finance & Mortgage Corporation, the National Holdings Corporation and the
National Securities Corporation.

Robert L. McGuire was born in Winchester, Virginia, May
12, 1895, a son of Saint George and Anna Marie (von Boehm)
McGuire, and a member of the historic McGuire family of Virginia, of which Dr. Hunter McGuire, distinguished surgeon of
the Confederacy, was a notable example, and a direct descendant
of the Lord McGuire, Baron of Enniskillen, of Ireland and

France. Saint George McGuire had a distinguished diplomatic career, ending with the inauguration of Woodrow Wilson to the presidency in 1913. He was sent on various diplomatic missions of importance to Germany, South America and Asia, and died of yellow fever at the age of forty years, while en route to Sumatra from China. His wife was born in Saxony, Germany, a daughter of Robert von Boehm, of an Austrian family, who had a distinguished record in the German army, and was decorated by the former Kaiser; and was a near relative of General von Boehm, who commanded a German division in the World war.

When still a child Robert L. McGuire accompanied his father to South America, where he studied under private tutors, and he continued his studies in the same manner in Europe and Asia, completing his quite extensive education with a legal course in the University of Leipsic, and still later had one year's work at LaSalle University. He was later a junior member of a German expedition into the interior of Brazil and subsequently was present at one of the earlier revolts in Nicaragua, Central America.

In August, 1917, Mr. McGuire enlisted for the World war in the field artillery, was commissioned a lieutenant, and went overseas, and because of linguistic ability and knowledge of the peoples was placed on duty with the Headquarters Staff in France. After the close of the war and his honorable discharge Mr. McGuire returned to civilian life and began handling real estate, as above indicated, in Richmond, becoming treasurer of the Northside Development Corporation and later vice president of Your Home Building Corporation. He then became president of the Westover Gardens Corporation and in July, 1927, he organized the National Finance & Mortgage Corporation, of which he is president. This latter corporation has a unique method to finance mortgages and developments for Richmond real estate men. This service provides the opportunity for public participation through authorizing the issuance of six and one-quarter per cent ten-year accumulative installment certificates for the investment of savings; and also used as sinking fund by other corporations, that wish to protect their stockholders from loss. The funds thus received will, in turn, be used for the purchase of superior mortgages and other negotiable paper.

Mr. McGuire married the Marchioness Wilmina Eleanora de Bonneville, of Bonneville, France, a daughter of the Marquis Arthur A. de Bonneville, of the French army, and a descendant of Cecelia de Treauneaux, who was lady-in-waiting to the Empress Josephine. Colonel de Bonneville, an engineer officer, representing the French army, came to America during the World war and assisted in establishing army camps, in which he was an instructor.

Through his financial company Mr. McGuire is not only aiding others in their development work, but he is going ahead with some enterprises of his own which promise to be more than usually successful. He has lately established a corporation for the purpose of taking over a large tract of land in the State of Tennessee and will form the Town of Bonneville, an industrial and residential enterprise. While not a native son of Richmond, he is a Virginian, and as such bears a deep love in his heart for the beautiful Southern city of such historic memories, and it is a source of great pride to him that he has been able to accom-

plish so much for it, and plans to greatly increase his benefactions in the next few years. He has contributed articles to trade
papers on phases of financing and promotions, and is author of
an extensive work on salesmanship.

REV. WILLIAM ARTHUR PEARMAN as a clergyman of the
Episcopal Church began his service in his native state of Ohio,
afterwards was in Missouri, and on coming to Virginia first
located at Richmond. He is now pastor of the church at Bedford City.

He was born on a farm in Noble County, Indiana, in 1868,
son of Benjamin F. and Adaline (Wittmer) Pearman, and a
grandson of William Pearman and John Wittmer. William
Pearman was a pioneer farmer of Indiana. John Wittmer was
born in Pennsylvania, became a miller by trade, and he walked
all the way from Niagara Falls, New York, to Northern Indiana, looking for, and where he finally found, a site for a mill.
Benjamin F. Pearman was born in Virginia and spent his active
life as a farmer in Indiana. He was a Methodist, a Democrat
and a member of the Masonic fraternity. His wife, Adaline
Wittmer, was born at Niagara Falls, New York. They had a
family of seven children and those now living are: Mrs. Mary
A. Bowser, of Elkhart, Indiana; Levi W., of Nappanee, Indiana;
Chloe, widow of W. B. Jacoby, living in California; Martha J.,
wife of H. S. Funk, of California; and William Arthur.

William Arthur Pearman was reared on a farm, attended
Indiana public schools and finished his literary education in the
old Lutheran College, Wittenberg College, at Springfield, Ohio,
graduating Bachelor of Arts in 1896. He completed his course
in the theological seminary in preparation for the Episcopal
ministry in 1899. His first church was at Mechanicsburg, Ohio,
where he remained four years. Going to Missouri he was rector
of a church at Clinton two years and at Warrenburg two years.
Rev. Mr. Pearman was assistant pastor of St. Paul's Church at
Richmond, Virginia, for two years. He was at Covington, Virginia, four years, and on October 1, 1918, came to Bedford. The
church at Bedford was established in 1847, and when Mr. Pearman began his work in the parish the congregation was still
worshipping in a very small building. He has succeeded in
erecting a handsome new church edifice costing approximately
$100,000, one that is an honor to the town and the parish. This
church was opened for worship June, 1924. St. John's Church
has over two hundred communicants.

Rev. Mr. Pearman married in 1900, Edith Keller Schindler,
a native of Springfield, Ohio, where she was educated in the
public schools. Her father, Charles Schindler, was an undertaker. Mr. and Mrs. Pearman had five children: Carl Schindler, born in 1902, now with a motor truck company at San Francisco; Benjamin Vincent, a graduate of high school and of the
University of the South at Sewanee, Tennessee, in 1926, now
with the American Pigment Corporation, of Bedford, Virginia;
Robert William, a chemist with the Frazer Paint Company, of
Detroit, Michigan; Frederick Keller, a student in Washington
and Lee University; and Edith Adaline, attending the Junior
high school at Bedford. Rev. Mr. Pearman is a Royal Arch
Mason, member of the Phi Gamma Delta, and all his sons are
members of the same fraternity in college. He also belongs to
the B. P. O. Elks.

John Wright

JOHN WRIGHT, an Englishman by birth, identified himself
with Richmond a few years after the close of the Civil war,
and for a quarter of a century was a prominent tobacco manufacturer, becoming one of the very successful men in an age
when that industry was largely under individual ownership and
control.

Mr. Wright was born in Lancashire, England, November 19,
1833, son of Thomas Anthony and Catherine Elizabeth (Knight)
Wright, both of whom represented the substantial landed gentry
of England. His father was a gentleman farmer.

John Wright, one of eight children, was educated by private
tutors in his father's home. When he came to America he
traveled on a sailing vessel and for a number of years made
his home in New York City. On coming to Richmond in 1875
Mr. Wright bought a country home in Henrico County. He
established his tobacco factory near Nineteenth and Franklin
streets, and for twenty-seven years he gave his close personal
supervision to his growing business there. He retired to his
farm in 1902, and lived quietly there until his death in 1907.
Mr. Wright was a member of the Tobacco Association and was
counted one of the most enterprising and public spirited citizens
of his time. He and all his family were members of the Episcopal Church.

His first wife was Miss Annie Helpin, who died shortly after
they came to Richmond, leaving no children. On November 17,
1893, Mr. Wright married Margaret Snell. Mrs. Wright, whose
home is now at 1715 Grove Avenue in Richmond, is a member
of the United Daughters of the Confederacy and Daughters of
the American Revolution, and has taken an active part in the
guilds and societies of the Episcopal Church. Her grandparents
were James and Millicent (Archer)Snell. Her father, James
Archer Snell, was born in Henrico County in 1818, was educated
by private tutors, and as a young man entered merchandising,
which he continued for over twenty years, and then retired.
He served three years in a Virginia regiment with the Confederate army. His business was located at Seventeenth and
Main streets, at that time Richmond being a comparatively small
city. James Archer Snell married Nancy Bibb Rison, of Amelia
County, and they had a family of eight children: James Archer,
Sallie Booker Snell, Millicent Jane, John Reighley, William
Booker, Nannie Irvin, Mrs. Margaret Ella Wright and Coakley.

To the marriage of Mr. John Wright and Margaret E. Snell
were born three children. The son Thomas Arthur, a distinguished scholar, was educated in the McGuire's School for Boys
at Richmond, took his Bachelor of Science degree at William
and Mary College, his Doctor's degree at Harvard University,
and for twelve years was principal of the Baker School in Richmond, and for the past ten years has been a member of the
faculty of Dartmouth College at Hanover, New Hampshire. He
is author of a book on Principles of Vocational Guidance.
Thomas Arthur Wright married Minnie Rowe, of Hampton, Virginia, and has two children, named Mary Morris and Margaret
Elizabeth. John Halpin Wright, the second son of Mrs. Wright,
graduated from William and Mary College and has since made
a great success in the real estate business, being one of the leading realtors of Washington, D. C. He is a member of the Real
Estate Board of Washington and belongs to several college and
other fraternities and civic organizations. John Halpin Wright

married Dorothy Jones, of Washington, and their three children are Margaret Madison, John Halpin, Jr., and Dorothy Knowles. Nancy Bibb Wright, the only daughter, was educated in Mrs. Morris' School at Richmond, and takes an active part in Sunday School work in the Episcopal Church. She is now the wife of Louis C. Adair, of Richmond, Mr. Adair being a brother of Cornelia Adair, president of the Virginia Teachers Association and one of the outstanding educational leaders in the state. Mr. and Mrs. Adair have three children, Nancy Bibb, Cornelia Storris and Catherine.

JOHN NOTTINGHAM UPSHUR, M. D., by his own life of service in the medical profession upheld the standards of a very distinguished Virginia family name.

Doctor Upshur was born at Norfolk, Virginia, February 14, 1848, and died at Richmond, December 10, 1924. He was a nephew of Abel Parker Upshur, who served as Secretary of the Navy under President Tyler, and then succeeded Daniel Webster as Secretary of State.

Doctor Upshur was a son of Doctor George Littleton Upshur and a grandson of Colonel Littleton and Anne (Parker) Upshur. Doctor George Littleton Upshur practiced medicine at Norfolk, and fell a victim to one of the yellow fever epidemics that overspread that city. Doctor George Littleton Upshur was a brother of the late John Henry Upshur, who became a rear admiral of the United States Navy and served with Commodore Perry in the expedition that opened Japan to commerce. He was on the Union side during the Civil war and had many important commands after the war, retiring after forty-four years of service.

Doctor John Nottingham Upshur was educated at Norfolk, attended the University of Virginia and graduated from the Medical College of Virginia in 1869. For more than half a century he pursued his professional routine with a skill and devotion that earned the admiration of thousands who were included at one time or other in his private practice, and he also reached eminence in the opinion of his professional associates. He was at one time president of the Virginia State Medical Association, and was founder of the Tri-State Medical Society, comprising the states of Virginia, North and South Carolina. He was also a member of the American Medical Association.

Doctor Upshur at the age of sixteen was a cadet at the Virginia Military Institute in Lexington, Virginia, and was severely wounded at the battle of New Market. He was always a staunch Democrat, and an active member of St. James Episcopal Church. He was affiliated with the Masonic fraternity.

Doctor Upshur married Miss Lucy Whittle, who died leaving one son, Doctor Francis Whittle Upshur. On December 10, 1879, he married Miss Elizabeth Peterkin, who survives him and resides at 1613 Grove Avenue in Richmond. Mrs. Upshur is a member of the Richmond Woman's Club. She is a native of New Orleans, daughter of William S. and Emma (Meeteer) Peterkin, who were born in Baltimore and lived for many years in New Orleans, where her father was a cotton broker.

Mrs. Upshur is the mother of three children. Her son, Colonel William Peterkin Upshur, graduated from the Virginia Military Institute, having previously attended the McGuire School for Boys in Richmond, and during the World war was in France, and he was awarded the Congressional Medal of Honor for bravery while on duty at Haiti. Colonel Upshur married

Lucy Munford. The daughter, Elizabeth Nottingham, is the wife of George J. Benson, a business man at Charlottesville, Virginia, and they have three children, Elizabeth Peterkin, Frances Day, and John Upshur Benson. The youngest child is Doctor Alfred P. Upshur, of New York, who attended the McGuire School at Richmond, the Virginia Military Institute at Lexington, and the Virginia Medical College, and is now associated with the Life Extension Institute of New York City. He is a member of the Virginia State and American Medical Associations. He served with many hospitals during the war as commandant.

Dr. J. N. Upshur was professor of Materia Medica and Therapeutics, and of the Practice of Medicine at the Medical College of Virginia. He was also chief medical examiner in Richmond, for the Equitable Life Insurance Company. He was a member of the Lee Camp, N. C. V., and served on the staff of the commanding General of that camp, as surgeon. During the World war, he was active as a speaker in behalf of recruiting, at many public gatherings.

ROBERT B. GRIGGS was born and grew up in Roanoke County, has been a participant in the development of the important city of Roanoke, and is founder and active head of the Griggs Packing Company, one of the large and important industries of the city.

Mr. Griggs was born in Roanoke County in 1861, son of Samuel and Eva (Kefauber) Griggs, his father a native of Floyd County and his mother of Roanoke County. Her father, Peter Kefauber, was a pioneer farmer of this section of Virginia. Samuel Griggs spent his life as a farmer and merchant, and was a Confederate soldier throughout the Civil war. He always voted as a Democrat, was a member of the Baptist Church, and in a quiet, unostentatious way achieved a great deal of life's most substantial rewards. He and his wife had eight children, six of whom are living.

Robert B. Griggs grew up on a Roanoke County farm and attended school at Big Lick, the village community which was the nucleus of the larger city of Roanoke. He began his career as a farmer, and as a farmer and stock raiser laid the substantial basis of his larger enterprises. Mr. Griggs retained large land holdings and farming interests in the vicinity of Roanoke until 1912, when he disposed of most of this property.

A number of years ago he started a small packing plant for hogs, and his individual push and enterprise have accounted for the remarkable growth of this industry, which now kills and packs ten thousand hogs annually, making a specialty of the manufacture of Virginia hams, widely sold all over the Roanoke territory. The great packing company is an incorporated institution with Mr. Griggs as president and active manager, and C. M. Griggs, vice president.

Mr. Griggs married, in 1891, Miss Hallie Mead, a native of Bedford County, daughter of Oliver Mead, and her maternal grandfather was Col. Richard Crenshaw, one of the extensive land owners of his day in Bedford County, and who gave each of his grandchildren a large farm. Mr. and Mrs. Griggs have had a family of five children: Mrs. Stewart Barber, whose husband is a contractor at Roanoke, and mother of one daughter, Lutitia, born in 1917; Robert C. Griggs, who died in 1926 at the age of twenty-three; Evelyn, who married Louis Hock, of Charlottsville, Virginia; Ruth Griggs, a student in Virginia College; and Hallie Mead, in high school. The family are members of the Trinity Methodist Episcopal Church, South. Mr. Griggs is a Democrat and a member of the Roanoke Chamber of Commerce.

BRANCH W. STONEBRAKER. The career of Branch W. Stonebraker, president and a member of the Board of Directors of the Roanoke Iron Works, possesses all of the elements so dear to the hearts of the lovers of self-made manhood. Starting life with only a common school education, his first experience in the business world was in a humble clerkship. Hard work, constant application, thorough assimilation of the details of the job which he held and fidelity to the interests of his employers carried him up the ladder, and at present he has the respect and esteem of his associates in one of the largest enterprises of its kind in Virginia.

Mr. Stonebraker was born February 26, 1886, in Washington County, Maryland, and is a son of J. C. and Sarah W. (Dalby) Stonebraker. His father, a native of the same county, was given good educational advantages and after leaving college turned his attention to literature, in which he has spent the greater part of his life, among his better known works being "The Unwritten South" and "Puritan and Cavalier." He is a member of the Reformed Church of the United States. A Democrat in politics, he served one or more terms in the State Legislature of Maryland, but is now living in retirement at Hagerstown. Mr. Stonebraker married Sarah W. Dalby, who was born near Farmville, Virginia, and graduated as salutatorian of her class from Farmville College, where later for several years she served as a teacher. She was a member of the first families of Virginia, being a descendant of the Mayos, Branchs, Worshams and Cabells, and is of the stock of the early French-Huguenots, the original settlers of eastern Virginia. She is also a direct descendant of William Mayo, who assisted in laying out the City of Richmond and surveyed the first boundary line between Virginia and North Carolina. To Mr. and Mrs. Stonebraker there were born eight sons and two daughters, of whom Branch W. was the third in order of birth, and five sons are now living.

Branch W. Stonebraker received his education in the public schools of Hagerstown, Maryland, and was seventeen years of age when he started work as a clerk in the offices of the Norfolk & Western Railroad at Roanoke. In 1908 he purchased an interest in the Roanoke Iron Works, Inc., of which he became assistant to the manager, and continued in that capacity until 1913, when he went to Chicago to become erection superintendent of one of the largest ornamental iron works plants in the United States. Returning to Roanoke, he became superintendent of the Roanoke Iron Works, and in 1917 was made general manager and a member of the directorate. On January 1, 1928, he became president of the company. This company manufactures ornamental iron work of all kinds and finds a ready and eager market for its product from Maine to Florida and as far west as Ogden, Utah. Mr. Stonebraker, who devotes his entire time and energies to the responsibilities of his office, is acknowledged to be one of the best informed and most capable men in his line in the country. He has won his way to his present position through hard and conscientious work, which has

met with well merited recognition and appreciation, and in his
labors has the full confidence of his associates and the friendship and co-operation of the men under his management. He
has found no time for public life or political activities, but gives
his support to movements for civic improvement. He is a past
president of the local Lions Club and a member of the Loyal
Order of Moose and the Travelers Protective Association.

In 1906 Mr. Stonebraker was united in marriage with Miss
Lula F. Via, a daughter of N. W. Via, an Albemarle County
farmer. She was educated in the schools of Roanoke and is an
active member of St. Paul's Reformed Church, in which Mr.
Stonebraker is a member of the Board of Elders.

JOSEPH WOLFE BEAR. One of the alert and enterprising
business men of Roanoke who has made his mark through his
own efforts and who stands deservedly high with all classes of
people is Joseph W. Bear, president of the Double Envelope
Company, and interested in other enterprises of the city. Mr.
Bear was born in Rockingham County, Virginia, February 26,
1896, a son of Decatur B. and Anna Virginia (Gibboney) Bear,
he born at Elkton, Rockingham County, where he died in 1919,
and she born in Wytheville, Virginia, survives and living at Elkton. During his younger life the father was a farmer, but
retired from that occupation early and gave his attention to
private matters and took some interest in politics, working in
conjunction with the Democratic party. Both he and his wife
were strictly religious people, but not of the same faith, as he
was a Methodist and she a Presbyterian. Of their eight children, all of whom are living, Joseph W. Bear is the second in
order of birth. His father's father, his paternal grandfather,
was Adam Bear, an extensive farmer and prominent citizen of
Rockingham County.

Until he was eleven years old Joseph W. Bear attended the
local schools, but at that tender age he left home and began to
earn his own living. But a child, with no backing or training,
he had to do the little jobs that he could find and it was not until
he was sixteen that he was able to get a start. At that time
he began making envelopes, and he has continued in this line of
business ever since. His initial work was done in Richmond. but
later he moved to Roanoke, and in 1917 organized the Double
Envelope Company, of which he is president and manager. The
plant, modern in every respect, is conveniently located at 532-
534 Luck Avenue, West, and the product is shipped all over the
United States. The company specializes in double envelopes
for church collections and prints them in eight different
languages.

In November, 1922, Mr. Bear married Miss Jean McDonald
Franklin, who was born in Roanoke, a daughter of M. C. Franklin, a broker of Roanoke. Mr. and Mrs. Bear have two children:
Joseph Wolfe, Junior, born August 7, 1923, and Clay Franklin,
born May 7, 1925. Mr. Bear is a member of the Second Presbyterian Church of Roanoke, and Mrs. Bear of the First Baptist
Church of Roanoke, and both are active in church work. Mr.
Bear belongs to the Shenandoah Club, Roanoke Chamber of
Commerce and the Country Club. His political convictions make
him a Democrat, and he exerts his right of suffrage but does not
aspire to public honors, for all of his time is taken up with his
company's affairs. He is a director of the Mountain Trust

Bank and of the Roanoke Mutual Building & Loan Association. Recognized as one of the really self-made men of Roanoke, Mr. Bear is accorded a great deal of credit because of what he has accomplished. Many were the obstacles that stood in his way, but he did not allow them to keep him from advancing; he worked long and faithfully at what he had undertaken, and gave the best service that lay in his power from the very inception of his business, and his rewards have proven that industry, thrift and strict integrity are valuable assets to any man no matter what he undertakes.

THOMAS ELMER JAMISON, president of Jamison's Chain Stores and of the Roanoke Grocery & Milling Company, is easily one of the leaders in the business life of his city and county, as he is along other lines, for his is a nature that naturally assumes control of affairs and carries them on to a successful completion. He knows exactly what he is aiming for and does not deviate from his planned course, and in his operations carries with him others, so that the rewards which come of enterprising industry and efficient thoughtfulness are not shared by him alone, but are also participated in by his associates.

The birth of Thomas Elmer Jamison took place in Franklin County, Virginia, May 4, 1865, and he is a son of John and Christana (Hartsell) Jamison. Growing to useful manhood in his native county, he attended the local schools and in them secured a solid foundation upon which to erect the superstructure of his after life, supplemented as this instruction was by the lessons inculcated in the home circle of the dignity of labor and the value of wise economy.

When he reached his majority the future capitalist left the shelter of the rooftree of his parents and went on the road as a traveling salesman for the Wrought Iron Range Company of Saint Louis, Missouri, his territory being the eastern part of Virginia. After a year on the road, in 1888 he came to Roanoke, arriving here at a time when the present city was little more than a village. However, with that faculty of looking into the future that is so characteristic of him he realized its possibilities, and commenced at once to plan to develop them. His first step in that direction was to secure congenial employment, and this was obtained with the P. L. Terry Milling Company as shipping clerk, and he continued to hold it for a couple of years, and while faithfully performing his allotted duties he was also learning the business, and when the company was reorganized as the Roanoke Grocery & Milling Company he was one of the old employes to be retained by the new management, and he was sent on the road. For the succeeding five years he visited the trade, building up wide connections and gaining favor for his company, and when he was recalled from the road it was to take charge of the sales department. Two years later he was elected vice president of the company, and after he had held that office for two years he was elected president of the company, and still retains that office. The Roanoke Grocery & Milling Company controls a large wholesale trade in Roanoke and throughout Virginia, West Virginia, North Carolina, Tennessee and a part of Kentucky.

Not content with what he had accomplished in one line, Mr. Jamison began to branch out and organizing the Roanoke Coffee & Spice Company, of Roanoke, the Salem Grocery Company, Salem, Virginia, and the Mullens Grocery Company, Mullens,

West Virginia, he carried these enterprises on as president of each one until they were placed upon a firm foundation. In the meanwhile he became impressed with the value of the chain store system, and September 9, 1921, established a chain of grocery stores known as Jamison's, there being at the opening of business seventy-six of these stores, but since that time the number has been increased to eighty-one. These stores are conveniently located in the states of Virginia, West Virginia, North Carolina and Tennessee, and it is the hope of Mr. Jamison to have the territory expanded in the near future so as to take in many other states. The Jamison Stores are conducted as subsidiaries to the Roanoke Grocery & Milling Company. In organizing this system Mr. Jamison had in mind the plan of furnishing the people of the different communities in which his stores are placed not only foodstuffs at a much lower price, but also to give them commodities of the very best quality, and so rigidly has he followed this plan that the name of Jamison's is now indissolubly connected with quality and fair prices, and the stores have become very popular. Through his parent company, the Roanoke Grocery & Milling Company, he is able to buy direct from the manufacturer in such immense quantities that necessarily he can place his goods on the market at prices that always prove attractive.

With the market furnished by the chain stores the Roanoke Grocery & Milling Company has steadily grown, from time to time, increasing its capital until it is now capitalized at one-half million dollars, and is the largest distributor of foods in Roanoke, if not in this part of Virginia. Not only does the Roanoke Grocery & Milling Company distribute foodstuffs to the general trade, but also to a number of public institutions of Virginia, to colleges and to hotels, the volume of business done annually being greater than any other company operating between Richmond, Virginia, and Cincinnati, Ohio. The work entailed upon Mr. Jamison is tremendous, but he not only attends to it in a most capable manner, but finds time to give considerable thought and attention to the affairs of the Magic City, and has succeeded in bettering conditions in a most remarkable degree. As the principal promotor of the ordinance which provides increased salaries for the fireman, he secured adequate fire protection, and lowered the insurance rate. It was he who began the agitation that resulted in the establishment of the Roanoke Chamber of Commerce, of which he was an organizer and first vice president. In all matters pertaining to improving and beautifying Roanoke Mr. Jamison can be depended upon to take the initiative, and in this connection special mention must be made of his work in purchasing the Terry property for park purposes. Mr. Jamison has served his city as an alderman, and while a member of the council was appointed by the president of the Chamber of Commerce to draft a plan for a better form of government for the city. For many years he served as president of the Wholesale Grocers Association, and was a member of the Manufacturers Association that was later absorbed by the Chamber of Commerce. The Presbyterian Church has in him an earnest and generous member. His fraternal connections are those which he maintains with the Knights of Pythias.

On November 10, 1892, Mr. Jamison married Miss Lillie Davidson, of Roanoke, and they have three children: Gladys Ann, who married D. R. Carpenter, a teacher in Roanoke College, Salem, Virginia; Thelma Virginia, who married H. K.

Adams, who is with the First National Exchange Bank of
Roanoke; and Frank Elmer, who has charge of the bakery of the
Roanoke Grocery & Milling Company. The children have all
been well educated, Gladys being a graduate of Hollins College;
Thelma was also educated at the same college, and Frank is a
graduate of the University of Virginia, class of 1926.

JOHN WILLIAM HANCOCK, division manager of the Appalachian Electric Power Company, is also president of the Roanoke
Public Library. This latter office is something more than a
casual duty of a successful business man. Mr. Hancock for
many years has been interested in books and the things they
represent, the broad range of literature, arts and sciences. The
life of the world and its people have always interested him, and
he has made one of the best private collections of books on Virginia history. He has been fond of hunting, fishing, moun-
taineering, nature study and amateur photography.

Mr. Hancock was born in Franklin County, Virginia, June
17, 1870, son of Benjamin Peter and Sarah Frances (Hutchinson) Hancock, grandson of William Thomas and Agnes (Booth)
Hancock. His ancestors, the Hancocks, Booths, Duncans and
Hollands, have been in Virginia since early Colonial times. Benjamin Peter Hancock was born in Franklin County, June 19,
1842, served in the Confederate army in Company D, Second
Virginia Cavalry, under Gen. J. E. B. Stuart, and was three
times wounded. After the war he followed farming in Franklin County until he retired. He died at Washington, February
19, 1925. His wife was also a native of Franklin County,
daughter of John C. and Lucy (Meredith) Hutchinson.

John William Hancock, oldest of the four children of his
parents, was reared on a farm, had a common school and academic education, and acquired a sound business training as
clerk in stores and employe of banks at Rocky Mount and
Roanoke.

His experience in the electrical public utility field covers a
period of over thirty years. From 1895 to 1899 he was accountant and cashier of the Roanoke Street Railway Company and
the Roanoke Electric Light & Power Company. Upon the reorganization and consolidation of these companies in 1899 as
the Roanoke Railway & Electric Company, Mr. Hancock was
made general manager and director, and in 1913 he also became
general manager of the Lynchburg Traction & Light Company,
which position he held until the formation of the Appalachian
Electric Power Company in 1926. He is president of the State
Association of Public Utilities, member of the American Institute of Electrical Engineers, National Electric Light Association
and American Gas Association.

During the Spanish-American war he was second lieutenant
of Company G, Second Virginia Volunteer Infantry, and acted
as assistant to the quartermaster of the Second Division, Seventh United States Army Corps, at Jacksonville, Florida. Mr.
Hancock is a fellow of the American Geographical Society, member of the Virginia Historical Society, Wisconsin State Historical Society, Sons of the American Revolution, Sons of Confederate Veterans, member of the Army and Navy Club of
Washington, Shenandoah Club of Roanoke, Roanoke Country
Club and Oakwood Country Club of Lynchburg. He is a member of the Grolier Club of New York and the California Book
Club.

He married at Roanoke, April 30, 1898, Miss Mary Carr
Leffler. Her ancestor, John Carr, of Loudoun County, was an
ensign in the Revolutionary army. The children born to Mr.
and Mrs. Hancock were: John William, Jr., who graduated as
a mining engineer from the Virginia Polytechnic Institute, took
a post graduate course at the Wharton School of Finance of the
University of Pennsylvania, and is now with an investment
banking house in New York City; Karl Bulow, now a student
of the University of Virginia; Mary Alice, who graduated from
Wellesley College; Elizabeth Dee; and Benjamin Philip, born in
1908 and died in infancy.

EDWARD L. JOHNSON is a talented physician and surgeon at
Bedford, where he has practiced a number of years, always
enjoying a large professional business, and has also established
connections in a business and civic way with his community.

Doctor Johnson was born on a farm in Bedford County, Virginia, December 19, 1879. His people have lived in Bedford
County for several generations. His parents, Jason and Mary
(Cottrell) Johnson, were natives of the same county. His
grandfather, John T. Johnson, was born in that county, as also
his maternal grandfather, James Cottrell. Jason Johnson spent
his life as a farmer and the old homestead is still owned by the
family. He was physically disqualified for service during the
Civil war, but rendered good service by helping neighbors who
had sons or husbands in the war. He was a Democrat and both
he and his wife members of the Baptist Church. Of their seven
children six are living.

Dr. Edward L. Johnson was educated at the old Jeter School
in Bedford County and from early manhood learned the lessons of self reliance. He had to earn the money and contrive
the means to complete his medical education. He determined to
become a doctor when a youth. Going to New York City he
found employment in the City Hospital on Blackwell's Island,
working there eighteen months and taking the course in nursing
at the same time. He was then employed as a nurse in another
hospital in New York, and had a certificate as a graduate nurse.
This work gave him opportunities for study and observation,
and he spent the greater part of each winter studying medicine. He went to New York with thirty-seven dollars and when
he came away he had increased that capital to sixty dollars and
had made large progress in his professional education. Doctor
Johnson graduated in medicine from the Medical College of Virginia at Richmond in 1907. He has since practiced in Bedford County. The day he established himself as a doctor he
had two professional calls. Since 1911 his home has been in
Bedford City, where in addition to his general private practice
he is surgeon for the Bedford Tire Company.

Doctor Johnson married in 1909 Ella Noell, a native of Bote-
tourt County, Virginia, who was educated there and at the Uni-
versity of Virginia, and taught school for a number of years.
She is very active in the Methodist Church and teaches the
Philathea class in the Sunday School. She is also matron of
Eastern Star. She is secretary of the local branch of the Daugh-
ters of the Confederacy. Her father, John Noell, was a farmer.
Dr. and Mrs. Johnson have one daughter, Eloise Noell, born
June 5, 1916. Both are members of the Methodist Church, and
Doctor Johnson is a past master of the Masonic Lodge, member
of the Royal Arch Chapter, Woodmen of the World, Benevolent

and Protective Order of Elks, Independent Order of Odd Fellows. He is a member of Bedford County Medical Society and the Medical Society of Virginia. Doctor Johnson owns a farm and orchard, is a director of the Citizens National Bank of Bedford, and is a member of the city council. He is also a director of the Bedford Tire & Rubber Company, and of the Nardin, Armstrong Corporation. He is the owner of the Johnson Service Station at Bedford, Virginia.

WILSON MILES CARY belonged to the generation that furnished some of the most youthful soldiers to the Confederate armies, and in the half century after the war he became a prominent figure in the tobacco industry at Richmond.

Colonel Cary was born at Williamsburg, Virginia, in 1843 and died at Richmond in April, 1919. He was the only son of Lucius Falkland and Anne (Henley) Cary, his father a merchant of Williamsburg. He was one of two children, his sister, Hattie Coke Cary, now being Mrs. William Christian, of Richmond.

Wilson Miles Cary was reared in the classical seat of learning at Williamsburg, attending William and Mary College. He left college to enlist in the Virginia troops, and gave four years to the service of the Southern cause. After the war he completed his college education, and then located at Richmond, entering the tobacco business.

He served with the rank of colonel on the staff of two governors of Virginia, Governor Philip McKinney \and Governor Fitzhugh Lee. Colonel Cary was an ardent Democrat and for many years held an official place in the Second Presbyterian Church of Richmond. He was a member of the Westmoreland Club.

His first wife was Anne E. Sublett, and by that marriage there are two children, Emily Sampson and Hunsdon. Emily married Thomas Marshall, great grandson of the Chief Justice Marshall, and has two children. Hunsdon married Mary Miller, daughter of George D. Miller, of Albany, New York, and a Richmond attorney.

Colonel Cary on October 10, 1878, married Lilias Blair McPhail, who survives him and resides at 19 North Boulevard in Richmond. She is a daughter of John Blair McPhail, who was educated at Yale College and was a Norfolk attorney, and married Ann Cabell Carrington. Mrs. Cary was educated by a private tutor at Mulberry Hill, the home of her ancestor, Judge Paul Carrington.

Mrs. Cary has a son and daughter, Lucius Falkland Cary, and Lilias Blair Cary. The son was educated at Hampden-Sidney College, graduated in law from the University of Virginia, and is now assistant city attorney of Richmond. He married Alma Cecil, daughter of Rev. Russell and Alma (Miller) Cecil, her father being pastor of the Second Presbyterian Church of Richmond, while her mother was a daughter of Dr. LaFayette Miller, a surgeon in the Confederate army. Mr. and Mrs. L. F. Cary have three children, Lucius F., Jr., now a student in the Virginia Military Institute, Elizabeth Cecil, and Miles Fairfax. Lilias Blair Cary married Rev. T. K. Currie, of Davidson, North Carolina, and now of Richmond, Virginia, and has two sons, Thomas Lauchlin and Albert LaDoux.

Thos. E. Payne D. D. S.

THOMAS E. PAYNE, D. D. S.   As a follower of one of the
skilled and learned professions, Dr. Thomas E. Payne, of
Roanoke, has achieved that success which comes to a man who
finds his vocation congenial and who invests it with determination, enthusiasm and natural talent.   The modern dental practitioner has ever before him the chance of making himself an
enormously important factor in the welfare of his community,
and a realization of this possibility has come to Doctor Payne
at Roanoke, of which city he has been a resident for about nineteen years.

Doctor Payne was born December 9, 1883, in Westmoreland
County, Virginia, and is a son of John T. and Ellen Cushen
(Jones) Payne. The Payne family is an old and honored one
in Virginia, having settled in the colony as early as 1620, at
which time the original ancestor took up his residence in what
is now Northumberland County.   John T. Payne was a son of
Thomas Ewell, a native of King George County, Virginia, who
had large farming interests and also carried on an extensive
mercantile business.   Mr. Payne was likewise a nephew and an
adopted son of Bishop John Payne, a noted dignitary of the
Episcopal diocese of Virginia.   John T. Payne was born in King
George County, Virginia, and was given good educational advantages in his youth, including preparation for the law.   He was
admitted to the bar and for some years in his early life practiced
with a measure of success, but eventually disposed of his practice, gave up his profession, and became a minister of the Methodist Episcopal Church.   For thirty-five years, or until his death
in 1918, he was a member of the Virginia Conference, filling
numerous pulpits and becoming widely known and greatly
beloved for his many good works, his zeal, piety, and humani-
tarianism.   He was laid to rest at Charlottesville, this state,
where Mrs. Payne, likewise a native of King George County,
still makes her home.   Mr. Payne was a member of the Masons
and the Independent Order of Odd Fellows, and was a Democrat
in his political allegiance, although he never sought public office.
He married Ellen Cushen Jones, a daughter of James Edward
Jones, a native of King George County, of which county he
served ably as treasurer for many years, and a member of a
family that settled in Virginia during Colonial days.

His father, John T. Payne, furnished Thomas E. Payne, who
was one of eleven children, with his early educational training,
following which he pursued a course at the New London Academy in Bedford County and the Bridle Creek Academy in Grayson County.   His dental studies were prosecuted at the Medical
College of Virginia, at Richmond, where he took the dental
course, and in 1909 was graduated with the degree Doctor of
Dentistry.   Doctor Payne commenced practice at Lynchburg,
but in 1910 located at Roanoke, where he has since attained
prominence in his profession as a general practitioner, and now
occupies well-appointed and perfectly equipped offices in the
Shenandoah Life Building.   He has all of the appliances and
instruments known to modern dental science, and is a careful,
kind, considerate and highly skilled operator, who has won the
confidence and esteem of a large patronage, which has been
attracted by his diligent attention to his work.   By keeping
himself fully abreast of all current developments and improved
methods in his art, he has maintained an excellent professional
standing, and meanwhile his amiable disposition and general

deportment have attracted to him many stanch friends. Doctor
Payne is a member of the Roanoke Dental Society, the Virginia
Dental Society and the National Dental Association, and his
religious connection is with Green Memorial Methodist Episcopal
Church, South. He is a past master of Lakeland Lodge, A. F.
and A. M., and a Scottish Rite Mason and Shriner, and is likewise prominent in the Knights of Pythias, being a past chancellor commander, a past grand chancellor of the state, a past
royal vizier of the D. O. K. K. and present imperial representative. He belongs to the Kiwanis Club and is an enthusiastic
supporter of all worthy civic movements. During the war he
served as a first lieutenant in the Dental Corps, was overseas
and was honorably discharged January 21, 1919, at Camp Stuart,
Virginia.

In October, 1920, at Roanoke, Doctor Payne was united in
marriage with Miss Katherine L. Lowry, who was born at
Lowry, Bedford County, and educated at Bedford City, and they
have one son, John Thomas, born March 19, 1922. Mrs. Payne
is a member of the First Baptist Church.

LEE R. GILLS of Bedford has had a remarkably successful
career. He grew up on a farm, started to work at an early age,
never had many or special opportunities conferred upon him and
from his own industry and genius for handling business affairs
has made himself an influence in a number of communities and
cities in southwestern Virginia.

He was born in Bedford County, April 13, 1856, son of Asa
and Caroline E. (Poindexter) Gills, grandson of Anthony Gills
and Richard Poindexter, the former a native of Nottaway
County and the latter of Bedford County. On both sides
the family have been farmers and planters for a number
of generations. His father was born in Nottaway County,
served four years in the Confederate Army, and in June,
1865, returned home to find his farm devastated, his negroes
gone, but he adapted himself to the new conditions and
gained some measure of substantial prosperity before his death.
He was always a Democrat and a member of the Methodist
Church. He and his wife had eight children and four are now
living: Eliza A., wife of Joseph Skinell of Bedford City;
Edward Gills, a farmer and canner of Bedford County; Lee R.;
and Munford C., who is in the real estate business at Bluefield,
West Virginia.

Lee R. Gills was about nine years old when the Civil war
closed. He had had a few terms of common schooling and after
the war he took his place in the fields working as his strength
permitted. Afterwards he attended a private school, the Hale
Ford Academy in Franklin County, and qualified himself for
teaching. He taught seven terms of school during winter
months, working on the farm in the summer. He early became
interested in saw milling and merchandising, and these two
lines have accounted for most of his years of energy and gave
him the foundation of his material prosperity. In this business
he was associated with his brother C. W. Gills and Mr. Johnson
for a period of twenty-six years. It was a very unusual partnership, unbusinesslike in a way, since each of the firm paid
his household running expenses out of the business cash drawer,
but in other respects it was a real partnership of interest and
work and commended its methods because of the success that

rewarded the members. The firm had different titles at different times, Gills Brothers, Gills & Johnson, at Rocky Mount, Gills and Holland, again Gills and Johnson and the Gills Grocery Company at Felicia. Mr. Gills has been a resident of Bedford for over thirty years. He was one of the organizers of the Peoples National Bank of Bedford in 1901 and was elected the first president and has served in that capacity for over a quarter of a century. During his active career he has traded in timberlands and bought millions of feet of lumber. His business operations extended to Roanoke where he began buying and building in 1907, and in recent years he has made a gift to his children of several pieces of property in that city but still owns other improved real estate there. For the last eighteen years he has been president of the Grand Piano Company. In 1925 he organized the Bedford Tire & Rubber Company of which he was president to January, 1928. This is a corporation capitalized at one million dollars, with $400,000 stock issued. Mr. Gills is a member of the Methodist Episcopal Church at Bedford and is on the Board of Stewards. He is a Democrat in politics.

He married, October 17, 1884, Cora M. Dudley, who was born in Franklin County, Virginia, daughter of William R. Dudley, a farmer and ex-Confederate soldier, who represented his district in the State Senate. Mr. and Mrs. Gills have four children. The oldest is Dr. W. L. Gills who was educated in the high school at Bedford, graduated from the academy there at the age of sixteen, took the regular four year course at the Randolph-Macon College at Ashland in three years, making the best grade credited to any student in a period of twenty-eight years. For three years he taught in the academy at Bedford, then entered Johns Hopkins University at Baltimore, taking the four years' medical course and winning a scholarship every year. On graduating he was offered an interneship in the Johns Hopkins Hospital, but declined to accept a post as interne he had won in a competitive examination with forty other young doctors at a hospital at Hartford, Connecticut. After twenty months there he was licensed to practice in Virginia, spent two and one-half years in general practice at Roanoke and since then has specialized in eye, ear, nose and throat at Hartford, Connecticut, where he is one of the outstanding physicians and surgeons. The second child, Bessie G. Gills, is the wife of Dr. W. P. Jackson, a physician at Roanoke. Clara E. Gills, married Major E. R. Richardson, an instructor in the Bedford Academy. Harry A. Gills, the youngest, a merchant at Bedford, married Roberta Moncure of Stafford Court House, member of the distinguished Moncure family of Virginia. She was educated at Nashville, Tennessee.

DAVID P. SCOTT, physician and surgeon at Lynchburg, is a member of the Scott family that settled in Caroline County, Virginia, in 1690, and is one of a long succession of physicians in the family.

Doctor Scott was born in Bedford County, Virginia, October 30, 1890, son of Dr. Hugh Donald and Evelyn (Davies) Scott, grandson of Dr. Samuel Burks Scott, a Bedford County physician, and great-grandson of Hugh Roy Scott. The founder of the Virginia branch of the family was James Scott, father of Col. Thomas Scott, who came from Aberdeen, Scotland, in 1690. There were six members of the family who held commissions under General Washington in the Revolutionary war. Dr. Hugh

Donald Scott was born in Bedford County, was educated in the
Medical College of Virginia and practiced for thirty-five years
in Amherst County. He was a member of the Episcopal Church,
a York Rite Mason and Shriner, and belonged to the B. P. O.
Elks. His wife was a daughter of Henry Landon Davies, a
native of Bedford County.

David P. Scott is one of a family of three children. His
brother Stuart Donald lives at Johnstown, Pennsylvania, and
his brother Samuel Burks, at Andover, New York. David P.
Scott was educated in the Hoge Military Academy, graduated
from the Medical College of Virginia in 1911, was an interne in
the Retreat for the Sick at Richmond and the Johnston-Willis
Sanitarium in that city. Doctor Scott engaged in practice at
Ashland, West Virginia, until 1915, and then took post-graduate
work in New York and at Harvard University and the Massachusetts General Hospital in Boston until 1917.

In April, 1917, he volunteered his services and was assigned
active duty at Washington in November. He was given various
advancements, and for a time acted as assistant chief medical
examiner at Camp Lee. He received his honorable discharge in
March, 1919, and soon afterward located at Lynchburg, where
he has practiced with a steadily growing reputation. He specializes in diagnosis. He is a fellow of the American College of
Physicians, member of the Medical Society of Virginia, the
Lynchburg, Southern Piedmont and American Medical Associations.

Doctor Scott married, February 14, 1914, Miss Beulah Davis,
who was born at Charlottesville and was educated there and in
the Blackstone Girls School. They have one daughter, Judith
Donald Scott, born in 1922. Doctor Scott and wife are members
of St. John's Episcopal Church.

FORREST W. WHITAKER is a veteran attorney of the Lynchburg bar, having practiced there for over thirty-five years. In
recent years he has also taken upon himself the responsibilities
and honors of judicial office, being a judge of the municipal
court.

Judge Whitaker was born in Halifax County, North Caro-
lina, October 6, 1865, son of Ferdinand H. and Louise (D'Berry)
Whitaker, both natives of North Carolina. His mother was a
daughter of Lemuel and Elizabeth (Staunton) D'Berry. The
D'Berrys came from France. The Whitakers have been in
America since Colonial times. His Revolutionary ancestor was
John Whitaker, who served under General Washington and was
a son of Richard Whitaker. John Whitaker was the father of
Wilson Carey Whitaker, grandfather of Judge Whitaker. Fer-
dinand H. Whitaker was a farm owner in Halifax County,
North Carolina, was a member of the Methodist Protestant
Church.

Forrest W. Whitaker was the eighth in a family of eleven
children, four of whom are living. He attended private school
in North Carolina, completing his literary education in the Oak
Ridge Institute. He studied law in the famous Dick and Dillard Law School at Greensboro, North Carolina, completing his
course in 1887. For several years he practiced in North Carolina, and in 1892 removed to Lynchburg, where his abilities as
a lawyer and other qualifications have made him an important
figure in the community. Since October 1, 1922, he has been a
judge of the Municipal Court, assigned to juvenile and domestic

J Frank Payne

relations division, and in that capacity has rendered a service that cannot be measured by any financial standard. To the examination of cases involving the delicate adjustments of family life and individual development he has brought a wide experience of humanity as well as a thoroughly seasoned knowledge of the law.

Judge Whitaker is active in the Democratic party and has been a delegate to state conventions. He is a steward in the Methodist Protestant Church, a member of the Masonic fraternity, and the Lions Club.

Judge Whitaker married October 4, 1900, Miss Carrie Kinnear, who was born at Lynchburg and was reared and educated there. Her father, George A. Kinnear, was for many years a merchant. Judge and Mrs. Whitaker have one daughter, Louise Kinnear, who attended the public schools and Salem College.

J. FRANK PAYNE, D. D. S. Included among the various branches of professional knowledge on which civilized humanity is more or less dependent for the maintenance of healthful conditions and the preservation of exemption from physical distress is the science of dental surgery. Careless habits of living and indulgences in articles of food and drink which are injurious to the teeth have become so general that in all communities skilled dental practitioners are indispensable factors. But, as in medicine and surgery, the science of dentistry is constantly developing new phases of usefulness, and in order to insure success the dentist of today must keep fully abreast of the latest achievements of his profession. He must add skill to thorough research and combine close application to his task with the ability gained through experience. A modern practitioner of this type is found in Dr. J. Frank Payne, of Roanoke, who while carrying on a general practice is somewhat of a specialist in the making of plates and crowns and of extraction.

Doctor Payne was born November 15, 1877, in Westmoreland County, Virginia, and is a son of John T. and Ellen Cushen (Jones) Payne, and a member of a family which came to Northumberland County, Virginia, as early as 1620. John T. Payne was a son of Thomas Ewell, a native of King George County, Virginia, who followed merchandising throughout his career, and a nephew and adopted son of Bishop John Payne, a noted Episcopal divine. John T. Payne was born in King George County, Virginia, where he was educated for the law, a profession with which he was identified successfully for a number of years. In the middle part of his life he became a minister of the Methodist Episcopal Church, and for thirty-five years, or until his death in 1918, was a member of the Virginia Conference. He was buried at Charlottesville, where Mrs. Payne, also a native of King George County, still makes her home. Mr. Payne was a member of the Masons and the Independent Order of Odd Fellows, and in politics was a Democrat. He and his wife became the parents of eleven children, of whom Dr. J. Frank was the second in order of birth. The maternal grandfather of Doctor Payne was James Edward Jones, a native of King George County, who was treasurer of that county for many years, and a member of an early settled family of Virginia.

J. Frank Payne attended public schools of Virginia, spent three years at Chesapeake Academy and a short time at Bowling Green Academy, and then for five years was an instructor at

the Gordonsville Female College and for a few months was a
teacher in the public schools, and then prosecuted his dental
studies at the Virginia Medical College, where he completed
the regular three-year course in two years. Eventually, in 1911,
he settled permanently at Roanoke, where he has since been in
the enjoyment of a large and constantly increasing practice. As
before noted, he practices general dentistry, but makes a specialty of crowns, plates and extraction work, and his offices in
the McBain Building are fully equipped with the latest appliances and instruments known to modern dental science. Doctor
Payne is a skilled operator and a man of kindly and gentle
personality. He was a member of the Roanoke Dental Society,
the Virginia State Dental Society and the National Dental Association, and fraternally is identified with the Knights of Pythias
and the Order of Owls. He is a Democrat in politics, without
political aspirations, and a consistent member of the Methodist
Church.

On February 24, 1904, Doctor Payne was united in marriage
with Miss Mary J. Mortimer, of Campbell County, Virginia,
who was educated in the public schools and at New London
Academy. They have two children: Caroline Mortimer, a
teacher in the public schools of Roanoke; and Ellen Cushen,
still attending school.

CHARLES A. METZGER. The name of Metzger has had honored associations with the industrial and business affairs of
Richmond for three quarters of a century. One of its representatives was the late Charles A. Metzger, whose widow, Mrs.
Metzger, resides at 1 South Boulevard in that city.

Charles A. Metzger was born at Richmond, December 12,
1862, and died in that city August 29, 1923. His father, Harry
Metzger, came from Germany and settled in Richmond about
1850. He established a cooperage business, and was a very
thoroughgoing business man and also much interested in local
politics, serving for a time on the Richmond City Council. He
married Caroline Meyer, of Germany. They were married in
Richmond in the late '50s, and of their six children Charles A.
was the second son.

The late Mr. Metzger attended school at Richmond and as a
very young man went to work in his father's establishment, and
after about six years was appointed manager. He had the
controlling interest in H. Metzger & Son, cooperage business,
after his father's death, and his two brothers, Lewis T. and
Edward H., were associated with him, and since his death these
brothers have continued it. It is one of the oldest firms of its
kind in Richmond or in the State of Virginia. The late Mr.
Metzger was a Democrat.

Mrs. Metzger is an active worker in St. John's Evangelical
Church and for thirty-two years has been a member of the
Ladies Aid Society. She also belongs to the Kings Daughters.
Mr. Metzger and Miss Elizabeth C. Frick were married at Rich-
mond, October 9, 1884. She was reared in that city, attending
St. Joseph's Academy. Her father, Theodore Frick, came from
Germany to Richmond in 1850 and organized the Theodore Frick
Packing Company, one of the early meat packing houses of Vir-
ginia. Theodore Frick married, in Richmond, Miss Christine
Wunsch, who also came from Germany. They had six children:
Mrs. Caroline Oeters, deceased; Theodore F., now deceased, who

continued the packing business after the death of his father;
Emma, whose first husband was Charles Frommer, and she is
now the wife of William H. Essig; Mrs. Metzger; Alvina W.,
who married J. H. Leisfield and has two children, J. H. Jr., and
Marie, wife of J. Cunningham and mother of a daughter, Elizabeth Cunningham; and Pauline, wife of W. P. Klein, a Richmond
merchant, and they have two daughters, Mrs. Robert Waldbauer,
who has a son, Robert, and Mrs. H. Waldbauer, whose two sons
are Walter and Henry. Mr. H. Waldbauer is a member of the
firm Boedecker Drug Company of Richmond.

RANDOLPH G. WHITTLE. Among the younger members of
the legal fraternity who are practicing at the bar of Roanoke,
one who has made rapid strides in his profession and is gaining
prestige and a large and important clientage is Randolph G.
Whittle. While his career has not been as lengthy as many
others of his fellow practitioners whose biographies appear in
this volume, he has made such good use of his opportunities and
has brought his natural abilities into play so energetically that
he has already attained a place in his profession beyond that of
many men who are his senior in years and experience.
Mr. Whittle comes of good legal stock, and was born May 4,
1900, at Martinsville, Virginia, a son of Judge Stafford G. and
Ruth (Drewry) Whittle. His father, a native of Virginia, and
a member of a fine old Southern family, received excellent educational advantages in his youth, at Washington & Lee University and at the University of Virginia, where he prosecuted
his legal studies. Judge Whittle commenced practice at Martinsville, where almost immediately he gained a position at the
bar. In a number of cases that attracted widespread interest
and attention he secured recognition, and as a consequence he
soon was elevated to the bench, where he rendered splendid
service. For many years he was judge of the Supreme Court of
Virginia, retiring in December, 1919, after a service of two
decades, during the last five years of which he was president of
the court. He is now living in comfortable and honored retirement at Martinsville, where Mrs. Whittle died in 1923. Few
Virginia judges have made a more favorable impression upon
the people of their day than Judge Whittle. A man of profound
learning in legal lore, he was possessed of the judicial temperament, and was wise, temperate and at all times fair-minded.
His retirement from the Supreme bench removed therefrom one
who possessed all the elementals of judicial distinction.
Randolph G. Whittle attended the grammar and high schools
of Martinsville, following which he entered Washington and Lee
University, and was graduated therefrom in 1924, with the
degree of Bachelor of Law. Immediately thereafter he engaged
in practice at Roanoke, where he has since continued with constantly increasing success. He has specialized in no subject, his
business being of a general civil character, and the success that
he has gained has come through constant industry and able
application of the knowledge gained through thorough preparation. Mr. Whittle is a member of the Roanoke City Bar Association, the Virginia State Bar Association and the American Bar
Association. He was president of the student body during his
last year at college, and is a member of the Phi Kappa Sigma
academic fraternity, Phi Delta Phi legal fraternity and Omicron
Delta Kappa honorary fraternity. Mr. Whittle is likewise a
Scottish Rite Mason, and in politics is a Democrat. While he is

greatly interested in civic affairs and is a modern citizen of enlightened views, he finds his practice sufficiently engrossing and interesting to take up all his time. He is unmarried and a member of St. John's Episcopal Church.

PROF. ELBERT MURRAY COULTER. The art of drawing out or developing the faculties, or the training of human beings for the functions in life for which they are destined, more commonly known as education, means the imparting or gaining of knowledge of every kind, good as well as evil, but specifically it signifies all that broadens an individual's mind, develops his tastes, corrects his manners and molds his habits. In a still more limited sense it means any course of training pursued by parents, teachers or a whole community to train the young physically, morally and mentally. In recent years, in answer to a constantly growing demand for training along commercial lines, there have come into existence many institutions which fit their students for the serious business problems of life. Among the leaders in this field is the National Business College of Roanoke, Virginia, of which Prof. Elbert Murray Coulter is president. Professor Coulter's own life is an inspiration to his students, as he started his career a poor youth and has worked his own way, unaided, to prosperity and position.

Professor Coulter was born July 31, 1871, at Pittsfield, Illinois, and is a son of John and Mary (Jones) Coulter. His paternal grandfather was John Coulter, who was born in Ireland and as a young man came to the United States and settled in Canada, later moving to Ohio and still later moving to Western Illinois, where he passed the remainder of his life in agricultural operations. His maternal grandfather, Isaac Jones, married Martha Preble, a descendant of Commodore Preble, U. S. N., a hero of the Tripolitan war between the United States and Tripoli in 1801-1805, which was caused by the refusal of this country to increase its payment for immunity from the depredations of the Tripolitan Corsairs. After several conflicts by sea and land peace was concluded June 4, 1805. John Coulter, the father of Professor Coulter, was born in Ohio, whence he removed in young manhood to Illinois and engaged in agricultural pursuits in the vicinity of Pittsfield. He later moved with his wife to Missouri, and there they passed the remainder of their lives. Mr. Coulter was a Republican in his political views, and he and his wife were faithful members of the Methodist Episcopal Church. Of their ten children only two are living, Elbert Murray being the second in order of birth.

Elbert Murray Coulter attended the public schools of Illinois and Missouri, and supplemented this by a course at a normal school in Kansas. He entered upon his career as a teacher at the Saint Joseph Business University, Saint Joseph, Missouri, and in 1896 came to Roanoke, Virginia, to take a professorship in the National Business College at a salary of sixty dollars per month. Aside from his meager salary he possessed nothing, but was thrifty and economical, and by 1898 had saved enough to buy a half-interest in the institution. Two years later he became sole owner by purchase and commenced his independent operations in a little building which was entirely inadequate for his needs, but the best he could afford in the circumstances. At the end of thirteen years he found himself in possession of sufficient capital to buy a lot and erect a building on Church Street, where he remained for ten years, and then bought his present quarters from the Fraternal Order of Eagles in 1919. Later he found it necessary to build an addition to this structure, and in 1928 another addition was constructed, so that at the present time the school has 40,000 square feet of floor space. Because of the able manner in which it has been conducted and the high standard which has always been maintained by Professor Coulter the school has prospered greatly, and is now one of the leading institutions of its kind in the country, having an average of from 700 to 800 students annually, and employing a teaching staff of fifteen able and experienced instructors. Its curriculum includes all of the regular branches, fitting its graduates to take well salaried positions in business life and equipping them in a modern and capable manner to meet and solve the problems of business life and self-support. Professor Coulter is greatly interested in civic affairs, but makes his home in the country on a farm located five miles from Roanoke, where the family enjoy the rural existence, and where he conducts a model dairy farm with Holstein cattle. He is a member of the Presbyterian Church and of the Board of Deacons thereof, and fraternally is a York Rite Mason and a member of the Mystic Shrine. He is a stanch Democrat in his political views, but has not cared for public office.

In 1902 Professor Coulter was united in marriage with Miss Mary Elva Keedick, who was born at Mount Vernon, Iowa, and educated at Cornell College in that community, and taught in the same schools where her husband was an instructor. To this union there have been born two children: Dorothy Viola, who attended high school at Roanoke, spent one year at the National Business College and two years at Hollins College, and is now completing her education at Columbia University, New York; and Murray Keedick, who is attending high school at Roanoke.

HON. MARTIN A. HUTCHINSON, secretary of the Commonwealth of Virginia, is truly a self-made young man, and through his own efforts, aided by the inspiration and helpfulness of his father and mother, has achieved his present success in life. While he has strong personal political influence at Richmond and throughout Virginia, he may justly take pride in the fact that his elevation to the important position he now holds is due solely to merit and as a reward for faithful and efficient service rendered, and not to the weight of this influence. As the *Richmond-Times Dispatch* said editorially in part of his appointment:

"Prompt elevation of Martin A. Hutchinson from chief clerk to secretary of the Commonwealth augurs well for the future appointments to be made by Governor Harry F. Byrd under the governmental reorganization plan adopted by the extra session of the General Assembly. Without permitting politics to enter into the selection of a successor of the late Colonel B. O. James, the Governor made an appointment which was a recognition of services rendered and an implied promise that faithful work will be rewarded in other departments.

"While one of the youngest men to occupy such an important post as secretary of the Commonwealth, Mr. Hutchinson is well qualified to perform the duties. He first came into the service of the State as assistant to James M. Hayes, Jr., then chief clerk to Colonel James. He soon had a fine grasp of the duties of the office, and on the elevation of Mr. Hayes to the post of Motor Vehicle Commissioner, Mr. Hutchinson stepped into his shoes.

"As chief clerk Mr. Hutchinson has been carrying the burden of the office for many months, owing to the physical condition of Colonel James, who could give little more than a cursory supervision of the work. In addition to the many duties of the office Mr. Hutchinson has found time to reorganize the Land Office, where untold history lies concealed in musty documents long forgotten. He holds the position of secretary to the State Democratic Committee, which he has filled with credit for several years."

Martin A. Hutchinson was born near Newport, Giles County, Virginia, September 13, 1892, a son of Daniel Mason and Theresa Viola (Jones) Hutchinson. The mother passed away in March, 1928. Mr. Hutchinson, Sr., still makes his home at Newport, Giles County. The Hutchinsons are of Scotch-Irish ancestry, the sturdy race that, migrating from Pennsylvania, founded and continued to maintain the forces of civilization in the Appalachian region of Virginia and the Carolinas.

For many years Daniel Mason Hutchinson was a country school teacher, and he is a man of scholarship, a fine type of citizen whose concern for the home, the church, the school and the state develops and maintains the truly Christian and civilized community. The home life of the Hutchinsons has been always ideal, and this ideal has been transmitted to the rising generation. The paternal grandfather of Mr. Hutchinson of this review was George W. Hutchinson, of Craig County, Virginia, a man of genuine prominence and great influence in his day. The maternal uncle of Secretary Hutchinson, the late Judge P. V. Jones, of Newcastle, Craig County, Virginia, was for several years judge of the Court of Craig County, and widely known in public life. Both the Hutchinson and Jones families in fact have been for many years very active factors in the public affairs of the Old Dominion.

Growing up in his native community, Martin A. Hutchinson attended the graded and high schools of Newport, after which he took a thorough commercial training in the Roanoke, Virginia, Business College. Following his graduation from the last named institution he entered the employ of the Bank of Pembroke, Giles County, Virginia. While with this bank he was appointed deputy county treasurer of Giles County, and was serving in both capacities when his career was interrupted by the call of his country, and he resigned from both to enter the service for the World war. He took his training in the Officers Training Camp, Fort Humphreys, Virginia, and was still stationed there when the armistice was declared. Honorably discharged from the army, he returned to Newport and civilian life.

In 1920 through the efforts of Governor Trinkle, then a member of the Virginia State Senate, he was appointed to a clerkship. During the regular session of 1922 and the extra session of 1923 Mr. Hutchinson had the honor of serving as clerk of the Virginia Senate. Following this service he was appointed to a position in the office of the late Col. B. O. James, first as assistant to the chief clerk and later as chief clerk, and finally, after the death of Colonel James, he was appointed secretary of the commonwealth, as already stated. As may be gathered from the editorial quoted above, this appointment met with general approval, for Mr. Hutchinson is a young man who has proven his

Walter Jameson M.D.

worth in whatever he has undertaken. He has not only ability, but initiative, and has never been content to rest upon the mere performance of the duties assigned him, but is ever reaching out for more opportunities for service, and a man is never doing better service than when he is trying to raise the standards of commercial or political morality. The condition of political morality is especially important, for its influence works downward through all the grades of society, and a country that is corrupt at the top cannot expect to be better at the bottom. Public service means that every department of public life shall be conducted in the best possible manner for the welfare of the largest number, and to accomplish this and to inspire others to follow his example Mr. Hutchinson is devoting his time, his ability and his whole heart.

Mr. Hutchinson married Miss Mary Estelle Givens, of Craig County, Virginia, and they have a daughter, Madge Givens Hutchinson. Mr. Hutchinson belongs to Newport Lodge No. 261, A. F. and A. M. He is a consistent member of the Methodist Episcopal Church, South. An ardent Democrat, he has given his party loyal support, and is serving it as secretary of the State Executive Committee.

On December 20, 1927, Mr. Hutchinson passed the bar examination and is now qualified to practice law. In order to do this he studied at night, and he has gained the reputation of being specially conversant with election laws, on which he is considered an expert. His office handles all such cases, and he is therefore well qualified.

WALLER JAMESON, M. D. The opportunities in medicine are are attractive to a certain type of man to whom they give an occupation in which he can use all the intellectual energy and faculties he has. It requires technical skill based on scientific knowledge to be a physician, but, unlike many scientific pursuits, does not take a man out of contact with the everyday world. On the contrary it puts him in contact with men in an unusually intimate way, appealing to the man who is interested in his fellows and who has an altruistic bent. Finally it gives him an honorable opening to make a living. The material rewards of medicine, however, never were and are not now commensurate with those of other vocations equally exacting and responsible. But the rewards, if not large, are dependable, and the conscientious practitioner has also the gratification that comes from a sense of social service and from the esteem and gratitude of those he serves. Such facts as the above apply directly to Dr. Waller Jameson, one of the able physicians and surgeons of Roanoke, a man of the highest standing, and a member of one of the old and honored families of Virginia. He was born in Lynchburg, Campbell County, Virginia, April 15, 1878, a son of Morton Clifford and Marie Frances (Ferguson) Jameson, natives of Stafford County and Franklin County, Virginia, respectively, both of whom are now deceased. For thirty-five years prior to his death in 1903 the father was connected with the Norfolk & Western Railroad, and rose to be its comptroller. The mother died in 1892, having borne her husband seven children, five of whom are living, and of them all Doctor Jameson is the youngest. The father was an Episcopalian, and a vestryman of the church. High in Masonry, he was advanced through all of the bodies of the Scottish Rite and to the thirty-second degree.

A strong Democrat, he worked hard for his party, and at one time was city collector of taxes in Lynchburg.

Doctor Jameson had the advantage of attending the excellent public schools of Philadelphia, where his father lived for twelve years, and he took his preliminary medical course in Randolph-Macon College, and his regular medical training in the University of Virginia, being graduated therefrom in 1903, with the degree Doctor of Medicine. For a year thereafter he was abroad studying in the East London General Hospital and the Rotunda Hospital, Dublin, Ireland. Returning to Virginia, he established himself in practice in Roanoke in 1905, and here he has since carried on a general practice, building up a large connection and winning and holding the confidence and affectionate respect of all with whom he is associated.

In 1905 Doctor Jameson married Miss Frances Chalmers, who was born in Lafayette, Kentucky, and educated in the public schools of Danville, Chatham, and in Chatham Institute. There are no children. Doctor and Mrs. Jameson have long been members of Saint John's Episcopal Church of Roanoke. While in college he made Sigma Chi, Pi Mu, the Tilka Club and the Thirteen Club, an honorary organization. He maintains membership with the Roanoke County Medical Society, the Virginia State Medical Society, the Tri-State Medical Society and the American Medical Association, and the Shenandoah Club of Roanoke, Virginia.

JOSEPH A. RUCKER, M. D. has a professional record in Bedford County covering a third of a century. He is an able doctor, and had likewise made himself indispensable as a citizen of his community.

Doctor Rucker was born in Bedford County, June 27, 1871, son of M. P. and Sallie Fannie (Parker) Rucker. The Rucker family came from France, and some of his ancestors were soldiers in the Revolution. His grandfather Anthony Rucker was a farmer in Bedford County. The maternal grandfather Joseph Parker was both a farmer and local Baptist Preacher. M. P. Rucker was born in Bedford County, spent his life as a farmer except for the four years he was a soldier in the Confederate Army and died in 1926. His wife was educated in the Roanoke Institute at Danville and died February 4, 1924. They were the parents of six children: Annie M., wife of William Southerland of Franklin County; David H. and William P., farmers and merchants in Bedford County; Dr. Joseph A.; Dr. M. P., a physician at Bedford; and Sallie Margaret wife of Ira P. Dixon of Covington, Virginia. Doctor Rucker's father was a Methodist and his mother a Baptist, both being active in their Church. He served for a number of years as superintendent of the Sunday school, and was also on the School Board and a justice of the peace.

Joseph A. Rucker was educated in the Sunnyside School near Bedford, the New London Academy, the University of Virginia where he began to study medicine and in 1893 graduated from the University of Louisville. For eighteen months he practiced and then returned to Bedford, where he has carried on his professional work thirty-three years. He is local surgeon for the Norfolk & Western Railway, physician to the Elks National Home and physician to the Randolph-Macon Academy, while the rest of his time is taken up with his duties as a general practitioner. He is now County Health Officer of Bedford County and for twenty years was secretary and has also served as president of the Bedford County Medical Society. He is a member of the Medical Society of Virginia and the American Medical Association. Doctor Rucker is a director of the Citizens National Bank of Bedford, is Independent in politics, is Past Master of Liberty Lodge of Masons at Bedford, past district deputy grand master of the B. P. O. Elks at Lynchburg.

He married in 1901, Miss Eliza Cauthorn, a native of Bedford, where her father Dr. George Cauthorn practiced medicine for many years. She was educated in the Belmont Seminary at Bedford. Doctor and Mrs. Rucker have four children: Joseph A. Junior, member of the class of 1928 and William Vincent, member of the class of 1929 in Washington and Lee University at Lexington; Ambrose A. and Virginia Browning, twins, both attending public school at Bedford. Doctor Rucker is a deacon in the Baptist Church and teaches an adult class of fifty members. This is a very brief statement of the principal activities and services of one of the best known citizens of Bedford County.

WALTER A. FITZPATRICK is a Bedford City banker, a native of Bedford County, grew up on a farm, has contrived his own opportunities and has made an important success of his career.

He was born on a farm in Bedford County in 1865, son of Hiram A. and Lucinda (Preston) Fitzpatrick, his father a native of Buckingham County and his mother of Bedford County. Hiram Fitzpatrick was a tanner and harness maker, and during the war between the North and South employed the resources of his business in making leather for the Confederate government. He served as a justice of the peace, was a Democrat and a member of the Methodist Church, while his first wife, who died in 1868, was a Baptist. She was the mother of five children, the two now living being Walter A. and Mrs. J. S. Saunders. By a second marriage there was a son, Burke Fitzpatrick, who is now an instructor in the State Teachers College at Radford, Virginia.

Walter A. Fitzpatrick while a boy attended one of the old Field schools in Bedford County, continuing his education in the Hales Ford College in Franklin County, and spent one session at the Virginia Polytechnic Institute at Blacksburg. Mr. Fitzpatrick in 1886, at the age of twenty-one, began clerking at Bedford in the Liberty Woolen Mills. He was there three years, for one year was employed in the county clerk's office, and one year with a commission house at Lynchburg. He returned to Bedford to become an employee of the Bedford branch of the Lynchburg Trust & Savings Bank. From that time to the present his best energies have been devoted to the banking business. In 1901 when the Peoples Bank was organized he was made its cashier. In 1919 this bank became the Peoples National Bank, and for the past five years Mr. Fitzpatrick has been the active vice president of the institution. He has other business interests in Bedford and conducts an insurance business.

He married in 1893, Mamie Turner, who was born in Bedford County and was educated there and at Lynchburg, and taught school for a time. Her father, Milton J. Turner, was a well known resident of Bedford County. Mrs. Fitzpatrick died in 1896. In 1907 he married Caroline White of Pittsylvania County, daughter of B. S. White. Mrs. Fitzpatrick finished her education in the Peace Institute at Raleigh, North Carolina. She is a member of the Presbyterian Church. He is active in the Methodist Church at Bedford, being a steward of the church and has been a regular attendant and worker in the Sunday school for a number of years.

MARTIN P. BURKS, JR. In the allotments of human life few individuals, comparatively, attain to true eminence. It is an interesting and curious study to note how opportunity waits on fitness and capacity, so that all at last fill the places for which they are best qualified. In the profession of law there is no royal road to promotion. Its high rewards are gained by diligent study and long and tedious attention to elementary principles, and are awarded only to those who develop, in the arena of forensic strife, characters of integrity and moral worth. All men generally fall into the niches of the elaborate edifice of life that they are qualified to fill. However "natural selection" may work in the production of species, there is a wondrous selection in the sifting out of the fittest from the mass of common material that crowds all the avenues of the law. In that most difficult and perplexing vocation the very occupation of superior position argues for its possessor solid ability, signal skill, sound learning and untiring industry. These are characteristics to be noted in the career of Martin P. Burks, Jr., a leading member of the Roanoke bar.

Mr. Burks was born April 3, 1882, at Liberty, Virginia, now Bedford, and is a son of Prof. Martin P. and Roberta (Gambrell) Burks, natives of Liberty, Virginia. A member of an old and honored family, Professor Burks was given the best of educational advantages, and after graduating from Washington and Lee University at Lexington, Virginia, pursued a law course at the University of Virginia. For a number of years he was engaged in the practice of his profession at Bedford, this state, appearing in litigated cases and developing an aptitude and capacity for forensic practice. Eventually, in 1899, he was called to a professorship at Washington and Lee University, where he was a member of the faculty of this noted institution for many years. He was accounted one of the best legists in the state and one who had no superior as an instructor of young lawyers.

Martin P. Burks the younger seems to have inherited his father's predilection and ability for the law and was given every opportunity to develop his talents. He attended Randolph-Macon Academy and the Episcopal High School at Alexandria, Virginia, for two years, following which he completed his preparations at Washington and Lee University and graduated in 1905 with the degree Bachelor of Law. Mr. Burks commenced the practice of his calling at Christianburg, Virginia, but after a short time went to Bristol and later to Big Stone Gap, subsequently returning to Bristol. Eventually, in 1912, he settled permanently at Roanoke, where he has since been engaged in a general practice, his present offices being located in the Boxley Building. He has attained a recognized position in his profession, and is a member of the Roanoke City Bar Association. While at the Episcopal High School he was a member of the debating society, and also of the Sigma Chi fraternity while at Washington and Lee University. He became a charter member of the Loyal Order of Moose at Roanoke when that order was established at this place, and has a number of civic and other

Thr. Fraser

connections. In politics Mr. Burks is a Democrat, but has preferred to devote himself to his profession rather than to the doubtful honors of public life or the constant bickerings and struggles of political activities. With his family he belongs to Christ Church, Episcopal.

On February 4, 1908, Mr. Burks was united in marriage with Miss Laura French Mangum Oglesby, who was born in North Carolina and educated at Randolph-Macon Woman's College, and taught school for two years prior to her marriage. To this union there were born four children: Martin P. III, a student at Washington and Lee University; Albert Oglesby, who graduated from high school in 1929; Laura French Mangum, who is attending school; and Edward Calohill, who commenced school in the fall of 1927.

THOMAS FRASER, who died at Richmond March 10, 1925, was prominent not only in that city but over the state as a doctor of veterinary medicine, and in the course of his long experience in private practice he did much to improve the standards of the profession throughout the state.

He was of pure Scotch ancestry on both sides and was born in Inverness, Scotland, June 2, 1864. His father was Robert Fraser, and he was the second son in a family of six children.

His early education was acquired in Inverness, Scotland, and several years later he came to America and located at Richmond in 1886, entering a partnership with Mr. F. Finlayson in the latter's blacksmith shop. He was made a member of the firm of Finlayson and Fraser, and when Mr. Finlayson died Mr. Fraser continued the business, finally selling it to his brother, who died in 1926. In the meantime Thomas Fraser turned his attention to veterinary medicine and in 1901 was graduated from the Veterinary College of Toronto, Canada. From that date until his death he carried on an extensive practice with headquarters at Richmond, and during that time he served as secretary of the Virginia State Veterinary Medical Association, and was also a member of the legislative committee of the State Board of Examiners. Doctor Fraser was an interested student of Masonry, served as master of Amity Lodge No. 76, A. F. and A. M., and was a thirty-second degree Scottish Rite Mason and Shriner. He and his family were Presbyterians.

He married, August 8, 1888, Miss Jessie Anderson Rankine, who was reared and educated in Lanark, Scotland. She was the seventh of the twelve children of James and Jessie (Anderson) Rankine. Mrs. Fraser survives her husband and resides at 2623 Hanover Avenue in Richmond.

ROBERT T. HUBARD, Virginia attorney, is a resident of Salem, and has served consecutively for over three terms as commonwealth attorney of Roanoke County.

He was born at Lynchburg, Virginia, July 7, 1881, son of Rev. E. W. and Julia L. (Taylor) Hubard. His father was born on a plantation in Buckingham, Virginia, in 1841, and when about twenty years of age he enrolled in the Buckingham Troop of the Fourth Virginia Cavalry. He was wounded early in his service and was unable to rejoin his command until 1863. After the war he studied in the Episcopal Seminary, was ordained in 1868, and for nearly half a century was active in the ministry, serving pastorates in Fincastle, Brandon, Lynchburg, Washington, Salem, and at Owensboro, Kentucky. He died August 8, 1915. He was a member of the Masonic Lodge at Lynchburg. Rev. E. W. Hubard, whose father was R. T. Hubard, married Julia L. Taylor, who was born in Caroline County, Virginia, daughter of Henry Taylor, a Virginia planter. She died November 16, 1918, at the age of seventy-six. They had three children: Julia T., deceased, E. B. Hubard, a civil and mining engineer at Livingston, Montana, and Robert T.

Robert T. Hubard, who has never married, was educated under his parents and also in private schools at Salem, graduated in 1901 with the A. B. degree from Roanoke College, and took his law course at the University of Virginia, graduating in 1907. During the four years between his college course and entering law school he worked in the oil fields of West Virginia. Mr. Hubard since 1907 has practiced law at Salem. In 1914 he was appointed to fill out an unexpired term as commonwealth attorney, and since then has been elected for three successive terms.

During the World war Mr. Hubard was United States appeal agent. He has interested himself in various movements for public improvement, particularly education and good roads. He is a past master of the Masonic Lodge, member of the Independent Order of Odd Fellows, and a Democrat in politics. His church home is St. Paul's Episcopal Church at Salem.

CHARLES HILTON WEBER has become one of the prominent figures in connection with public utility service in Virginia, maintains his executive headquarters in the City of Richmond, and here he served as division manager of the Chesapeake & Potomac Telephone Company from 1913 until May, 1927, when he was advanced to his present office, that of vice-president.

Mr. Weber is a representative of one of the old and influential citizens of Baltimore, Maryland, in which city he was born January 7, 1879. He is a son of the late August Weber, who was for many years president of the National Central Bank of Baltimore, an institution that was founded by his father, Charles Weber, and in point of continuous identification with this important line of financial enterprise August Weber held rank as the oldest banker in Baltimore at the time of his death, in October, 1926.

The earlier education of Charles H. Weber was acquired in private schools in his native city and was there advanced by his attending Baltimore City College and thereafter Marston's University School, he having been graduated from the Marston School as a member of the class of 1898.

Interesting data relative to the career of Mr. Weber are to be found in the following extracts from a newspaper article that appeared at the time of his election to the office of vice president of the Chesapeake & Potomac Telephone Company:

"Entering the service of the telephone company as chief clerk in Baltimore, in 1902, Mr. Weber has progressed steadily from position to position of increasing importance in the telephone organization. A few months after he was engaged as chief clerk he was made chief collector, and in 1903 he was appointed cashier. Shortly after this he was made manager for the City of Baltimore. Successively Mr. Weber was division manager, Baltimore district, and then division manager of Maryland, when he was transferred to Richmond in 1913. In the fourteen years that Mr. Weber has been in charge of the telephone matters in Virginia he has seen the company make substantial gains in telephone growth until today the system serves every section of the state. When he came to Virginia in 1913 there were only 45,000 telephones connected with the system. Today the Chesapeake & Potomac Telephone Company of Virginia serves about 130,000 stations.

"Besides being a director of the Petersburg Telephone Company at Petersburg and the Intermountain Telephone Company, whose headquarters are at Bristol, Tennessee, Mr. Weber is connected with a number of important financial organizations in Virginia. Principal among these are the Richmond Trust Company, of which he is a director, and the Richmond Trust Building Corporation, of which he is president."

In Virginia's capital city Mr. Weber has proven himself a most loyal and progressive citizen and man of affairs, and he is here actively identified with various civic and social organizations of representative order. He is a member of the Board of Governors of the Westmoreland Club, and has membership also in the Commonwealth Club and the Country Club of Virginia.

On April 11, 1908, in New York City, occurred the marriage of Mr. Weber and Miss Gladys Vereen McNair, daughter of Col. John Taylor and Mary Charlton (Strathy) McNair, of South Carolina.

REV. FRANCIS H. SCOTT, pastor of the First Christian Church of Roanoke, is one of the eloquent and scholarly divines of his communion, and a man whose zeal in behalf of his Master may be gleaned from the fact that ever since he was eleven years old he has steadily worked to become a minister of the Gospel and to remain faithful to his obligations. From one charge to another he has ascended in the importance of his labors until today he is ministering to a membership of 1,000 souls, and enjoying the warm support of his community in his efforts to better existing conditions. Rev. Mr. Scott was born in Essex County, Virginia, a son of Francis and Kate (Ware) Scott, natives of Virginia, he born in King William County, and she in Essex County. For many years he was a merchant at Dunnsville, Virginia, and a consistent member of the Baptist Church, but she was a member of the Christian Church. One of the leading Masons of his locality, he held membership in Arlington Lodge, A. F. and A. M., of Essex County. The following children were born to him and his wife: Anne Elizabeth, who married R. R. Rice, of Richmond, manager of the Slive store; Reverend Scott, who is the second in order of birth; Jeanette Latane, who married E. M. Lewis, a son of Dr. Frank Lewis, superintendent of education of Lancaster County, Virginia, and himself cashier of the Chesapeake Bank of Lively, Virginia; and Katherine Holt, who married J. P. Warren, of Richmond, connected with the Chesapeake & Ohio Railroad. The paternal grandfather of Reverend Scott was Rev. Azariah Francis Scott, a Baptist minister for a long period. The maternal grandfather was Robert Ware, a native of Essex County, and a farmer upon an extensive scale.

Reverend Scott attended the local schools of his native county and Johnson Bible College at Knoxville, Tennessee, and he completed his theological education in Lynchburg College, where he took special studies, but he returned to Knoxville for his degree, which he received in 1907. His first charge was that of assistant to Dr. Peter Ainslie, of Baltimore, Maryland, and during his

association with that outstanding figure in the church of the
Disciples of Christ he advanced considerably. After ten useful
years spent in Baltimore he came to Roanoke, October 1, 1917,
to take charge of his present church. Under his inspirational
leadership this church has made rapid progress, and has a membership of over 1,000.

On January 30, 1917, Reverend Scott married Imogene
Welck, born in Hagerstown, Maryland, and educated in an excellent private school of that city. Two children have been
born of this marriage: Francis H. Scott III, and Kathryn Virginia Scott. Rev. Mr. Scott is one of the valued members of the
Kiwanis Club and is now (1928) its president. During the
past ten years he has been reaching many people outside his
church through the medium of his lectures, the favorite one of
which, "An Evening in Dixie," he has given 250 times, and it is
still in great demand. He is president of the Virginia State
Conventon of Disciples of Christ, and a member of the Board of
Managers of the United Christian Missionary Society. During
1928 he served as president of the Roanoke Ministerial Association. It is not easy to overestimate the value of the work of a
man like Reverend Scott, for it is so far-reaching and comprehensive in its scope and effect. Deeply imbued with the spirit
of his sacred calling, he never spares himself, but works continuously to convert sinners and to keep Christians who are trying to live according to their vows in the straight and narrow
path. In all that he undertakes his upright honorable life is
an example others would do well to emulate, and Roanoke can
well consider itself fortunate in having him in its midst.

JOHN W. MCCAULEY. Roanoke has no more brilliant young
attorney than John W. McCauley, nor a man who devotes more
time and attention to his professional duties, and therefore his
undoubted success is not so remarkable. A very ardent Democrat, he has received recognition at the hands of his party's
leaders, and in 1927 was nominated on the regular Democratic
ticket for the office of state representative from Roanoke
County. Mr. McCauley was born in Sweetwater, Texas, March
21, 1900, a son of Claud and Ora May (Ward) McCauley, both
natives of Tennessee, who were taken to Texas in childhood.
In addition to being engaged in the practice of law in Sweetwater, in which he has attained to distinction, the father is a
banker. Two children have been born to him and his wife,
namely: John W., whose name heads this review; and Ray, a
Texas rancher, residing in San Antonio. The parents belong to
the Christian Church, in which they are very prominent. He is
a Mason and a Democrat, and at one time served as district
attorney of his county. His father, Jefferson McCauley, a native
of Tennessee, founded the family in Texas not long after the
close of the war between the states, in which he served as a
Confederate soldier, and received a serious wound in action,
but recovered and spent his life in farming. The maternal
grandfather, John W. Ward, went to Texas at an early day, and
as he was a man of large means had many interests, the most
of them centered in Waco.

John W. McCauley was graduated from high school in San
Antonio, and from the Virginia Military Institute, Lexington,
Virginia, in 1917, after which he studied law at home and was
admitted to the bar in 1921. For one year he was assistant
professor of mathematics in the Virginia Military Institute, and

at the same time was captain of infantry assigned to that institution during the World war, being honorably discharged therefrom in the early part of 1919. Upon his admission to the bar in 1921 Mr. McCauley entered upon the active practice of his profession in Roanoke, in partnership with Bruce Hunt, but a year later the firm of Woodrum, McCauley & Parsons came into existence as successor to Woodrum & McCauley.

On June 7, 1919, Mr. McCauley married Elisabeth Sayers, born in Wytheville, Virginia, where she attended school, but she completed her education at The Castle, New York. She is a daughter of Dr. W. S. Sayers, a retired physician residing in Roanoke. Mr. and Mrs. McCauley have two sons, William Sayers McCauley, who was born May 27, 1921, and Claud Ward McCauley, born February 22, 1928. Mr. McCauley belongs to the Christian Church, and Mrs. McCauley to Saint John's Episcopal Church. High in Masonry, he has been advanced through both the Scottish and York Rites, and he also belongs to the Mystic Shrine. He is a member of the Knights of Pythias, the Benevolent and Protective Order of Elks, the Loyal Order of Moose and the Woodmen of the World. As a lawyer he is a prodigious worker and he is making a most enviable record. Recognition of his standing has been given by his appointment to the staff of Governor Byard.

GEORGE E. MARKLEY. The advent of George E. Markley at Roanoke in 1884 was not a particularly auspicious one, as shortly after his arrival he was overtaken with ill health that caused him to return to his native Keystone State, but evidently the community had made a strong and favorable impression upon the young man who was then just entering upon his career, for the year 1887 saw him again a resident of the growing city, ready to take his place among its toilers and to accept such opportunities as came to his hand. By virtue of the possession of the homely qualities of industry and determination, overlying a strong strain of natural ability, he has since made a place for himself among the substantial and highly respected business men of the city.

Mr. Markley was born on a farm in Juniata County, Pennsylvania, in January, 1866, and is a son of Samuel and Mary J. (Harmon) Markley, natives of the same state. Samuel Markley came of a long line of agricultural stock, and after having secured a public school education adopted the vocation of his forefathers and for many years was a tiller of the soil in Pennsylvania. In the evening of life, after the death of his wife at Altoona, Pennsylvania, in 1898, he retired from active pursuits and moved to Virginia, where he died in 1913. They were consistent members of the Lutheran Church and highly respected people of their community.

George E. Markley was given the advantages of a public school education in his native state, where his boyhood and youth were passed on the home farm. Subsequently he was a clerk in a grocery store and was employed otherwise until 1884, at which time he first came to Roanoke. As before mentioned, not long after his arrival he was taken seriously ill and forced to return to his Pennsylvania home, but in 1887, at the time of the attainment of his majority, he left the parental roof and established himself in one of the largest retail grocery businesses in Roanoke with his brother, Chris Markley. After two years he left this business to accept the position of cashier of the Traders Loan, Trust and Deposit Company, an institution with which he continued to be identified for seven years, and in 1896 embarked in the plumbing business, being at this time the oldest plumber in point of consecutive years of service at Roanoke. During the thirty-two years that have followed the business of George E. Markley & Company, contract plumbers and jobbers, has grown to be one of the largest in this part of the state and has built up a reputation for high integrity and straightforward dealing. Mr. Markley also carries on an extensive roofing business, and some of the largest contracts for roofing and plumbing at Roanoke and the surrounding cities have been let to his concern. He is a Democrat in his political views, but has been so engrossed in business that politics has played only a small part in his career. However, as a public spirited citizen of civic pride he has given of his best in the support of all movements making for progress and advancement, be they civic, educational or religious. He is a consistent member of the Lutheran Church, as are the members of his family. Being a genial and sociable man, and one who enjoys the companionship of his fellows, he is a popular member of the Country Club and also a York Rite Mason and Shriner.

In 1894 Mr. Markley was united in marriage with Miss Flora B. Hooge, of Martinsburg, West Virginia, who was educated at her native place, a daughter of George H. Hooge, a machinist in the employ of the Norfolk & Western Railway for many years. Mr. and Mrs. Markley are the parents of two children: Herbert Ryneal, an electrician by trade, who is at present in the West; and Margaret Louise, aged fourteen years, who is attending school.

CHARLES M. ARMES. Among the self-made men of Roanoke County who by their ability, enterprise and industry have reached prominence in business life and at the same time have contributed to the welfare and prosperity of their several communities, one who is well entitled to mention in any history of Virginia is Charles M. Armes, for many years identified with the real estate business at Roanoke, but who now confines his activities to the business of real estate loans. Mr. Armes commenced his career when still a lad, and without financial support or friendly influence has made himself a leading business citizen, and one who has a number of prominent civic connections.

Charles M. Armes was born in Charlotte County, Virginia, March 6, 1866, and is a son of John W. and Mary A. (Anderson) Armes, natives of Prince Edward County, Virginia, both of whom are now deceased. His father was a railroad man for many years, and he and Mrs. Armes were faithful members of the Baptist Church. They were the parents of eight children, of whom six are living, Charles M. having been the fourth in order of birth.

Charles M. Armes received his education in the country schools of Charlotte County, and was only eleven years of age when he commenced work as a clerk in a small country store. Although his school attendance was decidedly limited, he has always made the most of his advantages and opportunities, and today has a reputation as a man of sound and practical education. When he had grown to sturdy young manhood he secured a position in the railroad service, and was thus employed for a number of years, in the meanwhile carefully conserving his savings. When he gave up railroading he became a bookkeeper for a wholesale house, but finally, in 1901, embarked in the real estate business, to which he subsequently added a real estate loan department. In 1906 Mr. Armes established the Columbia Savings and Loan Corporation, and in 1917 retired from the real estate field to give his entire attention to the loan business, in which he is now engaged, with offices in the Colonial Bank Building. Mr. Armes has large and important financial interests at Roanoke and in various other communities and stands high in the confidence and estimation of his business associates. In 1916 he established the Evergreen Burial Park, known as the most beautiful cemetery in the United States, of which he is the active head, holding the office of treasurer. Recently Mr. Armes was elected a member of the Board of Trustes of Roanoke College, and is a member of Green Memorial Methodist Church. Fraternally he is a member of the Knights of Pythias, and a York Rite Mason and Shriner, devoting considerable of his time to the work of the Shrine. Politically a Democrat, he is active and influential in the ranks of his party, although not as a seeker for personal preferment or public office. All public spirited civic movements have received his whole hearted support and cooperation.

In 1888 Mr. Armes was united in marriage with Miss Belle Norman, who was born at Mount Airy, North Carolina, but brought as a child to Virginia, where she received her education. They have no children.

JONATHAN C. WOODSON is active head of one of the oldest and largest organizations for handling real estate in the City of Lynchburg. Mr. Woodson has been in the real estate business thirty-five years, and his firm has developed and marketed the finest residential subdivisions in the community.

Mr. Woodson was born in Appomattox County, Virginia, January 30, 1853, son of John W. and Mary Elizabeth (Christian) Woodson. The Woodson family came from Scotland. His grandfather, Drury W. Woodson, was a planter in Appomattox County and also a tailor by trade. He married Louisa Hendrick. John William Woodson was born in 1823, learned the trade of tailor, taught school in order to complete his education at the University of Virginia, and after graduating from the Law School practiced his profession until the Civil war. He entered the army, was in the Quartermaster's Department, and died of typhoid fever July 4, 1864. His wife, Mary Elizabeth Christian, was born in 1827 and died in 1892. Her father, Jonathan Christian, was a native of Appomattox County. John W. Woodson and wife had five children. The three now living are: Mary Elizabeth, wife of L. D. Isbell, judge of the Relations Court of Huntington, West Virginia; Henry P., of Clearwater, Florida, and Jonathan Christian.

Jonathan Christian Woodson grew up in Appomattox County, attended the common schools there, and up to 1877 taught school. On locating in Lynchburg he clerked for a tobacco firm and was in the tobacco business for about twenty years. In 1893 he took up real estate, and since 1924 his firm has also had a department devoted to fire insurance.

Mr. Woodson married in May, 1885, Miss Fannie C. Binford, a native of Appomattox County. She died in 1887, leaving one

son, John William Woodson, who is associated with his father
in the real estate business and was educated at the Lynchburg
High School. He served four years on the Lynchburg City
Council. He married second, Miss Agusta Camm. They have
two sons, Jonathan Christian II and Henry Palmer. Mr. Woodson in 1890 married Miss Bennie M. Gipson, a native of Buckingham County. She died in 1911, leaving two sons, Thomas
Gipson and Richard Boatwright. Thomas Gipson was educated
in the Lynchburg High School and Washington and Lee University, and is with his father, in charge of the insurance department. Richard Boatwright is now studying public accounting at Atlanta. Both sons were in the World war, Thomas G.
in the Ambulance Corps until taken ill, and later joined the
navy on the *U. S. S. Pamlico*. He was honorably discharged
December 11, 1918. The other son was on transport duty during
the war.

Mr. Woodson and family are members of the Rivermont
Methodist Episcopal Church, South. He is affiliated with the
B. P. O. Elks and is a Democrat. The firm of J. C. Woodson &
Company has acted as brokers for city and farm property.
Some years ago they developed the Randolph-Macon Heights
property, the first high class subdivision at Lynchburg, and
later they opened the Peakland Division and also the Rivermont
Subdivision.

FREDERICK M. DAVIS. No profession or calling has ever
presented such opportunities for the really capable man as that
of the law, and from its ranks have come the ablest men of the
country. It has always been impossible for any man to rise to
distinction without a thorough preparation, even if self-earned,
and this study and thought naturally develop the reasoning faculties and broaden the understanding and character so that other
problems are more easily solved as they arise for disposal by
every public spirited citizen, and whenever, as is often the case,
a lawyer becomes interested in business as well he succeeds because of this professional training. Such training has brought
out in marked degree the varied capabilities of Frederick M.
Davis, able attorney and successful business man of Lynchburg,
well known to the people of his city and county because of his
valuable service as assistant commonwealth attorney in 1924
and 1925.

Frederick M. Davis was born in Lynchburg, February 28,
1893, a son of Micajah Preston and Maud (Mathews) Davis, he
born in Lynchburg and she in Rockingham County, Virginia.
His death occurred November 28, 1925, but she survives and
still resides in Lynchburg. After being graduated from the
Virginia Military Institute the father went into the insurance
business, which he built up to large proportions and through
which he became a well known man all over this part of the
state. He and his wife early united with the Westminster Presbyterian Church of which he was an elder at the time of his
death, and he was also a member of the Masonic Order. In
politics he was a Democrat. His father, George D. Davis, was
born in Bedford County, Virginia. The maternal grandfather,
John D. Mathews, was born in Port Republic, Virginia, but for
some years was a jeweler of Aberdeen, Mississippi, but returned
to Virginia, and continued to farm during the remainder of his
life. During the war between the states he was under the command of Gen. "Stonewall" Jackson. Both the Davis and

Ellen G. Kidd

Mathews families are old and aristocratic ones of the Old Dominion.

The only son of his parents, Frederick M. Davis was sent to Washington and Lee University after he was through his high school work in Lychburg, and he was graduated from that University in 1914. From 1914 to 1915 he was deputy clerk of the Corporation Court of Lynchburg, Virginia. He returned in 1915 to Washington and Lee University and in 1917 he graduated in law, but his service in the United States Navy during the World war as supply officer, with rank of assistant paymaster on board the *U. S. S. Gulfport*, prevented his entering upon his practice until 1919. Since then he has resided in Lynchburg, being engaged in the activities of his profession until the death of his father in 1925 when he took over his father's insurance business, conducting it in association with Norvell N. Holt. Mr. Davis is still a member of the legal profession. Unmarried, he resides with his mother. He belongs to the Rivermont Presbyterian Church. High in Masonry, he has been advanced through the Scottish Rite to the thirty-second degree. He belongs to Phi Delta Theta, and Phi Delta Phi, the legal fraternity, and is the national historian of Square and Compass, was president of Washington and Lee Square, and helped to organize the Square and Compass. At present he is secretary and treasurer of the Lions Club, of Lynchburg. He is service officer of the Lynchburg Post No. 16 of the American Legion. He has been scout master of Troop No. 1 since 1921, and takes a great deal of interest in the Scout movement.

MRS. ELLEN G. KIDD is the founder of the Pin Money Pickle Manufacturing Company, and while her home all her life has been in Richmond both she and her business have been given national and international recognition. Mrs. Kidd for twenty-eight years was the only woman member of the Richmond Chamber of Commerce, and for fifteen years she was a member of the Chamber of Commerce of Pittsburgh, Pennsylvania, these being slight tokens of the respect that has been paid her remarkable achievements as a woman in the field of commerce.

Ellen Gertrude Tompkins was born at Richmond, and her ancestry includes several notable families. She is a daughter of Edmund William and Julia Mosby (Burton) Tompkins, and a granddaughter of Harry and Fanny (Taylor) Tompkins. Through her mother she is in the sixth generation of descent from John Taylor, who came from Carlisle, England, and settled in Virginia. Another ancestor, in the fourth generation, was Major Day, a member of General Washington's staff in the Revolutionary war. Her father had two second cousins, one of whom became the wife of Carter Lee, a brother of Gen. Robert E. Lee, and the other married a sister of General Grant. Mrs. Kidd's father was at one time city treasurer of Richmond.

The old Tompkins home in Richmond was at 706 East Leigh Street, and it was in the kitchen of that home that Ellen Gertrude in the years following the Civil war made pickles according to an old recipe that had long been in the family. An old recipe like an old violin needs a capable performer to insure a perfect product, and the millions who have eaten Pin Money Pickles would probably agree that the quality and flavor are due at least as much to the skill and artistry of the woman who first gave her product that name and whose phenomenal ability as a business organizer has made possible the continuation of the standard of quality on large scale manufacturing, as to the special virtues of the original recipe.

It is said that Miss Tompkins only yielded after much urging to sell pickles from the kettle in her own kitchen, and then for the sake of "pin money," and so she happened upon the fortunate name for the product. She started the business on a very small scale, using her own kitchen as her plant, about 1872. The manufacture of Pin Money Pickles at Richmond is an industry that has been in existence for over half a century, and throughout its destiny has been carefully guided by Mrs. Ellen G. Kidd. For several years it was a seasonal occupation, depending upon custom orders. One of the first important orders she received was from the Pullman Company dining car department, for the sum of four hundred dollars. For many years Pin Money Pickles have been one of the few special brands of food products served on the standard menus of the Pullman dining cars, and this alone has made the name and the product familiar to the traveling public throughout America. Pin Money Pickles are served in hotels and other fine establishments in many foreign countries. From the small business that started in Ellen Tompkin's kitchen the business has been developed until it utilizes a large seven-story factory in Richmond. Besides this factory there is another monument to the business at Richmond, the Shenandoah Apartment Building, one of the largest and most exclusive and luxurious apartment houses in Virginia. Mrs. Kidd has her own home in that building.

Mrs. Kidd has attended many national conventions of the Business and Professional Women's Clubs and has served as vice president and treasurer of the League of Women Voters, and for over a third of a century she has been on the board of the Sheltering Arms Hospital. She has traveled extensively abroad, and many articles have been published concerning this remarkable Richmond business woman in the foreign as well as the American press. She is a member of St. James Episcopal Church, the King's Daughters and Musicians Club. Mrs. Kidd completed her early education in the Pegram School for Girls at Richmond.

A source of constant encouragement to her in the early years of her business as a manufacturer came from her husband, the late John Boulware Kidd. She had started the manufacture of pickles on a commercial scale before her marriage, and Mr. Kidd, an attorney by education, did everything in his power to assist and build up the business. John Boulware Kidd was born in King William County, Virginia, February 28, 1836, and died at Richmond in October, 1910. He was a son of John and Katherine (Boulware) Kidd, of King and Queen County. His mother was a sister of William Boulware, who was United States minister to Italy under President Tyler. John Kidd was an educator by profession.

John Boulware Kidd was educated by private tutor, graduated in law at Columbian College at Georgetown, D. C., but never practiced the profession. He taught school for some years, and his chief profession was insurance, which he followed until his death. He had studied law under Hon. James Lyons. The late Mr. Kidd was during the Civil war employed in the treasury department of the Confederate Government. He was a thorough Greek and Latin scholar.

Mrs. Kidd is the mother of four children. Her daughter Louise, who is a member of the A. V. P. A., Virginia League of

Fine Arts, Colonial Daughters of America, a member of the board of the Sheltering Arms Hospital, the League of Women Voters, and active in St. James Episcopal Church, is the wife of E. Henry Meanley. The second daughter, Caroline, married Thomas J. Foote, of Wilson, North Carolina, and they have three children, named Henry A., John Boulware and Ellen Tompkins. The son Leo Miller Kidd married Lydia Hamilton, and the younger son is Hugh Tompkins Kidd.

WILLIAM L. POWELL, M. D. Many of the biographies appearing in this publication, illustrating the growth and progress of the grand Old Dominion State, are those of early settlers or of the founders of great business enterprises, or of leaders in public life or in the professions. Such men through the circumstances of their coming, or of the period of their connection with affairs, possess a certain factitious advantage quite apart from their individual and intrinsic characters. Those following these, while they may possess equal or greater endowments, are in a measure overshadowed by the veneration in which men hold their elders, and are quite submerged in the vaster multitudes who, in great communities, compete with one another for prominence, crowding every avenue of business and filling every opening for fame. Nevertheless, the life of the state cannot be adequately illustrated without taking into account those who have assumed the work of their fathers and carried it on with success quite equal to and often exceeding theirs.

Dr. William L. Powell, a leading member of the Roanoke County medical profession, belongs to one of the later generations of citizens. He was born at Winchester, Virginia, August 31, 1876, and is a son of William L. and Eva C. (Magill) Powell, natives of Virginia, both of whom are deceased. His paternal grandfather was Humphrey Powell, a native of Loudoun County, Virginia, who passed his life on a large plantation which he owned and which was worked by his numerous slaves until the misfortunes of the war between the states swept away his fortunes. W. L. Powell, the father of Dr. William L. Powell, was born in Virginia and given good educational advantages, including a course at the Virginia Military Institute. He took up civil engineering as a profession and was thus engaged at the outbreak of the war between the states, when he entered the Confederate army and was made a captain. Following the close of that struggle, in which he established an excellent record, he again applied himself to his profession, in which he won prestige and success, and was engaged on many important improvements from Virginia to Florida. He was a Democrat in politics, although he never cared for public office, and his religious faith was that of the Presbyterian Church, in the work of which both he and Mrs. Powell were very active. She was a daughter of Doctor Magill, for many years a prominent physician and surgeon of this state, and at one time a professor of medicine in the University of Virginia.

The only child of his parents, William L. Powell received his early education in Washington and the Miller School in Albemarle County, following which he entered the University of Virginia, from the medical department of which he graduated with the degree Doctor of Medicine as a member of the class of 1900. For the next six years he was variously occupied in different hospitals at Philadelphia, Cleveland and other cities, and in 1906 took up his permanent residence at Roanoke. For the first two years he was in charge of the Roanoke Hospital, but since then has been engaged in a general practice, his present offices being located in the Shenandoah Building. Doctor Powell makes something of a specialty of surgery, a field in which he has gained well merited prominence, and is on the surgical staff of the Roanoke Hospital. He belongs to the Roanoke Medical Society, of which he formerly was president, the Virginia State Medical Society, the Southwestern Virginia Medical Society, the Southern Medical Society and the American Medical Association, and attends all possible meetings of these bodies, in addition to which he has done much post-graduate work in various cities. He is a close and careful student of his profession and keeps fully abreast of its various discoveries and inventions. Doctor Powell is a member of the Alpha Tau Omega fraternity, the Pi Mu honorary medical fraternity. During the World war he served for one year in the United States Medical Corps, being stationed at base hospitals at Philadelphia, Camp Sherman and Camp Greenleaf. He belongs to the Masons, the Independent Order of Odd Fellows and the Knights of Pythias, in all of which he has numerous friends, and his religious connection is with the Second Presbyterian Church, in which he is a member of the Board of Deacons. He is a public spirited supporter of all worthy civic movements and a contributor to charitable and religious enterprises.

In 1908 Doctor Powell was united in marriage with Miss Eleanor Kerr, who was born at Philadelphia, Pennsylvania, and educated in that city, where she was equipped for employment as a trained nurse, a vocation which she followed for several years prior to her marriage. Doctor and Mrs. Powell are the parents of one son, John Randolph, born in 1911, who is now attending high school at Roanoke.

HON. CLIFTON A. WOODRUM. Three generations of the Woodrum family have been identified with the practice of law in Virginia, and all have attained high places in their profession, as well as in public affairs. It would seem that the present representative of the family, Hon. Clifton A. Woodrum, had other plans in his youth, for he studied both pharmacy and medicine, but evidently the magnetic pull of hereditary traits proved too strong. In any case, that he made a wise choice finally is shown in the fact that he is senior member of one of the leading law firms of Roanoke, that of Woodrum, McCauley & Parsons, and is also a leader in public life, being at present a member of the national House of Representatives as representative from the Sixth Congressional District of Virginia.

Judge Woodrum was born at Roanoke, April 27, 1887, and is a son of Robert H. and Anna (Musgrove) Woodrum. His paternal grandfather, Jordan Woodrum, was born in that part of Virginia now included in West Virginia, but moved to Salem, Virginia, where for many years he was engaged successfully in the practice of law. His son, Robert H. Woodrum, was born in what is now West Virginia and received good educational advantages, attending Roanoke College and the law department of the University of Virginia. For a number of years he was engaged in the practice of his profession, and was also the first commonwealth's attorney at Roanoke, but in his declining years gave up his law practice and turned his attention to commercial pursuits, to which he was devoting his activities at the time of his demise in 1914. He was a man who was held in high esteem throughout the community, and during the period of his law practice was connected with much important litigation. He was a Democrat in his political allegiance, and a strong and active worker in the party, and his religious faith was that of the Lutheran Church. Mr. Woodrum married Miss Anna Musgrove, who was born in Texas, a daughter of Robert Musgrove, who for many years was a prominent stockman of Sweetwater, Texas. Mrs. Woodrum, who is now sixty-seven years of age, survives her husband and resides at Roanoke, where she is active in the work of the Lutheran Church. Four children were born to Mr. and Mrs. Woodrum: Clifton A., of this review; Robert J.; and two who are deceased.

The public schools of Roanoke furnished Clifton A. Woodrum with his early educational training, following which he became a student of pharmacy at the University of Medicine, Richmond. Eventually he turned his attention to the family profession of law at the University of Virginia, from which he was graduated with the degree Bachelor of Laws as a member of the class of 1908. He was admitted to the bar in the same year and at once commenced practice at Roanoke, where he is now senior member of the firm of Woodrum, McCauley & Parsons, general practitioners, with offices in the Shenandoah Life Building. Mr. Woodrum is equally conversant with all branches of his profession, and therefore has made a specialty of none. He is accounted a forceful, thorough and well-grounded lawyer, and bears an excellent reputation among his professional colleagues. He belongs to the Roanoke City Bar Association, the Virginia State Bar Association and the American Bar Association, the Phi Delta Phi law fraternity and the Sigma Chi fraternity. A Democrat in his political views, Judge Woodrum long has taken a prominent part in public affairs. He served as commonwealth's attorney and as judge of the Hustings Court, and in 1922 was elected to represent the Sixth Congressional District of Virginia in the national Congress. He was again elected to this body in 1926, and his work has been of a highly valuable and constructive character. He has been active and sincere in his support of all public-spirited measures launched in his community, and in every way has shown his civic pride and far sightedness as a citizen. Judge Woodrum is well known in fraternal circles, being a thirty-third degree Mason, and a past potentate of Kazim Temple, A. A. O. N. M. S.; and a member of the Knights of Pythias, the Benevolent and Protective Order of Elks and the Woodmen of the World.

In 1906 Judge Woodrum was united in marriage with Miss Lena Hancock, who was born at Bedford, Virginia, and educated in the public schools of that city and at Jeter Institute. To this union there have been born two children: Clifton A., Jr., attending Virginia Military Institute and Martha Anne, in the graded schools. The family belongs to the Green Methodist Episcopal Church, South.

WILLIAM B. HARRIS is active head of one of the largest lumber manufacturing organizations in the Southeast, the Williams McKeitham Lumber Company of Lynchburg.

Mr. Harris, who has earned a steady succession of promotions and important attainments in the commercial field, was born in Appomattox County, Virginia, in 1882, son of Tandy and Reberta Alice (Marks) Harris and grandson of John A. Harris, a native of Buckingham County, Virginia, who moved to Appomattox County, where he acquired a farm which, passing from son to son, has been in the possession of the family for three generations. Tandy Harris was born in Buckingham County, was two years of age when the family went to Appomattox County and he succeeded to the ownership of the old homestead and lived on it until his death in June, 1927. He was a Confederate soldier, joining the army at the age of fifteen, and served four years, until the final surrender. The homestead farm which has been in the family for three generations in Appomattox County is known as Locust Hill. He was a Democrat in politics and an active member of the Methodist Episcopal Church, South, serving as superintendent of its Sunday School. His wife, Alice Marks, was born in Botetourt County, Virginia, and died in 1919. Her father, Hudson Marks, was also born in Botetourt County. There were six children, three sons and three daughters, William B. being the oldest son and second child.

William B. Harris attended common schools while a boy on the home farm, and at the age of eighteen began his business career with C. I. Johnson, a prominent merchant and lumberman. He was in the service of Mr. Johnson for seven years and then located at Lynchburg and became a stenographer for the Williams McKeitham Lumber Company. In the consecutive service of this one organization he accepted larger responsibilities until he rose to the presidency of the company. It is a large manufacturing organization, owning and directing a number of plants in the two Carolinas and Florida.

Mr. Harris married in January, 1912, Ruby Smith, a native of Tennessee. Her father, Pryor N. Smith, was at one time president of the Smith-Briscoe Shoe Company of Lynchburg. Mr. and Mrs. Harris have twin sons, William Ballard, Junior, and Robert Smith. The family are members of the Episcopal Church, and Mr. Harris is affiliated with the Oak Wood and Piedmont Clubs.

ROBERT WITHERS MASSIE, a lumber dealer at Lynchburg, is a member of an old Colonial family of Virginia, and has contributed something to the honorable prestige enjoyed by the family in this state for several generations.

He was born in Campbell County, Virginia, April 24, 1858, and grew up in Nelson County. He is a son of Patrick Cabell and Susan C. (Withers) Massie, a grandson of Dr. Thomas Massie, a physician and surgeon who was in service in the American forces as a surgeon in the War of 1812. The maternal grandfather, Robert Walter Withers, was a planter and physician and married a Miss Alexander. Patrick Cabell Massie was born in Nelson County, Virginia, and died in 1877. His wife was born in Campbell County and died in 1903. Of their eight children two are now living, Robert W. and Mrs. L. P. Brown.

Robert Withers Massie was given good home educational opportunities and was a student in the Virginia Military Institute when the death of his father called him home to the responsibilities of the farm and head of the family, since he was the oldest child. During the next twenty years of his life he gave his time to the management of the farm, and after his brothers and sisters were all educated and established for themselves he located at Lynchburg, in 1897, and since that year has been in the lumber business. He has made the Massie Lumber Company, Incorporated, one of the largest manufacturing and whole-

Frank H. Hurd, M.D.

sale organizations in the Southeast, operating mills in South
Carolina and three mills in Virginia.   Mr. Massie is president of
the lumber company.   He is also a director of the First National
Bank of Lynchburg.

He married, in 1885, Miss Mattie W. W. Manson, who was
born in Bedford County, Virginia, daughter of Nathaniel C.
Manson, a Lynchburg attorney.   They have three children.
Robert W. Junior, who was educated in the Virginia Military
Institute, is associated with his father's lumber business.   By
his marriage to Wayatt McKinnon, of Red Springs, North Carolina, he has one son, R. W. III.   N. C. M. Massie, the second son,
a business man at Glasgow, Virginia, married Agnes Minne-
garode.   Martha W. is at home.

Mr. Massie and family are members of Saint Paul's Episcopal Church at Lynchburg.   He belongs to the Sigma Nu college fraternity, is a Democrat, and is president of the Board of
Visitors of Virginia Institute.   For three years he was elected
president of the Order of the Cincinnati.   He has membership in
this organization, made up originally of former officers of the
Revolutonary war, because of the service of his great-grandfather, Major Thomas Massie, who served with the rank of
major in the war for independence and was in service from the
beginning until the final surrender at Yorktown.   He was given
a large grant of land for his military services, and that land was
located near Chilicothe, Ohio, where the Massies were one of the
most conspicuous families in the early political history of that
state.

IRA H. HURT, M. D.   One of the brilliant young physicians
and surgeons of Roanoke who has already achieved distinction
in his profession, Dr. Ira H. Hurt, holds the confidence of the
public and the commendation of his associates because of the
able manner in which he discharges the heavy responsibilities
of his calling.   Both by inclination and intensive training is he
fitted for his work, and while giving it every possible attention,
he does not neglect his obligations as a good citizen, and few
men stand better than he.   Doctor Hurt was born in Franklin
County, Virginia, October 21, 1890, a son of Henry A. and Julia
(Huff) Hurt, natives of Virginia, he born in Franklin County
and she in Floyd County.   The mother is deceased, but the
father survives and is now living in Roanoke.   Formerly he was
a farmer, but after he came to Roanoke he worked in the car
shops for several years, later going into the bus business, and
finally becoming a grocer, in which line of business he is now
engaged.   Of the seven children born to the parents six survive,
and of them all Doctor Hurt was the first born.   All her life
the mother was an active member of the Baptist Church, to
which the father belongs, and he is also a Mason.   In political
faith he is a Democrat.   His father, Ira Hurt, was also a native
of Franklin County, Virginia, and at one time he was one of its
wealthiest men, and a very extensive planter.   The Methodist
Episcopal Church, South, had in him a devout member.   The
maternal grandfather, Isaac Huff, was born in Virginia, and he,
too, was a large landowner and planter.

Doctor Hurt attended the public schools of Roanoke, and
following his graduation from the high school course, had a year
of work in Roanoke College, after which he took two years in
the Medical College of the University of North Carolina.   He

was graduated from Jefferson Medical College, Philadelphia, Pennsylvania, in 1919, and interned for one year in the Presbyterian Hospital of the same city. In 1920 he established himself in general practice in Roanoke, where he has since remained with admirable results. In addition to his private practice Doctor Hurt is an assistant at the Shenandoah Hospital.

In 1923 Doctor Hurt married Miss Edith Jackson, born in Pittsburgh, Pennsylvania, and there educated. She was a trained nurse, in practice. One child has been born to Doctor and Mrs. Hurt, Phyllis Julia, born December 23, 1925. Doctor Hurt belongs to the Melrose Baptist Church, and he is a York Rite and Shriner Mason, and belongs to the Benevolent and Protective Order of Elks. For several years he has taken an active part in the work of the Roanoke Chamber of Commerce. He belongs to the Roanoke Academy of Medicine, the Virginia State Medical Society and the American Medical Association. During the World war he was in the Students Army Training Corps, and he now holds the rank of captain in the Medical Corps of the Virginia National Guard and the Officers Reserve Corps, U. S. A. He is commanding the Medical Detachment of the Two Hundred and Forty-sixth Coast Artillery, and attends its encampment every year. From the above brief review can be gathered the fact that Doctor Hurt measures up to the highest ideals of his profession and good citizenship, and that his future stretches out very bright before him.

HON. ROBERT C. JACKSON. For more than forty-six years Hon. Robert C. Jackson has been a member of the Virginia bar, and during the past two decades has been engaged in practice at Roanoke. For a large part of his career he has been the incumbent of positions of honor and trust, and at present is city attorney of Roanoke, an office in which he has discharged his duties with marked ability and conscientiousness. It has been his fortune to have attained well merited distinction in his profession, and to have been identified with many important movements that have contributed to the civic and general welfare.

Judge Jackson was born December 26, 1861, at Austinville, Wythe County, Virginia, and is a son of Thomas and Amanda (Porter) Jackson, and a grandson of Samuel Porter, a native of Wythe County, where the family was prominent for many years, its members for the greater part being planters. Thomas Jackson was born in England and came to the United States in young manhood, settling in Wythe County, where he spent the remainder of his life in agricultural pursuits. He and his wife, who was born in Wythe County, were the parents of seven children, of whom six are living, Robert C. being the youngest. Two of the sons were soldiers of the Confederacy during the war between the states: Samuel, who resides in Kansas, and John C., of Galax, Grayson County, this state. The parents were faithful members of the Methodist church.

Robert C. Jackson acquired his early education in the public schools of Wythe County, and was graduated from Emory and Henry College, Emory, Virginia, as a member of the class of 1879, receiving the degree Bachelor of Arts. He then entered the University of Virginia, where he spent three years, and in 1882 was graduated with the degree Bachelor of Laws. Commencing practice in Grayson County, he was elected county judge when he was only twenty-two years of age, and held that office for four years. When he resigned from that office he was elected commonwealth's attorney, in which capacity he acted for a like period, and continued to practice in Grayson County until 1896, when he moved to Wytheville. That community continued to be the scene of his professional labors until 1898, when he was elected judge of the Twenty-first Judicial Circuit, comprising the counties of Wythe, Pulaski, Giles, Carroll, Bland and Tazewell. Judge Jackson could have held this office indefinitely had he so desired, but resigned and moved to Roanoke County in 1908, where he has since made his home, his present offices being in the Shenandoah Life Building. He carries on a general practice and has attained to a high position in his profession, being the legal representative of a large and important clientage. In addition to his private practice he has served for several years in the capacity of city attorney. He is a member of the Roanoke County Bar Association, the Virginia State Bar Association and the American Bar Association, and has been a member of the Masonic fraternity for many years, having passed through the chairs of the York Rite. He likewise has been active in civic affairs and politics, and is a leading member of Trinity Methodist Episcopal Church, South, in which he is a steward and has been a Sunday School teacher for thirty years.

Judge Jackson married, in 1886, Miss Lelia Dickinson, who was born in Grayson County, Virginia, and to this union there were born three children: Hurd, who resides in the West; Elizabeth, who married a Mr. Anderson and resides in New Jersey; and Lelia, who married John Dechert, a resident of Harrisonburg, Virginia. The mother of these children died in 1893 and Mr. Jackson married, in 1900, Miss Marian R. Early, of Hillsville, Carroll County, Virginia, and has one son, Ralph, who resides in Florida.

CHARLES G. CRADDOCK. Lessons are daily brought home to us; tuition is ours for the asking in the various fields of human endeavor; we need no school or instructors to show us in which direction we must lay the course of our energies to gain position and success. It is true that study is needed, but the careers of the men who have tried and have attained furnish better instruction than can be gained through any other line. One of these lessons is that a real man does not allow himself to know that the word "quit" has found a place in our dictionary, our vocabulary or our personality. We may take a case in this connection and illustrate our point. Charles G. Craddock, president of the Craddock-Terry Company, has worked his way up in his present company from his initial position of clerk to that of president, and his thoughtful interest in other persons and things and his genial social qualities have well earned him the confidence and high esteem in which he is held by all who know him.

Charles G. Craddock was born in Lynchburg, Virginia, November 17, 1890, a son of John W. Craddock, a sketch of whom appears elsewhere in this work. Reared in his native city, Charles G. Craddock attended its graded and high schools and the Episcopal High School of Virginia, Alexandria, and had one year in the University of Virginia and another year in the University of Pennsylvania.

With the completion of his educational training Mr. Craddock entered the auditing department of his present company, and has steadily risen until today he is its president, which office he has held since 1924. Under his wise and aggresive administration the volume of business has expanded, while at the same time the quality of the product has been maintained, and today the company has a very high rating both commercially and industrially.

In 1916 Mr. Craddock married Miss Katharine Baker, born in Lynchburg, a daughter of Dr. W. H. Baker, the first eye, ear, nose and throat specialist of Lynchburg. Mrs. Craddock attended the schools of Lynchburg and Agnes Scott College, and is a finely educated lady of social graces. Three children have been born to Mr. and Mrs. Craddock: Eliza Deane Craddock, Charles G., Junior, and Frank Baker Craddock. Mr. Craddock is a member of the First Presbyterian Church of Lynchburg, and one of its most active workers. He belongs to the Delta Tau Delta Greek letter fraternity, the Rotary Club and the Country Club, as well as to other organizations of the city. In close touch with the progress of events he displays a thorough knowledge of public and business conditions, and brings it to bear in his skillful and systematic conduct of his affairs. From the start he has shown an appreciation of those traits of character which insure safe and sound business processes, and not only has endeavored to develop them in himself, but to surround himself with others who possess them, and because of this and other reasons already enumerated has kept his concern in the forefront of progress. Such men as he set the pace for others, and encourage development and expansion along all lines.

DAVID HAMPTON KIZER is an attorney, has practiced law at Lynchburg since finishing his course at the University of Virginia, and has made a good record in his profession and in the affairs and relationship of a citizen.

He was born in South Carolina, November 12, 1876, son of Ellis R. and Rosa (Shuler) Kizer, also natives of South Carolina. His mother was a daughter of Oliver Shuler, who was born in South Carolina and was a planter and slave owner before the war. The paternal grandparents were David Frederick and Elizabeth (Jackson) Kizer, the latter of whom died January 9, 1928, in her native State of South Carolina at the age of 103 years. David F. Kizer was a farmer. He and his wife reared eleven out of fourteen children, and all of them married and had sons and daughters. Ellis R. Kizer spent his life as a farmer, was a member of the Methodist Episcopal Church, South, the Masonic fraternity and a Democrat in politics. He was born December 27, 1853, and died October 20, 1913, while his wife was born in 1854 and died August 4, 1897. They had a family of ten children.

David Hampton Kizer attended the common schools in South Carolina, the Carlisle Fitting School at Bamberg, and in 1907 was graduated from the law department of the University of Virginia, having had several terms of experience as a teacher before finishing his law course. Mr. Kizer was admitted to the bar January 11, 1907, and in the same year established his offices in the Law Building at Lynchburg, where he has been for twenty years.

Mr. Kizer married, November 15, 1911, Miss Lucille Bullock, who was born in Russellville, Alabama, and was educated there and in the State Normal School at Florence, Alabama. She taught school before her marriage. Five children were born to their union: D. H. Junior, Shuler Anderson, William Bullock, Mildred Lawler and Charles Walter.

J. W. Simmerman M.D.

Mr. Kizer has served as steward of the Methodist Church of Lynchburg fifteen years, also as superintendent of the Sunday School and his wife takes an active part in the same church and its social and charitable agencies. Mr. Kizer is a past master of Marshall Lodge No. 39, A. F. and A. M., at Lynchburg, member of Lynchburg Chapter No. 10, Royal Arch Masons, DeMolay Commandery No. 4, Knights Templar, Kazim Temple of the Mystic Shrine at Roanoke, and is also affiliated with Lynchburg Lodge No. 17, Independent Order of Odd Fellows, is a past chancellor of Lynchburg Courtney Lodge No. 11, Knights of Pythias, and for the past twenty years has been treasurer of the Knights of Pythias Lodge and is a member of the D. O. K. K. He also belongs to the Junior Order of the American Mechanics and the Improved Order of Red Men, Tribe No. 96. He is a member of the Piedmont Club, the Delta Chi legal fraternity and is a Democrat in politics.

JOHN W. SIMMERMAN is an accomplished physician and surgeon whose most successful years in his profession have been spent at Roanoke.

Doctor Simmerman was born at Ivanhoe, Wythe County, Virginia, February 17, 1887, son of S. S. and Lula (Painter) Simmerman, natives of the same county. His parents reside at Wytheville, where his father is a farmer and banker. He is a Methodist and his wife a Presbyterian, and he belongs to the B. P. O. Elks. There were three children: Dr. John W.; S. S., Junior, a farmer at Wytheville; and Elizabeth, wife of C. P. Huff, a merchant at Pulaski, Virginia.

John W. Simmerman was educated in local schools in Wythe County, continued his education in the Virginia Polytechnic Institute at Blacksburg and was graduated in 1911 from the Maryland Medical College at Baltimore. He had his training as an interne at the Chesapeake and Ohio Hospital at Richmond and for two years practiced at McDonalds Mill. Doctor Simmerman in 1913 located at Roanoke, and has achieved a very excellent general practice. He is a member of the Roanoke Academy of Medicine, Medical Society of Virginia, American Medical Association.

Doctor Simmerman is a director of the Colonial National Bank of Roanoke and the Peoples Bank of Vinton. He is interested in community affairs, serving as a member of the School Board and is a York and Scottish Rite Mason and Shriner, member of the Knights of Pythias and its social adjuncts, the D. O. K. K. He and his family are members of Saint Peter's Episcopal Church.

He married, in 1910, Mae L. Quarles who was born in Halifax, Virginia. They have two daughters, Mary Louise and Mae Morrison, both attending school at Roanoke.

ROBERT T. LEMMON, M. D. Indelibly inscribed on the pages of the medical history of Campbell County and deeply graven in the hearts of those who know him is the name and personality of Dr. Robert T. Lemmon, of Lynchburg, whose modest deportment, kindness of heart and true beneficence mark him as a gentleman, while his strong intellect and experience directed in the channels of materia medica have gained for him distinction among the members of his profession in this part of Virginia. The salient features in the life of Doctor Lemmon may be deduced from the fact that he is beloved by all who know him, as much in professional circles as by those with whom he comes in contact in social relations. He has figured for a number of years as a prominent member of the medical fraternity of Lynchburg, which has always been distinguished for high rank in the profession, and he has not shirked his duty as a citizen, but has responded gladly to whatever calls have been made upon him.

Doctor Lemmon was born in Campbell County, Virginia, October 5, 1878, a son of Richard H. and Elizabeth (Maury) Lemmon, the former of whom was born near Charlottesville, Virginia, and the latter in Campbell County, and both are now deceased. The father was also a physician, and was prepared for professional work in the University of Virginia and the University of Maryland. Beginning his practice in Charlottesville, he later went to New Orleans, Louisiana, and from that far away city of the South he came to Lynchburg, and here he continued in active practice until his death in 1885. He was one of the old-time physicians, devoted to his profession and willing to sacrifice everything to it. For many years he was remembered as the "beloved physician" of Lynchburg, and there are those still living who were ministered to by him. The excellent wife and mother passed away in 1880, five years before her husband. After her death Dr. Robert Lemmon was taken into the home of Robert Massie, and there he was practically reared. He has one sister, Ann Maury, now the wife of John B. Lightfoot, Jr., of Richmond, an attorney, the two constituting the children of their parents. The elder Doctor Lemmon was a Democrat in political faith, but never an office seeker. A man ahead of his times, he realized the necessity for additional training and did post-graduate work in Johns Hopkins University, Baltimore, Maryland. His father, Dr. Robert T. Lemmon, was also a physician, a graduate of the University of Pennsylvania, and a general practitioner of Campbell County, so that Doctor Lemmon of this review is the third in direct descent to practice medicine in Campbell County. The great-grandfather on the paternal side was Reverend Lemmon, a minister of the Episcopal Church. The maternal grandfather, Jesse L. Maury, was born in Albermarle County, Virginia, and in addition to extensive operations as a farmer he built Piedmont, Virginia, and lived to be ninety-two years old.

Doctor Lemmon, of whom we write, first attended the Cleveland High School and that at Woodbury Forest. Still later he attended Kenmore High School, and in 1898 he entered the University of Virginia, and was graduated therefrom in 1902, with the degree of Doctor of Medicine. Going then to Norfolk, he was the first to serve as interne in the Sarah Lee Hospital of that city, and while there he took a six-months course in the New York Polyclinic Hospital. From there he went to Saint Joseph Hospital, Baltimore, Maryland. Entering the Medical Reserve Corps of the United States Army, he served as a first lieutenant in it for eight years, and for two years was in the Philippines. In January, 1913, he came to Lynchburg, and here he has since been engaged in practice, building up very wide connections in the city and county. While he carries on a general practice he specializes to a certain extent in genito-urinary diseases.

On November 5, 1918, Doctor Lemmon married Miss Mary Bigbie, a native of Lynchburg and a product of its public schools and seminary. Two children have been born to Doctor and Mrs. Lemmon: Robert T., Jr., and Richard H. Mrs. Lemmon belongs to the Episcopal Church. He is a member of Phi Kappa Psi, the Benevolent and Protective Order of Elks, the Campbell County Medical Society, the Virginia State Medical Society and the American Medical Association, and at one time he served the county medical society as secretary. Doctor Lemmon is a man who possesses depths of feeling, of purpose, of high resolve, that lead, when occasion demands, to virile action, and his associates know that he will devote time and energy to plan for and accomplish that which is best in civic life.

WILLIAM C. STEPHENSON. In the broad and intricate field of insurance success is the portion only of those who possess certain qualifications and characteristics. Contrary to ordinary belief, insurance is a highly specialized business, and its devotees must be men of sound character, keen knowledge of human nature, self confidence and untiring persistence. Diplomacy and tact are desirable concomitants, and above all the insurance man must be thoroughly conversant with his subject in its every detail, be able to "think on his feet" and one ready instantaneously to grasp an opportunity. Of the men who have possessed the above characteristics and through their use have gained success, one of the best known at Roanoke is William C. Stephenson, who is also widely known in other business activities, particularly those identified with the coal industry and with finance.

Mr. Stephenson was born July 13, 1872, at East Brady, Clarion County, Pennsylvania, and is a son of James B. and Katherine G. (Cowell) Stephenson. His father, who was born in New Jersey, became identified with the coal business at an early age, and was a pioneer in the Pocahontas fields of West Virginia, where he opened the fifth mine in this field at Bramwell, West Virginia. He eventually secured large and important interests and was one of the leading men in the trade at the time of his demise, which occurred at Roanoke, where he maintained offices for many years. He was a member of the Masonic fraternity and the Benevolent and Protective Order of Elks, and in his political convictions was a Republican. He belonged to the Methodist Episcopal Church, while Mrs. Stephenson, who was born in Pennsylvania, held membership in the Presbyterian Church, in the work of which she was very active. They became the parents of five children, of whom three are living; William C., of this review; H. L., a manufacturer of Buffalo, New York; and Nell J., wife of Dr. J. O. Boyd, of Roanoke, Virginia.

The early education of William C. Stephenson was acquired in the public schools of his native county, following which he pursued a course at the Clarion State Normal School. His first employment was with the Second National Bank of Pittsburgh, Pennsylvania. In 1893 he located at Roanoke, where he became interested in the various big business operations of his father. He now maintains well appointed offices at 112 Kirk Avenue, South West, and has a large and appreciative patronage which extends to all parts of the city and the surrounding countryside. Few men are better known to the coal trade of the city and state, and he is now president and treasurer of the Buckeye Coal and Coke Company. He is also vice president of the firm of Davis & Stephenson, Incorporated, and a director in the First National Exchange Bank of Roanoke and the Virginia Bridge and Iron Company, all of which concerns have profited materially by his ability, judgment and acumen. In his political views Mr. Stephenson is a stanch Republican, but has no desire for public office. However, few citizens are more public spirited or have contributed in greater degree to the welfare of their city by their constructive support of worth while measures. He has long been prominent as a York and Scottish Rite Mason, and served as high priest of his Chapter and eminent commander of his Commandery at the same time, in addition to which on another occasion he was grand commander of the state. With his family he belongs to Christ Episcopal Church.

In 1899 Mr. Stephenson was united in marriage with Miss Elizabeth M. Greenland, who was born in Clarion County, Pennsylvania, and educated at Wilson College, Chambersburg, Pennsylvania. To this union there have been born four children: William C., Jr., a medical student at the University of Virginia; Walter G., a traveling salesman for Castner, Currant & Bullitt, Incorporated; James B. II, and Richard C., attending school.

H. HERBERT HARRIS has given the best years of his life to the commercial interests of the City of Lynchburg, where under his experienced hand the Harris-Woodson Company, of which he is president, has become one of the largest manufacturing and wholesale confectionery firms in the South.

Mr. Harris was born at Charlottesville, Virginia, October 1, 1869, son of Henry Herbert and Emma (Bibb) Harris. His paternal grandparents, Henry and Susan (Hart) Harris, were residents of Louisa County, Henry Harris being a farmer and planter.

Henry Herbert Harris, a scholar and educator, for many years identified with Richmond College, was born in Louisa County December 17, 1836. Much of his early education was acquired from an older sister, a very gifted woman. He was graduated from the University of Virginia, and when the Civil war came on he served with the Engineering Corps. After the war he taught in a female seminary at Charlottesville, and left that to become professor of Greek in Richmond College, a chair he filled for twenty-nine years, and part of the time was also professor of modern languages and philosophy. He was an inspiring teacher, and hundreds of graduates of Richmond College have a most grateful memory for not only his scholarship and learning, but for his kindly and generous character. He was a member of the Baptist Church and for many years taught a Bible class in the Grace Street Baptist Church at Richmond. He resigned his position at Richmond College in 1895 to become identified with the Baptist Theological Seminary at Louisville. He died February 4, 1897, at Lynchburg and was buried in Hollywood Cemetery at Richmond.

He married, November 26, 1862, Miss Emma Bibb, daughter of William A. Bibb, of Charlottesville, William A. Bibb was a merchant and clerk of court. Professor Harris had six children: William A., who succeeded his father as professor of Greek at Richmond College, and has been with that institution a quarter of a century, having been educated in the college under his father and also at Johns Hopkins University. The second son is H. Herbert, of Lynchburg. Janet is the wife of R. E. Gaines, professor of mathematics at the University of Richmond. Dr. George T. Harris is a Lynchburg physician. Isabelle is a graduate of Richmond College and Columbia University, and is teaching mathematics in the West Hampton School at Richmond. The youngest of the family, Emma, married James H. Hancock, a coal operator at Lynchburg.

H. Herbert Harris was reared in Richmond, attended the McGuire Boys School, and graduated A. B. from Richmond College in 1888. For three years he clerked in a wholesale grocery store at Richmond, for two years was in the brokerage business, and removing to Lynchburg was with a wholesale grocery company there until 1901. In 1901 he established the Harris-Woodson Company, candy manufacturers, and during the past quarter of a century this has become one of the important commercial institutions of Lynchburg. The company maintains a force of fourteen traveling salesmen covering Virginia, West Virginia, Tennessee, North and South Carolina and Georgia, and also distribute a large amount of their confectionery products through brokers in other places. Mr. Harris is president of the company, T. A. Woodson, vice president, and R. A. Harris, vice president.

Mr. Harris is vice president of the Lynchburg City Savings and Loan Corporation, vice president of the Guaranty Title and Bond Corporation, and is a director in the First National Bank, the Lynchburg Mutual Building and Loan Association, the Pilot Building and Loan Association and a member of the Board of Directors of the Atlantic Life Insurance Company, of Richmond.

For many years he has taken an active part in civic affairs. He is treasurer and member of the board of the Baptist Hospital, the best equipped institution of its kind in the South. He is former president of the Lynchburg Chamber of Commerce and Lynchburg Rotary Club, member of the Virginia State Chamber of Commerce, is a member of the City School Board, and is a deacon in the Rivermont Baptist Church and superintendent of its Sunday School and chairman of the church building committee. Mr. Harris has membership in the United Commercial Travelers, the Beta Theta Pi college fraternity, and is a Democrat.

He married, October 25, 1902, Miss Annie Adams, a native of Lynchburg. They have three children. The son, Richard Adams Harris, was educated in the Episcopal High School at Alexandria, the University of Virginia, where he was a member of the Alpha Tau Omega fraternity, and is now vice president of the Harris-Woodson Company. He married Martha Latham, of Richmond, daughter of Rev. J. N. Latham, a Methodist minister, and has one son, Richard A., Jr. The two daughters of Mr. and Mrs. Harris are Annie Scott and Emma Maxwell Harris, who were educated in the Mary Baldwin Seminary at Staunton and Dana Hall at Wellesley, Massachusetts.

JAMES V. RAMOS, JR., was a Richmond pharmacist, and a well known member of a well known family in Virginia.

He was born at Richmond in September, 1854, and died in that city July 8, 1901. His father, Jose Ramos, came from the Azores Islands to Richmond, and married in that city Maria Kirby, a native of Virginia. Of their six children one was Miss Essie Ramos, a graduate of the Richmond Woman's College and a well known educator who taught for many years in the Richmond High School.

James V. Ramos, Jr., attended Richmond College and completed his course in pharmacy in the Medical College of Virginia. For a time he was employed by the Polk Miller Company and in 1881 engaged in the drug business at 8 Main Street under the firm name of Thornbury and Ramos, and it was one of the leading drug stores of the city for ten years. For a brief time before his death he had been interested in a drug business at Norfolk. Mr. Ramos practically all his life was a member of the Second Baptist Church of Richmond.

Mr. Ramos was survived by Mrs. Ramos and three children. Mrs. Lutie Page Ramos, whose home is at 2018 Grove Avenue, has in her ancestry some of the distinguished family names of old Virginia. Mr. Ramos and Miss Lutie Page were married January 8, 1884, at the St. James Hotel in Richmond, in the presence of her father, Major John M. Page, then on his death-bed, it having been his expressed wish and determination that the ceremony should take place before his death. They were married by Rev. Dr. James G. Armstrong, of the Episcopal Church, assisted by Rev. William W. Landrum, of the Baptist denomination, and Rev. J. W. Bledsoe. Major John M. Page, who died at the age of fifty years, was born in Campbell County, Virginia, and early in the war between the states became a first lieutenant in the Scottsville Greys commanded by Gen. James C. Hill. His company became a part of the Forty-sixth Virginia Regiment of Infantry in Wise's Brigade. He was made adjutant of the regiment and was conspicuous for his coolness and courage as well as for his qualities as a drill master. After the war he lived at Charlottesville, and several years before his death became proprietor of the St. James Hotel at Richmond. He was a member of the Charlottesville Lodge of Masons. Major John M. Page married Lucy Maria Flanagan, and they were the parents of six children: William Louis, John Leonard, cashier of the Peoples Bank of Charlottesville; James, who married Jennie Frazier and had three children, named Almira, John Leonard and Martha; Thomas L.; Fannie L.; and Mrs. Luttie Page Ramos.

Through her mother Mrs. Ramos is a descendant of the Payne and Flanagan families. George P. Payne, who died in December, 1744, was a justice of Goochland County in 1729-33, was sheriff of the county, 1734-37. He married Mary Woodson, daughter of Robert and Elizabeth (Feris) Woodson, and grand-daughter of Doctor John Woodson, who came from England to Virginia in 1619. A son of George P. Payne was Josias Payne, born October 30, 1705, and died in 1785. He was a member of the House of Burgesses from Goochland County during several sessions, from 1761 to 1765. He married Anna Fleming, daughter of Tarleton Fleming, Sr. Their son, William Payne, born February 10, 1732, and died March 2, 1822, married Mary Barrett, and of their nine children one was Col. James Payne, born April 2, 1762. Col. James Payne married Frances Dix, and the fourth among their eight children was Frances M. Payne.

Frances M. Payne, born February 8, 1791, and died December 14, 1873, became the wife of Capt. William Flanagan, of Fluvanna County. Their daughter, Lucy Maria Flanagan, born February 1, 1830, was the mother of Mrs. Ramos. William Payne, the great-great-grandfather of Mrs. Ramos, was commissioned a first lieutenant in Virginia troops March 22, 1776. Capt. William Flanagan was captain of Buford's Company of Militia in the War of 1812.

Of the three children of Mrs. Ramos the oldest is John Page, who married Pattie Haskins, of Mecklenburg County, and their two children are John Page, Jr., and Nathaniel Haskins. The

daughter Maria Vieria, now Mrs. W. R. Jones, is a graduate of Miss Coleman's School of Richmond. The third child is Jose Berrian Ramos.

The records of the Pension Bureau at Washington supply some further information concerning Captain Flanagan. He enlisted October 28, 1814, and was in service until January 13, 1815. His application for a pension was allowed January 18, 1872, when he was ninety years of age. He was born in Louisa County, Virginia, son of James Flanagan, whose first wife was Phoebe Simpson, and his second wife was the widow Mary Bowles Johnson. William Flanagan married in December, 1809, Sarah Curd Johnson, who died May 10, 1859, and his second wife was Anne E. Hughson, daughter of James and Mary Hughson.

EDWARD ROBERTS JOHNSON, president of the Roanoke Securities Corporation, has made his home at Roanoke almost continuously since he was fifteen years of age, at which time his father, the late Lucius E. Johnson, located at Roanoke to begin a service of more than twenty years as general superintendent and afterwards as general manager and president of the Norfolk & Western Railway Company. In transportation, industrial and financial affairs hardly any name in the present century has been accorded more prestige in Virginia than that of Johnson.

Lucius E. Johnson was born at Aurora, Illinois, April 13, 1846, son of J. Spencer and Eliza (Brown) Johnson. He was educated in public schools, served during the concluding months of the Civil war in Company C, One Hundred and Thirty-second Illinois Infantry, and in 1866 was working as a locomotive fireman, with headquarters at Aurora, the division point of the Chicago, Burlington & Quincy Railway. He was with that company, with headquarters at Aurora, for twenty years, rising to the position of master mechanic. In 1886 he was made superintendent of the Saint Louis Division of the Burlington System, two years later became superintendent of the Chicago Division, from 1890 to 1893 was superintendent of the Montana Central Railway, and from 1893 to 1897, superintendent of the Michigan Division of the Lake Shore and Michigan Southern, New York Central Lines, located at Toledo, Ohio.

On July 10, 1897, Lucius E. Johnson became a resident of Roanoke, having been called to the important responsibilities of the office of general superintendent of the Norfolk & Western, which at that time was in its formative stage of development as one of the great industrial railway systems of the East. As a practical railroad executive no man impressed his abilities more thoroughly on this system than Lucius E. Johnson. In 1899 he became vice president and general manager, on October 1, 1903, was elected president of the company, and on resigning that office January 1, 1918, was chosen chairman of the Board of Directors. From June 1, 1918, until March 1, 1920, during the United States Railroad administration, he was again president of the corporation, after which he resumed his post as chairman of the Board of Directors. Lucius E. Johnson died February 11, 1921.

An appreciation of what he did as a railroad man, particularly for the Norfolk & Western, is contained in the following paragraph: "Mr. Johnson came to the Norfolk & Western with a splendid reputation as a practical railroad executive. That reputation was greatly enhanced during his management of the Norfolk & Western. His administration wrought a great improvement in physical condition, increase of equipment, and betterment of its general transportation facilities and service. His mastery of the many technical problems involved in railroad operation enabled him to devise and put in force plans that placed every department in position to meet the requirements of a traffic, the continued growth of which has been one of the most remarkable in the railroad history of the country. An important direct result of this efficient management was the improvement of the financial status of the Norfolk & Western from year to year until its stock came to be regarded as one of the best rail- road securities in the United States. The Norfolk & Western was rendering efficient service not only from the technical operating standpoint, but as head of the company Mr. Johnson succeeded in developing a most cordial feeling between the public and the railway management, this factor of good-will being hardly less valuable to a transportation company than the more tangible asset."

Lucius E. Johnson married, April 10, 1869, Miss Ella Parker, of Aurora, Illinois, and they both lived to celebrate their golden wedding anniversary. The two sons of the marriage were George P. and Edward Roberts Johnson.

Edward Roberts Johnson was born at Aurora, Illinois, Sep- tember 10, 1882, and acquired his early education in public schools in that city, in Helena and Great Falls, Montana, at Toledo, Ohio, and after coming to Roanoke was a student in the Allegheny Institute of that city. He had a thorough technical education in Purdue University at Lafayette, Indiana. After his university career he was with the traffic department of the Norfolk & Western Railway at Suffolk, Virginia, resigning to engage in the coal business. From 1906 to 1910 he was vice president of the H. T. Wilson Coal Company at Detroit, and from 1911 to 1913 was president of the Borderland Coal Sales Company of Cincinnati. He became general manager of the Virginia Supply Company at Roanoke in 1914, and in 1917 was elected president of the company. Mr. Johnson is identified with other important interests and is a director in the Walker Machine and Foundry Company, the Securities Insurance Cor- poration and the Johnson-Carper Furniture Company. He served as president of the Roanoke Rotary Club from July 1, 1927, to June 30, 1928. He was president of the Roanoke Chamber of Commerce for 1928.

On account of his experience as a practical traffic man he was in a position to render special service of great value to the Government during the World war. On May 20, 1918, he was appointed fuel expert, Quartermaster Corps, as a dollar a year man; June 25, 1918, was commissioned captain, Quartermaster Corps, in charge of coal procurement branch, raw materials division; August 1, 1918, was made executive officer, raw ma- terials division; October 17, 1918, was commissioned major, Quartermaster Corps; December 14, 1918, was made chief, raw materials division; and was given his honorable discharge April 3, 1919. In the early months of the war he was employed under the auspices of the Young Men's Christian Association War Council at Atlanta, Georgia, and Camp Lee, Virginia.

Mr. Johnson organized in 1921 Johnson, Brown and Com- pany, which subsequently became the Roanoke Securities Corporation, of which he has since been president. He is also a director of the National Exchange Bank of Roanoke. Mr. Johnson is a Republican, member of the Phi Delta Theta college fraternity, is a Royal Arch, Council and Knight Templar York Rite Mason, also a Scottish Rite Mason and Shriner. He is a member of the Shenandoah Club, Roanoke Country Club, has served on the Official Board of the Greene Memorial Methodist Church and as president of the Roanoke Y. M. C. A.

He married at Toledo, Ohio, January 16, 1905, Miss Edith Grace Carson, daughter of Mr. and Mrs. C. F. Carson. They have two children, Lucius C. and Ruth Johnson.

REV. WILLIAM FRED LOCKE is a gifted minister of the Methodist Episcopal Church, South, known and loved in many communities, not only in Virginia but in Maryland and elsewhere.

His present pastorate is the Green Memorial Church at Roanoke, Virginia. Rev. Mr. Locke was born at Charles Town, West Virginia, in 1865, son of Thomas and Esther (Locke) Locke. Both parents were natives of Virginia and his father was a merchant and later a farmer. They were members of the Methodist Episcopal Church, South, and the father was a Democrat and a Mason. Of their eight children one son, William S., was killed at Ashland during the Civil war. Three are now living: Dr. T. F. Locke, a dentist at Woodstock, Virginia; Mrs. Sudie E. Lloyd, of Charles Town, West Virginia; and William F.

William F. Locke attended the Charles Town High School, continued his education in an academy conducted by Captain Cabell, and was also under the instruction of his brother, Austin M. Locke, a graduate of the University of Virginia. At an early age he began his studies preparatory for the ministry and was ordained in 1892. His first church was in the Springfield Circuit. For three years he was pastor at Piedmont, West Virginia, for two years had charge of St. James Church at Roanoke, and for four years was at Washington, D. C., with the Marvin Church. He was pastor three years at Front Royal, at Rockville, Maryland, at Mount Vernon Place Church in Washington three years, spent four years at Martinsburg, West Virginia, four years at Lexington, Virginia, six years in Baltimore, and five years at Fredericksburg, Virginia, and in October, 1927, was assigned pastoral duties with the Green Memorial Church at Roanoke, Virginia.

Rev. Mr. Locke married, in 1893, Daise E. Jamesson, who was born at Westernport, Maryland, and was educated in the Western Female Institute at Staunton, Virginia. They have one daughter, Dorothy Jamesson.

Rev. Mr. Locke is a York Rite Mason and Shriner, being a past master of the lodge at Front Royal. He also belongs to the B. P. O. Elks, is a Rotarian and a member of the Kiwanis Club.

WILLIAM F. LAWRENCE in his business career belonged to the Richmond of both ante-bellum as well as post-bellum times. He was one of the noteworthy men of his generation, and among other services to his credit was his record as a soldier of the Confederacy.

He was born in Henrico County July 4, 1830, and died at Richmond December 28, 1908, at the age of seventy-eight. His parents were William and Susanne (Ford) Lawrence, his father having been identified with planting and farming in Henrico County.

William F. Lawrence, oldest son of his parents, was educated in schools in Henrico County, grew up on a farm and plantation, and worked there until he took up a business career at Richmond. As a clerk he learned the grocery trade, and about 1858 engaged in the business on his own account. He left this when the war broke out and had three years of service with the Virginia troops, serving in a regiment of cavalry.

At the close of the war he returned to Richmond and re-opened a grocery store at Graham and Broad streets. At that time Richmond was under military rule, and he did an extensive business with the Northern soldiers who were camped in Monroe Park, across the street from his store. About 1874 he retired from merchandising, and gave his chief attention to the ownership and management of valuable parcels of real estate he owned in the business district, much of it on Broad Street, his keen knowledge in values bringing him a substantial fortune. He was always a Democrat in politics but never sought political preferment.

Mr. Lawrence first married Virginia Schumaker, who died in 1885, leaving no children. On March 6, 1895, he married Arlie R. Taylor, who survives him and resides at 22 North Boulevard. Mrs. Lawrence is a daughter of W. T. and Julia R. (Ford) Taylor. Her father was an early day merchant in Richmond, conducting a general store. Mrs. Lawrence was the oldest child of her parents. Her brother, W. T. Taylor, became a Richmond merchant and married Hattie Bowles. Her sister Kate Jane is now Mrs. C. M. Waldrop. Her brother Charles L. is deceased. Mrs. Lawrence's father served as a courier in the Confederate army and was once wounded in action.

Mrs. Lawrence became the mother of four children, the oldest, William F., being now deceased. Henry J. is a graduate of the University of Virginia and a successful architect at Houston, Texas; he married Helen Brook. Virginia C. Lawrence is the wife of J. C. Watson, secretary and treasurer of the Fire and Marine Insurance Company of Virginia, and has a daughter, Jeanne. Walter L. Lawrence, an employe of the State of Virginia, married Louise Boschen, daughter of Louis Boschen, a former member of the Virginia House of Delegates.

JOHN E. TOPPING both as a Doctor of Dental Surgery and as a business man and citizen has made himself a popular and prominent factor in the citizenship of Roanoke.

Doctor Topping was born in Middlesex County, Virginia, in 1886, son of F. E. and Mary F. (Purcell) Topping, both natives of the same county, and grandson of Edward Topping and John Purcell, likewise natives of Middlesex County and farmers and planters of that region. Doctor Topping's parents both died in 1925. His father was a substantial farmer and for twelve years held the office of sheriff of Middlesex County. They were members of the Baptist Church and he belonged to the Masonic fraternity.

John E. Topping was third in a family of five children. He grew up on the home farm in Middlesex County, attended public schools there and for three years acted as quartermaster on a boat on the Chesapeake Bay. He left that to study dentistry, paying most of his expenses while he studied. He took his degree of Doctor of Dental Surgery at the Baltimore Medical

College, which is now the Maryland University, in 1913. Doctor Topping for several years practiced at Fincastle and in 1917 located at Roanoke. He performs the general service of a well trained and capable dentist. In addition he is vice president of the Rutrough-Gilbert Motor Company, Incorporated, one of the largest and finest sales and service stations in Southwest Virginia.

Doctor Topping married, in 1921, Miss Jamie Arline Wilhoit, who was born in Albemarle County, Virginia, and was educated at Bedford and in North Carolina and taught before her marriage. Doctor and Mrs. Topping attend the Calvary Baptist Church. He is a Scottish Rite Mason and Shriner and is director of the Degree Team of the Shrine. He belongs to the Xi Si Psi dental fraternity and the B. P. O. Elks.

DAVID P. SITES. Strength of purpose, intelligently directed, results in almost every case in material advancement. The man who fluctuates from one line of endeavor to another seldom achieves lasting success. It is the man who, knowing well what he desires to accomplish, forges ahead, undeterred by obstacles, undismayed by the chances and changes of life, until he reaches his ultimate goal. It sometimes happens that in his enthusiastic endeavors he sacrifices health and strength and is gathered to his forefathers before his time, but even then in the brief span of years he has accomplished more than one who is content to sit still and idly watch the army of workers pass by. No man can reach heights of prosperity through his own efforts if he shirks duty or seeks to lay upon other shoulders the responsibilities belonging to him. Centers of industry develop men of large affairs, for competition acts as a stimulus to action and brings forth the best in a man, and so it is that David P. Sites, secretary and treasurer of Caldwell-Sites Company, Incorporated, wholesale and retail booksellers, stationers, paper dealers and office outfitters, has achieved a solid success in the work for which he is fitted and to which he has given his attention since 1897, or for more than thirty years.

David P. Sites was born in Rockingham County, Virginia, April 20, 1870, a son of Henry and Elizabeth (Helbert) Sites, both of whom were born in Rockingham County, and are now deceased. For many years the father was a cabinet maker and farmer, and worked very successfully at his trade. During the war between the states he served as a brave and valorous soldier of the Confederacy. Of the four children born to him and his wife David P. Sites is the third in order of birth. Both parents were members of the Methodist Episcopal Church, South, and the mother was always active in its good work.

After he had attended the common schools of his native county David P. Sites became a student of Cedar Grove Seminary and still later of Dunsmore College, Saunton, Virginia. For a time he worked as a stenographer for the general passenger agent of the Baltimore and Ohio Railroad in Washington, D. C., until he could get a start, and then, in 1897, coming to Roanoke, established a wholesale and retail book and stationery store, which from somewhat small beginnings he has built up to one of the largest concerns of its kind in this part of the state, and gives employment to forty people. The business is conducted under the name of Caldwell-Sites Company, Incorporated, of which C. R. Caldwell is president and David P. Sites is secretary and treasurer. Mr. Sites is the active head of the business, as Mr. Caldwell is a resident of Staunton.

In 1896 Mr. Sites married Miss Christine Harman, a daughter of John and Elizabeth Harman. Two children have been born to Mr. and Mrs. Sites, namely: Elizabeth, who married Gordon B. Macke, of Washington, D. C., an operator in tobacco; and Henry G., who is manager of the wholesale paper department of his father's company. Mr. Sites is an Episcopalian, and is serving his church as a vestryman. He belongs to the Roanoke Rotary Club, of which he is a past president, and served Rotary International as governor of the Fourth District, consisting of Virginia, North Carolina and South Carolina. He is a member of the Roanoke Country Club, and he has been president of the Roanoke Chamber of Commerce and of the Retail Merchants Association. He was the first president of the Lee Highway Association that sponsored Lee Highway, the transcontinental highway from Washington, D. C., to San Diego, California. During the World war he served as chairman of Unessential Industries in the district and was chairman of Virginia State Smileage Committee. At present he is a vice president and chairman of the board of the Mountain Trust Bank, and is on the directorate of several other banking concerns. Starting out in life as a poor boy, his advance has been steady and has come as a result of his own untiring industry and good management. At different times he has held the office of chairman of committees appointed to advance this locality. In fact it would be difficult to find a man more generally representative of the best interests of this section of the South than he.

DANIEL ROBERT HUNT. One of the most important offices in the government of any large and growing municipality is that of the city commissioner of revenue. This is a post that demands the utmost accuracy, the highest ability and the strictest integrity in order that the business of the city, as pertaining to this department, may move with the smoothness of well-oiled machinery. The City of Roanoke, therefore, is to be congratulated as possessing for the incumbent of this office such an able, energetic and honorable man as Daniel Robert Hunt, a resident of the city for thirty-three years, who has held his present office since 1913, it being a notable fact that he has had no opposition at the polls during the last four elections.

Mr. Hunt was born October 8, 1876, at Chatham, Pittsylvania County, Virginia, and is a son of Daniel Robert and Emma (Mebane) Hunt, the former a native of Pittsylvania County and the latter of the State of North Carolina. The parents of Mr. Hunt were both active members of the Presbyterian Church, and his father, who was a merchant at Chatham for many years, was a Mason fraternally and a Democrat in his political convictions. There were six children in the family, of whom Daniel Robert was the fifth in order of birth, and one child is deceased.

Daniel R. Hunt attended the public schools of Henry County and Ruffner Institute, but was only eleven years of age when he started to work in a tobacco factory. Following this for two years he worked on a farm in North Carolina, where he lived with an elder brother, Frank D. Hunt, a preacher of the Presbyterian faith. Following this he went to Charlotte, North Carolina, where he was employed on a farm for four years, and in 1895 came to Roanoke, which has since been his home and the scene of his unqualified success. At the time of his arrival he secured a modest position in the general offices of the Norfolk & Western Railway, and continued with that company for a period of eighteen years, during which time he rose steadily by reason of ability, great industry and fidelity until finally he was second in charge of the claim department of the auditor's office. He was holding this position in 1913 when he was elected city commissioner of revenue, a position which he still retains by virtue of four reelections, all without opposition in his party. Mr. Hunt has long been active in local Democratic politics and in movements which have contributed to the material welfare of his adopted community. In 1926, with C. H. Morrissett and J. Vaughan Gary, he was appointed by Governor Byrd to codify the tax laws of Virginia, this being one of the most progressive features of Governor Byrd's administration. Mr. Hunt is a member and elder of the Raleigh Court Presbyterian Church and teacher of a class in the Sunday School. Fraternally he is a York and Scottish Rite Mason and Shriner, belongs to the Knights of Pythias and is a life member of the Benevolent and Protective Order of Elks. He likewise holds membership in the Improved Order of Red Men, the Shenandoah Club, the Kiwanis Club and the Billy Sunday Club, and is a sociable man who enjoys the companionship of his fellows.

In 1922 Mr. Hunt was united in marriage with Miss Doris Huff, who was born in Floyd County, Virginia, and educated in the public schools of Roanoke and at Hollins College, where she carried off high honors. Prior to her marriage Mrs. Hunt taught in the public schools of Roanoke for several years. She is active in the social life of the city and a helpful member of the Raleigh Court Presbyterian Church.

SYLVESTER K. BITTERMAN. The wonderful growth in realty values in Roanoke during the past decade has brought to the forefront a class of men who for general ability, astuteness and driving force are unsurpassed in the annals of trade in this section. It may be well to say that conditions develop men, but it is better to say that men bring about conditions. Roanoke owes what it is today to the men who have had the courage to persevere, to act wisely and keep their operations clean in one of the most difficult fields of endeavor. Each section of the city can boast of a business man who has been practically its builder, and in the Church Avenue neighborhood is to be found Sylvester K. Bitterman, whose name is nearly as familiar as the proverbial household word. Since 1916 he has been operating in real estate with remarkable success. Starting out in life a poor boy, conditions of their own accord did not favor him; he made them what he wished them to be.

Sylvester K. Bitterman was born in Pennsylvania, August 1, 1864, a son of John and Harriet (Kehler) Bitterman, both of whom were born in Pennsylvania, but are now deceased. For many years the father was engaged in business in the Mahantango Valley, but died in 1865. The mother survived him for many years, passing away in 1926, aged eighty-four years. They had two children: Ellsworth, who is living retired in Pennsylvania, and Sylvester K., who is the younger.

The parents were conscientious members of the Evangelical Church, in which they took an active part, and they were held in high esteem by all who knew them. The paternal grandfather was John Bitterman, a native of Germany, who came to this country in young manhood, settled in Pennsylvania, and there, through his industry and thrift, became a prosperous farmer and highly respected citizen.

Sylvester K. Bitterman was educated in the public schools of Pennsylvania, and was early taught to work hard and save a portion of what he earned. His first business life came through his connection with the butchering industry, first in Pennsylvania and later in McDowell County, West Virginia, and later in Roanoke, to which latter community he came in 1886. After a short time spent in the city he went to West Virginia, but returned to Roanoke in 1889, and here he has since remained. From 1893 to 1916 he was in the retail liquor business, but in the latter year he went into the real estate field, in which, as already stated, he has been so strikingly successful.

In 1883 Mr. Bitterman married Miss Sallie E. Umlauf, who was born in Pennsylvania, and they became the parents of seven children, of whom five survive, namely: Sylvia, who is unmarried; Myrtle, who married Henry Scholz, a theatre manager; Edna, who married J. C. Johnson, Jr., of Roanoke, chief clerk in the motor power office; Virdie, who is a student at Beaver College, Jenkintown, Pennsylvania; and Margaret, who is also in the same college. Mr. Bitterman belongs to Christ Episcopal Church, and is active in church work. He is a life member of the Benevolent and Protective Order of Elks and of the Fraternal Order of Eagles. In addition to his extensive real estate operations and holdings Mr. Bitterman has other interests, and is a director and vice president of the Roanoke Industrial Loan Corporation. A man of many charities, he seldom lets the world know his benefactions, but his kindly heart can never let a case of destitution go unrelieved. His advice is oftentimes sought, for his sound judgment and knowledge of men and the motives which influence them are recognized, and it would be difficult to find one who is more closely identified with the progress of events than he.

CHARLES M. BROUN. It is sometimes found that efforts die away and enterprise becomes engulfed in inertia when the individual gains his desired goal, while, on the other hand, the chances for successful attainment continually encourage the exercise of perseverance and energy. In almost every case those who have reached the highest positions in public confidence and esteem and who are accounted among the most influential in business and professional lines are those whose lives have been devoted, without cessation, to deep study and close application. It is probable that the law has been the main highway by which more men of merit have advanced to prominence and position in the United States than any other road, and it is not unusual to find among the leading citizens of a community a legal practitioner. To respond to the call of the law, to devote every energy in this direction, to broaden and deepen every highway of knowledge, and finally to enter upon this chosen career and finds its rewards worth while—such has been the happy experience of Charles M. Broun, one of the learned legalists practicing at the bar of Roanoke. Mr. Broun has gained honor and position in his profession through the application of honesty, energy, perseverance, conscientiousness and self-reliance, and has kept abreast of his calling in its constant advancement; but it is not alone as a lawyer that he is known to the people of his city, for he has also attained to distinction in politics, is interested in business enterprises, and, perhaps, best of all, gives freely of his time and money in promoting religious and charitable movements.

Charles M. Broun was born in Middleburg, Loudoun County, Virginia, July 14, 1862, a son of Dr. James Conway and Ann Rebecca (McCormick) Broun, natives of Virginia, he born in Loudoun County and she in Clarke County. A physician, Doctor Broun received his professional training in the University of Virginia, and was engaged in the practice of his calling in Middleburg and Alexandria, Virginia. During the war between the states he served in the Confederate army, but, contracting a cold because of exposure, was stricken and died in 1864, leaving two children, of whom Charles M. Broun is now the only survivor. He and his wife, also deceased, were members of the Episcopal Church, and he was a Mason.

First attending the Shenandoah Academy, Charles M. Broun later became a student of the Kanawha Military Institute, Charleston, West Virginia, and took his professional training in the law department of the University of Virginia. His first experience in legal practice was gained in Berryville, Virginia, and he continued a resident of that community until 1908, during which period he steadily advanced in public confidence, and then came to Roanoke, and, forming the connection he now maintains, is engaged in a very large practice under the firm name of Broun & Price, with offices in the American National Bank Building.

In 1900 Mr. Broun married Miss Elizabeth Rice Page, who was born in Berryville, Virginia, and there educated. Two children have been born of this marriage: Charles Conway, and Elizabeth Page, the son attending Roanoke College at Salem and the daughter, a private school in Roanoke City. Both Mr. and Mrs. Broun are members of the Episcopal Church, of which he was a vestryman for many years at Berryville, Virginia. He is a past master of Treadwell Lodge, A. F. and A. M., of Berryville, and he belongs to Pleasant Lodge, A. F. and A. M., of Roanoke. Mr. Broun is also a member of the Knights of Pythias, the Improved Order of Red Men and the Benevolent and Protective Order of Elks, the Roanoke Country Club and the Shenandoah Club. For some years he served as commonwealth attorney of Clarke County, being elected on the Democratic ticket, and after coming to Roanoke he served as president of the Board of Alderman and mayor of the city. In fact he has always been active in the Democratic party, and one of the local leaders. Several years ago he organized the National Theatre Corporation, of which he is president. He is vice president of the Sun Investment Company and of the Consolidated Ice Companies, and president of the General Finance Small Loan Corporation. While still living in Berryville he organized the First National Bank of that town, and was its first president. Another enterprise in which he is largely interested is a power plant near Roanoke for the development of electric power, and his assistance is given to many other undertakings, for he is a man who believes in encouraging local enterprise, and proves it by investing his money at home. Beginning life with nothing, all that he has today has been earned by him in a legitimate way and his material success has been accompanied by the approval and warm friendship of all with whom he has been associated.

JOHN C. BURKS, M. D.   In noting the representative men
of Roanoke County, a prominent one in medical science is found
in Dr. John C. Burks, able and experienced physician and surgeon at Roanoke, where he is director and chief surgeon of St.
Charles Hospital, with which institution he has been identified
for sixteen years.   Doctor Burks has reached high place in his
profession, and has won confidence, consideration and esteem
throughout a wide area of his native state.

Dr. John C. Burks was born in 1873, in Rockbridge County,
Virginia, son of Dr. Charles Richard and Frances (Stoner)
Burks, both of whom were born also in Rockbridge County,
where their families had been early settlers and once owners of
large estates.   Dr. Charles Richard Burks, whose memory in
Rockbridge County as honorable man and faithful physician is
still preserved although many years have gone by since he
passed away, was born in 1833, in Rockbridge County, Virginia,
where he received his early schooling.   As a student of medicine
he spent one year in the Medical College of Virginia, and then
entered Jefferson Medical College at Philadelphia, Pennsylvania,
where he completed his course and from which he was graduated with his degree.   His life was one of faithful devotion to
his profession, both before and after the war between the states,
in which he played no insignificant part, being attached during
the entire period to the command of Gen. James E. Stuart, Confederate army, and took part as a cavalryman in the first battle
of Bull Run, and participated later at Chancellorsville and at
Gettysburg.   For some years he resided at Buffalo Forge and
then moved to Natural Bridge, where, until his death in 1904,
he carried on a large practice, both local and beyond, the number
of his patients being yearly augmented by tourists from all over
the world who came to view, wonder and admire one of America's most beautiful and picturesque regions.   To his marriage
with Miss Frances Stoner, who survived until 1916, four sons
and four daughters were born, John C. being second in order of
birth, and all were reared in the faith of the Methodist Episcopal
Church.

John C. Burks received his early educational training in the
public schools, later attended Fancy Hill Academy, and then,
whether influenced by heredity or not, Doctor Burks is the one
qualified to decide, he needed no urging to enter the Medical
College of Virginia to prepare for a future career.   From this
well known institution he was most creditably graduated in
1897, and shortly afterward established himself in medical
practice at Glasgow, Virginia, and practiced there and at Pocahontas until 1900, when he came to Roanoke, his object being a
wider field of professional opportunity and the scientific advantages close at hand in a large city.

Doctor Burks' judgment was not at fault.   Upon locating at
Roanoke he entered into partnership with Dr. C. G. Cannedy,
with whom he continued until the latter's death in 1908, after
which he operated the Rebecca Hospital until 1912.   In the
meanwhile, through further intensive scientific study, together
with attendance on numerous and important clinics in the great
medical centers of the country and Canada, Doctor Burks had
not only kept thoroughly abreast of the times in medical discovery, but had through personal investigation of many hospitals, both great and small, been able to plan satisfactorily the
present St. Charles Hospital at Roanoke, which he built in 1912,
and of which he has been chief surgeon ever since.   At that time

considered a model institution, later discoveries in mechanics have been taken advantage of and modern conveniences have been increased, and perhaps no city hospital of its size in the state offers better accommodation to the ill and afflicted or more reasonable expectancy of relief. Doctor Burks maintains thirty-three beds in the hospital and his patients come from all over the country.

Doctor Burks married Miss Lelia McCorkle, daughter of Dr. George B. McCorkle, a physician practicing at Covington and Glasgow, Virginia. Mrs. Burks, beloved by all who knew her, and a devoted member of the Presbyterian Church, passed away at Roanoke in January, 1927, leaving no issue.

Professionally connected with such organizations as the Virginia State Medical Society and the American Medical Association, Doctor Burks has a wide and appreciative acquaintance. He is a Scottish Rite Mason and a Shriner, belongs to the Elks and the Shenandoah Club, and since boyhood has belonged to the Methodist Episcopal Church.

DANIEL SAYLER GOOD. To succeed as a member of the Roanoke bar requires more than ordinary ability which has been carefully trained along the lines of the legal profession, as well as a vast fund of general information and keen judgment with regard to men and their motives. In a city of the size of Roanoke there is so much competition; events crowd each other; circumstances play so important a part in the shaping of events, that the lawyer has to be a man capable of grasping affairs with a competent hand to effect satisfactory results. Among those who have won enviable distinction as a member of the legal profession of this city is Daniel Sayler Good, with offices in the Mountain Trust Bank Building. He was born in Shenandoah County, Virginia, January 16, 1865, a son of Samuel and Sarah (Wampler) Good, both of whom were born in Rockingham County, Virginia, where they were reared. Mr. Good is of German descent but nevertheless tried to enlist in the late World war but was rejected on account of age limit. He did, however, enlist and served in Company A of Joe Lane Stern Battalion of Virginia Volunteers, Wm. S. Mounfield captain and R. F. Taylor being the major of the four Roanoke companies, A, B, C and D, and was honorably discharged when this company was merged with the National Guard.

His paternal ancester located in Pennsylvania according to a strong family tradition and had three sons, one of whom remained in Pennsylvania, another went West and the third came to Virginia.

William Good, the great-great-grandfather of the subject of this review, bought land in Dunmore, now Shenandoah County, Virginia, as early as May, 1772. Said William Good's eldest child was named Jacob and his youngest child was named Susanna, who married David Kaufmann, who served in the War of 1812. The said Jacob Good has a number of children: the younger also being named Jacob was the grandfather of the subject of this review. He married a young widow named Susanna Silvius, whose maiden name was Myers (sometimes spelled Moyers). The said widow had one son, Jacob, by her first marriage, and Samuel Good, the father of the subject of this review was her first child by this second marriage. The father Samuel was a farmer all of his life, and was a Democrat, and served as road commissioner of Shenandoah County, to which locality he and his wife moved after their marriage, buying a farm near New Market, on which both of them passed away. They are buried in Cedar Grove Cemetery in that neighborhood. For many years they were members of the German Baptist Brethren Church. Of their twelve children, ten lived to reach maturity, and of them all Daniel Sayler was the eighth in order of birth. The paternal grandfather of Attorney Good was Jacob Good, a farmer and wagonmaker, who married Susanna Silvius, as above stated. Both of them were born in Shenandoah County, Virginia. The maternal grandparents, John and Mary (Cline) Wampler, were both born near Timberville, Rockingham County, Virginia, and he was also a farmer by occupation.

Daniel Sayler Good attended the public schools of Virginia, and had a short course in the Polytechnic Institute, New Market, Virginia. Later he took a special course at Woodstock under J. Monroe Hottel and Worth Logan, as well as several courses at different normal schools, all being preparatory to entering the George Peabody College for Teachers, Nashville, Tennessee, from which he was graduated with the degree of Licentiate of Instruction, in 1887. That summer he taught grammar and penmanship in the State Normal school of Strasburg, Virginia. During 1887 and 1888 he was principal of the graded schools of New Market, and during the summer of the latter year he conducted a summer normal school at New Market. With that work concluded, in the fall of 1888 Mr. Good came to Roanoke, and entered the law offices of Griffin & Watts, where he read law, and during the summer session of 1890, attended the Law School of the University of Virginia, where he was under the preceptorship of John B. Minor, studying to such purpose that he was admitted to the bar in 1890, and established himself in a practice in Roanoke which he is still continuing with marked success.

Mr. Good is unmarried. He is a member of Calvary Baptist Church, and is secretary of the elementary department of the Sunday school. For years he has belonged to the Knights of Pythias, and he is a member of the Roanoke Country Club. Always interested in politics, he is a staunch Democrat, and, although never aspiring to office, preferring to work in behalf of his friends, he was alternate to the convention that nominated Charles T. O'Ferrell for governor of Virginia; and a delegate to the convention that nominated Governor Montague and Lieut.-Gov. Joseph E. Willard, the latter being a former law classmate of Mr. Good. He has also served as delegate to other state conventions, and was a delegate to the State Convention that elected delegates to the National Convention that first nominated Woodrow Wilson for the presidency and was a delegate to the State Convention held at Norfolk, that chose the delegates to the National Convention of 1924. Mr. Good has real estate holdings, as well as other local interests, which, together with his law practice, take up his time and attention.

He is a member of the Roanoke Chamber of Commerce and the Roanoke and the American Bar Associations. Essentially a self-made man, Mr. Good has every reason to be proud of what he has accomplished. His schooling was paid for by him, his course at George Peabody being paid for in part by a scholarship he won, and he has never ceased his interest in that body. Upon the occasion of its fiftieth anniversary he represented his class, and was historian of his class in 1909, when a directory of the alumni was published. When the drive for $20,000,000 endowment was made in 1926 in behalf of the college, he was local representative in Roanoke, and more than filled his quota. A man of distinction, learned, able, public-spirited, the personal friend of the great men of the state, Mr. Good occupies a high position, not only at the bar, but in his community, and confers honor upon whatever project he undertakes.

WADDIE PENNINGTON JACKSON is a physician at Roanoke, specializing in internal medicines, and his attainments and service have such as to give him a steadily mounting reputation all over Southwest Virginia.

Doctor Jackson was born at South Hill, Mecklenburg County, Virginia, February 18, 1888, son of Thomas J. and Elva (Ogburn) Jackson, natives of the same county. His grandfather, William Green Jackson, was a Mecklenburg soldier of the Confederacy, being a captain and later colonel, and was all through the war, though once captured in battle. The maternal grandfather of Doctor Jackson was Benjamin W. Ogburn, of Mecklenburg County. He was a graduate of Randolph-Macon College and for several years president of the Girls' School at Danville, Virginia. Doctor Jackson's parents were well-to-do farming people in Mecklenburg County, members of the Methodist Episcopal Church, South. Of their four children three are living: William Green, a merchant at Lawrenceville, Virginia; Julian A., a farmer at Baskerville; and Doctor Jackson.

Doctor Jackson attended high school at South Hill, graduated from Randolph-Macon Academy at Bedford in 1907 and from Randolph-Macon College at Ashland in 1910. After graduating from college he had to earn his own living, and during the several years before he was ready to enter medical college he engaged in teaching. He began his medical studies in Johns Hopkins University at Baltimore, where he was graduated in 1917 and during summer vacations had also taken additional work at the University of Michigan and Columbia University. After graduating he enrolled in the United States Navy, served on the *U. S. S. Galveston* and later was attached to the Naval Base Hospital at Hampton Roads, Virginia, until 1919. After the war and after being put on the inactive list Doctor Jackson spent a year in post-graduate work at Johns Hopkins University. Few doctors begin their careers with a more thorough training and ample preparation than Doctor Jackson. He located at Roanoke October 25, 1920. He is a member of the Roanoke Academy of Medicine, the Medical Society of Virginia, the Southwest Virginia, Southern and American Medical Associations and is an associate member of the American College of Physicians. He belongs to the Phi Chi medical fraternity.

Doctor Jackson married, September 16, 1918, Bessie Mae Gills, who was born at Union Hall, Franklin County, Virginia, and was reared and educated in Bedford County, finishing in Randolph-Macon Institute at Danville, where she was graduated in 1909. Doctor and Mrs. Jackson have two children: Elizabeth Harwell, born November 2, 1919, and Dudley Pennington, born April 1, 1924. Doctor and Mrs. Jackson are members of the Methodist Episcopal Church, South, and he is serving as a steward of the church. He is a member of the Masonic fraternity.

WALTER M. OTEY is a capable physician and surgeon practicing at Roanoke, having spent all the twelve years of his active experience in the medical profession in that city.

Doctor Otey was born in Bedford County, Virginia, February 8, 1891, son of Frank C. and Ossie (Slicer) Otey, both natives of Bedford County. His grandfather, Charles C. Otey, was born in the same county, became a captain in the Confederate army and was killed at the battle of Seven Pines. Frank C. Otey devoted his life to the farm, and died in 1925. His widow now resides with her son, Doctor Otey, at Roanoke. He was an active member in the Presbyterian Church and a Democrat in politics.

Doctor Otey was the second in a family of five children, four of whom are living. He was reared in a rural locality in Bedford County, and after the local schools attended Randolph-Macon College and the Virginia Polytechnic Institute at Blacksburg. He then entered the Medical College of Virginia at Richmond, was graduated in 1916, and for about a year was in the hospital at Roanoke under Doctor Slicer. Since 1916 he has engaged in a general practice as a physician and surgeon and a high degree of success has attended his efforts. He is a member of the Roanoke Academy of Medicine, the Medical Society of Virginia and the American Medical Association. In addition to his medical practice Doctor Otey superintends the management of the old homestead farm in Bedford County. He is a Scottish Rite Mason and Shriner, member of the B. P. O. Elks, Country Club and Shenandoah Club, and he and his family belong to Saint John's Episcopal Church.

Doctor Otey married, in 1914, Mary Hairston, a native of Henry County, Virginia, who was reared and educated at Danville. They have two children, Mary Elizabeth and Walter Maynard, Jr., both attending school in Roanoke.

LOUIS A. SCHOLZ is a veteran Roanoke business man and, having been identified with that city since 1889, participating in its growth from a small railroad town to a community of manifold industries and commercial prestige all over the Southeast.

Mr. Scholz was born at Freiburg, Germany, November 28, 1862, and spent his early years in that famous university town. His parents, Joseph and Pauline (Teichler) Scholz, lived all their lives in Germany, where his father was a blacksmith. They were Catholics. Of their seven children three are living, two sons, Louis and Fritz, being residents of Roanoke, while the only living daughter, Anna, is the wife of Martin Baier and lives in Germany.

Louis A. Scholz had a common school education in Germany and when fourteen years old began his apprenticeship to learn the brewing and malting trade. From the practical standpoint he was given very thorough instructions in every branch of the industry. When, in 1882, he came to the United States, a young man of twenty, he was thoroughly skilled in the brewing profession. His first six months in America were spent at Cincinnati, Ohio, where he was employed by Peter Schwab, after which he was with the Green Tree Brewery at Saint Louis for six months, then followed a journeyman experience in Kansas City, Omaha, Seattle and in San Francisco. At San Francisco in 1884 he brewed the first lager beer in that city for the National Brewing Company. His next location was at Baltimore, and in December, 1889, he arrived at Roanoke, thus ending his experience of

travel. Mr. Scholz was in the brewery business at Roanoke, active manager of the Virginia Brewing Company Plant from 1889 to 1916. In connection with the brewery he also engaged in ice manufacture, and he and his brother Henry became interested in quite a number of local enterprises and acquired a large amount of real estate.

Mr. Scholz is probably best known over Southwestern Virginia for his long and active identification with the Roanoke Fair Association, which he has served continuously as secretary since the fair was inaugurated in 1903. Mr. Scholz, a self-made business man, has prospered through his industry and the intent way he has applied himself to every undertaking. He owns an attractive country estate fifteen miles from Roanoke and makes his home there. Mr. Scholz and his family are Lutherans. He is one of the three surviving charter members of Roanoke Lodge, B. P. O. Elks, and is also affiliated with the Shenandoah Club and a life member of the Order of Eagles.

He married, in 1888, Henrietta Schaeffer, who was born at O'Fallon, Illinois. There are three children: Miss Pauline; Walter, a druggist at Roanoke; and Henrietta, wife of Stanley C. Weaver, a Roanoke real estate man.

HON. JACOB H. FRANTZ. After he had won the approval of his fellow citizens as a sound business man of undoubted financial ability in his operation of large real estate transactions, Hon. Jacob H. Frantz was elected city treasurer of Roanoke, and the manner in which he is handling the affairs of this important office proves the good judgment displayed in his selection. He was born in the vicinity of Roanoke, June 17, 1869, a son of Emory J. and Clarinda (Obenchain) Frantz, both of whom were born in Virginia, and are now deceased. The father was a farmer all his life, and was a substantial citizen of Roanoke County standing well with his neighbors, voting the straight Democratic ticket, and giving a splendid support to the Methodist Episcopal Church, South, in which work he was actively assisted by the mother. His fraternal connections were those which he maintained with the Masonic Order. During the last two years of the war between the states he served in the Confederate army, in which he enlisted at the age of sixteen years. Of the seven children born to the parents five are living, and of them all Jacob H. Frantz is the eldest. The paternal grandfather, Jacob Frantz, was born and reared on Mason's Creek. Early in life he was a farmer, but later became a tanner, and for many years operated a large tannery on Peters Creek. The maternal grandfather was a native of Botetourt County, Virginia, and he spent his life as a farmer. Both grandfathers were men of the highest standing, and gave a loyal support to progressive movements in their communities.

While his educational training was limited to the common schools, Jacob H. Frantz has since added much to his store of knowledge, and is today a very well informed man. Until he was thirty-five years old he was engaged in farming, but about 1905 he moved to Roanoke and embarked in the real estate business, conducting it until in 1925 he was elected city treasurer. Since then he has been devoting himself to the duties of his office.

In April, 1903, Mr. Frantz married Miss Mary K. Nelms, who was born in Bedford County, Virginia, a daughter of

Charles Dandridge Nelms, a farmer of Bedford County. Mrs. Frantz was educated in Roanoke County, and she is connected with church work as a member of the Methodist Episcopal Church, to which her husband also belongs, and of which he is a steward. They have had four children born to them, namely: Jacob Henry, who graduated from William and Mary College class of 1928; Mary Dandridge, attending Randolph-Macon College; Clarinda Ellen and Eben Nelms, who are attending the Roanoke High School. Mr. Frantz belongs to the Roanoke Lions Club. He is one of those who proves that the influence of a good and capable man is not confined to his own personal transactions, but rather is reflected in the lives of those with whom he becomes associated, and through them filters to the oncoming generation which shall contribute to the community's growth. Liberal in his views and in his contributions to worthy objects, Mr. Frantz has long been a decided addition to the citizenship of Roanoke and proven a notable increase of strength to the cause of public progress.

JOHN M. OTEY. In 1878 the late Col. Kirkwood Otey was made city auditor of Lynchburg. When he died in 1897 he was succeeded by his son, John M. Otey. The latter is still serving, thus making an uninterrupted succession of service of father and son in one municipal office for half a century. This is a noteworthy record in itself, and it is also significant of the citizenship of the Otey family, which for generations has expressed itself in terms of usefulness and self sacrificing devotion to community and state.

There have been many distinguished men of the Otey family in Virginia. At the corner of Eleventh and Federal streets in Lynchburg is the old Colonial home of the Otey family. The Revolutionary ancestor was John Otey, who had a son, Major Isaac Otey, who lived in Bedford County, Virginia, and married Elizabeth Matthews. Major Isaac Otey and wife had a son, John M. Otey, who in turn was the father of Col. Kirkwood Otey. Col. Kirkwood Otey married Lucy Dabney Norvell, and of their four children John M. Otey is the oldest. His sister Norvell is the wife of James A. Scott, of the insurance firm of Scott & Otey at Lynchburg. The second son, Kirkwood Otey, Jr., is in the automobile business at Charleston, West Virginia. The youngest of the four children died when eighteen years of age. John M. Otey also has the distinction of being a direct descendant of Sir John Pettus, who was one of the founders of the Virginia Colony established on the banks of the James River in 1607.

Col. Kirkwood Otey was born at Lynchburg October 19, 1829, graduated from the Virginia Military Institute and the University of Virginia, and before Virginia seceded from the Union helped organize and became first lieutenant of the Lynchburg Home Guard, which on April 22, 1861, was mustered into the Confederate service as Company G of the Eleventh Virginia Volunteers. He soon became captain of the company and under his command the company participated in thirteen battles and twenty-two skirmishes. Colonel Otey was three times wounded. He commanded his company as a part of Pickett's famous division in the charge at Gettysburg, and after that battle he was promoted to colonel in command of the Eleventh Regiment. After the war he was honorary captain of the Lynchburg Home

Guard, was also commander of the local camp of the Confederate Veterans, and he was buried with the Masonic and military honors that his career merited. Like many other prominent Virginians he was impoverished as a result of the war, and his wounds made him practically an invalid for a number of years. During this time his talented wife, daughter of a professor of the college at Lexington, Kentucky, supported the family by making tobacco bags. His mother during the war had bought an old warehouse at Lynchburg and converted it into a Confederate hospital. Mrs. Lucy Dabney Otey, who died August 25, 1903, was for many years active in charitable work, being the first member of the Salvation Army at Lynchburg, also active in the Florence Crittenden Home. Col. Kirkwood Otey after recovering from his wounds engaged in the insurance business, and in connection therewith performed the duties of city auditor from 1878 until his death. He and his wife were active members of the Court Street Methodist Episcopal Church, and he was a member of Marshall Lodge of the Masonic fraternity.

John M. Otey was born at Lynchburg February 5, 1866, and was educated in public schools and also in the academy conducted by Col. Thomas H. Carter. At the age of nineteen he went to work in his father's insurance office, and has been in that line of business ever since. The firm is now known as James A. Scott and John M. Otey, Incorporated, handling a general line of insurance.

Mr. Otey married, June 15, 1898, Miss Maggie Marshall Murrell, who was born at Lynchburg and was educated in public schools there and the Randolph-Macon Woman's College. Her father, Thomas E. Murrell, was a prominent tobacconist. Mr. and Mrs. Otey have one son, John M. Otey, Jr., who was educated in the Augusta Military Academy and the University of Virginia, and is now in the insurance business.

Mr. Otey for over thirty years was active in the Lynchburg Y. M. C. A., and for a number of years was its treasurer. He is one of the older members of Acca Temple of the Mystic Shrine at Richmond, and has membership in the various York Rite bodies of Masonry at Lynchburg, including the lodge to which both his father and grandfather belonged. He is also affiliated with the Independent Order of Odd Fellows and the B. P. O. Elks. He is a member of Grace Memorial Episcopal Church.

ALBERT SIDNEY NOWLIN, a prominent coal merchant of Lynchburg, with offices in the Peoples National Bank Building, is a member of one of the best known families of that city, one that has been closely identified with the history of Virginia since early Colonial times.

He was born in Appomattox County, September 8, 1878, son of Col. John H. and Sallie Louise (Woodson) Nowlin. He is a descendant of James Nowlin, a native of Ireland, who came to Virginia about 1700 and married Catherine Ward, a daughter of Bryan Ward. Their son James was the father of Abraham Nowlin, who married Mildred Watkins, and their son, Capt. Bryan Watkins Nowlin, married Mary Spencer and was the father of Col. John H. Nowlin.

Col. John H. Nowlin was a soldier and officer in the Confederacy during the Civil war and for many years followed planting and merchandising in Appomattox County. The home of

the Nowlins in the county was in the vicinity of Oakville.
Colonel Nowlin married Louise Woodson, daughter of John W.
Woodson, of another prominent Virginia family of Appomattox
County. Of their six children Albert Sidney Nowlin was the
oldest son.

Albert Sidney Nowlin grew up and received his early educational advantages in Appomattox County. He has been a resident of Lynchburg for thirty years, and has had a very successful career in the wholesale coal business, handling over an extensive territory in the Southeast the output of a number of coal
companies.

He married, February 28, 1915, Miss Annie Mosely Thornhill. They have one son, Albert Sidney, Jr., born January 30,
1917, and a daughter, Helen Thornhill, born November 21, 1924.

JOHN O. D. COPENHAVER, a resident of Roanoke, is president
of the Evergreen Cemetery Association. He was born in Tazewell County, Virginia, December 30, 1877, and is a son of Andrew J. and Eliza (Barnes) Copenhaver. The Copenhaver
family originated in Denmark, and the original immigrant settled in Pennsylvania, whence the family came to Virginia at a
very early day. The paternal grandfather of Mr. Copenhaver
was Samuel Copenhaver, a native of Virginia, who followed the
life of a planter throughout his career. Andrew J. Copenhaver,
the father of John O. D. Copenhaver, was born in Smyth County,
Virginia, and in young manhood enlisted for service in the Confederate army during the war between the states, at the close of
which he resumed his activities as a farmer. Later he removed
to Tazewell County, where he married a native of that county,
Eliza Barnes, a daughter of Robert Barnes, a Virginia farmer
whose family had come from Ireland at an early date and settled in the Old Dominion. Andrew Copenhaver and his wife
spent the remainder of their lives in Tazewell County, where
both passed away. He was a Republican in politics, and he and
his wife were faithful members of the Methodist Church, in
which he served as steward for forty-one years. Of their seven
children five are living, John O. D. having been the fifth in order
of birth.

John O. D. Copenhaver attended the country schools of Tazewell County, the Virginia Polytechnic Institute and Emory and
Henry College at Emory, Virginia, and after he finished from the
latter returned to the home place, where he was associated with
his father in the elder man's agricultural activities. At the age
of twenty-one years he went to Bluefield, West Virginia, where
he entered the employ of the Baldwin-Felts Detective Agency,
with which he continued to be identified for more than a quarter
of a century. This concern did much work for the Norfolk &
Western Railway Company, and Mr. Copenhaver was really
connected with the railroad company through the agency. In
March, 1926, Mr. Copenhaver resigned his position and took up
his residence at Roanoke, becoming president of Evergreen
Cemetery, which is conceded to be the most beautiful as well as
the best cared for cemetery in the United States. He has continued to act in this capacity and maintains offices in the Colonial
Bank Building. Mr. Copenhaver is a member of the Methodist
Episcopal Church, South, in which he has been a steward for ten
years. He is a thirty-third degree Mason, and in addition to
having been master of all bodies in the Scottish Rite has served
as potentate of the Mystic Shrine. He is also a member of the

Benevolent and Protective Order of Elks and the Kiwanis Club, and is a Republican in his political convictions.

In 1907 Mr. Copenhaver was united in marriage with Miss Letha A. Witten, who was born at Graham, Virginia, and received her education there and at Bristol, supplemented by attendance at Madison Hall, Washington, D. C. Two children have been born to this union: John Dresden, attending high school, and Martha Jane, attending public school.

JOHN GARNETT DEW was admitted to practice law in Virginia in 1867, and from that time until his death his career added many new associations and distinctions to the family names of Garnett and Dew. Judge Dew was a descendant of William Dew, who came from England in Colonial times and settled in Maryland. The Garnett family came from Essex, England, and there are many representatives of both names found in the military and professional annals of Virginia.

The father of Judge Dew was Benjamin Franklin Dew, an attorney, teacher and farmer of King and Queen County, who was a magistrate and a member of the County Court for a number of years. He was a brother of the notable educator, Thomas R. Dew, who was born in King and Queen County in 1802, son of Thomas R. and Lucy (Gatewood) Dew. Thomas R. Dew graduated from William and Mary College, and in 1826 was elected professor of history and political law in William and Mary College, and in that capacity he developed the chair of history and political science to real dignity and importance. He was elected president of William and Mary College in 1836, and the college enjoyed an unprecedented era of prosperity under him. He died in 1846. Benjamin Franklin Dew married Mary Susan Garnett.

She died when her son John Garnett Dew was ten years of age. The latter, with his brother, James Harvie, who later became a distinguished physician in New York City, attended school under Dr. Gessner Harrison. He was not yet sixteen when the war broke out between the states, and before it was over he had been in the service of the Confederacy for two years. He resumed his work at the University of Virginia during 1865-67 and took his degree Bachelor of Laws there in 1867. Judge Dew began practice in King and Queen County in 1868, and for over thirty years devoted his time to his large general practice and his public duties. He was a member of the County School Board from the time of its inception until 1884, and from 1884 to 1900 was judge of the County Court of King and Queen. In 1900 he became second auditor of State of Virginia and served in that office two term.

Judge Dew was a member of the Baptist Church and belonged to the Virginia State and American Bar Associations.

He married, October 28, 1875, Lelia Fauntleroy, descended from the distinguished Fauntleroy family of Virginia. The Fauntleroys have been prominent in their own name and many of them intermarried with other distinguished Virginia lines. Lelia Fauntleroy was born in King and Queen County, where her father, Dr. S. G. Fauntleroy, was a distinguished physician. Doctor Fauntleroy, who died in 1899, was highly educated in medicine, but it was not so much his vocation as an opportunity for useful service to his community. He owned three large plantations and before the war was a slave owner, and much of his practice was among his own people, and his service was rendered without compensation. He also held the office of overseer of the poor. Doctor Fauntleroy was eighty-one years of age when he died. He had four daughters and two sons. The son Dr. Claybrook Fauntleroy was a practicing physician and followed the worthy example of his father in his extensive charitable work. He died in 1924 after having practiced for forty years in King and Queen County. Dr. Claybrook Fauntleroy, his father and grandfather made up three generations who are represented on the list of alumni of the University of Pennsylvania.

Mrs. Dew, who resides at 1520 Grove Avenue in Richmond, is the mother of four children: Miss Mary Susan, a graduate of Hollins College; S. G. Dew, now deceased, who married Miss Nettie Thompson; B. Frank Dew, vice president of the State Planters Bank of Richmond, a Knight Templar Mason and Shriner and member of the Commonwealth Club, married Miss Gertrude Clark and has a son, B. Frank, Jr.; and Miss Elizabeth Dew.

Judge Dew was born at Newtown, King and Queen County, Virginia, July 23, 1845, and passed away at his home in Richmond in January, 1920.

JOHN WILLIAM SMITH, D. D. During the more than eight years that Dr. John William Smith has served as pastor of Greene Memorial Methodist Episcopal Church, South, of Roanoke, he has vigorously and continuously attacked ignorance, sophistry and error with the fearless loyalty to his honest convictions that is so characteristic of him. He has preached as he has lived, has been useful in all good works as a citizen and has borne himself in every position so that he has commended himself as an example for both young and old, and he is continuing in this work along the same lines with the prospect of many years of usefulness before him.

A native son of Virginia, for he was born in Loudoun County, his appointments have been held in Fairfax County, Virginia, Washington, District of Columbia, Baltimore, Maryland, and Roanoke, and he is deeply attached to the Southland, to which he so essentially belongs. His parents, John and America Smith, gave him a wholesome early environment in the home circle, and he attended the public schools of Washington City and Randolph-Macon College at Front Royal, Virginia. Upon his graduation from the latter he received his degree of Bachelor of Arts, and he has since carried on post-graduate work in George Washington University and Johns Hopkins University. In 1920 Randolph-Macon College honored him by conferring upon him the degree of Doctor of Divinity, and in 1925 he was given his Phi Beta Kappa key from the same institution because of his outstanding service and recognized leadership among her alumni. While in college he had distinguished himself as editor of the college annual, and in his preparatory school he won a medal as being its best debater.

From the beginning of his ministerial work Doctor Smith has proven his worth to his church, and honors have been conferred upon him with increasing frequency as he has become recognized as one of the outstanding figures in the Southern field, and of the Baltimore Conference, to which he is attached. In 1921 he was sent as a delegate to the Fifth Ecumenical Methodist Conference held in London, England, where he delivered the first of a series of addresses on "The Church and Modern Industrial Problems." From London he went on a trip through England and the continent, Mrs. Smith accompanying him. In 1924 he and Mrs. Smith made their second trip abroad, visiting Syria, Egypt, Greece and the Holy Land, and upon his return to Roanoke Doctor Smith gave many lectures upon his travels, especially those in the Holy Land, and brought vividly before his audiences conditions in these countries. However, these are not the first lectures he has delivered, for throughout his career he has appeared frequently upon the lecture platform, and is a very popular speaker. One of his lectures, the one on the Psalms and other portions of the Bible, is a special favorite, and he delivers it, and others, before minister's gatherings, summer conferences, young people's assemblies, Sunday School Training Institutes and similar church and lay meetings, his powerful oratory and flaming sincerity being particularly convincing. Doctor Smith does not confine his activities to his ministerial and lecture work, but branches out in many directions, and he is president of the Boy Scout's Council, president of the Children's Home Society, and a trustee of the Roanoke Hospital. For two years he was president of the Minister's Conference, and also served for several years as a director of the Roanoke Kiwanis Club.

Mrs. Smith belongs to an old and honored family, she being a daughter of Dr. W. E. Edwards, at one time a member of the Virginia Conference of the Methodist Church, and her grandfather, great-grandfather and brother were all clergymen. Doctor and Mrs. Smith have four children: Landon E., who is a business man of Roanoke; Emory E. and Ashby W., both of whom are attending Emory and Henry College; and Ethelbert Grake, who is a student in the local high school.

REV. THOMAS KAY YOUNG, D. D. No other profession makes such demands upon its members as does that of the ministry, and were it not for the fact that these "Men of God" are sustained by a power higher than their own many would fall fainting by the way. The intellectual attainments of the majority are beyond the ordinary, oratory plays an important part, and business acumen is frequently a necessary requisite, tact in marked degree must be present, but above all there must be a deep sincerity and steadfast belief in the divine origin of the call in order that the best results be obtained, and the Master's work be properly performed. But few of these ministers are adequately recompensed for their labors, their presence in times of deep sorrow and affliction, their influence in all uplift movements, and their example of godly living and speech, but they work on, "sustained by an unfaltering trust" and great must be their eternal reward. In Rev. Thomas Kay Young, pastor of the First Presbyterian Church of Roanoke, is to be found a man of the above described type, a man of learning, eloquence, business acumen and unblemished character, who is not only sustaining his church, but influencing his community in a manner that is attracting favorable comment from outsiders all over this part of the state.

Doctor Young was born in West Virginia, Fayette County, a son of William Wilsen and Elizabeth (Kay) Young, natives of Scotland, he born in Edinburgh and she in Lanark, and she survives and is living with her son, Doctor Young. The father was a miner, and was engaged in operating mines for big coal companies after coming to this country in 1880. He met his wife in Fayette County, West Virginia, although she had lived in Pennsylvania for some years, her parents having settled in that state upon coming to the United States in 1870, and they were married January 1, 1884. They had six sons and three daughters born to them, of whom five are living, and of them all Doctor Young is the second in order of birth. After he had secured his citizenship papers the father espoused the principles of the Democratic party, and continued to vote its ticket until his death. He was a Mason, an Odd Fellow and a Knight of Pythias, and both he and his wife early united with the Presbyterian Church, to which she still belongs.

Doctor Young attended the public school of Royal, West Virginia, and the West Virginia State Normal School at Athens, and later became a student of Hampden Sidney College, Virginia, from which he was graduated in 1908, with the degree Bachelor of Arts. His theological training was taken in the Union Theological Seminary, Richmond, Virginia, and he was graduated therefrom in 1911, with the degree Bachelor of Divinity. His first charge was a mountain mission at Holden, West Virginia, and he held it for eighteen months, his work there, difficult as it was, being productive of a real spiritual awakening, and a substantial increase in membership to the church. In October, 1912, he was sent to Covington, Virginia, and for the six succeeding years he labored faithfully and well, and when he left, March 1, 1918, he was followed by the regrets of his congregation. Sent to the Presbyterian Church at Lexington, Virginia, he repeated his good work there for six years, and January 1, 1924, was assigned to the pastorate of the First Presbyterian Church of Roanoke. This is an important charge with a membership of 1,100 souls, and the responsibilities are weighty, but Doctor Young is discharging them with inspired capability.

On September 21, 1907, Doctor Young married Miss Harriet Rebecca Cox, who was born in Farmville, Virginia, and educated in the Virginia State Normal School. She is a daughter of Benjamin Matthew Cox, for thirty-eight years manager of the above mentioned school, which position he held at the time of his death in 1924. Four children have been born to Doctor and Mrs. Young: Thomas Kay, Junior, who is a high school student; William Benjamin, who died in 1915, at the age of three months; Helen Laing; and Mary Elizabeth. Doctor Young was made a Mason in Petersburg, Virginia, and retains his membership with that lodge. He belongs to the Lions Club and the University Club. For several years he has been on the Board of Stewards of Jackson College, and for nine years he has been a trustee of Union Theological Seminary, Richmond, Virginia.

JOEL T. BANDY. It is said that the keynote of salesmanship, any kind of salesmanship, is sincerity, and that a salesman should not try to sell goods that he would not buy himself, and at the same price, same place and same time, and if it is true, as it is, then is it especially applicable to the real estate and investment business. In no other line does insincerity and lack of confidence prove obstacles as they do in that dealing with the selling of realty and the making of investments. These facts were long ago appreciated and approved by Joel T. Bandy, and in the years that he has been handling real estate and investments in

Roanoke he has been guided by them with very satisfactory results, and stands today in the fore front of operators in these lines. However, if a man is going to build up a profitable sales business in real estate over a term of years he ought to be more than a salesman; he ought to be an advisor in economics to the people with whom he deals. When a salesman has sold a client, the client ought to be so well pleased that he will go out and bring in his friends. The neglect of such suggestions Mr. Bandy has found will nearly always work to the disadvantage of the salesman himself, and is simply ruinous to the house which he serves, and therefore he has tried to train his men to accept them, and act accordingly, and the successful ones have done so. Starting in life without any capital, by safeguarding the interests of his clients he has advanced until he is one of the leading realtors of Roanoke.

Joel T. Bandy was born on a farm in Roanoke County, Virginia, December 12, 1860, a son of Thomas L. and Frances J. (Huddleston) Bandy, both of whom were born in Bedford County, where he was engaged in farming throughout his life. Throughout the entire war period of the sixties he served in the Confederate army. In political faith he was a Democrat. Both he and his wife were active members of the First Presbyterian Church of Roanoke. Of the four children born to the parents two survive: Mrs. E. S. McNanel, of Roanoke, where Mr. McNanel is now a retired railroad man, and Joel T. The paternal grandfather was George Bandy, born in Bedford County, a lifelong farmer. The maternal grandfather, Joel Huddleston, was also born in Bedford County. The Bandys are of Welsh extraction, and the Huddlestons are of English origin.

The local schools and Roanoke College educated Joel T. Bandy, and he earned his first money by farm work. Later he taught school, and after he located in Roanoke he was in the coal and feed business for several years. It was not, however, until he embarked in the real estate busines in 1900 that he found the vocation for which he was fitted, and in it he has steadily progressed and has to his credit some of the best of the development projects carried to successful completion in this region, notably that of Virginia Heights. He bought the land, put in the improvements, and built up what is recognized to be one of the most desirable residential suburbs of Roanoke. Regarding this property as a gilt-edged investment, he has retained ownership of several houses. Mr. Bandy is a director in the Colonial National Bank, and is otherwise interested in local enterprises. A strong Democrat, he works for his party's success, and served for twenty years as a member of the school board.

In March, 1891, Mr. Bandy married Miss Nannie P. Nelms, who was born in Bedford County, but reared in Roanoke County. After being graduated from Sullivan's College, Bristol, Virginia, she taught school until her marriage. Mr. and Mrs. Bandy have one child, Frances, who married W. M. Denny Taylor, of Roanoke, and they have two children: Nancy E. Taylor and Frances Taylor. Both Mr. and Mrs. Bandy belong to the Raleigh Courthouse Methodist Episcopal Church, South, of which he is a steward. A high Mason, he has been advanced through the Scottish and York Rites, and he also belongs to the Mystic Shrine. He is a member of the Knights of Pythias and the Roanoke Kiwanis Club, and is popular in all of these organizations.

ROBERT E. L. ABBOTT.   Like many men who have won success in commercial and industrial life, Robert E. L. Abbott, secretary, treasurer and general manager of the Virginia Lumber
Manufacturing Company of Roanoke, commenced his career as
a school teacher.   His experience in the educational profession
lasted for ten years, but his inclinations were always for a business career, and in 1906 he entered the employ of the firm with
which he is now connected, and in which he has gained promotion and success through the application of sound and substantial abilities.

Mr. Abbott was born May 4, 1868, in Craig County, Virginia,
and is a son of Sinclair C. and Lucinda Jane (Williams) Abbott,
natives of the same county.   His paternal grandfather was
James Abbott, who passed his entire life as a farmer in Virginia,
principally in Craig County, where he was held in high esteem
and respect by his fellow citizens.   Sinclair C. Abbott received
a public school education and as a youth learned the trade of
cabinet maker, which he followed until the outbreak of the war
between the states, when he enlisted in the Confederate army
and subsequently served throughout the four years of the war.
At the close of the struggle the young soldier returned to Craig
County, having recovered from a slight wound, and resumed his
activities as a cabinet maker, in which he was engaged during
the remainder of his life.   For some years he served as postmaster of the little Town of Abbott in Craig County, which was
named in his honor.   He was a Democrat in his political views
and a member of the Christian Church.   He married Lucinda
Jane Williams, a daughter of Rev. Philip Williams, a native of
Virginia and a minister of the Christian Church.   They had ten
children, of whom four are living, Robert E. L. having been the
fourth in order of birth.   One of the children, Dr. B. A. Abbott,
a prominent minister of the Christian Church, is editor of the
religious publication, the *Christian Evangelist,* of Saint Louis,
and in 1927 went to Lausanne, Switzerland, to attend the convention of members of all denominations for the general advancement of Christianity.   Some ninety churches representing
a score of different beliefs sent delegates to this world conference on faith and order.

Robert E. L. Abbott attended the local schools of Craig
County, following which he pursued a course at Kentucky University (now Transylvania) at Lexington, and after his graduation therefrom began teaching school.   During the following
ten years he was employed as a teacher in various schools in
Craig, Henry and Tazewell counties, but in the fall of 1906 accepted a position as bookkeeper for the Virginia Lumber Manufacturing Company of Roanoke.   He has been identified with
this concern for twenty-three years, and now acts as secretary,
treasurer and general manager, having risen to these posts by
industry and merit.   He is widely and favorably known in business circles and particularly in the lumber trade, and is known
as a man of the highest integrity and of broad information.   Mr.
Abbott has applied himself devotedly to his business affairs and
has few outside interests, although he is a Mason of the Scottish
Rite and a member of the Mystic Shrine.   He has cooperated
willingly and energetically in worthy civic movements, and with
his family belongs to the Christian Church.

In 1904 Mr. Abbott was united in marriage with Miss Bertie
Shelburne, who was born in Lee County, Virginia, and educated
at Milligan College, Tennessee, and to this union there have been

H. M. Stowe.

born three children: Elizabeth Christal, who resides with her parents; Robert Shelburne, who holds a position with the Virginia Lumber Manufacturing Company, and Edward Lee, who died when two years of age. The pleasant family residence is situated at 210 Wasena Avenue, Roanoke.

HENRY M. STOWE, postmaster of Bedford City, became a Virginian through his interest in the National Elks Home at Bedford. Few men among his contemporaries have had a career of greater variety of experience and association with prominent men than Mr. Stowe.

He was born at Cleveland, Ohio, September 10, 1854, son of Thomas A. and Maria (McKinzie) Stowe, and grandson of William Stowe, who was born at Middletown, Connecticut, November 15, 1795, and was an early settler in Ohio, where he married Emily Kelsey. This branch of the Stowe family was established in America by John Stowe, a native of England, son of John Stowe, the historian. John Stowe, the American, arrived in the United States April 9, 1734, on the ship *Elizabeth*, bringing with him six children. Thomas A. Stowe was born at Hudson, Ohio, July 23, 1827, was educated in Western Reserve College, became a printer and was connected with the *Cleveland Plain Dealer* from the establishment of that old and influential newspaper at Cleveland. He was on the staff of the *Plain Dealer* at the time of his death. For three years he was in a printing office in Iowa, but with that exception lived all his life in Ohio. He was a leading Democrat, served fifteen years on the board of education of Cleveland, and was president of the board when he died in 1877. At one time he was nominated for lieutenant-governor, and he served as a lieutenant in the Civil war. His wife, Maria (McKinzie) Stowe, was born January 1, 1834, and is still living at the age of ninety-four, making her home with a daughter in Los Angeles. She had a family of three children: Henry M.; Josephine Maria, a widow in Los Angeles; and Charles Brown, head of the Stowe-Fuller Corporation, fire-brick manufacturers at Cleveland. Thomes A. Stowe was an active Presbyterian, member of the church choir, served as grand master of the State of Ohio in the Ancient Order of United Workmen.

Henry M. Stowe was educated at Cleveland, as a boy sold newspapers on the streets, left school in 1871 at the age of seventeen to become a chainman with a surveying party. For five years he was in the news room of the *Plain Dealer*, but in December, 1877, left the printing office on account of lead poisoning. Three months later he became connected with the Worswick Manufacturing Company, manufacturers of plumbing and steam fitting supplies. He went to work for this company at thirty dollars a month.

In 1875 Mr. Stowe had married Angelina N. Worswick, daughter of the manufacturer. Two children were born to their union. The daughter, Winifred Olive, is the wife of Stanley L. Galpin, a member of the faculty of Trinity University in Connecticut. The daughter Marjorie is an art teacher living in Cleveland. The mother of these children died in 1922.

While with the Worswick Company Mr. Stowe acquired a thorough knowledge of the pipe fitting and plumbing business. He was put in the sales department and in January, 1880, was offered general supervision of the plant. Instead he organized the Union Machine Works, which did a prosperous business. In 1882 he had to give up his work on account of ill health, and spent three months on the salt waters on the coast of Florida. He then became a traveling salesman for the Macintosh Goode & Company, covering Ohio, Indiana and Michigan, and in 1886 went with the Continental Tube Works. Mr. Stowe in September, 1888, while in the employ of its Pittsburgh Tube Company, he located at Marion, Ohio, where he organized the firm of Cunningham & Stowe, heating engineers. This business later employed about twenty-five skilled workers. Owing to the panic of 1893 he returned to his plumbing business at Marion. He sold out in 1896, and for a time was identified with the work of the Monarch Cement Company in establishing a plant at Bronson, Michigan. Mr. Stowe in 1897 went to Alaska in the gold fields, but this was an experience without profit. He arrived in Chicago with only 25 cents, and through the friendship of a conductor was able to get back to Marion, Ohio. Mr. Stowe in February, 1899, went with the Forest City Electric Company, for nine months sold insurance, then resumed employment with the Forest City Company, and again took up insurance, a business he followed until 1918, when failing eyesight compelled him to seek a residence in the Elks National Home at Bedford, Virginia.

He remained there until he was appointed postmaster by his friend President Harding in 1918. He now gives all his time to his official work. Mr. Stowe in 1896 was president of the Bryan Silver Club in Ohio, but while living at Marion became interested in Warren G. Harding and was one of his local friends and admirers who brought him into politics.

Mr. Stowe married June 16, 1927, Camille Binnix Houston, a native of Philadelphia, daughter of John Binnix, general manager of the Central Iron Works at Harrisburg, Pennsylvania. Mrs. Stowe is a member of the Episcopal Church. Mr. Stowe has been actively identified with the B. P. O. Elks since 1888. For twelve years he was secretary of Cleveland Lodge of Elks, No. 18, being No. 5 on the membership roll and now the oldest member of that oraganization.

HUGH J. HAGAN, M. D., has practiced medicine in Roanoke since 1914. He was born in Atlanta, Georgia, December 11, 1888, a son of Hugh and Sallie Cobb (Johnson) Hagan, the latter of whom was born in Selma, Alabama, and the former in Richmond, Virginia. He studied medicine in the College of Physicians and Surgeons, New York City, and in Berlin, Germany, and Vienna, Austria, and upon his return to the United States was engaged in the practice of his profession in Atlanta, Georgia, for ten years. His death occurred in 1898, but she survives and is now living in Roanoke. They had two children: Doctor Hagan and Willis Cobb, the latter being a banker of Birmingham, Alabama. The parents belonged to the Episcopal Church from their youth up.

Doctor Hagan of this review attended school in Atlanta and Roanoke, and then entered Washington and Lee University, from which he was graduated in 1910. He then became a student of Johns Hopkins University, and was graduated therefrom in 1914, after having completed the four-year medical course, with the degree of Doctor of Medicine. His internship was taken in Jefferson Hospital, Roanoke. During the World war he served, with the rank of captain, in the Medical Corps from May 10, 1917, to January 30, 1919, being honorably discharged on the latter date. He was stationed at Monroe, Vale, Forrest, Devens and Dix camps, his service being entirely performed in this country.

On July 14, 1917, Doctor Hagan married Miss Barbara Fowle Campbell, who was born in Charles Town, West Virginia, and educated in that city and in a finishing school of New York City. Two children have been born to Doctor and Mrs. Hagan: Hugh Campbell and Robert Cameron. Doctor Hagan belongs to the Episcopal Church. He is a member of Kappa Alpha, Phi Beta Kappa, the Southwest Virginia Medical Society, the Medical Society of Virginia, the Southern Medical Association, the American College of Physicians, the Shenandoah Club, the Roanoke Country Club, the Dinner Dance Club and other local organizations, in all of which he is deservedly popular. His practice is internal medicine, and he devotes all of his time to it, not being connected with any business concerns.

PRESTON GARNETT HUNDLEY, physician and surgeon at Lynchburg, comes of a family of prominent professional people, being a brother of John T. T. Hundley, president of Lynchburg College, and his father was also an educator, though his outstanding service was in the upbuilding and extension of the influence of the Christian Church in Virginia.

Doctor Hundley was born at Dunnsville, Essex County, Virginia, March 14, 1880, son of John T. T. and Sarah Elizabeth (Garnett) Hundley, both natives of Essex County, and a grandson of Andrew Hundley, a planter and slave owner of Essex County who served as sheriff and treasurer of his county. Andrew Hundley married Nancy Trible. John Trible Thomas Hundley, Sr., was born in Essex County and was educated in Bethany College in West Virginia, the institution founded by Alexander Campbell of the Church of the Disciples. He began teaching in Essex County when little more than a boy, and kept up the work of teaching for over thirty-nine years in a two-room school known as the Dunnsville Academy, and his personal scholarship and inspiring influence made that an institution of the highest service in preparing young men for college entrance. He taught higher mathematics, surveying, Greek and Latin and other subjects. Throughout his life he was one of the most prominent laymen of the Christian Church in Virginia, and probably no ordained minister of the church did more for it than this educator. He died in 1890, at the age of fifty-nine years. His wife, Sarah Elizabeth Garnett, was a daughter of Judge Muscoe Garnett, who was a lawyer, for seventeen years a member of the House of Delegates, and an elder in the Christian Church. Sarah Elizabeth Hundley died in 1895.

Preston Garnett Hundley was the youngest son in a family of thirteen children. After the local schools he attended William and Mary College during 1897-99, and completed the work of the Virginia School of Pharmacy in 1903. From 1903 to 1905 he was manager of the Johnson Pharmacy at Hampton, and then entered the medical department of the University of Maryland at Baltimore and was graduated with the M. D. degree in 1909. Doctor Hundley practiced two years in the coal fields of West Virginia, for seven years at Pembroke, Virginia, and since 1921 has had his home and a busy practice at Lynchburg, a large amount of his work being in gynecology and obstetrics. Doctor Hundley is a member of the Lynchburg Medical Society, Medical Society of Virginia and American Medical Association. He is affiliated with the Knights of Pythias, the Lions Club, Independent Order of Odd Fellows, and is a deacon in the First Christian Church.

He married, November 24, 1909, Miss Mary E. Lyell, who was born in Richmond County, Virginia, and was educated in Baltimore College. They have three children: Robert Lyell, born in 1914; Preston Booker, born in 1915; and Olivia Anderson, born in 1917.

Mrs. Hundley is a daughter of John M. and Anna (Booker) Lyell. Her father served in the Ninth Virginia Cavalry in the Civil war and for a number of years was a member of the Legislature. He was a merchant in Richmond County, and owned the first automobile in the North Neck of Virginia.

JOHN OTTO BOYD, M. D. In sketching the career of one who has impressed himself by his versatile gifts upon the passing generation, one is pleased to find the unusual union of high philanthropic ends with such practical qualities as have made him a successful physician and surgeon. However rare may be such a combination of qualities, that they are not altogether incompatible is illustrated in the career of Dr. John O. Boyd, of Roanoke, who has a large practice and high standing in his profession, particularly in the field of his specialties, gynecology and obstetrics. With the exception of the period of his military service during the World war he has been located in the discharge of his professional duties at Roanoke since 1905, and during this time has established himself firmly in the confidence and esteem of the people.

Doctor Boyd was born March 12, 1881, at Winchester, Virginia, and is a son of Dr. P. W. and Fredericka (Schultz) Boyd. His paternal grandfather was Rev. Andrew Hunter Holmes Boyd, a well known early Presbyterian minister of Virginia, who filled many pulpits in various parts of the state and was a man who was held in great esteem and respect. Dr. P. W. Boyd was born in Frederick County, Virginia, where he received his early education, and as a youth entered Washington and Lee University, where he was graduated, and later graduated from the University of Maryland with the degree Doctor of Medicine. After engaging in practice for a few years he turned his attention to the hardware business, which he followed for many years at Winchester, both he and Mrs. Boyd, also a native of Frederick County, dying at that place. She was a daughter of Frederick Schultz, a native of Virginia and a larger planter, whose father, John Schultz, served in the American army during the War of 1812. Doctor and Mrs. Boyd were faithful members of the Presbyterian Church, in the work of which they were active, and Doctor Boyd was a Confederate soldier during the war between the states, serving as a private in Chew's battery. They had a family of eight children, of whom seven are living, Dr. John O. of this review being the last in order of birth.

John O. Boyd received his early education at Shenandoah Academy, Winchester, following which he pursued a course at the University College of Medicine at Richmond, and was graduated with the class of 1905, receiving the degree Doctor of Medicine. For a short time he served as an interne in the Virginia Hospital, but in 1905 located permanently at Roanoke, where he since has achieved remarkable success and high standing, his present offices being located in the Shenandoah Life Building. When the United States became embroiled in the great European struggle Doctor Boyd offered his services to the Medical Corps, and, being accepted, was sent to Camp Greenleaf, where he underwent intensive training. He was then assigned to Base Hospital No. 45, and subsequently was sent to the Base Hospital at Camp Pike, serving in surgical work in all its branches and also as acting chief surgeon. He finally was transferred to Hospital No. 23 at Philadelphia, whence he was discharged in 1919 and returned to his practice at Roanoke, after doing post-graduate work at Philadelphia and New York. Although he is equally at home in any branch of his profession, Doctor Boyd specializes as a gynecologist and in obstetrical cases, and is frequently called into consultation by his fellow practitioners for advice. He is a member of the Pi Mu honorary medical fraternity, the Roanoke Medical Society, the Virginia State Medical Society, the Southern Medical Society and the American Medical Association and is a fellow of the American College of Surgeons. He belongs also to the local Kiwanis Club and takes a keen interest in all that affects the welfare of the city, its institutions and its people. While he is an exceptionally busy man, he is much more than a professional drudge, for he is sociable by nature and enjoys the companionship of his fellows. He is a popular member of the Shenandoah Club and the Country Club, and his principal hobby and pastime is tennis, the Doctor being known as a very capable performer on the courts.

In 1912 Doctor Boyd was united in marriage at Roanoke with Miss Nellie J. Stephenson, who was born at Doylestown, Pennsylvania, and educated in the schools of Roanoke and at Wilson College, Chambersburg, Pennsylvania, and to this union there have been born four children: John Otto, Jr., Katharine Cowell, William Stephenson and Nellie Stephenson. The family belongs to the Presbyterian Church, in the work of which Mrs. Boyd is active and helpful.

DAVID DENTON HULL, JR., during a law practice covering a period of a third of a century early became identified in a professional capacity with the great iron and coal industries of the South, and for many years he has not only handled the legal affairs but has also served in an executive capacity for large corporations.

He represents the tenth generation of the American Hull family, one of the oldest of consecutive record from the time of the establishment of the original English colonies. His first American ancestor was George Hull, who was born in England in 1590 and was a member of the original Massachusetts Bay Colony, locating at Dorchester, Massachusetts, (now a part of Boston) and became a man of considerable local prominence, and was a representative in the first General Court of the Massachusetts Bay Colony. Members of successive generations of the family lives in New England, were soldiers in the Colonial Wars, business men and statesmen. The founder of the Virginia branch of the family was Samuel Hull, representing the sixth generation of the American family. Samuel Hull came from Ulster County, New York, to Virginia and settled in Smyth County in 1789. His son Norton Hull was born in Smyth County in 1792, and the only child of his first marriage was Thomas T. Hull, who was born in Smyth County, February 23, 1811, and died September 30, 1851.

He was the father of David Denton Hull, Sr., who was born at Marion, Smyth County, December 26, 1837, and who died June 19, 1919. Before the Civil war David Denton Hull, Sr., was a merchant, entered the Confederate army with the rank of lieutenant, and later was a captain in the Sixty-third Virginia Volunteer Infantry, General Humphrey Marshall's Division, and for a considerable time was with General Morgan's forces in Tennessee and Kentucky. After the war he became a man of extensive business enterprises at Marion, engaged in merchandising and milling, was one of the organizers and was successively vice president and until his death president of the Bank of Marion. He also served on the county board of supervisors, was a member of the board to supervise the erection of the Southwestern State Hospital, took a prominent part in maintaining educational facilities for Marion and his section of the state, being a member of the board of trustees of the Marion Female College and for over seventeen years chairman of the board of Emory and Henry College. He was a steward in the Methodist Episcopal Church. He married July 29, 1868, Mary A. H. Graham, of Wythe County, Virginia. Of their family of seven children David Denton, Jr., was the second child and second son.

David Denton Hull, Jr., was born March 26, 1872, and grew up in the attractive home which his father had established on a farm west of Marion. He attended private schools, and in 1891 was graduated valedictorian of his class at Emory and Henry College with the Bachelor of Arts degree. He spent about two years in the Law Department of the University of Virginia and in 1894 began practice at Pulaski. In 1900 he removed to Bristol and since 1908 has made his home at Roanoke. Mr. Hull in 1903 bceame general counsel and in 1917 also vice president of the Virginia Iron, Coal and Coke Company; a corporation that has owned and operated extensive coal and iron properties in the State of Virginia, Kentucky, Tennessee, Georgia and North Carolina. That relationship has been maintained ever since.

Mr. Hull takes an active part in the civic affairs of the community in which he resides. He is a member of the Roanoke, Virginia State and American Bar Associations, belongs to the American Steel and Iron Institute, the Trinity Methodist Episcopal Church at Roanoke, is a Kappa Sigma, a Pi Gamma Mu, a member of the Shenandoah Club of Roanoke, of the Roanoke Country Club and of the Westmoreland Club of Richmond. He served a term as president of the Roanoke Chamber of Commerce; is a member of the Board of Visitors of the University of Virginia; and is president and a member of the Board of Trustees of Hollins College Corporation.

He married June 16, 1923, Miss Elizabeth Duval Adams, daughter of Captain and Mrs. Richard Henry Toler Adams of Lynchburg. There are three children of this union: Annie Maxwell Hull, Susan Elizabeth Hull and Mary Graham Hull.

WILLIAM WISE BOXLEY. Prominent among the citizens of Roanoke who have risen from obscurity and poverty to high position and affluence solely through the medium of their own abilities is William Wise Boxley, known throughout Virginia and the adjoining states as one of the foremost railroad contractors in this part of the country. When he commenced his connection with railroad work Mr. Boxley was fresh from the farm, and his wage earning career began at the modest salary of one dollar per day. During the forty years that have passed since that time he has improved every opportunity that has arisen, and today is first vice president of the Colonial National Bank, an ex-mayor of the city, and a man universally looked up to and admired.

Mr. Boxley was born July 17, 1861, at the ancestral home, known as the "Great House," situated on the banks of the North Anna River, adjoining Spotsylvania, Louisa County, Virginia, and is a son of James and Sallie Ann (Lipscomb) Boxley. His paternal grandfather was Joseph Boxley, a native of Boxley, England, who came to the United States in young manhood and settled in Louisa County, Virginia, where he built the home above mentioned and passed the remainder of his life as a planter. His son, James Boxley, was born in his father's home, and followed in his father's footsteps as to the matter of a vocation, being a planter all of his life. He espoused the cause of the Confederacy during the war between the states and was active in securing food supplies for the army, but the misfortunes of war practically wrecked the family fortunes. Both he and his worthy wife were active members of the Baptist Church. Mr. Boxley married Miss Sallie Ann Lipscomb, who was born at Spotsylvania, a daughter of John Lipscomb, also born there, a farmer by vocation and a prominent leader in the Baptist Church. Five sons and three daughters were born to Mr. and Mrs. Boxley, of whom two sons survive: C. A., a retired capitalist of Charleston, West Virginia; and William Wise, of this review.

William Wise Boxley received only the advantages of a public school education and was reared on his father's farm, where he remained until the age of twenty-seven. In 1888, tiring of agricultural work and being attracted by the glamor and romance of railroading, he took a position as a common laborer in a construction gang, at wages of one dollar per day. It was not long before his employers took note of his industry and intelligence, and he was advanced to a foremanship and later to a superintendency. It was while thus employed that he embarked on a venture of his own, in the way of railroad construction, in 1892. At first, because of his limited capital, his operations were small, but with the accumulation of a larger source of income, as well as growing confidence, he increased and broadened his scope, and at the present time has to his credit many miles of railroad construction. He still continues in the same line of business and is interested in four of the most highly improved rock-crushing outfits obtainable. He maintains well appointed offices in his own building, bearing his name, which has eight stores and numerous offices, and was erected by him in 1923, although his headquarters have been at Roanoke since 1906. Mr. Boxley is first vice president and chairman of the executive committee of the Colonial National Bank of Roanoke, and in 1926 was president of the Chamber of Commerce. A Democrat in politics, he has been prominent in public affairs, and served four years as mayor under the first term of the city manager form of government. Mr. Boxley is a Scottish Rite Mason and a Noble of the Mystic Shrine. He belongs to the First Baptist Church of Roanoke, in which he is a member of the Board of Deacons, while his wife belongs to St. John's Episcopal Church.

In 1884 Mr. Boxley was united in marriage with Miss Fannie Haley, who was born in Louisa County, Virginia, and to this union there were born two children: William, who is deceased; and Littleburry James, a graduate of Washington and Lee University, who is associated in business with his father. Mrs.

Boxley met death by drowning in 1893, and in 1903 Mr. Boxley married Miss Willie Saunders, who was born in Louisa County, the marriage ceremony being performed at Richmond. Three children have been born to this union: Abney, a graduate of the Virginia Military Institute, in 1925, degree Bachelor of Science, who is now engaged in the contracting business with his father and half-brother; Mary Wise, a graduate of the National Cathedral, Washington, D. C.; and Cheyenne, a daughter, attending school at Gunston Hall, Washington, D. C.

J. BURTON NOWLIN, who has had a broad and successful experience in medical practice, now specializing in internal medicine at Lynchburg, is a member of an old Campbell County family, one that has been in Virginia for a number of generations.

The founder of the family was James Nowlin, who was born in Ireland in 1655. The name was spelled Nowlan in that country. James Nowlin on account of participation in religious wars came to America about 1700, and died in 1725. In order to pay his passage across the ocean he indentured himself to a Virginia planter named Bryan Ward, and he subsequently married Catherine Ward, the planter's daughter. One of their sons, Bryan Ward, married Lucy Wade, and their son, James Nowlin, a native of Pittsylvania County, married Rainey Downey. Mathew Bates Nowlin, son of James and Rainey (Downey) Nowlin, was born in Pittsylvania County, was a farmer, mill owner, and a man of large property interests, owning a hundred slaves before the war. At an early date he located on a large plantation in Campbell County, where he also operated a store. He died in 1856. He had served in the State Legislature. Mathew Bates Nowlin married Elizabeth Preston, and they were the grandparents of Doctor Nowlin of Lynchburg.

Doctor Nowlin was born in Campbell County in July, 1873, son of James Bowker and Susan Hamner (Burton) Nowlin. His mother was born near Lynchburg on her father's plantation "The Oaks." Her mother was Damaris Cobbs. Her grandfather, John Hudson Burton, who married Margaret Macon, was a descendant of Thomas Burton, who came from England in 1634 and settled in Henrico County, Virginia, being one of the pioneer planters in the vicinity of Richmond. James Bowker Nowlin spent most of his active life in the banking business at Lynchburg. He was a member of Kirkpatrick's Battery in the Confederate army. He was a Methodist, while his wife belonged to the Methodist Protestant Church. Of their four children two are now living, Dr. J. Burton and J. Graham, of Lynchburg.

Dr. J. Burton Nowlin was educated at the Lynchburg High School and graduated from the College of Physicians and Surgeons at Baltimore in 1896. For twelve years he practiced in Buckingham County, for two years was in Richmond specializing in children's diseases, and since 1910 has practiced at Lynchburg.

Doctor Nowlin married, September 21, 1898, Roberta Ellis Hall, daughter of Thomas B. Hall, a farmer. Doctor and Mrs. Nowlin have two children. The son, Preston Nowlin, was educated at the University of Virginia, graduating in medicine in 1924, spent twenty months as an interne in the Boston City Hospital and is now specializing in surgery. The second child, Ellis Nowlin, is the wife of George H. Cosby, Jr., a special insurance agent and insurance inspector at Charlottesville. Doctor Now-

lin and family are members of the Presbyterian Church. He is
a Scottish Rite Mason and Shriner, member of the Woodmen of
the World, and belongs to the Lynchburg and Campbell County
Medical Society and the Medical Society of Virginia.

DAVID HALBERT HOWARD. During the many years that he
was identified with the bar of Lynchburg, the late David Halbert Howard demonstrated the possession of splendid legal abilities, in the exercise of which he gained the right to be known as
one of the leaders of his profession in Campbell County. From
the time that he left college in young manhood until his death,
in 1925, he led an active, useful and successful career, and as a
member of the firm of Kirkpatrick & Howard was identified
with much litigation of a highly important character. While
he never sought office that would bring him to the forefront as
a public figure, in a quiet and unassuming way he exerted an
influence for good and was known as a man of public spirit and
civic pride.

Mr. Howard was born July 19, 1865, in Wythe County, Virginia, a son of J. Milton and Rhoda Jane (Allison) Howard. His
father, who spent his entire life in Wythe County, was an agriculturist, and the early environment of David H. Howard was
that of the home farm. After attending the rural schools he
took an academic course at King's College, Bristol, and then
became a law student at the University of Virginia, from which
he was duly graduated with his degree in 1890. He at once took
up his residence at Lynchburg, where he followed his profession with great success during the remainder of his life. He
was a member of the Virginia State Bar Association and the
American Bar Association, and carried on a civil practice, being
at all times an upholder of the ethics and amenities of his calling.
Mr. Howard was an elder in the First Presbyterian Church, and
belonged to the Masons, the Knights Templar and the Mystic
Shrine, and the Piedmont and Oakwood Clubs. Politically he
gave his allegiance to the Democratic party.

In 1897 Mr. Howard was united in marriage with Miss Nannie Vaughan, who was born at Danville, Virginia, and educated
in the schools of Lynchburg. She is a daughter of Dr. Egbert
G. and Lucie Guinn (Estes) Vaughan, the former a native of
Amelia County, Virginia, and the latter of Nelson County, Virginia. Doctor Vaughan received his medical degree from the
University of Pennsylvania and for many years was engaged in
practice in Halifax County, this state, where he became greatly
respected because of his skill and high personal character. He
is now deceased, but is survived by his widow, who resides with
Mrs. Howard, and who, although now at the advanced age of
ninety-five years, is in good health and both mentally and
physically active. Of the six children in the Vaughan family,
four are living: James Oscar, a traveling man, who resides at
Atlanta, Georgia; B. Estes, president of the First National Bank
of Lexington, Virginia, and also president of three other banking institutions in this state; Mrs. Janie V. Hudson, a widow
residing at Lynchburg; and Mrs. Howard. To Mr. and Mrs.
Howard there were born five children: Lucie, who completed
her education at the Agnes Scott School, at Atlanta, Georgia;
Nannie Vaughan, a graduate of Randolph-Macon College, who
studied art at New York City for one year and completed her
education at Paris, France, where she received the degree of
Interior Decorator and is now following her profession in New

York City; Rhoda, who graduated from Hollins College with the class of 1927; David Halbert, Jr., who graduated from Davidson College in 1928; and Estes Vaughan, who graduated from McCauley Preparatory School, Chattanooga, Tennessee, in 1928 and who is now attending the University of Virginia. Mrs. Howard has always been active in religious affairs, and belongs to the Woman's Auxiliary of the First Presbyterian Church.

CHARLES W. WOMACK is head of the firm C. W. Womack & Company, general contractors, whose work is found in a number of the prominent public buildings in Lynchburg.

Mr. Womack learned the contracting business thoroughly from a beginning as a building mechanic, and has long been one of the prominent representatives of business in the civic affairs of his home city. He was born on a farm in Campbell County, August 30, 1866, son of James and Mildred (Yancey) Womack, natives of the same county. His father spent most of his life as a contractor, largely in rural construction, and erected a number of the fine country homes around Lynchburg. He was quite active until his death at the age of eighty-one. He was a member of the Methodist Church and a Democrat in politics. Of ten children, five sons and five daughters, one son, Benjamin L., was a Confederate soldier in the Civil war.

Charles W. Womack attended public schools and learned the trade of carpenter under his father. He was associated with his father until the latter's death, and in 1887 removed to Lynchburg and there became associated with another veteran building contractor, John P. Pettyjohn, and was Mr. Pettyjohn's foreman twenty years. Mr. Womack in 1907 engaged in business for himself, organizing the firm of C. W. Womack & Company. Most of the important contracts handled by this firm have been in the City of Lynchburg. They include the Market House, the Christian Church, John Wyatt School, West End Shoe Factory, Lynchburg Hospital and many others involving similar amounts but less well known to the public.

Mr. Womack married in 1890 Miss Ellen A. Luck, who was born in Bedford County, Virginia, daughter of Marshall Luck. She attended schools in Bedford. Mr. and Mrs. Womack are members of the College Hill Baptist Church. He is a York Rite Mason and Shriner, member of the Grotto of Masons, and has filled all the chairs in James River Lodge No. 48, Independent Order of Odd Fellows. He and his wife are members of the Eastern Star and Rebekahs, and Mrs. Womack has filled the chairs in the Eastern Star Chapter. He is a member of the Lions Club, a Democrat, and is a former member of the Board of Aldermen of Lynchburg.

JOHN HUNDLEY HOSKINS, M. D., is a native Virginian, graduated from the Medical College of Virginia, and a large part of his professional service has been in the line of surgery, in connection with hospitals. He is one of the leading surgeons in the City of Lynchburg.

Doctor Hoskins was born in Essex County, Virginia, April 22, 1892, son of Willard Dunbard and Ella Garnett (Hundley) Hoskins, and grandson of William Hoskins and John T. Hundley. William Hoskins was born in King and Queen County, was a physician and practiced his profession in his native county for many years. John T. Hundley was born in Essex County, Virginia, spent most of his life as an educator, and was a Confederate soldier in the Civil war. Willard D. Hoskins was born in King and Queen County, and his wife, in Essex County, and both died on the same day and were buried in the same grave, in 1910. He was a merchant at Dunnsville, a member of the Christian Church, a Mason and Democrat. In their family of eight children, five sons and three daughters, Doctor Hoskins was the second.

Doctor Hoskins after the common schools attended William and Mary College for two years. He graduated with his medical diploma from the Medical College of Virginia in 1915 and had some special training at the Marine Hospital at Buffalo, New York. He began practice at Beckley, West Virginia, an important industrial community, leaving there at the time of the World war and was with the colors as a medical officer for nineteen months. He was stationed at Fort Oglethorpe, Georgia, and Metuchen, New Jersey, until discharged. After leaving the army Doctor Hoskins had post-graduate work in the great Bellevue Hospital of New York, then resumed practice at Beckley, and in 1923 bought a hospital at Hazard, Kentucky, which he conducted until 1925. Since 1925 he has practiced at Lynchburg, his work being almost exclusively in general surgery. He is a member of the Lynchburg and Campbell County Medical Society, the Medical Society of Virginia, the Piedmont and the American Medical Associations.

Doctor Hoskins married, January 5, 1918, Miss Emma Kelly, of Culpeper, Virginia. She was educated in the Cincinnati Conservatory of Music and was teaching at Beckley, West Virginia, when she met Doctor Hoskins. They have one daughter, Emily Hume Hoskins, born October 6, 1920, and they lost their only son, John H., Jr., who died in May, 1927. Doctor and Mrs. Hoskins are active members of the First Baptist Church of Lynchburg, and he is serving on the Board of Trustees. He is a Royal Arch Mason, member of the B. P. O. Elks, the Pi Kappa Alpha fraternity at William and Mary College, and the Phi Chi medical fraternity.

FRANK SCOTT COOPER, M. D. The son and grandson of physicians, it was but natural that Dr. Frank Scott Cooper, of Roanoke, should evidence an inclination for the profession of medicine in his youth and that he should apply himself thereto with success. However, versatility has always been one of his strong points, and as he is possessed of a degree of business judgment and foresight not always to be found among strictly professional men he has gradually drifted away from the moorings of his youth, and for many years has not been identified with medical or surgical science, various large business and financial interests having claimed his attention and interest to the exclusion of other activities. At present he is widely known in the automobile business, with which he has been connected since 1914, and in which he has attained an unqualified success and prestige.

Doctor Cooper was born at Fayetteville, Fayette County, West Virginia, March 22, 1878, and is a son of Dr. Calvin S. and Stella (Jones) Cooper. His paternal grandfather, Dr. John Cooper, was born in what is now the State of West Virginia, and was a country physician of the old-time type, who put his profession far above any emolument he might secure for his services, and who in the process of his practice covered an area of many miles in the vicinity of Fayetteville. His son, Dr. Calvin

S. Cooper, was born at Sewell, West Virginia, and received his medical education principally under the preceptorship of his father, although he also attended a medical school in Tennessee. For a time he was engaged in practice in West Virginia, but finally located at Roanoke, where he continued to follow his calling until his death in 1888. He was a Mason and a member of the Presbyterian Church, and a man who was held in universal esteem in his community. His worthy wife, a member of the Baptist Church, and a native of Amherst County, West Virginia, died in 1878, shortly after the birth of her son. There were two children: Mrs. Lottie C. Troegle, of Huntington, West Virginia, whose husband is a retired business man; and Dr. Frank Scott, of this review.

Frank Scott Cooper was but twelve years of age when he was forced to become partly self-supporting, his mother having died about the time of his birth and his father having passed away when the lad was only ten years old. He acquired a hardly-gained common school education, but seems to have inherited a heritage of love of learning from his father and grandfather, and spent what leisure time he could get in reading and study, when he was not employed in the coal mines in the vicinity of his home. He received some support from his maternal grandfather, Llewellyn W. Jones, who was born in Virginia and became a pioneer in Fayette County, West Virginia, where he acquired 10,000 acres of land and many slaves, but met a tragic death by drowning in the Mississippi River. Eventually Frank Scott Cooper accumulated sufficient funds with which to pursue a course at the University of West Virginia, following which he spent three years at the Medical College of Virginia, and then entered the College of Physicians and Surgeons at Baltimore, Maryland, from which he was graduated with the degree Doctor of Medicine as a member of the class of 1903. Having some knowledge of conditions in the coal regions, Doctor Cooper commenced his practice in the coal fields of Giatto, West Virginia, where he remained for about six years, and in 1908 took up his permanent residence at Roanoke. Here he opened an office and followed his profession as a physician and surgeon, and continued therein until 1914, building up an excellent practice and becoming recognized as a capable, thorough and reliable practitioner. During this time he had become increasingly interested in the automobile industry, and in 1914 formally gave up his practice to establish an agency, handling Overland, Dodge, Hudson and Essex cars. This he has developed into one of the largest enterprises of its kind in the state, and the Virginia Motor Car Company, Inc., of which he is the owner, now controls thirty-six successful and going agencies in the Old Dominion. Its remarkable growth may be attributed to Doctor Cooper's good business judgment, great industry and absolute integrity and to the thorough knowledge which he has gained through study and experience of the automobile industry in all its branches. Doctor Cooper also has a number of other important business connections and is a member of the Board of Directors of the First National Exchange Bank of Roanoke. He was one of the organizers of the large and handsome Patrick Henry Hotel, and has been vice president of the corporation since its inception. At all times he has had the civic welfare of the city thoroughly at heart, and formerly was vice president of the Chamber of Commerce. As has been noted, his career has been one of intense industry since boyhood, and he has made the most

of his opportunities, at all times preserving a love of high standards and ideals. Politics has played no part in his career and he maintains an independent stand, exercising his right of franchise by voting for the man rather than for the party. He is a York Rite Mason and Shriner and member of the Benevolent and Protective Order of Elks, and his religious faith is that of the Presbyterian Church.

In 1905 Doctor Cooper was united in marriage with Miss Elizabeth Williams, who was born in Bland County, Virginia, and educated in her native community, and to this union there have been born three children: Flora, attending the Flora McDonald School in North Carolina; Frank Scott, Jr., a graduate of Mercersburg (Pennsylvania) Academy, and now a medical student at Princeton University; and Paul S., born in 1916, who is attending public school at Roanoke.

MOSES PETER RUCKER, physician and surgeon, is a professional man of high standing, credited with many years of service in Bedford County, his home being at Bedford City.

He was born on a farm in that county June 27, 1876. The Rucker family came from France. Doctor Rucker is of Revolutionary ancestry. His parents were M. P. and Sallie Fannie (Parker) Rucker, and his grandfathers were Anthony Rucker and Joseph Parker. M. P. Rucker was a soldier in the Confederate army, and otherwise devoted his life to his farm in Bedford County, where he died in 1926. His wife passed away February 4, 1925. Of the four sons two became farmers and merchants and two physicians.

Moses Peter Rucker was educated in the Bedford High School, the New London Academy, and graduated with the M. D. degree from the Maryland Medical College in 1904. Since that year he has practiced steadily in Bedford, handling a general practice and also doing work as general surgeon for the Norfolk & Western Railway. He is a member of the Bedford County Medical Society, Medical Society of Virginia, and American Medical Association.

Doctor Rucker married June 28, 1910, Miss Mary Pryor Williams, who was born in Essex County, Virginia, descended from one of the first families in that county. Her father, William A. Williams, was an Essex County farmer. Mrs. Rucker finished her education in a girls school at Uniontown, Pennsylvania, and for two years taught at Norfolk. They have one daughter, Nancy Williams, now attending school. Doctor Rucker is a member of the Methodist Episcopal Church, is affiliated with the Masonic fraternity, Independent Order of Odd Fellows and Benevolent and Protective Order of Elks.

EDWARD L. STONE. While the art of producing impressions from characters or figures on paper or any other substance is of comparatively recent origin, less than five centuries having elapsed since the first book was issued from the press, there is proof that the principles on which it was ultimately developed existed among the ancient Assyrian nations. Printing from movable types was probably practiced in China as early as the twelfth or thirteenth century, as there are Korean books printed from movable clay or wooden types in 1317. The first book printed from cast, movable metal type was the Bible, printed by Gutenberg at Mainz, 1450-1455. Printing was taken to England in 1476 or 1477 by William Caxton, and the first

printing press set up in America was introduced by the Vicero
of Mexico, Antonio de Mendoza, in 1536.   The earliest press
in the British-American colonies was brought over for Harvard College in 1638.   In Philadelphia a press was set up in
1685 and in New York in 1693, and from that time to the present
the history of printing has been one of constant advancement and
marvelous improvement.   In this connection there is often too
much stress laid upon the inventors of new appliances, who, while
undoubtedly due to unqualified credit for their inventions, had to
have the support of the printing concerns themselves, and it is
in the latter connection that Edward L. Stone, president of the
Stone Printing and Manufacturing Company, past president of
the Chamber of Commerce, business man and book lover, of
Roanoke, should be given extended mention in any history of
Virginia.

Edward L. Stone was born at Liberty (now Bedford City),
Virginia, September 15, 1864, and after receiving a public
school education, at the age of eleven years took a job as
an apprentice in a small printing office located in his home
town.   Several years later he took a more promising position
with J. P. Bell, at that time the most progressive printer at
Lynchburg.   When the Shenandoah Valley Railroad was completed to Roanoke in June 1882, the former little way-station
took on new life, and Mr. Bell, a man of great foresight and business judgment, visioning the development and growth that was
to come, determined to open a printing office in the embryo city.
He arrived in July, 1883, bringing with him young Stone, and
they set up a printery in a small frame building on Commerce
Street, opposite the old Trout House.   The mechanical equipment of the plant consisted of two Gordon presses, a few cases
of body type, several dozen fonts of display type and the essential tools for a small office.   There had been two other small
printing offices at Roanoke, but these were soon passed by the
Bell concern, although the financial returns for the first few
years were far from satisfactory.   In 1885 Samuel G. Fields, of
Abingdon, the manager, died, and Mr. Bell appointed the twenty-
one-year-old Ed Stone to succeed him.   By 1887 the business had
expanded to such an extent that it was necessary to install two
new presses, a large amount of new type and a two horse-power
steam engine to operate the machinery.   On February 28, 1889,
the plant was entirely destroyed by fire, but this probably was a
blessing in disguise, for the firm decided to build more substan-
tially and permanently, upon Mr. Stone's advice, and a short
time after the conflagration leased the second and third floors of
the Gale Building, located on Jefferson Street, where new presses,
type and equipment were installed.   By 1890 a working force of
thirty-three persons was essential to handle the business, and in
1891, when J. P. Bell retired from the presidency, the controlling
interest was purchased by Edward L. Stone, J. B. Fishburn and
T. T. Fishburn.   At this time the capacity of the plant was
practically doubled, and Mr. Stone succeeded to the presidency,
under whose management the industry was developed into a
national business.   In September, 1891, the reorganized company removed to its own three-story brick building on Jefferson
Street, and in 1892 the corporate name of the firm was changed
to The Stone Printing and Manufacturing Company, which it
retains to this day.   Later the building on North Jefferson Street
was doubled and trebled in size to provide for the constantly
growing business, and in 1907 the present building was erected,

this being two stories and basement, with a frontage of 218 feet
and a depth of 110 feet.   At present the company employs from
150 to 200 skilled workers and is operating one of the best
equipped printing plants in America.   For many years the company has been specializing in such lines as railroad tariffs, business stationery, twelve-sheet calendars and commercial printing
in general.   Great quantities of printed matter are being produced for railroads, mining companies, banks and trust companies, and for big business concerns in general.   Recently the company added the 45-year continuous-service bar to Mr. Stone's
gold medal.

The company has long been noted for fine typography and
excellent quality of process color printing.   At the Jamestown
Tercentennial Exposition, held at Hampton Roads in 1907, the
company won the bronze medal for its exhibit.   At the Fourth
District Typothetae Federation Convention, held at Wilmington,
Delaware, April 17 and 18, 1925, the company was awarded
first prize for booklets and catalogues, and second prize for
printer's own advertising.   It also won prizes at other conventions of this organization at Winston-Salem in 1923 and at Norfolk in 1924.

Mr. Stone is an enthusiastic member and honorary vice president of the American Institute of Graphic Arts of New York
City, to the members of which the Stone Company, in 1926, presented "Keepsake No. 21," which consists of a facsimile of
"Typographia: an Ode on Printing," one of the earliest books
printed by William Parks, at Williamsburg, Virginia, and
dated 1730.   Mr. Stone with his own hands set the type matter for the introductory pages of this unique keepsake. Only
one copy of this book, which some authorities claim to have
been the first printed in Virginia, is known to be in existence,
this being in the John Carter Brown Library at Providence. By
special permission from this library Mr. Stone obtained the
photostat prints of this rare book, from which photoengravings
were made, and from these plates the keepsake was printed in the
plant of the company.   Mr. Stone's energetic work in behalf of
Typothetae and similar organizations is well known, he having
been one of the pioneers in perfecting and establishing the Standard cost system in the printing and other industries.   He was a
member of the executive council and cost commission of the
United Typothetae and Franklin Clubs of America, and is a
member of the Better Printing Committee.   For the U. T. A. he
has also served as a member of the executive committee, a member of the cost commission and a member of the legislative committee.   He was president of the Virginia Printers' Cost Congress, and was a member of the directorate of the same organization.

At his home Mr. Stone has a collection of rare books which is
quite unique and comprehensive.   The library is already famous
and is bound to become more renowned among book lovers.   Mr.
Stone knows the works of both the early printers and the great
modern printers as few other book collectors know them, and
to hear him talk on this subject is a pleasure for anyone interested in the "Art Preservative of all Arts."   Mr. Stone is a
member of the National Geographic Society; a life member of
the Virginia Historical Society, Richmond; Florida Historical
Society; Westmoreland Club, Richmond; Manufacturers' Club,
Philadelphia; Huntingdon Valley Country Club, Philadelphia;
American Institute of Graphic Arts (honorary vice president),

New York City; Grolier Club, New York City; director member
(honorary), University Club, Roanoke; Roanoke Country Club;
Roanoke Dinner Dance Club; Life Member Roanoke Realtors
Association (honorary); Associated Advertising Clubs of the
World; Bibliographical Society of London, England; Miami An-
glers' Club, Miami; Roanoke German Club, Roanoke; Interna-
tional Benjamin Franklin Society, New York City; a charter
member of the Lee Highway Association, Washington; Virginia
Historic Highway Association, Lynchburg; Board of Trustees,
Roanoke Community Fund; Board of Trustees, Committee to
Assist the Blind; The Virginia Academy of Science, Richmond;
Past-President, Chamber of Commerce, Roanoke; President,
Secretary, Treasurer, "an' everything," Quadraginta Club, New
York and Roanoke; Southwest Virginia Historical Society, Roan-
oke; Chairman City Planning and Zoning Commissions,
Roanoke.

Mr. Stone's activities are not confined to the printing com-
pany. He is a vice-president and director of the First National
Exchange Bank, Roanoke, the Walker Machine and Foundry
Corporation. He is also a director of the Virginia Bridge and
Iron Company, Roanoke; the Borderland Coal Corporation, the
Roanoke Auditorium Company, and many others. His civic ac-
tivities are numerous, and he is also identified with several civic
and fraternal organizations.

STONEWALL JACKSON GILL, M. D. For twenty-one years Dr.
Stonewall Jackson Gill has carried on a general practice in Roanoke, and when he came here it was as the experienced physician,
ripened by years of experience in his profession and service to
humanity. During the long period he has ministered to the
people of Roanoke he has won and holds their warm esteem and
approval, and there are very few men held as high as he by the
general public. He was born in Amherst County, Virginia,
December 16, 1861, a son of Curtis and Elizabeth (Martin)
Gill, both natives of Amherst County, now deceased. During
the earlier part of his life he was a contractor, and in addition
to erecting the first houses in Rockbridge and Elm Springs he
had contracts for building houses and milling plants all over
Virginia and West Virginia. After he married he bought a
farm on Indian Creek, and the remainder of his life was devoted
to farming. A man fond of outdoor life, during the last fifteen
years he lived he made it a practice to spend three months of
each year camping at the breakwaters of Big Piney River, a
number of his friends joining him in the outing. Of the nine
children born to him and his wife five are living, and Doctor
Gill is the youngest born. Both he and his wife were long very
active members of the Methodist Episcopal Church, South, and
he was a very real pillar of the church, and carried his faith into
his everyday life. Too old himself for military service during
the war between the states, his son, Thomas Gill, enlisted at
the age of sixteen years, during the latter part of the war. An
ardent Democrat, he took part in politics, although not an office
seeker. His father, Jonas Gill, was born in Chesterfield County,
Virginia, and became a prosperous farmer. The maternal
grandfather, Lowe Martin, was born in Amherst County, and
was a farmer by occupation. Although he owned many slaves,
one of the great-grandfathers of Doctor Gill was so impressed
by the evils of slavery that he set free 100 and sent those who
wished to go to Liberia at his expense.

Doctor Gill attended school in Harrisonburg, Virginia, and took his degree in medicine in Vanderbilt University, Nashville, Tennessee. Later he took post-graduate work in Georgetown University of Medicine, Washington City. He began the practice of his profession in Lowesville, Virginia, but after three years settled in Bedford County, Virginia, and there he remained in active practice for seventeen years, coming then to Roanoke, where he has found congenial surroundings and a large measure of success.

In 1887 Doctor Gill married Miss Lillian Page, who was born in Nelson County, Virginia, a daughter of James Page, a farmer. The following children have been born to Doctor and Mrs. Gill: Charlie Briggs, who died at the age of twenty-one years; Elizabeth H., who is in the hospital with her brother; Dr. Elburne G., a practicing physician of Roanoke; and Fannie Lou, who married Dr. W. H. Stryker, a dental surgeon of Williamsburg, Virginia. For four years Mrs. Stryker taught domestic science in William and Mary College, Williamsburg.

Doctor and Mrs. Gill belong to Cavalry Baptist Church. He is a Mason, a Knight of Pythias and an Elk. The Roanoke County Medical Society, the Virginia State Medical Society and the Southern Medical Society all hold his membership. During the past few years Doctor Gill has become very much interested in horticulture and owns an apple orchard in Bedford County which is bearing heavily, in 1927 producing about 18,000 bushels. When he bought the land he paid $2.25 per acre for it, and during the thirty-five years he has owned it, it has steadily advanced until today, with all his improvements upon it, this is a very valuable property.

ELBURNE GRAY GILL graduated from medical college in 1916, and has enjoyed a steadily growing reputation in his profession at Roanoke, and has also been active in the club and civic affairs of that city.

Doctor Gill was born at Sedalia, Bedford County, Virginia, October 21, 1891, son of Dr. Stonewall Jackson and Lillian Gill, and grandson of Mr. and Mrs. Curtis Gill of Amherst County, and of Mr. and Mrs. James W. Page of Nelson County.

Doctor Gill attended the Roanoke City High School and from 1912 to 1916 was a student in the medical department of Vanderbilt University at Nashville, Tennessee, where he obtained the degree Doctor of Medicine. In his work at Roanoke he has largely specialized in diseases of the eye, ear, nose and throat. In 1926 he was responsible for the construction of the Gill Memorial Eye, Ear and Throat Hospital, which is the only institution of its kind in Virginia.

Doctor Gill is a member of the American College of Surgeons and in 1921 was president of the Virginia Society of Ophthalmology and Oto-Laryngology.

He is a director of the Liberty Trust Company of Roanoke, was president of the University Club in 1921 and the Roanoke Lions Club in 1925. He is a Democrat, a Mason and Shriner, member of the Roanoke Country Club, and is a deacon in the Calvary Baptist Church and teacher of the Young Men's Bible Class, which has a membership of one hundred.

Mr. Gill married Miss Ruth Meals, a daughter of I. J. Meals, of Roanoke. She is a graduate of the Mary Baldwin Seminary at Staunton, Virginia. They have two daughters, Edith Page and Martha Vaughan Gill.

PAUL C. HUBARD. There are, unquestionably, men of natural force found in every prosperous community, who by reason of their inherent ability, by the use of their brains and the soundness of their judgment, attain distinction and acquire authority. They are men who industriously work for an end, and in helping themselves add to the sum of comfort and happiness for all about them. These quiet, resourceful men are the dependence of the whole social fabric, for their efforts not only bring into being the substantial industries that support commerce, but conduct along the safe and sane channels which assure public prosperity and general contentment. They may be men of versatile gifts and talents of a high order in many directions, but it is their soundness, their vitality and their steadfastness that sum up the whole and make them such important factors in the work of their communities. Such a man is Paul C. Hubard, proprietor of the Hubard Foundry & Machine Works, Incorporated, of which he is president.

Paul C. Hubard was born in Nelson County, Virginia, December 22, 1865, a son of William B. and Eliza (Callaway) Hubard, natives of Buckingham and Nelson counties, respectively, and both are deceased. The father was a planter and a man of prominence in Nelson County. Both he and his wife were active members of the Episcopal Church, and he was a member of the Masonic fraternity. In political faith he was a Democrat. Of the eleven children born to the parents three survive, those in addition to Paul C. Hubard being: Mrs. Sommerville, a widow, who lives on a farm, is the relict of Rev. George S. Sommerville, a clergyman of the Episcopal Church; and Anna, who is unmarried, is employed in the Forestry Department in Washington City.

Paul C. Hubard was educated in a local normal school and college, and his first work was done in the Glenmorgan foundry, where he learned draughting, completing his work in this line in Franklin Institute, Philadelphia, Pennsylvania. Returning to his old foundry, he remained there for a number of years, and was its designer. He also was a practical machinist, and became so adept that he also served as an instructor in the Virginia Polytechnic Institute for several years. During all of this time, however, he was steadily working toward the end of establishing his own business, and this he was able to do in 1896, when he opened the Hubard Foundry & Machine Works in Lynchburg. From the start the business was a success, and in 1904 he incorporated it, and is now president and general manager; C. W. Gooch, vice president; and A. B. Dabney, secretary and treasurer. A general line of machine work is done, and the quality is rated very high.

Mr. Hubard married in Richmond in the latter part of the last century Miss Louise Carrington, a native of that city, and a daughter of Dr. George Carrington, one of the prominent physicians and surgeons of Richmond and Rustburg until his death. Very prominent in Masonry, he at one time held the office of grand secretary of his order. Three children have been born to Mr. and Mrs. Hubard, but one only survives, she being Eleanor, who is attending school. A man of strong religious convictions, Mr. Hubard belongs to the International Bible Students Association. He is a Mason and a Knight of Pythias. While he votes the Democratic ticket and supports his party's principles, he is not an aspirant for political honors. A man of uncommon ability, kindly disposition and broad sympathies, he

Linwood D. Keyser

knows how to win the approval of men and earn and retain their friendship. His interest in Lynchburg and its development is warm and sincere and he has ever contributed generously toward the advancement of those measures which appeal to him as worthy ones. His success in life is all the more noteworthy in that it has been attained entirely through his own efforts.

LINWOOD DICKENS KEYSER, of Roanoke, took his A. B. degree at the University of Virginia in 1914, the M. D. degree at Johns Hopkins University in 1918, and has also been accorded a distinction readily recognized by all members of the medical and surgical profession, the degree Master of Science in Pathology from the University of Minnesota in 1921, bestowed in recognition of the several years of active connection with the Mayo Clinic.

Doctor Keyser was born at Victoria, Texas, September 26, 1893, but is a member of an old and well known family of Virginia. His great-grandfather, Christopher Keyser, was an elder and minister of the Baptist Church. Doctor Keyser's grandfather, Henry Marcellus Keyser, was a doctor of medicine and was born in Page County, Virginia, January 22, 1835. He graduated from the Cincinnati Medical College, later attended the Jefferson Medical College of Philadelphia, and in addition to practicing medicine was superintendent of schools in Page County, and for five terms a member of the State Legislature. He died in 1898.

The father of Doctor Linwood Dickens Keyser is Ernest Linwood Keyser, a well known business man of Roanoke. He was born in Page County October 21, 1868, attended the New Market Polytechnic Institute, graduated in pharmacy at Chicago in 1892, and for ten years was in the drug business at San Antonio and Victoria, Texas. In 1902 he located at Roanoke, and in recent years has given most of his time to drug and chemical manufacturing. He is president of the Keyser Chemical Company and has also been president of the Keyser-Warren Drug Company, and an official in the Keyser-Holback Drug Company. Ernest L. Keyser has been prominent in the Democratic party for many years, having been a delegate to the National Conventions of 1908 and 1912, was elected to the Virginia House of Delegates in 1910, and made himself especially valuable to Roanoke while in the Legislature. He is a Royal Arch thirty-second degree, Knight Templar and Shriner Mason, member of the B. P. O. Elks, and he is a member of the Baptist Church, while his wife is a member of St. John's Episcopal Church. He married, in 1889, Lillie Dickens, daughter of M. H. Dickens, of Bee County, Texas.

Their only son, Linwood Dickens Keyser, has spent most of his life at Roanoke, having been about six years of age when his parents established their home here on returning from Texas. Doctor Keyser graduated with the A. B. degree from the University of Virginia in 1914. He took his degree at Johns Hopkins University School of Medicine at Baltimore in 1918, and the degree Master of Science in Pathology was bestowed by the University of Minnesota in 1921.

During the World war Doctor Keyser was commissioned a first lieutenant in the Medical Reserve Corps, but was not called to active duty. From June, 1917, to March, 1918, he was an interne in the Church Home and Infirmary, Baltimore; June, 1918, to July, 1919, was an interne in the Johns Hopkins Hos-

pital at Baltimore, and from July to December, 1919, was
assistant resident surgeon at the Peter Bent Brigham Hospital
in Boston. He was resident surgeon at the New York Post-
Graduate Hospital from January to June, 1920, and on September 8, 1920, entered the Mayo Foundation as a fellow in pathology. He had a range of service and experience with the Foundation lasting several years, including nine and a half months
in surgical pathology, nine months in urology, three months in
general diagnosis, nine months in operative surgery, three
months in orthopedic surgery, and twenty-seven months in experimental surgery and pathology, this last work being carried
on in connection with his duties in other special departments.

Doctor Keyser on July 1, 1923, left the Mayo Foundation and
is now attending surgeon and surgical pathologist at the Roanoke Hospital. He is a member of the Roanoke Academy of
Medicine, Southwest Virginia Medical Society, Virginia State
Medical Society, Tri-State Medical Society, Southern Medical
Association and American Medical Association. He belongs to
the Association of Resident and Ex-resident Physicians of the
Mayo Clinics. He is a member of the American Urological Society
and belongs to the Sigma Xi honorary fraternity and Phi Chi
medical fraternity and is a fellow of the American College of
Surgeons. Doctor Keyser is one of the brilliant men of his profession in Virginia today. In addition to his work in laboratories, clinics and the general routine of his service he has contributed about twenty-five articles to various medical and surgical journals, chiefly on surgery and urological subjects.

While at the University of Virginia Doctor Keyser was a
member of the Raven Society and acted as student assistant in
chemistry during 1912-14. He is a Scottish Rite Mason and
Shriner, member of the Lions Club, Chamber of Commerce, University Club, Shenandoah Club, Country Club and St. John's
Episcopal Church. He is also assistant surgeon-in-chief to the
Sons of Confederate Veterans.

HOWARD SEVILLE HUNT for many years was in the railway
train service, being associated with some of the great trunk
lines of railway traversing Virginia and other eastern states,
was prompt, vigilant and efficient, and enjoyed the esteem of
both his associates and superiors.

He was born in North Carolina August 2, 1866,, and lost his
life while in the line of duty at Okonoko, West Virginia, in February, 1907. His father, Samuel H. Hunt, was born in Alabama,
entered the Confederate army when young, and at the end of
the war was mustered out in North Carolina, met his wife there,
Frances Ellerson, and after a few years in that state moved to
Virginia and spent the rest of his life as a merchant and farmer.
Howard S. Hunt was the oldest in a family of eight children,
seven sons and one daughter. He finished his education in the
Fishburne Military Academy at Waynesboro, Virginia. As a
youth he learned telegraphy with the Chesapeake & Ohio Railway at Lynchburg, spent two years there, and resigned from
that branch of the service to become a locomotive engineer. He
was an engineer for the Chesapeake & Ohio several years and
then with the Baltimore & Ohio, having an important run between Cumberland and Brunswick, Maryland, and lost his life
in a wreck on that division. He was a popular member of the
Brotherhood of Locomotive Engineers, belonged to the Masonic

fraternity, was a Democrat, and both he and his wife were active members of the Baptist Church.

He married at Crozet, Virginia, in February, 1892, Miss Dora Lee Wood, who survives him and resides at 1529 Morris Avenue in Norfolk. Mrs. Hunt was educated in the Gordansville Female Institute in Virginia and the Central Female Institute at Clinton, Mississippi. Her father, William H. Wood, was a merchant at Granada, Mississippi, and had served in the cavalry in the Confederate army during the Civil war. Her mother was Mary Elizabeth Robertson, a native of Virginia, and Mrs. Hunt is one of two living children. Mr. and Mrs. Hunt had five children: Samuel, who served overseas during the World war in the Signal Corps, is now an electrician living in New Jersey, and by his marriage with Amy Street has two children, Russell Hunt and Margarett Hunt; Harvey Lee, a chemist, who served two years in the Chemical Warfare Division in laboratory work during the World war, is a member of the firm Norfolk Testing Laboratories, and married May Hudson; William Hamilton, assistant manager of the Monticello, Norfolk's largest hotel, married Reva Hawkins, of Charlottesville, Virginia, and has one daughter, Marcia; Miss Eunice May lives with her mother, and James Wood is a student of aviation.

H. HILTON ANDERSON. Among the men prominently identified with the real estate, loan and insurance business of Fairfax County, one who has at all times maintained high ideals of business integrity is H. Hilton Anderson, of the firm of H. H. Anderson & Company of East Falls Church. His career has been signalized by participation in a number of large and important transactions and by strict adherence to the ethics and amenities of his business, and as a result he has not only won personal success and prominence, but has also attracted and held the confidence and esteem of the people of his community.

Mr. Anderson was born March 11, 1875, on a farm in Rappahannock County, Virginia, and is a son of H. B. and Eugenia (Griffin) Anderson, natives of the same county. H. B. Anderson was reared on a farm, on which he worked until the outbreak of the war between the states, at which time he, with his brothers Peyton and Joseph, enlisted in the Confederate army and went almost immediately to the field of conflict. Although Fort Sumter had been fired upon April 12, 1861, and the first blood had been shed April 19 in a street attack on the Sixth Massachusetts Regiment, which was on its way to Washington, it is thought that Peyton Anderson was the first soldier wounded in the war in actual conflict between forces of the South and North. His wound was not a fatal one, but his brother Joseph later met a soldier's death on the field of battle. Following the close of the war H. B. Anderson returned to Rappahannock County, where he resumed his farming operations, and also engaged in the operation of a sawmill. These activities he continued until his retirement several years before his death, which occurred February 17, 1909. Mrs. Anderson had passed away years before, February 18, 1886.

The education of H. Hilton Anderson was acquired in the public schools of Rappahannock County, and he was reared in a rural atmosphere. It was natural that he should adopt farming in his youth, and he remained with his parents until reaching the age of twenty-six years, at which time he moved to Fairfax County. In 1902 he took up his residence at Falls

Church, where he embarked in the feed and lumber business, and continued therein for about twenty years, with much success. In 1922 he received his introduction to the real estate loan and insurance business with Garland L. Kendrick, and in January, 1923, bought out the business, which he has conducted with much success to the present. While this is an old established business, it has prospered most materially since Mr. Anderson became its owner, and the firm of H. H. Anderson & Company now occupies a place among the leaders in its field in Fairfax County. Mr. Anderson applies himself strictly to his business and has few outside interests, not being a club or fraternity man. He is a staunch Democrat in his political convictions and a member of the Methodist Episcopal Church, while the members of his family are Baptists.

On February 21, 1905, Mr. Anderson married Miss Lulu Wileorbin, daughter of W. B. and Emma N. (Spillman) Wileorbin, natives of Rappahannock County. Mr. Anderson's father-in-law has always been a farmer, and is now eighty-four years of age, his worthy wife also surviving. He is a Confederate veteran of the war between the states. To Mr. and Mrs. Anderson there has come one son, E. James, born May 16, 1913, who is attending school.

WILLIAM POWER TYREE. Although unknown to the present generation of business men of Virginia, his death having occurred in 1906, the late William Power Tyree was one of the strong and forceful men of his day at Danville, where he was engaged for a number of years in the wholesale brokerage business. His career, cut short by death when he was only forty-five years of age, was an active, varied and useful one, and in each of his several avenues of activity he won the respect of men who admire and appreciate the abilities of others.

Mr. Tyree was born at Danville, Virginia, in April, 1861, and was a son of David and Hannah (O'Brien) Tyree. His parents were born and married in Dublin, Ireland, where David Tyree was a merchant, and following their union immigrated to the United States and settled at Danville, where Mr. Tyree continued his business as a merchant until his death. William Power Tyree was the fourth child in a family of eight children, among whom was a son Tom, who rose to a captaincy in the Confederate army during the war between the states, and another son, David, who was engaged in business affairs at Danville for many years.

The public schools of Danville, as well as a private school, furnished William Power Tyree with his educational training, following which he became teacher of mathematics at the Baptist College of Danville, a position which he retained for two years. He then entered the Commercial Bank of Danville, with which he remained until elected city tax collector of Danville. When he left that office four years later he embarked in the wholesale grocery business as a broker, and continued therein until his death May 2, 1906. Although he was a Democrat in his political views, Mr. Tyree was a life long fighter in the cause of temperance and for many years was the head of the prohibition party at Danville. Fraternally he was a popular member of the Knights of the Maccabees. As a man of civic pride and public spirit, he was one of the enthusiastic workers in the Chamber of Commerce and the Board of Trade, and his associates in the business world frequently came to him for counsel and guidance. He belonged to Epiphany Episcopal Church of

C. L. Robinson.

Danville, in which he was superintendent of the Sunday school
and missed only one Sunday in thirteen consecutive years.

On July 2, 1891, in Halifax County, Virginia, Mr. Tyree was
united in marriage with Miss Jennie C. Clarke, of that county,
daughter of E. H. Clarke, a prominent plantation owner. The
Clarke family is descended from an ancestor who sat in the
House of Burgesses, and the family resided in Cumberland
County, Virginia, prior to the War of the Revolution. E. H.
Clarke was a member of the Home Guards stationed at Rich-
mond during the war between the states, and he and his wife,
Mary Robinson, of Campbell County, Virginia, were the parents
of three sons, Frank, Thomas and Samuel, all of whom were
soldiers of the Confederacy, and all now farmers of Halifax
County. To Mr. and Mrs. Tyree there was born one son, William
Power, who was educated at Danville and Norfolk and since
his twenty-first year has been manager of the tractor department of the Ford Motor Company at Norfolk. He married Mary
Elizabeth Pritchard, of Pantego, Beaufort County, North Carolina. Since the death of her husband Mrs. Tyree has resided at
Norfolk, where she has an attractive home at 533 Maryland
Avenue. She is a member of the Episcopal Church, and has been
active and helpful in its work.

CHARLES LEE ROBINSON. To the civic and industrial advancement and prestige of the City of Winchester, judicial center of
Frederick County, the late Charles L. Robinson made splendid
contribution. He was a business man of remarkable initiative
and executive ability, and had the courage to carry forward
important industrial enterprises to success in the face of objec-
tive predictions of his failure. He developed two of the leading
industries of Winchester and was one of the most valued and
honored citizens of this historic old city at the time of his death,
which occurred April 1, 1922. It is obvious that a tribute to
his achievement and to his memory will be a fitting contribution
to this publication.

Mr. Robinson was born in the State of Indiana, January 1,
1855, and was a boy when the family home was established at
Fairmont, Marion County, West Virginia, which state was at the
time still a part of Virginia. His father, Francis Harrison
Robinson, came to West Virginia as a representative of the
construction and service of the Baltimore & Ohio Railroad, with
which he long continued his alliance, both he and his wife having continued their residence to Fairmont until their death.

To the public schools of Fairmont the subject of this memoir
was indebted for his early education, and even as a boy he manifested exceptional mental alertness, self-reliance and tenacity
of purpose—attributes that distinctly marked and conserved
the success of his later business career. His early experience
in business affairs was gained at Fairmont, and there he initiated his independent activities by engaging in the retail coal and
ice business on a modest scale. He made this venture a success,
but he constantly was on the outlook for broader opportunities,
with the result that eventually, in 1902, he removed with his
family to Winchester, Virginia, and entered upon the vigorous
and constructive business career that led to his advancement
to the status of one of the leading figures in the industrial and
commercial life of this community. He came to Frederick
County before the apple industry of this section of the state
had developed to its present large and important proportions.

Though discouraged in such action by other men of affairs at Winchester, Mr. Robinson here purchased a small ice manufacturing plant that had been operated with negligible success. In his initial stage of developing this enterprise he encountered many perplexities and discouragements, but he had faith in himself and his judgment and, as ever, refused to be baffled or dismayed by adverse conditions. He built up a prosperous ice and storage business and likewise turned his attention to developing other enterprises that had been semi-failures under previous control. He believed in Winchester and its great future, and proved that he had a reason for this faith. In 1907 Mr. Robinson bought the Winchester Steam Laundry, and under his resourceful and vigorous policies this likewise was made a success. The Snapp Foundry next attracted him as an investment. This likewise had proved a waning industrial enterprise, but he promptly infused his characteristic energy and progressiveness into its management, with the ultimate result that it now stands as one of the leading industrial concerns of this section of Virginia. He purchased this property in 1910, and in the upbuilding of the business he had the effective co-operation of his sons, under whose control the business has been successfully continued since his death.

It was in April, 1902, that Mr. Robinson made his initial business venture in Winchester, by purchasing the modest ice plant that as to prove the nucleus around which has been developed the substantial and important enterprise now conducted under the corporate title of the C. L. Robinson Ice & Cold Storage Corporation. The original manufactory of this concern had a production capacity of only ten tons of ice daily, and the output was used almost exclusively in local consumption. The capacity of the present modern plant in 100 tons of ice daily. In connection with the enterprise Mr. Robinson proceeded with the development also of a cold-storage plant, to meet the demands of apple-growers of this section of the state. In 1905 he established a cold-storage plant with a capacity of 20,000 barrels, and this was used almost entirely for the storage of apples for market demands. By subsequent expansions the capacity of the Winchester storage plant has been increased to 200,000 barrels, and the scope of the business has been increased through the operation of a well equipped storage plant at Berryville, Clarke County, Virginia, and another at Charles Town, West Virginia. In 1912 Mr. Robinson and his sons assumed control of the Berryville Ice & Refrigerating Company, and later developed the prosperous ice and storage business at Charles Town, both of these plants being of modern equipment and large capacity. In 1911 was effected the incorporation of the business under the present title of C. L. Robinson Ice & Cold Storage Corporation, the stock of which is retained entirely by the Robinson family. Of this corporation, the service of which has been of inestimable value in affording market outlet for the great apple industry, Mr. Robinson continued the president until his death, and its operations are based on a capital stock of $150,000. In 1917 Mr. Robinson bought the entire capital stock of the business at Berryville and also of the holdings at Winchester and Charles Town. The association of the Robinson family with the apple industry became still closer when, in 1910 the subject of this memoir acquired his first orchard, and since that year the family holdings of bearing orchards have been increased to 1,200 acres,—in Frederick

County, Virginia; Jefferson and Berkeley counties, West Virginia; and Washington and Allegany counties, Maryland. In these splendid orchards are produced the finest types of apples, including New Town Pippins, Grimes Golden, Golden Delicious, Stark's Delicious, King David, Jonathans, Stayman Wine Saps, York Imperials, Ben Davis, Yellow Transparent, Dutchess, Wealthy, McIntosh, Rome Beauty, etc.

In 1910 Mr. Robinson purchased the Snapp Foundry, which is now incorporated under this title and the stock of which is owned by his family. The Snapp Foundry was established in 1865, by F. R. Snapp, and the original plant stood on the site of the present large and modern plant. Mr. Robinson acquired the property from the heirs of the founder of the business, and as owner he entrusted the operations of the foundry to efficient managers, this arrangement having continued until his death. From a run-down status he developed the business into a substantial and important industry, and the work of progress has been effectively carried forward by his sons since he himself passed away. After the death of Mr. Robinson the business of the Snapp Foundry was reorganized and incorporated, and his widow became its president, his daughter Mary E. was made vice president, and his son Charles A. became secretary and treasurer. The capital stock of the Snapp Foundry is $15,000, and the son Frank B. is now president of the corporation, while the son Charles A. continues not only as secretary and treasurer but also as general manager. The major development of this enterprise has occurred within the past eight years, and the foundry now maintains a corps of thirty employes, most of whom are skilled workmen. The establishment manufacturers gray-iron castings, and these are shipped over a wide territory, from Albany, New York, to New Orleans, Louisiana, and as far west as Butte, Montana. In the machine shop are maintained the best of modern facilities for the handling of general repair work for the industries of this section of the state, and the corporation has also provision for the fabrication and erection of structural steel, in which connection it has executed important contracts and provided service that previously had required recourse to concerns in outside cities. The company figures likewise as jobbers of machine supplies and material, and this effective service obviates former expenditure of time, with incidental financial losses, in connection with providing supplies that formerly had to be shipped from distant points.

The late Charles L. Robinson is survived by his widow, whose maiden name was Marie Elizabeth Barnes and who was born and reared at Fairmont, West Virginia, she being still a resident of Winchester and being a loved figure in the social life of this community. Of the five children the eldest is Frederick A., who is now vice president of both the Snapp Foundry and the C. L. Robinson Ice & Cold Storage Company; Frank B. is president of these companies and maintains his home at Charles Town, West Virginia; Harry D. is treasurer of both corporations; Charles A. is secretary, treasurer and general manager of the Snapp Foundry; and Miss Mary Elizabeth remains with her widowed mother in the attractive home at Winchester. All of the children were born at Fairmont, West Virginia. Frederick A. married Miss Mamie Brown, of Winchester; Frank B., married Miss Blanch Boxwell, of the same city; and Harry D. married Miss Louise Hall, of Fairmont, West Virginia. Charles A., youngest of the sons, is familiarly known by his second personal name, Arthur, and he married Miss Reba Beam, of Carlisle, Pennsylvania, in which city he and his brother Harry D. attended Dickerson College. All of the sons are affiliated with the Masonic fraternity, including the Mystic Shrine.

The late Charles L. Robinson was a zealous member of the Methodist Episcopal Church, as is also his widow, and he was a Knight Templar Mason, besides being a Noble of the Mystic Shrine. He was affiliated also with the Knights of Pythias, the Independent Order of Odd Fellows and the Improved Order of Red Men. He was a business man of exceptional ability, was loyal and public-spirited as a citizen, and his sterling character found expression in kindly and generous human helpfulness, ever extended in an unostentatious way. His genial and buoyant personality gained to him the high regard of all who came within the sphere of his influence.

HON. WILSON MAHONE FARR, commonwealth's attorney of Fairfax County, and one of the ablest men practicing at the bar of Fairfax, is a man fortunate in his choice of a profession. Its employments are congenial to him, and he follows them with unflagging interest and zest. To him the work of the law is not drudgery, but a source of keen intellectual pleasure, and its controversies afford him frequent opportunities to show his ability to meet his opponent upon any ground. It is his rare good fortune to be a man in love with his work and to find in it adequate and satisfying occupation for all his faculties. So generally recognized are his unusual capabilities, his uprightness and his unflinching courage that he is regarded as the ideal man for the important office he holds, a fact attested by his election and reelection to it during a period of over six years.

Mr. Farr was born in Henrico County, Virginia, October 17, 1884, while his parents were residing there temporarily, but his family belongs to Fairfax County. He is a son of Richard Ratcliffe Farr, born at Farr's Crossroads, Fairfax County, Virginia. During the second year of the war between the states, when only a little over sixteen years old, his father enlisted in Company B, of General Mosby's command. Seriously wounded in the Blazer fight, he was paroled at the close of the war, at the time being only in his eighteenth year. After the close of the war he took a prominent part in local affairs, was active in politics, and served in the State Legislature for a number of terms. Another honor was his, that of being one of the early state superintendents of public instruction, holding that important office for the term beginning January 1, 1882, and ending January 1, 1886. He married Miss Margaret E. Malone, born in Buncombe County, North Carolina, a daughter of John and Ann Rebecca (Gooding) Malone of Fairfax County.

Growing up in Fairfax, Wilson M. Farr attended its public schools, and later the Central High School, Washington City, after which he entered Roanoke College, Salem, Virginia, and remained there through the sophomore year. His legal education was taken in Georgetown University of Law, Washington, and he was graduated therefrom in 1907, with the degree of Bachelor of Laws. For the term of 1906-07 Mr. Farr taught school in the town of Fairfax, and in 1906, he passed the state bar examinations and was admitted to the bar. From then on he has been engaged in a general practice with offices in Fairfax, with increasing success. In 1922 he was appointed commonwealth's attorney to fill out an unexpired term, was reelected without opposition in 1924, and again reelected in 1927, and is the present incumbent of the office.

On November 24, 1915, Mr. Farr married Miss Edith Wiley, a daughter of Robert Wiley (a member of Jackson's Corps) and Mary E. (Lee) Wiley, and they have two daughters: Edith Malone Farr, who was born September 7, 1923; and Ann Ratcliffe Farr, who was born November 22, 1924. Mr. and Mrs. Farr maintain their home in Fairfax, and here they welcome their many friends with true Southern hospitality. Mr. Farr belongs to the Belle Haven Country Club, the Fairfax Chamber of Commerce, the Sons of Confederate Veterans, the Virginia State Bar Association and is a director of the National Bank of Fairfax.

ROBERT LEE STRANGE. The late Robert Lee Strange was given but a little more than half a century in this world, but during that time he accomplished much, and left behind him the memory of a life well spent, of duty faithfully discharged, and of good citizenship proved and sustained. He was born in Fluvanna County, Virginia, in 1866, and died in Richmond, Virginia, in November, 1923. He was a son of William George Strange, a commission merchant, saw-mill owner and prominent business man of Richmond for many years. Descended in direct line from Gen. John Bony Strange, of Revolutionary fame, Robert Lee Strange was proud of the connection and that other members of the family were notable, one of them more nearly in his generation being his father's cousin, who was clerk of the County Court of Fluvanna County for many years.

Educated in the public schools of his native county, Robert Lee Strange grew up to useful manhood, and when old enough for its responsibilities went into the saw-mill business with his father in Dinwiddie County, Virginia, maintaining that connection until after the death of his father, when he went to Goochland County and engaged in farming for himself. He also bought and sold and fattened cattle for market. Still later he reentered the saw-mill business and remained in it for ten years, and then he and H. S. Holland began quarrying stone from the quarry in Goochland County, and in this occupation he completed his business career, retiring in 1922 and locating in Richmond. While he was in the last named line he served as postmaster and freight agent for the Chesapeake & Ohio Railroad at the station adjacent to his quarry. In political faith he was a Democrat, and quite active locally. However, he was not a man who sought publicity, but rather tried to do his duty as privately and unostentatiously as possible. His home and his family came first with him, and with his loved ones he found his greatest happiness. A devoted husband, a careful father and a kind friend, he was a man whose loss was deeply felt when death removed him from the midst of those who knew and appreciated him.

On December 28, 1899, Mr. Strange married Miss Kathrine Tillman, a daughter of P. R. and Sarah Virginia (Brown) Tillman, and granddaughter on her mother's side of James Dabney Brown, a private courier for Gen. Robert E. Lee during the war between the states, an honor his descendants deeply appreciate. Mrs. Strange was educated in public and private schools in Goochland County, and she is a lady deeply interested in current events, a good mother and neighbor. Four children were born to Mr. and Mrs. Strange: Virginia, who married Elmer Kiser, of Tazewell, Virginia; Bernice, who is a registered nurse, graduated from the Retreat of the Sick Hospital, Richmond, class of 1925, and engaged in the practice of her profession; Catherine, who is in the employ of the Chesapeake & Ohio Railroad; and Robert Lee, Junior, at home, aged ten years.

HENRY LOUIS SMITH since 1912 has had the distinction of presiding over one of the South's finest institutions of learning, Washington and Lee University at Lexington.

Doctor Smith was born at Greensboro, North Carolina, July 30, 1859, son of Jacob Henry and Mary Kelly (Watson) Smith and a great-grandson of Henry Louis Smith, a pioneer of the Shenandoah Valley of Virginia. Jacob Henry Smith was born in the Shenandoah Valley and his wife was a daughter of Judge Egbert R. Watson, long a member of the bar of Charlottesville. Jacob Henry Smith gave his life to the Presbyterian ministry in Virginia and North Carolina. He was the father of five sons who gained eminence in the ministry and in the learned professions, all five listed in "Who's Who in America." One of them was Dr. Samuel M. Smith, of Columbia, South Carolina, who was known as a scholar, preacher and orator in the Southern Presbyterian Church; another was the late Dr. Charles Alphonso Smith, at one time professor of English in the University of Virginia and in the United States Naval Academy, who died in 1924; another is Dr. Egbert Watson Smith, secretary of Foreign Missions of the Presbyterian Church in the United States since 1911; and a fourth is Dr. Hay Watson Smith, of Little Rock Arkansas.

Henry Louis Smith was reared in a home of high ideals and of religious influences, and learned to appreciate the qualities of intellectual culture when a boy. He also had the interests of a normal boy, participating in all outdoor sports both in school and college. He received his early education at Greensboro, entered Davidson College of North Carolina in 1877, and was graduated in 1881 with the A. B. degree maxima cum laude and winning gold medals for his work in Greek, mathematics and English essay. For five years he was principal of a classical academy at Selma, North Carolina, and in 1886 Davidson College bestowed upon him the Master of Arts degree and called him to the chair of physics and geology. He held that chair until 1901. From 1898 to 1901 he was vice president of the college, and from 1901 to 1912, president. In the meantime he had continued his post-graduate studies at the University of Virginia, which awarded him the Doctor of Philosophy degree in 1891, his major work being in physics and geology. He is credited with being the first scientist in the United States to use the X-Ray in medical and surgical cases, and made the first X-Ray photograph ever taken in the South. He did laboratory work at Cornell and Harvard Universities in 1893 and 1894. He was president of the North Carolina Teachers Assembly in 1889, and of the Association of Virginia Colleges in 1914-15. The University of North Carolina awarded him the honorary LL. D. degree in 1906. He has been vice president of the American College Association, is a member of the American Academy of Political and Social Science, American Society for Broader Education, American Association for the Advancement of Science, and is a Phi Beta Kappa, Phi Delta Theta and Omicron Delta Kappa.

In the closing months of the World war much influence was credited, in the weakening of the German popular morale, to the widespread distribution of pamphlets behind the lines, dropped from balloons. This device was originated by Doctor Smith, who for it was awarded the prize offered by the National Security League for the best means of distributing among the German people such propaganda. Doctor Smith is the

W. Lewis Schafer, M.D.

author of many articles and bulletins on educational and scientific subjects and a widely known lecturer on educational and scientific subjects. He has for many years been a ruling elder in the Presbyterian Church. In 1921, representing the governor of Virginia, he headed the delegation which formally presented to the government and people of Great Britain in Trafalgar Square, a bronze duplicate of Houdon's statue of Washington.

He married at Davidson, North Carolina, August 4, 1896, Julia Lorraine Dupuy, a descendant of Bartholomew Depuy and his wife, the Countess Susanne Lavillon, Huguenots, who came to Virginia from France during the era of religious persecution. Doctor and Mrs. Smith had the following children: Jacob Henry, deceased; Helen Lorraine, Raymond Dupuy, Julia Dupuy, Louise Watson, Opie Norris and Francis Sampson.

WILLIAM LEWIS SCHAFER, M. D. Were all the good deeds of the members of the medical profession to be published the pages of this work would be crowded with nothing else, for no class of men are so innately charitable and self-sacrificing as those who take upon themselves the responsibilities of this most exacting as well as noble calling. No physician lets his charities be known to the general public. Where the need exists, he gives of his care, experience and knowledge without thought of a return, and a very few of the profession rise to great wealth through their practice. The requirements of the profession are such as to demand the highest class of characteristics, and the development of character is very pronounced. In many communities the medical men are the leading factors in municipal life, and always they give their support, usually taking the initiative, in inaugurating sanitary reforms and improvements. Such a man is Dr. W. Lewis Schafer, one of the brilliant young physicians of Alexandria, whose success is marked, and who has won and holds the confidence of his fellow citizens.

Doctor Schafer is not only carrying on a large private practice, with offices at 511 Prince Street, but he is serving as city bacteriologist with exceptional capability. He was born in Alexandria, February 22, 1899, a son of W. Lewis and Effie L. (McCracken) Schafer, natives of the same city. The father is manager of the Doremus Machine Company, having charge of the company's electric plating shop in Washington City, a responsible position.

Following his graduation from the Alexandria High School in 1916 Doctor Schafer entered George Washington University, Washington, and had been there but a year when he enlisted, in 1917, as a private in the regular army, and was assigned to the Medical Corps. He served for ten months overseas, was gassed twice, and was invalided for six months on account of his injuries from the gassing, but upon his recovery and honorable discharge he returned to the University, and was graduated therefrom in 1925, with the degree of Doctor of Medicine. For the subsequent year he interned in Stuart Circle Hospital, Richmond, and in the latter part of 1926 came to Alexandria and entered upon the practice of his profession, in which he has succeeded so wonderfully. Almost immediately he was made bacteriologist, and has since continued to so serve the city. He is unmarried. Doctor Schafer belongs to the Alexandria Medical Society, the Virginia State Medical Society and the American Medical Association. On January 1, 1929, he was appointed to the position of city health officer. He still holds the rank of first lieutenant in the Six Hundred and Ninth Coast Artillery Reserve Corps. The Masonic Order, the American Legion, the 40 and 8, and the Old Dominion Boat Club hold his membership. He is numbered among the stalwart Democrats of Alexandria, although his various professional responsibilities prevent his participating as actively in politics as he might otherwise. The Episcopal Church is his religious home.

HON. BRYAN GORDON. Among the men who have contributed to the dignity and stability of public affairs at Clarendon, few have rendered more valuable and capable service than Hon. Bryan Gordon, justice of the peace and assistant police judge at Clarendon, with offices at the Arlington County Court House. For more than thirty-two years a member of the bench and bar of Virginia, West Virginia and Oklahoma, his experience had been broad and varied, and he has been successful in building up a substantial reputation for legal ability and personal probity.

Judge Gordon was born August 7, 1873, in Albemarle County, Virginia, and is a son of Dr. John C. and Mary (Pigram) Gordon. His father, a native of Orange County, Virginia, was educated for the profession of medicine, which he followed throughout his life in Albemarle County, with the exception of his service with the Confederate army as a surgeon during the war between the states. He was a man of high standing in his calling, who won respect no less by his high character than by his professional ability, and was an honored member of the Albemarle County Medical Society, the Virginia State Medical Society and the American Medical Association. He also had several business connections, and in his death in 1919 his community lost a valuable member of society. Mrs. Gordon, who is also deceased, was a native of Norfolk, this state.

In his boyhood Bryan Gordon's parents took up their residence at Charlottesville, where the youth received his early educational training at Major Jones' University School. He then entered the University of Virginia, in the law department of which institution he took the three year course with the exception of C. and T., and immediately engaged in the practice of his profession at Charlottesville. Subsequently he went to Morgantown, West Virginia, where he remained for five years, removing to Oklahoma City, Oklahoma, and this was followed by twelve years of practice at Manassas, Virginia. On leaving Manassas Judge Gordon accepted a position in the United States Internal Revenue Department at Washington, D. C., and at the end of six years, in 1924, took up his residence at Arlington County Court House, where he has since become a prominent figure in his profession. For several years Judge Gordon served very capably as justice of the peace, a position which he still holds, and January 1, 1928, was appointed assistant police judge. He is able, courageous and thoroughly learned in all departments of the law, and is a member of the local bar association and the Virginia State Bar Association. He belongs to the Blue Lodge of Masonry and the Monarch Club and politically is a Democrat. In his youth Judge Gordon joined the Baptist Church, and at present is a member of the Board of Deacons and also teaches a class of boys in the Sunday School. He has always been a staunch supporter of all measures fostered for the benefit of the community, and has the reputation, well earned, of being a public spirited and constructively inclined citizen.

In December, 1913, Judge Gordon was united in marriage with Miss Elise Stevens, a daughter of Dr. William L. and Eloise P. (Gibson) Stevens, of Orange County, Virginia. Doctor Stevens served as a contract surgeon during the Spanish-American war, and for many years was successfully engaged in the practice of his profession at Orange, where his death occurred in 1921. To Judge and Mrs. Gordon there have been born two children: Bryan, Jr., born in 1916 and Julia Lindsay, born in 1920. By a former marriage Judge Gordon has one daughter: Mary Frances, who is a student at the University of Pittsburgh.

KENNETH H. GAYLE was born shortly before the inception of the great Civil war that brought much of distress and devastation to his native state of Virginia, and the period of his boyhood was marked by the depressed and inconsistant conditions that prevailed during the so called period of reconstruction after the close of the war. He passed his entire life in Norfolk County, Virginia, was long and actively concerned with business affairs in the City of Norfolk, and was one of the sterling and honored citizens of Norfolk at the time of his death, in October, 1926.

Mr. Gayle was born at Portsmouth, judicial center of Norfolk County, June 7, 1860, and thus was sixty-six years of age at the time of his death. He was the fifth in order of birth in the family of eight children born to Robert F. and Sarah B. Gayle. The public schools of Portsmouth afforded Kenneth H. Gayle his early education, and after having been employed about two years in a grocery store he formed the business association that was to continue during the remainder of his earnest and worthy life. He was still little more than a boy when he entered the employ of C. C. Billups & Son, engaged in the agricultural implement business in Norfolk, and with this representative concern he continued his alliance fully half a century, that alliance having been terminated by his death. In his inviolable loyalty and efficiency Mr. Gayle contributed much to the upbuilding of the large and important business of this concern, and every stage of his career was marked by his retention of the confidence and the esteem of his business associates, the while his circle of friends in his native county and state was limited only by that of his acquaintances.

Mr. Gayle was loyal and public spirited in his civic attitude, was a staunch supporter of the cause of the Democratic party, but he never manifested any ambition for political office. In his youth he served as a member of the Old Dominion Guards of Portsmouth, in which military organization he was a member of Grimes' Battery. He was long and actively affiliated with the Royal Arcanum, and was an earnest member of the Methodist Episcopal Church, South, as is also his widow. The subject of this memoir was a member of the Gayle family that was founded in Mathews County, Virginia, many years ago, and it may be noted that he was a brother of Rev. Finley Gayle, D. D., a distinguished clergyman of the Methodist Episcopal Church, South.

On the 6th of April, 1885, was solemnized the marriage of Mr. Gayle and Miss Irene R. Young, who was born and reared in Portsmouth, where she received the advantages of the public schools. She is a daughter of the late Joseph L. and Caroline E. Young, she having been the third in their family of eight children. Joseph L. Young long gave service as a clerk in the United

States Navy Yards at Portsmouth and was one of the honored and public spirited citizens of that city, where he was for a number of years a valued member of the Board of Education. The Young family, of French and Welsh lineage, made settlement on the Slashes plantation, near Richmond, Virginia, prior to the War of the Revolution. The father of Mrs. Gayle was a gallant young soldier of the Confederacy during virtually the entire period of the Civil war, and in that service his brother George was killed in battle. Joseph L. Young in his earlier career followed the printing trade and was for a number of years employed in the office of the *Richmond Enquirer*, in the fair old capital city of Virginia. After the close of his service in the Civil war he was for many years manager of the Old Landmark Publishing Company at Norfolk, and it was after his experience that, under civil-service regulations, he initiated his effective clerical service with the United States Navy Yards at Portsmouth, where he and his wife passed the remainder of their lives.

Mr. Gayle is survived by his widow and their two children. Irene Y., elder of the children, is a graduate in music and is a popular figure in the social and cultural circles of her home city of Norfolk, where she was born and reared and where she received the advantages of the public schools, including high school. She now is retained as an efficient private secretary in Norfolk. Kenneth H. Gayle, Jr., younger of the two children, was graduated from the Virginia Military Institute with the degree of Civil Engineer, and is now executive head in the New York City office of the Ingall's Iron Works. He married Miss Mary Jackson, of Montgomery, Alabama.

FREDERICK RIDINGS SAVAGE. One of the very sound financial institutions of James City County is the Peninsula Bank & Trust Company, and its patronage and high standing is sustained by the character of the men associated with its management. Of them none is of more moment in the world of business and finance than Frederick Ridings Savage, its vice president and treasurer.

The birth of Mr. Savage occurred in Berlin, Maryland, October 7, 1884, and he is a son of Thomas T. and Emma (Ridings) Savage, he born in Accomac County, Virginia, and she born in Maryland. The father was a hotel proprietor of Berlin, Maryland, all of his life, and for years he was a well known figure to the traveling public, for his hotel was noted for its excellent accommodation. His death occurred in April, 1916, but he is survived by the mother, who makes her home with a daughter in Dover, Delaware.

His boyhood and youth passed in Berlin, Maryland, Frederick Ridings Savage went into the local bank when he left school, and was also in one of Accomac County, and in these connections he learned the banking business from the bottom up. In 1903 he came to Williamsburg and organized a branch of the banking house of L. L. Dirickson & Company that is now the First National Bank of Williamsburg. Although at that time he was but eighteen years old, he was made its first cashier, and discharged his duties in a most satisfactory manner. The bank was incorporated in 1909 and nationalized in 1916, and during these changes Mr. Savage continued with it. On May 1, 1917, he resigned and February 11, 1918, was made secretary and treasurer of the Peninsula Bank & Trust Company of Williamsburg, and in 1928 was made its vice president and treasurer. This bank was organized in 1897 and reorganized in 1917 by William A. Bozarth. In 1918 the present modern banking home was erected, which furnishes every facility for the conduct of a general banking business. The bank is capitalized at $100,000; has a surplus of $55,000, and deposits of $1,500,000. Within the last year the deposits have been doubled in proportion to the growth of the bank in public confidence. At the time Mr. Savage came into it the bank was in bad condition, and its deposits were only $260,000. A level-headed business man and experienced banker, Mr. Savage knew just how to build up his institution and win and retain the confidence of the people of this section, and that he has done so the financial statement last issued proves. Mr. Savage's fellow officers are: George P. Coleman, president; F. R. Savage, first vice president; H. M. Clements, second vice president; A. D. Jones, secretary and assistant treasurer. Some of the leading business men of Williamsburg are on the directorate of this bank.

On July 11, 1912, Mr. Savage married Miss Lorna Daley, a daughter of Thomas R. and Minnie (Cole) Daley, he born in the State of Wisconsin and she born in the State of Maine. They are now residents of Leesburg, Florida. Mr. and Mrs. Savage have two children: Minnie Cole, who was born in July, 1913; and Thomas Daley, who was born in December, 1917. A Democrat both by inheritance and conviction, Mr. Savage has always given his party loyal support, and has been honored by being its successful nominee for the City Council a number of times, his period of service with that body covering some years, during which he has given an excellent account of himself. Active in Masonry, he has served several times as master of his lodge, and he is a member of the Mystic Shrine, also of the Odd Fellows, and is a life member of the Elks. Interested as he is in the welfare of the city, he cooperates with the Rotary Club, of which he is a member, in forwarding public spirited movements, and is a valuable citizen in many ways. He is an Episcopalian.

CHARLES C. BOWE is now the senior member of the representative Richmond real estate firm of N. W. Bowe & Son, and in this connection, as well as in his civic loyalty, he is well upholding the high honors of the family name. This business was established by his father in Virginia's capital city nearly sixty years ago, and the firm now has prestige as one of the oldest and most important in the domain of real estate operations in this section of the Old Dominion.

Mr. Bowe was born in Richmond, July 2, 1884, and is the son of Nathaniel Woodson Bowe and Emma Lewis Bowe, the former of whom died March 14, 1914, at his home in Richmond.

Nathaniel W. Bowe was born in Hanover County, Virginia, and received in his youth excellent educational advantages. When the Civil war was precipitated on a divided nation he gave loyal and gallant service as a soldier of the Confederacy, as a member of the First Virginia Infantry, which became a part of the Army of Northern Virginia, commanded by the revered Gen. Robert E. Lee. After the war he did well his part in reviving the depressed civic and industrial affairs of Virginia and in overcoming the chaotic conditions that resulted from the misrule of the so-called reconstruction period. After the war he served one term as sheriff of Hanover County, and upon removal to Richmond he here assumed a clerical position in the office of Grubbs & Williams, a leading real estate firm of that period. Upon the death of Mr. Grubbs he was admitted to partnership in the business, which thereafter was conducted under the title of Williams & Bowe. Later Mr. Bowe operated as N. W. Bowe until 1902, when his son Bruce was taken into partnership under the title of N. W. Bowe & Son. In 1914, after Mr. Bowe, Sr., died, the business was incorporated with Bruce Bowe as president and Charles C. Bowe vice president.

Nathaniel W. Bowe was a man whose life was ordered on the highest plane of integrity and honor in all its relations, and thus it was that he brought to his real estate firm not only constructive service but also a reputation for inviolable fidelity to trust, he having insisted that at all times the interests of the buyer must be held on a parity with those of the seller. His careful and honorable policies gained to his firm a large and representative clientage, and year after year he had charge of properties and investments of many of the oldest and most influential families in Richmond. He thus functioned in connection with the historic Ravensworth and Whitehouse estates of the Gen. Robert E. Lee family, and since his death his sons have continued the same safeguarding of all of these varied interests. The sons were by their honored father thoroughly schooled in the business and in the sterling policies he had adopted therefor. There has continued to be a close and mutually appreciative social and business relationship between the Lee and the Bowe families, and in this connection it is interesting to note that Charles C. Bowe, immediate subject of this review, was chosen to act as godfather at the baptism of Robert E. Lee IV in 1924, the youngster who thus perpetuates for his generation one of the most distinguished names in American history, being a son of Dr. George Bolling Lee of New York City, who is a son of William Fitzhugh Lee and a grandson of Gen. Robert E. Lee.

Bruce Bowe, son of the late Nathaniel W. Bowe, was, as previously stated, the first of the number to be admitted to partnership in the old established real estate business, and he continued his close executive connection with the firm until his death March 26, 1923. Like his father, he was uniformly respected and trusted by all who knew him, and his death was a distinct loss to the business circles of the Virginia capital, as well as a source of sorrow to his host of friends. Since his death the business has been conducted by the younger sons, Charles C. and Nathaniel W., Jr.

Charles C. Bowe was graduated from Richmond College as a member of the class of 1901, and received therefrom the degree of Bachelor of Arts. His entire active career has been marked by close and effective association with the real estate business of N. W. Bowe & Son, and he is now senior member of the firm, which has membership in the National Association of Real Estate Boards, in which Mr. Bowe is a member of the committee on code of ethics. Governor Trinkle appointed Mr. Bowe a member of the Virginia Real Estate Commission at the time of its organization in 1924, and subsequently advanced him to the position of chairman of this commission. He was reappointed by Governor Byrd, and continued his service as chairman until 1926, when he resigned the post, owing to the insistent demands placed upon him by his private business interests. Mr. Bowe is secretary of the Union Stockyards Company of Richmond, his father having having held this office many years and having been the incumbent of the same at the time of his death.

HENRY PHINEAS THOMAS. Efficiency is the keynote of success in every profession, along all lines of endeavor. It is the symbol, the co-related sign and working feature of the marvellous accomplishments of every age and of all people. Without it civilization today would never have passed beyond the state of the cave man. None of the learned professions would have been developed from the faint beginnings of people striving for mental advancement, nor would the air, the earth, the water and even the Heavens above all be bound together to produce power and place for each generation. Half-way methods cannot succeed in anything. To raise anything beyond the low level of mediocrity requires skilled and carefully trained knowledge and the power to use this to the highest degree. In nothing is this truer than in the practice of the law. The attorney without efficiency is a dead letter; his progress is measured by his lack of this important quality, and his failure is a foregone conclusion from the beginning. Among those who have forged to the front among the members of the bar of Alexandria none deserves higher praise than Henry P. Thomas, for he is a man who has always striven to develop his natural and acquired talents and add to his store of knowledge until he has reached the highest degree of efficiency in each line, and this policy, inaugurated at the beginning of his professional career, still continues to animate his actions.

Mr. Thomas was born in Leesburg, Loudoun County, Virginia, May 22, 1894, a son of William Phineas and Sallie (Bitecor) Thomas, both of whom were born in Loudoun County. After the close of the war between the states the father, who had been a soldier of the Confederacy, engaged in farming, and following that occupation the remainder of his life, became one of the well known agriculturists of his county, and he died in Loudoun County in July, 1915, aged sixty-nine years. The mother died in November, 1919, aged sixty-nine years.

Reared in Leesburg, Henry P. Thomas was graduated from High School in 1915, after which for two years he was a student of the University of Virginia. In 1917 he enlisted in the United States Navy, and served in that branch of the country's forces until May, 1919, when he was honorably discharged. With his return to civilian life Mr. Thomas entered the National University of Law, Washington, District of Columbia, and was graduated therefrom in June, 1923, with the degree of Bachelor of Laws, and the following year received his degree of Master of Laws from the same institution. In 1923 he came to Alexandria and became associated with Judge C. E. Nicol in the practice of law, continuing with him until Judge Nicol died two years later, since which time he has practiced alone, and has built up a very large clientele, and has been markedly successful. In addition to attending to his law practice Mr. Thomas has other interests and is president of the Alexandria Realty, Investment, Finance Corporation. He is an officer in George Washington Lodge, A. F. and A. M., and he has been advanced to the Mystic Shrine in the Masonic order. The Alexandria Bar Association and the Virginia Bar Association hold his membership, and he belongs to the American Legion and the Belle Haven Country Club. As a director of the Alexandria National Bank he is becoming well known in banking circles. For several years he has been an enthusiastic member of the Kiwanis Club, and he has also had charge of the Boy Scouts of Alexandria for about the same length of time. His support in politics is given to the Democratic ticket, but he is not one who seeks public honors. Long a consistent member of the Presbyterian Church, he is active in its different bodies, and is now treasurer of the Men's Bible Class. Mr. Thomas is unmarried. He resides at 428 North Washington Street, and maintains his office at 115 North Fairfax Street, Alexandria. A public-spirited man, and one who has the welfare of his fellow citizens at heart, he is always ready and glad to assist them as far as lies in his power.

HON. RICHARD C. L. MONCURE. During the past several decades there has been undoubtedly no single factor that has played such an important part in the advancement and success of young business men of ambition and energy as the automobile industry. The marvelous growth of this business, which still is going forward to such an extent that no man can predict the size of its future, has furnished the opportunity for young men from all walks of life to secure positions which, in proportion to their importance, were formerly held only by men many years their senior. In this relation mention should be made of Hon. Richard C. L. Moncure, mayor of Falls Church, Fairfax County, and president of the Moncure Motor Company, Inc., who is the authorized Ford dealer for his community and who has already achieved a success that many men would consider desirable if gained only after a lifetime of effort.

Mr. Moncure was born at Macon, Georgia, March 30, 1903, and is a son of R. C. L. and Irene (Winship) Moncure. His father, a native of Stafford, Virginia, was given good educational advantages, and for a number of years was engaged in the successful practice of law at Arlington County Court House and Washington, D. C. He made his home at Falls Church for a number of years, and was a man of high ability in his profession, whose promising career was cut short by death at the age of forty-three years, April 23, 1918. Mrs. Moncure, who was born at Macon, Georgia, now lives at Falls Church.

The education of Richard C. L. Moncure was thorough and comprehensive, including attendance at the public schools of Falls Church and the high schools of Macon, Georgia, and Washington, D. C. After studying French abroad he entered New York University, and then returned to Washington and entered George Washington University, from which he was graduated with the degree of Bachelor of Laws in 1925. Mr. Moncure commenced his career as a lawyer and was well on his way toward the attainment of a large and representative practice when he decided to enter the automobile industry as a dealer. He accordingly secured the Ford agency, in March, 1926, taking over the Moses Motor Company, which he renamed the Moncure Motor Company, Inc., of which he has since been president. He deals in Ford and Lincoln cars and Fordson trucks and in addition maintains an up-to-date service station and repair department and deals in equipment and accessories of all kinds. Mr. Moncure has made a success of his business and is accounted one of the successful young men of his community. In local affairs he has also taken an active part, and March 1, 1927, was elected to the office of mayor of Falls Church. Although probably one of the youngest mayors in the United States, he has given his city a splendid administration, which has included the installing of a number of improvements.

Mr. Moncure is unmarried. He is treasurer of the Falls Church Fire Department, and a member of the Masonic Order, the Order of the Eastern Star, the Washington Golf and Country Club and the Episcopal Church. His mother, with whom he makes his home on Brown Avenue, is a Christian Scientist.

WILLIAM AARON GAYLORD, JR., passed his entire life in Norfolk and gained status as one of its progressive business men, he having for many years represented in this seaboard section a large English concern and having had supervision of the loading and unloading of tramp steamers in the interests of this English corporation. He became widely and favorably known in ocean navigation circles, and as citizen and business man in his native county he commanded unqualified popular confidence and esteem.

Mr. Gaylord was born in Norfolk on the 23d of January, 1875, and here his death occurred in October, 1919, his early education having been received mainly in St. Mary's Academy in this city. He was the second of the seven children born to William Aaron Gaylord, Sr., and Anna Theresa (Farrell) Gaylord, his father having here given many years of service as foreman of the Reid Bakery, one of the leading concerns of this kind in Norfolk. The original American representatives of the Gaylord family came from France and settled in Virginia in the Colonial era. The paternal grandfather of the subject of this memoir was a loyal soldier of the Confederacy in the Civil war. Reuben Nicholls Farrell, an uncle of Mr. Gaylord on the maternal side, served many years as high constable of Norfolk County. Richard Gaylord, a brother of the subject of this sketch, was a loyal and efficient member of the Norfolk fire department and as such sacrificed his life at the post of duty in the great fire that swept the city in 1918. He was killed while on duty in that conflagration, his death having occurred June 30, 1918. Edward T. Smith, a brother of Mrs. Gaylord, is likewise a brave and honored member of the Norfolk fire department, at Station No. 2, on Battle Street, and while on duty at the fire that destroyed the Monticello Hotel he was so severely burned he was for many months incapacitated and in the care of physicians.

At the age of fifteen years Mr. Gaylord found employment in the bakery of which his father was the foreman, and he was thus engaged about two years. At the age of seventeen years he entered upon an apprenticeship to the trade of wheelwright, which he followed until he was nineteen. At the age of twenty years he initiated his service with the English concern previously mentioned, and with this service he continued to be identified during the remainder of his life. He had supervision of the unloadng of tramp steamers from all parts of the world and laden with all manner of cargoes, his activities in this connection having gained to him a wide acquaintanceship among those engaged in the shipping trade touching the maritime ports of America's Atlantic coast.

Mr. Gaylord was a Democrat in political allegiance, was affiliated with the Improved Order of Red Men and the Fraternal Order of Eagles, and his widow is a member of the Ladies of the Maccabees.

On the 12th of February, 1895, was solemnized the marriage of Mr. Gaylord and Miss Susie Smith, who was born and reared in Norfolk. Of the children of this union five survive the honored father: William James, who is a city employe of Norfolk; Myrtle Louise, who is the wife of Henry Lewis Farrell, a civil engineer in the service of the Virginian Railway; Edward L., who is a printer by trade and vocation; James L., who likewise resides in Norfolk; and Seabright, who is the wife of Thomas O. Downing. Mr. and Mrs. Downing reside in Norfolk, where Mr. Downing is connected with the American Oil Company, and their one child is a son, Thomas O., Jr.

Mrs. Gaylord is a daughter of James L. and Maria (Warren) Smith, both natives of Virginia, where they were reared and educated and where the father became a substantial business man in Norfolk. The first American representative of this Smith family came from Ireland and settled in Virginia prior to the Revolution, and five generations have lived in the Norfolk community. Settlement was here made more than 200 years ago, and members of the family were patriot soldiers in the War of the Revolution. Andrew J. Smith, an uncle of Mrs. Gaylord, was wounded while he was serving as a soldier of the Confederacy in the Civil war, as were also two of her maternal uncles, William and Major Warren. Mrs. Gaylord still resides in her native city, where her attractive home is at 428 Twentieth Street, and where her circle of friends is limited only by that of her acquaintances.

JOHN W. MOORE, one of the leading realtors of Richmond, and a member of the Virginia Real Estate Commission, was for many years a member of the Common Council of Richmond, and an active figure in politics and civic affairs. He has the honor at present of being state president of the Ancient Order of Hibernians, and he belongs to other fraternal organizations, in all of which he is highly regarded. Mr. Moore was born at Richmond, in 1874, a son of Michael and Catherine (Kane) Moore, the former of whom was born in Ireland.

Growing to useful manhood in his native city, John W. Moore attended the parochial schools, and when old enough went into a grocery business, later leaving it to engage in handling real estate, in which he found his life work. For some years he has been senior member of the old and reliable realty firm of Moore & McGranighan.

Always a Democrat, Mr. Moore has been for many years a forceful figure in local politics, and for twenty-two years, ending in 1928, he was a member of the Common Council of Richmond, first of the City of Manchester on the South Side of the James River from Richmond, and following the consolidation of the two cities in 1910 he continued a member, representing after that the Madison Ward in the Richmond Common Council. He has always been a progressive in municipal affairs, and was among those who brought about the city manager plan for municipalities, which originated in Virginia. For several years Mr. Moore was also president of the Virginia League of Municipalities, and he is still carrying on the same line of work, for his heart is centered in his home city, and he is deeply interested in continuing its prosperity and advancing still further its progress.

In addition to his other interests Mr. Moore is a director of the Mechanics & Merchants Bank. In May, 1927, he was signally honored by appointment by Governor Byrd to membership in the Virginia State Real Estate Commission. He belongs to the Benevolent and Protective Order of Elks, the Fraternal Order of Eagles, which he formerly served as state president in Virginia, and the Ancient Order of Hibernians, of which he is state president in Virginia, having held the office since 1922.

A. B. Nicol.

Mr. Moore married Miss Annie M. Kain. They maintain their residence at 1509 Porter Street, where they have a very pleasant home, one of the most desirable in Richmond. Mr. Moore's business address is 18 North Seventh Street, and here he has been located for some years. It would be difficult to find a man more thoroughly representative of the best interests of Richmond and Henrico County than Mr. Moore, and his personal popularity is at its height and his commercial standing is unquestioned. All that he today possesses has been won through his own efforts, and great credit is due him for what he has accomplished.

AYLETT BAUDER NICOL. The legal profession is one that demands much and requires of its devotees implicit and unswerving devotion to its exactions. Long and continued study, natural ability and keen judgment with regard to men and their motives are all required in the making of a successful lawyer. That so many pass beyond the line of the ordinary in this calling and become figures of note in political life demonstrates that this profession brings out all that is best and most capable in a man. For ages the most brilliant men of all countries have turned their attention to the study of the law, and especially is this true in the United States, where the form of government gives opportunity for the man of brains to climb even into the very highest position within the gift of the people, and it is a notable fact that from among the lawyers have more of our great men come than from all the other callings combined. One of the men who is already giving promise of great things in his part of the state, Aylett B. Nicol, of Alexandria, is measuring up to the highest ideals of his profession, and is enjoying a very large and constantly augmenting practice. He was born in Prince William County, Virginia, August 5, 1883, a son of Charles Edgar and Mary Louise (Bauder) Nicol, natives of Prince William and Port Royal, Caroline County, Virginia, respectively. The father was engaged in the practice of law in Brentsville, Virginia, and in Manassas until 1908, when he moved to Alexandria, and here he continued in his law practice until his death. He was elected judge of the Circuit Court of the Sixteenth Circuit in 1894, and served in that capacity until 1907, when he resigned to become a candidate for Congress. While he made an excellent running, he was defeated, and resumed his law practice, in which he continued until October 21, 1924, when he was claimed by death, at the age of seventy years. His prominence was not confined to the domain of the law, however, for he served for two or three terms in the House of Burgesses, and he was one of the leaders of his political party. The mother died December 31, 1901.

Growing to manhood in his native state, Aylett B. Nicol attended the public schools of Manassas, and had some instruction in an excellent private school, and attended the high school of that city and also Richmond College. His professional training was gained in the University of Virginia, and he was admitted to the bar in 1905, and that same year entered upon the practice of his profession in Alexandria. After the retirement of his father from the bench he practiced with him. After his father's death he continued the work of the firm alone, and has never taken another associate. In all of his practice he has been eminently successful. A man of unusual capabilities, Mr. Nicol is a valued addition to the legal fraternity and to the

City of Alexandria, and is, without doubt, one of the best types of a Virginia gentleman and professional man.

On June 16, 1926, Mr. Nicol married Miss Mary Prudence Terry, a daughter of Frank F. and Mary Terry, natives of Massachusetts, the former of whom is retired and a resident of Assonet, Massachusetts. The latter died in February, 1926. On September 4, 1928, Mrs. Nicol died. There are no children. Mr. Nicol is substitute civil and police justice of Alexandria, and he belongs to the Virginia and Alexandria Bar Associations. Fraternally he maintains membership with the Fraternal Americans and the Improved Order of Red Men. He belongs to the Belle Haven Country Club and the Alexandria Chamber of Commerce. During the World war he was in training, but was not sent overseas as the armistice was signed before he was fully prepared. In political faith he is a Democrat. The First Baptist Church of Alexandria holds his membership, and he is one of its trustees. His father left a large estate, principally in real estate, and Mr. Nicol as one of the five children inherited some very valuable residential and business properties, and he has invested in others. All of the father's six children are now living with the exception of one. Mr. Nicol has a most desirable residence at 112 Myrtle Avenue, and possesses one of the finest law libraries in the state, which reflects his originality, profound grasp of the law and his studious habits.

J. FRANKLIN MCLAUGHLIN has been since May, 1927, the vice president in charge of operations of the Virginia Electric & Power Company, of which important corporation more specific record is given on other pages of this work, in the personal sketch of its president, William E. Wood, so that a repetition of the data is not here required.

Mr. McLaughlin claims the historic old Bay State as the place of his nativity, as he was born at Hingham, Massachusetts, his early education having been acquired in public schools and having been supplemented by his special courses in Brown University, Providence, Rhode Island. In 1912 he initiated his association with the Stone & Webster Management Corporation, the headquarters of which are in Boston, Massachusetts, and with this great corporation he has since continued his alliance. He won successive promotions and was finally assigned by this corporation to take charge of the Norfolk division of the Virginia Electric & Power Company, and he thus continued his residence at Norfolk, Virginia, until May, 1927, when he was elected vice president of the company and assigned to take charge of operations at the company's headquarters at Richmond. Prior to coming to Norfolk, Virginia, in the interest of the Stone & Webster Management Corporation, which assumed control of the Virginia Electric & Power Company at that time, Mr. McLaughlin had represented the corporation in effective service in Boston, Massachusetts; Providence, Rhode Island; El Paso, Texas; and Baton Rouge, Louisiana. Concerning his loyal civic attitude while he was a resident of Norfolk the following estimate has been written: "He accomplished much progressive work in Norfolk. He was chairman of the industrial commission, a vice president and director of the Norfolk-Portsmouth Chamber of Commerce, and was a director of the Rotary Club, the Maritime Exchange, the Norfolk National Bank of Commerce & Trusts, and of the Boys Club of that city."

In the period of the nation's participation in the World war Mr. McLaughlin made a record of loyal and efficient service in the aviation department of the United States Army, in which he won the rank of captain. His initial training for this service was gained at Kelly Field, San Antonio, Texas, and thereafter he was sent to England as a staff officer with a squadron of army flyers, he having there continued on staff duty until the close of the war. He came to Norfolk, Virginia, June 30, 1925, and there remained until his transfer to Richmond in May, 1927, as previously noted in this review. In the historic old capital city of Virginia Mr. McLaughlin has become a member of the Commonwealth Club, the Westmoreland Club, the Hermitage Club and the Country Club of Virginia. He is a progressive and popular accession to the civic, business and social circles of the fair old capital city.

FRANK ST. CLAIR in the later years of his life was identified with Norfolk, a prominent figure in real estate circles there. The foundation of his successful life had been laid as a journalist in Southwest Virginia, particularly at Wytheville, where he and his father were in the newspaper business for a long period of years.

Frank St. Clair was born at Wytheville May 15, 1857, son of David and Sarah V. (Walker) St. Clair. His father for many years was a newspaper publisher at Wytheville. Frank St. Clair was the oldest of seven children and was reared and educated in Wytheville. As a boy he worked in his father's newspaper office, learned the trade of printer and had experience in all departments. In 1885 he established the *Wytheville Enterprise*, and that newspaper has now had a continuous existence for forty-three years. It has been one of the most popular newspapers in Southwest Virginia, and today it exemplifies the progressive policy given it by its former publisher, Frank St. Clair. Mr. St. Clair about 1888 also established the *Farmers Alliance*, a newspaper for the rural population and expressing the doctrines of the Farmers Alliance organization. It continued to be printed for several years. Mr. St. Clair sold both newspapers in 1903 and at that time moved to Norfolk, where he engaged in the real estate business. He spent his last years in retirement and died September 21, 1925. He was as successful in the real estate field as he had been as manager, editor and owner of the *Wytheville Enterprise*.

He married at Norfolk October 2, 1889, Miss Alice Genevieve Smith, who was reared and educated in that city, daughter of Thomas and Mary Jane Smith. Mrs. St. Clair, who resides at 400 Raleigh Avenue in Norfolk, is a member of the Catholic Church. Her grandfather came from Ireland and settled in Virginia. Her father was in the wholesale dry goods business for many years at Norfolk. Mr. and Mrs. St. Clair had two children, Frank, Jr., and Robert.

RANDALL DAVISSON TAYLOR ELLIOTT was born in Loudoun County, Virginia, August 30, 1897. After completing his primary schooling in the public schools and the Western High School of Washington, D. C., he attended the University of Virginia, where he took one year of academic work, followed by a law course, from which he graduated in 1923 with the degree of Bachelor of Laws (LL. B.). Mr. Elliott is the son of Henry Randall and Elizabeth (Taylor) Elliott.

Mr. Elliott is admitted to practice before all of the courts of Virginia and the District of Columbia and before the Court of Claims. He was admitted to the bar of the State of Virginia in 1922 and to the bar of the District of Columbia in 1925. He maintains his offices at 1331 G Street and at 119 South Fairfax Street, Alexandria, Virginia. From 1925 until 1928 Mr. Elliott was senior member of the law firm of Elliott & Nelms, being associated with Henning C. Nelms, of Washington.

Mr. Elliott has specialized in the practice of corporation law, having gained prominence through his representation of corporations which have retained him as general counsel, among which may be mentioned: Washington—Shenandoah Valley Motor Lines, Inc., a subsidiary of the Eastern Public Service Corporation; the National Biographical Society, Inc.; Lee Jackson Caverns, Inc.; Automatic Railroad Inspector Corporation; Battlefield Crystal Caverns, Inc.; Allied Brokerage Corporation and the Hotel Development Corporation.

On November 16, 1926, Mr. Elliott married Miss Gladys Mary Berry, daughter of William Wallace and Gladys (Kelsey) Berry, natives of Bedford, Virginia. Mrs. Elliott is a graduate of Columbia University of New York. Mr. and Mrs. Elliott have one child, Randall Davisson Taylor Elliott, Jr., born October 24, 1927.

During the World war Mr. Elliott served in the United States Railroad Administration as Assistant to the Title Examiner.

Mr. Elliott belongs to the International Association of Cosmopolitan Clubs, the City Club of Washington, the University of Virginia Club of New York City, and the Board of Trade of Washington. He holds the rank of Assistant Deputy Commissioner of the District of Columbia Council of the Boy Scouts of America. Mr. and Mrs. Elliott reside at 3315 Garfield Street, N. W., Washington, D. C.

CHARLES FREDERICK PETRIE for forty years was a resident of Norfolk, and in his profession as a civil engineer had an extensive practice that kept him in touch with many of the great landed and industrial interests of the Atlantic Seaboard.

Mr. Petrie was born in Dundee, Scotland, May 24, 1860, and died at Norfolk May 13, 1928, at the age of sixty-eight. His father, David R. Petrie, was a broker in the jute business at Dundee, Scotland. The only son of the family now living is Dr. Reginald O. Petrie, a physician in England. One other son, Alexander, was a shipping agent at Calcutta, India, and another, David, was a ship owner in Scotland.

Charles Frederick Petrie was educated at Dundee, graduated from a technical school as a civil engineer, and after some years of experience in his native country came to New York City in 1888, and in 1889 established his home at Norfolk. At Norfolk he was associated with the firm of W. D. Murray Company as a partner for six years. After selling his interest in this firm he established himself in practice under his own name, and for thirty years looked after an extensive business as a civil engineer and surveyor. He retired from Business in 1927. Mr. Petrie was a member of the Presbyterian Church.

He married Helen Williamson, of Edinburgh, Scotland, who died at Norfolk in 1908. At Norfolk October 27, 1910, he married Ella Landrum Rice, daughter of W. L. and Sallie C. (Wingfield) Landrum. Her father was a carriage manufacturer for many years and served in the Confederate army. The Landrum

family came from England and settled in Albemarle County, Virginia, before the Revolutionary war. The Wingfields were also a distinguished Colonial Virginia family. Sallie C. Wingfield's father was a captain in the Confederate army. Mrs. Petrie, who resides at 112 West Twenty-eighth Street in Norfolk, by her first marriage had two children, Lillian May and Edward A. Rice. Lillian May is the wife of James R. Guy, superintendent of the Southern Transportation Company, and his two children, Laluce, wife of Irving H. Dwyer, and Louis Lee. Edward A. Rice, assistant superintendent of the Richmond office of the Otis Elevator Company, married Mamie G. Bransford and has two sons, Adolph and Ralph E. Rice.

HON. PAUL MORTON, city manager of Alexandria, is a civil engineer by profession, and served for two and one-half years overseas during the World war, so that he is a man of broad vision, wide experience and trained ability, and in his present office in rendering an excellent account of himself. He was born in Louisville, Kentucky, December 24, 1894, a son of Thomas B. and Margaret (Williams) Morton, natives of Kentucky and Tennessee, respectively. The father is president of the Armored Car Company of Louisville, Kentucky, and a man of considerable prominence in that city.

Reared and educated in Louisville, Kentucky, Paul Morton was graduated from the Dupont Training School of that city in 1913, and for the succeeding year was a railroad engineer on the Louisville & Nashville Railroad in Alabama, where he was connected with Railway construction. In 1914 he came to Virginia and was engaged in building double tracks for the Southern Railroad from Charlottesville to Orange. Later he went with the Chesapeake & Ohio Railroad in West Virginia, and was stationed in different parts of the state, during the last two years having his headquarters in Richmond. In January, 1922, he came to Alexandria as director of public safety, and in May, 1925, was made city manager, in which office he has since continued with eminently satisfactory results. While serving as city manager he still looks after the public safety, and his time is fully occupied.

In December, 1919, Mr. Morton married Miss Elizabeth R. Smith, a daughter of Russell and Mamie (English) Smith, natives of Virginia and New Jersey, respectively. Mr. English was an admiral in the United States Navy for many years. For the past thirty-five or forty years Mr. Smith has served as treasurer of Culpeper County, Virginia. Two children have been born to Mr. and Mrs. Morton, namely: Paul, Junior, and Earlena English, the former born in November, 1920, and the latter in February, 1923. Mr. Morton is a member of Washington Lodge, A. F. and A. M., No. 22 and of the Benevolent and Protective Order of Elks.

In June, 1917, Mr. Morton volunteered for the World war, and was sent overseas with the unit commanded by General Dawes, now vice president of the United States. He enlisted as a civil engineer, and served overseas until the month of May, 1919, when he was returned to the United States and honorably discharged. The American Legion, the Belle Haven Country Club and the Kiwanis Club, of which he is a director, and the Chamber of Commerce hold his membership. His political convictions make him a Democrat, but he has never aspired to public honors. In religious faith he is an Episcopalian. Mr.

Morton maintains his residence at 122 Walnut Street. With his enlightened mind and strong intellect, coupled with his knowledge upon many subjects, Mr. Morton is a valuable asset to his community, a fact that is heartily appreciated by his fellow citizens.

WILLIAM WALLACE WILLS is a Fluvanna County farmer who has had a prominent part in promoting the planting industry in this section of Virginia. Mr. Wills lives at Palmyra on a farm a mile south of town. The property has been in the family for generations. Originally it comprised a great estate, but has been reduced until the property now owned by Mr. Wills consist of 464 acres.

Mr. Wills was born there August 11, 1860. The farm for many years was called "Falling Gardens," but in later years has borne the name "Solitude." Mr. Willis is a son of Dr. Albert J. and Martha (Coodington) Wills. His grandfather was John Wills. His mother was born in Cumberland County on the old Hatcher estate, being a descendant of the prominent Hatcher family. Dr. Albert Wills was born at Chatham, practiced medicine for many years at Palmyra, and when he died left his estate to his children, and it subsequently came into the possession of William Wallace Wills. Doctor Wills was on the medical board of the Confederate army. He was a Democrat but not active in politics. In his later years he removed to Texas for his health, and one or two of his sons also went out to that state. There were five children in the family: Virginia, wife of Penbrook Pettit, of Palmyra; Albert, now deceased; William Wallace; John; and Mattie Q. The son John in 1884 went to the Panhandle of Texas and was one of the founders of what is now the outstanding city of the Panhandle, Amarillo. He was connected with the United States Government survey in laying out a route for express and mails across the southwest plains.

William Wallace Wills attended school at Palmyra, and practically all his life has been spent on the old homestead. He early took part in the management of the property, and has been one of the progressive and far-seeing farmers who have sought to develop good markets for the products of this rich section. He was instrumental in having numerous canning factories established over Fluvanna County and owned and operated three of his own. For many years he shipped canned tomatoes to midwest centers such as Chicago, Omaha, Kansas City, but of late years the local canneries have been compelled to develop other markets partly through the competition of the western state canneries and also on account of the high freight rates from Virginia.

Mr. Wills has been quite active in the Democratic party, though never seeking a public office. He is a steward of the Methodist Episcopal Church, South, and for many years was superintendent of the Sunday School. He belongs to the Independent Order of Odd Fellows. He married, October 1, 1890, Miss Alice B. Bell, of Fluvanna County, daughter of Askley and Hardenia (Leslie) Bell. Her parents are still living, her father being a planter. Mr. and Mrs. Wills had three children, Askley, now deceased, Cora and John. Cora is the wife of W. N. Hannah, of Palmyra, and her three children are William N., Jr., Askley Bell and Alice Rebecca. John Wills, connected with the Virginia State Highway Department at Richmond, married Miss Jessie Campbell, of Wellington, Virginia.

JAMES HATTON WATTERS. The late James Hatton Watters, president of the wholesale hardware house of Watters & Martin, the only concern of its kind in Norfolk, was a public spirited man, active in political and civic affairs, and prominent in financial circles. Very charitable, he gave generously wherever he saw the need of assistance, and he was a zealous church worker and popular with all classes. He was born in Norfolk, Virginia, July 13, 1840, and died at Virginia Beach, Virginia, July 9, 1918.

James Hatton Watters was a descendant of William Woodhouse, the father of the Episcopal Church in Princess Anne County, who died in 1774. His son, Jonathan Woodhouse, was a soldier of the American Revolution, and for his services in that war was commissioned a major in the Virginia State Militia by the governor. The parents of Mr. Watters of this review were James and Georgiana (Martin) Watters. She was a daughter of Alexander Martin, of Norfolk, and a member of the oldest family of that name in Norfolk.

When war was declared between the states James Hatton Watters enlisted in the Confederate army and served for four years with the Norfolk Light Artillery Blues. While he was wounded in the battle of Chancellorsville, he recovered, rejoined his regiment, and was with General Lee at the time of the surrender at Appomattox.

Returning to Norfolk at the close of the war, he entered the wholesale hardware business under the name of Taylor, Martin & Company, which firm was composed of Walter H. Taylor, S. Martin and Thomas Elliott. Mr. Watters later bought Mr. Martin's interest and the name was changed to that of Taylor, Elliott & Watters. Still later the firm became Watters & Martin, was incorporated, and Mr. Watters continued to serve it as president until his death. His son James Watters is general manager of the business, and it is located at 110 Water Street, Norfolk. A Mason, Mr. Watters belonged to Owens Lodge, A. F. and A. M. He belonged to Epworth Methodist Episcopal Church, South, of Norfolk, and served it as steward for many years. Banking also attracted his attention and for a long period he was a director of the Marine Bank of Norfolk. The city benefited by his work in its behalf and he served at different times as chairman of the Finance Committee, chairman of the Waterworks Committee and chairman of the Police Commission.

After the death of his first wife, who bore the maiden name of Margaret Garrett, Mr. Watters married Miss Mattie Lee Watts, who was born in Richmond, Virginia, a graduate of Norfolk College, the ceremony taking place January 21, 1893. She is a daughter of Joseph Granberry Watts, a prominent business man of Norfolk, who had been engaged in the manufacture of brick in Richmond prior to moving to Norfolk. The following children were born to Mr. Watters: Garrett, who was graduated from the Law School of the University of Virginia, is connected with his father's hardware business, and is a prominent Elk; James H., who is vice president of the New York Air Brake Company of New York City, married Miss Pearl Luthy; Martha, who married William C. Griffiths, a business man of Narberth, Pennsylvania; and Elizabeth, who for two years was a student of Goucher School, after which she entered Teachers' College, Farmville, Virginia, and was graduated therefrom. Mrs. Watters still resides in Norfolk, her home being at 315 Fairfax Avenue, and here she and her daughter are enjoying life surrounded by the comforts provided for them by Mr. Watters, and the companionship of their many friends. They are active church workers, and continue many of the charities of the good husband and father.

EDMOND CARY LINDSAY. During the more than forty years that the late Capt. Edmond Cary Lindsay followed the sea he passed through many experiences and vicissitudes of fortune, but when his life ended at his home at Norfolk in September, 1921, it could be said of him that his career had been a worthy and useful one, characterized by a high sense of Christian obligation and featured by numerous instances of sheer bravery and indomitable courage. The life of the captain of a sea-going tug or United States revenue cutter is necessarily a hard one, tending to coarsen many men's nature, but Captain Lindsay always preserved the manner and actions of a gentleman, while at no time allowing the finality and sternness of his discipline to be abated.

Captain Lindsay was born March 19, 1858, in York County, Virginia, a son of William J. and Martha Ann (Elliott) Lindsay. His father was a native of Scotland, who came to the United States and settled in York County, where he passed the remainder of his life in agricultural operations. Edmond Cary Lindsay acquired his education in the country schools of York County, and his early boyhood was passed in an agricultural atmosphere and environment, but he had inherited an adventurous nature and a natural love for the sea. Accordingly, when he was still a young lad he shipped as a mess boy, and in the years that followed visited many ports of the world. He gradually worked his way upward until when only twenty years of age he secured his master's papers and took the title of captain. For the greater part of his life he was captain of a tug boat, but during his later years was captain of a United States revenue cutter, and held this position at the time of his retirement from active service in 1919. As before noted, he had many experiences. On one occasion he was captain of a tug stationed at Old Point Comfort, where he saved the life of a small girl from drowning, and at another time, when he was captain of the tug *Matt White* and that vessel blew up, he saved a man from drowning, these two being the only survivors of the ill-fated vessel. Captain Lindsay was a popular and highly respected member of the Captains and Pilots Association, and in his political convictions was a stanch Democrat.

On November 14, 1878, Captain Lindsay was united in marriage with Miss Mary R. Conkle, of Richmond, daughter of Gottlieb and Fredericka Conkle, natives of Germany. Ten children were born to this union: William Lee, captain of a tugboat, who married Gertie Harrington; Bessie May, the wife of Edward William Winder, a farmer of Norfolk County, who has two daughters, Mary and Elizabeth; Francis Edward, who follows the profession of a marine engineer; Lottie Pearl, the wife of Ed Smith, a locomotive engineer; Edmond Cary, a commanding officer in the United States Navy during the World war, who was in the coast service for twenty-six months, and is now a captain in the service of the Old Dominion Steamship Company, who married Mary Petty; John Laurence, an ensign in the United States Naval Reserves for twenty-two months during the World war, in which he made many trips between the United States, England and France, and is now engaged in business at

R. C. Bowton

Norfolk as a flour miller, married Eugenia Manuel and has three sons, Charles Vernon, John Laurence and Cary; Claudius Maynard, Ralph Stewart and Allen Earleston, all members of the Norfolk police department; and Annie Madeleine, who married Howard Lambert and has one child, Beverly Ann. Mrs. Lindsay, who survives her husband and resides at 327 Poole Street, Norfolk, is an active member of the Methodist Church.

REESE CHARLES BOWTON is giving a most constructive and progressive administration as city superintendent of schools in Alexandria, and has been the incumbent of this office since 1923.

Mr. Bowton is able to advert to the staunch old Hoosier State as the place of his nativity, his birth having occurred at Lawrenceburg, Indiana, April 28, 1876. He is a son of James and Eleanor (Reese) Bowton, both of whom were born and reared in Indiana, the parents of James Bowton having come to the United States from London, England, and having gained pioneer prestige in Indiana. The father of Mrs. Eleanor (Reese) Bowton was a native of Pennsylvania, and her mother was born in Virginia. James Bowton became and long continued one of the substantial exponents of farm industry in his native state, but passed the closing years of his life in Illinois, where he died in March, 1925, his birth having occurred August 19, 1844. His widow, now (1929) seventy-eight years of age, is a loved member of the family circle of her son Reese C., subject of this review.

The childhood and early youth of Reese C. Bowton were compassed by the influences of the old home farm in Dearborn County, Indiana, and in the public schools of that county he continued his studies until he was graduated from the high school at Lawrenceburg. Thereafter he completed a course in the University of Indiana, in which he was graduated as a member of the class of 1911 and with the degree of Bachelor of Arts. Through his post-graduate work in the University of Wisconsin he received from the latter institution in 1915 the supplemental degree of Master of Arts, and in Columbia University, New York City, he has thus far taken eighteen months of the work that will lead to his reception of the degree of Doctor of Philosophy. Mr. Bowton taught his first term of school when he was twenty years of age, in 1896, and he continued his pedagogic service at intervals while he was pursuing his university courses. Mr. Bowton is an enthusiast in all that pertains to the work of his profession, and his service therein has been cumulative in its success. He has taught in the public schools of Indiana, Illinois and Missouri, and has been in active educational work in Virginia during a period of ten years. He gave five years of service as superintendent of the public schools of Clifton Forge, Alleghany County, Virginia, and since July, 1923, he has been superintendent of the city schools of Alexandria. He is a member of the National Education Association, is affiliated with the Phi Delta Kappa college fraternity, is an active member of the Kiwanis Club in his home city, is a Democrat in his political allegiance, and his religious faith is that of the Methodist Church, of which he has been a member since his boyhood and in which he and his wife now maintain active affiliation with the local organization of the Methodist Episcopal Church, South. He has valuable farm interests in Iroquois County, Illinois, where his father passed the closing years of his life. The one other child of the family was Alma T., who likewise became a successful and popular teacher, her death having occurred November 13, 1903.

In July, 1918, was solemnized the marriage of Mr. Bowton and Miss Edna Iddings, who likewise was born and reared in Indiana, as were also her parents, Charles and Martha (Wilson) Iddings, who there passed their entire lives. Mr. Iddings was long and successfully engaged in farm enterprise in Indiana, and there his death occurred in March, 1922, his widow having survived him about three months, as her death occurred in June of the same year. Mr. and Mrs. Bowton have four children, Reese C., Jr., Forrest Lowell, James Russell, and Virginia Elder. Mr. Bowton purchased from the City of Alexandria the fine and historic old home now occupied by him and his family at 323 South Fairfax Street. The house was erected more than a century ago, and this venerable residence has as its popular chatelaine a gracious and cultured woman, Mrs. Bowton, who is well upholding the social prestige that has attached to it for many years.

WILLIAM OTIS BAILEY, specialist in eye, ear, nose and throat, is a resident of Leesburg and has had an interesting career in his profession, and particularly as an officer in the Medical Corps of the United States Navy during and subsequent to the World war.

He was born September 12, 1889, at Charleston, South Carolina, son of Ephraim Mikell and Helen (Trenholm-Prentiss) Bailey, his father a native of Edisto Island and his mother of Cheraw, South Carolina. His father, for several years a prosperous hardware merchant of Charleston, died in that city in February, 1910. The mother lives with her son at Aldie.

After attending public schools in Charleston and Washington, D. C., William Otis Bailey entered Emerson Institute at Washington, graduating with the class of 1907. In 1912 he graduated from the medical department of George Washington University, was an interne in the public health service at Boston, Massachusetts, and at the Providence and Casualty Hospitals at Washington. He took post-graduate work in the Army Medical School in 1914 and at the Naval Medical School in 1917 and 1920. Doctor Bailey during 1914-15 was on active duty with the Medical Reserve Corps, U. S. A., and following that spent six months in the Indian service in Arizona and Minnesota. During 1916-17 he practiced as an eye, ear, nose and throat physician at Washington. In 1917 he joined the Medical Reserve Corps of the navy, with which he was connected for about two months, and upon America's entrance into the World war was commissioned a lieutenant, junior grade, later becoming a lieutenant commander (T.).

Capt. C. S. Butler, of the United States Naval Medical School at Washington, has furnished an interesting account of Doctor Bailey's World war service. He was on duty in connection with the naval establishment in the Virgin Islands from September, 1917, to about the same date in 1920. Shortly after reporting at St. Thomas in September, 1917, he was ordered to assume charge of the medical work of the Island of St. Croix, as chief municipal physician. As he was the senior naval medical officer on the island he was responsible for all medical work and sanitation for the entire island and its population, about 16,000 souls. This is the largest of the three islands purchased from Denmark and officially transferred to the United States in February, 1917. He found at St. Croix two run-down municipal hospitals, a poorly equipped leper asylum, an insane asylum, and everywhere ordinary sanitary provisions neglected. With the trained personnel furnished him by the naval government Doctor Bailey during the three years of his stay in St. Croix accomplished results that make Americans proud. The municipal hospitals and other institutions were organized along modern lines, brought to a high degree of working efficiency, the natives were taught in the training schools how to care for their sick, and sanitation as a whole was perfected so that the entire population experienced benefits. These constructive measures resulted in a great decrease in infant mortality, in the better care of women in child-bed, in the treatment of internal disease, in the establishment of the means to carry out modern procedures in surgery as well as the actual work of surgery, and in sanitation and prophylaxis. To this work Doctor Bailey took, in the words of Captain Butler, an honesty of purpose, a desire to serve, a disarming approachableness and a happy disposition, and consequently he at all times enjoyed the esteem of his subordinates and made great headway in winning the affection of the natives.

Doctor Bailey resigned his commission in March, 1924, and then took up his residence at Leesburg, where he has since carried on the routine of his private practice as a specialist and has charge of the eye, ear, nose and throat work at the Loudoun County Hospital and the Fauquier County Hospital. He also has offices at Warrenton and Charles Town, West Virginia, Manassas and Culpeper.

Doctor Bailey is a member of the District of Columbia Medical Society, the Maryland and Virginia Medical Societies, the Loudoun County and Fauquier County Societies, and the American Medical Association. During the fall of 1928 he was abroad studying at Vienna and Budapest. He is a member of the Loudoun County Golf and Country Club, is a Democrat and a member of the Episcopal Church. Associated with him in charge of the offices at Warrenton, Culpeper and Manassas is his brother, Dr. M. Prentiss Bailey.

Doctor Bailey married, March 24, 1917, Miss Mary Hardin Parker, daughter of Edwin Pearson and Mary Lillington (Hardin) Parker, her father a native of Portsmouth, Virginia, and her mother of Hickory, North Carolina. Mr. Parker is now in the insurance business at Washington, D. C. Doctor and Mrs. Bailey, whose home is at Aldie, have three children: William Otis, Jr., born December 28, 1917, Mary Lillington, born August 10, 1923, and Edwin Pearson, born May 7, 1928.

THE PORTSMOUTH STAR, a newspaper that has reflected the modern spirit in the Virginia Tidewater country, bringing daily to its readers the life of the outside world and at the same time providing a medium for the expression of the views and interests of the home people, and using its influence first and last and all the time for a better and greater Portsmouth and Eastern Virginia, was founded September 3, 1894, just a century after the first beginnings of journalism in Norfolk County.

The founders of the *Star* were Paul C. Trugien and William B. Wilder. They made the *Star* a modern newspaper from the start, publishing the full afternoon report of the old Southern Associated Press. After the retirement of Mr. Wilder, Mr. Trugien carried on for many years, steadily building a news-

paper of power and influence. In 1900 he incorporated the
Portsmouth Star Publishing Company, enlarged and modernized
the plant, putting in the first typesetting machines and the first
perfecting press used by any newspaper in Tidewater, Virginia.
He brought into business and financial cooperation with him
many of the prominent men of Portsmouth of that day. Mr.
Trugien in 1906 sold the majority stock in the company to
A. McK. Griggs, who had been associated with the paper since
1900. He was its editor and publisher for twenty years.

Early in 1917 the Portsmouth Star Corporation, with Norman R. Hamilton as president, acquired the business and interests of the Portsmouth Star Publishing Company. Norman R.
Hamilton was one of the first subscribers to the original *Star*
while he was a student in the Portsmouth High School and for
Messrs. Trugien and Wilder secured its first subscription lists.
Later he became the *Star* representative in Norfolk, and it may
be said he has had an interest in the *Star* throughout the third
of a century of its history. Under the new ownership in 1917
improvements and developments were inaugurated to give the
Star increased influence and power among Virginia newspapers.
One was the establishment of the *Sunday Star*. Mr. Hamilton in
1924 acquired the controlling ownership of the *Star*, and during
the past five years the equipment and the facilities of the paper
have been steadily enlarged and improved.

In addition to realizing its primary function as a daily newspaper circulated throughout Tidewater, Virginia, the *Star* has
also adhered to a notable tradition of public service and public
duty. The achievements standing to its credit comprise a chapter in constructive journalism. It was instrumental in the organization of the Kings Daughters Hospital while Mr. Trugien
was in charge; in the formation of the original Business Men's
Association of Portsmouth, in establishing the Home for the
Aged, and twice used the full power of its public influence in
preventing the removal of the general offices of the Seaboard
Air Line from Portsmouth. It has given valuable publicity to
the work of the Navy Yard, to the city in campaigns for physical
betterment and moral improvement, to schools, churches and
other institutions, and a number of years ago it did much to
arouse sentiment for the construction of the George Washington
Highway between Portsmouth and Eastern North Carolina. The
Portsmouth Star is an independent newspaper, published every
afternoon and Sunday morning, devoted to the interest and welfare of the people it serves. It is the people's paper, standing
fearlessly for that which it believes to be right, independent of
influences of every kind, except those of the best.

NORMAN R. HAMILTON. In the history of Portsmouth's only
newspaper, the *Portsmouth Star*, brief reference was made to
its owner and publisher, Norman R. Hamilton. Mr. Hamilton
was born at Portsmouth November 13, 1877, was educated in
the public schools of that city and has had practically a life long
experience and contact with newspaper work. His early training was at Norfolk and for a number of years he has figured
in the history of the *Portsmouth Star*.

Mr. Hamilton is a son of Richard Dabney Hamilton, printer
and journalist, and the great-grandson of Rev. William Hamilton, who with Rev. Gideon Ousley was one of the earliest pioneer
Methodist missionaries sent out to Northern Ireland by John
Wesley, founder of Methodism. Mr. Hamilton's ancestors fought

in the Revolutionary war, in the Mexican war, in the Seminole-Indian wars in Florida, and were in the Confederate army and navy.

Mr. Hamilton in addition to being a publisher has a noteworthy record in politics and public affairs. In 1912 he was Democratic presidential elector from Virginia. In 1914 President Wilson appointed him collector of customs for the district of Virginia, and he served two terms in that position. Before America entered the war Mr. Hamilton as collector of customs at Norfolk and Newport News, was charged with the enforcement of American neutrality in the waters of Virginia, and it became his duty to handle difficult diplomatic problems in connection with the arrival in Hampton Roads, first, of the German raider Prinz Eitel Frederick, next, the Krom Prinz Wilhelm and later, the German prize ship Appam. All of these ships he interned, along with other enemy vessels that had taken haven in Virginia waters and which were there when the United States entered the World war.

For this and other conspicuous service rendered the Government as collector of customs and as representative of the treasury and state department at Hampton Roads Mr. Hamilton received the commendation of President Wilson, and at the close of his term as collector was similarly commended by President Harding.

Mr. Hamilton in 1924 was a delegate from Virginia to the Democratic National Convention at New York. The Democratic State Convention at Roanoke June 21, 1928, named him delegate to the Houston convention. As a result of automobile injuries received while attending the state convention at Roanoke he was unable to go to Houston and the Virginia State Convention named as alternate in his stead his son, Richard Douglas Hamilton, a student at Washington and Lee University, just of voting age, who in consequence served as the youngest member of the National Democratic Convention at Houston.

Mr. Hamilton and Miss Adelaide Etheredge were married October 10, 1901, in the First Presbyterian Church of Portsmouth. Among Mrs. Hamilton's ancestors were members of the Madison family of Virginia. The two sons of Mr. and Mrs. Hamilton are Norman Etheredge, a young Norfolk business man, and Richard Douglas Hamilton.

JAMES HOGE TYLER, member of a family that has conferred so many distinctions upon old Virginia, was in his long career a soldier of the Confederacy, a business man and farmer, and climaxed his service to the State as governor from 1898 to 1902.

He was born at his father's old home "Blenheim" in Caroline County, August 11, 1846. He died at East Radford, Virginia, January 3, 1925, when in his seventy-ninth year. Blenheim, his birthplace, had been the home of the Tyler family for 170 years. His parents were George and Eliza (Hoge) Tyler, his mother a daughter of Gen. James Hoge. His mother dying at his birth, James Hoge Tyler was reared by his grandparents, General and Mrs. James Hoge, at their home "Belle Hampton" in Pulaski County. There at an early age he became assistant to his grandfather, who was stricken with paralysis. He was instructed by private tutors and by his grandfather, and after the death of General Hoge in 1861 he joined his father in Caroline County and attended the school of Franklin Minor in Albemarle County. He also attended Schooler's Academy. He enlisted as a private in the Confederate army and served throughout the war with characteristic courage and fidelity. After the war he engaged in farming in Pulaski County, and through his writings for the press and his individual influence had much to do with awakening the need of the country to manufacturing and mining development and the bringing in of necessary capital for that purpose. In 1877 he was elected a member of the State Senate and in the Senate urged the reduction of state taxes and made another early contribution to economy as a member of the commission which settled the state debt. He also served as a member of the Board of Public Buildings at Blacksburg and Marion, and was made rector of the Virginia Agricultural and Mechanical College, now the Virginia Polytechnic Institute at Blacksburg. This position he resigned to become lieutenant governor, having been elected in 1889. He was a member of the commission to examine into the disputed Virginia-Maryland boundary line, and was elected chairman of the joint committee of the two states.

Governor Tyler from early youth was affiliated with the Presbyterian Church, being chosen a deacon at the age of eighteen and an elder at twenty-three, and for three times was delegate to the General Assembly, attending the Pan-Presbyterian Council at Toronto, Canada, and at Glasgow, Scotland, where he presided over the session.

In 1897 he was given the nomination for governor by acclamation and was elected by a majority of more than 52,000. His administration was a triumph in its combination of economy with constructive progress. The state debt was reduced by more than a million dollars without hampering any important public interest, and at the same time the public school fund was increased, and at the close the public treasury contained more than $800,000.

In the words of an editorial in the *Norfolk Ledger-Dispatch*: "Assuming the governorship of Virginia when the commonwealth was just recovering from the transitory stages following the reaction to the reconstruction regime, James Hoge Tyler was a chief executive of the State who set a pace which may have well been followed by some of his successors. A young man, virtually a youth coming out of the Confederate army, he entered business life and was the last governor of Virginia who had seen service under the stars and bars, and in that way in particular may be designated as the connecting link between the old and the new Virginia. It was during Governor Tyler's administration that the call for a constitutional convention was submitted to the people and the document of the 1902-03 was the result. He urged many reforms in the operation of the State government which failed of adoption, but the establishment of a Bureau of Labor was one achievement, while the State tax rate was reduced and appropriations for State institutions increased, an accomplishment that is almost paradoxical. Governor Tyler was perhaps not a brilliant executive, but of all of Virginia's leaders past and present no man stands higher for rugged honesty, integrity and fidelity to the State's interests, and displayed a desire to put his administration on the road to substantial constructive achievement. Perhaps, judged by modern ideas, he did not go as far as he might have done, but nevertheless he initiated ideas that have been accepted since the time of his active participation in State affairs and have been taken up

J Brooke Howard

by his successors with more or less credit to themselves. Norfolk feels that it has been linked with Governor Tyler's family
for many years. His son, the present mayor of the city, exemplifies many of the qualities that characterized the public life
of the father."

Governor Tyler was in a great measure a representative of
the agriculture side of Virginia's life. He was interested in
farming and served as president of the Virginia State Farmers
Institute and as president of the Southwest Virginia Live Stock
Association. He was a trustee of Hampden-Sidney College, was
on the board of the Union Theological Seminary and the Synod-
ical Orphans Home at Lynchburg.

Governor Tyler married, November 16, 1868, Miss Sue M.
Hammet, of East Radford. His children were: S. Heth Tyler,
of Norfolk; E. H. Tyler, of Pulaski County; James Hoge Tyler,
Jr., of Roanoke; Hal C. Tyler, of East Radford; Mrs. Frank P.
McConnell, of East Radford; Mrs. Robert W. Joplin, of Lan-
caster, South Carolina; and Mrs. Henry Wilson, of Harrisburg,
Pennsylvania.

THOMAS BROOKE HOWARD, one of the brilliant young attorneys practicing at the bar of Alexandria, has achieved a distinction that has brought his name into favorable notice all
over Virginia and at the national capital, and he is not only
recognized because of his professional attainments, which are
somewhat remarkable, but also because of his high personal
character and pleasing personality. He was born in Alexandria, Virginia, September 28, 1902, a son of Thomas Clifton
and Minnie (Stansbury) Howard, natives of that part of Alexandria County that is now Fairfax County. While he is in
business as a merchandise broker in Washington City, Thomas
Clifton Howard still maintains his residence in Alexandria,
where he is regarded as one of the leading citizens of this historic city.

Growing up in Alexandria, T. Brooke Howard attended the
local schools, including the high school, from which he was
graduated in 1919, and even thus early displayed abilities that
led his teachers to advise his developing them along the line of
professional training. Encouraged by his wise and helpful
parents, he took a course in law in the University of Virginia,
and was graduated therefrom in 1924. In October of the succeeding year he established himself in practice in Alexandria,
his offices being at 105 South Royal Street, and his residence at
207 South Washington Street. He is a young man who from
the start has deeply impressed others with his unshakable honesty as well as his ability to lay hold of the essentials of a
situation, and has won and holds the respect too often withheld
from beginners in any line. His influence is and has been invariably for enlightened progress, for his sympathies are true
and his judgment sound. He represents in character and accomplishment the qualities which raise and dignify democratic
citizenship and are the foundation of our best leadership. In
addition to his careful and masterly professional services he is
ever ready to give the best that lies within his unusual powers,
his qualities of heart and brain.

Mr. Howard is unmarried. He is a member of the Virginia
State Bar Association and of the Alexandria Bar Association.
One of the social leaders, he finds relaxation and congenial com-

panionship as a member of the Belle Haven Country Club and the Old Dominion Boat Club. While he has not entered public life, he is a staunch Democrat, and gives his support to his party's principles and candidates. The Presbyterian Church has in him a consistent member.

HENRY WOOD CAMPBELL, Doctor of Dental Surgery, F. A. C. D., who has practiced dental surgery at Suffolk since 1889, was born at Amherst, Virginia, July 9, 1866, son of an old and prominent Virginia family.

His father, Rev. Thomas Horace Campbell, a native Virginian, was born December 18, 1838, and was a soldier of the South in the Confederate army, being in the command under Gen. George E. Pickett. A bullet received in the battle of Gaines Mills he carried to his grave. After the close of the war he entered the ministry of the Methodist Episcopal Church, South, and was distinguished by his eloquence, his devotion to the church and humanity, and for thirty-two years carried on his labors as a pastor, from 1874 until his death on July 14, 1906. Rev. Thomas Horace Campbell married Miss Henry Virginia Wood, whose father, Rev. Henry D. Wood, was a Methodist minister who died in Georgia. Henry Virginia Wood was born April 12, 1843, in Buckingham County, Virginia, was married at "Spring Garden," Amherst County, Virginia, April 16, 1864, and died January 5, 1920, at her home, "The Oaks," in Amherst County. She was interred at Lynchburg, Virginia.

After completing his early education in the schools of Amherst and under private tutors Henry Wood Campbell entered the University of Maryland, from which he was graduated with the degree Doctor of Dental Surgery in 1889. In the same year he established an office at Suffolk, Virginia. His professional work has always had a broader range than that of routine practice. He has been influential in setting higher standards in the profession generally. From 1896 to 1918 he was president of the Virginia State Board of Dental Examiners, retiring in that year from the board. He was reappointed to the state board in 1920 by Governor E. Lee Trinkle of Virginia, and was reelected its president, in which capacity he still serves. He was honored with election as president of the Virginia State Dental Association for the year 1894-95, and was chairman of its legislative committee from 1909-11. It was largely through his influence that the General Assembly of Virginia passed a bill recognizing dentistry as a specialty of medicine in the same class with the other specialties of medicine which required the degree of M. D. This bill was passed in 1910, and became effective in 1914. This standard, if continued, would have required a complete medical education for all dentists practicing in Virginia. He is a member of the American Dental Association, and has the honorary degree of "Fellow of the American College of Dentists." He is a member of the committee of the National Association of Dental Examiners in conjunction with the Carnegie Educational Foundation working to create a National Board of Dental Examiners. He served as president of the National Association of Dental Examiners in 1905-06. He also is an honorary member of the North Carolina Dental Society, the South Side Virginia Dental Society, and a member of the Virginia Tidewater Dental Association, and for many years he has been a contributor to periodicals and journals of his profession.

Aside from his profession Doctor Campbell is president of the Suffolk Mutual Building & Loan Association, a director of the American Bank & Trust Company, Inc., and from 1903 to 1919 he was a member of the Suffolk City Council, being its president from 1914-16, and chairman of the finance committee in 1918. During the World war he was appointed a member of the Medical Advisory Board, and was secretary of this board during its existence. Doctor Campbell is affiliated with the Masonic fraternity, is a member of the Country Club, former president of the Lions Club, a member of the Association for the Preservation of Virginia Antiquities, a member of the Virginia State Chamber of Commerce, is a Democrat and a Methodist.

On June 4, 1895, he married Miss Emmeline Eley, of suffolk, daughter of Richard Seth and Eliza Priscilla (Riddick) Eley. Her parents were native Virginians, and her father was a lieutenant in the Confederate army, and was imprisoned upon Johnson's Island. After the war he was a retail merchant in Suffolk until the time of his death in 1893. Her mother died in 1924, at the age of eighty-seven. Both are interred at Suffolk, Virginia. Doctor and Mrs. Campbell have a family of four children: Seth Eley, an electrical engineer with the General Electric Company; Dr. T. Wood Campbell, associated with his father in practice; Margaret Elizabeth; and Emily Louise.

CLAUDE L. YOWELL, principal of the Hampstead High School, Hampstead, Maryland, is a member of an old and prominent family of Madison County, Virginia.

Mr. Yowell was born in Madison County, March 7, 1898, son of Casper and Mary (Weaver) Yowell. The Yowells came from England and the Weavers from Germany, settling in Virginia in Colonial times, and both families were represented by soldiers in the War of the Revolution. The Weavers were Lutherans and helped establish the first Lutheran Church in the state in 1726. Mr. Yowell's grandfather Weaver enlisted at the age of seventeen in the Confederate army, serving with the Reserves. His grandfather Yowell served in the Madison cavalry under General Lee. Casper Yowell has been a noted stock farmer and breeder in Madison County, having a farm specializing in Black Angus cattle, Poland China hogs and Shropshire sheep. He is a deacon in the Baptist Church and active in the Sunday School. Casper Yowell and wife had two sons, Claude L. and Russell W. Russell was born March 23, 1908, and is a student in the University of Virginia.

Claude L. Yowell grew up on the home farm in Madison County, attended local schools and in 1922 graduated Bachelor of Science from the University of Virginia. He took the Master of Science degree at the University in 1927, and is now doing work on a Doctor of Philosophy degree in the summer sessions at Johns Hopkins University. He has been teaching for the past six years, two years at the Handley High School, Winchester, Virginia; three years as principal of the Stanardsville High School. For his theses in taking the Master's degree he wrote a history of Madison County which is now on the market and is the first work of this nature finished on the history of this county. The publication of this book led to his becoming a member of the Pi Gamma Mu, honorary social science fraternity, of which he is now an active member.

Mr. Yowell married, June 30, 1925, Miss Grace T. Yowell, of Rappahannock County, daughter of Weldon A. and Mazie

(Leathers) Yowell. Her father is a farmer and stock raiser in Rappahannock County. Mrs. Yowell is one of five children, Gladys R., Susie G., Kelsey A., Grace T. and Hugh A., being the only one of these now married. Mrs. Yowell graduated from the Harrisonburg Teachers College in 1925, and was engaged as a teacher in the Stanardsville High School for the next three sessions. Mrs. Yowell is active in the clubs of her adopted town.

JOHN W. DARDEN. No better illustration of the value of industry, perseverance and determination, guided by integrity and probity and directed by natural and developed ability, could be found than the career of the late John W. Darden. Left an orphan at a tender age, he faced life with but a meagre education and without the aid of friendly alliances or other adventitious circumstances worked his way to a position among the substantial men of his community, being long a well known figure in railway, mercantile and agricultural circles in Nansemond and Southampton counties. He was a man of high character and public spirit, and in his death, which occurred in October, 1914, his community lost one of its reliable and valued citizens.

Mr. Darden was born at Southampton, Virginia, July 16, 1847, the oldest of six children of John Wilson Darden, a farmer, and his wife, Nannie (Norfleet) Darden. He was descended from a family which originated in Scotland, whence the American progenitor immigrated to this country during the early Colonial period and settled in Virginia. John W. Darden was only twelve years of age when his parents died and he was forced to leave school at Southampton to face life's responsibilities on his own account. He was variously employed at such honorable employment as he could find until he reached the age of seventeen years, and then enlisted in a regiment of Virginia volunteer infantry, with which he served bravely until the close of the war between the states, seeing much active service and receiving a wound in the arm, the scar of which he carried until his death. At the close of his military service he sought railroading as a means of livelihood, and through industry and fidelity rose to be section master of the Seaboard Airline Railway in Southampton County. Later he held a like position with the Southern Railway, and during its construction was in charge of the leveling of rails. Resigning from this position, Mr. Darden embarked in mercantile affairs and for several years was the proprietor of an establishment at Franklin and subsequently at Southampton, but following his marriage sold his business interests, purchased a farm in Nansemond County, and from that time forward until his demise was successfully engaged in agricultural pursuits. Mr. Darden was a man of high character and a consistent member of the Baptist Church. While he took much interest in public affairs, he never sought office, but supported generously the movements that his good judgment told him would benefit his community.

In November, 1874, Mr. Darden married Miss Margaret Jane Edney, a descendant of a family which originated in England and settled in Virginia prior to the Revolutionary war. She was educated at private schools and is a daughter of Jonathan and Margaret (Spence) Edney, her father being originally an inventor and manufacturer of machinery in Camden County, North Carolina, who later moved to Franklin, Virginia, and spent the rest of his life in the lumber and grain milling business. Mrs. Darden was the fifth in order of birth in a family of ten

children. To Mr. and Mrs. Darden there were born ten children: Junius Willard, who is deceased; John W. H., a merchant of Branchville, Virginia, who married May Taylor and has one son, John Taylor; Nancy Norfleet, who married Thomas Ewre, of Camp Mill, Franklin, and has three children, Oretha, Margueritte and Thomas; Lucy Emma, who is deceased; Margaret Indiana, the wife of Robert L. Harper, of Raleigh, North Carolina, and has one child, Darden; William Mosby, of California, who has two children, Sarah and William Mosby, Jr.; Wallace Alexander, who is deceased; Annie Asenath, the wife of John E. Coggin, a lumberman of Philadelphia; Dr. St. Clair, a medical college graduate and specialist in tuberculosis, in charge of the Healthwin Sanitarium at South Bend, Indiana, who has two children, Thomas and Robert; and Sarah Mabel, who married Rochelle Harrell, of Suffolk, Virginia, and has two children, Sarah and Rochelle. Mrs. Darden, who survives her husband and resides at 615 Colonial Avenue, is one of the highly esteemed ladies of Norfolk, and is active in the work of the Baptist Church.

CARTER PERKINS, D. D. S., was one of the veteran and honored representatives of his profession in his native state of Virginia at the time of his death, which occurred in the city of Newport News December 7, 1926. Not only his professional skill and precedence but also his sterling character and high communal standing make specially consistent the memorial tribute here accorded to him.

Doctor Perkins was born in Middlesex County, Virginia, August 13, 1832, and thus he had attained to the patriarchal age of ninety-four years when his earnest and worthy life came to its close. Aside from the marked success that he gained in the practice of his profession Doctor Perkins became a leader in real estate development and exploitation after he had established his residence in Newport News, and as a young man he gave loyal service in defense of the cause of the Confederate states in the Civil war.

The subject of this memoir was a son of Col. Carter Perkins and Mary Ann (Humphrey) Perkins, of whose six children he was the fourth in order of birth. Colonel Perkins was owner and operator of a fine plantation estate in Middlesex County, and he made a record of gallant service as a soldier in the War of 1812, in which he held the rank of colonel.

Doctor Perkins gained his early education mainly in private schools and under the direction of private tutors. In fortifying himself for the work of his chosen profession, before the era of regular dental colleges, he was favored in gaining technical and practical instruction under the preceptorship of Doctor Cowlen, of Baltimore, Maryland, who was one of the eminent dental practitioners and authorities of that period. After completing his through course in dentistry Doctor Perkins returned to Virginia, and thereafter he continued in the active practice of his profession in Middlesex and Lancaster counties until 1858, when he removed to Charles City County, where he continued in practice until the inception of the Civil war, when he promptly subordinated all personal interests and enlisted for service in the Confederate army. On the 5th of July, 1861, when he was twenty-nine years of age, he enlisted at Jamestown in Company K, Fifty-third Virginia Infantry, and soon afterward he was detailed to duty as quartermaster clerk. In September, 1861, he was assigned to a clerkship in the commissary department, and in 1862 he was placed in hospital service, supply department, in the city of Richmond. Before the close of 1862 he was honorably discharged, by reason of physical disability.

After the close of the Civil war Doctor Perkins engaged in the lumber business in Charles City County, and there he continued operations on an extensive scale until 1889, when he sold his interests in the lumber business and removed to Newport News, where he resumed the practice of his profession. In 1894 the Doctor retired from practice and turned his attention to the real estate business. He became president of the Newport News Development Company, which promoted the development of the east end of the city, and after a few years of association with this line of enterprise he became associated with his son Robert W., in the furniture business, under the title of Newport News Furniture Company. He sold his interest in this business in 1901, and for the ensuing five years he was cashier and a substantial stockholder of the Newport News Savings Bank. In 1906 the Doctor here resumed the practice of his profession, from which he did not retire until 1920, when he was eighty-eight years of age. He thereafter lived in gracious and well earned retirement in Newport News until his death at the venerable age of ninety-four years. Doctor Perkins long held membership in the American Dental Association and the Virginia State Dental Association, and as author he made valuable contributions to the standard and periodical literature of his profession. He was a stalwart advocate of the principles of the Democratic party, and he served as a member of the City Council of Newport News, as well as a member of the Board of Education. He was an earnest member of Trinity Methodist Episcopal Church, South, as is also his widow, who continues a gracious figure in the social and cultural circles of Newport News, where she is a member of the Woman's Club and also of the American Legion Auxiliary.

In May, 1858, Doctor Perkins was united in marriage with Miss Mary Minge Graves, of Charles City County, and of this union were born five children: Robert W. became one of the representative business men of Newport News and served as a member of the Virginia Legislature. Carter, William C., and John Freeman likewise became actively identified with business enterprises, and the only daughter was Mary Minge. The death of Mrs. Perkins occurred prior to the removal of the Doctor to Newport News, and he was still a resident of Charles City County when his marriage to Miss Mary Sue Richardson was there solemnized in Charles City Chapel of the Methodist Church, November 25, 1885. Mrs. Perkins is a daughter of the late Dr. Pryor Richardson and William America (Christian) Richardson, the former of whom was born in New Kent County and the latter of whom was a member of the influential Christian family that was founded in Virginia in the Colonial days. Dr. Pryor Richardson was graduated from William and Mary College as a member of the class of 1837, and thereafter he took a course in a leading medical college in Baltimore, Maryland. He became one of the leading physicians and surgeons in Charles City County, where he likewise owned a large and valuable plantation estate, and he was influential in the councils of the Democratic party during the course of many years. Ann, eldest of the children of Dr. Carter Perkins and Mary S. (Richardson) Perkins, is the wife of William E. Scruggs, a Government employe at Newport News, and they have one child, Ann Carter. Pryor Richardson Perkins, second of the children, sacrificed his life in the World war, he having been killed in action while with his command at the Argonne front in France, October 3, 1918.

He held the rank of first lieutenant in the Twentieth Aerial Squadron. This gallant young Virginian had received preliminary training at the University of Ohio, Columbus, and was of the first contingent of Americans to receive training with the school of the Royal Air Force at Oxford University, England, where he was graduated as a technical expert in air service early in 1918, his commission as first lieutenant having been received by him in May of that year. Margaret, next younger of the children, is the widow of Benjamin C. Flannagan, who was in the service of the Norfolk Southern (electric) Railway, and their two children are Margaret Perkins Flannagan, and Richard Perkins Flannagan. Elizabeth, youngest of the children, is the wife of Frank E. Kuhn, an employe of the Chesapeake & Ohio Railroad, and their one child is Frank E., Jr.

LEMUEL CORNICK SHEPHERD, M. D., was through a period of forty years one of the able representatives of his profession in the City of Norfolk. He was a doctor of broad and liberal culture, of progressive ideas, enjoyed not only a successful private practice, but was also a leader in public health work.

He was born at Petersburg, Virginia, January 26, 1864, son of John Camp and Susan (Land) Shepherd. At the time of his birth his mother was living as refugee from Norfolk, which was the home of the family. After the war John Camp Shepherd became a merchant in Princess Anne County, Virginia, and was also a farmer. He served in the Confederate cavalry throughout the period of the war.

Doctor Shepherd was one of a family of six children and was educated in country schools in Princess Anne County, attended the Episcopal High School at Alexandria, and was graduated from the Bellevue Hospital Medical College of Long Island in 1886. A few years later he interrrupted his private practice to go abroad and spent portions of the years 1892-93 in study at Vienna and Berlin. For several years Doctor Shepherd was a member of the Norfolk Board of Health and also served as city bacteriologist. He was a member of the Norfolk and American Medical Associations and the Medical Society of Virginia. Doctor Shepherd was a Democrat in politics, and he and his wife were active members of St. Paul's Episcopal Church.

Doctor Shepherd was still a comparatively young man when he died April 4, 1926. He married, September 6, 1894, Emma Cartwright. Mrs. Shepherd, whose home is at 1219 Westover Avenue, Norfolk, was born in Nantucket, Massachusetts, and was reared and educated in that state, attending the State Normal School at New Britain, Connecticut. Her father, Benjamin Cartwright, was an old time whaling captain who sailed out of the Port of New Bedford. Her mother was Agnes Hamilton, and Mrs. Shepherd was one of four children. Mrs. Shepherd is an active member of the Norfolk Society of Arts. She is the mother of three children. Her son Lemuel C. II was educated in the Norfolk Academy and the Virginia Military Institute and is a captain in the United States Marine Corps. Captain Shepherd married Virginia Tunstall Driver, of Norfolk, and has two sons, Lemuel III, and Wilson Driver. Edith Shepherd, who was educated in the Randolph-Macon Woman's College at Lynchburg, is the wife of James Vass Brooke, a civil engineer, and they have two daughters, Mary Goode Brooke and Edith Shepherd. The youngest child, Miss Virginia Hamilton, attended school at Norfolk and Skidmore College at Saratoga Springs, New York.

ADAM ADDISON WENDEL, sheriff of Norfolk County, is a prominent type of the new Virginian, a western man who was attracted to this section of Tidewater, Virginia, many years ago. He has taken a prominent part in the development of its industrial resources, and has given an administration of the office of sheriff which has been approved three times by the votes of the people.

Mr. Wendel was born at Washington Court House, Fayette County, Ohio, July 8, 1869. His people were early settlers in Ohio. Mr. Wendel was reared and educated in that locality, and as a young man became interested in the lumber industry. It was his connections with lumbering which brought him to Norfolk County in 1901 as superintendent and manager of an organization which had secured ten thousand acres of timber land in the famous Dismal Swamp region. He and his associates put up a saw mill which had a daily cut of sixty thousand feet of lumber. This inaugurated the production of lumber in a region which for centuries had been practically waste land, and for twenty years Mr. Wendel gave his time and energies to this business. Besides clearing away the timber and utilizing it for lumber, some eight hundred acres were turned into valuable and productive farming land. For this drainage was essential, and this was secured through the formation of a drainage district. Besides its possibilities for farming the region is a natural game preserve, abounding in deer, bear and other prizes of sports. All these advantages have made Mr. Wendel very much attached to the region, and he spends a considerable part of the year in that recreation ground.

He has never been a seeker for office, but the possibilities of a real public service led him to become a candidate for sheriff in 1919. He was elected, was reelected in 1923, and in the August primaries of 1927 was nominated by a large margin of votes. The three hundred square miles of territory in Norfolk County, with six hundred miles of road, demand utmost vigilance on the part of the sheriff and his nine full-time deputies in the enforcement of the laws providing for peace and good order.

Mr. Wendel is a member of the B. P. O. Elks and the Izaak Walton League, and is deeply interested in the fish and game conservation work with a view to making the Dismal Swamp a nationally known game preserve. Mr. Wendel married Olive Durnell, of Washington Court House, Ohio. She is active in church and social life at Portsmouth.

LUTHER SPURGON BALLARD was for many years well known in business circles in Portsmouth, a leader in the insurance field there, and had a great many friends and business associates who keenly felt his loss when he died December 15, 1925.

He was born in North Carolina, in 1875, one of the thirteen children of Stephen Ballard, a planter of the old North State. Luther S. Ballard was educated in public schools, and learned the insurance business by several years of active experience at Philadelphia. From there he removed to Portsmouth, and built up a large business as general agent for the Mutual Insurance Company of Richmond. He always voted as a Democrat and was a member of the Court Street Baptist Church at Portsmouth.

He married in September, 1909, at Portsmouth, Mrs. Ella (Scott) Savage, widow of William Savage and daughter of David and Sarah (Bunting) Scott. Her father was a Norfolk County

Paul Lyne Delaney   Martin D. Delaney, M.D.

farmer and Mrs. Ballard was reared and educated in that county. She was left a widow with one small child, Russell Scott Savage, who also took the name of his step-father, and is now continuing in the insurance business in Virginia, being one of the leaders in that field. He married Minnie Allen and has two children, David Savage and Jack Allen.

Mrs. Ballard, who resides in Portsmouth, at 225 North Elm Avenue, is a member of the Central Methodist Church, is president of its aid society and treasurer of the Earnest Workers Society. She is also a member of Stonewall Chapter, United Daughters of the Confederacy.

MARTIN DONOHUE DELANEY, M. D., has been established in the practice of his profession in the City of Alexandria more than a quarter of a century, and his unqualified success offers the best evidence of his professional skill as well as of his secure place in popular confidence and esteem in the community that has profited by his earnest and able ministrations. He gives special attention to the surgical branch of his profession, and in the same has attained to high reputation. He maintains both his residence and office headquarters at 131 North Washington Street.

Doctor Delaney was born in the City of Toledo, Ohio, April 28, 1874, and is a son of Dennis William and Josephine (Donohue) Delaney, both of whom were born in Ireland and both of whom were young at the time of the coming of the respective families to the United States. They lived in Philadelphia and he served three years under General McClellan. During the greater part of his active career Dennis W. Delaney was a successful contractor and builder in Prince William County, Virginia, and there his death occurred February 5, 1911, his wife having passed away on the 12th of January of the following year and both having been devoted communicants of the Catholic Church. Doctor Delaney is a direct descendant on his mother's side of Commodore Barry, the father of the old American Navy. On his father's side he is descended from the nobility of France.

As a boy and youth Doctor Delaney attended the Christian Brothers School of Philadelphia, Pennsylvania, and thereafter continued his studies in St. John's Academy in his present home City of Alexandria. His higher academic education was acquired in Mount St. Mary's College at Emmettsburg, Maryland, from which he received the degrees of both Bachelor and Master of Arts. His technical education for his chosen calling was gained in the medical department of Georgetown University, District of Columbia, from which he was graduated as a member of the class of 1898. After thus receiving his degree of Doctor of Medicine he gained fortifying experience by serving two years as an interne in Columbia Hospital, Washington, D. C., and he then, in 1900, established himself in the practice of his profession in Alexandria, where he has since continued his ministrations with marked success and where he specializes in surgery, with many delicate operations to his credit, both of major and minor order. Recognition of his special skill as a surgeon is attested by his being a fellow of the American College of Surgeons, the representative national organization. He has membership also in the American Medical Association, the Virginia State Medical Society, the Northern Virginia Medical Society and the Alexandria Medical Society. He is surgeon for the Southern Railway, Richmond, Fredericksburg & Potomac

Railroad, and the Chesapeake & Ohio Railroad. Doctor Delaney
is a member of the Virginia Governing Committee of the Gorgas
Memorial Institute of Tropical and Preventive Medicine. He
is also a life member of the Service Veterans of the United
States.

The political allegiance of Doctor Delaney is given to the
Democratic party, and both he and his wife are zealous communicants of the Catholic Church. The Doctor is affiliated with
the Knights of Columbus and the Benevolent and Protective
Order of Elks, is a charter member of the Washington Society,
and in his home community is a member of the Belle Haven
Country Club. Ancestors of Doctor Delaney were gallant
soldiers in the War of the American Revolution, though his parents were natives of Ireland, and he is thus eligible for affiliation with the Sons of the American Revolution, while by similar
ancestral heritage Mrs. Delaney has eligibility for membership
in the Daughters of the American Revolution and also the
Colonial Dames, she being a descendant of Col. John Fitzgerald,
who served as an aide-de-camp on the staff of Gen. George
Washington in the great struggle that gained American Independence.

On the 4th of June, 1906, was solemnized the marriage of
Doctor Delaney and Miss Catharine O'Donoghue, a daughter of
Martin and Margaret (Lyne) O'Donoghue, of Georgetown, District of Columbia, where her father was a wholesale merchant,
both he and his wife having been born in Ireland. Mr.
O'Donoghue died at the age of fifty-two years, June 28, 1888,
and his widow attained to the age of seventy-five years, she
having passed to the life eternal on the 9th of September, 1917.
Martin O'Donoghue was descended from the O'Donoghues of
Ross Castle, Ireland. Martin Donohue, eldest of the children
of Doctor and Mrs. Delaney, was born June 5, 1907, and is now
(1928) a student in the Virginia Military Institute; Paul Lyne
was born April 5, 1909, and is attending Georgetown University, where he is pursuing studies in both the literary and law
departments; Catharine, the only daughter, was born November 28, 1913, and is a student in the Alexandria High School;
William Morgan, youngest of the children, was born February
20, 1916, and is attending school in his home city.

EUGENE MARCELLIS POLLARD. A veteran of the Confederate
service and a business man of unquestioned ability, the late
Eugene Marcellis Pollard, after years of faithful service as a
railroad man and druggist retired to Richmond, and here, in the
capital city of the South, he passed away in 1913, beloved and
honored by all who knew him. He was born in Chesterfield
County, Virginia, July 27, 1845, and was educated in its schools
up to the age of sixteen years. He was a son of Joseph and
Lydia Frances (Bottom) Pollard, who had five children.

The school days of Eugene Marcellis Pollard were interrupted by the tocsin of war, and in spite of his youth he enlisted in the Confederate army, and remained in the service
for four years, during which period he was wounded in action,
and rose to the rank of sergeant. After the close of the war he
entered the employ of the Norfolk & Western Railroad, and
remained with that company for three years, leaving to go into
the drug store of Dr. W. B. Conway, and rose, during the fifteen
years he remained with him, to be manager of the business.
Never very strong as a result of his war experience, he then

retired, and, coming to Richmond, here passed the remainder of his life. He was a member of Virginia May Lodge, A. F. and A. M., and Stonewall Jackson Post, Confederate Veterans. He and all his family were Presbyterians, and earnest church workers and supporters.

On December 13, 1871, Mr. Pollard married Miss Virginia M. Jones, a daughter of David T. and Martha Ann (Beville) Jones, and granddaughter of John Archer Beville, a French Huguenot who came from France to Virginia. For several generations the Jones family has resided in Chesterfield County, Virginia. David T. Jones was a planter, and served as a captain of a company of Virginia militia in the ante-bellum days. He and his wife had two children, Mrs. Pollard's brother, Ulysses Bolling Jones, being her senior. Mrs. Pollard was educated in the Masonic Female Institute in Blacksburg, Virginia. Of the children born to Mr. and Mrs. Pollard eight lived to reach maturity, namely: Maude, who is the owner of the Poe Court Book Shop and an authority on antiques, married Joseph Kelly Hull, a railroad man connected with the Chesapeake & Ohio Railroad; Mrs. Virginia May Wright, widow of the late John Wright, formerly with the Chesapeake & Ohio Railroad, and mother of five children, John Caskie, Randolph, Evelyn, David and Charles; Stella Frances, who is cashier of the Postal Telegraph Company and lives in Richmond; Parke P., an electrical contractor of Richmond, who married Eva Lee Russel, of Mecklenburg County, Virginia, and has two children, Parke P., Junior, and Dorothy Elizabeth; Lulu, who is the wife of T. W. Graves, manager of the Wilson Packing Company, Danville, Virginia; Edith Argyle, who is the wife of Howard Mann Morecook, traveling freight agent for the Chesapeake & Ohio Railroad, and mother of Howard Mann Morecook, Junior; Glenna Leville Pollard, who is with the Chesapeake & Ohio Railroad; and Eugenia Minon Pollard, who resides in Richmond.

WILLIAM EDWARD REESE. In recalling the life and activities of those who once trod the old familiar ways with ourselves but have now passed from the scene of life, their characteristics are remembered, their generous impulses are recollected and the real value of their influence is determined. In such a review a loving and appreciative light shines on the life and personality of William Edward Reese, who for many years was one of the honored citizens of Richmond, where his widow is still residing. He was born in Virginia, September 23, 1868, and died in Richmond April 15, 1924. His father, William Reese, was a farm owner and planter of Halifax County, Virginia, a man well and favorably known throughout a wide region, and his mother's first name was Rebecca. They had three children: Albert, who is a truck farmer upon an extensive scale; Mrs. Eliza Dawson; and William Edward, who was the youngest of the family.

The public schools of Halifax County educated William Edward Reese, and when he completed his education he became a clerk in a hardware store at Cody, Halifax County, but after several years he left that employment to enter the sawmill business. Selling his mill later on, he engaged in the wholesale lumber business in Lynchburg, Virginia, and at the same time he was interested in a stone quarry. When he sold these interests he located permanently in Richmond, and for two years handled scrap iron, and for two years more he was in the bag business. He was also interested in a fertilizer plant in Ellerson, Virginia,

that is still in operation. However his health failing, he found
it necessary to dispose of all his holdings, and for several years
prior to his death lived retired. He was an enthusiastic member
of the North Side Baptist Church, but outside of that connection
his interests were centered in his family. A public spirited
citizen, warm hearted and generous, anxious to help others and
to sustain through his contributions the higher things of life, his
influence lives on.

In November, 1900, Mr. Reese married Miss Dollie McDaniel,
a daughter of James W. and Dolly (Ridgeway) McDaniel, who
had seven children, of whom Mrs. Reese was the third in order
of birth. She was educated in Halifax County, and is a very
fine lady, a good mother and kind neighborhood visitor, no
trouble or calamity coming to those in her vicinity without her
offering her sympathy and material help. One child, Dr. Clyde
Bishop Reese, was born to Mr. and Mrs. Reese. He was educated in the public schools of Lynchburg, Virginia, and the Virginia Military Institute, from which he was graduated in 1923
with the degree of Doctor of Dental Surgery, and since then has
been engaged in the practice of dentistry in Richmond. Doctor
Reese married Miss Vernesse Cecelia Batterfield, of Virginia.
His fraternal connections are with the Masonic order and the
Odd Fellows, and his professional ones are with the Virginia
State Dental Association. A young man of undoubted ability,
well trained, he has forged ahead, and is today one of the leading
dentists of the city, and a man of whom the best is spoken, for
he stands well with the public.

JOHN O. GAMAGE was born at Norfolk, Virginia, in January,
1837, and here he maintained his home until his death, which
occurred in February, 1910. He was an honored representative
of one of the sterling and influential pioneer families of Norfolk,
here succeeded to the control of a large and important wholesale
merchandise business that had been founded by his father fully
ninety-five years ago, and here he continued as a leading citizen
and business man until the close of his long and worthy life.
The business founded by his father, Elisha Gamage, nearly a
century ago is still continued under the family name and its executive head at the present time is Miss Nancy C. Gamage, who
is a daughter of the subject of this memoir and who provided the
data on which this tribute to her honored father is based.

John O. Gamage was reared and educated in Norfolk and
was the first of three generations of the Gamage family to be
educated at the Norfolk Academy. He was a son of Elisha and
Mary Ann (Fulton) Gamage, of whose seven children he was
the third in order of birth. The Gamage family was founded in
America in the early Colonial period, and its lineage is one of
ancient and distinguished order in France and England. The
French branch spelled the name, De Gamache. The family record traces back to 900, A. D., and it was one of royal status in one
of the minor kingdoms of ancient France, whence representatives went into England with William the Conqueror. It was
from England that came the original representatives of the family to America, where settlement was made in the Massachusetts colony long prior to the war of the Revolution, members of
the family having later been established in the State of New
York.

Elisha Gamage, the pioneer merchant of Norfolk, Virginia,
was born and reared in the State of New York and was a son

of Samuel Gamage II, who was a large landowner in that commonwealth and whose father, Samuel, Sr., went forth from Massachusetts as a patriot soldier in the Revolution, he having been a member of the Massachusetts troop commanded by Col. Thomas Croft, and another member having been Paul Revere, whose historic ride has made him a famed figure in American history. Subsequently this first Samuel Gamage became a lieutenant of marines on the frigate *Dean*, and on this war vessel he served under Capt. Samuel Nicholson in the naval arm of the Continental service in the Revolution. Samuel Gamage II was a gallant soldier in the War of 1812.

It was in the year 1833 that Elisha Gamage established himself in the wholesale general merchandise business in Norfolk, and the business has been continued under family name and control to the present time, though changing conditions in the passing years have brought both modification and expansion of its varied functions. It was about 1834 that Elisha Gamage became executive head of the Farmers Bank of Norfolk, and he continued the president after the reorganization under the title of Merchants & Mechanics Bank. He was long one of the most progressive and influential business men of Norfolk and was a citizen who commanded unqualified popular esteem and confidence, the high prestige of the family name having here been maintained by his son John O. after he himself had passed from the stage of his mortal endeavors.

As a young man John O. Gamage became actively associated with his father's wholesale mercantile business, and his diversified experience well fitted him for assuming eventual control. The enterprise is now conducted under the title of John O. Gamage, and its present functions are the handling of lime, cement and other building supplies and accessories. The business is one of substantial order and representative character, and is the oldest business in this line in Norfolk to be continuously conducted by one family. Since the death of her father in 1910 Miss Nancy C. Gamage has been active president of the company and has directed the business with marked ability and success.

John O. Gamage was a man of fine character, loyal and public spirited as a citizen, and progressive and resourceful in the handling of business interests of importance. He was significantly loyal to the cause of the Democratic party, though never a seeker of public office, and was a valued member of the Norfolk Board of Trade and the local Chamber of Commerce. His original religious affiliation was with the Presbyterian Church, but he later became an active member of the Methodist Episcopal Church, South. He was a member of that splendid old organization, the Norfolk Light Artillery Blues, which was founded in 1828, and with this command he served as a loyal soldier of the Confederacy in the Civil war, as a member of Capt. C. R. Grandy's Battery, Garnett's Battalion of the army corps commanded by Gen. A. P. Hill. Mr. Gamage was wounded and captured, and was for some time held as a Federal prisoner of war at City Point, near Petersburg, Virginia.

In 1859 was solemnized the marriage of Mr. Gamage and Miss Bell Sarah Williams, daughter of Rev. Peter Williams, of Northampton County, Virginia, her father having been a clergyman of the Methodist Church and having been a descendant of Henry Williams, who settled on the Dale Grant in Northamton County, he having been a brother of Roger Williams, the founder of the State of Rhode Island. Mrs. Gamage, venerable in years, continues to maintain her home in Norfolk and was long a gracious figure in its social and cultural activities, besides being a devout member of the Methodist Church. She is a grand-daughter, on the maternal side, of Thomas Clay, who bought part of the historic Arlington estate from the Custis family.

John W. Gamage, eldest of the children of Mr. and Mrs. John O. Gamage, married Miss Fannie Camp, of Petersburg, Virginia, and he continued as a representative business man of Norfolk until his death. Albert E., the second son, was asso-ciated with his father in business and was about forty years of age at the time of his death. Mary Bell, eldest of the daugh-ters, died at the age of twenty-five years. Miss Nancy Clay Gamage assumed control of the business interests of her father at the time of his death and is now president of the John O. Gamage business, which was established many years ago, and is engaged in the building material business of wholesale order. Miss Gamage has proven herself amply able to maintain the honors of the family name in both civic and business affairs and is a popular figure in both social and business circles in her native city, where she is a member of the Woman's Club and of the Chamber of Commerce, besides being a zealous member of the Methodist Episcopal Church, South. Ida B., next younger of the daughters, was graduated from the Maryland Institute of Art and was twenty-three years of age at the time of her death. Miss Edna Sue, youngest of the children, was graduated in 1916 from the training school for nurses maintained by the Protestant Hospital in Norfolk, and as a nurse she served with the University of Virginia Corps in the World war period. She and her sister Nancy C. maintain a home in Norfolk, Virginia.

SAMUEL HORACE HAWES, whose record as one of the leading merchants and business men of the City of Richmond for over fifty years is recalled by all the older residents of the city, was a fine example of Virginia citizenship and a man of distinguished family connections.

He was born in Powhatan County, Virginia, June 5, 1838, and died at Richmond February 13, 1922, at the age of eighty-four. His father, Samuel Pierce Hawes, was born in Dorchester, Massachusetts, in 1799, and was sixteen years of age when he came to Richmond in 1815. In 1845 he established a coal busi-ness in the city, and was active in that line of commercial work until his death. Samuel Pierce Hawes married Judith Ann Smith, of Virginia. They had a family of eight children. One of these was Rev. Dr. Herbert H. Hawes. Another, Mary Vir-ginia, was one of the most widely known American women of letters, under the pen name Marion Harland. She married the Rev. Edward Payson Terhune.

Samuel Horace Hawes was educated in public schools in Richmond and as a youth became associated with his father's coal business. He took active charge of the business at his father's death. At the outbreak of the Civil war he enlisted in the Richmond Howitzers, and was in the service four years. During the last thirteen months of the war he was a prisoner at Fort Delaware and later at Morris Island, South Carolina. He held the rank of first lieutenant. After the war he returned to Richmond and thereafter gave his active attention to his busi-ness affairs.

He was a director of the State Planters Bank of Richmond for many years and for two terms president of the Chamber of

Charles McCulloch M.D.

Commerce. He was on the Police Benevolent Association board and for many years a member of the board of the Male Orphan Asylum. Mr. Hawes used the prosperity gained in business in many ways for the benefit of the community in which he lived. He was a member of the Westmoreland Club and of Lee Chapter No. 1, United Confederate Veterans.

On October 3, 1867, he married Miss Martha C. Heath, of Newark, New Jersey, where she was born and educated. She died February 13, 1897. Her father, S. R. W. Heath, was a merchant and president of the Firemen's Insurance Company of Newark. Mr. and Mrs. Hawes had three children. Horace Sterling Hawes, the oldest, was educated in Rutgers College at New Brunswick, New Jersey, and is a merchant at Richmond. He married Mary McCaw, daughter of William McCaw, of Richmond, and has two children: Mary McCaw, wife of Randolph Carter Harrison and mother of two children, Randolph Carter, Jr., and Mary Ann; and Ann Sterling, wife of A. E. Willson Harrison and mother of a son, Horace Hawes. The second son, Heath Woodruff Hawes, is deceased. The daughter, Miss Katharine H. Hawes, who resides at 3211 Chamberlayne Avenue in Richmond, was educated in the Ely School in New York City. She is a member of the Richmond Woman's Club, is a life member of the Association for the Preservation of Virginia Antiquities, and for seven years was president of the Richmond Y. W. C. A.

Samuel Horace Hawes' second wife was Mrs. Mary Mayo Blair Fitts, widow of James Henry Fitts.

CHARLES McCULLOCH, physician and surgeon, is one of the prominent citizens of Lexington and has practiced medicine in the state nearly thirty years.

Doctor McCulloch is a grandson of one of the most distinguished figures in American finance, Hugh McCulloch, who was a native of Maine and in 1833 located at Fort Wayne, Indiana, where he soon became cashier and manager of the Fort Wayne branch of the State Bank of Indiana. In 1856 he was made president of the Bank of the State of Indiana, and from that post resigned in May, 1863, to become comptroller of the currency under Secretary of Treasury Chase, and had the task of enormous responsibility of organizing the newly created bureau and putting into operation the National Banking System. He was given the chief credit for making that transition without friction or delay, and he was also given high credit for funding the national debt at the close of the Civil war. In March, 1865, he was appointed secretary of the treasury by President Lincoln, serving until March, 1869, and in October, 1884, was again appointed secretary of treasury at the close of President Arthur's term, being the only man who ever held that office by two appointments. He was the founder of the Hamilton National Bank of Fort Wayne, and his son Charles succeeded him in the bank, and his grandson, Ross McCulloch, is still head of the institution.

Dr. Charles McCulloch was born at Fort Wayne, Indiana, June 2, 1873, son of Frederick H. and Caroline (Riddle) McCulloch, his father a native of Fort Wayne and his mother of Cincinnati. Her father, Adam Riddle, was also born at Cincinnati and was a leading lawyer of that city. Frederick McCulloch was in business as a merchant at Fort Wayne and after coming to Virginia followed farming for over forty years. He was a

vestryman in the Episcopal Church and a member of the
Masonic Order. Of his three children two are living: Doctor
Charles and Elizabeth, the latter of whom is the wife of Dr.
James Morrison, of Lynchburg.

Charles McCulloch was given liberal educational advantages.
He was a student in the University of Virginia during 1891-92,
and while there became a member of the Phi Kappa Psi fraternity. His first call to a professional career was in veterinary
surgery, and he graduated in that subject in New York in 1894.
He practiced for a short time and then entered the medical
department of George Washington University, taking his
diploma in 1897. He first practiced at Howardsville, Virginia,
and after two years became a member of the faculty of the
Virginia Polytechnic Institute at Blacksburg, where he remained
three years. From 1901 to 1922 he was busy with a very extensive country practice, with home at Howardsville, his professional work taking him over three counties. Doctor McCulloch
in 1922 retired from his profession and during the next five
years lived on a farm near Lexington. He resumed general
practice in 1928. He is a member of the Rockbridge County,
Virginia State and American Medical Associations.

Doctor McCulloch married Rosa Bruce Anderson, of Richmond, Virginia. They have two children, the son Hugh McCulloch, a graduate of the Virginia Polytechnic Institute, being a
salesman for the Frigidaire and Delco Light products. The
daughter, Nancy B., is a student in St. Hilda's Hall at Charleston, West Virginia. The mother of these children died in 1914,
and Doctor McCulloch later married Ruth Floyd Anderson, of
Lexington, daughter of Major William A. Anderson, former
attorney-general of Virginia.

JOHN THOMAS WHITE. The late John Thomas White, of
Norfolk, was a well known figure in its business and civic life,
and in addition to managing his large oyster planting and packing business, he was concerned with other matters of general
importance, in all of his operations showing keenness of perception, excellent judgment and coöperation in public effort. He
was a man of broad and abundant sympathies, always working
for better conditions wherever public need was recognized, and
his memory is tenderly cherished by those who knew and appreciated him.

John Thomas White was born in Mathews County, Virginia,
December 4, 1845, and died in Jacksonville, Florida, March 7,
1919. He was a son of John and Sarah (Bohanon) White, grandson of Capt. James White, captain of a company in the War of
1812, and great-grandson of John C. White, who was a Revolutionary soldier. Through his mother John Thomas White
descended in a direct line from Ambrose Bohanon, who settled
in Virginia in 1660, taking up a land grant in Kingston Parish,
now Mathews County. Ambrose Bohanon, a son of the above,
was quartermaster in General Washington's army during the
American Revolution. Joseph Bohanon held the rank of colonel
in the Continental army. He and his wife had eight children
born to their marriage.

Growing to manhood in his native county, John Thomas
White attended its schools, and after his education was completed
he went to the eastern shore of Maryland and was there engaged
in merchandising until 1886, when he sold his interests and,
coming to Norfolk, engaged in the oyster planting and packing

R L May

tic loyalty as a member of the City Council. He was a stalwart in the local ranks of the Democratic party, and was affiliated with the Benevolent and Protective Order of Elks, the Independent Order of Odd Fellows and the Royal Arcanum. Mr. Broughton was a son of William Broughton, who was born in Princess Anne County, Virginia, in 1804, and whose father was one of four brothers who came from England, and one settling in Georgia, one in North Carolina and two made settlement in Virginia prior to the War of the Revolution. His mother's maiden name was Penelope Jarvis. Since the death of her husband Mrs. Rhea has continued to maintain her home in her native city, where she has ever been a popular factor in social circles, and her residence is at 119 West Eleventh Street. The subject of this memoir is survived also by one child, Virginia Broughton, who is the wife of Frank Porter Lawler, her husband being employed in the Norfolk National Bank of Commerce and Trust. Mr. and Mrs. Lawler have a son, Beverley Rhea, born November 3, 1925.

ROBERT LEE MAY, vital and progressive business man and loyal citizen of Alexandria, has shown exceptional initiative ability and versatile resourcefulness in the development of the virtual public utility service represented in the Alexandria-Barcroft-Washington Rapid Transit Company and the Richmond-Washington Motor Coaches, Inc. Of the former modern line of motor-coach transports Mr. May is the owner, and of the latter corporation he is the president. Through the admirable service given by the two concerns, thus founded and developed by Mr. May, Alexandria and Barcroft are given direct motor transportation facilities to the national capital and similar service is extended between the nation's capital city and the historic old city that is the capital of Virginia.

Mr. May was born in Spotsylvania County, Virginia, March 13, 1882, and is a son of Martin Luther and Susie A. (Clore) May, both likewise natives of the county. Martin L. May was engaged a number of years in the work of his trade, that of carpenter, prior to entering service as a member of the police force in the City of Washington, D. C., and after his retirement from this constabulary service he resumed work at his trade. He was in the Dominion of Canada at the time of his death, and his widow died in 1920.

Robert Lee May was a lad of twelve years at the time of the family removal to Washington, D. C., and in the schools of that city he received the major part of his youthful education. As a young man he there gave five years of service as car conductor on the lines of the Capital Traction Company, and he then joined the metropolitan police department in Washington, his service with which continued eleven years. He resigned his position at the time of the nation's entrance into the World war, joined the secret-service department of the Government and had the distinction of serving as bodyguard to President Woodrow Wilson during the period of the war, his resignation having occurred after the armistice had brought the great conflict to a close. It was while he was thus engaged that a sequence of circumstances led to his initiation of the motor-transport enterprise through the medium of which he has since gained splendid success and prestige. While engaged in Washington he had shown his loyalty to his native state by retaining his residence at Barcroft, a little Virginia hamlet about five miles distant from the White House, and in making his daily trips between his home and the capital he utilized a motorcycle. A casual accident to the somewhat decrepit Ford automobile used by his wife led him to the train of thought that brought him to a decision to establish and operate a motor-bus line between Barcroft and Washington for the accommodation of the people of the village and those residing along the Columbia turnpike. Mr. May, with a Reo chassis, fitted up a sort of rudimentary transport that would accommodate about twenty persons when crowded, and this he placed in commission on the route, while he himself officiated as driver. The first trip was made June 27, 1921, and thus was given inception to what has become a large and important enterprise in the field of interurban motor transportation. The year 1928 finds five motor busses in operation on the Barcroft-Washington line, and July 1, 1924, Mr. May expanded his business by establishing his line between Washington and Alexandria, fine de luxe cars being operated on this line and express service provided during rush hours. Mr. May encountered opposition in the latter project, but popular sentiment was with him, as the pioneer, and he eventually gained control of the interests of his competitors and is now sole owner of the Alexandria-Barcroft-Washington Rapid Transit Company, the service of which is maintained at the best modern standard. The service of the line is used by fully 3,000,000 persons annually.

It was in 1926 that Mr. May effected the organization of the Richmond-Washington Motor Coaches, Incorporated, and the de luxe service given by this admirable line between the national capital and the Virginia capital has met with unqualified popular approval and support, the while it constitutes a valuable public utility for the communities through which the line passes. Of this corporation Mr. May has been president from the beginning, and his progressive policies have been the force through which the service has been developed and perfected. Mr. May has been able to translate his thoughts into constructive action and has made an outstanding record in the domain of national motor transportation. He is chairman of the executive committee of the Virginia Motor Bus Association, at the time of this writing, in the summer of 1928, and is a member of the transportation committee of the Alexandria Chamber of Commerce. He maintains his home in Barcroft and his busses activities have contributed much to the remarkable development and progress of that place. His executive headquarters are established at 127 North Pitt Street in the City of Alexandria.

Mr. May is a Democrat in politics, is a member of the Rotary Club of Alexandria, as well as of the Old Dominion Club, is affiliated with the Knights of the Maccabees, and he and his wife are members of the Baptist Church, though he was reared in the faith of the Methodist Episcopal Church, South. He is a stockholder in the American Fidelity and Casualty Company of Richmond.

The two transportation concerns of which Mr. May is the executive head maintain at Alexandria a monster garage, with a floor space of 20,000 square feet, and this is equipped with all facilities for the repairing of the motor coaches of the two lines, more than fifty busses being now in operation, employment being given to seventy persons, and a smaller garage being maintained in the City of Washington.

October 12, 1904, marked the marriage of Mr. May and Miss Lulu Jackson Barr, daughter of Lewis J. and Virginia (Jackson) Barr, both of whom were born in Virginia and the latter of whom was a descendant of Gen. Stonewall Jackson. Mr. Barr is now a member of the A. B. & W. Rapid Transit Company, his wife having died in November, 1887. Mr. and Mrs. May have two children: Beverly Cornell, who was born in November, 1905, is now associated with his father's business in the capacity of traffic manager and as vice-president of the Richmond-Washington Motor Coaches, Inc. He married Miss Margaret Louise Curtis, and they have two children, Robert Marshall, born October 15, 1925, and Martha Lou, born November 4, 1926. Sidney Alice, younger of the two children of the subject of this review, was born January 1, 1907, and is the wife of Virgil Gaines, who is a director and second vice-president of the Richmond-Washington Motor Coaches, Inc.

GEORGE ALLISON, JR., was one of the valued local executives of the Virginia Electric & Power Company in the City of Norfolk at the time of his death, which here occurred in September, 1912. He had been long and prominently concerned with public utility service in Virginia and had made a record of successful achievement in this connection, the while his sterling characteristics gave him a strong hold upon the confidence and good will of all who knew him.

Mr. Allison was born in the City of Knoxville, Tennessee, in November, 1870, the Allison family having been established at Charleston, South Carolina, prior to the Civil war and the ancestral line having been marked by kinship with the distinguished Harrison family that gave two Presidents to the United States, Gen. William Henry Harrison and Benjamin Harrison. The subject of this memoir was a son of George and Margaret (Parham) Allison, his father having been a skilled electrician and having been for a long period in navy yard service.

Mr. Allison received most of his early educational discipline in the City of Richmond, Virginia, where the family home was maintained in the period of his boyhood and early youth. His father was for some time a construction foreman for the Western Union Telegraph Company, and the subject of this memoir gained practical experience by assisting his father in this connection. Thereafter he was for ten years in the employ of the Southern Bell Telephone Company, his next connection, with the Southern States Telephone Company, was of about equal duration, and finally he entered the service of the Virginia Electric & Power Company, with which he continued his association until the time of his death.

Mr. Allison gained high reputation as a technical and practical expert in the various phases of applied electricity, and his service in this connection was ever marked by loyalty and efficiency. He had no ambition for the activities of practical politics, but was a staunch supporter of the cause of the Democratic party. He was a communicant of the Protestant Episcopal Church, and his widow, who still resides in Norfolk, is a member of the Presbyterian Church, in the faith of which she was reared.

In June, 1892, Mr. Allison was united in marriage to Miss Minnie Martin Davis, who was born and reared in Prince Edward County, Virginia, a daughter of John W. and Sarah Elizabeth Davis, her father having been a substantial farmer of that county and a scion of a family that was founded in Virginia in the early Colonial period, the lineage tracing back to sterling Scotch origin. Prior to the Civil war members of the Davis family held large landed estates and were extensive exponents of plantation industry in Charlotte County. The father of Mrs. Allison gave loyal service in support of the Confederacy during the period of the Civil war, his assignment having been to the commissary department of the Confederate army. Concerning the children of Mr. and Mrs. Allison the following brief data are available: Percy E. is in the service of the Virginia Electric & Power Company, as is also the next younger son, George L., who likewise maintains his home in Norfolk, the maiden name of his wife having been Mildred Dillon and their two children being daughters, Mildred and Jane. Robert, who is, like his older brothers, associated with the same utility company, as was the honored father, married Miss Rae Lipschutz, and their one child is Frank. Minnie, older of the two daughters, is the wife of Vincent Thomas, who is engaged in the mercantile business in Norfolk, and they have two children, Vincent, Jr., and William. Margaret, the younger daughter, is the wife of Erskine Blackburne, who is in the service of the Norfolk Loan & Bank Company. Frank, youngest of the sons, likewise is connected with the Virginia Electric & Power Company.

LUTHER PAUL BAUM. The knowledge that a man is judged for what he accomplishes and the effect his work has on others, not alone with reference to himself, should encourage the average American to put forth his best efforts so that when he has passed from this earthly sphere he will be remembered with kindly interest and respectful regard. Many opportunities are within the grasp of every man who is determined to live an honest and upright life, and among the men of Norfolk who during his lifetime set an example to his fellow citizens not only as a private citizen, but also as an able public official was the late Luther Paul Baum. For some years he was connected with the Norfolk County engineer's office, and his service in this particular is sufficient evidence of his ability and fidelity to duty, but it is but due to his memory to state that he in his public capacity displayed only the same traits which characterized his private life—strict attention to the details of his work and thoughtful and intelligent management, qualities which could not fail to bring about satisfactory results.

Luther Paul Baum was born in Princess Anne County, Virginia, in October, 1861, and died in Norfolk in April, 1904. He was educated in Reynoldson College, Gates County, North Carolina, but he did not complete his collegiate course, as he returned home and began farming on the portion of his father's estate that he had inherited at the time of his father's death. There he remained until 1887, and in that year came to Norfolk County, Virginia, and here he continued his farming, but subsequently moved to the City of Norfolk to assume the duties assigned him in the office of the county engineer, and it was while he was in office that he died.

In February, 1884, Mr. Baum married Miss Penelope Jackson, of Norfolk County, Virginia, a daughter of William A. and Penelope (Pendleton) Jackson. Mr. Jackson was a landowner and lumberman of Norfolk County, and one of the leading citizens of this section of the state. Eight children were born to Mr. and Mrs. Baum, namely: Renan C., who is an electrical engineer, married Miss Emma Patterson, of Pittsburgh, Pennsyl-

\ania, and they have two children, Elizabeth and Marjory; Mary
Pendleton, who married Temple L. Gatewood, of Richmond, Virginia, an extensive drayman and transfer man, owning his own
business, has no children; Harvey A., who is vice president and
general manager of the Atlantic Commission Company, married
Miss Gladys Lanning, and they have three children, John Minch,
Harvey A., Junior, and Phyllis Matilda; Lillie, who married
John Plant, of Boston, Massachusetts, has two children, John
and Elizabeth; Christie, who is a business man of Norfolk, is
a veteran of the World war, during which he served overseas
with the One Hundred and Sixteenth Infantry, A. E. F., was
wounded and gassed in the Argonne offensive, married Miss
Carolyn Rapeltz, and they have one child, Carolyn Penelope;
Nellie Bryan Baum; Luther Paul, who is a business man, married
Miss Hattie Schultz; and William A. Jackson Baum.

Mr. Baum was a member of the Royal Arcanum and the
Independent Order of Odd Fellows. For years he belonged to
the Baptist Church, of which his wife is still a member. She
is very active in the Woman's Club and the Art Club Society.
The Baum family is of German origin, and was established in
Virginia when it was still a colony of England. The Pendletons
came to Virginia from England at a very early day, and took
possession of a grant of 12,000 acres of land in New Kent County.
From that time to the present those bearing the name have been
active factors in the professions and public life, and all of them
have been honorable and upright gentlemen. The Jackson family was early established in Norfolk County, and its members
have also been in the public eye ever since, holding positions
of importance and acquitting themselves most creditably. During the summer months Mrs. Baum maintains her residence at
204 Nineteenth Street, Virginia Beach, but after October 1 of
each year she lives at 1017 Colonial Avenue, Norfolk. Her
position in society is well established and she is most highly
regarded by all with whom she is associated. The children are
a credit to her and her husband, and she is naturally very
proud of them and what they are accomplishing.

REV. JOHN WILLIAMSON DAUGHERTY. Both at Richmond and
in Norfolk County the name of the late Rev. John Williamson
Daugherty is held in affectionate memory for the zeal and earn-
estness of his ministry and the work he did in building up the
institutions of organized Christianity.

Doctor Daugherty was born at Williamsburg, Virginia, in
January, 1856, and died at Richmond in April, 1909. His grandfather was a native of Ireland and came to America and settled
in Maryland after the Revolutionary war. The Daughertys were
for several generations identified with the sea. Doctor Daugherty's father, John Fenton Daugherty, was a sea captain. The
mother of Rev. Doctor Daugherty was Lucy Bassett, member
of the old Colonial family of Bassetts of Williamsburg, a family
that gave soldiers to the Revolution and men high in poltical
station.

John Williamson Daugherty was the oldest of three children.
For several years he clerked in stores, and at the age of twenty-
four engaged in the commission business. He followed an active
business career until he was thirty years of age, when he left
commercial pursuits to enter the ministry, and was ordained
and had as his first charge the Court Street Baptist Church of
Portsmouth. Later he was assigned to the South Street Baptist

Church for six years. While in those pastorates he was able to raise practically all of the donation for the addition to the Court Street Baptist Church Sunday School building and secured most of the fund for the original building of the South Street Baptist Church. On leaving Portsmouth he became pastor of the Fulton Baptist Church at Richmond. In 1896 Doctor Daugherty withdrew from the Baptist communion and organized the Apostolic Church at Fulton, in Richmond, and devoted his full time and energies to this denomination until his death. He was a Democrat in politics.

Doctor Daugherty first married Margaret Guy, of Portsmouth. She died leaving five children: Lucius; John Williamson, Jr., now a physician at Flushing, Long Island; Thomas B., a physician engaged in practice at Fayetteville, West Virginia; Elizabeth B., wife of Frank B. King, of Orlando, Florida; and Margaret H., wife of Fred Bates, of Richmond. The son, John W., Jr., served with the rank of first lieutenant in the Medical Corps of the United States Navy during the World war, continuing in the service altogether for three and a half years.

Doctor Daugherty married in January, 1894, at Portsmouth, Miss Minnie Lee Fulford, of Portsmouth, her father being a descendant of Sir John Celestus Fulford, who was with the King's Court of James II, and who later settled on the Virginia coast, acquiring a grant of land. Capt. John C. Fulford was captain of the Portsmouth Grays in the Confederate army, and married Virginia C. Davis. Mrs. Daugherty was the oldest of four children. Mrs. Daugherty, who now makes her home at Portsmouth, at 1055 Ann Street, is the mother of six children: Richard F., who served as a chief yeoman with the United States Navy during the World war, is now an employe of the Standard Oil Company at Norfolk, married Ruth Wainwright and they have one daughter, Ann Lee; Paul C., a dental technician at Norfolk, married Percy Ethel York; Emily J. is the wife of Malcolm F. Beazley, a railway engineer, and has a son, Malcolm F., Jr., Mary P. is the wife of W. T. Beck, a railway employe, and they have two sons, W. T., Jr., and Richard Edward; Daniel, with the Burrow & Martin Drug Company, married Mary R. Unser; and James B., dental technician at Portsmouth, married Isabel Hooks and has one daughter, Jane Lee.

JOHN CARY CURLING was a prominent business man of Norfolk County, winning his own way from an early age and in a comparatively brief lifetime secured more than a normal prestige and degree of success.

He was born in Norfolk County in October, 1886, and died at Portsmouth in July, 1921, son of J. W. and Virginia F. (Grimes) Curling. He was four years old when his father died and had to face the prospect of working to make his own opportunities. He attended the schools in Norfolk County and for several years he and his brother operated the home farm for their mother. From seventeen to nineteen years of age Mr. Curling was with the Roper Lumber Mill. At Portsmouth for several years he was in the furniture business and also in the fish business, leaving that to become associated with J. E. Norman in a merchant tailoring business known as the Silver Dollar Tailoring Company. From one shop this business steadily grew until they were operating stores in twelve cities of Virginia and North Carolina. Mr. Curling gave all his time to this business for ten years, when he sold out to his partner and then

concentrated his attention on a clothing store at Portsmouth. He was also interested in the fish business during his later years.

Mr. Curling married Rosa Hanrahan, of Portsmouth, daughter of J. W. and Sarah Frances Hanrahan. Her father was a Portsmouth business man and was descended from a family that settled in this section of Virginia shortly after the Revolutionary war. Mrs. Curling is a Methodist. Her brother, Frank C. Hanrahan, is a prominent Portsmouth business man, now serving his second term as city manager of Portsmouth. Mrs. Curling, who resides at 416 Webster Street in Portsmouth, has one daughter, Ruth Elizabeth, now deputy city collector.

HOWARD MALCOLM SMITH is one of the progressive young business men of the City of Alexandria, metropolis of Arlington County, where he is engaged in the real estate and general insurance business and is regional superintendent for the Provident Relief Association of Washington, D. C. His office headquarters are at 624 King Street, in the Smith Building.

In the picturesque little mountain city of Staunton, Virginia, Howard M. Smith was born January 15, 1896, and he is a son of Howard M. and Margaret (Bacon) Smith, the former of whom was born in Nelson County, this state, and the latter at Waynesboro, Augusta County. Wilson Smith, grandfather of the subject of this review, operated wagon trains between the City of Richmond and the Shenandoah Valley prior to the Civil war. Howard M. Smith, Sr., was long and successfully identified with the insurance business, and at the time of his death was deputy superintendent of the Metropolitan Life Insurance Company at Staunton, Virginia, where he died January 15, 1924, and where his widow still maintains her home.

Howard M. Smith of this sketch was reared and educated in his native city and there gained his youthful experience in the insurance business as an associate of his father. In 1916, as a member of a Virginia regiment of the National Guard, Mr. Smith entered military service on the Mexican border, where his command was inducted into the United States Army and where he held the rank of sergeant until he received his honorable discharge in May, 1917. Thereafter he continued his association with the insurance business in his native city of Staunton until May, 1920, when he established his headquarters in Alexandria, where he has built up a substantial real estate and insurance business and is superintendent for the Provident Relief Association of Washington, D. C., which issues health, accident and life insurance. As a general underwriter of insurance Mr. Smith likewise represents other important insurance corporations in the various lines of indemnification. In his real estate operations Mr. Smith has figured as manager of development and exploitation for all of the Alexandria subdivisions of F. C. Goodnow, has given similar service in connection with the Washington & Kane subdivisions and also has a most attractive subdivision of his own, called Westwood and situated near Mount Vernon, the historic George Washington estate. He is a director of the Alexandria Realty Investment Corporation, of which he served as secretary three years. His political allegiance is given to the Democratic party, he and his wife are communicants of the Protestant Episcopal Church, and he is affiliated with the American Legion.

February 3, 1916, recorded the marriage of Mr. Smith and Miss Mary L. Smith, daughter of John D. and Ida V. (Clements) Smith, the latter of whom died at the birth of her daughter Mary L., who was doubly orphaned by the death of her father when she was a child of three years. Mr. and Mrs. Smith have two children: Dorothy Ann, born January 18, 1917, and Nancy Lee, born February 2, 1919.

JAMES IREDELL. Probably no family has played a more prominent or conspicuous part in the history of North Carolina than that which bears the name of Iredell. It has not been alone in public and miltary life that it has shone brightly ever since the birth of the nation, but in the professions and arts and sciences, in finance and in business. Among the brilliant men of this distinguished family, one who chose banking and the marts of commerce and trade as the medium through which to attain success was the late James Iredell of Norfolk, long identified with banks and railways, but at the time of his death an important factor in the business of nitrate shipping.

Mr. Iredell was born in 1868, at Raleigh, North Carolina, and was a son of Cadwallader James and Martha (Southgate) Iredell. He was a direct descendant of the historical character, Justice James Iredell, who held his office under President George Washington, and who was his great-grandfather, while his grandparents were Governor James and Frances (Tredwell) Iredell. A complete review of the career of Governor Iredell will be found elsewhere in this work. Cadwallader Iredell was for many years a banker of South Carolina, making his home for the most part at Columbia, although he also resided for some years at Raleigh, North Carolina. He was a man of high character who upheld the best traditions of the family. During the war between the states he held the rank of captain of a company of North Carolina volunteer infantry.

James Iredell was a child when taken by his parents to South Carolina, and there acquired his early education in public schools. Following this he went to Columbia College, from which institution he was graduated with the degree of Bachelor of Arts, and not long thereafter entered the Bank of Columbia, South Carolina, where he arose to the position of cashier. He remained with that well known banking house in the same capacity for a period of fifteen years, during which time he formed a wide acquaintance among men high in finance and prominent in other lines of industry. In 1903 Mr. Iredell resigned his position and changed his scene of operations to Norfolk to become treasurer and auditor of the Norfolk Street Railway Company, and retained this position until 1917, in which year he became interested extensively in the shipping of nitrate. He was engaged in this line of business at the time of his death, which occurred in July, 1919. Mr. Iredell was a Democrat, but did not seek public office or political preferment. He was a citizen of public spirit and civic pride, however, and always a supporter of worthy movements for the betterment of his community. He had a number of social and fraternal connections, and his business interests were many and varied.

In September, 1905, Mr. Iredell was united in marriage with Miss Laura Merle Higgs, of Raleigh, North Carolina, who was educated at St. Mary's College and is a daughter of Jacob and Laura (Sorrel) Higgs, both the Higgs and Sorrel families being well known in North Carolina, where they are of worthy pioneer stock. Jacob Higgs was for many years a merchant at Raleigh, where he had an excellent reputation for integrity and good citizenship. Mrs. Iredell survives her husband and resides at 5A Weynoke Apartment, Colley and Princess Anne avenues, Road W. She is a consistent member of the Episcopal Church and has been active in its work. There were three children born to Mr. and Mrs. Iredell, James Iredell IV, born July 15, 1906, connected with the Texas Oil Company at Norfolk, Virginia; Martha Southgate Iredell, born August 4, 1909, and Ann Stith Iredell, born September 22, 1918.

IRA JEFFERSON BROOKS II. Practically the entire career of the late Ira J. Brooks II, of Portsmouth, was passed in connection with railroad work, and from 1900 until his death in 1919 he was car inspector for the Norfolk & Portsmouth Belt Line Railway. During his life he depended solely upon his own ability and resources to win promotion and success, and it was his fortune so to conduct himself as to win the esteem and respect of his associates and fellow citizens.

Mr. Brooks was born in Dinwiddie County, Virginia, January 23, 1856, a son of Ira W. and Sarah (Mays) Brooks. His father, a native of Petersburg, this state, enlisted in the Confederate army during the war between the states, in which he suffered a wound while in the cavalry service, but fought until the close of the great struggle. Following his return to the pursuits of peace he took up the business of contracting, and followed that line with success until the time of his demise. He and Mrs. Brooks, who was a native of Dinwiddie, were the parents of nine children, of whom Ira J. was the eldest.

Ira J. Brooks received his education under private teachers in Dinwiddie County, and as a young man was employed for a time at Petersburg. In 1877, at the age of twenty-one years, he secured a position with the Norfolk & Western Railroad, and remained with that line for a period of twenty-three years. In 1900 he took up his residence at Portsmouth to accept the position of car inspector for the Norfolk & Portsmouth Belt Line Railway. As before noted, he continued with this concern until his death June 10, 1919, when he was sixty-three years of age. Mr. Brooks was a thorough master of every detail of his business, and at all times had the full confidence and respect of his associates and fellow citizens. He was a member of the Knights of Pythias, the Woodmen of the World, the Junior Order United American Mechanics, the Improved Order of Red Men and the Independent Order of Odd Fellows, in all of which orders he had many friends and took a profound interest in the work. He was a stalwart Democrat in his political allegiance and was active in his support of the principles and candidates of his party. His religious connection was with the Methodist Church.

On June 30, 1896, in Nansemond County, Mr. Brooks was united in marriage with Miss Rosa Saunders, who was reared and educated in that county and was a daughter of Benjamin Saunders, a farmer and lumberman, and a Confederate veteran of the war between the states, in which he was wounded. He was a son of Edward Saunders, a plantation owner, and the latter was a son of George Saunders, a soldier of the War of 1812, while the latter's father was a member of the Virginia troops during the War of the Revolution and was present at the surrender of Yorktown. The men of the Saunders family have been planters almost without exception. The mother of Mrs. Brooks was Emily Hunter, and she and Mr. Saunders were the parents of fourteen children. To Mr. and Mrs. Brooks there were born four living children: George Henry, who is employed by P. D. Guathmey, of Smithfield, Virginia; Miss Florence Catherine, who is preparing for a career as a professional nurse, and will graduate from the Provident Hospital of Norfolk in the class of 1929; Miss Ida Laurine, who has a position with the Seaboard Air Line Railway; and Ira Guy, who is attending school. Mrs. Brooks, who survives her husband and resides at 459 Maryland Avenue, Portsmouth, belongs to the ladies' auxiliary of the Woodmen of the World and the Pythian Sisters, and is also active in the work of the Methodist Church.

JOHNSTON PETTIGREW COFFIELD. From the time of his arrival at Portsmouth in 1898 until failing health necessitated his retirement in 1919, the late Johnston Pettigrew Coffield was one of the substantial citizens of his community and was widely known in the risk and indemnity field as the capable manager of the Portsmouth office of the Virginia Life Insurance Company. His career was one in which he engaged in a variety of pursuits, in all of which he displayed ability and versatility, and while his connection with civic affairs was only that of a good citizen, he so comported himself in all walks of life as to be remembered as a man whom his community could ill afford to lose.

Mr. Coffield was born at Edenton, Chowan County, North Carolina, August 18, 1864, and was a son of William Henderson Coffield, the owner of "Green Hall," one of the largest plantations of the Old North State, which was conducted with all the hospitality that characterized the pre-war South. This plantation comprised thousands of acres of land, and was worked by slave labor, while its owner was a true type of the old Southern gentleman. A large part of his wealth was swept away by the misfortunes of war, but up to his death he always maintained "open house" and was known far and wide for his generosity and benefactions.

Johnston Pettigrew Coffield attended private school at Edenton, although his education was somewhat curtailed by the early death of his father. He was still little more than a youth when he was called upon to take charge of the great plantation, which consisted of land extending for eight miles on each side of the road to Edenton. After a few years the plantation was sold and the estate settled, and Mr. Coffield engaged in the fish packing business at Edenton, an industry to which he applied himself for six years. In 1895 he removed to Norfolk, where he entered the employ of the Virginia Life Insurance Company, and several years later was sent to the Portsmouth office in the capacity of superintendent. Here he greatly increased the volume of the company's business and built up a substantial reputation as a capable and energetic insurance man. Failing health caused his retirement in 1919, and from that time forward until his death, December 12, 1922, he lived quietly at his home, although still superintending the details of his large interests. Mr. Coffield was a Democrat, but in no sense a politician. His religious faith was that of the Baptist Church.

In November, 1888, at Petersburg, Virginia, Mr. Coffield was united in marriage with Miss Roberta Powell, the youngest of the nine children of John H. and Mary (Wescott) Powell. Mr. Powell, who was born at Edenton, North Carolina, moved to Petersburg, Virginia, where he spent a long and successful career in merchandising. Four children were born to Mr. and Mrs. Coffield: Mary Louise, who died unmarried; Minnie Petti-

A. M. Nelson.

grew, the wife of Fletcher Smith, a business man and Mason and Elk of Petersburg, who has twin children, John Fletcher and John Newsome; Dr. John Albert, a practicing dental surgeon of Portsmouth, who served in the hospital service during the World war; and Roberta Powell, a teacher in the public schools of Portsmouth, and a member of the Virginia State Teachers' Association. Mrs. Coffield, who survives her husband and resides at 200 Florida Avenue, is an active member of the Woman's Club and the Monumental Methodist Church.

ALEXANDER M. NELSON, president of the Nelson Hardware Company, and connected in an official capacity with a number of other important business enterprises of Roanoke and its vicinity, has achieved a really great success. As a poor boy, without resources except his clean hands, high ideals, strong purpose and an ability to make friends, he began his business career. From the first he put such vision, understanding and fidelity into his work as to attract the favorable attention of those engaging him. Soon he was by himself, beginning in a small way, but an independent merchant. There were years of hard struggle; there were critical periods, and there were moments when his courage almost failed, but always there was a definite policy reaching into the years ahead; there was a clearly defined program, and there was a magnificent purpose always pushing behind policy and program, and this condition still prevails. For fifty-two years Mr. Nelson has been engaged in the hardware business, and out of the 20,000 hardware stores in the United States he is one of the eighty-nine that has been continuously in operation for half a century.

The subject of this review was the second born of one of those fine, prolific unions so popular before birth control propaganda became a factor in the domestic life of the country. His parents, William J. Nelson and Sally Harrison (Rodes) Nelson, respectively of Port Republic and Lynchburg, Virginia, settled and reared their children a few miles south of Staunton, in Augusta County, Virginia. Both parents and seven of the twelve children are now deceased. William J. Nelson and his wife were life time members of the Presbyterian Church, the former being an elder in the church that Woodrow Wilson's father served as pastor. After an academic course at Washington and Lee University he graduated in law at the University of Virginia, leaving his profession to accept a lieutenancy in the Confederate army. After Appomattox he returned to Staunton and the practice of law, serving for a number of years as a member of the City Council. His wife's father marched under the Stars and Stripes in Mexico, but, later on, her brother, Gen. Robert Rodes, was killed fighting against this emblem at the battle of Winchester in the Civil war.

Alexander M. Nelson attended the public schools of his native place, and was graduated from its high school in 1875. When only sixteen years old, however, he had begun working in a hardware store, receiving fifty cents a day at Lexington, Virginia, and in 1883 was able to go into business for himself at Culpeper, Virginia. In 1888 he came to Roanoke and established a retail hardware store under the name of Nelson & Myers, and the partners continued to operate as retail merchants until 1902, when Mr. Nelson took over the business and established a wholesale hardware store which he operates as the Nelson Hardware Company. Associated with him in this business, of which he is president, are John M. Nelson, vice president; Robert R. Nelson, secretary-treasurer, and Alexander M. Nelson, Jr., purchasing agent. This is a close corporation, the stockholders being members of the Nelson family, each of the six sons being stockholders and actively engaged in the business. Mrs. Stout, sister of Mr. Nelson, and widow of the late Judge Stout of Augusta County, and Mrs. Sublett, another sister of Mr. Nelson, and widow of the late Ed Sublett, a former wholesale produce dealer, are the only others owning stock in the company. Mr. Nelson is also vice president of the First National Exchange Bank, and a member of its executive committee, and he is president of the Nelson Coal Corporation. The Nelson Hardware Company covers Virginia and portions of West Virginia and North Carolina, keeping four men on the road all the year. It is capitalized at $400,000 and is the largest and oldest house in Roanoke, and one of the leading ones of the state. The name of Nelson was connected with Washington and Lee University for many years, as Prof. Alexander L. Nelson, an uncle of Alexander M. Nelson, held the chair of mathematics in that institution of learning for fifty years.

In 1888 Alexander M. Nelson married Miss Sallie Hart, who was born in Charlottesville, Virginia, a daughter of the late John Hart, a prominent educator. Eight of their ten children are living: John M., who was educated in Washington and Lee University; Alexander M. Nelson, Jr., who attended the Roanoke High School; Coleman H., who was educated in the Roanoke schools and the University of Virginia; William J., who was educated in the Roanoke schools; Robert R., who attended Virginia Polytechnic Institute; Katherine, who married Junius P. Fishburn; Elizabeth, who is unmarried, and her twin brother, Charles L. The family was well represented in the World war, three of the sons serving in combat divisions of the A. E. F., while a fourth was on guard duty in this country. His family all belong to the Second Presbyterian Church, of which he has been a trustee for many years. He is a member of the Shenandoah Club and the Roanoke Country Club. Very active in the local Democratic party, he served for several years as a member of the Roanoke City Council, and has been useful to his city in many other capacities. The success Mr. Nelson has achieved is no little thing. It is in no sense the fortuitous result of a combination of favoring circumstances, but the working out of a policy long held and definitely followed, often against great difficulties and discouragement, and such a success is the mark of a big man.

JOSEPH H. FABER. From 1880 until his death in May, 1922, the late Joseph H. Faber was identified with the photographic business at Norfolk, where through his high character and great integrity he won the confidence and esteem of his fellow citizens. In no department of human activity have greater strides been made in recent years than in photography. The man who succeeded several decades ago would find himself hopelessly in arrears should he, with no additional equipment, attempt to cope with the conditions of the present. Photographic portraiture is an art which admits of infinite conception and requires varied knowledge and great painstaking in its development. The men who maintain its highest artistic methods necessarily have a thorough knowledge of human nature and are artistic and scholarly in their inclinations, and it was to this class that the late Mr. Faber belonged.

The Faber family originated in Germany, whence came the first American progenitor at an early day, the family taking up its residence in the vicinity of Charleston, South Carolina, where they became large planters prior to the war between the states. Joseph H. Faber was born at Charleston, South Carolina, and was reared and educated in his home community. In young manhood he removed to Fredericksburg, Virginia, where he and his brother established themselves in business as the proprietors of a photographic studio. After a few years Mr. Faber married and in 1880 moved to Norfolk, where he passed the remainder of his life. He was at the time of his death the senior member of the photographic firm of Faber & Son, and a man who was held in the highest esteem.

Mr. Faber married Miss Emma J. Freeman, and they became the parents of three children: George Lewis, of whom more later; Thomas L., a commercial photographer and member of the Masonic fraternity; and Fred, a graduate of the University of Virginia, who was on the staff of engineers who built the Mount Royal tunnel in Canada, and now a consulting engineer of Crowley, Louisiana, married Tillie Ficklin and has two children, Ann and Jane.

George Lewis Faber was born at Norfolk, Virginia, in September, 1886, and received his education at Norfolk and Richmond College. At the close of his college career he returned to Norfolk to join his father in the firm of Faber & Son, of which he became the owner at the elder man's death, and which he conducted successfully until his own demise in December, 1925. He was a good business man and one who enjoyed the confidence and respect of those with whom he came in contact, and his death lost to his community a reliable and public spirited citizen. He belonged to the Rotary Club and the Princess Anne Country Club and was a Mason and Shriner. For several years he taught a class in the Sunday School of the Freemason Baptist Church.

In July, 1914, George L. Faber was united in marriage with Emily Sherrer LaBlanc, who was born at Philadelphia, Pennsylvania, a daughter of Samuel and Sadie LaBlanc, and a member of a family which originated in France and settled at Philadelphia prior to the war between the states. Samuel LaBlanc fought as a soldier in a Pennsylvania volunteer infantry regiment during that struggle, following which he followed the profession of a construction engineer during the remainder of his life, his death occurring in 1907. He married Sarah (Sadie) Sherrer, of Reading, Pennsylvania, and Mrs. Faber is the oldest living child of this union. Her brother, Charles Wesley LaBlanc, was district manager in Westchester County, New York, for the Hoover Vacuum Cleaner Company, is a veteran of the World war, in which he enlisted as a private and rose to a lieutenancy in France. In July, 1929, he was appointed to the office of assistant general manager of the same company at Philadelphia. He married Anne Dobson, of New York City, and they have one son, Charles Wesley, Jr. Another brother, Samuel LaBlanc, Jr., was in the engineering department at the Newport News Shipbuilding Company, was a well known baritone singer and in 1906 he died in the height of his career.

Mrs. Emily Faber, one of Norfolk's most talented women, attended school at Norfolk, and began her musical education in

New York City, where she took organ and piano under Gaston Detheir. She then went abroad, where she studied organ under Alexander Guilmont in France and Dr. Varley Roberts in England. She also attends the studio of Frank La Forge of New York City. She is now organist and choir director of the Freemason Baptist Church and organist and director of Ohef Sholom Temple of Norfolk, and conducts a musical studio. She was one of the organizers of the Mifane Trio, a musical organization consisting of violin, Marian Carpenter Miles; piano, Emily LaBlanc, and 'cello, Philip O. Nelson, and is a member of the Norfolk Country Club, the Princess Anne Country Club, the Norfolk Society of Arts, and the Freemason Street Baptist Church. She is a past secretary of the Virginia Music Teachers State Association and is a member of the National Federation of Music Clubs, representing the Emily LaBlanc Faber Junior Club. She is also a member of the American Guild of Organists.

WILLS COWPER was a merchant before the Civil war, having a reputation all over the Norfolk district. Members of his family still reside in that city.

He was born in Gates County, North Carolina, son of Thomas Cowper, also of Gates County, and grandson of John and Louise (Godwin) Cowper.

Dr. Thomas Cowper acquired a thorough education and in his youth was sent abroad, studying and completing his medical course in France. He remained abroad five years and after returning to the United States settled at Portsmouth, Virginia, where he took up the practice of his profession. He carried the routine work of a physician there until he fell a victim to a scourge of the yellow fever in 1858, dying in the line of duty.

Wills Cowper married Dizer Saunders, who was born in Nansemond County, Virginia, daughter of Robert and Sarah (Hedges) Saunders, natives of the same county, and of English and Scotch ancestry. Mrs. Cowper became the mother of thirteen children: Thomas, John G., Walter G., Elizabeth Ann, Emma Frances, Clarence, Laura, Anna, Virginia, Wills, Richard, Louise and James P.

Of these children Laura Cowper became the wife of John N. Dewell, who was born at Garysburg, North Carolina, and from early manhood was a merchant at Norfolk and Portsmouth, where he lived until his death at the age of seventy-two. Mrs. Dewell and her sister Anna now reside at 314 East Free Mason Street in Norfolk. Their brothers, John Gilbert, Clarence and Walter G., were all soldiers in the Confederate army. Clarence lost a finger in one battle. John, though participating in fifty-two battles and in the war from beginning until the surrender at Appomattox, was never wounded or captured.

ARMISTEAD PLUMMER PANNILL, commissioner of revenue for the City of Norfolk, is descended from an old Colonial Virginia family. The Pannills have been active in the public life of Norfolk for a great many years.

Mr. Pannill was born at Petersburg, Virginia, a great-grandson of William Pannill, who was born in Orange County, Virginia, February 1, 1768, and married Martha Ann Morton, who was born at Greenville, North Carolina, December 12, 1762.

Their son, Col. William Pannill, was born at Oxford, North Carolina, July 6, 1794, located at Petersburg, was educated in William and Mary College, and during the war between the states was provost marshal at Petersburg. He became the first president of what is now the Norfolk & Western Railway. Colonel Pannill married Eliza Binns Jones, who was born at Petersburg July 3, 1804. Her father, George Hamilton Jones, was born at Petersburg, May 1, 1775, being a lineal descendant of John Jones, who represented Brunswick County in the House of Burgesses. George Hamilton Jones married Elizabeth Binns, of a family that settled in Sussex County as early as 1652.

Capt. Thomas Pannill, father of Armistead P. Pannill, was born at Petersburg March 8, 1834, and enlisted in the Third Regiment of Virginia Infantry, commanded by Roger Prior. This regiment was attached to Pendleton's Brigade. The brigade held a position on the south side of the James River at the time of the McClellan raid on Richmond, and members of the brigade witnessed the battle between the *Merrimac* and the *Monitor* in Hampton Roads. Captain Pannill participated in the battle of the Crater in the siege of Petersburg. After the war he engaged in business handling real estate, was an auctioneer, and died in 1919. He and his wife reared the following children: Henry; Eliza Otey, who married George M. Pollard; James Knox; William; Robert Houston; Armistead Plummer; Samuel Weisiger; Louise Barlow, who married James H. Johnston; and Charles Jackson, who married Ethel World.

Armistead Pannill was educated in public schools, and as a young man became identified with the real estate business. In 1898 he was appointed assistant health officer and in 1917 became commissioner of revenue for the City of Norfolk, an office he has filled for eleven years. He is affiliated with Atlantic Lodge No. 2, A. F. and A. M., John Waters Chapter No. 1, Royal Arch Masons, Grice Commandery of the Knights Templar, Khedive Temple of the Mystic Shrine, Norfolk Lodge No. 38, B. P. O. Elks, and Norfolk Lodge No. 39, Independent Order of Odd Fellows.

Mr. Pannill married in 1901 Lillian Burke Archer. They have a daughter, Martha Archer, who is the wife of Robert W. Ribble and has a son, Robert W., Jr.

REV. EDWARD TURNER DADMUN. A gentle spirit, a splendid intellectual equipment, a deep and abiding human sympathy and tolerance, and a significant consecration to human service were expressed in the personality and achievement of the honored subject of this memoir. Mr. Dadmun was a leader in the work of the Y. M. C. A. in Virginia, served in this splendid organization in its overseas activities in the World war, and as a clergyman of the Methodist Episcopal Church, South, he made his powers a force in advancing Christian work and the aiding and uplifting of his fellow men. Mr. Dadmun was sixty years of age at the time of his death, which occurred in the City of Norfolk, Virginia, December 5, 1923, and a tribute to his memory consistently finds place in this publication.

Mr. Dadmun was born at Watertown, Massachusetts, in May, 1863, and was the eldest of the three children of William Henry and Charlotte (Turner) Dadmun, the former of whom was born in Boston, Massachusetts, and the latter in Ontario, Canada. William Henry Dadmun was long and prominently concerned with the lumber industry, and both he and his wife continued to reside in Massachusetts until their death.

The subject of this memoir gained his earlier education in the public schools of Massachusetts and under the private preceptorship of Prof. Henry Loomis. He early became animated with the spirit of constructive service in connection with the finer ideals of human thought and action, and he was twenty-one years of age when he came to Virginia to enter service as the first secretary of the Y. M. C. A. in the City of Norfolk. He acted as a general supervisor in the erection of the first building of the association in this city, and made a trip to the North to purchase furniture and other accessories for the new instiution. He here continued his faithful and constructive service about four years, and thereafter he served a few years as secretary of the Y. M. C. A. in the City of Staunton, this state. He was next advanced to the position of assistant secretary of the Virginia state organization of the Y. M. C. A., and about five years later he resigned this office to enter active work in the ministry of the Methodist Episcopal Church, South, in which he was duly ordained a clergyman. His work as a minister and evangelist was principally in the tidewater region of Virginia, and he served some time as presiding elder of the Farmville district of his conference. Sincere, earnest and loyal, a strong and brilliant pulpit orator, Mr. Dadmun labored zealously and effectively and brought many converts into the fold of the Divine Master whom he served.

When the nation entered the World war Mr. Dadmun resumed his active association with the work of the Y. M. C. A. and was assigned to service at Camp Johnson, Florida, where he remained six months as camp secretary of the Y. M. C. A. As an overseas secretary of his organization he made one voyage to France, and upon his return he was assigned to duty at Hoboken, New Jersey, where he had supervision of selecting men for Y. M. C. A. overseas service. Later he became port secretary of the Y. M. C. A. at Newport News, Virginia, and there he did valuable work in connection with assigning Y. M. C. A. workers to the transports that bore them to overseas service. After the armistice brought the war to a close Mr. Dadmun resumed his work in his conference of the Methodist Episcopal Church, South, and he held a pastorate at Lynchburg one year, he having then been assigned to the pastorate of the church at Hampton, where he continued his labors until he suffered the health impairment that resulted in his death. He was virtually a pioneer in Y. M. C. A. work in Virginia, and did much to infuse in the organization that vitality and usefulness that have continued to characterize it in the intervening years. He was an implacable adversary of the liquor traffic and a resolute worker in behalf of the prohibition cause. His widow continues a zealous member of the Methodist Episcopal Church, South, and also of the W. C. T. U. In a basic way Mr. Dadmun gave allegiance to the Democratic party, and he was affiliated with the Improved Order of Red Men and the Junior Order United American Mechanics. His unfailing kindliness and his perfervid zeal in human service gained to him the affectionate regard of those who came within the sphere of his benignant influence.

On the 21st of July, 1891, was solemnized the marriage of Mr. Dadmun and Miss Olive Leigh Morgan, daughter of Olive Branch and Hope Alice (Davis) Morgan, of Petersburg, Virginia, where the father was a representative business man. Since the death of her husband Mrs. Dadmun has maintained her residence in Norfolk, where her home is at 418 West Nineteenth Street. Of the five children of this union the eldest is Miss Hope Alice, who was educated in the City of Richmond

and who remains with her widowed mother, as does also the next younger daughter, Charlotte, whose education was acquired in the Norfolk schools. Edward Henry, the eldest son, attended the Virginia Military Institute, and he entered World war service with the Norfolk Light Artillery Blues when that fine organization was mustered into the United States Army, he having been in active service in France one year and having reecived his honorable discharge after the armistice brought the great conflict to a close. He and his wife, whose maiden name was Julia Whitmore, maintain their home in Richmond. Branch Morgan, next younger of the sons, received the advantages of the Virginia Military Institute, is a civil engineer by profession and maintains his home in Norfolk. Robert, youngest of the children, is associated with business in this city.

ALVIN T. DULANEY. Emerson said "I cannot even hear of personal vigor of any kind, great power. of performance, without fresh resolution. This is the moral of biography." Measured according to that standard how inspirational is the life of Alvin T. Dulaney, who in the short span of his mature years has made himself the wealthiest man in Greene County, and while thus gaining large material rewards he has not failed to win and hold the respect and confidence of his associates. Accounts of achievements like his encourage the disheartened to hold on when they are ready to let go; they induce them to persevere when they had decided to go back; they give them fresh help and renewed confidence in themselves. Ambition requires a great deal and a great variety of food to keep it vigorous, and perhaps one of the reasons for Mr. Dulaney's success has been that he has branched out and, not resting content with his progress in merchandising, entered the oil industry, in both rising to high position.

Alvin T. Dulaney was born in Greene County, Virginia, June 3, 1881, a son of James Fillmore and Lou Alice (Wilhoit) Dulaney, and grandson of John G. Dulaney, a native of Greene County, and Ezekiel F. Wilhoit, a native of Albemarle County. Both grandfathers were farmers, and that was also the occupation of James Fillmore Dulaney, who was born in Greene County and who through his efforts developed a valuable property in his home farm. He died March 14, 1914, and his widow, who survives him, was born in Albemarle County. James Fillmore Dulaney was a Democrat in politics. They had five children: Charles Q., who owns and operates the home farm; Alvin T.; Mrs. E. D. Ott, wife of a practicing attorney at Harrisonburg, Virginia; John E. F., associated with the State Highway Department at Richmond, Virginia; and Cary B., with the Sanitary Grocery Company at Washington, D.C. Both parents were strong church members, the father a Methodist and the mother a Baptist, and they took their religion into their every day lives, and the influence they exerted among their children and in their community was of an uplifting character.

Alvin T. Dulaney acquired his education in local public and private schools and in several excellent academies. At the age of eighteen he left home and secured a position as salesman in the dry goods and notion store of Charles E. Hughes at Charlottesville. In the fall of 1900, going to Covington, Virginia, he and his brother, C. Q. Dulaney, and F. M. Beale opened a small dry goods and notion store under the name Covington Bargain House. This business was sold out the following year, when

Mr. Dulaney and his brother opened at Ruckersville, Virginia, a general merchandise store under the firm name of Dulaney Brothers. This was operated as a partnership until 1919, and since then Mr. Alvin T. Dulaney has been sole owner, operating a department store carrying everything required for the home, farm and automobile. Realizing the market that existed for certain lines not then handled, the partners in 1903 established the Ruckersville Implement Company, handling a general line of farm implements, machinery, wagons, buggies, harness, et cetera. After the death of T. B. Jennings, a partner in 1912, the business was incorporated in the general business of Dulaney Brothers. In 1908 they established a firm at Barboursville, comprising C. Q. Dulaney, Alvin T. Dulaney and M. H. Williams, under the name Dulaney, Williams & Company, handling a general line of machinery, vehicles and farm supplies of all kinds. In 1913 the interest of Dulaney Brothers was sold to M. H. Williams, who later sold it to his nephews, Williams & Company, under which title the business is still operated.

In 1914 the Dulaney Brothers added to their Ruckersville business a Ford agency. At that time there was one car in Greene County. They continued the operation of the agency until the fall of 1925, and during the twelve years it became the outstanding country automobile agency in Virginia. The success they had with the Ford business at Ruckersville caused the Ford Motor Company to request the Dulaney Brothers to establish another agency at Gordonsville, Virginia. This was started as the Gordonsville Motor Company, Incorporated, in 1921, and the business was a success from the start. Mr. Alvin T. Dulaney was vice president and principal stockholder of the Gordonsville business until 1924, when he sold his interest to the remaining stockholders, who still carry it on. The first venture in oil made by Alvin T. Dulaney was the Gordonsville Gas & Oil Company at Gordonsville, a small distributing company formed in 1923 and continued until 1926, at which time Mr. Dulaney sold out to his partners and then formed the Shenandoah Park Oil Company, of which he is the manager. He is also a director in the Peoples National Bank of Charlottesville.

On June 10, 1910, Mr. Dulaney married Buford J. Stephens, born in Standardsville, Virginia, a daughter of Doctor Stephens, one of the beloved physicians of Standardsville. Mr. and Mrs. Dulaney have three sons: James Fillmore, who is attending school in Standardsville, and Alvin T., Jr., and Albert Stephens, who are attending the Ruckersville schools. Mrs. Dulaney is a valued member of the local Methodist Episcopal Church, South. While Mr. Dulaney votes the Democratic ticket, he has not had the time or inclination to go into politics, his business interests absorbing all of his energies, but he is interested in the advancement of his home city and county, in which he takes great pride.

DENHAM ARTHUR KELSEY is a prominent Norfolk attorney, with offices at 111 East Main Street in that city. He came to Norfolk from the Piedmont section.

He was born at Bedford, son of Oswald W. Kelsey and grandson of Alfred Kelsey. His father was born in the Cathedral Close near Salisbury, England. Alfred Kelsey spent all his life in England, a very devout member of the Established Church. Oswald W. Kelsey was educated in Christ Church School and about 1872 came to the United States, being the only representative of his family to come to America. He bought a farm near

Bedford, in Bedford County, Virginia, but did not find farming profitable and subsequently engaged in the real estate business at Bedford. He died at the age of forty-seven. He married after coming to Virginia, Rosalie Bell, who was born at Bedford, which at that time went under the name of Liberty. She was a daughter of Alfred and Mary (Lowry) Bell, of English ancestry. D. Arthur Kelsey was one of two children. His sister, Gladys is the wife of William W. Berry and has two children.

D. Arthur Kelsey attended public schools, including the Bedford High School, and was a young man when he came to Norfolk. He was deputy clerk in the Federal Court until 1907, and while in that position studied law. After being admitted to the bar in 1907 he engaged in practice and later was appointed chief deputy clerk of the Norfolk District Court. He resigned this office in 1920 and has since engaged in a general law practice, to which he gives all his time.

Mr. Kelsey married in 1919 Nelle Buchanan, who was born at Richmond, daughter of H. L. and Elizabeth Buchanan. Mr. Kelsey by a previous marriage has two sons, D. Arthur, Jr., a student at the University of Virginia, and Sidney Harrison, a student at William and Mary College. Mr. Kelsey is a member of St. Luke's Episcopal Church, and in politics is a Republican.

SIGMUND MITTELDORFER BRANDT, Norfolk lawyer, member of a family that has been identified with the commercial interests of Eastern Virginia for many years, was born at Norfolk in 1880.

His parents were Henry and Pauline (Mitteldorfer) Brandt. Henry Brandt, in 1876 established at Norfolk the foreign banking business which is yet in successful operation. The late Joseph Brandt, brother of Sigmund M., was admitted to partnership in 1906. Henry Brandt was born in Neustadt, Germany, son of Joseph Brandt, of the same city, and grandson of Herman Brandt, also of Nuestadt. The first of this family to come to America was Leon Brandt, who built up a name and reputation in American journalism, and died shortly before the Civil war, being buried at Albany, New York. It was through the influence of Leon Brandt that Henry Brandt, his brother, came to this country at the age of fifteen. Henry Brandt finished his education in schools in North Carolina, living in Fayetteville, that state, until the outbreak of the Civil war. As a member of the North Carolina Militia he entered the Confederate army with his brother George Brandt, who had come to Fayetteville at the instance of Leon Brandt several years earlier, and who also served in the Confederate army. Prior to the war George Brandt was connected with cotton mills in the vicinity of Fayetteville, and also was interested in sailing vessels operating between the ports of Wilmington and Liverpool.

Henry Brandt's wife, Pauline Mitteldorfer, was born in the City of Nuremberg, Bavaria, and was a very young girl when her father died. She came to Richmond, Virginia, living with her uncle, Moses Mitteldorfer, who had settled in Richmond many years earlier. She was followed by her mother, Mrs. Cecilia Mitteldorfer. The first Mitteldorfer located at Richmond about 1840. Henry Brandt and wife were married in Norfolk, and they lived to celebrate their golden wedding anniversary April 3, 1921. They were married in what is known as Olaf Sholem Temple, and they held membership in that temple for half a century. Henry Brandt was a member of Ruth Lodge, A. F. and A. M., forty years.

Sigmund M. Brandt was educated in Norfolk Academy, spent one year in the Virginia Polytechnic Institute, and in 1901 was admitted to the bar by the Supreme Court of Appeals of Virginia. He qualified in the Supreme Court of the United States April 25, 1913. Mr. Brandt is a member of the Virginia State and American Bar Associations. He is a member of the Croatan Country Club.

He married, April 10, 1918, Miss Juliette Heller, of Atlanta, Georgia, daughter of Max and Clara (Kaufman) Heller. They have one daughter, Claire Pauline Brandt, born June 17, 1919.

CLAUDE EUGENE HERBERT. The Herbert family have lived in and around Norfolk for generation after generation. The family were established in this section of Virginia in the early Colonial period.

As early as 1659 John Herbert was a resident of Norfolk County. His will was probated in Norfolk in 1675. His son, John Herbert, was born at Norfolk and was a landed proprietor. His will was probated in 1679. He left two children. One of them, Thomas Herbert, was born at Norfolk in 1679, and married Margaret Dale, daughter of Henry and Frances (Ballentine) Dale. He was a ship builder and owned and operated a ship yard, and took a prominent part in local affairs, bearing the title of captain. He died at the age of seventy-nine, his will being probated in 1749. Of his family of six sons and one daughter the son Henry, born at Norfolk about 1715, married Abigail Carson, daughter of Jonas Carson, of Accamac County, Virginia. Henry succeeded to the ownership of the ship yard and conducted it as a successful business. He was a vestryman of St. Brides Parish. His will was probated in 1778.

His son, Caleb Herbert, one of nine children, was born in Norfolk about 1745 and was the chief representative of the family in this generation in the Revolutionary war period. He was a member of the committee of safety during the war and was listed on the committee as a master ship builder, owning a ship yard. He married Ann Nicholson, daughter of James Nicholson. His will was probated in 1796, and he reared five children.

His son Maximilian Herbert was born in Norfolk about 1772, succeeded to the ownership of the ship yard and also conducted a large plantation. He died in 1828. By his first marriage he had four children and one by his second marriage. A son of his first marriage was Maximilian II, born at Norfolk in 1806, and who followed planting, employing slave labor on his farm. He organized a company for service in the Confederate army and was commissioned a captain, serving in General Mahone's Brigade. He died in the camp at Petersburg in 1862. His wife was Lydia Herbert Nash, daughter of Thomas and Sarah Nash. He was survived by five children.

His son Maximilian Herbert III was born in Norfolk March 18, 1834, and became a farmer in Southampton County, but later returned to Norfolk and died there in 1903. He married Mrs. Eugenia (Briggs) Pace, daughter of Bennett and Louise Pace. They reared a family of eight children, one of whom was Claude Eugene Herbert.

Claude Eugene Herbert was born in Southampton County, October 18, 1869. He attended a one-room schoolhouse in his

native county and since 1895 has been a resident of Norfolk.
He learned the wholesale grocery business by several years of
experience as a clerk, and later he and J. W. Hough formed a
firm handling wholesale groceries. Later the Southern Distributing Company was organized and he became its secretary and
treasurer, and is now president of that successful Norfolk business.

Claude Eugene Herbert married Eva Parrish Beale, who
was born in Norfolk. Her father, Cype Beale, came from Hertford County, North Carolina, to Norfolk County, and for a
number of years was in the dairy business and later a wholesale
grocer. Cype Beale married Julia Ann Raboteau, who was
born in Fayetteville, North Carolina, daughter of John Samuel
and Esther (Barclay) Raboteau. Claude E. Herbert and wife
reared two sons, Eastwood Davidson and Claude Page. Mr.
Herbert is a member of Corinthian Lodge No. 266, A. F. and
A. M., has membership in the various Scottish Rite bodies and
Khedive Temple of the Mystic Shrine. He is a member of the
Park Place Methodist Episcopal Church, South. He has always
been keenly interested in the public affairs of Norfolk and has
been a member of the City Council continuously since 1918.

His son Eastwood Davidson Herbert, a prominent young
Norfolk attorney, with offices in the Bank of Commerce Building, was born at Norfolk, was educated in public schools in that
city, attended the Episcopal High School at Alexandria, and
in 1917 entered the University of Virginia, where he took his
A. B. degree in 1920 and his degree in law in 1922. He was
admitted to the bar and at once engaged in practice at Norfolk,
where he has made himself an attorney of recognized ability and
with a splendid practice. He is a member of the Park Place
Methodist Episcopal Church, and of Corinthian Lodge No. 266,
A. F. and A. M.

WILBUR CURTIS HALL has practiced law at Leesburg since
1915, and for ten years has been a representative of Loudoun
County in the Virginia Legislature.

He was born at Mountain Gap, Loudoun County, February
5, 1892, descended from a family of Halls that settled in Virginia shortly after the close of the Revolutionary war. His
grandfather, James M. Hall, was a native of Loudoun County,
spending his life there as a farmer. John W. Hall, father of
the Leesburg attorney, was born in 1857, and was engaged in
farming until he retired in 1917. He married Annie E. Holli-
day, who was born in Loudoun County in 1869. Their two sons
are Wilbur Curtis and Stilson Hutchins, both prominent citizens
of Leesburg.

Wilbur C. Hall attended a two-room school at Mountain
Gap, graduated in 1910 from the Leesburg High School, and
as a means of financing himself in law school he worked in a
printing office. He was a student in Washington and Lee University during 1913-14, was licensed to practice in 1914, and
in 1915 took his law degree at Georgetown University.

During most of the time since he started his law practice
he has engaged in some form of civic or patriotic service. July
10, 1918, he joined the colors, being honorably discharged December 4, 1918. He held the rank of petty officer in the navy
and later was one of the organizers of the American Legion of
Virginia, serving on the State Executive Committee and as

delegate at large to national conventions. He served as colonel on the staff of Governor Davis.

He was elected to represent Loudoun County in the House of Delegates in November, 1917, and has been regularly reelected, his increasing experience making him one of the most influential members of the Lower House of the Virginia Legislature. Among other measures he has been actively identified with legislation in behalf of soldiers of the World war and the enforcement of the prohibition laws. He is the author of Virginia insurance code, having instigated the fire insurance investigation and wrote the bill providing for revocation of the license of any driver of an automobile convicted of driving while intoxicated.

Mr. Hall is unmarried. He is a member of St. James Episcopal Church at Leesburg, Olive Branch Lodge No. 114, A. F. and A. M., of which he is a past master, Loudoun Chapter No. 25, Royal Arch Masons, of which he is a past high priest, Piedmont Commandery No. 26, Knights Templar, Acca Temple of the Mystic Shrine at Richmond, Loudoun Lodge No. 26, Independent Order of Odd Fellows, of which he is a past grand, Hamilton Council No. 24, Junior Order United American Mechanics. He is a member of the University Club of Washington.

HUGH CAPERTON PRESTON. Among the men of Virginia who wielded with equal energy and ability the implements of peace and the weapons of war, the late Hugh Caperton Preston, of East Radford, was a striking example. Coming of a long line of distinguished ancestors who had established splendid records as patriots, soldiers and statesmen, it was natural that he should inherit military ability, while in no less a degree did he rank high as a real estate dealer at East Radford, where his death occurred January 3, 1905.

Mr. Preston was born at "Elmwood," the old Caperton estate in West Virginia, September 5, 1856, and was a son of Col. James Francis and Sarah (Caperton) Preston. Old records show the fact that one John Preston came from England to Virginia in 1745 and settled on a land grant at Tinkling Springs, Augusta County. His son, William Preston, after taking part in the Indian wars as a captain, became a colonel in the Colonial army during the War of the Revolution, following the close of which he became the founder of Smithfield Plantation, a tract of some 7,000 or 8,000 acres on a part of which is located the Virginia Polytechnic Institute. James Patton Preston, son of William Preston and grandfather of Hugh Caperton Preston, was a colonel during the War of 1812, and afterward became governor of Virginia. Among his sons was Hon. William Ballard Preston, a famous lawyer and statesman, who in 1849 was secretary of the navy in President Taylor's cabinet, and during the war between the states a member of the Confederate Senate. Another son, Robert Taylor Preston, served as a colonel in the Confederate army.

Col. James Francis Preston was born in Virginia and as a youth secured a commission to West Point Military Academy, from which institution he was duly graduated. During the Mexican war he volunteered for service, equipped and organized a complete company at his own expense, was commissioned a captain, and after the close of that struggle he returned to his estate, "White Home," in Montgomery County, Virginia. When the trouble broke out between the forces of the North and South he espoused the cause of the Confederacy and became colonel of the Fourth Virginia Infantry, a part of the great "Stonewall" Brigade, which won deathless fame on many a hard-fought field. Colonel Preston did not live to see the fall of the Confederacy, his death occurring in 1862, caused by the exposure incidental to his military service. He married Sarah Caperton, of Elmwood, Monroe County, Virginia (now West Virginia). One of their sons, William Ballard Preston, enlisted for service in the Spanish-American war under his brother, Hugh C., and received a commission as first lieutenant. Later he went to the Philippines, where he was commisisoned a captain on the Island Panay at Iloilo, and then was appointed governor of one of the group of islands, but died before assuming office. He married Elizabeth Scott.

The education of Hugh Caperton Preston was completed at Virginia Military Institute, from which he was graduated as a senior captain and adjutant as a member of the class of 1877. As a young man he became head and master of his mother's estate, known as "White Thorn" in Montgomery County, Virginia, but sold this in 1892 and went to East Radford, where he entered the real estate and insurance business, also serving two terms in the capacity of mayor. At the outbreak of the Spanish-American war he lived up to the family traditions by enlisting as a captain in the volunteers, Company M, Fourth Virginia Volunteer Infantry, under Colonel Petit, and saw one year of service in Cuba. One month after his return the regiment was mustered out of the service, but he secured a commission in the Thirty-first United States Volunteers, and with the rank of first lieutenant went to Mindanao, Philippine Islands, where for two years he served as captain of the post. In 1901 Mr. Preston returned to the United States and again took up the real estate business at East Radford, in which he continued to be engaged until his death. He also had various other business connections, was widely and favorably known in business circles, and served as secretary of the Southwest Virginia Live Stock Association. He was a Democrat in his political convictions, was fraternally affiliated with the local lodge of the Independent Order of Odd Fellows, and was a member of the Episcopal Church.

On April 30, 1878, at Staunton, Virginia, Mr. Preston was united in marriage with Miss Cary Marx Baldwin, of Winchester, Virginia, who was educated at Dunbar Institute and Mary Baldwin's School at Staunton, a daughter of Dr. Robert Frederick and Cary (Barton) Baldwin, the former of whom was a distinguished surgeon of his day who held the rank of colonel in the Confederate army during the war between the states. Seven children were born to Mr. and Mrs. Preston: James Francis, who died in infancy; Robert Baldwin, county engineer of Norfolk County, who married Merle Page and has three children, Robert Baldwin, Jr., Edwin Page and John Baldwin; Cary Baldwin, the wife of Hartwell Henry Gary, a mechanical engineer of Norfolk and president of the Norfolk Tank Corporation, and has two children, Cary Preston and Hartwell Henry, Jr.; Sarah Caperton, president of the Preston School of Dancing and director and owner of the Camp Carybrook for Girls; William Ballard, who enlisted for service on patrol duty on the Mexican border and served as sergeant until the United States entered the World war, when he was appointed first lieutenant and sent to Camp Lee, and in May, 1918, went to France, where he was

promoted to the rank of captain of a machine gun company on
the battlefield, and who married Lelia Harrison Dew and has
two children, Bettie Harrison Braxton and William Ballard IV;
Hugh Caperton, identified with the National Highway Commission, who married Ann Cahill and has one child, Hugh Caperton
III; and Katherine Stuart, a registered nurse, who is a member
of the McGuire clinical staff of St. Luke's Hospital at Richmond.

JOHN HENRY NININGER is a Norfolk attorney, has practiced
law there a number of years and represents one of the prominent
families of Southwestern Virginia.

He was born at Hollins in Roanoke County, son of Christ
Nininger and grandson of Peter Nininger. Peter Nininger was
a farmer in Botetourt County and also a preacher in the German
Baptist Church. He married Lydia Gish, member of an old
Virginia family. She died at the age of eighty-nine and he
passed away at the age of eighty-seven.

Christ Nininger was born at Daleville, Botetourt County,
Virginia, in 1835, grew up on a farm, and from Botetourt moved
to Roanoke County, where he acquired a plantation of 650 acres.
He engaged in general farming and also established and conducted a cannery for fruits and vegetables. He was a lay
preacher of the Progressive German Baptist Church and died
at the age of seventy-three. Christ Nininger married Nannie
Frantz, who was born near Salem in Roanoke County, daughter
of Jacob Frantz. She was reared a Methodist. She died at the
age of seventy-two, having reared nine children, named Rosa B.,
Letcher, George M., Lula G., Frank P., John H., Staples V.,
Harry C. and Charles M.

John H. Nininger grew up on a farm in Roanoke County,
attended a one-room country school, and afterwards entered the
National Normal University at Lebanon, Ohio. He received a
thorough academic training in that splendid school and subsequently for two years attended the law department of the University of Virginia. Mr. Nininger was admitted to practice in
1894 and first established his law offices at Bluefield, West Virginia. In 1898 he went to Washington to become a clerk in the
treasury department, but after one year resigned and located
at Norfolk, where he has become permanently established as a
citizen and attorney, engaged in a general law practice. He
is a man of wide experience, learned in the law, resourceful in
the handling of his professional work, and has been deservedly
successful.

He married in 1903 Emily L. Eggleston, who was born in
New Kent County, Virginia, daughter of William T. and Sarah
(Williams) Eggleston. Mr. and Mrs. Nininger have three children, Mary Eggleston, Louise Fisher and John Henry, Jr. Mary
is a student in William and Mary College. Mr. and Mrs. Nininger
are members of the Park Place Baptist Church of Norfolk.

WILLIAM BROOKS SMITH. In those sections where the agricultural interests are important, many of the men who serve in
public office come from the farming class, and rightly so, for it
is their work and their property which support the machinery
of the law, and they are the logical officeholders. There is another reason, and it is that they, living as they do close to the
soil, know the needs of the people, their resources and possibilities, and they can therefore give a better and more comprehensive service than an outsider no matter how capable or experi-

enced he might be along other lines. As a case in question attention is called to William B. Smith, one of the leading agriculturists of Mathews County, now serving as county clerk. In his office he is rendering a service that is appreciated by all who have reason to call upon him, and his fellow citizens are satisfied that in him they have a friend and able representative, one who will safeguard their interests.

William B. Smith was born at Mathews Court House, Virginia, February 27, 1888, a son of Sands and Carrie W. (Diggs) Smith, natives of Mathews County. When war was declared between the states Sands Smith was one of the gallant young men who enlisted in the cause of the Confederacy, and served with the famous Black Horse Cavalry throughout the war period, winning distinction for his intrepid bravery. After the close of the war, and his return to Mathews County, he served it as sheriff for a number of years, or until 1886, when he was appointed clerk of the county, and at the following election was elected to the office. From then on he was continued as county clerk through successive elections until his death November 10, 1914. The mother died September 23, 1923.

Reared and educated in Mathews County, William B. Smith attended its public schools and Randolph-Macon Academy, Bedford City, Virginia. Returning home, he became deputy clerk of Mathews County, and November 16, 1914, after his father's death, was appointed his successor to fill out the unexpired term. With its expiration he was elected to the office, and has been reelected every eight years since that time. This is a somewhat remarkable case, as for forty-two years the office of county clerk of Mathews County has been filled by a father and son. Mr. Smith is unmarried. He resides in Mathews County, where he has 600 acres of valuable farming land, 150 acres of which he operates himself, and is a scientific farmer. His fraternal connections are numerous and include membership with Oriental Lodge No. 20, A. F. and A. M.; the local lodge of the Junior Order United American Mechanics; and Naoman Tribe, Improved Order of Red Men. In political faith he is a Democrat, and he is very active in the local party. While he is not a member of any religious organizations, he was reared by parents who were zealous members of the Methodist Episcopal Church, South, and is a liberal donor to different churches in his neighborhood.

HON. L. SUMTER DAVIS. When Newport News was but a small town of no special importance, Hon. L. Sumter Davis came into its midst, and from thenceforward until his death, July 21, 1920, he continued to take a most important part in its development. On the day of his death the following appeared editorially in the local press:

"Newport News has sustained a genuine bereavement in the death of Sumter Davis, one of its pioneer citizens and a man devoted to the best interests of the community. As citizen and member of the common council he discharged his duties with fidelity and he enjoyed the respect and good will of his fellows. We chronicle this record in the public print as a mark of respect, and we point to his character, his career and the esteem in which he was held as an incentive to good citizenship in others."

L. Sumter Davis was born in Williamsburg, Virginia, in 1861, a son of Philip and Rosa Davis, the former of whom was a farmer and Confederate veteran. The parents had ten children, of whom L. Sumter Davis was the youngest child. As a boy he assisted his father on the farm, and at the same time attended school in Newmarket, Virginia. When he was eighteen years old he came to Newport News, entering the employ of the ship yards, and he maintained that connection the remainder of his life, and when he died was manager of one of its important departments, a position he held for many years.

In September, 1891, Mr. Davis married Miss Cora Puckett, a daughter of Walter and Virginia (Lee) Puckett. Mr. Puckett was a resident of Richmond, and later of Newport News, and while living in the former city he served on the school board. He was a Confederate veteran, having served in the Southern army during the war between the states. Of the four children born to Mr. and Mrs. Puckett, Mrs. Davis is the third in order of birth.

Five children were born to Mr. and Mrs. Davis, namely: Horace, who is a draughtsman in the ship yard; Sumter, who is instructor of apprentices in the ship yard; Emerson, who is timekeeper in the ship yard; Evelyn, who is the wife of Russel Cooper, a business man of Newport News; and Lois, who is attending the public schools of Newport News.

Mr. Davis was a charter member of Newport News Lodge No. 92, I. O. O. F.; an energetic and helpful member of the Junior Order United American Mechanics, and for years he was in the City Council, practically serving from the incorporation of the city until his death.

The funeral of Mr. Davis was held in his late residence, Rev. W. P. Stuart of the Hampton Baptist Church officiating, and his remains were interred in Greenlawn Cemetery. The active pallbearers were two members of the Odd Fellows Lodge, Dr. F. B. Longan and H. B. West, of the Board of Aldermen, R. W. West and A. E. Lowder. The honorary pallbearers were D. S. Jones, R. Lee Davis, E. F. Piland, Floyd Hudgins, C. C. Smith, Dr. R. B. Gary, W. B. Yost, Arthur Davis and Minor Manning. The floral tributes were numerous and beautiful, attesting the high esteem in which he was held. A multitude attended, many more people than could be accommodated in the house in East End, where for many years he had made his home.

The following is quoted from a local newspaper after the death of Mr. Davis:

"L. Sumter Davis was one of those pioneer citizens of middle age who are peculiar to a young city.

"He will be missed acutely because though a pioneer in residence, he was one of the men who kept step in the march of village to city, who put his shoulder to the wheel, gave himself unselfishly to the service of his town and was never surprised at the good and development that came because he believed in his city and in himself.

"It is citizenship of that character which will remain the hope of the city, however much it grows and develops with the years."

At the regular meeting following the death of Alderman Davis, the City Council of Newport News appointed the following as a committee on resolutions: Guy P. Murray, H. B. West and James D. Bohlken. The following resolutions were drawn up by the committee and approved by the Council:

"Whereas, God, in His infinite wisdom, saw fit to call from our midst to His eternal reward, Mr. L. Sumter Davis, one of the most active, faithful and conscientious members of the Board of Aldermen of Newport News; therefore, be it resolved,

E. S. Adrian

"First, That the city has sustained a great loss in the death of our fellow alderman.

"Second, That we extend to the bereaved wife and children our deepest sympathy, and pray that they may be comforted by Him who doeth all things well.

"Third, That a copy of these resolutions be sent to the family, a copy to the press, and a copy be spread on the minutes of the board of aldermen.

> "Guy P. Murray,
> "H. B. West,
> "J. D. Bohlken."

In conclusion it may be said of Mr. Davis that he peacefully, honorably and capably met and discharged all of the obligations of life; honored and beloved he passed away, sincerely mourned by all who knew him. As a successful business man he was honorable, prompt and true to every engagement; he was always a warm friend of education, and the supporter of all worthy movements which have their root in unselfish devotion to the best interests of the country. As an alderman he left his impress indelibly inscribed upon the history of Newport News, and to his friends and family his memory will ever remain enshrined in a halo of gracious presence and kindly spirit.

HON. EUGENE SILVESTER ADRIAN. The man who honorably discharges the duties of the office of sheriff in these days of many perplexities and dangerous criminals must possess more than an ordinary amount of personal courage, and be a man of unflinching honesty. Within the past decade so many problems have arisen which must be handled by the sheriff of a county that the office carries with it onerous duties, and the qualifications are of necessity much higher than formerly. In Eugene S. Adrian, Loudoun County possesses one of the best men to serve as its sheriff it has ever had, and each day adds to the prestige he enjoys. The lawless element understand that in him they have a relentless enforcement officer, and that his bailiwick is not a desirable field for operations of a criminal character. However, on the other hand he is a man who insists on a fair deal for everyone, and protects the rights of his charges no matter what may be the crime of which they are accused. All of these qualities are appreciated by his fellow citizens, and they intend to keep him in his present office.

Sheriff Adrian was born near Ashburn, Loudoun County, Virginia, September 6, 1878, a son of James Alexander and Olivia E. (Havner) Adrian, he born in Philadelphia, Pennsylvania, and she in Loudoun County. During the war between the states he served in the Confederate army, and after peace was declared he returned to Loudoun County, from which locality he had enlisted in the artillery branch of the service, and was engaged in farming until his death, which occurred in May, 1915. The mother survives and resides with her children.

Reared and educated in Loudoun County, Sheriff Adrian remained on the farm with his parents until he reached his majority, at which time he went into pump and well work, drilling wells all over this neighborhood, and this continued to occupy him for twenty-six years. He then became deputy sheriff of Loudoun County, and after serving in that capacity for seven years he was elected sheriff of the county, taking office January 1, 1924. So admirable was his administration that he was elected to succeed himself, taking office for his second term January 1, 1928.

On August 6, 1902, Sheriff Adrian married Miss Mary Lillian Hummer, a daughter of Maurice A. and Catherine (Brown) Hummer, natives of Loudoun County. After serving as postmaster for many years, Mr. Hummer is now living retired in Sterling, Virginia, and receives a pension from the United States Government. Sheriff and Mrs. Adrian have had thirteen children born to them, namely: Keith F., who is in the employ of the Washington-Potomac Electric & Power Company of Washington City; Allen M., who is with the Roberts Construction Company, Falls Church, Virginia; Helen C., who is in the employ of the Bell Telephone Company; Alma and Elsie, both of whom are attending Leesburg High School; and Etta, Howard, Ruth, Dorothy, Nellie, Alice, James and Fred. Sheriff Adrian is a Mason, and he belongs to the International Sheriffs Association, the Business Men's Association of Leesburg, the Rotary Club and the Sons of Confederate Veterans, and Mrs. Adrian belongs to the Daughters of Confederate Veterans and the order of the Eastern Star. He is a staunch supporter of the Democratic party. In religious faith he is a Presbyterian. Sheriff Adrian's office is in the courthouse at Leesburg, and he lives at the county seat, his home being one of the comfortable ones of the city. Both he and Mrs. Adrian have many friends throughout the county and enjoy a pleasant social life. It can be truly said of him that no man ever had cause to regret his faith in him, nor has anyone any reason to feel that his confidence is misplaced, for Sheriff Adrian is an admirable, upright and conscientious official and true Christian gentleman of the highest personal character.

JUNIUS FRANCIS LYNCH, Norfolk physician and surgeon, is a former surgeon general of Virginia and was a division surgeon with the American Expeditionary Forces in the World war.

Doctor Lynch has had many ancestors who served with distinction in the army and navy. His people on both sides have lived in Virginia for a number of generations. However, Doctor Lynch himself was born in Alabama, December 2, 1865, son of Col. Francis Edward and Mary Knox (Buford) Lynch. The founder of the Lynch family was Francis Lynch, who came to this country about 1790, settling at Petersburg, Virginia. He acquired a fortune as a tobacco exporter. The old Lynch home is still standing on High Street in Petersburg.

Doctor Lynch's grandfather was William F. Lynch, a captain in the United Staes Navy and later a commodore in the Confederate States Navy. As a captain and under the auspices of the United States Government he made the first and only authentic exploration of the Dead Sea and the Jordan in 1848. His book, *Lynch's Expedition to the Dead Sea and the Jordan*, was published shortly after this and attracted wide attention and was the source of most of the reliable information published in different accounts of these features of the Holy Land. The French Geographical Society awarded him a medal for the work. As a commodore of the Confederate States Navy he commanded the Confederate naval forces in the battle of Roanoke Island February 2, 1862. Commodore Lynch married Virginia Shaw, a daughter of Capt. John Shaw of the United States Navy. Captain Shaw came from Ireland, and was also an officer of high standing in naval circles.

Francis Edward Lynch, who attained the rank of colonel in the Confederate army, was a physician by profession. He was born at the Brooklyn Navy Yard, was educated in Georgetown University and the College of Physicans and Surgeons at Baltimore. At the time of the war between the states he entered the Confederate army as a captain and before the close was a colonel in Wheeler's Cavalry Corps. His wife, Mary Knox Buford, was a daughter of William Knox Buford, of Virginia. The oldest son of their marriage is Dr. Junius Francis Lynch.

Doctor Lynch graduated from the Medical College of Virginia in 1888. He has always been a leader in his profession. For twenty-five years he was on the staff of Saint Vincent's Hospital at Norfolk. He was the founder, is a former president and now an honorary member of the Seaboard Medical Association of Virginia and North Carolina. He is a member of a number of other professional societies and in the course of his work covering forty years has used his experience and research as the source of a number of articles he has contributed to medical journals. He is former vice president of the Medical Society of Virginia.

Doctor Lynch continues the tradition of the family in the military affairs of his home state and nation. For twenty-five years he has been identified with the Virginia National Guard, in service all the way from enlisted man to surgeon general of Virginia. In 1910 Governor William Hodges Mann commissioned him surgeon general, and he held that position at the time of the World war. He entered the Federal service as major, was made assistant division surgeon in the Twenty-ninth Division at Camp McClellan, Alabama, was transferred to the Ninety-third Division as division surgeon at Camp Stuart, Virginia, in December, 1917, and shortly afterward sailed for France. In France the Ninety-third Division was broken up and Doctor Lynch was attached to the Forty-second or Rainbow Division until July, 1918, when he was put in command of a hospital at Saint Maixent, France. After the armistice he was ordered to Paris as chief of surgical service in the United States Army Hospital No. 57, the largest American hosiptal in Paris. He was discharged in Hoboken, New Jersey, in the fall of 1919. He went into the army as a major in the Medical Corps, was promoted to lieutenant colonel in France and was commissioned a colonel in the Medical Reserve Corps shortly after his return from service abroad.

Colonel Lynch is a past department commander of the American Legion, a past national executive committeeman of that organization, and founder and commander of Post No. 35. He is president of the Department of Virginia Reserve Officers' Association of the United States and member of its executive council. Doctor Lynch has never held a political office, though deeply interested in the Democratic party. During the campaign of 1924 he was president of the local Davis-Bryan Club.

He married at Orange, Virginia, in 1891, Miss Lucy Virginia Kemper, who died in 1915. She was a daughter of James L. and Belle (Cave) Kemper. Her father for many years prior to the Civil war was speaker of the House of Delegates in the Virginia Legislature, and is best known in Virginia history as governor of the state from 1874 to 1878. He was the first Democratic governor of Virginia after the Civil war. He was one of Virginia's sons to reach the rank of major-general in the Confederate army. While commanding a brigade in Pickett's memor-

able charge at the battle of Gettysburg he was desperately
wounded at the head of his men and was left on the field for
dead. He survived, and was commissioned a major-general. He
died in Orange County in 1895. Doctor Lynch in 1921 married
Mary Shield, of Hampton, Virginia, widow of Harvey L. Wilson
and daughter of Dr. Mallory Shield, of "Little England," Hampton. Doctor Shield entered the Confederate army at an early
age, was severely wounded in action, and after the war took up
the study of medicine, graduating from the University of Virginia. Doctor Shield married Florence Winder Booker, a woman
of rare charm and beauty, whose life was devoted to good works.

Doctor Lynch's only child is a daughter by his first marriage,
Virginia Kemper Lynch, who was married in 1916 to Lyman
Millard, of Norfolk. Mr. and Mrs. Millard have two children,
Lyman Millard, Jr., and Virginia Kemper Millard.

MILTON BENJAMIN AMES, well known in life insurance circles
at Norfolk, represents some of the oldest and most prominent
families of the eastern shore of Virginia.

Mr. Ames himself is a native of that section of Virginia. He
was born in the Village of Pungoteague in Accomac County.
His father, Samuel W. Ames, was born in the same village
August 25, 1862. The grandfather, Leonard H. Ames, was born
in the same locality, son of Levin Sneed Ames, grandson of
Joseph Ames. Joseph Ames was a son of Levin Ames, grandson
of Joseph Ames. The Ames family came from England and
settled in Accomac County in early Colonial times, and through
every generation since then they have played a prominent part
in the civic, business, professional and social life of that section.
The family was represented by soldiers in the Revolutionary
war, the War of 1812 and in the Confederate army. Mr. Ames'
great-great-grandfather, Capt. Joseph Ames, commanded a company in the War of 1812. His grandfather, Leonard H. Ames,
was a soldier in the Confederate army, rising to the rank of
lieutenant. Leonard Ames married Virginia Joynes, another
name of distinction in the eastern shore. She was a daughter
of Edward Joynes, granddaughter of William R. Joynes, great-
granddaughter of Reuben Joynes. The Joynes family is of
Scotch ancestry. Reuben Joynes was a planter and land owner
who served as a lieutenant in the Ninth Virginia Regiment in the
War of the Revolution. He married Margaret Dunton. William
R. Joynes was a life long resident of Accomac County, a planter
and slave owner, and married Hester Rogers. Edward Joynes,
father of Virginia Joynes, was a planter and merchant, conducting a business at Old Warehouse Point in Accomac County. He
married Catherine Scott.

Samuel W. Ames was liberally educated, but chose a business
rather than a professional career. As a young man he was a
merchant at Pungoteague, and subsequent years brought an
accumulation and enlargement of his commercial interests. At
the present time he is president of the Accomac Farm Land Association of the Federal Land Bank, is vice president of the
Eastern Shore Banking Company, vice president of the Eastern
Shore Agricultural Association, the oldest agricultural society in
the United States, and he individually owns a large amount of
land in that rich section of Virginia.

Samuel W. Ames married Nannie Edmonds Mears. She was
born at Keller in Accomac County. Her father, Benjamin W.
Mears, was a son of William Mears, grandson of William Mears,

great-grandson of John Mears, and great-great-grandson of John Mears, whose father was William Mears. The records of the Mears family in Accomac County run back to 1755, and they have constituted a long line of planters and business men. Benjamin W. Mears was a planter and merchant, a Confederate soldier, and always deeply interested in educational matters, serving as a member of the local school board. He married Emma S. Mapp, daughter of George B. Mapp and granddaughter of George Thomas Mapp, great-granddaughter of Howson Mapp, who was a son of Howson Mapp and grandson of John Mapp, the earliest representative of this well known family in Accomac County. Ann Edmonds, the mother of Emma S. Mapp, was a daughter of James and Nannie (Wharton) Edmonds. Nannie Wharton was a daughter of James and Susanna Wharton, granddaughter of John and Elizabeth (Bagwell) Wharton and great-granddaughter of Francis W. Wharton.

Samuel W. Ames and wife reared the following children: Milton B., Susie M., Virginia Emma, Nannie Wharton, Lucy Mears, and Cora Byrd.

Milton Benjamin Ames attended the Accomac High School, continued his education in Randolph-Macon College, taught one year in Accomac County, then entered Lehigh University in Pennsylvania and graduated from the Eastman Business College of Poughkeepsie, New York, in 1907. Mr. Ames had the benefit of an extended experience in banking in New York, clerking in a Fifth Avenue Bank, and during the two years he was there he also attended night classes of New York University.

After returning to Accomac County he engaged in banking. For several years he had been a student of life insurance, and he took up that business on the conviction that a much larger percentage of young people should invest in life insurance, not only for the protective feature, but in order to secure a competency for old age. Mr. Ames after taking up life insurance removed to Norfolk and for many years has represented the Mutual Benefit Life of Newark, New Jersey, in this district.

He married in 1912 Miss Mabel Jordan Roberts, a native of Norfolk, daughter of Leonard P. and Ruth (Handy) Roberts. Mr. and Mrs. Ames have three sons, Milton B., Jr., William Jordan and Samuel Roberts. Mr. Ames is a member of the Colonial Avenue Methodist Episcopal Church, and for several years he was on its Official Board and superintendent of the Sunday School. Mrs. Ames is a member of the First Baptist Church. Fraternally he is affiliated with Atlantic Lodge No. 2, A. F. and A. M., Norfolk, United Royal Arch Chapter No. 1, Grice Commandery No. 16, Knights Templar, and Khedive Temple of the Mystic Shrine.

RICHARD BUCKNER SPINDLE, JR., judge of the City Police Court of Norfolk, has had a very successful career as a lawyer since beginning practice. He is a native son of Virginia and member of a family that has been in this state since Colonial times.

Judge Spindle was born at Christiansburg, Montgomery County, Virginia, and is a descendant of Robert Spindle, a native of England, who came to America in the period of Colonial settlement and located in Virginia. He was the father of William Spindle, who married Elizabeth Alsop, and they were the parents of Benjamin Spindle, a native of Spotsylvania County, Virginia, where he lived out his life as a planter. Benjamin Spindle was twice married; first to Maria Claiborne Wigglesworth, daughter of Thomas and Matilda (Foster) Wigglesworth, granddaughter of John and Philadelphia Claiborne (Fox) Wigglesworth, and great-granddaughter of John Wigglesworth, who came from England when a young man and settled in Virginia; and, second, to Sarah Hill Buckner, a daughter of Col. Richard Buckner, of Hazel Grove, Caroline County, and a descendant of Richard Buckner, of Essex County, planter and clerk of the House of Burgesses in 1714.

Richard Buckner Spindle, Sr., son of Benjamin and Sarah Hill (Buckner) Spindle, was born near Spotsylvania Court House in 1854. The ancestral home was burned during the battle of Spotsylvania Court House, and he was only a boy when both his parents died. He was educated by his uncle, Cuthbert Buckner, principal of a boys' school at Fredericksburg, and at the age of sixteen went to Christiansburg and entered the service of his older brother, Capt. Thomas Wigglesworth Spindle, a merchant. He afterwards entered business for himself, in which he remained until his death in September, 1928. He married Bessie Gertrude Wardlaw, who was born in Oglethorpe, Georgia. Her father, Rev. John Wardlaw, was a minister of the Methodist Episcopal Church, South. Her aunt, Mrs. O. S. Pollock, was the principal of the Montgomery Female College in Christiansburg, and Bessie Gertrude Wardlaw attended that school, acquiring a thorough culture and education, and she herself for several years conducted a private school in Christiansburg. She and her husband reared seven children, named Gertrude, Daniel H., now deceased, John W., William Henry, Katherine, deceased, Theodore and Richard Buckner, Jr. The daughter Gertrude is the wife of Alfred Randolph Wilson, president of the Amicable Life Insurance Company of Waco, Texas.

Richard Buckner Spindle, Jr., received his preparatory training in his mother's school. He graduated with the A. B. degree at Washington and Lee University in 1906, then was an instructor for two years at the Augusta Military Academy. In 1910 he took his law degree at Washington and Lee, acting as instructor in English while pursuing his studies in the law school. In the same year he located at Norfolk, and has been busy with his general practice and his official duties. He was assistant city attorney from 1918 to 1922, and was elected judge of the City Police Court in 1923, and reelected in 1927. He has been particularly interested in the traffic problem, inaugurated the first distinct Traffic Court in Norfolk, was a member of the National Conference of State and Highway Safety, popularly known as the Hoover Conference, which promulgated the Uniform Traffic Code subsequently adopted by the General Assembly of Virginia and the Model Municipal Traffic Ordinance. He is a director of the National Highway Traffic Association sponsored by the Automobile Club of America, and of the Tidewater Automobile Association.

Judge Spindle married, October 20, 1914, Lettie Mae McRoberts who was born at Lancaster, Kentucky, daughter of Robert E. and Annie (Ware) McRoberts. She is of old Virginia ancestry and has membership in the Daughters of the American Revolution. Judge and Mrs. Spindle have two children, Marjory Ware and Richard Buckner III. Successful as lawyer and judge, he has found time to be interested in varied outside activities. He is a Mason and a Shriner, a member of the local and state bar

associations, president of the Norfolk Saddle Club, one of the trustees of the Norfolk Public Library, vestryman of Christ Church, and has membership in the Virginia Historical Society.

FRANCIS PATTERSON LANDON.   A man of sterling integrity and worth, possessing in a high degree the esteem and confidence of the entire community, Francis P. Landon, the genial and accommodating postmaster at Hopewell, is well worthy of representation in this biographical volume.   A true Virginian, he was born in Salem, Roanoke County, Virginia, a descendant, several generations removed, of one of three Landon brothers, James, John and William, who immigrated from England to America in early Colonial days and settled in Virginia.   His father, George Hopkins Landon, was a son of Alvin Landon, a life long resident of the "Old Dominion."

Alvin Landon, who possessed not only good business ability, but keen foresight, owned and operated stages along the boundary line between Virginia and Tennessee, the line extending from Lynchburg to Bristol. This stage route was well patronized by people on business or pleasure bent, among the passengers of prominence having been Andrew Johnson, who frequently travelled over it, both as vice president of the United States and as president of our country.   Alvin Landon married Candace Rogers, and into their household three sons were born, namely: James M., Thomas and George Hopkins.

As a youth George Hopkins Landon served an apprenticeship in a printing establishment, becoming familiar while thus employed with the art preservative of all arts. During the Civil war his sympathies were with the Southern people, and during the last years of the conflict he enlisted in the Confederate service, took part in several engagements, and when Lee surrendered was doing guard duty at New River Bridge.   Soon after his return to Virginia he embarked in the drug business at Salem. He met with good success, and continued as a druggist the remainder of his active life.   He far outlived the allotted period of three score and ten years, dying at the age of seventy-eight years.   His wife, whose maiden name was Mary J. Acton, was born in Philadelphia, Pennsylvania, a daughter of James and Elizabeth (Wood) Acton, well known families, both the Woods and Actons having been among the early settlers of Virginia. She, too, attained a ripe old age, passing away at the age of seventy-two years.

One of a family of seven children, Francis P. Landon obtained his elementary education in the public schools of Salem, Virginia, in the meantime spending his leisure hours as a clerk in his father's store.   At the age of sixteen years, having a decided taste for pharmaceutics, he entered the Philadelphia School of Pharmacy, from which in 1892 he was graduated with the degree of Phar. D.   Locating then in Richlands, Virginia, Mr. Landon was there associated with Doctor Roberts, a physician and druggist, for a few years. He was afterward engaged in the drug business in different places, including Bluefield, West Virginia, Tazewell and Pocahontas, both in Virginia, Keystone, West Virginia, and Charlottesville, and Lynchburg, Virginia.

In 1916 Mr. Landon located in Hopewell, Prince George County, Virginia, where he remained in the employ of a leading druggist until 1922.   In that year he was appointed postmaster at Hopewell, and at the expiration of his term of service was reappointed to the same responsible position by Calvin Coolidge.

Mr. Landon has been twice married. He married first, in 1892, Lata Frances Tuttle, who was born in Brooklyn, New York, a daughter of Charles and Elizabeth Tuttle. She died in 1907, leaving four children, as follows: Bertha Groge, Gertrude Acton, George Kemlo and Francis P. Bertha G., wife of J. C. Walters, has four children, all boys, Jesse C., Frank, William and Douglas. Gertrude Acton, who married Theodore Benning, has four children. George Kemlo married Mary Taylor Eggleston, and they are the parents of two children, Ann Taylor and George K., Jr.

While a resident of West Virginia Mr. Landon was appointed by Governor Dawson a member of the State Board of Examing Pharmacists, and was one of the organizers, and a charter member of the West Virginia State Pharmaceutical Association. Prominent in public affairs, he was vice president and secretary of the Keystone Board of Trade and vice president of the West Virginia State Board of Trade. He is a member of the Chamber of Commerce, of the Kiwanis Club, and is a thirty-second degree Mason and a Noble in the Mystic Shrine, Potentate representative for Hopewell, Virginia, a past Master Mason, a past chancellor commander of the Knights of Pythias and a past noble grand of the Independent Order of Odd Fellows. He is a member of the National Geographic Society and is author of the Woman of the Clan. Mr. Landon has one of the finest reference libraries in the state. He is building a fine home at Broadway and Wilson, opposite Abbott Park.

WILLIAM MARVIN MINTER is an attorney practicing at Mathews, and was born in Mathews County November 26, 1886, son of J. Willie and Lillian Ethelyn Minter.

Mr. Minter finished his education in the College of William and Mary, and has been practicing law since 1916. He was also a newspaper man, having been proprietor of the *Mathews Journal* from 1908 to 1923. In November, 1917, he was commissioned a second lieutenant in the Officers Training School at Fort Myer and served in home camps until his discharge in December, 1918.

He married, December 5, 1917, Eva M. Armistead, daughter of A. L. and Mary Virginia Armistead.

GEORGE EDWARD PICKETT. Far back, even to Colonial days, reach authentic records of a notable Virginia family, the Picketts, one that has contributed much to the state's prestige, particularly along military lines. The name of Col. William Pickett, once owner of a great estate in Farquier County, is memorialized for his valor and activity in the early Colonial, French and Indian wars, and no less distinction is accorded Col. Robert Pickett, of the next generation, who was a member of General Washington's staff in the Revolutionary war and later identified with military affairs in the War of 1812. That same spirit of personal courage and determined independence has prevailed uninterruptedly in the family ever since. A worthy member of this old family is found in George Edward Pickett III, of Washington, District of Columbia, lawyer, business man, historian and honored overseas veteran of the World war.

George Edward Pickett was born October 23, 1893, at Washington, District of Columbia, second son of Maj. George Edward and Ida (Christiancy) Pickett, and grandson of Maj-Gen. George Edward Pickett, a distinguished officer both in the Mexican war and later in the Civil war. Maj. George Edward Pickett was born at Richmond, Virginia, as was his father, whom he greatly resembled. He was a graduate of the Virginia Military Institute, and in 1898 entered military life as a major in rank in the United States Regular Army, and went to the Philippine Islands, where he remained until 1911, when he started on his return to the United States but did not survive to reach his home, his death occurring in mid-ocean on April 18, 1911. He married Miss Ida Christiancy, who was born in Monroe County, Michigan, and is now a resident of the City of Detroit. Their two sons survive: Christiancy and George Edward, both of whom are overseas veterans of the World war.

Christiancy Pickett served in France as a member of the 13th Field Artillery, Fourth Division, and, although in imminent danger throughout the entire period, was fortunate enough to escape all injury and returned at the end of the war practically unharmed. He is now a captain in the Regular Army, stationed at Fort Sill, Oklahoma, and as a specialist on tractors and trucks has compiled valuable statistics on army motor transportation. He married Miss Eula Mae Cherry, and they have two children: Christiancy, Jr., and Marguerite, aged four and two years, respectively.

George Edward Pickett enjoyed superior educational advantages during boyhood and youth, not only in Washington and Richmond, but also in San Francisco, California, in which city he was graduated from high school. He then accompanied his parents to the Philippine Islands, and while there attended Bishop Brent's Boys School, and after returning to America entered the Virginia Military Institute at Lexington, from there going to Harvard University and taking a classical course. For some time he then was a student in Hobart College at Geneva, New York.

Thus well equipped educationally for the future, Mr. Pickett turned his attention to the business field, accepting a clerkship in the National City Bank of New York in 1916, and received rapid promotion, filling the position of an assistant manager when in May, 1917, he hastened to Washington City in order to enlist for service in the World war. In this he was sadly disappointed, as a disability of color blindness caused his rejection by army, navy and Marine Corps officials. Although he did not permit himself to be entirely discouraged, he returned temporarily to the banking business, with the Riggs National Bank at Washington. In the meanwhile the great war, in which his heredity and instinct constantly urged his taking part, developed into more and more of a calamity, and when an opportunity came in December, 1917, to enlist as a private in the 20th Engineers he took advantage of it gladly, attended the Officers Training School at Camp Johnson and was graduated ninth in a class of 350. After serving as sergeant and seargeant-major he received his commission as second lieutenant, and on April 6, 1918, when Company H, Quartermaster Supply, set sail from Newport News, Virginia, he accompanied this body, as second in command, for France, and after reaching Depot No. 1 was assigned as personal officer, mess officer and semi-court officer, the duties of which he performed with the utmost efficiency, and largely because of this unremitting attention to duty he met with his first serious war injury. In his official capacity it was his custom to frequently visit the front lines, and on one of these dangerous trips he received a bullet in his arm. He did not permit this painful wound to limit his activities materially, but a subsequent injury ended his military service in France and almost closed his brave young life. It occurred when he was on duty as a mess officer, when his truck ran into a tree and was demolished, causing permanent injury to the bones of his knee. He was not able to leave France until July 18, 1919, when he returned to the United States and immediately went under treatment in Walter Reed Hospital, Washington City, from which he was honorably discharged from military service on August 18, 1921, with the surgical dictum of permanent total disability. This opinion, however, has been proved faulty, for since then he has improved seventy-five per cent.

Upon his release from the hospital and with marked evidence of returning health, Mr. Pickett put into operation a business enterprise in which he is still interested, this being an information brokerage business, by which reports were prepared for clients on any desired subject. It was not until 1924 that he began the study of law, and applied himself so closely that in 1926 he was graduated from the National University at Washington with his LL. B. degree, and in June, 1927, received his LL. M. and his M. P. L. degrees. He maintains his law office in the International Building on F Street, Washington City, and was also licensed to practice in North Carolina on January 30, 1928. As resident manager in Washington, Mr. Pickett is identified with the Blackstone Institute, Chicago, Illinois, an institution of merit that prepares and sells law courses to non-resident students. Along additional lines Mr. Pickett is successfully engaged in literary work, as he is department historian of the Disabled American Veteran organization.

Mr. Pickett married on August 10, 1920, Miss June D. Oglesby, daughter of Capt. Milton Landis and Ella (Drewhl) Oglesby, the former of whom was born in Kentucky and the latter in Illinois. Captain Oglesby is a captain in the Army Reserve Corps and formerly, during the World war, was a captain in the Ordnance Department. His present headquarters are in New York City, he being special representative and lecturer for the Bureau of Explosives for the American Railway Association. Mrs. Pickett is a highly educated lady and a member of the Daughters of the American Revolution. The two little children of the family are: George Edward, fourth, born in 1921; and Virginia, born in 1924.

Mr. Pickett belongs to a number of clubs and organizations, including such bodies as the American Legion, the American War Veterans Club, Sons of the Loyal Legion, Sons of the Confederacy and the Military Order of the Aztecs. He is a member of St. Stephen's Episcopal Church and teaches the boys' class in the Sunday School. In political life he is independent.

CLIFFORD WILLIAM BANKS has for many years been associated with one of the greatest organizations in the world for the handling, transportation and marketing of fruit products, the American Fruit Growers Association. Mr. Banks is sales manager for that association, and as such has his business offices at Norfolk and also at Rural Retreat, he and his family spending the greater part of the year at Norfolk.

Mr. Banks is a native Georgian, and comes of a family that has been prominent in the state for a number of generations, and several communities carry the family name. Mr. Banks was born at Macon October 28, 1881, son of James A. and Lula (Asbury) Banks. His father was born and reared in Macon, graduated from Emory College, now Emory University, of Atlanta, and at the age of thirteen was accepted as a soldier of the Confederacy. Three of his brothers were killed in action during the war. Following the war he became a farmer and fruit grower and merchant. He was interested in military affairs, being a captain in the Georgia State Militia, and while attending an encampment at Chickamauga he exposed himself and contracted pneumonia, from which he died. He is buried at Forsyth, Georgia. His wife, Lula Asbury, was born and reared at Forsyth, was educated in the Monroe Female College, now the Bessie Tift College, and has been distinguished by some unusual accomplishments, has been an artist, musician, a fine singer, and has used her talents in music in the Baptist Church for many years. She is now eighty-one and lives at Macon. Her family has been closely identified with the cause of female education in Georgia. Her parents were Richard T. and Katie (Peteet) Asbury. Richard T. Asbury was a splendid type of the old time southern gentleman, a lawyer by profession, and after the Civil war was in the same law office with the great southern statesman, Alexander H. Stephens. He turned from the law to educational work, and he donated many acres and founded the Monroe Female College at Forsyth, and for many years served as president of the institution, now the Bessie Tift Female College. He died in 1914 and his wife in 1919. James A. Banks and wife had five children: Mattie Lou, Clifford W., James A., Bessie and Richard T. James A. is head of the St. Johns River Terminals of Jacksonville, Florida.

Clifford W. Banks attended public school at Macon, Mercer University of Georgia, and after his college career was in the service of the American National Bank of Macon for about eight years. He was assistant cashier when he left. As a financier and business man he has long made a study of conditions effecting the marketing of the great volume of fruit grown in the southeastern states. He left the bank to become associated with the Georgia Fruit Exchange as sales manager. For ten years he was instrumental in providing adequate and profitable marketing facilities for the hundreds of carloads of choice Georgia peaches and other fruit. Mr. Banks for seven years was in the fruit and produce business for himself, with headquarters at Saint Louis. In 1921 he became associated with the American Fruit Growers Association as sales manager, with head offices at Norfolk and with branch offices at Staunton, Winchester, Rural Retreat and Cheriton, Virginia, and Martinsburg, West Virginia. This organization probably handles more fruit in the course of a year than any other similar organization in the world.

Mr. Banks is a member of the Norfolk Kiwanis Club, is affiliated with the Knights of Pythias, is a Democrat and a member of the Episcopal Church.

He married at Macon, Georgia, September 17, 1907, Miss Marion Lane, who was reared and educated at Macon and attended the Wesleyan Female College there. She is a member of the Society of Colonial Dames, Daughters of the American Revolution and United Daughters of the Confederacy, but her chief interest is in her home and her two talented daughters. She. is a daughter of Gen. Jeff and Marion (Reese) Lane. Her grandfather was a general in the Confederate army and for many years after the war a leading figure in railroad transportation in the South, being at the time of his death general manager of

the Georgia Southern & Florida Railway, part of the Southern
Railway System. He died in 1905, and both he and his wife are
buried at Macon. The original Reese family home is still standing at Athens, Georgia, and every American is interested in that
home because it was there that John Howard Payne wrote his
immortal song "Home Sweet Home," and the copy in his own
handwriting was in the hands of the family until recent years.
Mr. and Mrs. Banks had four daughters, two of whom died in
infancy. The two now living are Lillian Williams and Marion
Lane, both attending school at Norfolk. Lillian is a member of
the class of 1929 in the Maury High School, and is one of the
editors of the *Maury News*.

ALBERT MICOU SNEED, M. D., chief surgeon for the Peninsula
Transit Corporation, coroner of James City County, and a member of the County Board of Health, is one of the ablest members
of his profession in this region, and he maintains his residence
and office at Toano, Virginia. He is a man who has always
placed professional ethics above personal convenience, and who
has given freely of his skill and time to the furtherance of public
health measures and the treatment of those unable to afford
proper care. As a result he stands deservedly high in public
esteem, and it is a matter of record that since he took charge
of the affairs of the coroner's office are in better condition than
ever before.

Doctor Sneed was born in Albemarle County, Virginia, July
9, 1889, a son of Dr. Edgar Morris and Stella Virginia (Stark)
Sneed, natives of Albemarle County. Dr. Edgar Morris Sneed
has been engaged in the practice of medicine in Stafford County,
Virginia, since 1902, having previously practiced in Albemarle
County from 1889, and is one of the eminent members of his profession in that neighborhood. His father was a Confederate
veteran, having served in the Southern army throughout the
war between the states. The mother is also living.

The early education of Dr. Albert Micou Sneed was secured
in several private schools of Albemarle County and Stafford
County, and he later became a student of William and Mary College, and while there became a member of Pi Kappa Alpha fraternity. Upon leaving William and Mary College he entered
the Medical College of Virginia, Richmond, and was graduated
therefrom in 1912, after taking the full course, with the degree
of Doctor of Medicine, and as a member of Phi Chi, the medical
Greek letter fraternity. For the subsequent two years he was
one of a staff of eight doctors connected with the hospital maintained at Stonega, Virginia, by the Stonega Coke & Coal Company. When he left that company Doctor Sneed went to New
York City and for one year was associated with Dr. H. L. Winter,
nervous diseases. In December, 1915, Doctor Sneed came to
Toano, James City County, where he has since been very successfully engaged in practice.

On October 9, 1912, Doctor Sneed married Miss Lucy Harrison Wade, a daughter of Dr. William and Annie F. (Powers)
Wade, natives of Virginia, the father born in Albemarle County
and the mother in Richmond. Doctor Wade was engaged in the
practice of dentistry in Richmond until his death, which occurred
June 11, 1918. Mrs. Wade followed him in October of the same
year. Doctor and Mrs. Sneed have three children: Ann Harrison, who was born in January, 1914; Emily Gresham, who was
born in February, 1916; and Mary Micou, who was born in Jan-

G. H. Musgrave M. D.

uary, 1920. He is a member of the University Club of Richmond, and he and his wife belong to the Williamsburg Cotilion Club. Professionally he maintains membership with the Virginia State Medical Society, the American Medical Association, the Walter Reed Medical Society and the James City County Medical Society. A very active Democrat, he is a member of the James City County Central Committee of his party. For years an Episcopalian, he is now serving as vestryman of Hickory Neck Episcopal Church. During the World war he served as a member of the Medical Advisory Board of James City County. Mrs. Sneed is the first of her sex to be elected a member of the James City County School Board, and she is also motor vehicle agent for James City County and the City of Williamsburg. For several terms she has served as president of the Toano Woman's Club; she is president of the Guild of the Episcopal Church; State chairman of illiteracy, for the Parent-Teachers Association and is a past vice president of the State Parent-Teachers Association. Both Doctor Sneed and his wife, as will be seen from this brief review, are very potent factors in the life of James City County, and they are accomplishing a vast amount of good along many lines of endeavor.

GEORGE HARRISON MUSGRAVE, M. D. A member of the medical profession of Virginia for eighteen years, it is not at all unlikely that Dr. George H. Musgrave, of Leesburg, owes the selection of his profession and much of his success therein largely to heredity, inasmuch as both his grandfather and great-grandfather were physicians. However that may be, he has honestly earned his present position as a skilled, conscientious and reliable practitioner through industry and faithful fidelity to the highest ethics of his calling, while his success in the care of his large practice has won him universal confidence and esteem.

Doctor Musgrave was born July 12, 1884, in Southampton County, Virginia, and is a son of R. N. and Sallie H. (Pope) Musgrave. His great-grandfather was Dr. Robert T. Musgrave, one of the pioneer physicians of this section of Virginia, and his old ledger, showing his accounts from the years 1825 until 1832, inclusive, are not only kept by his great-grandson as a keepsake, but as a valuable historical record of those early days and as matter indicative of the activities of the pioneer devotees of medicine. The grandfather of Doctor Musgrave, Dr. George N. Musgrave, was likewise an early country practitioner, whose practice extended over an area of many miles of territory and who was beloved and respected during his day.

R. N. Musgrave was born in Southampton County, Virginia, and in young manhood adopted the lumber business, which he followed for a long period of years in his native locality. At this time he has an office at Norfolk, whence he conducts his numerous activities in this line of business. He has been successful in his operations and is known as one of Norfolk's substantial business men and reliable citizens. Mrs. Musgrave passed away at Norfolk August 17, 1926.

George H. Musgrave acquired his early education in the public schools of Southampton County, following which he pursued courses at Bedford Academy and Randolph-Macon College. He matriculated at the University of Virginia, from which institution he was graduated with the degree of Doctor of Medicine as a member of the class of June, 1908, and then served his interneship at the Norfolk Protestant Hospital. Doctor Musgrave commenced practice at Capron, Virginia, January 1, 1910 this being contract lumber practice, and then went to Boykins, Virginia, where he had his headquarters until he enlisted in the Medical Reserve Corps in April, 1917, for service during the World war. Securing a first lieutenant's commission, he saw twenty months of service overseas, and was honorably discharged with the rank of major in April, 1919. He then returned to Boykins and resumed practice, continuing until January, 1924, when he became a member of the Virginia State Department of Health, and was identified therewith until October, 1926, since when he has been engaged in general practice at Leesburg, his well appointed offices being located in the Orr Building. Doctor Musgrave has a splendid practice and has acquired a substantial reputation for reliability as a diagnostician, skill as a practitioner and ability as an operator. He is a member of the Loudoun County Medical Society, the Virginia State Medical Society and the American Medical Association, and is a conscientious student of his profession, keeping fully in advance of its discoveries and developments. He is affiliated with the Masonic Order and belongs to the American Legion. Politically he is a Democrat, and his good citizenship is evidenced by his willing support of civic movements of a worthwhile nature. He belongs to the Methodist Episcopal Church.

In June, 1919, Doctor Musgrave was united in marriage with Miss Bessie D. Ridley, daughter of John W. and Bettie (Goodwin) Ridley, natives of Southampton County, where Mr. Ridley resides as a retired agriculturist, Mrs. Ridley having passed away in 1920. Doctor and Mrs. Musgrave have had three children: Bettie Goodwin, born April 26, 1920; George Harrison, Jr., born February 5, 1927, who died January 4, 1928, and Nancy Harrison, born February 7, 1929.

ISAAC TALBOT WALKE, proprietor of an insurance agency at Norfolk which has been in existence and under the ownership and management of the Walke family for six decades, is descended from one of the very first families to establish homes in what is now Norfolk County.

He is a direct descendant of Thomas Walke, a native of England, who first went to the Barbadoes in 1622 and later moved to Virginia, establishing himself at Fairfield in Princess Anne County. He married Mary Lawson, whose father, Col. Anthony Lawson, was one of the eminent lawyers of Virginia Colony. Thomas Walke held the rank of colonel of militia under King Charles II. He was a vestryman in the Lynnhaven Parish Church, one of the famous churches of old Colonial Virginia.

His son, Anthony Walke, married Anna Lee Armistead, a granddaughter of Capt. Hancock and Mary (Kendell) Lee. Mary Kendell was a daughter of Col. William Kendell, who served as collector of revenues at Accomac in 1660. Hancock Lee was a son of Col. Richard Lee, the ancestor of Richard Henry Lee, known as the champion of American Independence. In William Forest's sketches of Norfolk the statement is made that Anthony Walke purchased 150 acres of land on which at a later date the City of Norfolk was laid out, the first plat of the city being made in 1682. Anthony and Anna (Armistead) Walke had as one of their children Anthony Walke, who married Jane Randolph, and they were the parents of William Walke, who married Mary Calvert. The next generation was represented by William Walke, who married Elizabeth Nash, and they in turn were the parents of Richard Walke, who married Diana Talbot. Richard and Diana were the grandparents of Isaac Talbot Walke.

Mr. Walke was born at Norfolk. His father, William Talbot Walke, was also a native of that city, where he was reared and educated, and served in the Confederate government during the Civil war. Afterwards he took up the insurance business and followed it until his death. His wife was Sally Gary, born at Garysburg, North Carolina. They reared the following children, William Talbot, Richard Gray, James Newsom, Mary Diana, Sally Willoughby, Isaac Talbot and Herbert Nash.

Isaac Talbot Walke after completing his course at Norfolk Academy entered Eastman's Business College at Poughkeepsie, New York, and with this training became associated with his father in the insurance business. In later years he acquired that business. This insurance agency was established by his father in 1869. It is located at 203 Granby Street in Norfolk.

Mr. Walke married Linda Harrell, a native of Murfreesboro, North Carolina. They have three children, Isaac Talbot, Jr., Linda Harrell and Gertrude Willoughby. The family are members of Christ Episcopal Church in Norfolk.

WILLIAM THOMAS ELLETT. The late William Thomas Ellett, long one of the substantial business men of Richmond, and an active factor in the furniture industry, had a career typical of the period in which he lived when the South was recovering from the disastrous effects of over four years of warfare, and he participated in much of the constructive work of his city. His youth and young manhood spent on a Virginia farm, he came to Richmond at the age of twenty-two years, and followed the path of ambition and gave his native qualities of character and practical ability to assist in whatever came to hand. It is upon such men as he, their accomplishments and their strong faith, do those of the rising generation build their confident hope of the American future.

William Thomas Ellett was born in New Kent County, Virginia, in February, 1861, and he died in Richmond, Virginia, July 7, 1922, a son of Cornelius and Mary Ann (Lacey) Ellett, the former of whom was a farmer and planter. Mrs. Ellett was a lady of superior education and in the absence of adequate schools taught her children, of whom there were ten, not only the lessons to be found in books, but those which come from the heart of a loving mother and good Christian woman.

Farming in his native county until he was twenty-two, the ambitious young man sought a wider horizon in the capital city of the South, and here, in Richmond, he learned the carpenter trade, followed it for a few years, and then became a contractor and builder. The strenuous character of his work brought about a breakdown and he was forced to seek a change of occupation, returning to farming, and was engaged in that occupation for ten years, when once more he came to Richmond, entered the furniture business, and continued in it until 1920. He retired from it, and later entered the grocery field, but a few months later his death occurred.

On April 27, 1887, Mr. Ellett married Miss Evelyn Thomas Long, a daughter of Andrew Jackson and Martha Ann (Blake) Long. Her father was a farmer and carpenter, and he and the mother had ten children born to them, of whom she was the eighth in order of birth. Mrs. Ellett was educated in King William County. During the latter part of the war between the states Andrew Jackson Long served in the Confederate army. The Long family came to the United States from Ireland and settled in Caroline County, Virginia. The Ellett family settled in King William County, Virginia, just after the close of the American Revolution, so that both it and the Long family are old ones in the state.

Of the children born to Mr. and Mrs. Ellett there are five now living, namely: Pearl Blake, who married Joseph Alexander Barlow, a farmer and planter, and they have two children, Joseph Alexander, Junior, and William Edward; Chastine Clyde, who married Annie Laurie Gordon, and has two children, Mary Evelyn and Lester Earle; William Wyatt, who is engaged in the plumbing business in Richmond, married Elizabeth Ruby Thorpe, and they have two children, William Wyatt, Junior, and Lowell E.; Andrew Cornelius, who is an automobile salesman, married Lelia E. Anderson, and they have one child, Gay Nelle; and Evelyn Inez, who married Walter Dewitt Smith, a Government employe. Of the above children William Wyatt is the veteran of the World war, for which he volunteered, and served in the United States Navy for eighteen months, and had nine months of active service on the sea.

Mrs. Ellett is a consistent member of the East End Baptist Church, to which Mr. Ellett belonged in line. He was a Mason and belonged to the Shrine in that order, and to the Owls, Junior Order United American Mechanics, and the Odd Fellows.

JOHN WALKER DOWN was well known as a lumberman in Virginia, manufacturing large quantities of timber products that entered extensively into the coastwise trade and also went to foreign markets.

Mr. Down was born in Gloucester County, New Jersey, April 21, 1840, and died in Mathews County, Virginia, in November, 1917. His father, John Walker Down, Sr., was in the lumber industry in New Jersey for many years. The Down family came in Colonial times to New Jersey. A town in Gloucester County, Downstown, was named for one of the family. Several monuments in that county refer by name or otherwise to the conspicuous services rendered by members of the Down family in the Revolutionary war and Colonial affairs.

John Walker Down was the youngest in a family of five children. He attended common schools and at the age of twelve years was driving a team for his father. When he was twenty-three years old he engaged in general merchandising, but after a few years left that to continue in the lumber business. From New Jersey he extended his interests down into Virginia, in Mathews County, and at one time had three mills in operation in this state, shipping lumber by the shipload to New Jersey and Philadelphia markets, and also large quantities to Europe. He retired four years before his death. He was a Democrat, a member of the Masonic fraternity, and he and his wife were Methodists.

His first wife was Matilda Miller, of New Jersey, who died five years after their marriage. Of the two sons born to this marriage the one now living is Everett, a banker at Atlanta City. His second wife was Miss Anna McGonigall, who died twenty years later. Two of their three children are living. Lena

Chas R Dawley

Hester is the wife of Harry L. Nelson and has three children, Harry, Jr., William W., and Anna M.; and Hannah R. married Herbert Ingram, of Hagerstown, Maryland, who was killed in action in France in the early part of the World war.

Mr. Down in 1893 married Nannie Simpson Cromwell, of Petersburg, Virginia, who was reared and educated at Norfolk and who resides at 701 West Thirty-eighth Street in that city. Mrs. Down's father, John A. Simpson, was a farmer, and served all through the Civil war in the Confederate army. He was captured and was a prisoner when the war ended. Her mother was Sarah Hendren, and Mrs. Down was the third in a family of nine children. Mrs. Down has two daughters, Bessie Vernon and Sarah Louise. Bessie Vernon is the wife of William Waugh, of Bedford County, Virginia, and her four children are named Vernon, Lester, Merlyn and Elizabeth. Miss Sarah Louise Down is in the employ of the state government at Norfolk, with the Society for the Prevention of Cruelty to Children.

HON. CHARLES ROBERT FAWLEY, sheriff of Rockingham County, is one of the substantial men of that region, and has served not only as sheriff but as deputy under four other sheriffs. He has lived a life of action and responsibility and has proven his courage and resourcefulness innumerable times. His administration as sheriff has been one in keeping with the strength and integrity of his character, and has been attended by strict law enforcement and reduction of criminal activities.

Sheriff Fawley was born on a farm in Rockingham County, Virginia, May 8, 1875, son of George W. and Sarah J. (Fulk) Fawley. Both the Fawley and Fulk families have been in Virginia for many generations. The Fawleys were of Irish descent, and first established homes in Pennsylvania and then moved down into Virginia, into Loudoun County. His grandfather, Jacob Fawley, was a native of Loudoun County and spent all his life as a farmer.

George W. Fawley was for many years a farmer and blacksmith. He served as a justice of the peace, was the first postmaster at Fulk's Run, when the office was established in 1870, and he taught in the Fulk's Run district. He was a local leader in the Democratic party, and a member of the Baptist Church, while his wife belonged to the Church of the Brethren.

Sarah J. (Fulk) Fawley was a descendant of Matthew Fulk, who was of Scotch-Irish descent and came to America about 1735. He was with Colonel Lewis in an expedition to treat with the Indians and he married an Indian woman. Not long after the Indians were removed from Rockingham County he also went west, but left a large family of boys and some girls who settled in the vicinity of Broadway in Rockingham County. Sarah J. Fulk was a daughter of John G. Fulk, who was a son of Daniel Fulk and a grandson of John Fulk. John Fulk, a son of Matthew, was born in 1760, and married a Miss Bible. He moved to Brock's Gap in 1785.

Sheriff Fawley was the youngest of ten children, seven of whom are living. He grew up in a rural neighborhood, attended school there, and farming was the business he first learned and the occupation he followed until 1912. For twelve years he was in the employe of the Virginia State Highway Commission and for years was district supervisor of the Seventh Congressional District for the Virginia State Game Commission. Mr. Fawley in November, 1927, was elected sheriff by a majority of over 1,400 votes and assumed the duties of his office in January, 1928. He had been a deputy sheriff for a quarter of a century.

In December, 1899, he married Augusta V. Siple, who was born in Pendleton County, West Virginia, and educated in the common schools of her home neighborhood. Sheriff and Mrs. Fawley have one daughter, Lucile Virginia, attending the Junior High School. He is a member of the United Brethren Church, while his wife is a member of the Methodist Episcopal Church, South. Mr. Fawley is a member of the Masonic fraternity and Independent Order of Odd Fellows. He owns a farm in Rockingham County, and is interested in its operation. A man of high principles, upright and honorable in everything he undertakes, he is making an excellent record as sheriff, and law breakers have recognized his sturdy qualities in the enforcement of the laws.

HON. BATHURST DAINGERFIELD PEACHY, commonwealth's attorney of James City County, and one of the most brilliant of the able attorneys practicing at the bar of Williamsburg, although still in the full flush of vigorous manhood, has a remarkable record of achievement behind him, and holds the confidence and respect of his professional associates as well as the public generally. He was born in Williamsburg, Virginia, July 5, 1893, a son of Bathurst Daingerfield and Mary Garnett (Lane) Peachy, natives of Williamsburg.

The elder Bathurst Daingerfield Peachy was also an attorney, and was engaged in practice in Williamsburg, and his father, Samuel Peachy, was a member of the same learned profession. For a number of years the office of commonwealth's attorney was filled by the older Bathurst Daingerfield Peachy, and he attained to a distinguished position among his associates in the law. His death, which occurred July 23, 1916, when he was fifty-eight years old, removed from Williamsburg one of its most distinguished citizens, and from his family a devoted husband and father. Mrs. Peachy survives her husband and is still living in Williamsburg.

The younger Bathurst Daingerfield Peachy grew up in Williamsburg, and enjoyed the normal life of any lad of his locality while attending the local schools, and, being an apt pupil, he was graduated from the high school in 1908, when he was but fifteen years old. Entering William and Mary College, Williamsburg, he was graduated therefrom in 1914 with the degree of Bachelor of Arts. For the succeeding year he was an instructor in his *alma mater*, and then took legal training in the law department of the University of Virginia, and was admitted to the bar that same year, in 1916. Establishing himself in practice in Williamsburg, Mr. Peachy showed from the beginning of his career the same admirable qualities which had advanced both his father and grandfather at the bar, and has built up a very large and lucrative practice. For four years he served as judge of the Juvenile Court and the Domestic Relations Court, handling the difficult problems brought before him with masterly tact and kindly authority. On January 1, 1928, he assumed the duties of the office of commonwealth's attorney, to which he had been elected the preceding fall, and already has proven his courage, his thoroughness and his unflinching, uncompromising attitude toward offenders against the law. He has as one of his most cherished possessions the splendid law library of his grandfather, and this, in addition to his own large collection of law books, gives him one of the best law libraries, of a private character, in the state.

On June 16, 1919, Mr. Peachy married Miss Grace Bozarth, a daughter of William A. and Flora (Weeks) Bozarth, native of New Jersey. Mr. Bozarth is a lumber dealer and president of the Peninsula Bank & Trust Company of Williamsburg, and he has been a resident of Williamsburg for thirty years. Mr. and Mrs. Peachy have two children: Grace Monro, who was born February 14, 1922; and Bathurst Daingerfield, Junior, who was born December 30, 1924.

For some years Mr. Peachy has been a valued member of the Virginia State Bar Association and the American Bar Association. He belongs to the Williamsburg Rotary Club and the American Legion. His fraternal connections are those which he maintains with the Masonic Order and Kappa Sigma. In political faith he is a Democrat, and he is one of the leaders of his party in this section. He is an Episcopalian. During the World war Mr. Peachy enlisted in the Aviation Corps of the Marine branch of the service and was stationed at the Boston Institute of Technology. His honorable discharge bears the date of February 1, 1919. When he was released from military service he returned to Williamsburg and resumed his practice. Judge Peachy maintains his office in the First National Bank Building.

REV. THEODORE WHITFIELD, D. D., an eminent Baptist divine, whose last years in the ministry were spent in Richmond, Virginia, was born in Hinds County, Mississippi, January 31, 1834, and died at Richmond May 28, 1894.

The Whitfields came from England in the early part of the seventeenth century, settling in Elizabeth City and Nansemond counties, Virginia. They intermarried with the Bryan and Hatch families. His parents, Rev. Benjamin and Lucy (Hatch) Whitfield, were natives of North Carolina, from which state they moved to Mississippi. Theodore was the eighth in a family of twelve children.

"Rev. Theodore Whitfield, D. D., was converted in the church next to his father's home 'Magnolia,' Hinds County, Mississippi, when thirteen years of age. * * * Reared in a lovely Southern home, he was educated in the fine arts as well as in the more substantial sciences and classics; entered the University of North Carolina 1852, A. B., 1854; entered the Baptist ministry, studied at the Theological Seminary, Newton Center, Massachusetts. * * * His pastorates were in Danville, Kentucky, Aberdeen and Meridian, Mississippi, Charlotte, Goldsboro and Newbern, North Carolina, and Fulton, near Richmond, Virginia, where he served for seven years before his death. He received the degree of D. D., from Wake Forest College, North Carolina, 1878. While in Greensboro, North Carolina, at the time of the war between the states, he preached for the Baptist Church and did local services for the Confederate States. While ministering to soldiers of both armies in Goldsboro, North Carolina, he contracted camp fever, from which he was desperately ill for a long time. Later he was superintendent of the State Institute for the Blind at Jackson, Mississippi, until removed when General Ames of Boston became governor of Mississippi.

"Born of wealthy and distinguished parents, he was a gentleman both by breeding and culture. * * * His life was devout. * * * As a theologian he stood without a rival among the Baptist ministers of Richmond and was called by them 'the Sage' of their Conference. For some years he served as North Carolina vice president of the Foreign Mission Board of the Southern Baptist Convention. Singularly guileless, he was courteous and dignified in deportment. A concise preacher, indefatigable pastor, a facile writer, a beloved friend, he bequeathed to his wife and children the priceless legacy of an unsullied name and saintly memory. He died May 28, 1894." (Extract from a memorial volume published at the time of his decease.)

Doctor Whitfield married into one of the oldest and most distinguished families of North Carolina, the Moreheads. He and Miss Annie Eliza Morehead weer married at Greensboro, North Carolina, October 11, 1859. Mrs. Whitfield was a daughter of Hon. James Turner and Mary Teas (Lindsay) Morehead. Charles Morehead, founder of the Morehead family in the South, settled in the Northern Neck of Virginia about 1630. Joseph Morehead married Elizabeth Turner, a daughter of James Turner and Keren-Happuch Norman, of Spotsylvania County, Virginia. Their son, John Morehead, married Obedience Motley, of Amelia County, and settled in Rockingham County, North Carolina. John Morehead was a soldier of the Revolution. John Morehead and his wife, Obedience Motley, had two distinguished sons. One of them, John Motley Morehead, born in 1796 and died in 1886, became governor of North Carolina.

The other son, James Turner Morehead, was born in Rockingham County, North Carolina, January 11, 1799, and died at Greensboro May 5, 1875. He was a lawyer, served in the State Senate 1935-42, and the United States Congress, 1851.

Doctor and Mrs. Whitfield had three children: James Morehead Whitfield, George H. Whitfield and Miss Emma M. Whitfield.

James Morehead Whitfield graduated from the University of Virginia with the degree of M. D. He became a medical chemist and for some years served as city chemist and coroner of Richmond. He married Mary Graham Mathews, of Virginia, and has three living children: James M., Jr., a physician now practicing in Richmond; Theodore M., a graduate Ph. D., of Johns Hopkins University, a teacher; and Philip Whitfield, a lawyer. All these sons were born in Richmond and all graduated at the University of Richmond.

George H. Whitfield, at present director of the Department of Public Utilities of the City of Richmond, graduated at Richmond College with the degree of A. B. and at Cornell University, New York, 1896, as a mechanical and electrical engineer. During the World war he was for several years connected with the International Arms & Fuze Company, Bloomfield, New Jersey, part of this time as manager of the shell factory. Previous to this he was one of the directors of the Virginia Railway & Power Company of Richmond. He married Laura Merryman Crane, of Baltimore, and has two daughters, Clare Merryman and Anne Morehead, both born in Richmond.

Miss Emma Morehead Whitfield, of Richmond, was born at Greensboro, North Carolina, graduated at the Woman's College of Richmond, studied at the Art Students' League of New York and in Paris. Examples of her work as a portrait artist are to be found in the Confederate Battle Abbey and the Governor's Mansion at Richmond; the Supreme Court Building at Raleigh, and at Greensboro, North Carolina, etc. Miss Whitfield is a member of the Woman's Club, Society of Colonial Dames of America in the State of Virginia, United Daughters of the Confederacy, Daughters of the American Revolution, and is historian of the Baptist Woman's Missionary Union of Virginia.

SIDNEY THOMPSON. In the thriving town of Middleburg, Loudoun County, is a financial institution that gives the most effective of service in safeguarding and advancing communal interests along all lines, and of this substantial and well ordered institution, the Middleburg National Bank, Sidney Thompson is the cashier.

Mr. Thompson was born in Washington, D. C., on the 13th of October, 1893, and is a son of John L. and Anne (Price) Thompson, the former a native of North Carolina and the latter of Maryland, and both representatives of old and influential families that were early established in these respective commonwealths. Dr. Jacob Thompson, grandfather of the subject of this review, was a loyal surgeon of the Confederacy during the course of the Civil war, and was a son of Sidney Thompson, an influential citizen and extensive exponent of plantation industry in North Carolina. Jacob Thompson, like his father, was also a tobacco-grower on an extensive scale on his plantation estate in North Carolina. On the maternal side Sidney Thompson of this review is a scion of the Price family that was long one of prominence and influence in Southern Maryland.

John L. Thompson was born and reared in North Carolina and received his education in that state. He finally established his residence in Washington, living there until he met his death in a railroad wreck at Danville, Virginia, in September, 1903, his widow having not long survived him, as her death occurred in August, 1905.

Sidney Thompson was reared in the capitol city of the nation and there received his early education, and after his graduation from a military academy he was employed in the Poolesville National Bank, Poolesville, Maryland, the attractive little town in which he now maintains his home and from which he makes trips to and from Middleburg, Virginia, for the discharge of his executive duties as cashier of the Middleburg National Bank.

Mr. Thompson has devoted his career to bank work since he graduated from school and in 1914 assumed his present executive office, that of cashier of the Middleburg National Bank. Mr. Thompson has made a close study of financial affairs pertaining to practical banking, and his advancement has come through his own ability and loyal service. He is also now the financial advisor for the Foxcroft School for Girls, one of the exclusive girls' schools in America, located near the town of Middleburg.

The Middleburg National Bank was established and chartered in 1924. When the bank was organized Mr. Thompson became its cashier through the recommendation given by E. F. Rorebeck, then the chief national bank examiner of the Fifth Federal Reserve District.

The political allegiance of Mr. Thompson is given to the Democratic party, and he and his wife are communicants of the Protestant Episcopal Church.

In September, 1915, was solemnized the marriage of Mr. Thompson and Miss Katherine Walling, who was born and reared in Maryland and who is a daughter of Dr. Byron W. Walling, for fifty years a representative physician at Poolesville, Maryland, where he is now living retired from active practice, he having been born in Maryland, as was also his wife, whose family name was Poole and who was a representative of the family in honor of which Poolesville was named. Mr. and Mrs. Thompson have two fine sons, Byron Walling and Sidney, Jr.

REGINALD L. NIXON. Among the men who have contributed to the good government of Virginia during recent years, through faithful and conscientious service in the discharge of the duties and responsibilities of the offices to which they have been elected by their fellow citizens, Reginald L. Nixon, of Leesburg, is worthy of more than passing mention. His career has been typical of the self-made man, and the success he has gained is another exemplification of the fact that industry and fidelity find their just rewards. For the last five years Mr. Nixon has been before the people of his community as a public servant, and during this period has won the confidence and respect of his fellow citizens in a marked degree, his present activities being carried on in the capacity of commissioner of revenue of Loudoun County.

Mr. Nixon was born at Leesburg, December 26, 1881, and is a son of George H. and Virginia E. (Milbourne) Nixon, the latter a native of Hamilton, Virginia. George H. Nixon was born at Leesburg, where he received a public school education, and when a mere lad volunteered for service in the Confederate army during the war between the states. He came through that struggle unscathed and returned to his native place, where after several other ventures he established himself in the hotel business. He became well known to the traveling public as the popular host of a modern hostelry, and bore an excellent reputation among his fellow townsmen for high character and good citizenship. He passed away in 1903, and is survived by his widow, who still makes her home at Leesburg.

Reginald L. Nixon was given good educational opportunities in his youth, first attending the public schools of Leesburg, later pursuing a course at Randolph-Macon Academy, and finally being a student at a military academy at Danville, Virginia. He began his career as a bookkeeper in the employ of Chapin & Sacks of Washington, D. C., and later was with Golden & Company, also of the capital, then becoming identified with the banking business as a bookkeeper for the Loudoun National Bank of Leesburg. He remained with this institution, gaining steady promotion, for seven years, or until 1924, when he was elected commissioner of revenue of Leesburg. During his two-year term of office he discharged his duties in such a capable and expeditious manner that in 1926 he was elected commissioner of revenue for Loudoun County, and is still acting in that capacity. Mr. Nixon is a member of the Independent Order of Odd Fellows and the Rebekahs, and in his political allegiance supports the candidates and principles of the Democratic party. A member of the Methodist Episcopal Church since his youth, he is active in its work, and is now lay leader and teacher of the Men's Bible Class in the Sunday School.

In February, 1920, Mr. Nixon was united in marriage wtih Miss Naomi Galleher, a daughter of W. R. and a Miss (Webb) Galleher, both natives of Loudoun County. Mr. Galleher has

been a traveling salesman all of his life and makes his home at Leesburg, where he and his wife are held in high esteem. Mr. and Mrs. Nixon have no children. Mrs. Nixon is active in the work of the Methodist Episcopal Church.

CECIL CONNOR, Leesburg attorney, is the present representative of the Twenty-ninth Senatorial District in the Virginia State Senate. He has practiced law thirty years, and few men have been more diligent in making use of the opportunities for individual accomplishment and public service.

Mr. Connor was born at Philomont, Loudoun County, Virginia, February 4, 1871. His grandfather, John T. Connor, was also a Virginian, a farmer, and married Susan A. Lyne, representative of another well known family name in Loudoun County. John T. Connor, father of Senator Connor, was born in Loudoun County in 1844, was a shoemaker, farmer, shoe merchant and postmaster at Philomont and Paxon. He died at Bluemont, Virginia, in May, 1916. His wife, Mary E. Brown, was born near Lincoln, in Loudoun County, in 1847.

Cecil Connor, one of the children of these parents, grew up on his father's farm in Loudoun County, attended rural schools, and beyond those advantages had to contrive his own opportunities. At the age of eighteen he became a teacher, and teaching gave him the financial means and also some of the leisure required for his private law studies. Later he spent a year in Washington and Lee University, graduating from the Law School in 1896. He was licensed to practice in June, 1898, and since that year has been a busy member of the bar at Leesburg, handling a general practice, and has also represented several banks and other corporations in his clientage.

Mr. Connor prior to his election to the State Senate served four consecutive terms in the office of commonwealth attorney of Loudoun County. He was in that position during the World war, which brought a large addition of responsibilities to his official routine. He also served as counsel and appeal agent of the Local Draft Board. Senator Connor is a member of the Leesburg and Virginia Bar Associations, and is a member of the Knights of Pythias.

He married at Washington, D. C., November 8, 1905, Miss Edna F. Fadeley, daughter of Henry J. and Mary Estelle (Johnson) Fadeley. They have one son, Cecil Fenton, born May 6th, 1907. He is now practicing law in the law office of Charles Henry Smith at Alexandria, Virginia.

GEORGE MASON DILLARD is a member of the Norfolk bar, and has brought to his profession a ripe scholarship, integrity of character and a resourcefulness that have stood the test of many years of successful practice.

He was born at Charlottesville, Virginia. His father, George Walden Dillard, was born in Caroline County in 1812 and at an early age was left an orphan, being reared in the family of an uncle. He had a fair education and at Scottsville became a merchant, invested in farm land in that vicinity and owned a country home four miles from Scottsville. He died in 1896, at the advanced age of eighty-four. George Walden Dillard married Lucy Jane Dillard, who was born in Spotsylvania County, daughter of William and Elizabeth (Mason) Dillard. In a local history of Henry County, Virginia, the statement is made that George Dillard of Wiltshire, England, settled at Jamestown in

1660, being then twenty-six years of age. He had a son, James Stephen, two years old. This George Dillard was granted 250 acres for services in fighting Indians, and later 25,000 acres were granted to James Stephen Dillard, his son, and the Carys, Wises and Pages, a tract that became known in history as the Williamsburg Plantation.

George Walden Dillard reared a family of nine children: Alice E., James Daniel, Julia B., William B., Mary E., Martha F., Benjamin L., George Mason and Nora L.

George Mason Dillard was educated at Scottsville, and graduated in law at the University of Virginia in 1882. Soon afterward he moved to Norfolk, where he has practiced law for over forty-five years, being one of the oldest members of the bar of that city.

Mr. Dillard married, in 1904, Elizabeth Allyn, who was born at Norfolk, daughter of Joseph T. and Mary R. (Bell) Allyn. They have four children, Allyn, George Mason, Mary Walden and Elizabeth Allyn. The son Allyn was educated in the Woodbury Forest School, graduated in law at the University of Virginia and is now practicing in New York City. The son George Mason graduated from the Maury High School at Norfolk, attended the Woodbury Forest School and the Virginia Military Institute, and is now associated with the Cleveland Illuminating Company at Cleveland, Ohio. The members of the family that remain at Norfolk are communicants of St. Paul's Episcopal Church.

WILLIAM FREDERICK LOW. The really useful men of a community are those on whom their fellow citizens can rely in matters of import, especially those of finance; men who have won this confidence by the wisdom of their own investments and by the honorable lives they have led in every field of effort and as neighbors and friends. Such a man in every particular is William F. Low, cashier of the First National Bank of Williamsburg, a prominent representative of the financial interests of his city and James City County.

William F. Low was born April 1, 1891, in Richmond, Virginia, a son of Fred and Mary Alice (Day) Low, natives of Richmond. During a large portion of his mature life the father was with the city fire department, and was a man highly respected by all who knew him. His death took place December 18, 1903. The mother is still living and resides in Williamsburg.

Growing up in Richmond, William F. Low attended its public schools, but, as there was necessity for him to become self-supporting, he did not plan for a collegiate training, but entered the American Locomotive Company as a mechanical draughtsman, and held that position for about five years. When he left that company it was to enter the banking business, first as runner for the Broad Street Bank. His faithfulness and reliability brought about promotions, and during the ten years he was connected with this bank he rose to be assistant manager of the savings department. In March, 1918, he left Richmond and the Broad Street Bank and came to Williamsburg to assume the duties of assistant cashier of the First National Bank, and one month later was made cashier, which position he still holds. The bank was organized about 1903, and has a capital of $30,000, a surplus of $30,000, and total resources of over a million dollars. Mr. Low is a stockholder in the bank. His associates are: L. W.

Lane, president; J. W. Jones, vice president; and T. L. Sheppard, assistant cashier.

An active Democrat, Mr. Low is a member of the City School Board, and a friend of education. He is a thirty-second degree Mason, and belongs to the Rotary Club. Long an Episcopalian, he is now connected with Bruton parish, and is one of its vestrymen. Mr. Low is unmarried. Few men in banking circles in this section of the state have established a reputation broader and more striking than has he; few have gained a higher reputation for efficiency, fidelity and faithfulness, and as a man of marked intellectual activity his labors have given an impetus to business life and educational progress.

GEORGE SCHLEY DESHAZOR, JR., is clerk of the Circuit Court and county clerk of Warwick County, with home and headquarters at Denbigh.

His family have been identified with Virginia since Colonial times. Mr. DeShazor was born at Newport News, Virginia, September 19, 1899, son of George S. and Mary A. (Dugan) DeShazor. His father was born at Nashville, Tennessee, and a year after his birth his parents returned to Virginia. He was a son of John A. DeShazor, a native Virginian, who during the Civil war was a contractor for the Confederate government, building fortifications and other military works. Two of the brothers of George S. DeShazor, Sr., were soldiers in the Confederate army. Mary A. Dugan was born in Philadelphia and her father was a Union soldier in the war.

George S. DeShazor, Jr., attended school at Newport News, graduating from high school in 1916. This was followed by a business course at Newport News, and his first employment there was clerk in the postoffice. After a year and a half he was made deputy clerk of Warwick County, January 9, 1924, and on August 2, 1927, was elected to the office of Circuit Court clerk and clerk of the county for a term of eight years.

Mr. DeShazor is unmarried. He is affiliated with Lodge No. 1514 of the Loyal Order of Moose, and is a Democrat in politics.

DAVID MINOR MCDONALD. Leesburg has its full representation of men who, starting on their independent careers without financial resources or other adventitious aids, have forced their way through sheer energy and native business talent to positions of independence and prestige, but it is doubtful if a better illustration could be found than David Minor McDonald, proprietor of the McDonald Auto Service. Losing his father when he was but nine years of age, his education was necessarily curtailed by the need of his assistance in contributing to the family support, but this proved no hindrance to the ambitious and determined youth, whose energies have since carried him so far. At present he is accounted one of the substantial citizens of the younger generation, and is contributing to the civic welfare of Leesburg in the capacity of vice president of the Rotary Club.

Mr. McDonald was born July 22, 1892, in Loudoun County, Virginia, and is a son of Capt. John B. and Virginia C. (Lyon) McDonald. His father, a native of Scotland, came to the United States in young manhood and took up his residence in Loudoun County. Eventually he became captain of a tugboat plying the waters of Alexandria Bay, and there lost his life by drowning during a storm in 1901. Mrs. McDonald, who was born in

Loudoun County, survived him until April, 1922, and passed away at Leesburg.

David Minor McDonald received a public school education in Loudoun County, and was still a youth when he started soliciting insurance. This business he followed with a measure of success for some years, but he did not feel that he was making the progress that he should, and in 1918 took a position as an automobile mechanic for the Lambert Motor Company. During the six years that followed he applied himself to the fullest extent in learning every detail of the business, and in the meantime saved his earnings carefully and added to them by several well placed investments. Finally he decided that he was equipped and ready to embark upon a venture of his own, and in 1924 he founded the McDonald Auto Service, of which he has since been the proprietor. So successful was this business under his direction and management that from practically nothing it had grown within four years to an enterprise valued at $160,000. Mr. McDonald handles Chevrolet automobiles, and maintains a commodious salesroom and service station, making a specialty of repair work and the recharging and repairing of batteries. He also handles tires, equipment and accessories, and has one of the most modern establishments of its kind in this section of the state, his present building, erected in 1927, being 100 by 50 feet, and his accessory building 36 by 16 feet. He now gives employment to ten people, including skilled mechanics. Mr. McDonald has an excellent reputation in business circles and is vice president of the Rotary Club and master of the Leesburg Hunt Club. He votes the Democratic ticket, and he and Mrs. McDonald are members of the Methodist Episcopal Church.

On January 17, 1917, Mr. McDonald was united in marriage with Miss Pauline Lambert, daughter of J. D. and Sallie B. (Weeden) Lambert, natives of Virginia. Mr. Lambert is a retired merchant of Ashburn, this state, where Mrs. Lambert died in 1925. Four children have been born to Mr. and Mrs. McDonald: Marie Louise, born December 20, 1917; Ann Elizabeth, born November 19, 1921; Eda Lee, born January 20, 1926; and David Minor, Jr., born November 1, 1928.

HON. JOHN PENDLETON LEACHMAN, treasurer of Prince William County, is one of the substantial farmers of the county, his finly developed property lying near Manassas, and there he resides, although he has his offices in the Farmers Bank Building, Manassas. He was born in Prince William County, Virginia, December 18, 1853, a son of John Thomas and Elizabeth Ann (Lewis) Leachman, also natives of Prince William County. Although not an enlisted man, the father served as a guide during the first battle of Manassas, and he continued farming after the close of the war, being so engaged at the time of his death. His father was John Leachman, for many years sheriff of Prince William County and owner of the farm now owned and operated by Treasurer Leachman. The father passed away in December, 1912, and the mother in 1902, and both were most excellent people, highly esteemed by all who knew them.

While he remained with his parents on the farm until he was twenty-five years old, John Pendleton Leachman attended the local schools and Bethel Military Academy near Warrenton, Virginia. When he left the homestead it was to begin operating his present farm of 160 acres, and here he raises pure bred Shorthorn cattle. During the period he was getting his farm

in good shape he served for ten years as sheriff, and when he
left office it was to become assistant cashier of the National
Bank of Manassas. In 1911 he was elected treasurer of the
county, and has continued to serve in this office ever since, his
present term expiring in 1931, at which time he will have been
county treasurer of Prince William County for twenty consecutive years. In 1897 he had a little preliminary experience
in his office, as he served at that time as deputy treasurer.

Mr. Leachman married Mary Virginia Strother in October,
1884. She is a daughter of Thomas and Mildred (Childs)
Strother, natives of Fauquier County, Virginia. He died in
1861, but she survived him many years and passed away in
1916. Ten children have been born to Mr. and Mrs. Leachman,
namely: Mildred, who is the wife of D. B. Smith, of Warrenton,
Virginia; Edith May, who is the wife of Robert H. Smith, of
Manassas, Virginia; Olivia, who is the wife of Allen L. Oliver,
of Cape Girardeau, Missouri; Lillian, who is the wife of J. L.
Hinson, of Manassas; Marie, who is the wife of Douglas Janney,
of Clarksburg, West Virginia; William H., who is a traveling
salesman, residing in Manassas; John P., who died in New
Mexico when he was twenty-three years old; Thomas Keith,
who was accidentally killed in New York City by a railroad
when he was twenty-one years old; James Lewis, who died at the
age of eighteen months; and one child, who was born dead.
Mrs. Leachman died in 1918. In November, 1925, Mr. Leachman married Miss Emma Shisler, of Philadelphia, Pennsylvania,
a daughter of John Shisler, a native of Pennsylvania, who with
his wife resides in Philadelphia. Mr. Leachman is a thirty-
second degree Mason, and belongs to Acca Temple, A. A. O. N.
M. S., Richmond. He belongs to the Manassas Kiwanis Club,
is active in the local Democratic party, and is a member of the
Episcopal Church. His farm four miles southwest of Manassas
is, as already stated, a magnificent property, and is interesting
historically as having been in the Leachman family for many
generations, and on it is buried the paternal great-grandfather
and great-grandmother of Mr. Leachman of this review. It
was from Prince William County that his uncle, William Leachman, enlisted for service in the Mexican war, and others bearing
the name have been prominent in both war and peace in this
and other regions of the state.

HORACE BLUFORD effectively upheld in all the relations of
life the honors of a family name that has been worthily linked
with the annals of Virginia history since the Colonial era. He
passed his entire life in Norfolk and was one of the representative business men and influential citizens of this community at
the time of his death, which occurred April 6, 1905. Through
his wide and constructive activities in fraternal circles Mr.
Bluford became specially well known throughout his native state,
and his circle of friends was limited only by that of his
acquaintances.

Horace Bluford was born at Norfolk September 6, 1861, and
was a son of George A. and Margaret Ann (Cooke) Bluford,
both representatives of old and honored Virginia families.
George A. Bluford likewise was born and reared in Norfolk, and
he became one of its most progressive and influential citizens,
many of the streets of the city having been laid out by him
and his other contributions to civic and material advancement
having been of noteworthy order, besides which he here built

up an important hide and leather business that received his close attention many years.

The schools of his native city afforded Horace Bluford his youthful education, and his initial business experience was acquired by his serving a short time as clerk in a local mercantile establishment. He finally engaged independently in the produce commission business, and in this connection he developed one of the largest and most important enterprises of the kind in Norfolk. At the time of his death the business was conducted under the title of H. Bluford Company, and since he passed away the business has been effectively carried forward under the control of his son Vernon, while the title of the concern has been changed to Crocker-Bluford Corporation.

Mr. Bluford served as a gallant soldier in the Spanish-American war, he having been a member of Company B, Fourth Virginia Volunteer Infantry, and having been with this command in active service in Cuba. His company was commanded by Captain Higgins. The political allegiance of Mr. Bluford was given unreservedly to the Democratic party, and his religious faith was that of the Presbyterian Church, of which his widow likewise is a zealous member. Mr. Bluford was specially prominent in fraternal circles and was the organizer and first president of the Virginia Grand Aerie of the Fraternal Order of Eagles. He organized also the Norfolk Lodge of the Benevolent and Protective Order of Elks, and he was prominently affiliated also with the Royal Arcanum and the Improved Order of Red Men. He took deep interest in all that concerned the civic, social and material welfare of his native city and was one of its progressive and public spirited citizens. His fraternal relations included his membership in the Virginia organization of the veterans of the Spanish-American War, and he was one of the loyal and influential members of the Norfolk Chamber of Commerce.

On the 13th of June, 1883, was solemnized the marriage of Mr. Bluford and Miss Annie Lee Fowler, who was born at Petersburg, this state, but who was educated in the schools of Norfolk. Mrs. Bluford is a daughter of Thomas Henry and Elizabeth V. (Bolsam) Fowler, the former of whom was born in Maryland and the latter of whom was born and reared in Norfolk, Virginia, the Bolsam family having been founded in Norfolk County prior to the War of the Revolution and having given patriot soldiers to the Continental Line in that great struggle for national independence. Thomas Henry Fowler gave loyal service to the Confederacy in the Civil war period, and for a time was in a hospital at Petersburg. He was active as a representative of the drug business for some time after the close of the war and later was an executive with the Old Dominion Steamship Company, with headquarters at Norfolk, in which city he and his wife continued to reside until their death. Mrs. Bluford is the gracious and popular chatelaine of one of the attractive and hospitable homes of Norfolk, where she resides at 323 West Fourteenth Street. Mr. Bluford is survived also by three children, the eldest of whom is Vernon, who is his successor in business as president of the Crocker-Bluford Corporation. Vernon Bluford received the advantages of the Norfolk public schools and also those of a business college. He is one of the popular and progressive business men of his native city, his Masonic affiliations include his membership in the local Commandery of Knights Templar and also the Mystic Shrine, and he is a member also of the Benevolent and Protective Order of Elks and the Fraternal Order of Eagles. His wife, whose maiden name was Lillian Ellis, was born and reared in Maryland, and their one child is a daughter, Jean Ellis. Horace, Jr., the second son, is likewise a representative business man of Norfolk, and he is a member of the local lodge of Elks. He married Miss Capitola M. Prince, and they have five children: Marguerite, Doris K., Gloria Lee, Barbara A. and Frances Elizabeth. Nellie Virginia, the only daughter, is the wife of Robert M. Boyd, who is president of the Twin City Tobacco Company, with his residence and executive headquarters in Norfolk, where he has served two terms as city treasurer. Mr. and Mrs. Boyd have two children, Robert M., Jr., and Patricia Lee. Mr. Boyd is affiliated with the Masonic fraternity, including the Ancient Arabic Order Nobles of the Mystic Shrine.

J. GREEN CARTER has become one of the influential and progressive representatives of the real estate and insurance business in the county in which he was born and reared, and at the county seat of which, the thriving city of Warrenton, he maintains his residence and business headquarters.

The birth of Mr. Carter occurred at Casanova, Fauquier County, Virginia, February 11, 1876, and he is a son of Cassius and Frances (Scott) Carter, the former of whom was born in Prince William County and the latter in Culpeper County, this state. When the Civil war was precipitated on a divided nation Cassius Carter loyally cast in his lot with the Confederacy, and his service in that conflict was with a fine black-horse company of cavalry that was recruited at Warrenton. He took part in the various engagements in which his command was involved and made a record of gallant and faithful service. After the close of the war he engaged in farm enterprise in Fauquier County, and he continued to give his supervision to his well improved farm estate near Casanova during the remainder of his life, his death having occurred December 25, 1914, and his wife having passed to the life eternal October 10, 1893. Cassius Carter was one of the substantial and honored citizens of Fauquier County, was a stalwart supporter of the cause of the Democratic party, was affiliated with the United Confederate Veterans, and he held the faith of the Protestant Episcopal Church. Both were representatives of sterling families that were early founded in Virginia.

The public schools of Fauquier County were the medium through which J. Green Carter acquired his earlier education, and this discipline was supplemented by his course in the Virginia Polytechnic Institute at Blacksburg, where he studied civil engineering and became skilled in its various phases. This profession he followed a number of years, during a portion of which he was in government service, and in the period of 1910-15 he was assistant manager of the Fellsmere Farms Company at Fellsmere, Florida, in which locality the corporation controlled a large and valuable landed property. During the period of the nation's participation in the World war Mr. Carter did his part in patriotic service, as he was retained as supervisor of the Bartlett-Hayward munition plant at Baltimore, Maryland. Since 1918 he has been successfully established in the real estate business at Warrenton, and he has handled both city and farm properties in such degree and such manner as to make his operations count much in furtherance of civic and material progress in his native county. In connection with his real estate business he maintains a well ordered insurance department.

The political allegiance of Mr. Carter is given loyally to the Democratic party, he is a communicant of the Protestant Episcopal Church, and in his home city he has membership in the Chamber of Commerce, the Rotary Club and the Fauquier Club, besides being a popular and appreciative member of the Warrenton Country Club. Mr. Carter still permits his name to appear on the roster of eligible bachelors in his native county, where his circle of friends is limited only by that of his acquaintances.

JAMES LOUIS EARLY graduated from medical college in 1901 and has had a progressive record in the work of his profession, with a steadily increasing range of responsibilities and professional honors. For many years he practiced at Saltville, but is now one of the leading men of his profession at Radford.

Doctor Early was born at Woodlawn in Carroll County, Virginia, September 14, 1876. His people have been in Southwest Virginia for a number of generations. His grandfather, James W. Early, was born in Wythe County in 1806, and for many years followed farming in Carroll County, where he died in 1889. The father of Doctor Early was William Kenny Early, who was born in Carroll County in 1847 and at the age of sixteen entered the Confederate army, serving with the cavalry until the end of the war. After the war he graduated from Roanoke College, was a farmer in Carroll County until 1908, and then moved to Galax, where he became a lumber manufacturer. Both he and his wife are now deceased. His wife, Mary Louise Belo, was born at Salem, Virginia, in 1853. Dr. James L. Early had a brother, George B., who for many years was in the service of the Newport News Ship Building & Dry Dock Company and another brother, Charles William, is a graduate of the United States Naval Academy at Annapolis and was a commander in the navy during the World war. Harry Edward Early is an electrical engineer.

James Louis Early was educated in private and public schools in Carroll County, graduated from the Woodlawn Normal Institute in 1895, and in 1901 graduated from the University College of Medicine at Richmond. For several years he practiced at Woodlawn and Galax, and for a time was surgeon for the Carolina, Clinchfield & Ohio Railroad while it was in course of construction. Doctor Early in 1905 located at Saltville, where in addition to a general practice acted as surgeon and physician to the Norfolk & Western Railroad and several industrial organizations. In October, 1926, Doctor Early moved to Radford, and has a fine suite of offices in the Farmers & Merchants Bank building. For a number of years, up to January, 1929, he was a director in the Mountain Trust Bank of Roanoke. He is a director of the Peoples State Bank of Radford.

Doctor Early is a member of the Southwest Virginia, the Southern and American Medical Associations, the Medical Society of Virginia and the Association of Norfolk & Western Railway Surgeons. During the World war he was chairman of the Examining Board of Smyth and Grayson counties. He is a director of the Kiwanis Club of Radford, a Royal Arch and Knight Templar Mason and Shriner, having filled a number of offices in Masonic bodies, and is also affiliated with the Indepen-

dent Order of Odd Fellows and B. P. O. Elks. He is a member of the Presbyterian Church.

Doctor Early married, June 29, 1910, Miss Melita Rorer Wilson, daughter of Dr. William A. and Mary (Miller) Wilson, of Radford. Mrs. Early finished her education in the State Teachers College at Farmville.

GEORGE FRANKLIN SIMPSON, M. D., D. D. S. In the case of Dr. George Franklin Simpson, of Purcellville, is shown the effects of determination, hard work and aspiring ambition, for he worked his way through college and later on attended night classes while practicing dentistry during the daytime, for he is a graduate dental surgeon as well as a physician and surgeon. The fact that he was without money or influence did not discourage him, rather it braced him and enabled him to overcome obstacles and achieve success where one less persistent might have failed. This hard and intensive training has brought out admirable characteristics, broadened his viewpoint and made him a most desirable citizen, and one always willing to assume civic responsibilities.

Doctor Simpson was born at Woodgrove, Loudoun County, Virginia, June 19, 1869, a son of John Thomas and Rose Anna Agnes (Allder) Simpson, natives of the same county as their son. During the war between the states John Thomas Simpson fought in the Twelfth Virginia Cavalry under the command of General Ashby. At one time he served as a member of the Charleston, West Virginia, Militia. After the close of hostilities he settled down to farming in Loudoun County, where he died on his ninetieth birthday. The mother and wife died at the age of eighty-three years, February 6, 1912.

Doctor Simpson was reared in Loudoun County and went to school held in a one-room schoolhouse. However, during that period he had been able, at different times, to get a little schooling in the public schools of Washington City, and was also under a private tutor. Beginning his studies for a professional career, he took dentistry and medicine, and was graduated in the former June 6, 1900, and was licensed to practice. In August, 1901, he was graduated in medicine, his courses having been taken in the National University, Washington. He was president of his graduating class. He was engaged in the practice of dentistry in Washington for a year and taught dentistry during 1901, 1902 and 1903 in his *alma mater* and had charge of the dental infirmary of that institution. Until 1908 he was engaged in the practice of both dentistry and medicine in Washington, but in the latter year came to Loudoun County, first locating in Hillsboro, but coming to Purcellville January 26, 1916, and here he has built up a very large and valuable medical practice.

While a resident of Washington, Doctor Simpson married Miss Maude Evelyn Garner, of Washington, a daughter of George Thomas and Mary C. (Claggett) Garner, natives of Virginia and Maryland, respectively. For a good many years Mr. Garner was in the Government employ, but is now deceased. He is survived by Mrs. Garner, a lady seventy-nine years old, and a resident of Norwood, Massachusetts. Doctor and Mrs. Simpson have no children.

Doctor Simpson has served on the Town Council of Purcellville, as he did on that of Hillsboro. He is an ex-president of the Purcellville Chamber of Commerce, having held the office for two successive terms. He is a director of the Loudoun

Light & Power Company and vice president of Loudoun Hospital. During the World war he was chairman of the Medical Advisory Board of Loudoun County. In Masonry he is a past master and a past district deputy grand master of the Blue Lodge; belongs to Leesburg Chapter No. 55, R. A. M.; Piedmont Commandery, K. T., of Plains, Virginia; and Acca Temple, A. A. O. N. M. S., and the Shrine Club, of Alexandria, Virginia. He is a charter member of the Loudoun County Golf and Country Club, and belongs to the Virginia State Medical Association, the District of Columbia Medical Association, the Northern Virginia and Maryland Medical Society, the Loudoun County Medical Society, and the American Medical Association. He is local surgeon for the Washington & Old Dominion Railroad. In politics he is a Democrat. A very zealous Methodist, he is chairman of the building committee now constructing the new church edifice, and is a steward of the church. Lee Camp, Sons of Confederate Veterans, at Leesburg, holds his membership, he being eligible because of his father's military service in behalf of the Confederacy. The beautiful Simpson residence and office, one of the finest in Purcellville, was built by Doctor Simpson in 1915, and here he and his wife welcome their many friends on all occasions.

CHARLES ADAMS HUBBARD, of Denbigh, is commissioner of revenue of Warwick County, and has performed the duties of that responsible position for a period of twenty years.

He was born at Yorktown, Virginia, January 20, 1874, son of Judge James Filmer and Emily C. (Adams) Hubbard. His mother was born in Massachusetts, while his father was a native of James City County, Virginia, and was an able and successful lawyer. For thirty-five years he served in the office of commonwealth's attorney of York County, and just prior to his death had been appointed circuit judge, dying before taking office. His death came in December, 1903, at the age of sixty-four. He had been a lieutenant in the Confederate army during his youth, was in the cavalry and served during the entire conflict. The wife of Judge Hubbard died in 1882.

Charles A. Hubbard was reared and educated at Yorktown, attended Lee Hall and William and Mary College at Williamsburg. After his college training he managed his father's farm until 1902, in which year he took employment with S. R. Curtis, the county treasurer, a railway contractor, and was identified with that line of business until 1908, when he accepted appointment as commissioner of revenue, the office in which he has served continuously. He has made a splendid record in handling the finances of Warwick County.

Mr. Hubbard married, April 23, 1909, Miss Georgia Eller Garrow, daughter of James Toomer and Cornelia Nelson (Wright) Garrow, the former a native of Warwick County and the latter of Surry County. Her grandfather, John Toomer Garrow, was at one time sheriff and a justice of the peace of Warwick County, and died as a result of his service in the Civil war. Mrs. Hubbard's father served as deputy sheriff and for many years was a merchant in Denbigh, being at the time of his death, February 3, 1929, the oldest business man of the community, dying at the age of eighty years. Mrs. Hubbard's mother died in November, 1922, at the age of sixty-three.

Mr. Hubbard is affiliated with the B. P. O. Elks. He has been a practiced rider since a small child, and for forty or forty-

five years has kept fox hounds and has indulged in the sport
of fox hunting. He knows and is known by all the followers
of that sport in Eastern Virginia. The Hubbards are active in
the Methodist Church, Mrs. Hubbard teaching an intermediate
class in the Sunday School. She is a member of the United
Daughters of the Confederacy and is secretary of the local
chapter, Comte de Grasse, of the Daughters of the American
Revolution, and is also a member of the Ladies Auxiliary of the
Veterans of Foreign Wars. Mr. Hubbard's father was a leading
Mason. Mrs. Hubbard was a teacher for several years before
her marriage. Recently they have completed one of the fine
homes in Denbigh.

JEREMY PATE WHITT is a prominent educator whose work
for a number of years has been familiarly associated with the
Radford State Teachers College and through that institution a
large body of active school workers have learned to appreciate
his ability and his fine personal character.

He was born near East Radford, September 25, 1879, son
of Hezekiah and Ellen (Cecil) Whitt. His great-grandfather
was one of the early settlers of Montgomery County. His grandfather was also named Hezekiah Whitt. His father was born
and reared in the Meadow Creek settlement near East Radford,
attended private schools, was a Confederate soldier, and after
the war followed farming and stock raising until his death. He
owned and operated one of the first flour and corn mills in his
community, known as Whitt's Mill. He was eighty-two years
of age when he died in 1913, and is buried in the old Laurel Hill
Church Cemetery. His wife, Ellen Cecil, was born and reared
in Pulaski County, and was one of the first students of Martha
Washington College at Abingdon. Her father, J. G. Cecil, had
much to do with early educational affairs in Pulaski County,
serving as the first county superintendent of schools, and was
one of the founders of Emory and Henry College. He was in the
Virginia Legislature during the Civil war. The mother of
Jeremy P. Whitt taught school before her marriage. She was
a member of the Christian Church. Her death occurred March
26, 1906. Both of these parents had been married previously.
The first wife of Hezekiah Whitt was Miss Mollie Harman, of
Montgomery County, and the two children of that marriage were
Walter Whitt, of Lockney, Texas, and Minnie, wife of A. H.
Finks, of Roanoke, Virginia. Professor Whitt's mother first
married Alford Goodykoontz, of Floyd County, Virginia, and
her one son of that marriage, John, died in 1897.

Jeremy Pate Whitt was the only child of his parents' second
marriage. He attended public schools in Montgomery and
Pulaski counties, and in 1902 was graduated with the degrees
A. B. and A. M. from Milligan College of Tennessee. For twenty
years he taught school in North Carolina, Tennessee, Kentucky,
Florida and Virginia, being superintendent of the Radford city
schools from 1911 until 1920. During 1920-21 he spent a year
in post-graduate study in the Peabody Normal College at Nashville, Tennessee, and then came to the Radford State Teachers
College as registrar and director of the training school of the
department of education.

Mr. Whitt is a member of the Pi Gamma Mu fraternity, is
a Democrat, and an elder in the Christian Church, a teacher in
the Sunday School and chairman of the Official Board of the
church. He married at Milligan College, Tennessee, March 26,

1904, Miss Jaynie Clyde Shumate, of Danville, Kentucky. She was educated in private schools in Kentucky, graduated from girls' college in that state, and afterwards attended the University of Tennessee. She taught in public schools, was instructor in English in Sullins College in Bristol, Virginia, and in Milligan College, Tennessee, and from 1911 to 1920 was principal of the Radford High School and instructor in English. For several years she has taught in the summer schools of the Radford State Teachers College. Mrs. Whitt is active in church, and has been secretary and president of the Radford Woman's Club. She is a member of the United Daughters of the Confederacy, an associate member of the American Association of University Women, and is eligible to membership in the Daughters of the American Revolution. Her parents were Francis Marion and Elizabeth (Higginbotham) Shumate, of Danville, Kentucky. He and his wife after retiring moved to California, and he now resides at Glendale, where his wife died in 1924.

WILSON R. BOWERS, head of the department of mathematics in the Radford State Teachers College, had as the background of his experience before coming to the college many years of work as a teacher in country and town schools over Southwestern Virginia.

Mr. Bowers was born near Galax, in Carroll County, Virginia, March 3, 1875, son of William and Sarah (Gallimore) Bowers. He is a grandson of William Bowers and a great-grandson of George Bowers, who came from Germany and was one of the early settlers in Carroll County, Virginia. William Bowers, his father, was born and reared in Carroll County, attended private schools and at the age of sixteen was drafted for service in the Civil war, but the war closed before he was called to active duty. He spent his active career as a farmer and stock raiser and died May 10, 1917, being buried in the family cemetery near Galax. His widow, who survives him at the age of seventy-four, has always been a regular member of the Christian Church. She was born and reared near Austinville, Virginia, and attended private schools. She lives with a daughter at Hopewell, Virginia.

Wilson R. Bowers was the oldest in a family of eleven children. He attended public schools and private schools in Carroll County, the Stuart Normal School and Woodlawn Institute, and in 1900 graduated with the degrees Bachelor of Science and later Bachelor of Arts from Milligan College of Tennessee. Lynchburg College gave him the honorary degree Master of Arts. For three summers he did graduate work at the University of Virginia and for one and a quarter years at Columbia University of New York, where he won his Master of Arts degree in 1919. He has since done one and a quarter years work toward his Ph. D. degree. Mr. Bowers for eighteen years was engaged in grade and high school work in Virginia, all except the first three years as principal of high school. For several years he was head of the schools at Rural Retreat, and while there was instrumental in securing the erection of a handsome new high school building. Mr. Bowers in 1919 came with the Radford State Teachers College as head of the department of mathematics. He owns his home in Radford, other real estate and a farm in Carroll County.

He is affiliated with Virginia May Lodge No. 38, A. F. and A. M., and the Knights of Pythias and Knights of the Mystic Chain,

Eppa S. Cox.

VIRGINIA 277

is a member of the Kiwanis Club, Chamber of Commerce and the Southwestern Virginia, incorporated. He is independent politically and a member of the Methodist Episcopal Church, South. Since 1921 he has been superintendent of the Grove Avenue Sunday School, Radford.

He married at Rural Retreat Miss Nannie Brown Eiffert, who attended public school there and the Hawkins Institute and Milligan College. She was a teacher of music in the Rural Retreat High School for several years before and after her marriage, and she took an active part in choir work at East Radford. She is a daughter of Henry A. and Susan (Brown) Eiffert. Her father for many years was a farmer and stock raiser at Rural Retreat and then engaged in business as a merchant there. After retiring he moved to Cleveland, Tennessee, where he died in 1927 and where his widow lives with her youngest daughter, Mrs. Max Fouts. Mr. and Mrs. Bowers have two children, Eleanor Randolph and Warren Brown Bowers, the former a member of the class of 1929 and the latter in his first year in the Radford High School. Mr. Bowers is author of the following pamphlets and articles: America's Discontent, A Factor in Her Development; Martin Luther's Contribution to Modern Education; School Hygiene; Principles and Methods in Teaching Primary Arithmetic; The Relationship of the Practical and the Cultural in Modern Education. He is now beginning to write a book on the "Teaching of Elementary Mathematics."

HON. EPPA SHERMAN COX, county treasurer of Fauquier County, has a long and honorable career behind him in the service of his county, and has built up a reputation second to none for faithful performance of duty and strict adherence to high ideals of good citizenship. He was born near Elk Run, Fauquier County, Virginia, January 6, 1869, a son of James W. and Alvernon T. (Lake) Cox, natives of Virginia. During the war between the states James W. Cox served as a clerk in the commissary department at Richmond, and after the war was over he returned to Fauquier County and for thirty years was a teacher of the county and at the same time he was engaged in farming. His death occurred when he was fifty-seven years old, in 1889, but he was survived by the mother until 1902. Through his mother Treasurer Cox belongs to the Lake Clan, which has a membership of 300 in the different states of the Union, all of whom trace back to three brothers by the name of Lake who came to the American colonies prior to the Revolution, in this hemisphere, and in the Old World to forebears for 1,000 years. The clan holds annual meetings, and it is a source of interest and pleasure to those belonging to it to have the privilege of keeping in touch with those of common family ties and connections. The pride of race is something that lies very close to the heart of everyone, and when the family record is as honorable as that of the Lakes, then those allied to it ought to give every assistance in keeping it up to the high standards already reared, and this Treasurer Cox is doing.

Reared and educated in Fauquier County, Eppa S. Cox had his father for his teacher during the greater portion of his school days. Subsequently he took a correspondence school business training course, but he continued on the farm with his parents until he was thirty-three years old, after which he farmed on his own account for two years. In 1899 he was elected commissioner of revenue for the Cedar Run District, and held that office for twelve years, at the termination of that period receiving appointment as deputy county treasurer, and holding the office from 1911 to 1915. In 1923 he was elected county treasurer and reelected to the same office in 1927, without opposition, and is still the incumbent of the office.

On September 25, 1901, Mr. Cox married Miss Carrie May Lee, a daughter of James E. and Sarah Virginia (Lee) Lee, natives of Bedford County, Virginia, and Missouri, respectively. Mr. Lee was a Confederate veteran, and a distant relative of Gen. Robert E. Lee, and served with the rank of sergeant. Returning home after the close of the war, he was engaged in farming in Bedford County the remainder of his life, and died there in 1899. Mrs. Lee survived him until 1901, when she, too, passed away. Mr. and Mrs. Cox have had four children born to them: Virginia Alvernon, who was born January 15, 1903, is a trained nurse, and is now superintendent of a hospital at Sheridan, Wyoming; Gilbert Lee, who was born March 2, 1906, is a graduate of the Virginia Polytechnic Institute, class of 1928; James Edwin, who was born October 5, 1908, is a student of the Virginia Polytechnic Institute; and Ida Louise, who was born December 25, 1912, is a student of Calverton High School. Mr. Cox belongs to the Independent Order of Odd Fellows, of which he has been a member for thirty years, and to Black Horse Camp, Sons of Confederate Veterans. His political views make him a Democrat, and he is a strong supporter of his party's principles. For years a member of the Methodist Episcopal Church, South, he is a trustee of the church at present, and also superintendent of the Sunday school. While his office is in Warrenton, he continues to reside at Calverton, and he is held in the highest esteem by the people of both communities and throughout Fauquier County. The welfare of the county is dear to him and he has worked hard both as a public official and private citizen to do everything within his power to keep things abreast of the times, and it would be difficult to find anyone more universally respected or more highly honored.

ADAM MONROE TURNER, whose home is at Broadway, Rockingham County, was born on the top of the Shenandoah Mountains in the same county March 2, 1859. His career has been made up of commendable industry and honorable relations with his fellowmen.

He is a descendant of James Turner who came from Sweden and settled at Greencastle, Pennsylvania, about 1790. He was a very successful farmer, and while never in politics he wielded an important influence in the promotion of schools and churches. He was of the Dunkard faith. In 1803 he removed to Rockingham County, Virginia, settling about two miles above Brock's Gap on a little stream known as Lambs Run, a tributary of the north branch of the Shenandoah. He married a Fronkfodder, and among their children were John Turner, born in 1798, Jacob, born in 1800; Andrew, born in 1803; Joseph and James and also four daughters. Of the sons John married a Pear, Jacob, a Cherryholes, Andrew, a Zetty, Joseph, a Bible.

James Turner, who was born on Lambs Run after his parents settled in Rockingham County, grew up with a farm training and a fair education so that he qualified for teaching school. He was a member of the Christian Church, a Republican and in 1861 served with the Virginia Militia. He married Mary Fulk, a daughter of John G. Fulk and a descendant of Mathew Fulk, who was of Scotch-Irish descent and came to America about 1735. He was with Colonel Lewis in an expedition to treat with the Indians, and he married an Indian woman. Not long afterward the Indians were moved from Rockingham County and he also went, but left a large family of boys and some girls, who lived or settled about two miles west of Broadway in Rockingham County, at a place called Trissels Church. John Fulk, a son of Mathew Fulk, was born in 1760 and married a Miss Bible. He moved to Brock's Gap in 1785. One other member of the family was Adam Fulk, who moved to Ohio when it was still the Northwest Territory, and Adams County in the southern part of the state of Ohio was named for him, and he became prominent in county affairs. Another member of the family, Jacob Fulk, was an early settler near Fort Wayne, Indiana, and George Fulk figured in the early settlement of the South Branch Valley of West Virginia. John Fulk had a son, Daniel Fulk, who was the father of John G. Fulk and grandfather of Mary (Fulk) Turner.

Another descendant of Mathew Fulk is Charles R. Fawley the present sheriff of Rockingham County. The sheriff's father, George W. Fawley, married Sarah J. Fulk, a daughter of John G. Fulk. George W. Fawley was a school teacher and for many years a justice of the peace, and in 1860 as a Union man voted for Douglas of Illinois and died a Democrat. He was a son of Jacon Fawley, who married a Minnick and settled at Brock's Gap about 1800 from Loudoun County, having come originally from Pennsylvania.

Adam Monroe Turner, a son of Adam Monroe Turner, a son of James and Mary (Fulk) Turner, derived his education from the common schools and as a young man took up farming and lumbering. He owns about 800 acres of farming land, mostly in Rockingham and Shenandoah counties, besides several thousand acres of mountain land.

Mr. Turner in his public relations with the community has always been guided by a desire to better the conditions of the people, providing better schools, churches and good roads. One of his outstanding services was his work in bringing about the construction of the Brock Gap State Highway for the purpose of developing the northwestern section of Rockingham County, the greater part of which lies within Brock's Gap. He devised a plan by which this road could be built and paid for by the traffic, and this was the plan followed in its construction. In promoting this plan Mr. Turner was under the handicap of being a Republican, while the legislative board of supervisors of the county and district were all Democratic and the officials themselves opposed to the project. In spite of all this Mr. Turner persisted until his ideas were adopted and the plan carried out, and the result has more than justified all his expectations, the highway having paid for itself and given revenue to the rest of the county. The road is about seventeen miles long and has since been taken over by the state as a part of the national system of highways leading into West Virginia. It was Mr. Turner's motion that put the Valley Pike in the hands of the state and he cast the first vote to that end.

Mr. Turner taught seven terms under the free school system, and of the eleven children in his father's family eight became school teachers. In after years he built a house which he turned over to the county for a public school, and this has been the means of giving a large number of men and women the fundamentals of an education.

Mr. Turner since early boyhood has been an enthusiastic sportsman. He has enjoyed hunting as a pastime for over half a century, and during that time has killed 154 bears besides many deer and other wild animals and wild fowl. The deer became extinct about 1900, and about six years ago he restocked a part of the mountain with deer and these are now accumulating fast. In politics Mr. Turner has always been a Republican in national affairs, and also in the state except once when he supported and helped nominate Governor Byrd. He votes a mixed ticket in the county. He was twice elected to the Board of Supervisors, serving eight years, was twice appointed land assessor, holding that office until the law was changed, and only by a small majority was defeated for the House of Delegates, carrying the county but losing the city of Harrisonburg. Mr. Turner, his friends declare, is a thorough practical Christian, though not a member of any denomination. He has helped build every church in the western part of his district, and has given his time and means generously in behalf of other worthy institutions and charities.

He married, December 25, 1879, at Fulks Run in Rockingham County, Miss Mary Catherine Ritchie. Her father, Jonathan Ritchie, was a farmer and served in the Confederate army from 1861 to 1865. This branch of the family is distantly related to that of Governor Ritchie of Maryland. Her mother was a Sprinkle, descended from Peter Sprinkle, a soldier in the War of 1812, and a niece of John C. Sprinkle, a Confederate officer. Mr. and Mrs. Turner are the parents of two daughters. Hallie Hester, born September 27, 1881, near Fulks Run in the Brock's Gap community, is well educated, taught in public schools and is now the wife of Lahone Clutteur, a farmer living near Broadway. Alice Virginia Dare, the second daughter, was born on Shenandoah Mountain in December, 1883, was educated in the common schools and is the wife of John W. Fulk, a farmer near Singers Glen in Rockingham County.

ERWIN GROVER HALL, physician and surgeon, since locating at East Radford, has specialized in eye, ear, nose and throat, and is one of the outstanding specialists in that field in Southwest Virginia.

He was born at Willis in Floyd County, Virginia, December 18, 1886, son of Isaac Thomas and Leah (Young) Hall. His father was born and reared in the same locality, attended private schools, and spent his life as a farmer. He died in 1912 and is buried in Rockingham County. His wife, Leah Young, was born and reared in Floyd County, attended private schools, and now lives with her son, Doctor Hall, at Radford. She is an earnest member of the Baptist Church. Of the ten children born to the parents of Doctor Hall six died in childhood from diphtheria. Another, William, died at East Radford at the age of twenty-one, and Luther was drowned at East Radford when eleven years old. The two surviving children are: Addie, wife of A. H. Jennings, of East Radford; and Doctor Erwin.

Erwin Grover Hall attended public schools at East Radford, spent one year in the University of Richmond, and this was followed by the full four years course in the University College of Medicine at Richmond. He was graduated in 1911 and for ten years conducted a general practice in medicine and surgery in Rockingham County. On giving up his work there he went to Baltimore, and for a year devoted his time to post-graduate work with the Presbyterian Eye, Ear, Nose and Throat Hospital. With this special training and his years of general medical practice he located at East Radford in 1922, and his office hours have been crowded with work in his special line. Doctor Hall is a member of the Medical Society of Virginia and the Southwest Virginia Medical Association. He was for a number of years a member of the Rotary Club, and is affiliated with Virginia May Lodge No. 38, A. F. and A. M. He is a Democrat and is on the Board of Deacons in the Baptist Church and teacher of a men's Bible class.

He married at Eclipse, Virginia, September 23, 1911, Miss Clara Earle Harrison, of Nansemond County, where she was reared and educated. She is a member of the Baptist Church and the Woman's Club of Radford. Her parents were William Allen and Lelia (Sweeney) Harrison. Her father, who died in 1914, was for many years engaged in the oyster industry at Eclipse. Her mother is a resident of Eclipse. Doctor and Mrs. Hall have three sons, Stewart Harrison, Robert Allen and E. G., Jr., all attending the public schools of East Radford.

JOHN CALVIN HOPKINS is associated with his brother, Robert S. Hopkins, as joint owners of the Hopkins Pharmacy at East Radford, and both brothers are graduate pharmacists, masters of that profession and very capable and energetic young business men.

John C. Hopkins was born at Tazewell, Virginia, March 14, 1890, son of O. E. and Rebecca W. (Peery) Hopkins, and grandson of John Calvin Hopkins, who spent many years of his life as a merchant at Tazewell. O. E. Hopkins was born in Tazewell, attended public schools there, and for many years has been engaged in farming and stock raising. He and his wife live at Tazewell and are members of the Methodist Episcopal Church, South. His wife, Rebecca Peery, was born at Tazewell Court House and is a graduate of the Martha Washington College of Abingdon. Her parents were Albert and Sarah (Smith) Peery. Her father was a merchant at Tazewell and died about thirty years ago. Her mother is now eighty-six years of age. O. E. Hopkins and wife had seven children: Alice, wife of M. Zeigler; Elizabeth, wife of A. S. Greybeal; Albert; John C.; Robert S.; Martha, wife of J. A. Stimson; and Edward.

John Calvin Hopkins attended public schools in Tazewell and took his degree in pharmacy at the Medical College of Virginia in 1919. For the past ten years he has been associated with his brother in the drug business at East Radford, and the Hopkins Pharmacy there is a very popular trading place, and especially enjoys the confidence of the medical profession because of the skill in pharmacy of both the proprietors. Mr. Hopkins is also a director of the Peoples Bank. He is affiliated with Virginia May Lodge No. 38, A. F. and A. M., is a member of the Rotary Club, and is serving on the local school board. He is a Democrat and a member of the Methodist Episcopal Church, South.

He married at Tazewell, February 21, 1912, Miss Stella Vermillion, of Tazewell, who finished her education in Martha Washington College at Abingdon. For a number of years she has been a teacher of art and holds a position as art instructor in the Radford State Teachers College. She is a Methodist, a mem-

ber of the Music and Art Clubs, and is very popular in the
college community. Her parents were W. I. and Elizabeth
(Williams) Vermillion, residents of Tazewell. Her father has
carried on an extensive business as a road and stone contractor.
Mr. and Mrs. Hopkins have one daughter, Elizabeth, who graduated in 1929 from the Radford High School.

Robert S. Hopkins was born at Tazewell October 27, 1892,
was educated in public schools and Randolph-Macon College, and
graduated from the School of Pharmacy of the Medical College
of Virginia at Richmond in 1917. He has a war record, having
enlisted in January, 1918, in the United States Marine Corps.
He was trained at Paris Island, South Carolina, and at Quantico,
Virginia, and in April, 1918, went overseas with the Third Re-
placement Battalion, Second Division, and joined the Marine
Headquarters in France. In September, 1918, he was invalided
home, was honorably discharged on January 14, 1919, and soon
afterwards removed to Radford, and in April joined his brother
in the drug business.

Robert S. Hopkins is affiliated with Virginia May Lodge No.
38, A. F. and A. M., Peyton Coles Chapter No. 27, Royal Arch
Masons, Bayard Commandery No. 15, Knights Templar at Roanoke, and Kazim Temple of the Mystic Shrine at Roanoke. He
is a member of Harvey Howe Post No. 30 of the American
Legion, the Kiwanis Club, is a Democrat and a Baptist.

He married at Radford, October 24, 1919, Miss Agnes Johnson, daughter of Albert Sidney Johnson, and member of a very
prominent family in this section of the state. Mrs. Hopkins
attended high school at Radford and is a graduate of the State
Teachers College, after which she taught school for several
years before her marriage. She is a Baptist and a member of
the United Daughters of the Confederacy and Daughters of the
American Revolution.

CHARLES H. STIMPSON throughout his residence in Virginia
was identified with some phase of the maritime interests center-
ing around Norfolk and Portsmouth. He lived all his life close
to and in touch with the affairs of the sea.

He was born at Bath, Maine, in 1831, and died at Berkeley,
Norfolk, in 1885. The Stimpsons were of English ancestry.
His mother was a Lamont, of French Huguenot extraction.
Charles H. Stimpson attended school at Bath, Maine, and as a
young man came to Virginia, working in ship yards, but for the
greater part of his active life was associated with Captain Baker
in the business known as the Baker Ship Salvage & Wrecking
Company, one of the largest organizations of its kind on the
Virginia coast.

Mr. Stimpson married, December 19, 1877, Ann J. Simpson,
of Toronto, Canada, daughter of Samuel and Mary Simpson.
The Simpsons were of Scotch-Irish ancestry, coming to Canada
from Ireland. Her father was a pioneer lumberman in Canada,
where the family settled about 1830. He did an extensive business in exporting lumber to the United Kingdom. Mrs. Stimpson now resides at 309 Dinwiddie Street in Portsmouth. She
is a member of the Episcopal Church and her husband was a
Mason. She has two children, Harry L. and Miss Mary. Harry
L. is mate of a steamship on the Pacific Ocean, and married a
western girl. Miss Mary Stimpson has become well known in
educational and social service work, is a member of the Virginia
State Teachers Association, and is a graduate of Columbia University of New York City.

WALTER GORDON TROW, M. D., has been engaged in the successful practice of his profession at Warrenton, judicial center of Fauquier County, since 1911, save for the interval of his service in the Medical Corps of the United States Army in the World war and the subsequent period of his recuperation from the effects of being gassed while with his command at the front with his unit in France.

Doctor Trow was born in the City of Washington, D. C., December 16, 1879, and is a son of Gordon Winthrop Trow and Fidelia Harriet (Bundy) Trow, who were born in the State of Vermont, of Colonial American ancestry. For a long term of years Gordon W. Trow was in Government service in the national capital, and there his death occurred in 1903, his venerable widow being now a loved member of the family circle of her son, Dr. Walter G., of this review.

After his graduation from the Eastern High School in Washington, D. C., Doctor Trow soon initiated his preparation for the exacting profession of his choice, and in 1905 he was graduated from the medical college of George Washington University. After thus receiving his degree of Doctor of Medicine he fortified himself further by devoting much of the ensuing year to post-graduate work at the Hahnemann Hospital in the City of Philadelphia. Thereafter he was engaged in practice in his native city one year, and during the ensuing four years the stage of his professional activities was at Hallwood, Accomac County, Virginia. He then, in 1911, removed to Warrenton, where he has since continued in active and successful general practice save for the period of his World war service, and where he has been retained since 1916 as local surgeon for the Southern Railway. When in the spring of 1917 the nation became involved in the World war, Doctor Trow soon volunteered for service in the Medical Corps of the United States Army, gained therein the rank of first lieutenant, later was promoted to captain and finally was advanced to the rank of major. He was with his unit in overseas service from April, 1918, until the following December, and in the meanwhile the armistice had brought the great conflict to a close. He suffered a severe gas attack while at the front, and after his return home he went to Camp Lee and then received treatment at the Walter Reed Hospital, Washington, D. C., where he was confined until July, 1919. He has not as yet recovered fully from the effects of the gas attack, and February 9, 1929, he was retired under the Emergency Officers Retirement Act with the rank of major.

After measurably recuperating in a physical way and after receiving his honorable discharge, Doctor Trow resumed his professional ministrations at Warrenton, where he controls a large and representative practice and has standing as one of the representative physicians and surgeons of this section of the Old Dominion State.

Doctor Trow has membership in the Northern Virginia Medical Society, the Virginia State Medical Society, the Virginia, Maryland and District of Columbia Medical Societies, the American Medical Association, the Southern Railroad Surgeons Association, besides being an influential member of the Fauquier County Medical Society. He is affiliated with the American Legion, the Independent Order of Odd Fellows and the Royal Arcanum, and in his home city is a member of the Chamber of Commerce and the Community League. He and his wife are members of the Presbyterian Church, and Mrs. Trow is eligible for affiliation with the Daughters of the American Revolution and also the Colonial Dames. The Doctor has had neither time nor desire to enter the arena of practical politics, but he is a staunch advocate and supporter of the cause of the Democratic party.

In November, 1910, Doctor Trow was united in marriage with Miss Elizabeth Edmonds Harper, who was born near Leesburg, Virginia, and who is a daughter of Robert and Roberta (Parrott) Harper, the former of whom was born in Stafford County, and the latter of whom was born in Petersburg. For a long term of years Robert Harper was engaged in the dry goods business in Alexander, and thereafter he was long engaged in the same line of enterprise at Leesburg, Loudoun County. He finally retired to his farm in Loudoun County, and he died in May, 1908, at the age of eighty-three years. His widow attained to the same age, and her death occurred in February, 1926. Mr. Harper served as a member of the Confederate Home Guard in the Civil war period, he was a lifelong member of the Presbyterian Church and in the same served many years as an elder, an office of which he was still the incumbent at the time of his death, besides which he had served a long period as Sunday school superintendent. He was twice married and became the father of fourteen children. Doctor and Mrs. Trow have five children: Walter Gordon, Jr., and Robert Harper (twins), born September 26, 1911; Randolph Edmonds, born March 7, 1914; William Newton, born April 20, 1916; and Roberta Parrott, born May 13, 1922. At the time of the preparation of this review Robert H. is a student in the military academy at Danville, Virginia (summer of 1929), and his twin brother, Walter G., Jr., is a student in the Warrenton High School, as is also Randolph E.

AMBROSE WILSON, senior member of the firm Wilson Brothers, druggists at East Radford, was born in that Southwest Virginia community September 6, 1893. Both he and his brother are World war veterans, and Mr. Wilson has had a wide and diversified experience in business.

The Wilsons have long been prominent in and around Staunton, Virginia, and they are of the same stock as that from which was descended the World war president, Woodrow Wilson. Mr. Wilson's grandfather was a pioneer circuit riding Presbyterian minister. John A. Wilson, father of Ambrose, was born near Staunton, attended public schools and spent many years in the service of the Norfolk & Western Railway Company. He was foreman at Radford, general foreman at Roanoke, then was made master mechanic of the Radford Division, and after his health failed so that he was unable to keep up with the heavy responsibilities of this position he was made foreman in the shops at Radford and held that position when he died, April 1, 1910. He is buried in the Central Cemetery at East Radford. His wife, Mary Catherine Locke, was born and reared in Virginia. Her parents, Frederick and Wilhelmina Locke, came from Darmstadt, Germany, living for a time at Baltimore, later at Fredericksburg, then near Staunton, and made their final home near Lynchburg and Radford. Mrs. Mary Catherine Wilson attended school at Lynchburg. She is a member of the Episcopal Church. Of her twelve children the daughters Ethel and Sue are deceased; Frederick; Louise, wife of E. Demming Lucas, a Petersburg attorney; Robert L., of Radford, foreman in the Norfolk & Western Railway shops, married Stella Ross, a descendant of the famous Betsy Ross; Rev. John A., Jr., an Episcopal minister at Richland, Virginia, married Bess Gillespie; Henry R., general foreman of the Norfolk & Western Shops at Shenandoah, married Bessie Lucas, of Radford; Frank S., of Detroit, Michigan, married Margaret Fink, of Radford; Louis L., district manager at Huntington, West Virginia, for the Reliance Life Insurance Company, married Lillian Dorsey, of Hurricane, Putnam County, West Virginia; Ambrose; Edward, with the Foster Sumner Corporation at Radford, married Addie Painter; and Hugo L. Wilson. Hugo L. Wilson is the junior member of the firm of Wilson Brothers. He was born in East Radford in 1898, graduated from high school and was with the colors three years, going with the First Virginia Field Hospital Corps, which subsequently was made a part of the Twenty-ninth Division. He returned from overseas in July, 1919, and at that time became associated with his brother in business. He is a charter member of Harvey Howe Post of the American Legion and is a member of the Episcopal Church.

Ambrose Wilson attended the grade and high schools at Radford, leaving school to take work as a clerk with the Goodykrantz Drug Company. Later he was with Scott Brothers at Charleston, West Virginia, for two years with the Frederick Pharmacy at Huntington, a year and a half with the Dow Drug Company at Cincinnati, for two years with the Van Lear Drug Store in Roanoke, two years with the Pearisburg Pharmacy and a year and a half with the Gus Washington Drug Store at Logan, West Virginia, and a year with the Covington Pharmacy at Covington, Virginia.

In June, 1916. he enlisted and was sent to the Mexican border at San Antonio, Texas. In March, 1917, he returned home, but was almost immediately recalled for service in the World war. He was in training at Camp McClellan, Alabama, until June, 1918, when he sailed for overseas, landing at Cherbourg, France, as a member of the One Hundred and Fifteenth Field Hospital, Twenty-ninth Division. He was in the Haute Alsace Sector and in the Meuse Argonne campaigns and received his honorable discharge at Camp Meade, Maryland, June 19, 1919.

It was shortly after his return from overseas that he and his brother established the firm of Wilson Brothers in East Radford. Both of them are very competent business men, and have given the town a very up-to-date establishment, affording a splendid service and also carrying a varied stock of goods that makes their store a very popular center of trade. Besides the regular stock of a drug store they handle the Atwater Kent, Fada and Kolster radio sets and equipment, and also phonographs and records.

Mr. Ambrose Wilson took the lead in organizing the Radford Kiwanis Club, and was secretary and director four years. He is a director and secretary of the Retail Merchants Association, and in 1926-27 was on the executive committee of the State Department of the American Legion. He is a Royal Arch Mason, member of Harvey Howe Post of the American Legion, belongs to the Kiwanis Club, and is a Democrat in politics. He is a vestryman in the Radford Episcopal Church.

Mr. Wilson married at Winston-Salem, North Carolina, March 7, 1922, Miss Epsie Celina Rike, of Randleman, Randolph County, North Carolina. She attended public schools and the North Carolina Woman's College of Greensboro. Mrs. Wilson is a member of the Episcopal Church, the Music Club and Woman's Club, and the American Legion Auxiliary. Her father, Samuel R. Rike, has for many years been a leading farmer and tobacco grower in Randolph County, North Carolina, where both her parents reside.

JOHN B. SPIERS is an attorney, a World war veteran and since locating at Radford has accumulated a very satisfactory business and is enjoying a high degree of prestige in his profession and as a public official.

He was born at Newport News, Virginia, June 29, 1897, son of Louis H. and Nora (Belcher) Spiers. The Spiers and Belcher families lived in North Carolina and over the line in Southern Virginia. His maternal grandfather, John E. Belcher, was a Confederate soldier. Louis H. Spiers was born in North Carolina, and for many years was a lumber inspector, being employed by the Newport News Ship Building and Dry Dock Company. In 1920 he was held up and robbed and killed by a highwayman. His wife, Nora Belcher, was born and reared in Chesterfield County, Virginia, and was a member of the Christian Church. She died in 1907. The five children of these parents were: Helena O., wife of W. G. Avery, of Newport News; Anna F., wife of Fred L. Brucker, of Gary, Indiana; John B.; Louis J., of Greenville, South Carolina; and Norma, wife of Ernest Fisher, of Norfolk, Virginia.

John B. Spiers passed his boyhood days at Newport News, attended the grade and high schools there and engaged in some self-supporting activities before he entered the University of Virginia. In October, 1917, he resigned his position in Richmond to join the colors, and was trained at Fort Monroe with the Sixtieth Regiment of the Coast Artillery Corps. In the spring of 1918 he was commissioned a second lieutenant, went overseas with the Fifty-fourth Coast Artillery Corps, and while in the Officers Training School at Saumur, France, was injured, sustaining a broken foot, and during the remaining months of the war he was in Base Hospital No. 27 and other hospitals in France and finally was sent home and given his honorable discharge at Camp Lee in March, 1919. For about six months after leaving the army he was employed at Richmond and in the fall of 1919 began his studies at the University of Virginia. He is a member of Harvey Howe Post of the American Legion.

Mr. Spiers graduated from the law department of the university in 1922. He had been admitted to the bar in 1921 and he first practiced at Lynchburg. In March, 1923, he removed to Radford, where he opened an office and quickly made his abilities recognized in his profession and was accorded a large general practice. His law offices are now in the First National Bank Building. In 1923 he was appointed commonwealth's attorney of the city of Radford and in 1924 was elected to that office. His administration as commonwealth's attorney has been one highly satisfactory to the good people of the county and has brought increased prestige to him both as a lawyer and man.

Mr. Spiers is a director of the Radford Veneering Lumber Company, Inc., is president of the Radford Kiwanis Club, is a member of the Virginia Bar Association and a Democrat in politics. He is affiliated with Ginter Park Lodge, A. F. and A. M., at Richmond, Virginia; May Lodge of the fraternity at Radford, Chapter No. 27 of the Royal Arch Masons, and the

Order of the Mystic Chain, Modern Woodmen of America. He belongs to the college fraternities Delta Upsilon and Delta Theta Phi. He is a deacon of the Christian Church.

Mr. Spiers married in Orange County, Virginia, June 7, 1924, Miss Maxine Graves, of Liberty Mills, Virginia, where she grew up and where she attended public schools and later continued her education in the Episcopal School at Chatham and is a graduate of West Hampton College of Richmond in the class of 1923. She taught in the high schools at Gordonsville, Virginia, and Danville, West Virginia, before her marriage. Mrs. Spiers is a member of the Christian Church, is a member of the Music Club at Radford and belongs to the Daughters of the American Revolution. Her father, L. W. Graves, was for over four years a member of the House of Delegates, representing Orange and Madison counties. He was one of the leading farmers of Orange County, was president of the Gordonsville National Bank and president of the Charlottesville Lumber Company. Mrs. Spiers' mother died in 1923. To the marriage of Mr. and Mrs. Spiers was born one son, John B., Jr., in 1925.

COL. FRANK P. McCONNELL, prominent banker at Radford, is a native of Alabama, son and grandson of two distinguished citizens of that state, but in his home at Radford is closely associated with that section of Virginia where his earlier ancestors lived for several generations. One of his first ancestors in Southwestern Virginia and on the border country in Eastern Tennessee was John McConnell, who married Martha Campbell. Their son, Major John P. McConnell, was born at Fayetteville, Tennessee, and married Martha Campbell Kennedy. Major John P. McConnell was the great-grandfather of Frank P. McConnell of Radford. Major John P. McConnell's mother was a sister of General Lewis of Virginia.

Felix Grundy McConnell, the grandfather, was born at Nashville, Tennessee, April 1, 1809, and moved to Talladega County, Alabama, in 1834. He rose to prominence as a lawyer, served in both Houses of the Alabama Legislature, and in 1843 was elected to represent the Fourth Alabama District in Congress. He was reelected and died while still a member of Congress at Washington, September 10, 1846. He married in 1835 Elizabeth Jennings Hogan, who was a great-granddaughter of William Jennings, a captain in the Revolutionary war. Felix Grundy McConnell had two daughters, Kathleen and Olivia, who were respectively the first and second wives of Gen. Charles M. Shelley, a brigadier general in the Confederate army and a member of Congress.

Col. William Kennedy McConnell, father of Col. Frank P. McConnell, was born in Talladega County, Alabama, March 25, 1841. He left LaGrange College to join Company B of the Sixteenth Alabama Infantry as a private, was made color bearer, drill master, and later transferred to the Thirtieth Alabama Infantry and participated in a long list of well known battles of the war and became a colonel of infantry in the Confederate service. After the war he spent two years in Mexico, then located at Selma, was appointed commandant of the University of Alabama, for seven years was tax collector of Dallas County, and in 1884 became agent for what is now a branch of the Southern Railway Company at Talladega and served in that capacity until his death, January 16, 1891. He married, May 7, 1868, Martha Ellen Smith, of Columbia, Tennessee, who was educated in the Columbia Female College, graduating with high honors in 1867. She died January 25, 1914. She possessed a decided literary talent and contributed a number of short stories and other articles to magazines. She was active in the Methodist Episcopal Church, South, the United Daughters of the Confederacy and Daughters of the American Revolution. Of her children the oldest is Felix G. McConnell, of Oklahoma City, and Col. Frank P. is the second son. William K., Jr., died in infancy. Dr. Ray M. McConnell became a noted scholar, a graduate of Southern University of Greensboro, Alabama, of Vanderbilt University of Tennessee, and the University of Chicago, took his Master and Doctor of Philosophy degrees at Harvard University, and won a traveling fellowship at Heidelberg, Leipsic and Bonn, Germany, and at the University of Paris, Paris, France. He traveled extensively abroad and was professor of philosophy in Harvard University when he died in June, 1911, being buried in the Professors Plat in Mt. Auburn Cemetery at Cambridge, Massachusetts. The daughter Lena married Capt. Clifton L. Sitton, a captain in the Spanish-American war, who died about 1900, and she is now engaged in missionary work as matron of the Methodist Orphanage at Raleigh, North Carolina.

Col. Frank P. McConnell was born at Union City, Tennessee, July 1, 1870. He attended public and private schools at Selma and Talladega, graduated in 1890 from the Alabama Polytechnic Institute at Auburn, and later attended the Law School at the University of Richmond. At the age of sixteen he became associated with his uncle, Houston Isbell, in the Isbell National Bank, and he was cashier of that institution in 1908, when he married. For several years he was actively associated with a group of banking interests in Oklahoma and Arkansas, and still has large holdings in the banks of those states. In 1911 Colonel McConnell removed to Richmond, Virginia, and became president of the Manchester National Bank, president of the South Richmond Bank and vice president of the Bank of Commerce and Trust. In 1920 he took up with the State Banking Department as state bank examiner, but in 1922 resigned to become associated in the organization of the Peoples Bank of Radford, of which institution he has since been president and cashier and a director. A number of prominent Virginia men are associated with this bank, including Hon. Hal C. Tyler as vice president, Judge R. L. Gardner, vice president, and another vice president is Harry S. Walker. Colonel McConnell is a director in the Radford Real Estate and Insurance Corporation.

He derived his military title from his service of four years as colonel in command of the Third Regiment of the Alabama National Guard. Colonel McConnell is a Royal Arch and Knight Templar and thirty-second degree Scottish Rite Mason, member of Acca Temple of the Mystic Shrine at Richmond, is a past exalted ruler of the B. P. O. Elks, member of the Independent Order of Odd Fellows, and for fifteen years was grand purser of the Kappa Alpha Fraternity. He is a member of the Army and Navy Club of New York. He is a Democrat and an elder in the Presbyterian Church at Radford.

One of the interesting news dispatches published in Richmond, Virginia, newspapers, in the fall of 1908, may be quoted as the introduction to Colonel McConnell's family life: "Culminating a romance which had its origin at Virginia's executive mansion years ago will be the wedding of Miss Belle Norwood Tyler, daughter of ex-Governor and Mrs. J. Hoge Tyler, to Col.

Frank P. McConnell of Talladega, Alabama, at the Tyler home in East Radford, on November 16, 1908. The happy romance had its origin at a notable gathering of distinguished members of the Kappa Alpha fraternity in the executive mansion in 1901. The social affair was a reception given at the mansion to the Kappa Alpha convention and the naval hero, Capt. Richmond Pearson Hobson, by the Governor and his wife. The bride-to-be is one of the most prominent young ladies of Virginia society. She is a fine type of that queenly beauty which made Virginia famous."

Mrs. McConnell as a girl lived at Governor Tyler's country home, Belle Hampton, and was educated by private tutors and governesses at Radford. She is an active member of the Presbyterian Church and is well known in social circles in Southwest Virginia. She is a member of the United Daughters of the Confederacy and Daughters of the American Revolution. Colonel and Mrs. McConnell have one son, J. Hoge Tyler McConnell, now attending the Radford High School.

DANIEL COX SANDS, president of the Middleburg National Bank at Middleburg, Loudoun County, is not only one of the substantial capitalists and loyal and progressive citizens of the historic Old Dominion, but is also doing a splendid service in maintaining Virginia's prestige in the breeding and exploiting of fine track horses. He has in this section of Virginia a splendid landed estate of 3,000 acres, given over primarily to the raising of thoroughbred horses and fine Guernsey cattle.

Mr. Sands was born in New York City, in November, 1875, and is a son of Daniel C. and Martha (Titus) Sands, both likewise natives of the old Empire State of the Union. Daniel C. Sands became a successful manufacturer of woolen goods, but lived virtually retired for many years prior to his death, which occurred in March, 1917, his widow having passed away in February, 1926.

The public schools of New York City afforded Daniel C. Sands his early education, which was there supplemented by his attending Columbia University. After leaving the university he gave two years of service as a civil engineer and he then turned his attention to farm industry and incidentally initiated his activities in the raising of turf horses of the best type. In March, 1908, Mr. Sands established his residence in Loudoun County, Virginia, where he has since continued to give supervision to his valuable landed estate, which he has made one of the finest of American stock farms, and his civic loyalty was further shown when he became, in 1924, one of the organizers and incorporators of the Middleburg National Bank, of which he has since continued the president. He is likewise president of the Goose Creek Lime Grinding Works, and his influence and tangible aid are always to be counted upon in the furtherance of measures and enterprises tending to advance the communal welfare. Mr. Sands is an enthusiast in hunting and also in the game of polo, and at the time of this writing, in 1928, he is the popular master of the Middleburg Hunt Club. In New York City he has membership in the Union League Club and the Riding Club, besides being an influential member of the Turf and Field Club. In his home community in Loudoun County he is a popular figure in both business and social circles, and at Warrenton, Fauquier County, he has membership in the Country Club and the Fauquier Country Club. His political

allegiance is given to the Democratic party, and though he is a
birthright member of the Society of Friends, he attends and
supports the Protestant Episcopal Church in his home town of
Middleburg, his wife being an active communicant of this parish.
In the World war period Mr. Sands was a zealous worker in
behalf of patriotic activities and served as chairman of the
various committees in charge of war work in Loudoun County.

Mr. Sands is a prominent figure in leading turf circles and
has exploited many of his fine horses on the American turf. He
is the owner of "Playfellow," who has made a splendid track
record, and is associated with Admiral Grayson, of the United
States Navy, in the ownership of "My Own," another famous
race horse. On his Loudoun County estate he has a stable of
twenty selected brood mares of the best lineage and type, and
maintains also a herd of purebred Guernsey cattle, representatives of which have been prize winners at local stock shows.
Mr. and Mrs. Sands maintain their residence on their ideal
rural estate four miles north of Middleburg, and the beautiful
home is known for its gracious hospitality.

In October, 1908, was solemnized the marriage of Mr. Sands
and Miss Edith M. Kennedy, daughter of the late David Kennedy, who was born in England and whose wife was born in the
State of New York. David Kennedy was a successful contractor
and builder, and both he and his wife were residents of New
York City at the time of their death. Mr. and Mrs. Sands have
no children.

JOHN JACOB GIESEN, physician and surgeon, in the Hopkins
Building at East Radford, is a native of Southwest Virginia,
and is a man of splendid equipment for his profession. He completed his medical course just in time to go into training and
service with the Government during the World war.

Doctor Giesen was born at Roanoke, Virginia, October 26,
1891, son of Anthony and Emilia (Rossa) Giesen. His father
was born and reared at Buffalo, New York, attended public
schools there and from early manhood worked in and followed
the business of ice manufacturing. About 1890 he became
interested in an ice plant at Roanoke and in 1900 moved to Radford, where he established the Radford Ice Corporation and
was active head until 1928, when he sold the plant to the Central Atlantic States Service Corporation. He has not entirely
retired from business, being associated with his sons in the
automobile business at Radford. He is an active member of the
Lutheran Church, and his wife was also identified with that
church. She was born in Germany and attended school there,
and came to this country with her parents, who located at Baltimore, where she finished her education. She died in 1926. Of
their eight children one died in infancy, and the others are:
Dr. John T.; W. L. A. Giesen, of Radford; Catherine, wife of
H. H. Lowman, of Radford; Dr. Andrew F., now practicing
medicine at Konowa, Oklahoma; Anthony Jr., of Radford;
Arthur R., of Radford; and Virginia, wife of J. L. Sharp, of
Pottsville, Pennsylvania.

John Jacob Giesen attended public schools at Roanoke and
also at Radford, took his preparatory course at St. Albans
Academy and was also in the National Business College at Roanoke. In 1913 he received the A. B. degree from Roanoke College
of Salem and followed that with his professional studies in the
University of Maryland at Baltimore. The university conferred

upon him the M. D. degree in 1918. In the meantime he had enlisted with the 115th Field Hospital, Twenty-ninth Division, and was in training at Fort Oglethorpe, Georgia, and at Camp McClellan, Alabama. On July 1, 1918, he was commisioned a first lieutenant in the Medical Corps, was assigned duty with the Maryland General Hospital and remained there until January 1, 1919.

After leaving the service of the Government Doctor Giesen became a member of the staff of the St. Albans Sanatorium at Radford, and his work was with that institution from June 1, 1919, until April 1, 1925. For two years his health was such that he retired from the active work of his profession, and on June 1, 1927, opened his private offices in the Hopkins Building at East Radford, and a large volume of practice has come to him.

Doctor Giesen is a member of the Grand Chapter of the medical fraternity Chi Zeta Chi, is a member of the Medical Society of Virginia, the Southwest Virginia, Southern and American Associations. He is a past secretary and now president of the Rotary Club, is an Independent Republican, and is president of the council of the Lutheran Church at Radford. He is also affiliated with Virginia May Lodge No. 38, A. F. and A. M., and a lodge of Elks at Baltimore.

Doctor Giesen married at Elkton, Maryland, May 5, 1919, Miss Goldie Mae Miles, of Mathews County, Virginia, where she grew up and attended school. She is a graduate of the Nurses Training School at the Maryland General Hospital. Mrs. Giesen is a member of the Methodist Episcopal Church, South. Her father, James A. Miles, was for many years active in the fish and oyster business in Mathews and Westmoreland counties, and is now retired at Mathews Court House. Her mother died about 1903. The three children of Doctor and Mrs. Giesen are Jane Miles, Ann Elizabeth and John Williams, Jane being a student in the grade schools of Radford. Doctor Giesen is the present commander of Harvey Howe Post No. 30 of the American Legion.

FRANK Y. CALDWELL, city treasurer of Radford, was born in that city, where he is a member of a family that has been long and prominently identified with business and public affairs. In his official career he continues the traditions of public service set by his father.

His father is Milton M. Caldwell, now retired, who was born in Craig County, Virginia, attended public schools and the Virginia Polytechnic Institute at Blacksburg, and in early years was a merchant at Radford. For seventeen years he held the office and performed the duties of clerk of courts and for twelve years was city treasurer. He has lived retired since 1921. His father, George C. Caldwell, served in the Confederate army four years. Milton M. Caldwell married Carrie Yingling, who was born and reared at Radford, attended school there, and was always a devoted member of the Methodist Episcopal Church, South. She died October 24, 1926, and is buried in the East Radford Cemetery. Her parents were George W. and Sallie (Cofer) Yingling. George W. Yingling for many years was employed as a machinist with the Norfolk & Western Railroad. Milton M. Caldwell and wife had five children: Frank Y.; Paul R., a Norfolk & Western Railway employe at Bluefield, West Virginia; Miss S. Lorena, a teacher at Radford; Katherine, widow of T. W. Lawford, and a teacher in the public schools of Radford; and Wilda May, who died in infancy.

Frank Y. Caldwell was born at Radford February 23, 1895, and was educated in the grade and high schools, graduating from high school in 1914. That was followed by four years at the Virginia Military Institute, where he was a member of the class of 1918, but on June 12, 1917, he answered the call to the colors and went for training to Fort Myer, Virginia, for two months, and on August 15, 1917, was commissioned a second lieutenant and transferred to Camp Lee. He remained there until May 25, 1918, when he went overseas with the 317th Infantry, Eightieth Division, in Company F. He was put with the British and French troops south of Calais, France, until August 8, 1918, when he was returned home and given duties in the training camp at Greenville, South Carolina, and Charlotte, North Carolina, and received his honorable discharge at Camp Greene at Charlotte on March 15, 1919.

Mr. Caldwell after his return home engaged in the mercantile business in April, 1920, and on January 1, 1922, began his term of service as city treasurer of Radford. He was reelected to this office in 1925. Mr. Caldwell is a Democrat, member of the Methodist Episcopal Church, South, the Kiwanis Club, and is affiliated with Virginia May Lodge No. 38, A. F. and A. M., East Radford Chapter No 27, Royal Arch Masons, and Harvey Howe Post No. 30 of the American Legion.

He married at Belspring, Virginia, January 9, 1926, Miss Pauline Perfater, who attended public school there and is a graduate of the Radford State Teachers College with the class of 1921. Prior to her marriage she taught in schools at Portsmouth, Virginia, and in Pulaski County. Mrs. Caldwell is a member of the Methodist Episcopal Church, South, the American Legion Auxiliary, and takes a helpful part in the life of her community. She is a daughter of A. T. and Dora (Sifford) Perfater. Her parents reside at East Radford, her father for many years having been a locomotive engineer with the Norfolk & Western Railway. Mr. and Mrs. Caldwell have one son, Frank Y., Jr., born May 3, 1928.

JAMES A. PAINTER is a native of Southwest Virginia, and has given the years of his manhood to merchandising, the real estate business, and in later years to his duties as clerk of the Corporation Court of the city of Radford, where he and his family reside.

He was born in Wythe County, Virginia, August 23, 1875, son of James Bell and Sallie (Gillespie) Painter, and grandson of Isaac Painter, who was a farmer and stock raiser in Wythe County. James Bell Painter grew up in Wythe County, served four years as a Confederate soldier, taking part in many of the great battles of the war, part of the time as a member of the Stonewall Jackson Brigade. After the war he engaged in farming and stock raising, and finally sold his property in Wythe County and moved to a farm in Tazewell County, where he lived until his death. His first wife, Sallie Gillespie, was born and reared in Tazewell County, daughter of Reese Gillespie, who for many years was clerk of the County Court there. Mrs. Sallie Painter attended public schools and private schools in Tazewell County, and was always a member of the Methodist Episcopal Church. She died in 1880. The second wife of James Bell Painter was Mary Jane Davis, of Rural Retreat, Virginia. There were six children by each marriage, those of the first union being: Warren G., of Harrisonburg, Virginia; Jesse H., of Dallas, Texas; Lina Belle, who married Sidney Brown and is deceased; Temple E., of Hopewell, Virginia; James A., of Radford, Virginia, and Charles S., of Kingsport, Tennessee. The children of the second marriage were: Ida, wife of Tyler Witten, of Pearisburg; William L., of Tazewell; Francis Neal, of Bristol, Virginia; Cary, of Bluefield, Virginia; Mrs. Lillian Brown, deceased; and George Whitefield, of Pearisburg.

James A. Painter grew up in Tazewell County on his father's farm and had the advantages of public schools there. His first work after leaving school was clerking in a store at Tazewell for the firm of Britton and Greaver. This experience and that of five or six years with W. W. Jeter, of Pocahontas, Virginia, gave him a fundamental knowledge of business, and he then embarked his experience and capital in a general store at Narrows, Virginia, and was a merchant in that town for ten years. After selling his business he removed to Newport News, lived there about six years and was in the furniture business. On selling out he returned to Southwest Virginia and located at Radford in 1906, and for four years was a furniture merchant, and since then has conducted a real estate business, chiefly operating with his own properties. He is a director of the Peoples Bank of Radford.

Mr. Painter was appointed clerk of the Corporation Court of Radford on January 31, 1910, and has performed the duties of that position consecutively for nineteen years, having been three times elected without opposition. Mr. Painter is a past master of Glencoe Lodge No. 148, A. F. and A. M., member of Royal Arch Chapter No. 27 at Radford, the Independent Order of Odd Fellows, Modern Woodmen of America and the Order of the Mystic Chain. He is a Democrat and a Presbyterian.

He married in Giles County, Virginia, December 2, 1893, Carrie Morrison Priddy. She attended school at Narrows. She is a member of the Methodist Episcopal Church, South, the United Daughters of the Confederacy and the Daughters of the American Revolution, her ancestors having been in Virginia since Colonial times. She is a daughter of Frank Nelson and Melvina (Stanley) Priddy. Her mother's people as well as her father's were Colonial Virginians. Her father spent most of his life as a merchant at Narrows and was a soldier of the Confederacy. Mr. and Mrs. Painter had a family of eight children, two of whom died in infancy. Eileen A., who was educated in the Radford High School, is the wife of B. C. Addington, a commercial traveler living at Bluefield, West Virginia. James Frank Painter was educated in the public schools of Radford, in 1917 enlisted in the navy, and was in training at the Norfolk Navy Yard until honorably discharged because of disability in 1918, and has been more or less an invalid ever since, though for four years he carried on an insurance business and was deputy clerk under his father until 1925. He married Catherine DuBay, of Mount Clemens, Michigan, and they have two children, Jane Morrison, born in 1925, and James F., born in 1927. Miss Mary Belle Painter graduated in 1928 from the Radford High School, Miss Virginia Wilson finished high school work in 1927, Miss Evelyn Elizabeth was a member of the high school class of 1929, and the youngest of the family, Thomas Wesley, is still in high school.

LEO S. HOWARD, city judge of East Radford, is representative
of the younger group of attorneys and citizens of Southwest
Virginia, and his career so far has been in line with the many
distinguished attainments of the Howard family running back
through the various generations.

This is a family connection equally well known in England
and America. The Howards of Virginia were a branch of a
very wealthy family of England, and the Virginia descendants
today are among the claimants to a great estate which for many
years has been a subject of prolonged chancery adjudication,
and in the meantime is held in trust by the Bank of England.
The founder of the Howard family in Montgomery County, Virginia, was a Presbyterian minister who came from England.
At one time the sum of 25,000 pounds, English money, was sent
to New York for the Virginia relatives, and a son of the Presbyterian minister rode all the way on horseback to that city for
the money, but so much time had been consumed in preparations for the journey and the journey itself that the money had
in the meantime been sent back to England.

Judge Howard's grandfather, William Howard, was a merchant, farmer and stock raiser in Pittsylvania and Floyd counties, and he and his wife are buried in the Floyd Court House
Cemetery.

Leo S. Howard was born at Floyd Court House, September
23, 1901, son of B. G. and Katherine (Sutherland) Howard.
His father was born and grew up in Floyd County, attending
public schools and the Virginia Polytechnic Institute and University of Virginia. He has been a member of the bar for
thirty-five years, practiced at Floyd Court House, at Stewart and
Hillsville, Virginia, and has had business in all the courts. For
a number of years he has been president of the Peoples Bank
of Floyd County, and has done a great deal in promoting good
road building in that county. He and his family reside at
Floyd Court House. He is owner of two farms, one comprising
250 acres near the Court House and partly within the corporation limits, and another of 250 acres of blue grass grazing land
on the top of the Blue Ridge Mountains. His wife, Katherine
Sutherland, is a daughter of Capt. W. H. Sutherland, who was
an officer in the Confederate army and served for thirty-six
years as clerk of Carroll County. Mrs. Katherine Howard attended public schools in Carroll County and a girls' school at
Wytheville. She is a member of the United Daughters of the
Confederacy and is active in the Methodist Episcopal Church,
South. There are two sons in the family, B. G. Howard, Jr.,
and Leo S., both of whom have followed the law as a profes-
sion. B. G., Jr., was educated in the Virginia Polytechnic
Institute and Washington and Lee University, is associated in
practice with his father, married Miss Alice K. Smith, of Floyd
Court House, and has two children, Katherine and William
Joseph.

Leo S. Howard graduated in 1919 from the high school at
Floyd Court House, but from August, 1918, had been with the
Students Army Training Corps at the Virginia Polytechnic
Institute until the armistice. For two and a half years he was
a student in Roanoke College, took the three years law course
at Washington and Lee University, graduating in 1925, but was
admitted to the bar in December, 1923. Mr. Howard has been
in practice at East Radford since February, 1926, associated
with the well known attorney Hal C. Tyler, a son of the late

O. A. Ryder, M. D.

Governor Tyler. Mr. Howard in October, 1928, was appointed city judge, and gives most of his time to his judicial functions. He is a member of Floyd Lodge No. 329, A. F. and A. M., is a member of the Knights of the Mystic Chain, the Rotary Club, is a Democrat and a Presbyterian.

He married at Christiansburg, Virginia, January 14, 1929, Miss Evelyn Gerald. Mrs. Howard graduated from the Christiansburg High School, and afterwards attended the Marion Female College, the Lynchburg College, the University of Virginia and the Radford State Teachers College, and was a teacher for about a year before her marriage. She is active in the Christian Church. Her parents are Walter Crockett and Mary (Hawley) Gerald. Her father is one of the leading farmers and stock men at Christiansburg.

OLIVER ALLISON RYDER, physician and surgeon at 115 South Columbus Street, Alexandria, located in that city for private practice shortly after the close of his military service as a medical officer during the World war.

Doctor Ryder is a descendant of Isaac Ryder, who was given a grant of land from the King of England in Orange County, New York. His descendant, Oliver Ryder, was born in Rockland County, New York, in 1827, was a successful building contractor, and died in 1917. He married a Miss Van Voort, of Holland Dutch ancestry. Their son, Rev. Oliver Ryder, was born at Fort Montgomery, New York, May 5, 1860, and on account of his health when a boy was sent to Yadkin College in Yadkin, North Carolina, where he graduated. He became a minister of the Methodist Episcopal Church, South, holding pastorates in North Carolina and Virginia, and died at Norfolk May 21, 1912. He married Martha Allison Russell, who was born in Union County, North Carolina, January 26, 1864.

Oliver Allison Ryder, one of a family of three sons, was born at Siler City, Chatham County, North Carolina, September 3, 1887. He was educated in private schools, graduated from the Richmond High School in 1906, was clerk in the Richmond office of the Chesapeake & Ohio Railway for three years, for two years attended the University of Richmond, and in 1913 took his M. D. degree from the Medical College of Virginia. He had his internship in the Chesapeake & Ohio Railway Hospital at Huntington, West Virginia, and in 1914 located for practice at Cambria, Virginia.

Soon after America declared war on Germany he was commissioned a first lieutenant in the Army Medical Corps, was called to active duty September 20, 1917, and for six months was in the United States Army X-ray School at Richmond, one month in the Officers' Training School at Fort Oglethorpe, two months at Camp Forest, Georgia, and one month near Allentown, Pennsylvania. He was himself in a hospital for two months recovering from appendicitis, and was then put in charge of the X-ray Department of the Attending Surgeons' Office at Washington. On May 1, 1919, he was commissioned a captain.

After leaving the army Doctor Ryder did work in the New York Children's Hospital, and during the summer of 1919 was in the New York Post Graduate School specializing in children's diseases and X-ray work. In his general practice at Alexandria since October, 1920, Doctor Ryder has given the community the benefit of his unusual training and early experience. He is

a member of the American X-Ray Society, Medical Society of
Virginia, Northern Virginia and District of Columbia, and
Alexandria Medical Societies, and the Southern and American
Medical Associations.

Doctor Ryder is a member of Andrew Jackson Lodge No.
20, A. F. and A. M., Mount Vernon Chapter No. 14, Royal
Arch Masons, Virginia Consistory No. 2 of the Scottish Rite at
Alexandria, and is also a Shriner. He has affiliations with the
Independent Order of Odd Fellows, Knights of Pythias, B. P. O.
Elks, Modern Woodmen of America and Woodmen of the World.

He married at Portsmouth, Virginia, October 8, 1921, Miss
Anne Elizabeth Potts, daughter of Rev. Reginald H. and Anne
(Moore) Potts. Her father was at one time pastor of the Monu-
mental Methodist Episcopal Church, South, at Lynchburg. Mrs.
Ryder was a graduate of Randolph-Macon Woman's College of
Lynchburg. She died at Alexandria April 14, 1927. Mr. and
Mrs. Ryder had two children, Oliver Allison Ryder IV, born
December 12, 1922, and Oscar Potts Ryder, born June 18, 1925.

ROY WATSON ARTHUR, city manager of Radford, came to his
present position after a long and varied experience with some
of the great industrial organizations operating in Virginia. He
possesses a great knowledge of technical details, has an able
executive record, and has done a great deal of valuable work
for the community of Radford.

Mr. Arthur was born at Motleys in Pittsylvania County,
Virginia, November 6, 1878, son of William C. and Theresa Watson (Laughon) Arthur. The Arthur family came from England
about the time of the Revolution. William C. Arthur was born
and reared in Bedford County, attended private and public
schools there, and was a Confederate soldier in the war between
the states. For many years he was an employe of the Southern
Railway Company, both in construction work and in train operation. He died in January, 1925, and is buried at Lynchs Station.
His wife, who died in August, 1926, and is buried in the same
place, was born and reared in Campbell County, near what is
known as Lynchs Station. Both she and her husband were
active members of the Methodist Episcopal Church, South.
The Laughon family has been in Virginia for a number of
generations and some of her ancestors were in the Revolution.
Her father was John Edward Laughon. William C. Arthur
and wife had a family of seven children: Ernest L., deceased;
William K., deceased; James S.; Lillian, who died in infancy;
Roy W.; Esther B.; and Lizzie M.

Roy Watson Arthur acquired his early education in the public schools of Campbell County, attended the Piedmont Business
College at Lynchburg and the University College of Medicine
at Richmond for two and a half years. Ill health caused him to
leave medical school and give up the training for a professional
career. Soon afterward he found the opening opportunity that
brought him many successive relationships with the great mining and industrial organizations of the state. For three years
he was employed as cashier of the Cranes Nest Coal & Coke Company at Toms Creek. From 1906 to 1914 he was with the Lane
Brothers Company, contractors of Alta Vista and their subsidiaries companies, part of the time in clerical duties, later in
charge of operations. He left that to go with the Boyd-Smith
Mines, Incorporated, at Mineral, Virginia, and when these properties were sold to the Dupont Company Mr. Arthur remained

and eventually was made superintendent of operations, serving in that capacity until 1919, when he was transferred to the Dupont plant at Hopewell, Virginia, becoming assistant power supervisor and later shipping supervisor during the dismantling of the plant. He was at Hopewell until 1922 and for two years remained there with the Gibson Appliance Company as manager. For about a year Mr. Arthur was in the real estate business and in 1925 accepted the call to Radford as city manager, in charge of the practical operations of the city government.

Mr. Arthur is interested in two farms, one in Campbell County and the other in Louisa County. He is a member of Orange Chapter No. 47, Royal Arch Masons, the Kiwanis Club, is a Democrat and a Methodist.

He married near Christiansburg, Virginia, March 16, 1907, Miss Verna Mae Pelter, of Montgomery County. Mrs. Arthur was educated in public schools, attended the Concord State Teachers College at Athens, West Virginia, and was a teacher before her marriage, in Montgomery County. Mrs. Arthur is a member of the Methodist Episcopal Church, South, the United Daughters of the Confederacy and the Woman's Club. Her parents were J. E. and Josephine (Childress) Pelter. Her father was a Confederate soldier and after the war engaged in farming and stock raising. He had acquired part of his early education in the University of Virginia. He always took a keen interest in politics. He died in 1874 and is buried in Franklin County, Virginia. Her mother passed away in 1917 and is buried in Montgomery County. Mr. and Mrs. Arthur have a family of three children, Audrey Mae, Lucille Pelter and Roy William. Audrey was educated in high school in Louisa County and Hopewell, graduated in 1929 from the Radford State Teachers College and is teacher of English and mathematics at War, West Virginia. Lucille attended school in Louisa County, the high school at Hopewell and Radford, and is a member of the class of 1930 in the Radford State Teachers College. The son Roy is a seventh grade pupil at Radford.

GORDON McNEELY ROBERTS is one of the active business leaders of the Radford community of Southwestern Virginia, active manager of the M. L. Harrison Tie & Lumber Company.

He was born at Stoneville, North Carolina, March 16, 1885, of old Southern antecedents and a son of William M. and Louise (McNeely) Roberts. His grandfather, George W. Roberts, was a farmer in North Carolina and married a Miss Strong. William M. Roberts was born and reared in North Carolina, attended private schools and spent his active career as a farmer. He died in 1923 and is buried in the McNeely Cemetery. By an unusual coincidence he was born, was married and was buried on the 14th of April. His wife, Louise McNeely, was born and reared near Stoneville, North Carolina, and attended private schools in Caswell County. She also died in 1923. Her father, Rev. George W. McNeely, was a minister of the Primitive Baptist denomination, preaching in North Carolina and in Southwestern Virginia. The children of William M. Roberts and wife included one that died in infancy; Jesse Howard, who died in Texas in 1910; Myrtle, wife of T. P. Poole, of Stoneville, North Carolina; and Gordon M.

Gordon M. Roberts attended public schools in North Carolina, the Massey Business College at Richmond and after leaving college in 1906 spent two years with the Norfolk & Western Rail-

way Company as a clerk. Since 1908 he has been in the cross
tie and lumber business, associated with the M. L. Harrison
Tie & Lumber Company. He started as bookkeeper for the organization and since 1912 has been general manager of this
business at the Radford headquarters. He is financially interested in the company and is also a director of the Taylor-Col-
quitt Company of Spartanburg, South Carolina, and is interested in several other business enterprises in Southwestern Virginia.

Mr. Roberts is a past president of the Radford Rotary Club,
is a Thirty-second degree Scottish Rite Mason and Shriner,
being a member of Kazim Temple at Roanoke. He is a Democrat, and is on the board of deacons of the Presbyterian Church.
He married at Radford November 26, 1912, Miss Willie Trolinger Harvey. She was educated by private instructors and
in Hollins College, and is a member of the Presbyterian Church.
She is a daughter of Lewis and Bettie (Trolinger) Harvey,
residents of Radford, her father being a well-to-do farmer and
stock raiser. There were eight children in the Harvey family: Mrs. Roberts; Robert B. Harvey, of Radford; Henry M.;
James of Bluefield, West Virginia; Margaret M., wife of Emory
Mitchell, of Bluefield, West Virginia; Lieutenant Fred who was
killed in action in France during the World war; Miss Elizabeth and Miss Frances, both of Radford. Mr. and Mrs. Roberts
have two daughters, Margaret McNeely and Bettie Gordon.

JAMES SAMUEL BRANCH, SR., a descendant of Col. John
Branch, governor of two states, North Carolina and Florida,
was a native of North Carolina, became a well known figure in
the lumber business in the southeastern states, and Mrs. Branch
and some of her children reside at Norfolk, her home being at
643 West Thirty-fourth Street.

Mr. Branch was born at Enfield, Halifax County, North Caro-
lina, April 17, 1863, and died at Florence, South Carolina, Janu-
ary 26, 1917. He was a son of John Richard and Josephine
(Hunter) Branch. His father was a merchant and planter at
Enfield, North Carolina, and a soldier in the Confederate army.
Mrs. Josephine Branch is now living in Rocky Mount, North
Carolina. Her father, Doctor Hunter, was a Florida planter.
Col. John Branch, governor of North Carolina and Florida and
also a member of the United States Senate from Florida, was
the great-grandfather of the late James Samuel Branch.

James Samuel Branch was a boy when his father died and
he early assumed responsibilities in assisting his mother in the
management of the home farm. He was educated at Wake Forest Preparatory School and Bingham College in North Carolina.
On leaving the farm he became associated with the Cape Fear
Lumber Company at Wilmington, North Carolina, as a lumber
inspector, and after the plant was burned in 1906 he went with
the Camp Lumber Manufacturing Company at Marion, South
Carolina. He retired from business about six years before his
death. He attended the Methodist Church, was a Democrat,
and Mrs. Branch is an active member of the Baptist Church.

Mr. Branch married at Franklin, Virginia, in August, 1893,
Alice Eliza Wiggins, who was reared and educated at Suffolk,
Virginia. Her parents were John Bowers and Mary Sarah
(Parker) Wiggins, of North Carolina and Virginia. Her father
was a merchant. Her great-grandfather, Thomas Oliver, was
sent by the King of England on a special mission to the Colonies.

Her uncle, Capt. Irvin C. Wills, was an officer in the Confederate army. Mrs. Branch's brother, Jasper L. Wiggins, is now in his third term as mayor of Edenton, North Carolina, and also served in the Spanish American War. Mr. and Mrs. Branch had four children. The son John Richard, now connected with the Texas Asphalt Company at Richmond, Virginia, was in France two years during the World war and is a member of the Masonic fraternity. Samuel C. Branch, an employe of the city of Norfolk in the water department, is a member of the Masonic Order, married Elsie Burns and has a daughter, Norma. Linwood O. B. Branch, in the service of the Seaboard Air Line Railway, was for four years, 1922-26, city assistant purchasing agent, served eighteen months in the navy during the World war, and by his marriage to Iris Godfrey has a son, Linwood O. B., Jr. James S. Branch, Jr., the youngest of the four sons of Mrs. Branch, was secretary to Col. Charles Borland in the city safety department, served as a first lieutenant in the Norfolk Home Guard, and is now connected with the Virginian Railway.

WALTER ADGATE WARFIELD, M. D. The City of Alexandria, metropolis of Arlington County, has its due quota of able and successful physicians and surgeons, and among the number is Doctor Warfield, whose technical skill and personal popularity have conspired to gain to him a substantial and important general practice and give him rank among the leading representatives of his profession in his native city and county.

Doctor Warfield, who maintains his office at 908 Cameron Street and his residence at 910 that thoroughfare, was born in Alexandria on the 4th of February, 1884, and is a son of Frank and Cora M. (Smith) Warfield, the former of whom was born at Alexandria and the latter in the City of Richmond, this state. Frank Warfield was reared and educated in Alexandria and in his native city he has been actively identified with the drug business during virtually his entire career, as has also his uncle, Edgar, who is still actively engaged in this line of enterprise, though he celebrated in 1928 the eighty-seventh anniversary of his birth, his being the distinction of having been a gallant young soldier of the Confederacy in the Civil war.

In the Alexandria High School Doctor Warfield was graduated as a member of the class of 1898, and thereafter he was a student in the National School of Pharmacy, Washington, D. C., until he decided to broaden the scope of his studies and prepare himself for the medical profession. With this ambition in view he attended the George Washington University for three years, then entered the medical department of the University of the South at Sewanee, Tennessee, and in that institution he was graduated in 1905. In the year that thus marked his reception of the degree of Doctor of Medicine he opened an office in Alexandria, and here he has continued in successful general practice during the intervening period of nearly a quarter of a century, save for the interval of his service on the Mexican border during the troubles that there occurred in 1916-17. In this military service the Doctor went forth as a member of a Virginia regiment in which he was accorded the rank of first lieutenant in the Medical Corps, this rank having been retained by him after the regiment was mustered into the United States Army, from which he resigned and was accorded honorable discharge in January, 1917. The Doctor has mem-

bership in the American Medical Association, the Virginia State
Medical Society, the District of Columbia Medical Society and
the Alexandria Medical Society. His political allegiance is given
to the Democratic party, he and his wife are communicants of
the Protestant Episcopal Church, he is affiliated with the Kappa
Sigma college fraternity, and is a member of the Belle Haven
Country Club. His home in Alexandria is one of the beautiful
places of the city, and he maintains also a fine summer home on
Belmont Bay, where he erected a beautiful residence, which
with its surrounding estate of more than 500 acres makes the
place rank well with historic Mount Vernon in beauty. The
ancestral lineage of Doctor Warfield traces back to both England and Sweden.

On the 19th of March, 1919, was solemnized the marriage of
Doctor Warfield and Miss Ruth Barkley, who was born at Weldon, North Carolina, the daughter of James E. and Sarah
(Parker) Barkley. Her father was born at Tallahassee, Florida,
while her mother was born at the "Meadows" in Northampton
County, North Carolina. Doctor and Mrs. Warfield are prominent figures in the representative social and cultural circles
of their home city, and both the city and country homes are
known for their gracious hospitality under the regime of Mrs.
Warfield as the popular chatelaine thereof.

HON. JAMES M. BARKER. Whether considered from the
standpoint of his professional attainments or from the viewpoint
of progressive citizenship, Hon. James M. Barker is a young lawyer of pronounced character. For four years, from 1923 until
1927, he occupied the office of commonwealth's attorney of Washington County, and established a record for sterling accomplishments that would have assured his retention in that capacity as
long as he desired, but, preferring to return to private practice,
he refused to stand for reelection. He now has an excellent practice at Abingdon, where he is a prominent factor in all civic
movements and enterprises.

Mr. Barker was born at Turkey Cove, Lee County, Virginia,
November 6, 1888, and is a son of John B. and Susan (Slemp)
Barker, and a grandson of Charles Barker, a native of Washington County, who for many years was engaged in planting in Lee
County, where his death occurred. John B. Barker was born in
Lee County, where he received a public school education, and
during the war between the states enlisted in the Confederate
army, with which he fought valiantly until the close of the
struggle. He then returned to his home, where he followed the
life of a planter until his death in March, 1926. In addition to being a successful agriculturist he was active in Democratic politics, and was a man of high character and considerable influence
in his community. Mrs. Barker, who was also born in Lee
County, died in 1925. She was a daughter of Hugh Alley Slemp,
who had a plantation at Turkey Cove, and was a first cousin of
Congressman Slemp, the elder, and a second cousin of Hon. Bas-
com Slemp, for many years a member of Congress and subsequently private secretary to President Coolidge.

James M. Barker was given excellent educational advantages
in his youth, attending the grammar and high schools of Cleveland, Virginia, and Emory and Henry College of Emory, this
state, from which he was graduated with the degree of Bachelor
of Arts in 1910, winning the Robertson medal for oratory. Mr.
Barker has always been a good speaker, and is well known for

his work on the stump during political campaigns, his services as a speaker also being in constant demand on all public occasions. After leaving Emory and Henry College he pursued his professional studies at the University of Virginia, from which he was graduated with the degree of Bachelor of Laws in 1913, and immediately entered upon the practice of his profession at Hazard, Kentucky. While there he had a large practice and also served as a member of the school board. At the end of six years, during the greater part of which time he was attorney for the Virginia Iron and Coke Company, doing their title and abstract work, he moved to Abingdon, which has since been his home and the scene of his really remarkable success. Soon after his arrival at Abingdon he entered Democratic politics, and in 1923 was elected commonwealth's attorney for Washington County, an office in which he established a record of securing about 90% of convictions out of all persons indicted, being at all times an active, vigorous and fearless prosecutor. He was urged to accept the nomination for reelection in 1927, but his private practice had grown to such proportions he felt that he owed it his entire attention. He still is a leading member of the Democratic party, was manager for the national committee in Washington County during the last presidential election, and on several occasions has been a delegate to congressional conventions. He maintains offices at Abingdon, and is a member of the Virginia Bar Association. Mr. Barker is active in all matters pertaining to the welfare and advancement of his community, and he and his family are members of the Methodist Episcopal Church, South.

On June 3, 1916, Mr. Barker was united in marriage with Miss Olletha May St. John, of Washington County, daughter of D. S. and Annie St. John, members of old and distinguished Virginia families, and residents of Washington County, where Mr. St. John is engaged in extensive operations as a planter. Mrs. Barker was educated at Martha Washington College, Abingdon, and is active in club circles at Abingdon, and in the various charities of the Methodist Episcopal Church, South. Mr. and Mrs. Barker are the parents of two children: James M., Jr., born February 16, 1917; and Joseph Kelly, born November 10, 1919.

JOSEPH A. McGUIRE, surgeon, founder and proprietor of the Norton Hospital at Norton in Wise County, has enjoyed a distinguished service in his profession for over a quarter of a century. During that time he has lived in his native locality of Southwest Virginia, and for some years also practiced on the other side of the state line in West Virginia.

Doctor McGuire was born at Cedar Bluff, Tazewell County, Virginia, March 17, 1876, son of James M. and Maggie (Hurt) McGuire, and grandson of James McGuire. James M. McGuire was born in 1839, was a farmer and merchant, and died in 1893. His wife, Maggie Hurt, was born in 1857.

Dr. Joseph A. McGuire is a graduate of Emory and Henry College, taking the Bachelor of Science degree there in 1896. He was graduated in medicine from the University of Virginia in 1900 and began practice in Wise County. After four years he went to Texas, and for six years made his home at Dallas, where he enjoyed a favorable professional record. In 1910 he located at Princeton, West Virginia, and in connection with his private practice became one of the promoters of the Virginian General Hospital and served as surgeon for the Virginian Railway.

Doctor McGuire disposed of his hospital and other professional interests at Princeton in 1920 and, locating at Norton,
Virginia, erected the Norton Hospital. This is a three-story
brick structure, with a thirty-five bed capacity, and in its general
equipment comprises practically every facility found in a modern
standard hospital. Doctor McGuire since its founding has been
manager of the hospital and chief of its surgical staff.

An honor that is significant of his high standing in the surgical profession of Southwest Virginia came with his appointment
as a member of the Virginia State Board of Health. He is a
member of the Wise County Medical Society, Medical Society of
Virginia, American Medical Association, Southern and Clinch
Valley Medical Associations. Doctor McGuire is a member of the
Kiwanis Club, is a Knight Templar Mason and Shriner, member
of the Elks, and is a Methodist.

He married, June 5, 1907, Miss Gertrude Flanary, who was
born at Wise Court House February 26, 1885. Her father, C. F.
Flanary, was a business man and state senator of Virginia, and
died in 1910. Doctor and Mrs. McGuire's children were: Joseph
A., Jr., born September 14, 1909, and died in 1918; and Ruth
Flanary, born October 23, 1912.

ROBERT SWANSON KYLE, M. D. Prominent among the leading members of the younger generation of physicians and surgeons of Wise County is Robert Swanson Kyle, M. D. who is engaged in the successful practice of his profession at Big Stone
Gap. Prior to taking up the active duties of his calling he prepared himself thoroughly, having a full realization of the responsibilities as well as the opportunities devolving upon the
devotees of medicine and surgery, and has continued to be a
faithful student of his vocation, with the result that he is rapidly
becoming one of the skilled practitioners of his section.

Doctor Kyle was born in Carroll County, Virginia, June 14,
1898, and is a son of S. D. and Mary J. (Howard) Kyle. The
Kyle family is of Scotch origin and came to America at an early
date, having been for many years well known in Carroll County,
where was born Madison Kyle, the grandfather of Doctor Kyle.
Madison Kyle was a successful planter of his locality and an active Democrat, as well as a devout member of the Methodist
Episcopal Church, South. S. D. Kyle, the father of Doctor Kyle,
was born in Carroll County, where he received a public school
education, and as a young man adopted the vocation of planter,
which he has followed with industry and success to the present.
He is a Democrat without political aspirations, and he and his
wife are members of the Methodist Episcopal Church, South, in
the work of which both are active.

Robert Swanson Kyle was graduated from Woodlawn High
School in Carroll County in 1917, following which he was a
student in William and Mary College for two years, and then
enrolled as a medical student in the Medical College of Virginia,
Richmond. He was graduated from that institution as a member
of the class of 1923, receiving the degree of Doctor of Medicine,
and served his interneship of one year at the Lewis-Gale Hospital, Roanoke. In 1924 he commenced the practice of his profession at Galax, Virginia, where he remained for two years, and
then settled permanently at Big Stone Gap, where he has since
built up an excellent practice in general medicine and surgery.
Combined with his skill and learning is a pleasing personality,
which has made him many friends, and in addition to his regu-

lar practice he is acting as medical examiner for all of the leading life insurance companies represented at Big Stone Gap. He is a member of the Wise County Medical Society, the Virginia Medical Society and the American Medical Association, and as a fraternalist belongs to Clinch Valley Blue Lodge, A. F. and A. M., and the Phi Beta Pi fraternity. He is a Democrat in his political convictions and a member of the Methodist Episcopal Church. As one of the rising young men of his community he takes an active part in all worthy civic movements, and during the World war attended the Army Students Training Camp.

In June, 1926, Doctor Kyle was united in marriage with Miss Vera Sue Hampton, of Grayson County, Virginia, a member of an old and distinguished Virginia family and a daughter of Kemper and Annie Hampton, residents of Grayson County, where Mr. Hampton is a leading figure in the lumber industry. Mrs. Kyle, a woman of superior attainments and accomplishments, was educated at Martha Washington College and the Atlanta Conservatory of Music of Atlanta, Georgia. She is a leader in the club and social life of Big Stone Gap and an active member of the Methodist Episcopal Church. Doctor and Mrs. Kyle are the parents of one daughter, Mary Ann, who was born March 13, 1927.

ANTHONY GIESEN has for years been one of the leaders in business and public affairs in the community of Radford, where he is president of A. Giesen & Sons.

Mr. Giesen was born at Buffalo, New York, November 28, 1869, son of Andrew F. and Katherine (Nobb) Giesen. His parents were natives of Germany, and on coming to the United States in 1845 settled in Buffalo, and in 1888 moved to Baltimore, Maryland, where both of them are buried. After the death of the father the widowed mother spent her last years at Roanoke. There were fourteen children in the family, and twelve of them grew up: Mary, John, Anthony, Adam, three deceased sons, Andrew, Conrad and George, Annie, Gertrude, and three other children are deceased, Jacob, Katherine and Christine.

Anthony Giesen attended public schools in Buffalo and learned the machinist's trade there. He followed the trade of machinist with various companies and organizations until 1901, in which year he established an ice factory and bottling plant at Radford. He has been prominently identified with the commercial life of the city ever since. In 1928 the ice plant was sold, but the bottling business is still carried on, making a specialty of the manufacture and distribution of the King Cola drinks. Mr. Giesen branched out into another line in 1923 when he established A. Giesen & Sons, automobile dealers, having the distribution over this locality for the Chrysler and Plymouth cars. The company owns and operates a modern garage and shop, with repair, oil and gas service. Mr. Giesen has numerous other investments in the city and for a number of years was an active stockholder in the Peoples Bank. He owns local real estate.

Both he and his sons are popular citizens and take a keen interest in local politics. Mr. Giesen was for two and a half terms a member of the City Council. In the last election he ran for city commissioner, and in spite of the fact that he was away from the city during the campaign, he was defeated by only eleven votes. Mr. Giesen is a member of the Independent Order of Odd Fellows, B. P. O. Elks, Improved Order of Red Men, Modern Woodmen of America. He is a Republican and for many years was a member of the council of the Lutheran Church.

He married at Baltimore, Maryland, July 19, 1892, Miss Emelie Rossa, of Baltimore. She was born and spent her early years in West Poland, being sixteen years of age when her parents came to America and located at Baltimore. She regularly attended the Lutheran Church, but was all in all devoted to her home and children. She died August 20, 1926, and is buried in the Radford Cemetery. Her parents were Carl and Elizabeth Rossa, who settled at Baltimore in 1887, and both are buried in the Forest Lawn Cemetery of that city. Her father was an employe of the Baltimore & Ohio Railroad Company.

Mr. and Mrs. Giesen were the parents of eight children, one of whom died in infancy. The oldest son is Dr. John J. Giesen, a well known physician at Radford. William L. A. Giesen, associated with his father in the A. Giesen & Sons, is an aviator, owning his plane at Cooks field, and married Miss Grace French, of Radford. The daughter Katherine is the wife of H. H. Lowman, of Radford, and has two children, Robert Anthony and Rebecca. Dr. Andrew Giesen was educated in Roanoke College, spent one year in the University of Virginia and finished his medical studies in the University of Oklahoma, and is now practicing in that state. He married Virginia Vaughan, of Radford, and has a son, Andrew F., Jr. Anthony G. Giesen attended high school at Radford, graduated from Roanoke College in 1925, is secretary and treasurer of A. Giesen & Sons, and is one of the prominent young business men of the city, being a Rotarian, a member of the Pi Kappa Phi and Modern Woodmen of America. Arthur Rossa Giesen, the next son, graduated from the Virginia Military Institute in 1927, holds a commission as second lieutenant in the Reserve Officers Training Corps, and is with his father and brothers in the automobile business. The youngest child, Virginia Gertrude, is the wife of Jack Lee Sharp, who is connected with the coal industry at Pottsville, Pennsylvania.

HENRY C. BOLLING. Occupying a position of prominence in his profession in Wise County, and a specialist in real estate and corporation law at Norton, Virginia, Henry C. Bolling is recognized as one of the ablest younger members of the bar in active practice in Southwest Virginia. He worthily bears an old and nationally distinguished family name, one that is linked to centuries of American history and to Virginia's earliest Colonial settlements. From the founding of Jamestown in 1607 has come down the beautiful story of Pocahontas, one that still thrills the school children over the entire country, and a romantic story that is seldom in after life entirely forgotten. The Bollings of Wise County are in the ninth generation of descent from Pocahontas, who became the wife of the Virginia planter, John Rolfe, and was the grandmother of the maiden espoused by Robert Bolling, the only Englishman by that name to come to America, and from whom all the Bollings in America have sprung. Henry C. Bolling's direct line of descent is traced to the Bolling who married Martha, sister of President Thomas Jefferson, while the John Randolphs of Virginia were also kindred.

Henry C. Bolling was born at Flat Gap, Wise County, Virginia, September 21, 1902, son of George Washington and Ellen (Kiser) Bolling, and grandson of Amos Bolling and of Abednego

Kiser. The maternal grandfather was a native of Virginia but of German parentage. At one time he was an extensive planter in Russell County, and was a soldier in the Confederate army during the Civil war. The paternal grandfather, Amos Bolling, was born at Wytheville, Virginia, and from there came to the Big Sandy River in Wise County, where he owned much land and operated large plantations before the war between the states. He was active in the Democratic party, served in local offices and with his family belonged to the Baptist Church.

George Washington Bolling, father of Attorney Bolling, has practically spent his entire life at Flat Gap, where he was born and where he has always had important business interests. For many years he was the leading merchant at Flat Gap, and now gives attention ond oversight to agricultural affairs. He is a Confederate veteran of the Civil war, and has always been active in Democratic politics in Wise County, and a supporter of the Baptist Church. He married Miss Ellen Kiser, who also survives, and they had a family of five sons and three daughters born to them, Henry C. being sixth in order of birth. All survive except the eldest, Pearl, who was the wife of Floyd Caldwell, of Kentucky, and Mary, the fourth child, who died in infancy; Samuel A., the eldest son, who served on the military police force at Camp Lee, Petersburg, Virginia, during the World war, resides at Esserville, Virginia, and is deputy sheriff of Wise County; Rufus A. and Walter D. who are in the Government mail service and lives at Flat Gap; Ethel E., who is the wife of Will Riddle, of Jenkins, Kentucky; and Luther, who resides with his parents. Another highly considered close relative is that beautiful and gracious lady, Mrs. Woodrow Wilson, formerly Bolling, with similar descent from Pocahontas.

After completing his course in the Flat Gap High School Henry C. Bolling attended the Virginia State College at Radford for a time and then taught school in Wise County for five months. Even then he had commenced to cherish an ambition to study for the law, but circumstances were not favorable just then and he bravely turned his attention in another direction and accepted a clerkship in the store of the Blackwood Coal & Coke Company at Blackwood in Wise County, and three and a half years later was advanced to the position of store superintendent, in which capacity he continued with the company for two years longer. During this time, in addition to attending to his business duties most satisfactorily, he had advanced himself intellectually by taking correspondence courses in business administration, photo and play writing, business english, and business psychology, and when he resigned the position with the Blackwood Company, which he had won and retained through personal merit, it was in order to enter the University of Richmond to secure higher educational advantages. There also he neglected no opportunities, during his first year attending classes in general literature in the evening and law classes during the daytime, necessarily making rapid progress through such diligence, and subsequently spent two years as a student of law in the University of Richmond and a general review course on all the subjects of law at the University of Virginia. On passing his bar examination in June, 1927, Mr. Bolling located at Norton, Virginia, as a general law practitioner, and has made real estate and corporation law a specialty. His unusual legal talent and his thorough knowledge have been recognized and he has a satisfactory number of important clients throughout the city and county already showing

confidence in his professional judgment. He is a member of the
Wise County and the Virginia State Bar Associations, and a
member of the Commercial Law League of America.

Mr. Bolling married at Norton, Virginia, February 29, 1925,
Miss Nell Elizabeth Mann, daughter of Robert L., and Ellen
(Osdorne) Mann, the former of whom is interested in the furni-
ture business at Norton. The Mann family, of which Governor
Mann of Virginia is also a member, is an old and distinguished
one of the state. Mrs. Bolling is a graduate of the Norton High
School, an active member of the Methodist Episcopal Church,
South, in which he is a Sunday school teacher, and has a wide
and appreciative social circle in her native city. Mr. Bolling be-
longs to the Masonic fraternity and the Modern Woodmen of
America, and is very active in Democratic political circles.

HON. EMBREE W. POTTS.   Among the men of notable professional achievement at Abingdon, Virginia, none are held in
higher personal regard than Hon. Embree W. Potts, a leader
of her bar and formerly judge of the Juvenile and Domestic
Relations Court of Washington County. Additionally, he has
long been an influential factor in Democratic politics in Washington County, and both in public affairs and professional effort is numbered with the worth-while citizens of Southwest
Virginia.

Judge Potts was born at Gainesville, Texas, October 21,
1886, son of Hugh Frank and Lura (Hagy) Potts. His paternal
ancestry came from North Carolina and his maternal ancestry
from Virginia, but during the life of the paternal grandfather
the Potts family removed to Alabama, and in that state the late
Hugh Frank Potts was born and reared. Later he became established at Gainesville, Texas, as a banker and merchant, and
he is credited with being one of the early clear-headed business
men to make practical the idea of chain-store merchandising.
He was a faithful supporter of the Methodist Episcopal Church,
South, and was a member of the Masonic fraternity. He married Miss Lura Hagy, whose father, Judge Pleasant Hagy, and
whose grandfather, Martin Hagy, were both born in Washington
County, Virginia. The latter was an extensive planter at one
time, and a member of the Presbyterian Church.

Judge Pleasant Hagy, maternal grandfather of Judge Potts,
was a man of remarkable character, and the occurrences of his
eventful life linked him with both Virginia and Texas. Early in
the war between the states he enlisted in the Confederate army,
in an organization called the Glade Springs Rifles, in Washington County, Virginia, in which he proved the possession of soldierly qualities including daring, which probably brought about
his capture by a Federal force. Shortly afterward, however, he
was exchanged, when he made his way to Texas and reenlisted
there and served until the close of the conflict as captain of his
company. He then joined the Texas Rangers and assisted with
that brave organization in preserving peace and safety on the
frontier. Some years later he lead important land surveys over
the country, and still later was called to the Circuit bench, because of his upright character and sound judicial qualifications.
Until the close of his life he was active also in Democratic political circles in Cooke and other counties of Texas.

Embree W. Potts received his early educational training in
the public schools of Gainesville. In 1903 he was graduated from
the Webb School at Bellbuckle, Tennessee, and later entered

Vanderbilt University at Nashville, from which he was graduated in 1908 with his A. B. degree, continuing in the study of
law. While there Mr. Potts was not only a satisfactory student
and unusually proficient in many of his studies, but took an active interest in the Delta Kappa Epsilon Greek letter fraternity,
and in such interests as represented by the Commodore Club, of
which he was made president and also president of the Senior
Class.

Upon leaving Vanderbilt University Mr. Potts entered upon
the practice of law at Abingdon, Virginia. In the years that
have followed he has built up a large civil and corporation practice, has taken an important part in notable cases of litigation
and has won legal victories that have brought him well deserved
professional distinction. He was appointed the first judge of the
Juvenile and Domestic Relations Court in Washington County,
and served three years, but then retired in order to resume his
private practice.

In 1915 Judge Potts married Miss Victoria Ayers Eaton, of
Bristol, Virginia, daughter of A. B. and Ann J. Eaton, the late
Mr. Eaton having been a prominent business man at Bristol and
Big Stone Gap for many years. Mrs. Potts is a niece of Attorney-General Rufus A. Ayers of Virginia, and a direct descendant of Governor Wingfield, the first governor of the Virginia
colony. She was educated in the schools of Bristol and at Sullins
College, is a member of the D. A. R., and is interested in the social life at Abingdon. Judge and Mrs. Potts have one daughter
and one son, Mary Victoria and Embree William, Jr., aged respectively ten and eight years.

Judge Potts grew up under Democratic political training, and
old party principles have always governed his convictions and
received the approval of his judgment. He has served as a member of the Sinking Fund Committee of Washington County and
on the Abingdon City Council. He belongs to the Virginia State
Bar Association and is a Knight Templar Mason and a Shriner,
and is a past master of his lodge at Abingdon, and belongs also
to the order of Odd Fellows and to the Civitan Club, of which he
is a past president. Both the Judge and Mrs. Potts are active
members of the Methodist Episcopal Church, South, in which he
is both church and district steward.

WILLIAM A. BAKER, M. D. Not only is Dr. William A. Baker,
of Big Stone Gap, a well-known figure as a general practitioner,
but he is also achieving a wide reputation in pediatrics, his success in the disease of children fast making him a specialist in
that branch of his profession. His broad sympathy, his thorough
understanding of children, and his deep study of the maladies
with which they are stricken, all combine to make him the ideal
children's doctor, and it will not be long before he will become
one of the leaders in pediatrics in Virginia.

Doctor Baker was born in Jonesville, Virginia, April 4, 1863,
a son of W. A. M. and Ellen A. (Hamblin) Baker. Mr. Baker is
deceased, and Mrs. Baker died at the age of eighty-three in Dallas, Texas. During his life time he was a farmer, and a very
active Democrat. During the war between the states he served
most bravely in the Confederate army, and for some years he
was deputy sheriff of Lee County, Virginia. The Methodist Episcopal Church, South, held his membership. The Baker family is
of English descent. The Hamlin family descent is traced from

the Hamblin who established Fort Blackburn in Scott County, Virginia, a man of historical fame.

From Jonesville Institute Doctor Baker went to the University of Maryland, and still later to the Louisville Medical College, Louisville, Kentucky, from which he was graduated in 1891 with the degree of Doctor of Medicine. He returned to Jonesville and established himself there in a general practice, which he continued to carry on for fifteen years, but then went to Pennington Gap, Virginia, for a year, after which he located permanently at Big Stone Gap, where he has enjoyed a large and lucrative practice and become one of the very prominent men of his profession in this part of the state. He belongs to the Wise County Medical Society, which he has served as president, the Clinch Valley Medical Society, the Virginia State Medical Society, Southern Railroad Surgeons Association and the American Medical Association. For two years he has been surgeon for the Southern Railroad, and he is examiner for all the leading insurance companies for this district. He has been advanced to the Chapter in Masonry, and is a past master of the Blue Lodge and a past high priest of the Chapter, and he also belongs to the Modern Woodmen of America. During the World war he served on the Volunteer Medical Board and the Medical Advisory Board. For many years he was a member of the board of Jonesville Institute. Not only does he frequently read papers before the different medical societies to which he belongs, but he has had many of them published in the medical journals of the country, and is regarded as an authority upon numerous subjects. He sponsored a bill before the Legislature to place student nurses in this state on an eight hour shift, but it failed of passage, although his idea has been adopted by all the hospitals and schools in Virginia. Like his father, he is an active Democrat, and served as health officer for Big Stone Gap until the county system was adopted. A man who appreciates the value of keeping abreast of the progress that is being made in his profession all the time, he makes it a practice to attend clinics at frequent intervals, usually going to Louisville, Kentucky, for that purpose. Whenever the opportunity offers he lectures before civic bodies, taking these openings to bring before the public his progressive ideas with reference to health conservation, sanitation and the care of children. Long a member of the Methodist Episcopal Church, South, he is now serving the local church as steward.

Doctor Baker married Miss Elizabeth D. Duncan, of Jonesville, a daughter of Col. C. T. Duncan, one of the distinguished men of Lee County, a noted attorney, commonwealth attorney, judge of the Circuit Court, and in later life counsel for the Louisville & Nashville Railroad. During the war between the states he served under Gen. "Stonewall" Jackson with the rank of colonel. Mrs. Baker was educated in the Female College of Asheville, North Carolina, and the Female College of Lynchburg, Virginia, and she is now one of the valued members of the Methodist Episcopal Church, South, of Big Stone Gap, and very active in its missionary work. Of the children born to Doctor and Mrs. Baker, two died in infancy, Fanchi and Billy Baker. Thelma, who was graduated from the high school of Big Stone Gap, married R. H. Engel, of the same place; Mary E., who was graduated from the high school of Big Stone Gap, died in 1918, while a pupil nurse of the University of Maryland; Eleanor, who was graduated from the high school of Big Stone Gap, is a pro-

F. B. Fitzpatrick

fessional nurse; Duncan McLaurin is an engineer with the State Highway department at Richmond, and Margaret, who was graduated from the high school of Big Stone Gap, is a stenographer.

FRANCIS BURKE FITZPATRICK, who holds the chair of education in the Radford State Teachers College, came to that institution with a record of successful work as a teacher and administrator, and educators all over Virginia know him as the author of numerous text books and educational bulletins, and as a pioneer in the introduction of improved efficiency methods in school work.

Mr. Fitzpatrick, who holds the degrees A. B. and M. A., was born at Fancy Grove in Bedford County, Virginia, March 15, 1872. His grandfather, Thomas Fitzpatrick, moved from the vicinity of Scottsville, Virginia, to Bedford County, where he lived out his life. Hiram A. Fitzpatrick, the father, was born in Rockingham County, Virginia, was fifteen years of age when the family settled in the Goose Creek Valley of Bedford County, and during the Civil war he was employed as a saddle maker by the Confederate government. After the war he became identified with an extensive establishment as a merchant at Kaseys, Virginia, and was also postmaster there, and operated a tannery and saw mill. He died about 1907 and is buried in Fairview Cemetery at Roanoke. By his first marriage he was the father of five children: W. T. Fitzpatrick, deceased; B. N. Fitzpatrick, deceased; W. A. Fitzpatrick, a banker at Bedford City; Celia, deceased; and Minerva, of Goodview, Bedford County, widow of J. S. Saunders, who died in 1928. The second wife of Hiram A. Fitzpatrick was Frances Johnson, daughter of Benjamin and Fannie (Preston) Johnson, a family of farming people in Bedford County. Frances Johnson was born and reared in that county, near Fancy Grove, and was educated in private schools. She died in 1872, at the birth of her son Francis Burke.

Francis Burke Fitzpatrick was educated in public schools in Bedford and Pittsylvania counties, graduated from Randolph-Macon Academy of Bedford City, and took his A. B. degree at Randolph-Macon College at Ashland in 1898. During the past thirty years he has been a constant student, and has come in contact with eminent educators in various institutions. For several summers he pursued research work in Columbia University of New York, and in 1919 took his Master of Arts degree at the University of Chicago. Practically all of his residence work has been completed preparatory to the Doctor of Philosophy degree, the only requirement being the preparation of his thesis. Mr. Fitzpatrick for several years taught in grammar and high schools in Bedford and Pittsylvania counties. For six years he was principal of the high school at Gate City, formerly known as Shumaker College, for two years was high school principal at Pulaski, and for three years principal of the Roanoke High School. In 1913 he was elected superintendent of schools at Bristol, Virginia, resigning in 1919 to become professor of education in the Radford State Teachers College.

Mr. Fitzpatrick in 1908 was honored with election as president of the Virginia State Teachers Association, and has been vice president for a number of years and one of the active leaders in the organization. Some of his text books include *Present Day Standards for Teaching, Present Day Standards for Supervision and Teaching.* As principal of schools and through his influence at the State Teachers College he has done much to bring about the use of standard tests. He made thorough surveys of the schools of Bristol, Lynchburg, and in Page County, and the results of his researches have been issued in a number of bulletins, one of the most important being *Present Standard and Practices of Virginia School Superintendents,* published by the Radford State Teachers College. His text books are published by the F. A. Owen Company of Dansville, New York. Mr. Fitzpatrick for many years was a member of the State Board of Examiners.

During the World war he was a director of the Red Cross work in Southwestern Virginia and has been president of the Radford Chapter. He is a member of the National Education Association, the Southwestern Virginia, Incorporated, the Knights of the Mystic Chain, is a Pi Gamma Mu, member of the Kiwanis Club. He is a Democrat, and for years has taught in the Sunday School of the Methodist Episcopal Church, South, and is a lay leader of the church, frequently filling pulpits for pastors of different churches.

He married at Christiansburg, Virginia, December 24, 1903, Miss Mary Douglas Wade, daughter of Col. Hamilton and Bettie (Earhart) Wade. Her father was a colonel in the Confederate army under Lee, and after the war for many years filled the office of county clerk of Montgomery County. He died in 1907 and his wife in 1914, and both are buried at Christiansburg. Mrs. Fitzpatrick was educated in the grade and high schools of Christiansburg, was a member of the class of 1900 in Marion College at Marion, Alabama, and taught in public schools in Virginia, for several years before her marriage teaching art in the Jeter Institute at Bedford. She finds a diversity of interests in church work, is a former president of the Woman's Club of Radford, former president of the United Daughters of the Confederacy, and also of the Chapter of the Daughters of the American Revolution. Mr. and Mrs. Fitzpatrick have three children: Frances Elizabeth was educated in the Radford High School, graduated in 1926 from the State Teachers College, and is now teacher in a public school at Richmond; Hamilton Douglas graduated from the local high school, from Randolph-Macon College at Ashland in 1927, and is teacher and athletic director of the high school of Pocahontas, Virginia; and Evelyn Margaret graduated from Radford High School and is a member of the class of 1929 in the Radford State Teachers College.

NICHOLAS F. HIX, physician and surgeon, graduated from medical college in 1900, and during the greater part of his professional career has been a resident of Wise. His thorough training, natural gifts and long experience have brought him well deserved leadership in his profession.

Doctor Hix was born in Prince Edward County, Virginia, December 8, 1876, son of Dr. Thomas W. and Bettie (Gough) Hix. His father was born in Appomattox County, Virginia, in 1832, grew up there on a farm, served all through the war as a Confederate soldier, graduated from Jefferson Medical College of Philadelphia, and practiced for some years at Appomattox and later in Prince Edward County. He was at the height of his career of usefulness when he died in 1884. He was a member of the Baptist Church and the Masonic fraternity. The wife of Dr. Thomas W. Hix was born in Campbell County, Virginia, in 1834 and died in 1915. Their children were: William G., an educator, who died at Greensboro, Alabama, in June 1929, Jennie, who married W. R. Bracy; Mary A., who married Benjamin Hooper and died at Sheppards, Virginia, in 1926; Thomas B., a farmer; John W., a business man of Roanoke; Elizabeth, deceased; Lucy A., deceased wife of Charles Garden; and Nicholas F.

Nicholas Flood Hix attended public school in Prince Edward County, continuing his education in Randolph-Macon Academy at Bedford, and in 1894 graduated from William and Mary College. For two years he was principal of the high school at Rustburg in Campbell County, and then entered the medical department of the University of Virginia. He was graduated with the M. D. degree in 1900, and from 1900 to 1904 practiced at Gate City, Alabama. He returned to Virginia and since 1904 has made his home and professional residence at Wise. Doctor Hix has kept in touch with professional interests by post-graduate study, having attended the Chicago Post-Graduate College of Medicine in 1916 and has frequently attended clinics at Louisville and elsewhere. He is a member of the Wise County Medical Society, Medical Society of Virginia, and during the World war was medical examiner for the Wise County Draft Board.

Doctor Hix has been chairman of the Board of Welfare of Wise County, and is interested in the coal industry and owns and operates several farms in the county. He is a Democrat, member of the Independent Order of Odd Fellows, and is a deacon in the Baptist Church at Wise.

Doctor Hix married, February 9, 1908, Miss Ethel Mae Fulton, daughter of Judge Elbert and Sophronia (Dotson) Fulton. Mrs. Hix was educated in Randolph-Macon Woman's College at Lynchburg. They have three daughters, Elizabeth Jacquelin, Margaret Fulton and Ethel Mae.

EUGENE P. COX, physician and surgeon at Norton, is a native Virginian, was a medical officer overseas during the World war, and had had a very interesting range of service and experience since getting his medical degree.

He was born in Scott County, Virginia, September 27, 1887. His great-grandfather, David L. Cocke, settled at Fort Blackmore during the time of Daniel Boone. Doctor Cox's grandfather, Robert K. Cocke, was born at Fort Blackmore, became a physician and surgeon, doing a great deal of country practice in the early days around Fort Blackmore, where he lived until his death in April, 1887. His wife, Nancy Buster, died in 1896. Joseph N. Cox, father of Doctor Cox, was born at Fort Blackmore December 8, 1854, grew up and married there, and in 1887 moved to Wood, Scott County, where he was a farmer and stock raiser until his death on December 19, 1913. He served three terms as county supervisor. He was a Mason and member of the Free Will Baptist Church. His wife was Victoria McClelland, a native of Scott County, born October 1, 1854.

Eugene P. Cox was one of a large family of children and grew up with his brothers and sisters on the home farm at Wood. He attended public school there, and in 1911 graduated with the A. B. degree from Emory and Henry College. With a substantial literary education he entered the University College of Medicine at Richmond. This college two years later was combined with the Medical College of Virginia, and in 1915 he was given his M. D. degree by this institution, completing four years work. He is a member of the Kappa Psi medical fraternity. Doctor Cox

spent most of the year 1915 as an interne in the Lewis Gale
Hospital at Roanoke. He began practice at Clinchport, soon lo-
cating at Rye Cove, Virginia, and was there at the time of the
World war.

Doctor Cox volunteered in October, 1917, was commissioned
a first lieutenant in the Medical Corps December 8, and in January, 1918, was called to the colors at Fort Oglethorpe and six
weeks later was transferred to Camp Wadsworth, Spartanburg,
South Carolina. In August, 1918, he went overseas as assistant
regimental surgeon of the Fifty-fourth Pioneer Infantry. He
landed at Brest September 12, was sent to the Argonne sector
in the same month and remained there until after the armistice.
During several months after the armistice he was with the American forces at Coblentz, Germany. On June 26, 1919, he returned home, and received his honorable discharge at Camp
Lee July 18, 1919.

Doctor Cox resumed his practice at Rye Cove, remaining
there until September, 1922, when he removed to Norton, and
has become one of the recognized leaders of his profession in that
community of Wise County. He has his office in the Kemmerer
Building. Doctor Cox is a member of the Wise County, Virginia
State and American Medical Associations. He is a Democrat in
politics, and a member of Norton Post No. 143, American Legion.

He married, February 8, 1916, Miss Myrtelle Mitchell, daughter of William and Venus (Fugate) Mitchell. Her father was a
farmer and Hereford cattle breeder. Mrs. Cox finished her education in Sullins College at Bristol, Virginia. They have a son,
Joe Mitchell Cox, born April 28, 1918.

WILLIAM R. CULBERTSON, M. D., was for a number of years
successfully engaged in the general practice of medicine in
Southwestern Virginia. Then came the World war, he became
a medical officer, and at its close he entered the United States
Public Health Service, and as county health officer of Wise County he has for several years devoted all his professional experience and ability to the tasks and responsibilities of leadership
in one of the broadest and most salutary movements in our nation's history.

Doctor Culbertson was born in Scott County, Virginia, July
21, 1879, son of Joseph and Mary (McConnell) Culbertson. His
father spent his active life as a merchant in Western Virginia.
Doctor Culbertson grew up in the home of a business man, had
the advantages of the public schools of Scott County, and as a
young man taught there for three years. His preparation for a
career in life came as the result of his own earnings and efforts.
Doctor Culbertson for two years attended the Medical College of
Virginia at Richmond and in 1904 he was graduated from the
Baltimore University College of Medicine at Baltimore, Maryland.

After graduating Doctor Culbertson located at Coeburn, Virginia, and had all the routine service of a village and country
doctor there for a number of years. He was commissioned a first
lieutenant in the Army Medical Corps and in 1918 was sent for
duty to Camp Wadsworth, South Carolina, remaining until after
the armistice.

He was honorably discharged in December, 1918, and was
then assigned under the United States Public Health Service to
duty at Norton, Virginia, having charge of the campaign
against venereal diseases in this section of Virginia. A year

Victor L. Flay

later he was appointed county health officer of Wise County under the State Board of Health, and at the same time was put on the reserve list in the United States Public Health Service. Since becoming county health officer he has totally reorganized the work of his office, placing it on a basis of efficiency, measured not only by his individual capacity and zeal in the work, but he has set in motion the routine of work which coordinates with the State Public Health Service and affords Wise County a remarkable degree of protection and at the same time giving the people the constant influence of health and sanitary propaganda.

Doctor Culbertson is a member and secretary of the Wise County, Southern, Clinch Valley and American Medical Associations, the Medical Society of Virginia, is former president of the County Society, member of the American Public Health Service Association. He is a Knight Templar Mason and Shriner, member of the American Legion and Kiwanis Club, and is a Presbyterian.

Doctor Culbertson married Miss Mazela Dingus, of Scott County, daughter of Philip Dingus, a well known planter. Mrs. Culbertson finished her education in Sullins College at Bristol. She is a member of the Civic Club of Norton, the Eastern Star Chapter, and the Methodist Episcopal Church, South. They have three children: Joseph, born August 10, 1907, a graduate of the Norton High School, now attending the University of Virginia; Leon, born May 14, 1910, member of the class of 1928 in the Greenbrier Military School at Louisburg, West Virginia; and William, born May 16, 1916.

VICTOR LEVIN FLOYD. One of the few retail commercial houses that have had a continuous existence and service since the close of the Civil war is the V. L. Floyd Grocery Company of Richmond, a business that was founded by the late Victor Levin Floyd, and which remains today a growing concern conducted by members of his family.

Victor Levin Floyd was born in Northampton County, on the Eastern Shore of Virginia, December 7, 1837, and died at Richmond in February 13, 1911, when in his seventy-third year. This branch of the Floyd family came from England, there being two brothers who arrived in the seventeenth century, and one of whom settled on the Eastern Shore. His father was Captain Berry Floyd, a plantation owner and sea captain, who owned and operated a boat from Cape Charles to Boston Massachusetts, making a great number of voyages up and down the coast, until finally he lost his life at sea. Captain Berry Floyd married Lavinia Nottingham, of Virginia, and of their seven children Victor L. was the third.

Victor L. Floyd attended private schools in Accomac County was a farmer for several years, and before the war owned a large plantation and a number of slaves. When the War between the States came on he joined the Hampton Grays, and was in the war from beginning to end, a period of four years. Twice he was wounded in battle and once was taken prisoner. He was finally released after the end of hostilities. Before the war he had sold his plantation and his slaves and for two years was in business as a wheelwright. In 1865 he established a retail grocery business in Richmond, located on Brook Road, and he made his store an important institution of a prosperous city community and gave to it the most active years of his life.

However, not all his time was taken up with business. He served two terms, eight years, as a local magistrate, was influential in the Democratic party, was a member of the Robert E. Lee Camp of Confederate Veterans, and he and all his family belonged to the Episcopal Church. He and his sons became Masons and the daughters joined the United Daughters of the Confederacy.

Mr. Floyd married, December 1, 1869, Miss Lucy Dabney Walton, of Henrico County, Virginia, who was reared and educated there, attending private schools. Her father, Robert G. W. Walton, was a land owner in Henrico County and had served as a soldier in the War of 1812. Her mother was Frances Blackburn. Mrs. Floyd was the ninth in a family of twelve children.

Mrs. Floyd, whose home is at 5016 New Kent Road in Richmond, is the mother of eight children. Her son James Herbert, a city employe, married Lulu Harris and had two children, Ruby Camille, who is the wife of J. N. Bowen, and Henry Page, a postal employe. Victor Levin, Jr., died in 1905. He married Inez Vaughan and had two children, Walker Bryan and Victor Levin III. Harry Lee Floyd and his next younger brother, Garnett Floyd, are merchants at Richmond, being associated in carrying on the grocery business of V. L. Floyd Grocery Company, founded by their father in 1865. Harry Lee married Emma Foster and has three children, Emily Florence, now Mrs. W. Moore, Harry Lee, Jr., and Lavinia Louise. Garnett married Jennie Pyper, and they had six daughters, the oldest, Lillian Frances, being the wife of J. E. Lindsey and the mother of a daughter, Dorothy Keith, while the other children are Marion Hope, Vera Belle, Lucy Virginia, Jeanne Garnett and Elizabeth Keith. Marion Edward Floyd is a city employe at Richmond, and by his marriage with Mrs. Marie Lystand has two children, Marion Edward, Jr., and Eleanor Belle. Miss Lulu Belle Floyd and Miss Winnie Davis Floyd both reside in Richmond. The youngest of the family is Nannie Estelle, wife of W. W. Buran, a merchant at White Sulphur Springs, West Virginia, and they have two children, Wilburn Wright and Lucy Floyd.

AVERY BRYAN GRAYBEAL, physician and surgeon, is a resident of Marion, Smyth County, where he conducts a general practice and also acts as physician to several industrial organizations in that section.

Doctor Graybeal was born at Clifton, North Carolina, December 31, 1895, and he grew up and began his professional career in one of the most interesting of the mountainous districts of Western North Carolina. His grandfather, John Graybeal, was a farmer and slave owner in Ashe County, North Carolina. David Graybeal, father of Doctor Graybeal, was born in Ashe County September 11, 1845, and was member of a North Carolina Regiment of Infantry during the last three years of the Civil war, and in after years was affiliated with the United Confederate Veterans. He spent his active career as a farmer in Ashe County, and died March 8, 1925. He was a Democrat and a member of the Methodist Episcopal Church, South. He married Bethana Ashley, who was born at Warrensville, North Carolina, May 21, 1853, and died February 9, 1926. They had a large family of children: Martha, who married Marion F. Miller; Mary Ann, who married Scott Genry; Joseph, who died in 1897; Evelyn, who died in infancy; James M., who became an eye, ear, nose

and throat specialist in Montana; William Reece; Charles E.;
Minnie Ethel, who married Guy Eller; Albert; and Avery B.

Avery B. Graybeal was reared in Ashe County, attended local schools and graduated in 1912 from the Appalachian Training School at Boone. During 1913-14 he was a student at the
North Carolina Medical College at Charlotte and in 1917 took
his medical degree from the Medical College of Virginia at Richmond. Doctor Graybeal practiced at Clifton, North Carolina,
two and a half years, and then two years at Grassy Creek in his
old home neighborhood. During the World war he was medical
examiner of the Draft Board of Ashe County. In 1922 he located at Grant in Grayson County, Virginia, and since September, 1925, has practiced at Marion in Smyth County. He is a
well trained physician and surgeon and also has the facilities
for the practice of electro therapy. He acts as examiner for life
insurance companies and is physician to the Virginia Table
Company, the Lincoln Company, Knight Brothers Brick and
Tile Company. Doctor Graybeal is a member of the Southwest
Virginia Medical Society, the Medical Society of Virginia and
the American Medical Association.

Fraternally he is affiliated with the Lodge and Royal Arch
Chapter of Masonry, is a Democrat and a Methodist, and in the
Kiwanis Club is chairman of the committee on child welfare.
He married at Boone, North Carolina, August 21, 1917, Miss
Mary Frances Payne. Her father, James M. Payne, was a Bap-
tist minister. Doctor and Mrs. Graybeal have two children:
Avery Bryan, J., born March 8, 1919, and Kent Payne, born May
15, 1922.

CHESTER ARTHUR HUTCHINSON, physician and surgeon at
Appalachia, Wise County, was born in that section of Virginia,
and in his professional career and as a private citizen has done
honor to one of the old and prominent names in the Virginia
Highlands.

The Hutchinson family was transplanted from Ireland to
Virginia in the early Colonial period. Doctor Hutchinson's great-
grandfather, Emanuel Hutchinson, was a native of Scott County,
Virginia, but as a minister of the Protestant Episcopal Church
went about over a large section of Southwestern Virginia, and
died in Wise County. He married Nancy Carter, a native of
Scott County. Their son, Francis Hutchinson, was born in Scott
County in 1825, in early life was a school teacher, later a farmer,
and was a Union soldier during the Civil war, enlisting in 1861
in Kentucky and saw service under General, after President,
Garfield. He was in the siege of Vicksburg. He died in Wise
County February 14, 1907. His wife, Matilda Howell, was born
in North Carolina in 1837, and died in April, 1887.

They were the grandparents of Doctor Hutchinson. The latter's father was Peter F. Hutchinson, who was born in Wise
County May 4, 1860, and throughout his active career was a
farmer and fruit grower. He has voted as a Republican, is a
member of the Methodist Episcopal Church and the Independent
Order of Odd Fellows. Peter F. Hutchinson married Jane Freeman, who was born in Wise County June 26, 1857, and died October 11, 1920. The Freeman family is of German ancestry, was
established in Virginia in Colonial times, and her father, Joseph
Freeman, was born in Wise County in 1832 and died in 1899,
having been a farmer and shoemaker. He was a Confederate
soldier in the last two years of the Civil war. Joseph Freeman

married Sarah Powers, who was born in 1828 and died in 1906.
Her father, Jeremiah Powers, was one of the prominent old time
citizens of Wise County, a farmer, was the first justice of the
peace and held the first court convened in the county. Peter F.
Hutchinson and wife had the following children: Mary, who
married Stephen Davis; Elizabeth, who married Calvin B. Stallard; Joseph Francis, who became a minister of the Methodist
Church; Chester A.; Charles Wesley; Julia, wife of Alvin Mul-
lins; Pearl Adeline, who married Stewart Jessee; Ava, wife of
Emory Davis; Maude, who married David Davis; Mrs. Manilla
Davis; Thomas; and Troy Howell who graduated from the University of Virginia in Medicine in 1929.

Chester Arthur Hutchinson was born in Wise County, February 14, 1887, graduated from high school at Clintwood in
1906, spent two years in the University of Chattanooga and in
1912 graduated Doctor of Medicine from the Atlanta College of
Physicians and Surgeons. As a graduate of this school he is an
alumnus of Emory University. Doctor Hutchinson has had a
wide experience in surgery and general medicine, and in addition to the opportunities presented by his practice he has attended various clinics and post-graduate courses, spending some
time with the Mayo Brothers at Rochester, Minnesota. After
graduating from college he practiced one year at Athens, Tennessee, one year at Pittsburg, Georgia, for four years was surgeon for the Stonega Coal & Coke Company in Wise County,
Virginia, and for four years chief surgeon for the Blackwood
Coal & Coke Company at Blackwood. His home and professional
connections have been established at Appalachia since January
1, 1923. He is a member of the Wise County, Virginia State
and American Medical Associations.

Doctor Hutchinson is affiliated with Appalachia Lodge No.
229, A. F. and A. M., Stevenson Chapter No. 19, Royal Arch
Masons, Cyrene Commandery No. 21, Knights Templar, Acca
Temple of the Mystic Shrine at Richmond, Roanoke Consistory
of the Scottish Rite, and is also a member of the Knights of
Pythias. He is a Republican and member of the First Presby
terian Church at Appalachia.

Doctor Hutchinson married, September 6, 1909, Miss Viola
Hamilton, daughter of J. Hopkins and Sallie Ann (Neal) Hamil-
ton. Mrs. Hutchinson graduated from the Clintwood High
School and for several years taught in Wise County. They have
three children: Joseph Newell, born June 14, 1910, Georgia
Leigh, born October 20, 1915, and Claudia, born July 8, 1919.

CAPT. ABEL L. HUNTLEY is one of the veterans of the maritime transportation interests who have found home and business
connections in the Norfolk section of Virginia. Captain Huntley
is a New Englander, but married his wife in Virginia, and he
represents some of the old and prominent lines of Virginia
descent. Their home is at 714 Reservoir Street in Norfolk.

Captain Huntley was born at Black Hall, Connecticut. His
father was a Connecticut farmer and a veteran of both the Mexican and Civil wars. His mother was Jane (Waters) Huntley.
Captain Huntley was educated in the Black Hall schools and at
the age of fourteen began employment with the Thames Tow
Boat Company, and remained in the service of that organization
forty-four years. Later he joined the Thomas J. Howard Company of New York City, and is now master and captain of their
tow boat, *William G. Howard,* which claims Norfolk as its home

port. Captain Huntley is a member of the Master Mates and Pilots Association.

He married, August 23, 1911, at Norfolk, Mrs. Bettie Frances (Dabney) Johnson. She was born in Albemarle County, Virginia, daughter of John and Sarah Elizabeth (Proffitt) Dabney. Both the Proffitt and Dabney families have been in Virginia since Colonial times. The Proffitts were of French Huguenot origin. The Dabneys were early settlers around Richmond, and many of them have been prominent in business and professional life. Mrs. Huntley was the seventh child in a large family of twenty-five children of her father. She was first married, December 27, 1891, to John Walter Johnson, of Louisa County, Virginia. By that marriage she had three children: Albert Mason Johnson, a Government employe, married Edna Lee Dobbs, of Norfolk, and has a son, Albert Mason, Jr.; Daisy Pleasents is the wife of Dr. James L. Carmony, of Baltimore, who served as first lieutenant in the army during the World war; and Roy Dabney Johnson, married Virginia Cutler, of Newport News. Mrs. Huntley is a member of the Methodist Episcopal Church, South.

HON. WILLIAM ROBERTSON MCKENNEY. A student by nature, taking an especial interest in educational and political affairs, Hon. William Robertson McKenney, late of Petersburg, held an assured position in legal circles, and while a member of Congress did much to promote the healthy growth of city, county and state. A son of Robert Armstrong McKenney, he was born December 2, 1851, in Petersburg, of substantial Scotch and English ancestry. For a few generations prior to locating in Virginia the McKenney family, it is said, resided in Maryland, and were citizens of prominence.

Robert Armstrong McKenney married Virginia Robertson, a great-great-great-granddaughter of Alexander Spotswood, who served as governor of the Colony of Virginia for a number of years. On the maternal side she was of distinguished lineage, her father, William Robertson, having married Ann Spotswood, a daughter of Capt. John and Sallie (Rowzie) Spotswood, and granddaughter of John and Mary (Dandridge) Spotswood, the said Mary Dandridge having been a daughter of William Dandridge, who served as a captain in the English navy. After leaving the navy he came to this country, locating in Virginia, where he was subsequently appointed as one of the commissioners to locate the boundary lines of Virginia.

Receiving excellent educational advantages when young, William Robertson McKenney was a pupil in the first class organized after the establishment of McCabe's Preparatory School. Entering the University of Virginia in the fall of 1872, he studied there a year, after which he taught for a year in the McCabe School. Returning then to the university, he completed the academic course and subsequently entered the law department of the University of Virginia, from which he was graduated with the degree of LL. B. in 1876.

Immediately beginning the practice of his profession in Petersburg, Mr. McKenney met with good success in his labors, his practice widening year by year, his counsel being sought not only in his native city, but in surrounding communities. Becoming active in public affairs, he served as a member of the Common Council many years, a part of the time being its president, and was also for many terms a member of the local Board of Education. In 1895 he had the honor of being elected to represent the Fourth Virginia Congressional District, and while there performed the duties devolving upon him most faithfully. Physically and mentally alert and strong, his sudden death on January 2, 1916, from that dread disease pneumonia was a shock to the entire community, and deeply deplored by old and young.

Mr. McKenney married, December 2, 1878, Miss Clara Justine Pickrell, who was born in New Orleans, Louisiana, a daughter of Addison and Justine (Lockett) Pickrell, and granddaughter of Henry and Amelia (Fontenelle) Lockett. Having been a young child when her parents died, Mrs. McKenney was brought up by her paternal grandparents. She is a woman of culture and refinement, practical and generous in the expenditure of her money, placing it where it will be of the greatest benefit to the general public. In 1924 Mrs. McKenney presented the McKenney home on Sycamore Street to the city, said home to be used as a Free Library Building, for which it is admirably adapted, the library itself being now known as the William Robertson McKenney Free Library.

At this writing, in 1927, Mrs. McKenney still resides in Petersburg, where she has the love and respect of the entire community. Of her marriage with Mr. McKenney five children were born, namely: Anne Pickrell, William Robertson, Jr., Virginia Spotswood, Clara Justine and Robert Armstrong, of whom a brief account appears elsewhere in this volume.

ROBERT ARMSTRONG MCKENNEY. A man of excellent character, and a most congenial companion, Robert Armstrong McKenney has followed the professional footsteps of his father, the late William R. McKenney, and is rapidly gaining a stable position among the active and able attorneys of Petersburg. He was born in Petersburg, Virginia, August 9, 1893, coming on both sides of the house of honored ancestry.

His paternal grandfather, Robert A. McKenney I, married Virginia Robertson, a daughter of Williaim and Ann (Spotswood) Robertson. Through this grandmother he is a direct descendant of William Dandridge, who served for a time as captain of a vessel belonging to the English Navy, but subsequently immigrated to America, becoming a pioneer settler of Virginia. Taking an active part in the public affairs of the new colony, he was one of the commissioners appointed to establish the boundary line between Virginia and North Carolina. Further ancestral history may be found elsewhere in this volume, in connection with the sketch of the late William R. McKenney.

Fitted for college in Hall and Arrington's Academy in Petersburg and in the Woodbury Forest School at Orange, Virginia, Robert Armstrong McKenney studied for a time at the University of Virginia. He subsequently entered Dartmouth College at Hanover, New Hampshire, and was there graduated in 1917, with the degree of A. B. On March 28, 1917, Mr. McKenney enlisted for service in the World war, and was assigned to the navy, which was then making strenuous efforts to clear the ocean of mines and destroyers. Much of his time was therefore spent on foreign waters, serving first as a third class quartermaster, but later being promoted to the first class, a rank he maintained until his honorable discharge from the service on June 6, 1919.

Very soon after his return to Petersburg Mr. McKenney became assistant secretary-treasurer of the Banking Trust and

Mortgage Company, a position he retained until 1924. In that year, having a decided inclination for legal work, he entered the law department of the University of Virginia, from which he was graduated in 1927. Immediately opening an office in Petersburg, he met with encouraging success from the start, his unsparing pains and patience in behalf of his clients being sure to win him an extensive patronage.

Mr. McKenney married, in 1920, Miss Katherine Friend Jones, who was born in Petersburg, a daughter of William Bland Pryor and Mary Nowlen (Meacham) Jones. One child, Ann Pickrell McKenney, has blessed their union. Fraternally Mr. McKenney belongs to two college fraternities, the Phi Alpha Delta and the Phi Beta Kappa (honorary). He is also a Mason, and a member of the American Legion. Both he and his wife are faithful members of Saint Paul's Episcopal Church.

JOSEPH B. WOLFE, JR., physician and surgeon, with home at Coeburn, Wise County, is an eminent representative of his profession in Southwestern Virginia. He has practiced over thirty-five years. He brought to his work a thorough education, natural gifts, and also the traditions of a family many of whose members have been doctors in the previous generations.

Doctor Wolfe is a native of Kentucky, but his family has lived in Virginia for many years. His grandfather, Ezra M. Wolfe, was a native of Pennsylvania, of German ancestry, and for many years was in business as a merchant at Charlottesville, Virginia. His wife, Lucy Bishop, was a daughter of Dr. Joe Bishop, a physician at Patrick County, Virginia.

The father of Doctor Wolfe of Coeburn was Joseph B. Wolfe, Sr., who was born at Charlottesville, Virginia, February 18, 1832. He took the degree in medicine from the University of Virginia, practiced in Scott County until 1862, and from that year until 1870, in Wolfe County, Kentucky. He then resumed his professional connections with Scott County, Virginia, and had practiced fully half a century when he retired in 1903. He lived in Joplin, Missouri, until his death on June 19, 1906. He was for twelve years superintendent of schools of Scott County, was a staunch Democrat, member of the Masonic fraternity and the Christian Baptist Church. Doctor Wolfe, Sr., married Sarah Horton Wilson, who was born in Russell County, Virginia, December 25, 1841. There were nine children in the family: Dr. Thomas J., who graduated from the College of Physicians and Surgeons of Baltimore; Lucy, who married Logan L. Banner, a physician; Mollie, who married James O. Kennedy; Ezra M., of Lebanon, Virginia; Joseph B., Jr.; Lindsay C., who became a Baptist minister; John J., a lawyer at Joplin, Missouri; Dr. Isaac E., a physician at Coeburn; and Annie, who died in childhood.

Joseph B. Wolfe, J., was born in Wolfe County, Kentucky, March 7, 1869. He was reared in Scott County, Virginia, attended a private school in Tennessee for a time, and in 1891 was graduated from the Louisville Medical College. In the same year he began practice at Coeburn, and for many years that community has learned to rely upon him for his professional skill, his rich experience in diagnosis, his resourcefulness in emergencies, and his boundless sympathy and kindliness. For many years he has enjoyed a great reputation as a surgeon, though his practice is of a general nature. He has frequently absented himself for brief periods of time to come in touch with

the eminent physicians and surgeons of the great medical centers. He did post-graduate work at the Philadelphia Polyclinic
in 1908, 1910, 1912 and 1914, and at the New York Polyclinic in
1900. He is a member of the Medical Society of Virginia and
the Southern and American Medical Associations.

Doctor Wolfe is prominent in the Masonic fraternity, being
affiliated with Coeburn Lodge No. 97, A. F. and A. M., Craig
Chapter No. 31, Royal Arch Masons, Cyrene Commandery No.
21, Knights Templar, Acca Temple of the Mystic Shrine at
Richmond. He is a Democrat and a member of the Methodist
Episcopal Church, South.

He married at Coeburn, September 22, 1892, Miss Julia
Carico, daughter of William A. and Sarah (Minton) Carico. Her
father was a Coeburn merchant. Mrs. Wolfe attended Tazewell
College of Virginia. Doctor and Mrs. Wolfe have four children:
Annie, who married Willard Kilgore; William, who became a
druggist; Mary, who married Burney H. Body; and Louise, who
died at the age of two years.

CLAUDE B. BOWYER is an eminent surgeon, and for many
years has specialized in industrial practice for some of the great
coal mining organizations of Southwestern Virginia. His home
is at Stonega in Wise County, where he is surgeon in charge of
the local hospital and the general medical and surgical facilities
of the Stonega Coal & Coke Company.

Doctor Bowyer comes of a long line of professional men, and
his family has been one distinguished by personal attainments
and services in many fields of effort. The Bowyers have been in
Virginia since Colonial times. His grandfather, Dr. Henry Quincy Adams Bowyer, was born in Franklin County, Virginia, was
a graduate in medicine from the University of Pennsylvania at
Philadelphia, and served as a surgeon in the Confederate army.
After the war he practiced at Rural Retreat in Wythe County
until his death at the age of sixty-five.

The father of Dr. Claude Bowyer was Dr. Henry L. Bowyer,
who was born in Franklin County October 8, 1853. He was
reared in Wythe County, attended local schools and after the
war began preparation for the medical profession. He attended
Roanoke College at Salem, graduated Doctor of Medicine from
the University of Louisville, Kentucky, and first practiced in
Grayson County. He subsequently located at Emory, and was an
outstanding member of his profession in that community until
his death on January 28, 1927. For many years he was physician and surgeon to Emory and Henry College, and during the
World war had charge of the Students Army Training Camp of
the college. He was an active member of the Presbyterian
Church and a Democrat in politics. Dr. Henry L. Bowyer married Mary Catherine Painter, a native of Wythe County, Virginia, where she was born in 1861. There were ten children in
the family, Claude B. being the oldest; Helen M.; Warren H.;
Clarence P., Henry L. and W. Roscoe were all in service during
the World war, and the latter two died as a result of their service; Miranda married Robert M. McKinney; Mamie J.; Thomas;
and Douglas. Thomas Bowyer is a graduate of the Medical College of Virginia and is now an interne in St. Agnes Hospital at
Baltimore.

Claude B. Bowyer was born in Grayson County, Virginia,
December 25, 1880. He grew up in a home of culture and refinement, and had every incentive for a professional career in

Chas. L. Morris

the dignified character and usefulness exemplified by his father. He was reared in the scholastic atmosphere of Emory and Henry College, graduated with the A. B. degree from that institution in 1902, and in 1906 took his degree in medicine at the Medical College of Virginia at Richmond. He was in New York in 1911 and 1914, in the Post-Graduate Medical School, and specialized in industrial medicine at Harvard University in 1921 and 1922. He was an interne in the Memorial Hospital of Richmond during 1909-10. Practically all his professional service has been given to the community at Stonega, and for several years he acted as surgeon for the Stonega Coal & Coke Company, for the Interstate Railroad Company and the Southern Railroad Company, and he now has charge of all the collieries operated by the Stonega Company, and as chief of the medical and surgical service has eleven physicians acting under him in Virginia and West Virginia. He has given the Company Hospital at Stonega an enviable reputation.

Doctor Bowyer for six years was secretary of the Wise County Medical Society, is a member of the Southern, Virginia State and American Medical Associations, and is a charter member of the Industrial Physicians and Surgeons of the American Medical Association. Besides his professional connection he is a stockholder in the Stonega Coal & Coke Company and is a director of the First National Bank of Appalachia, president of the Lonesome Pine Country Club, and on the board of trustees of Emory and Henry College. On account of the importance of his connections with the essential coal industries his application for active military service was declined during the war. Doctor Bowyer is a Democratic voter, and has served as steward in the Methodist Episcopal Church, South, at Stonega.

CHARLES LEE MORRISS. No profession to which man can devote his time, thought and attention requires more dignity, kindness of spirit and genuine sympathy than that of funeral director, and with these essential qualities Charles Lee Morriss, of Petersburg, is amply supplied, his kindly attention to the minor details of the last services to the dead alleviating in great measure the sorrow of relatives and friends. A son of James Tollerson Morriss, Jr., was born in Petersburg, Virginia, of Welsh ancestry, being a lineal descendant of Charles Julius Morriss, a native and life long resident of Charles City County, Virginia.

James Tollerson Morriss, Sr., grandfather of Charles Lee Morriss, was born January 10, 1797, on a plantation in Charles City County, Virginia, and there the birth of his son, James Tollerson Morriss, Jr., occurred on April 7, 1836. James Tollerson Morriss, Sr., owned an extensive plantation, which he operated with the help of his many slaves. The maiden name of his first wife, grandmother of Charles Lee Morriss, was Sarah Ann Howle. She was born in Charles City County, Virginia, May 12, 1793, a daughter of Charles and Ann Howle. She died in middle life, and her husband married again.

Quite young when his mother died, James Tollerson Morriss, Jr., left home after the advent of his stepmother, and from the age of sixteen years was self-supporting. Going first to Richmond, Virginia, he was employed as a pattern maker in a foundry. Locating in Petersburg in 1848, he served as an apprentice at the cabinet maker's trade under James Caldwell, in whose employ he continued until 1856. He then engaged in the furniture and undertaking business on his own account on Bolling Street. Subsequently enlarging his operations, Mr. Morriss established the business of funeral director, which he continued until his death, June 8, 1890.

The maiden name of the wife of James Tollerson Morriss, Jr., was Parthenia Lee Ladd. She was born in Dinwiddie County, Virginia, February 9, 1853, a daughter of William LeRoy Ladd, who was born in New Kent County, Virginia, where his father, LeRoy Stith Ladd, the son of David Ladd, a Quaker, who owned a plantation which he managed with slave help. At the outbreak of the Civil war William LeRoy Ladd enlisted in the Confederate service and while in camp was stricken with typhoid fever and there died. To James T. Morriss and his wife, whose maiden name was Parthenia Lee Ladd, five children were born, Charles Lee, Ella Gale Humphreys, Martha Lee Bell, Alice Randolph Hood and Annie Rebecca Guthrie. Ella Gale, the oldest daughter, is the wife of Charles Gilbert Humphreys, and Martha Lee is the wife of Dr. Haney Hardy Bell. Alice Randolph was the wife of W. M. Hood and Annie Rebecca was the wife of C. L. Guthrie.

Charles Lee Morriss obtained his first knowledge of books in the Anderson School, afterwards attending the old high school on North Union Street. When seventeen years old he began working with his father who had established an undertaking business in 1856, and subsequently succeeded to the business, which he is carrying on very successfully. He has made rapid progress in his profession, keeping abreast of the times in every respect, having one of the most complete, up-to-date funeral director establishments to be found in all Virginia.

Mr. Morriss married, January 3, 1912, Sarah Grant Triplett, who was born in Chester County, South Carolina, a daughter of Grover and Claudia (Grant) Triplett, and granddaughter of Amzi Triplett of Chester County, South Carolina. Both the Triplett and Grant ancestors were pioneer settlers of Virginia, some of them coming from England, settling in South Carolina rather than in Virginia.

Mr. and Mrs. Morriss have two children, James Tollerson Morriss IV and Sarah Triplett Morriss. For upwards of a quarter of a century he has served on the Official Board of Trinity Methodist Episcopal Church, of which he and his family are active members. Mr. Morriss is a Knight Templar Mason and a member of the Rotary Club, local Chamber of Commerce and Country Club.

SAMUEL H. YOKLEY, M. D. Standing high in medical science in Southwest Virginia and foremost among his professional brethren in Washington County is Dr. Samuel H. Yokley, physician and surgeon at Meadow View, Virginia, and formerly health officer. He is a veteran of the World war, and since its close a captain in the United States Medical Reserve Corps. Doctor Yokley is of Revolutionary stock. The Patriot soldier and the founder of his family in America came from France in 1770 and settled in what was then Rowan County, North Carolina, and here took part in the battle of Guilford Court House under Gen. Nathaniel Greene against Lord Cornwallis.

Dr. Samuel H. Yokley was born at Thomasville, North Carolina, October 15, 1879, son of Judge Samuel and Janie Catherine (Tackett) Yokley, and grandson of Lewis Yokley. The grand-

father acquired an extensive tract of land in what is now Davidson County, North Carolina, and under the old regime before the
Civil war was a wealthy planter and a local magistrate.

Samuel Yokley, father of Doctor Yokley, justice of the peace
and a member of the County Court, was a prominent man in
North Carolina all his active life. He owned large plantations in
Davidson County, where he reared a family that had many social
connections of worth. He was active in the old Whig party and
was one of the founders of the Republican party in his section,
which many times called him to positions of public responsibility. Throughout his life he was a faithful member of the German
Reformed Church. He married Miss Janie Catherine Tackett,
who was born in North Carolina, her Irish ancestors having been
early settlers there.

Samuel H. Yokley received his early educational training at
Thomasville and then took a course in the Yadkin Valley Institute at Boonville, which prepared him for college, and in 1904
he was graduated from Wake Forest College at Wake Forest,
North Carolina, with his A. B. degree, and in 1905 he won his
A. M. degree. Of versatile talents and well prepared for a professional future, Mr. Yokley entered upon the study of law, but
after a year of application and more mature thought he came to
the realization that another profession, medicine, rather than
the law, appealed to him more urgently. Later he completed his
medical course with credit in the University College of Medicine
at Richmond, Virginia, from which he was graduated in 1909,
and spent one and a half years as an interne in the Sheltering
Arms Hospital at Hansford, West Virginia.

Doctor Yokley first established himself in medical practice at
Buena Vista, Virginia, but one year later came to Meadow View,
where he has continued active ever since with the exception of
his period of war service, during which he was attached to Base
Hospital at Camp Custer, Michigan, entering as a first lieutenant
and emerging with the rank of captain.

In 1911 Doctor Yokley completed a post-graduate course in
Tulane University, New Orleans, and has attended important
clinics and conventions in many other medical centers. Well read
and experienced in every branch of medical science, he has always been a general practitioner. For fifteen years he has been
surgeon for the Norfolk & Western Railway, and belongs to this
system's Railway Surgeons Association, and also to the Southern
Railway Surgeons Association, and is examiner for twenty-three
life insurance companies.

In June, 1922, Doctor Yokley married Miss Marie Layman,
of Botetourt County, Virginia, daughter of George W. and Mary
(Moomaw) Layman, prominent residents of Troutville, Virginia, Mr. Layman being a retired banker. Mrs. Yokley was educated at Daleville College and Brandon Hall, is talented in music
and a member of the Meadow View Music Club, belongs to the
American Legion Auxiliary, and is a leader in the social, club
and cultural movements that promote enjoyment and benefit in
community life. She is active also in the religious body in which
she was reared, the Church of the Brethren.

Doctor Yokley has never been unduly active in political life,
but formerly he served as health officer at Meadow View. He is a
past commander of American Legion Post No. 12, Abingdon, belongs to the Masonic fraternity, leading medical bodies and the
Baptist Church.

ROBERT W. HOLLEY, M. D. There is no period in the world's history which fails to demonstrate that exceptional ability and knowledge rightly applied are invariably triumphant and lasting, and live in further achievement long after poor finite clay has returned to its original elements. In medicine, that noble science to which men of the finest and best on earth have devoted their lives, wonderful progress has been made, but each marvelous discovery and surprising achievement have been the result of the intelligent, scientific study and experiment of the physicians and surgeons who, each one during his span of life, added to the sum of knowledge to a greater degree as circumstances permitted. Beyond the time of the ancient Egyptians a knowledge of medicine was considered essential. In the Mosaic law we find medical and sanitary advice. The Greeks defied Æsculapius as the Father of Medicine, and on down through the ages to the present day there have been men of renown whose lives and abilities have been given over unselfishly to wresting from nature the secrets so necessary to the general preservation of health. A distinguished member of the medical profession of Virginia, honored and beloved, whose useful and well rounded life, rich in good deeds and high endeavor, measures up to the above mentioned standards is Dr. Robert W. Holley, of Appalachia.

Doctor Holley was born in Mendota, Virginia, June 14, 1877, a son of Henry C. and Martha J. (Hamilton) Holley, natives of Virginia, he born in Franklin County and she in Mendota, and she is still living, but he died in 1901. For years he was a farmer and lumberman, and for a time he was in the Government service. During the war between the states he served in the Confederate army. The Baptist Church had in him a devout member and faithful worker. The maternal grandfather, John M. Hamilton, was in the cattle business in Mendota for many years, was an active Democrat, and postmaster there during several presidential administrations. He was a Mason and a Methodist, and one of the well known men of his times and locality.

Doctor Holley attended the Mendota High School, the Medical College of Virginia, Richmond, from which he was graduated in 1899 with the degree of Doctor of Medicine, and the New York Lying In Hospital, where in 1925 he took post-graduate work in obstetrics. For two years after securing his degree Doctor Holley was engaged in a general practice in Mendota, but then became contract surgeon for the Virginia Iron and Coal Company, and was located at Toms Creek, Virginia, for a short time, but was later sent to Inman, Virginia, where he continued for fifteen years. When he was elected treasurer of Wise County he resigned his position as surgeon and held his elective office, to which he had been elected as the regular Republican nominee, for four years. Upon the completion of his four years he came to Appalachia, and here he has since remained in private practice, having become one of the really great men in his profession. Doctor Holley belongs to the Wise County Medical Society, the Clinch Valley Medical Society, having been president of the former at one time, the Virginia State Medical Society, and is physician for the Standard Oil Company and examiner for all of the leading insurance companies for this district. He is a director of the First National Bank, the Appalachia Hotel Corporation, president and director of the Appalachia Realty Corporation, president and director of the Old Dominion Drug Corporation, a director of the Wise County Mutual Building &

Loan Association, and a trustee and member of the staff of the
Appalachia Masonic Hospital. He is a thirty-second degree and
Shriner Mason, is a past master of the Blue Lodge, and deputy
grand master of Virginia. A staunch Republican, in addition to
the office already mentioned he has been elected to the City
Council, of which he is now a member, and to the office of school
trustee. For two years he was chairman of the Republican
Central Committee of Wise County, and he is a recognized leader
of his party. Reared a Methodist, he has continued in that faith,
and is now a steward of the Methodist Episcopal Church, South,
of Appalachia.

Doctor Holley married Miss Nila Williams, of Cumberland
Gap, Tennessee, a daughter of Marion Williams. Mrs. Holley
was educated in Oberlin College, Ohio, and is a cultured lady of
many social graces, an ardent member of the Baptist Church.
Doctor and Mrs. Holley have two children: Marian, who was
graduated from Intermont College, Bristol, Virginia, in 1926,
married J. Frank Richmond, of Gate City, Virginia; and Ruth,
who is also married.

HON. LUTHER E. FULLER. In the biographies of men who
have attained merited distinction in American law there are combined charm and force that commend them to every sound think-
er. It is but natural to feel an interest in tracing the footsteps
of those who have reached high positions in public confidence,
and who have wielded their influence for public good; who, loving truth and integrity for their own sakes, have undeviatingly
followed their dictates, no matter what the personal conse-
quences might be. Records of this character are calculated to
be important factors in the raising of the ministrations of law
in public estimation, and should serve as plain guide posts for
the junior members of the profession in their pursuit of reputation, position and distinction. Although yet in the very heyday
of life, Hon. Luther E. Fuller, commonwealth's attorney of Russell County, has already made just such a record, and his life
has been a succession of honors and he may look forward to
many more, for he is not only a very able lawyer, but a popular
man, and the only Republican to be elected to any county office
for twenty years in Russell County.

Luther E. Fuller was born in Council, Buchanan County,
Virginia, January 15, 1897, a son of James M. and Louisa Grace
(Woosley) Fuller, the latter of whom is deceased, but the former
survives, being a retired merchant of Honaker, and one of the
most active Republicans of the county. For years he has been
one of the moving spirits in the Independent Order of Odd Fellows, of which he is a past grand, and he is a valued member
of the Missionary Baptist Church. The paternal grandfather,
James Harvey Fuller was a Russell County planter, an active
Republican, and collector of taxes in his part of Virginia during
the war between the states. His church was the Missionary
Baptist. The Fuller family was established in the American
colonies by Sir Edward Fuller and his wife, Rose, who were
among the passengers of the Mayflower. The maternal grandfather, Thomas Woosley, although now eighty-three years old,
is still active in the ministry of the Christian Church, resides in
Buchanan, and is beloved by all who know him. From its organization a member of the Republican party, he has always worked
for its success and is still one of its leaders in his home community. He is of Scotch-Irish descent. Few men have any

better background than Attorney Fuller, and he is proud of his
forebears, and it has always been his desire to live up to their
standards and prove himself worthy of them.

Luther E. Fuller was educated along very liberal lines, for
after he had completed his high-school work in Buchanan County
he attended the Mission School at Council, Virginia, and later
William and Mary College, and was graduated from the latter.
His law training was taken in the University of Richmond, from
which he was graduated in 1923 with the degree of Bachelor of
Laws. For one year thereafter he was engaged in private
practice by himself at Honaker, but in 1924 he formed a partnership with Hon. A. T. Griffith, and this association continued for
eighteen months, and was then severed, Mr. Griffith going to
Lebanon, and Mr. Fuller continuing alone. He is a member of
the Russell County Bar Association, Virginia Bar Association,
Delta Theta Pi, the Quill and Scimitar, the Commercial Law
League of America and the Civitan Club, of which he is president. He is a Blue Lodge Mason and a member of the Missionary
Baptist Church. Like his father and grandfather, he is a zealous Republican and served for four years as chairman of the
Republican County Central Committee, resigning from that office
when he became the candidate of his party for the office of
commonwealth's attorney in 1927. At the time he was mayor
of Honaker, but resigned to take office January 1, 1928, as commonwealth's attorney, to which he was elected in the fall of 1927.
He has also served as a member of the City Council of Honaker.
A speaker of power and eloquence, he has been in great demand
in party campaigns, and is a forceful pleader at the bar and
noted as a criminal lawyer. Mr. Fuller is attorney for the Potomac Joint Land Bank of Washington City, and is also actively
engaged in the insurance business in partnership with his uncle,
owners of the Honaker Insurance Agency. He owns large tracts
of coal land in Dickenson County, has large holdings of timber
land in Buchanan County, and owns a big farm in Russell
County, which he has cultivated.

On July 16, 1927, Mr. Fuller married Miss Jennie Wood
Warren, of Lancaster County, Virginia, a daughter of Thomas
F. and Ethel May (Wood) Warren, the latter being a native
of New Jersey and the former of Virginia, he being a member
of one of the very famous families of the Old Dominion. Mr.
Warren is engaged in the furniture and real estate business in
Lancaster County and New Jersey, and is an Odd Fellow and a
Baptist. J. C. Warren, the paternal grandfather of Mrs. Fuller,
was an officer in the Confederate army during the war between
the states, and both before and after the war was a planter
upon an extensive scale. The maternal grandfather, Auley B.
Wood, moved from New Jersey to Virginia, and in the latter
state located at Ottoman, where he was engaged in the practice
of medicine, and was a prominent Odd Fellow and Baptist. The
Warren and Wood families are of English origin.

Mrs. Fuller was educated in the Ottoman High School, White-
stone High School and William and Mary College, and prior to
her marriage she taught in the Honaker public schools. She is
a member of Kappa Kappa Gamma, the Honaker Literary Society, Young Woman's Christian Association's Student Council,
R. N. P. Club, and the Baptist Church. In the latter connection
she is a Sunday School teacher and leader in the Baptist Young
People's Union. Both Mr. and Mrs. Fuller are social leaders,
and deservedly popular with all classes. As a man Mr. Fuller

Philip D. Stout, M.D.

is upright and straightforward in all his transactions in life; as a lawyer he is capable, discerning and trustworthy, and a convincing pleader, gifted with talents that make for success. In political affairs he depends largely upon his inborn friendliness of nature, being successful without being bitterly partisan, and strangely and admirably free from that venom which characterizes so many in public life. While he has a just desire for office and power, he cannot be tempted by the glitter of gold. In the truest sense of the word Mr. Fuller is a gentleman, just as he is an able lawyer and honest public official.

PHILIP D. STOUT, M. D. Although one of the younger medical practioners well established at Bristol, Virginia, Dr. Philip D. Stout, specialist in internal medicine, and a veteran of the World war, is recognized as unusually able professionally, commanding the confidence and high regard of many scientific organizations and other learned bodies. Doctor Stout belongs to an old Southern family of English extraction, the founder of which came to the United States very many years ago, and the Stouts in several adjoining Southern States are direct descendants of his six worthy sons, all men of industry, thrift, religion and conspicuous good citizenship.

Dr. Philip D. Stout was born October 19, 1894, in Johnson County, Tennessee, son of David and Martha (Norris) Stout, third born in their family of seven children, four of whom survive, his one sister and two brothers being: Emma, who is the wife of J. Frank Stout, of Mountain City, Tennessee; George W., who is now operating the family estate in Johnson County, Tennessee; and J. Blaine Stout, who is a merchant at Doeville, Tennessee.

David Stout, father of Doctor Stout, was born in Johnson County, Tennessee, son of Godfrey Stout, farmer and dealer in lumber and produce, and grandson of Major Stout, who was an extensive farmer and stock dealer there. David Stout was both farmer and merchant during his active years, but now lives comfortably retired in Johnson County, Doeville, Tennessee, where both he and wife have long been faithful members and liberal supporters of the Baptist Church. The maternal grandfather of Doctor Stout was a native of North Carolina, but spent the greater part of his life as a farmer in Eastern Tennessee.

The excellent public schools provided Philip D. Stout's early educational training preparing him for Wautega Academy at Butler, Tennessee, and upon completing his academic course he entered the East Tennessee State Normal College at Johnson City, where his diligence in study and versatility of talent greatly pleased his instructors. It was about this time, perhaps, that he began to think seriously of a future medical career, although he determined that decision could wait until after he had won several coveted college degrees.

Before entering Wake Forest College, Wake Forest, North Carolina, for more advanced instruction, Doctor Stout found time to complete a commercial course in Piedmont Business College at Lynchburg, Virginia. In due course of time he was graduated from Wake Forest College with his A. B. degree, and subsequently through post-graduate work there earned his A. M. degree, and had also been exceedingly prominent in the Euzelian Literary Society at Wake Forest College.

With intelligence thus quickened and mind broadened, Doctor Stout now turned his attention to what he had decided his real business in life, the knowledge and practice of medicine. Entering Vanderbilt at Nashville, Tennessee, he soon found absorbing interest in his studies, but this was a memorable period of change, and as the menacing war clouds came closer and closer, the change came to himself, the student becoming the soldier. Early enlisting for service in the World war as a member of the Medical Reserve Corps, he enlisted additionally, in May, 1918, in the Medical Division at Fort Oglethorpe, Camp Greenleaf, Georgia, where he remained three and a half months, when he was sent to the non-commissioned officers training school with the rank of corporal, but shortly afterwards was recommended for the R. O. T. C. at Camp Hancock, Augusta, Georgia, and on completing his training was offered a rating of second lieutenant or an honorable discharge, and as the war had ended he accepted the latter, which was made official on December 6, 1918.

In January, 1919, Doctor Stout returned to Vanderbilt University to continue his medical studies, some time later removing to the University of Maryland at Baltimore, from which he was graduated with his medical degree in 1922. Then followed one year of service as interne and house surgeon in St. Thomas Hospital at Nashville, Tennessee, and a post-graduate course at Harvard University in internal medicine. Since then he has been engaged in active practice, first for a few months at Bluff City, Tennessee, then at Bristol, Tennessee, and since 1927 has been established at Bristol, Virginia, with convenient offices in the Reynolds Arcade Building, this city.

The soundness and extent of his professional knowledge has made Doctor Stout widely acceptable as a medical writer and speaker. He is attached to Kings Mountain Hospital as clinical pathologist and lectures on clinical pathology before the Nurses' Training Class, and belongs to the medical societies of Sullivan, Johnson and Carter counties, Tennessee, the Tennessee State Medical Society, the Southern Medical Society and the American Medical Association and lesser bodies. He is examiner for many leading life insurance companies and many fraternal organizations, is a member of the local Federal Pension Examining Board, belongs to the Masonic fraternity and to the Elks, Kiwanis Club, Chamber of Commerce and is a member of the Bristol Country Club. He takes a good citizen's interest in civic affairs and is identified with Republican politics but is not an active partisan.

Dr. Philip D. Stout was united in marriage June 20, 1928, with the charming daughter of Mrs. Margaret McAllister Barron, of Huntsville, Alabama. They lived happily together until his wife, Elizabeth Barron Stout, was fatally injured in an aeroplane accident May 31, 1929, while visiting her family at Huntsville, Alabama. No children were born to this union.

CHARLES N. DAVIDSON. Among the early settlers in Southwest Virginia of pure Irish extraction were the Davidsons, the McClellans and the McConnells, a vigorous, sturdy group that proved industrious, reliable and, when occasion arose, intensely loyal to the state. From such an honorable ancestral background came one of Wise County's prominent men of today, Hon. Charles N. Davidson, commander of revenue for Wise County. Although for a number of years Mr. Davidson has been serving in public office, he is also an experienced business man and has important banking interests at Appalachia, Virginia, his home city.

Charles N. Davidson was born on the old home plantation in Scott County, Virginia, November 25, 1882, son of William M. and Mary L. (McClellan) Davidson, both of whom were born in Scott County and passed their lives there. They were faithful members of the Methodist Episcopal Church, in which William M. Davidson was a steward for many years. During the war between the states he served as a soldier in the Confederate army as a member of Company C, 25th Virginia Volunteers, of which organization his father, Hiram Davidson, and his two brothers were also members.

The maternal grandparents of Commissioner Davidson were Andrew Jackson and Susanna (McConnell) McClellan, the former of whom was a soldier in the Confederate army all through the war. He was a planter and later deputy sheriff of Scott County, and all his life active in Democratic politics. The father of his wife was the first sheriff of Scott County, and both of her two brothers were distinguished men in their day, Major S. P. and Dr. A. D. McConnell. During the early part of the war between the states the elder brother served as a major in the Confederate army, but later, when urged to accept the office of clerk of the court of Scott County, resigned his military office and it is related that shortly afterward, when the near approach of the Federal troops caused apprehension concerning the safety of the countyseat, it was through the strategy of Major McConnell that none of the papers, books or county records were lost or endangered, for he kept guard over them in a mountain fastness. The other brother, Dr. A. D. McConnell, a prominent physician, represented Scott County in the Virginia House of Delegates for two terms.

Charles N. Davidson received his educational training in the schools of his native county, assisted his father and remained with his parents until he was twenty-one years old, since which time he has been a resident of Wise County. Inclined toward a commercial life, he came to Wise and accepted a clerkship with the firm of Head and Sloan, changing three years later to the Stonega Coal and Coke Company, where he filled a responsible position for seven years, during which time he had become so well and favorably known to the citizens of Stonega that they petitioned and in June, 1914, he was appointed postmaster there. This office he continued to fill until February 1, 1922.

Since early manhood Mr. Davidson has taken a deep and intelligent interest in public affairs and has participated in local politics, seldom accepting political preferment for himself, but ever loyal to his party and helpful to his friends. Since 1910 he has been recognized as a leader in the Democratic party and practically ever since has been a member of the Wise County Democratic Committee. In 1923 he was nominated for the office of commissioner of revenue from this district, was elected by a large majority over his opponent, and served in that office for the next four years, under the old law that provided for four commissioners. In the meanwhile the law was changed, and when he was reelected in 1927 and entered upon his duties on January 1, 1928, it was with heavier responsibilities than before, for he is now sole commissioner of revenue for Wise County, his long experience in this office making his services of inestimable value to the public.

In 1908 Mr. Davidson married Miss Zoie Quillin, who was born in Scott County, daughter of the late Rev. James M. and Virginia (Frazier) Quillin, the former of whom for many years was a leading minister in the Primitive Baptist Church in Southwest Virginia. Mrs. Davidson is a well educated lady, companionable, understanding and sympathetic, and, with her husband, has a wide circle of friends. They both are active members of the Methodist Episcopal Church, South. Commissioner Davidson belongs to the Masonic fraternity and other representative organizations. He has business interests at several points, and a leading one is the Peoples Bank of Appalachia.

KENNETH CARTRIGHT PATTY is an attorney and former mayor of Bluefield, Tazewell County, one of the prominent younger men in the professional and civic affairs of that important industrial locality of Southwest Virginia.

Mr. Patty was born at Parrottsville, Cocke County, Tennessee, and some four or five generations of the Patty family have lived in East Tennessee. William Patty was born there, of Irish ancestry, and was a pioneer Methodist minister. He was the father of Rev. Raphael W. Patty, a minister of the same church. Elbert S. Patty, son of Raphael W., enlisted for service in the Confederate army and and died of typhoid fever while in the service. His wife, Mattie Robeson, was born in 1842 and died in 1918. These were the grandparents of the Bluefield attorney. The father was Rev. William M. Patty, who was born in Buncombe County, North Carolina, July 2, 1862, but was reared in East Tennessee, and as a young man entered the Methodist ministry, as a representative of the third generation of the family in that calling in East Tennessee. He is now retired. He married Minnie Bushong, who was born at Knoxville, Tennessee, January 20, 1866. Their oldest son, Graydon K. Patty, became a Methodist minister.

Kenneth Cartright Patty received his early schooling under his aunt, Lena Bushong, and later attended high school at Clintwood, Virginia, and Tazewell, graduating from the latter in 1910. For several years he clerked in a store at Tazewell, studied law, and was a student in the law department of Washington and Lee University until he answered the call to the colors in February, 1918. He was licensed to practice law in Virginia December 27, 1917. He was assigned duty with the University of Virginia Base Hospital No. 41, spent four months at Camp Sevier, South Carolina, embarked for overseas July 5, 1918, and was with the Base Hospital near Paris until after the armistice. He received an honorable discharge, with the rank of sergeant, May 1, 1919.

In June, 1919, Mr. Patty began the practice of law at Graham in Tazewell County. On September 1, 1924, he was elected mayor of Graham, and served until August, 1926. It was during his administration and with him as the leader that the campaign was made to change the name Graham to Bluefield, Virginia. He also led the fight to annex more territory to the city, increasing the population by over a thousand. More concrete sidewalk construction is credited to his administration than to all the previous ones combined in the history of the town. During these years Mr. Patty has carried on a general law practice, and has served as officer and director of local industrial and banking corporations.

He is a Democrat, is a member of the Methodist Episcopal Church, South, is affiliated with Harman Lodge No. 222, A. F. and A. M., at Bluefield, is a past high priest of the Royal Arch Chapter No. 28 at Bluefield, and a past district deputy grand

Judith A. Smith

high priest of District No. 12. He is also a past chancellor of
Graham Lodge No. 150 of Knights of Pythias. He is a member
of Graham Commandery No. 22, Bluefield, Virginia.

He married at Scottsburg, Halifax County, Virginia, October
15, 1921, Miss Ruth Friend Lacy, daughter of James T. and Ada
(Crews) Lacy. Her father is a retired farmer and banker and
former member of the Virginia State Senate. Mrs. Patty attended the Richmond Woman's College and graduated from the
New England Conservatory of Music at Boston. They have one
daughter, Ann Holman Patty, born March 2, 1928.

MRS. JUDITH A. (RIDDICK) SMITH. Left a widow with two
small children to care for, Mrs. Smith bravely faced the problem,
and having selected the educational field as one of promise has
met with such success in the various departments of the public
schools of Petersburg that she eventually became the supervisor
of drawing for all of the schools of that city, serving ably and
creditably until resigning the position.

Mrs. Smith was born in Nottaway County, Virginia. Her
father, the late Rev. James A. Riddick, inherited in a large
measure the characteristics of his thrifty Scotch ancestors. He
acquired a good education, and having been converted in his
youth became a preacher in the Methodist Episcopal Church,
South. Joining the Virginia Conference, he held pastorates in
various places, and during one term served as presiding elder
of the Norfolk District. Subsequently as a circuit rider he
established churches in both Virginia and North Carolina. In
1861 he bought a residence at Stony Creek, Sussex County, where
during the Civil war that section of the state was invaded by
both armies, and all of the houses in the village, with but two
exceptions, were burned. At the close of the conflict he returned
with his family to Petersburg, and there resided until his death
at the ripe old age of nearly ninety years.

Rev. James A. Riddick married Judith A. Gregory, who was
born in Amelia County, Virginia, a sister of Maj. W. F. C. and
Crab Gregory, both of whom served during the Civil war on
the staff of Governor Wise. She died at the comparatively
early age of fifty-nine years, leaving seven children.

Born in 1850, Mrs. Judith A. Smith gleaned her first knowledge of books in private schools, later advancing her education
at Kittrells, near Oxford, North Carolina. In 1872, at the age
of twenty-two years, she became the wife of Dr. Joseph W.
Smith, who was born in 1827 in Chesterfield County, Virginia,
a son of Jabez Sidney Smith, who was a native of New York and
of English ancestry.

As a young man Joseph W. Smith decided to enter the medical profession, and after being graduated from the Jefferson
Medical College in Philadelphia, with the degree of M. D., he
located at Petersburg, Virginia. Meeting with well earned success from the first, he continued there until his death, when but
fifty-two years of age. As a physician and surgeon the Doctor
held a position of note, his services both before and after the
Civil war having been in much demand, especially in severe and
critical cases. His brother, Jabez Sidney Smith, was a prominent lawyer and Mason of Washington, D. C. Doctor Smith
was an uncle of Oscar W. Underwood, United States senator
from Alabama. In 1872 Doctor Smith was united in marriage
with Miss Judith A. Riddick, and into their pleasant home two
children were born, Jabez Sidney and Joseph W.

Left a widow when young, with two small children to care for, Mrs. Judith A. (Riddick) Smith bravely faced the problem by entering the educational field, the need therefor having arisen from the fact that her husband's entire fortune had been swept away. Securing a position as a teacher in the Petersburg public schools, she met with such merited success that she was subsequently made principal of the Anderson School, which stood on the site now occupied by the City High School. Her artistic tastes and ability becoming recognized, she was elected supervisor of drawing in all of the schools, a position she filled most acceptably to all concerned until her resignation which she requested at the close of her thirty-three years of service in the Petersburg schools. She is now living retired from active pursuits at her attractive home on West Washington Street. For fifty years she has been an active member of the Episcopal Church.

Mrs. Smith's oldest son, Jabez Sidney Smith, who, like his brother, served in the Spanish-American war, lost his health while in the army, and for three years prior to his death, when but twenty-seven years old, was an invalid. The younger son, Joseph Walworth Smith, is well established in business at Petersburg. Joseph W. Smith was educated in public schools at Petersburg. At an early age he became identified with the hardware business, starting at its very bottom. Through industry and application he has risen to the position of member of the firm of Charles Leonard Hardware Company, Inc., one of the largest firms of its kind in the South. He, like his mother, is a consistent member of the Episcopal Church. He has had numerous opportunities to engage in similar business elsewhere, but refuses to leave his home and his mother. He served in the Spanish-American war and is unmarried.

Talented and accomplished, Mrs. Smith is a gifted artist, noted for her pencil, landscape and portrait work, and having an excellent command of the English language tells many interesting and thrilling incidents of the Civil war. Although she has outlived the Psalmist's prescribed three score years and ten, her physical health and mental faculties are seemingly unimpaired, a visit with her being a pleasure to both the old and young.

BENJAMIN FRANKLIN BUCHANAN, of Marion, is a lawyer with the prestige of over forty years of active and successful practice, and the position of leadership he early acquired in his home community has been extended over the state at large, particularly through his many terms in the State Senate and as former lieutenant governor. In the alignment of political honors and responsibilities in the year 1928 Senator Buchanan is regarded as the next successor to the office of governor of the great commonwealth of Virginia.

The Buchanan family has lived in Smyth County, Virginia, since Colonial times. Senator Buchanan is a descendant of James Buchanan, a native of County Donegal, Ireland, who on coming to America settled in the Cumberland Valley of Pennsylvania. Senator Buchanan is a descendant in the fifth generation from this ancestor. John Buchanan, his son, was born in Pennsylvania, and as a young man moved down to the Valley of Virginia to the locality known as Rich Valley in Smyth County, where he acquired and began the development of large holdings. He married a distant relative, named Martha Buchanan. John Buchanan was killed while serving as captain of a company in the Continental Army during the Revolution, having previously participated in the important battle of Kings Mountain. His son, Patrick Buchanan, was born in Rich Valley and spent his life there as a farmer. He married Elizabeth Haytor, a native of Tazewell County, Virginia.

Their son, Patrick Campbell Buchanan, was born at Rich Valley December 12, 1818, and died July 7, 1877, having lived all his life on the same farm, fifteen miles north of Marion. He was an A. B. graduate of Emory and Henry College, and for five years was assistant professor of methematics in his alma mater. During the Civil war he was collector of internal revenue, and also served as treasurer of Smyth County and for several terms as sheriff. He was a member of the Methodist Episcopal Church, South. Patrick Campbell Buchanan married Virginia Copenhaver, who was born in Smyth County May 21, 1830, and died July 2, 1871.

Benjamin Franklin Buchanan, the oldest of the children of Patrick Campbell Buchanan and wife, was born at Rich Valley October 4, 1859. He attended private schools, and graduated with the A. B. degree from the University of Virginia in 1880. He is a member of the honorary scholastic fraternity Phi Beta Kappa, also the Phi Delta Theta social fraternity. He graduated with the law degree from the University of Virginia in 1884, and since 1885 has given attention to an extensive private law practice.

His first service in the State Senate as representative of the First Senatorial District was from 1893 to 1897. He was again elected to the Senate in 1915, and during 1915-17 was one of the members of the Virginia Tax Commission, revising the tax laws of the state. He was lieutenant governor of Virginia from 1917 to 1921, and in recognition of his service to the state in that position and also his legal scholarship Hampden-Sidney College made him an honorary Doctor of Laws in 1921. Since the close of his term as lieutenant governor he has been in the State Senate by repeated reelections, the last time having been chosen to office without opposition.

Senator Buchanan owns a farm near Marion, is director of several banks, and during the World war was general counsel for the comptroller of currency at Washington. He is a member of the Virginia Bar Association, the American Bar Association, and has long been prominent in Masonic circles, being a past master of Marion Lodge No. 31, A. F. and A. M., a past high priest of Marion Chapter No. 54, Royal Arch Masons, a past commander of Lynn Commandery No. 9, Knights Templar, a past grand commander of the Grand Commandery of Virginia, and a member of Kazim Temple of the Mystic Shrine at Roanoke. He is a member of the Marion Rotary Club.

He married, March 2, 1887, Miss Eleanor F. Sheffey, daughter of Judge John Preston and Josephine (Spiller) Sheffey. Her father was at one time judge of the Circuit Court, a successful lawyer, merchant and farmer. Mrs. Buchanan is a graduate of Marian College and of Stonewall Jackson College at Abingdon. They have five children: John Preston, who was educated in the Virginia Military Institute, Washington and Lee University and the University of Virginia, after which he became associated with his father in law practice; Josephine, who graduated A. B. from Hollins College; Virginia Campbell, who became the wife of Major Guy B. Dent, of the United States Army, a World war veteran; Eleanor Fairman, who graduated with the A. B. degree from Agnes Scott College at Decatur, Georgia; and David Haytor, a graduate of the Greenbrier Military School at Lewisburg, West Virginia, and West Point Military Academy.

ORRIN K. PHLEGAR, M. D.   In these days of wonderful mechanical inventions the world at large is learning, as never before, how brave, courageous and determined a spirit dwells oftimes beneath a quiet and inconspicuous exterior. This spirit, however, is not, of itself, either a new or modern development, although its daily manifestation in a public way has become so phenomenal. Every individual who has achieved success in life through his own efforts has possessed this indomitable spirit, a gift of Nature that he seldom parts with. Such a spirit enabled one of Tazewell County's prominent men of medical science, Dr. Orrin K. Phlegar, physician and surgeon at Bluefield, Virginia, to overcome hindering circumstances in early life, and to finally reach the goal of his ambition, high standing in the medical profession.

Orrin K. Phlegar comes of old and substantial families of German extraction, long settled in Floyd County, Virginia. His birth took place at Newbern, Virginia, May 5, 1876, son of Tazewell T. and Flora (Overstreet) Phlegar, and grandson of Jacob Phlegar and Tillman Overstreet, all natives and life long residents of Floyd County, the only survivor being the mother of Doctor Phlegar. His father, the late Tazewell T. Phlegar, was a cabinetmaker and wheelwright in early business life, having learned these trades under his father, who was known far and wide for his mechanical skill, and maintained large shops of his own at Jacksonville. Later Tazewell T. Phlegar became interested in telegraphy, and became a skilled telegraph operator, a position he filled at the time of his death. All his life he was an industrious, practical man and worthy citizen, a Democrat in politics and a member of the Lutheran Church.

Orrin K. Phlegar received his early educational training in the public schools of Pearisburg, Virginia, where he qualified as a satisfactory student, with talents indicating success in professional life if properly developed, but just at that time the subject of higher education could not be considered in the family, and, taking his father's advice, Mr. Phlegar learned the art of telegraphy, and for thirteen years was a telegraph operator for the Norfolk & Western Railroad. Although his early hopes of a medical education had to be given up, they were in no wise abandoned, and as soon as practicable, in relation to his other work, he began the study of medicine by himself, found opportunity to continue his reading under local practitioners, and at length, with capital earned and prudently saved, felt free to resign his telegraphic position and enter the University College of Medicine at Richmond, and from this institution he was graduated in 1906 with his degree. For one year afterward he was physician for the Boxley and Carpenter Railroad Contractors at Gladys in Campbell County and then for nine months in Scott County, and then embarked in a general medical practice at Crandon in Bland County, where he remained three years, removing then to Radford, and one year later, in 1912, to Graham, Virginia, now the city of Bluefield.

In 1903 Doctor Phlegar married Miss Bertha May Collins, of Pearisburg, Virginia, daughter of John Collins, a descendant of one of the early Colonial families of the state. She was care-

fully reared and liberally educated, and is active in the Baptist Church. Doctor and Mrs. Phlegar have one daughter, Thelma, who is not only known and beloved at Bluefield for her beautiful character and social graces, but is sincerely admired for her unusual intellectual achievements. Although she has but just passed her twenty-fourth birthday, she fills a high position as an educator in the Concord State Normal School at Athens, West Virginia, and since childhood has won scholastic honors in every institution she has attended. She is a graduate of the Graham High School; a graduate of Intermont College at Bristol, Virginia; an A. B. graduate of West Hampton College, Richmond, Virginia; and won her A. M. degree at Columbia University.

In the sixteen years that have passed since Doctor Phlegar came to Bluefield his life has been a busy and beneficent one, devoted entirely to his profession. He has so demonstrated not only his scientific knowledge and skill but the other qualities that belong to a physician that Nature sets apart at birth, that possibly no other practitioner in the county enjoys greater confidence and personal esteem. He is assistant surgeon for the Norfolk & Western Railroad and physician for the New York Life, the Metropolitan, the Jefferson Standard and other leading insurance companies. He belongs to the Masonic fraternity and to both State and County Medical Societies. Politically in national matters he is a Democrat.

EDWARD A. BAIN. Among the enterprising men associated in some manner with the manufacturing and mercantile interests of Petersburg the name of Edward A. Bain, bottler of temperance drinks, may well be mentioned. He and his father, James Bain, were both born in Petersburg, while his paternal grandfather, Rev. George Bain, was a native of Dinwiddie County, and a well known Methodist Episcopal minister.

As a young man James Bain was a clerk in William Spotswood's drug store, a position he filled until after his marriage. Settling then on land that had come to his wife by inheritance, he operated her large plantation with slave labor. During the period of the Civil war he made a specialty of raising food stuff for the Confederate army. He continued his agricultural work until his death, when but sixty-three years of age. His wife, whose maiden name was Nannie Greenway, was born on a plantation in Dinwiddie County, a daughter of Dr. Robert Greenway, a large and prosperous landowner, and a successful physician. She died ere the infirmities of age overtook her.

One of a family of six children, Edward A. Bain began the battle of life on his own account as a clerk in the Moore Warehouse, a position he held some time. Going then to North Carolina, he remained there a year. Returning to Petersburg in 1887, Mr. Bain established himself in business as a bottler of temperance drinks, beginning in a small way, with a very limited capital. Succeeding in his venture from the start, he gradually enlarged his operations, investing his savings in desired improvements. In 1927 at an expense of several thousand dollars, Mr. Bain installed in his plant the latest improved and approved machinery for bottling, at the same time making sure that the sanitary conditions are all that can be desired in any establishment of the kind.

On July 22, 1882, Mr. Bain was united in marriage with Miss Josephine D'Alton, who was born in Petersburg, Virginia, a daughter of Henry and Julia (Karney) D'Alton, both of whom

were born in Ireland, of honored French ancestry. Six children
have been born of the union of Mr. and Mrs. Bain, as follows:
Irene, wife of William P. Atkinson, has one child, Josephine
Nash, by her first marriage to George Templeton; Edwin, asso-
ciated in business with his father; Theresa June, who married
Webster Whitten, has two sons, James Webster and Edward
Bain; Charles Leonard married Bess Chick, and they have one
child, Elizabeth Ormond; Willis Robinson married Susie Chieves
Smith, and their only child, a daughter, is named Anne Green-
way, in honor of her paternal grandmother; and Eugene Anthony
was recently graduated from the medical department of the
University of Virginia.

PATRICK HENRY DREWRY, Petersburg attorney, is prominently known as an able and successful lawyer all over southern
and eastern Virginia, where he has practiced for over a quarter
of a century, also has one of the names best known over the
state as a public man, chiefly due to his important service in the
Virginia Senate and as representative of the Fourth Virginia
District in Congress.

Mr. Drewry was born at Petersburg May 24, 1875. The
consecutive record of his ancestors goes back unbroken to Samuel Drewry, of Southampton County, living there at the time
Southampton was formed in 1748. In England the Drewry family has been distinguished by many honors and achievements
since the first Drewry went over from Normandy, France, with
William the Conqueror in 1066. He was knighted on the battlefield of Hastings and granted land in the south of England, at
Drakelowe and Thurston, where the Drewrys lived for over six
hundred years. Two members of the Drewry family were charter members of the London Company, to whom Virginia was
originally granted. Mr. Drewry is probably a descendant of
Robert Drewry, who came to Virginia in 1635, when he was
sixteen years of age, settling in York County. Samuel Drewry,
a son of the Samuel named above, was a soldier in the American
Revolution. His son, Humphrey Drewry, a soldier in the War
of 1812, was a great-great-grandfather of the Petersburg
attorney.

His father, Emmett Arrington Drewry, was born in 1837
and died in 1891. His home was at Drewrysville in Southampton
County. He was educated under private tutors, graduated from
Randolph-Macon College, from the Medical College of Virginia,
and Jefferson Medical College of Philadelphia. His medical education was completed just before the war between the states,
and he became an officer in the Confederate army, at first in the
line and later, after the battle of Gettysburg, in the Medical
Corps. He entered as a lieutenant, coming out with the rank
of major. He practiced medicine at Drewrysville and otherwise
had a prominent part in the affairs of Southampton County,
helping get the Atlantic and Danville Railroad built through
the county, and was at one time superintendent of county
schools. He was a charter member of the Medical Society of
Virginia. Dr. E. A. Drewry married first Miss Laura Roney,
daughter of Major Roney, of Dinwiddie County, by whom he
has one son living, Dr. Herbert R. Drewry, of Norfolk, Virginia.
After her death he married Alta Laughton Booth, by whom he
had two sons, the subject of this sketch and Hunter Leigh
Drewry of Martinsburg, West Virginia. She was the daughter
of P. H. Booth, granddaughter of Col. Samuel Booth, of Surry

County, whose father, Beverly Booth, was a soldier in the War of the Revolution and a Baptist minister. Rev. Beverly Booth was a son of Robert Booth, Jr., and a grandson of Robert Booth, Sr., who in 1653 represented York County in the House of Burgesses.

In passing from this brief account of his forefathers there is no diminution in intellectual vigor, in the spirit of high idealism, in forceful action and in public spirit as manifested in the career of Patrick Henry Drewry. He had an excellent groundwork of preparation in school and the experiences of his young manhood. He attended McCabe's University School at Petersburg, took his A. B. degree at Randolph-Macon College at Ashland and for a time held the chair of English and Greek at Centenary College at Palmyra, Missouri. He was graduated from the law department of the University of Virginia in 1899, and while teaching in Missouri passed the bar examination in that state. Subsequently he qualified for practice in Virginia, and in 1902 began his individual work as an attorney in Petersburg. In 1907 he became associated with one of the able lawyers of the city, C. T. Lassiter, in the firm of Lassiter & Drewry. Their partnership was discontinued in 1921. Since 1923 Mr. Drewry has practiced with William Old as senior member of the firm Drewry & Old. These firms in corporation practice as well as in general practice before courts and juries enjoyed unqualified leadership and distinction among the law firms in their section of the state.

Mr. Drewry became a participant in politics when a young man, not for rewards and honors of office, but through a sincere conviction that every properly qualified citizen should make his influence felt in public affairs and government. When he finally accepted the responsibilities of office he brought to his service the accomplishments of a successful lawyer and a mature judgment and large familiarity with public men and public interests. In 1911 he became a candidate for the State Senate, and was elected and entered that body in 1912, serving continuously until 1920. The outstanding feature of his record in the Senate was in connection with the change in the financial system of the state. He originated the measure known as the Budget Bill, a bill that was largely the product of the Economy and Efficiency Commission, of which he was chairman, and afterwards by appointment of the governor he served as chairman of the Advisory Board on the Budget and as chairman of the State Auditing Committee.

Mr. Drewry was elected April 27, 1920, to fill the unexpired term in Congress of Walter A. Watson. He was elected for the regular term in 1920 and has been reelected without opposition to each succeeding Congress. He represents one of the important agricultural districts of Virginia, and has interested himself primarily in matters affecting agriculture, particularly the agriculture of the southeastern states. He voted for the cooperative marketing bill, the bill to relieve depression in agricultural sections, the Muscle Shoals legislation, and various other bills and amendments affecting the farm section of the country. Mr. Drewry is a member of the Naval Committee and was a member of the Board of Visitors of the Naval Academy at Annapolis in 1926. He has also served on such important committees as insular affairs, territories and naval expenditures. He succeeded Hal Flood as a member of the Democratic National Congressional Committee and became a member of the Executive

Committee of that organization. Mr. Drewy was a delegate to
the National Democratic Convention of 1916 at Saint Louis, and
has been a delegate to all state conventions since 1912, and was
chairman of the Resolution Committee in the State Convention
of 1924.

Mr. Drewry during the World war served on the committee
of preparedness, was director for the Fourth District of the
Minute-Men and worked in behalf of the Liberty Bond, Red
Cross and other campaigns. He was Government appeal agent
for the Petersburg District during the World war. He is a
member of the Board of Stewards of the Washington Street
Methodist Episcopal Church, South, at Petersburg, member of
the Petersburg Country Club, Westmoreland Club of Richmond,
is a Phi Beta Kappa, also belongs to the Sigma Chi fraternity
and the B. P. O. Elks.

He married at Palmyra, Missouri, April 18, 1906, Miss Mary
E. Metcalf, daughter of Judge J. Q. A. and Harriet (Hanley)
Metcalf, her father a native of Virginia, of a Maryland family,
while her mother was a member of the well known Philadelphia
Hanleys. Mr. and Mrs. Drewry had three children, Patrick
Henry, Jr., John Metcalf and William Emmett. Patrick Henry,
Jr., was born at Petersburg March 21, 1907, attended high school
there, graduated in 1928 from Randolph-Macon College with the
Bachelor of Science degree, and then entered Johns Hopkins
University at Baltimore for the study of medicine. At Randolph-
Macon he was assistant instructor in biology. The other two
sons are attending the Petersburg High School.

WILLIAM V. BIRCHFIELD, JR. Only a mind of unusual
strength, persistent grasp and broad sweep of abilities can earn
signal success in a special field already crowded with keen competitors, and at the same time retain fresh and balanced faculties
for the consideration and advancement of public and social problems. The character of William V. Birchfield, Jr., is cast in no
ordinary mold, for he not only stands among the leading lawyers
of Southwestern Virginia in the construction and application of
corporation law—a legal domain surcharged with countless details and of such vast importance to the ingenious, practical
American—but has also obtained much more than a local reputation as a clear and broad exponent of the most vital questions
of industrial and social reform.

Mr. Birchfield was born August 24, 1884, at Marion, Smyth
County, Virginia, and is a son of William V. and Ollie M. (Bonham) Birchfield, of Marion, the former a native of Washington
County, Virginia, and the latter born in Smyth County. William
V. Birchfield, Sr., died in 1927. He was identified with the Reynolds Tobacco Company, and in his younger days was broadly influential in Democratic politics. He was a Mason and an active
and generous supporter of the Methodist Episcopal Church. He
and his wife had two sons: William V., Jr., of this review; and
James F., who is attending the Virginia Military Institute.

William V. Birchfield, Jr., attended public schools in Marion
County, and was graduated from Marion High School as a member of the class of 1910. He then entered Randolph-Macon Academy, but in 1911 left that institution to enter Emory and Henry
College at Emory, Virginia, where he remained two years. He
became a student of law at Washington and Lee University,
from which he received the degree of Bachelor of Laws as a
member of the class of 1916, and immediately thereafter went

to Roanoke, where he became identified with the law firm of Hall, Wingfield & Apperson, with which he continued to be connected for three years. For the four years that followed he practiced alone at Roanoke, where he also did a large abstract and loan business, and in 1924 settled permanently at Marion, where he now occupies commodious offices on Main Street. Since locating at Marion Mr. Birchfield has been successful in building up a large corporation practice and is now accounted one of the leaders in the field. He represents the Knight Brick and Tile Company, the Maryland Casualty Company and the Federal Land Bank of Baltimore, Maryland, and has also done a large business in loaning money to agriculturists. In addition to great erudition in his profession Mr. Birchfield is a fine speaker, and his services are much in demand as an orator during the campaigns of the Democratic party, of which he has been a leader in Southwest Virginia. In 1927 he was his party's candidate for the office of commonwealth's attorney of Smyth County and met with defeat by only a few votes. He belongs to the Roanoke Bar Association and the Virginia State Bar Association, is prominent in the Kiwanis Club, and also hold membership in the Phi Kappa Alpha and Phi Alpha Delta fraternities, in which he was very active while at college.

In 1922 Mr. Birchfield was united in marriage with Miss Virginia Semple, a member of an old and distinguished Virginia family, and a daughter of R. B. Semple, of Roanoke. Mrs. Birchfield was educated in the schools of Roanoke and is one of the leaders in the club and social life of Marion. Mr. and Mrs. Birchfield are the parents of one child, Bettie B., who was born in 1924.

WILLIAM HENRY FREY. A man of sterling integrity and worth, possessing from early boyhood a decided mechanical inclination, probably inherited, William Henry Frey devoted his talents to the study of medicine and pharmacy. A son of Andrew Frey, he was born in 1869 at Georgetown in the District of Columbia, the family home having been located on Washington Street. Since that time the city limits have been extended, street names and numbers have been changed, his birthplace now being found at 1224 Thirtieth Street.

John Jacob Frey, Mr. Frey's paternal grandfather, was a well known and successful building contractor, working in different cities and spending the later years of his life in the District of Columbia. He reared a large family, and two of his sons, Andrew and John William, succeeded to his business.

Andrew Frey, in company with his brother, became a successful contractor, and at one time owned considerable valuable real estate in Washington, D. C., where he resided for some time. He died at the age of sixty-nine years, and his wife, at the age of forty years, leaving three sons, John J., William H. and Andrew R.

After graduating from the Western High School in Washington William Henry Frey spent a year in the medical department of Columbia University, New York City, after which he completed a full course in pharmacy, being graduated in 1889. Returning to Washington, he located at the corner of Seventh and B streets, in a building belonging to his father. Subsequently removing to the corner of Ninth Street and New York Avenue, he continued there until the death of his father in 1902, when he came to Dinwiddie County, settling in Petersburg, on the south side of West Washington Street. He soon bought property on the north side of West Washington Street, remodeled the buildings, and there built up a prosperous business, which he conducted until his death, November 28, 1920.

William Henry Frey married Miss Laura Polk Nalle, who was born on a large plantation located on Bethel Pike, quite near the Bethel School, and five miles from Warrenton, Fauquier County, Virginia. Her father, James Polk Nalle, was born in Culpeper County, Virginia, where he grew to manhood. John William Nalle, Mrs. Frey's grandfather, operated his plantation with slave labor, residing upon it until his death, at the venerable age of ninety years. His wife, whose name before marriage was Caroline Jeffress, was a member of one of the old and honored Virginia families.

James Polk Nalle inherited a plantation, but as a young man he acquired a wide knowledge of architecture and moved to Washington, D. C., where he drew plans for and superintended the erection of many residences, apartment houses and public buildings, including among others the Evans House. He spent the later years of his life in Washington, dying there at the age of sixty-one years. He married Mary Virginia Nalle, who was born in Fauquier County, Virginia, a daughter of Robert and Elizabeth (Keyes) Nalle and a very distant relative of John William Nalle. She died at the age of four score years, her body being laid to rest in the Blandford Cemetery. To her and her husband eight children were born, namely: William Walter, who died in infancy, Norman Nicholas, Laura Polk, John Robert, Arthur James, Bertha Mary, Lillian Estelle and Leila Grace.

Mr. and Mrs. Frey have two children, William Henry, Jr., and Florence Elizabeth Frey. William H. Frey received the degree of A. B. at Hampden-Sidney College and that of M. A. at the University of Virginia. He married Elizabeth Sullivan, and with his wife and two children, Nancy Polk Frey and Betty Ann, resides at La Jolla, California. Florence E. Frey married Bernard A. Davey, who died at the early age of thirty years. Mr. Davey was educated in the Northwestern University, Chicago, where he took a course in journalism, and for a while was advertising manager for the *Washington Times*, later being associated with the *Chicago Tribune*. Removing from Chicago to Birmingham, Alabama, he was connected with a leading daily paper of that city until his death at the age of thirty years. Mrs. Davey and her son, Bernard Frey Davey, are now living with her mother, Mrs. Frey. Mrs. Davey, who took lessons in vocal music at the Baltimore Conservatory of Music, is now an accompanist at Petersburg, Virginia, and is soloist at Grace Episcopal Church at Petersburg, Virginia.

MAX JOHN ALEXANDER, M. D. Tazewell County, Virginia, can lay claim to many men of high merit and definite achievement in both professional and business life, and an interested visitor is not long left in doubt concerning the confidence and esteem reposed in Dr. Max John Alexander, physician and surgeon at Pocahontas, formerly mayor of this city, and member of the County Board of Health.

Dr. Max John Alexander was born at Darlington, in Darlington County, South Carolina, March 28, 1887, son of C. and Minnie Carrie (Hymes) Alexander, the latter of whom still resides at Darlington, where her father, Henry Hymes, was a leading merchant for many years. The father of Doctor Alexander was born in the city of New York, where his father, Henry Alexander, had settled when he had come from Germany, and continued to make his home there. C. Alexander received his schooling and early business training in New York but later removed to South Carolina, where he was engaged in the mercantile business until his death at Darlington in 1924.

Max John Alexander grew up in a home of family affection, plenty and morality, and was afforded liberal educational advantages. After completing his course in the Darlington High School he continued his studies in St. John's Academy at Darlington, subsequently entering the Medical College of Virginia, from which he was graduated in 1910 with his degree. After serving one year as an interne in the Johnston-Willis Hospital at Richmond he became a member of the Hospital Staff, where during his service of over two years he made a fine record professionally.

Doctor Alexander then established himself in medical practice at Pocahontas, where he has maintained his headquarters ever since, although he is a licensed practitioner over a large area, including Virginia, West Virginia and South Carolina. He is physician for the Pocahontas Fuel Company, which operates with a labor force of 5,500 employes, an especially responsible position, not only including his caring for the general health of this large body, but he also is the absolute authority in cases of accident when hospital treatment is necessary. Through his efforts many of the Fuel Company's worthy men, during periods of illness, have been given an opportunity to recuperate in the famous sanitarium at Bluefield, West Virginia. Additionally, a large private practice demands constant attention. He is surgeon for the Norfolk & Western Railroad Company, is examiner for all the leading life insurance companies, and for an extended period has been a member of the County Board of Health.

In 1910, at Richmond, Virginia, Doctor Alexander married Miss Margaret Palmer, daughter of Charles and Alice (Cavel) Palmer, of that city, of a well known family of the Old Dominion. Mrs. Alexander completed her education in the Virginia State Normal School at Farmville, and has many social and cultural interests both at Pocahontas and Richmond. She is a member of the Episcopal Church. Doctor and Mrs. Alexander have two sons: Charles Palmer, born May 12, 1914; and John McConnell. born August 12, 1923.

Doctor Alexander has attended many clinics in leading medical centers, including the Mayo Brothers at Minneapolis, has an extensive library and occasionally finds time to contribute to medical literature. He is a member of the Tazewell County, the Clinch Valley, the Virginia State Medical Societies, being an official of the Clinch Valley body and of the American Medical Association. During the World war he was a member of the United States Medical Reserve Corps, but was never called into active service. With his versatile talents, both politics and business claim some attention, and in 1914, on the Democratic ticket, he was elected mayor of Pocahontas, in which office he served with marked efficiency for two years. It has always been his aim as a loyal and faithful citizen to lend support to substantial local enterprises, and his influence has not been without result. At present he is a director of the Citizens Drug Company of Pocahontas, and is also one of the directing board of the White Pharmacy at Bluefield, West Virginia. In addition to belonging to scientific research bodies that are giving an added interest to modern medical science, he has membership in such fraternal organizations as the Knights of Pythias and the Benevolent and Protective Order of Elks.

JAMES CLYNE HONAKER. Anywhere in the district around Rocky Gap in Bland County the name of Honaker is immediately identified by the family of that name, which for over a hundred years, through four generations, has been active in the commercial life of the community as merchants. No other one family has supplied such a consecutive service in one field of business in Bland County.

James Clyne Honaker was born near Princeton and Bluefield, West Virginia, March 2, 1869. The Honakers came at a very early date to Southwestern Virginia, and his great-grandfather was Abe Honaker, who moved to Bland County from Pulaski County. Abe Honaker's son, Peter C. Honaker, was for many years a merchant at Rocky Gap, and also owned and operated a farm there. The father of James C. Honaker was James D. Honaker, who was born at Rocky Gap, attended a private school, and carried on the family business as a merchant, and was also a farmer. He represented Bland and Smyth counties in the Lower House of the State Legislature in 1881, being at that time the youngest member of the Legislature, and later he was a member of the session of 1900. He died May 17, 1919, and is buried in the Rocky Gap Cemetery. He married Sally B. Bailey, who was born near Princeton, West Virginia, was well educated and taught school before her marriage. She was a member of the Methodist Episcopal Church, South. She died August 3, 1903. Of her four children two died in infancy, and the two now living are James C. and John D. The latter was for a number of years in the mercantile business and is now an automobile dealer at Bluefield, West Virginia. He married Edna Nottingham, of Cape Charles, Virginia, and their three children are James Luther, Thomas H. and Clara Belle.

James C. Honaker attended the public schools of Rocky Gap and was a student in the Virginia Polytechnic Institute until 1887, when at the age of eighteen, he became associated with the family business at Rocky Gap and has carried it on for forty years, though much of the active management now devolves upon his son, representing the fourth generation of this family as merchants. This son is James Eugene Honaker. They have a large store, supplying an extensive territory around Rocky Gap. Mr. Honaker also owns several fine blue grass farms and is extensively engaged in stock raising in Bland County. He is a director of the Bank of Rocky Gap and for some years was director of the First National Bank of Narrows, Virginia. For five years he was treasurer of Bland County.

Mr. Honaker is a Royal Arch Mason, member of the B. P. O. Elks at Bluefield, West Virginia, is a Republican and a trustee of the Methodist Episcopal Church, South.

He married, April 20, 1890, at Ingleside, West Virginia, Miss Sallie Jarrell, who was educated in Marion Female College and taught school for several years before her marriage. She is active in church and community affairs. Her parents were George W. and Elizabeth (Harman) Jarrell, of Ingleside. Her father was a farmer and stock raiser in Augusta County, Virginia, and Mercer County, West Virginia, and was killed by lightning in 1881. Her mother subsequently became the wife of

John W Harrison

John B. Hern, who died at Salem, Virginia, in 1927, and she survives at the age of eighty-three.

Mr. and Mrs. Honaker are the parents of eight children. The daughter Eula Lee is the wife of H. G. Helvey, of Rocky Gap, and their eight children are named William, James, Sallie, Virginia, Henry, Lucille, Dorothy and Wayne. Gaston S., the second child, was drowned at the age of twelve years in Wolfe Creek. James E. Honaker, the active associate of his father in the general mercantile business at Rocky Gap, was educated in Emory and Henry College, and is a member of the Board of Supervisors of Bland County. He married Miss Seretna Graham. Miss Eloise Honaker, living at home, was educated in the Marion Female College. Miss Mary is also at home. Juanita is deceased. Elizabeth C. is the wife of Raymond D. Williams, of Pembroke, Virginia. John B., the youngest, attended the Rocky Gap schools and is at home.

JOHN WILLIAMS HARRISON belonged to an active generation of Richmond business men who broadened and extended the influence of Richmond as a great wholesale and distributing center for the Southeast. He was a native Virginian, a descendant of the famous family of Harrisons whose lives are so intimately identified with the state in every generation since the founding of the colony. His great-great-grandfather, Carter Harrison, was a son of Benjamin Harrison of Berkeley and a brother of Benjamin Harrison, one of the signers of the Declaration of Independence and later governor of Virginia.

John Williams Harrison was born at Elkora, Cumberland County, February 13, 1857, and died at Richmond in August, 1918. His father was Maj. Carter Henry Harrison, and his grandfather, Randolph Harrison, whose home was Clifton Plantation. Randolph Harrison married Janetta Fisher.

Maj. Carter Henry Harrison was a planter and slave owner, and during the Civil war rose to the rank of major in the Confederate army and recruited a company of the Black Hawk Infantry. He was mortally wounded at the battle of Bull Run July 18, 1861, and died July 19, 1861, aged thirty years. He married Alice Burwell Williams, of the Orange County family of that name.

John Williams Harrison was educated by private tutors in Cumberland County and finished his education in the Virginia Polytechnic Institute. At the age of sixteen he was working in the wholesale grocery house of his uncle, Robert F. Williams, at Richmond, and at Richmond began his independent career as a coffee broker. After fifteen years in the brokerage business he became an importer of coffee, and handled a business of steadily increasing volume year after year, building up an organization and a trade which are still in existence. He had a number of traveling salesmen covering all of the southeastern states.

Not all his life was taken up with business. He enjoyed a wide association with men of affairs, belonged to the Wholesale Grocers' Association, the Richmond German Club, was a charter member of the Commonwealth Club, and belonged to the Country Club. He and his wife and children were all members of St. Paul's Episcopal Church.

He married at Uniontown, Pennsylvania, September 17, 1890, Miss May Kennedy Willson, who was reared in Pennsylvania and finished her education at Baltimore, Maryland. Her father,

Alpheus Evans Willson, was a distinguished Pennsylvania lawyer and jurist, graduated from Princeton University in 1847, and in 1873 was appointed judge of the Fourteenth Judicial District of Pennsylvania and served on the bench for twelve years by appointment and election, and finally refused a seat on the Supreme bench of the state. Judge Willson married Catherine Harrison Dawson, of Brownsville, Pennsylvania. They had three children: Eliza Evans, who married R. H. Lindsey, of Uniontown, Pennsylvania; Catherine Dawson, who married Harry W. Hazard, of Elizabeth, New Jersey; and Mrs. Harrison. Mrs. Harrison's mother was a lineal descendant of Governor Stone and Verlinda Cotton, the latter a sister of Rev. William Cotton of Williamsburg, Virginia, while Governor Stone was the first Protestant governor of Maryland.

Mr. and Mrs. Harrison had a family of three children. Their daughter, Eliza (Elsie) Willson, is the wife of Anthony C. Adams, a Richmond banker, and he has two children, Catherine Dawson Willson and Anthony Crease, Jr. Randolph Carter Harrison, vice president of the State Planters Bank of Richmond, married Mary McCaw Hawes, of Richmond, and has two children, Randolph Carter, Jr., and Mary Anne. Alpheus Evans Willson Harrison, in the trust office of the First and Merchants National Bank. He married Anne Sterling Hawes and has two children, Horace Hawes and Anne Willson.

Randolph Carter Harrison graduated with the A. B. degree from the University of Virginia in 1916, and during the World war was a lieutenant of military observation in the Aviation Corps, at first with French troops and later with the American forces. He is a member of the Richmond German, Commonwealth and Country Clubs. The second son, A. E. Willson Harrison, was also educated at the University of Virginia and spent two years with the colors during the war, being captain of a machine gun company. He is a member of the Commonwealth Club, German Club and Country Club and the Deep Reed Hunt Club. Mr. Adams belongs to the Commonwealth Club, German Club and Country Club. He was a lieutenant, being on duty on the Mexican border as well as in France during the World war. Mrs. Randolph Harrison and Mrs. Willson Harrison are members of the Junior League and of the Country Club. Mrs. Adams is also a member of the Country Club.

JOHN G. GILLESPIE. A prominent family of Tazewell County that can trace its ancestral line many generations back in Southwest Virginia bears the name of Gillespie, for many years a name familiar in the professions, in military and commercial life and agriculture, and in the political field. The Gillespies were people of wealth and importance long before the war between the states, and today, as of old, they are active in business and public affairs. A worthy and highly esteemed member of this old Tazewell County family is found in John G. Gillespie, postmaster at Bluefield, Virginia.

John G. Gillespie was born in Tazewell County, Virginia, September 5, 1866, son of Rev. James Harrison and Mary E. (Crockett) Gillespie, and grandson of Thomas H. Gillespie and John I. Crockett, all of whom were born and practically spent their entire lives in Tazewell County. Both grandfathers of Postmaster Gillespie were men of large possessions before the Civil war, Grandfather Crockett owning many acres of valuable coal lands, and Grandfather Gillespie being a leading banker, but both lost heavily in the war. Grandfather Gillespie later became a planter, and subsequently was elected a member of the Virginia Legislature from Tazewell County.

Rev. James Harrison Gillespie, father of Postmaster Gillespie, was an exceptional man both in war and peace. It so happened that he was a vigorous, robust youth of sixteen years when the war between the states came on, and probably due to his physical fitness, despite his youth, he was accepted as a soldier in the Confederate army and served throughout the war under Capt. D. B. Baldwin, his soldierly qualities bringing him promotion to a first lieutenancy. Later for forty years he served in the ministry of the Christian Church. He was widely known for his Christian zeal and benevolence, and was a member of the Masonic fraternity.

Although John G. Gillespie was not reared under circumstances that afforded him educational advantages beyond those of the common schools, these in combination with an alert mind and natural inclination and interest in public events and business enterprises have brought him a large measure of business success and have made him acceptable and valuable to his fellow citizens in public positions of responsibility. He remained at home giving his father assistance until he was twenty-one years old, and then went into business for himself as a merchant at Tip Top, Virginia. He continued there until public interests demanded his entire time, when he removed his business to Bluefield, where it is still carried on by his sons, under the style of R. P. Harman Mercantile Corporation, of which corporation Mr. Gillespie is vice president.

In 1887 John G. Gillespie married Miss Sallie McMullin, daughter of James H. McMullin, of an early settled family of Tazewell County, and Postmaster and Mrs. Gillespie have a family of five sons and three daughters, all useful members of society and highly esteemed in their several communities. The eldest, James H., who was educated in the public schools of Tazewell County, and Lynchburg College, is a traveling salesman, with home at Bluefield; Jesse S., who, like all his brothers, attended public schools of Tazewell County and Lynchburg College, is manager of the Harman Mercantile Corporation at Bluefield; Thomas W., who completed his course in pharmacy in Richmond, is a druggist at Oak Hill, West Virginia; Robert G., is manager of the stores of the Leckie Colleries Company at Aflex, Kentucky; Henry B., the youngest son, is a student in Graham High School; Sallie E., who attended the Graham High School and the State Teachers College at Lynchburg, is an instructor in the Bluefield High School; Elma F., who is a graduate of the State Teachers College at Lynchburg, is the wife of Robert Peirle, a druggist at Holden, West Virginia; and Elizabeth is now a student in the State Teachers College at Harrisonburg, Virginia. During the World war Jesse S. served one year in the United States Navy; Thomas W. spent thirteen months with the A. E. F. in France; and Robert G., when the war closed, was in a military training camp.

For many years Postmaster Gillespie has been active in Republican politics in the Ninth Congressional District. While still a resident of Tip Top, Virginia, he was elected commissioner of revenue for the Graham District of Tazewell County, and was continued in that important office twenty years, and it is worthy of note as indicative of the confidence and personal esteem in which he is held that his elections to office have been outside of partisanship, as his district has been normally and unchangeably Democratic. In March, 1927, he was appointed postmaster at Bluefield, and his time is now entirely devoted to the duties of his office, for Mr. Gillespie is one who regards a public office as a public trust and acts accordingly. He is a Royal Arch Mason, and while residing at Tip Top served six terms as master of Keystone Lodge, A. F. and A. M. He has membership also in other fraternal bodies, including the Odd Fellows and the Knights of Pythias, and in civic bodies that work for the substantial welfare of the city. Both he and wife belong to the Christian Church, in which he is an elder.

FRED H. KING. As far as lies in the power of this age to trace back into the misty records of the past the manners and customs of the peoples of all ages have been brought to light, and in every instance there is to be found definite traces of the respect paid to the dead. The countries of Asia and Africa show countless instances of the care taken to preserve the bodies of the dead, and to hand down to future generations a record of their deeds; while in the New World the same evidences prevail. However, never before in the history of man has such care been given the dead as that afforded by the modern undertaker. He is a professional man of skill, carefully trained, licensed under the state in which he operates, and in many instances he possesses artistic ability of a high order, and a proper comprehension of the dignity of the occasion. There are many men of this high class in Virginia, and one of them worthy of much more than passing mention is Fred H. King, of Norton, whose funeral parlors are conveniently located at 927 Virginia Avenue.

Fred H. King was born in Barrackville, West Virginia, September 29, 1884, a son of John W. and Helen (Toothman) King. The father died January 2, 1929, but the mother is still living and residing in West Virginia. For years the father was a master mechanic, but later living retired. He was an active Republican, and a consistent member of the Methodist Episcopal Church. The paternal grandfather, William King, was born in Wales, but he was brought to the United States by his father, William King, who also brought his eleven other sons, twelve in all. They settled in Virginia, and from them have descended the majority of those in this country bearing the name of King. When West Virginia was formed during the war between the states the Kings found themselves in the new division.

The public schools of West Virginia grounded Fred H. King in the fundamentals of an education, and when he left the schoolroom he entered the employ of the Consolidated Coal Company, and for the following fifteen years was in the mercantile department of this corporation in West Virginia and Kentucky, and had charge of their store and undertaking in different places. Leaving the company, he went with the Seattle Hardware Company, which he represented in Alaska, and then for a time he was with the Seattle Mercantile Association. His experience in undertaking led him to decide to go into that line for himself, and after he had taken a course in embalming in the Hohenschuh College of Embalming, Des Moines, Iowa, he came to Norton and opened his present parlors. Here he has one of the finest establishments in the state, his equipment being of the latest design, and motorized. His chapel, parlors and stock of goods are such as to enable him to offer the most satisfactory and dig-

nified service. As an embalmer he is accepted as one of the best
in the demo-surgery line, and makes this work one of his specialties. He has been treasurer of the Virginia State Funeral
Directors Association, is a member of the National Funeral Directors Association, and is vice president of the Southwest Virginia Funeral Directors Association, which embraces all the
counties west of Roanoke, Virginia. High in Masonry, he has
been advanced through all of the bodies of the York Rite, and is
treasurer of the Blue Lodge, Chapter and Commandery, is a past
high priest of the Chapter and a past commander of the Commandery, and he also belongs to the Mystic Shrine. For two
years he was a director of the Norton Kiwanis Club, of which he
is still a member. Active in politics, he is now a member of the
City Council of Norton. The Christian Church holds his membership, and his wife also belongs to this church.

On March 29, 1904, Mr. King married Miss Viva Riblett, of
West Virginia, a daughter of Jackson F. and Gertrude (Nay)
Riblett, both of whom are living and residents of Centralia,
Washington, where Mr. Riblett is a ranchman, but they were
born in West Virginia. The paternal grandfather of Mrs. King
was Daniel Riblett, who served in the Union army during the
war between the states. Mrs. King was educated in the high
school of Shinnston, West Virginia. One child, Pauline King,
has been born to Mr. and Mrs. King, and she is now attending
school in Norton.

MARGARET BUCHANAN JARRATT is a resident of 311 South
Jefferson Street, Petersburg, and represents some old and honored Virginia families, both those from whom she is descended
and those with whom she is related by marriage.

She was born in Greensville County, Virginia, daughter of
John and Richetta (Peter) Cole and granddaughter of William
and Elizabeth (Cocke) Cole. John Cole inherited large tracts
of land in Prince George and Greensville counties, and also
plantations in the State of Mississippi, and it was his practice
once a year to visit these plantations, which were operated by
overseers. He died in Greensville County at the age of seventy-
one. John Cole married Richetta Peter, daughter of John and
Martha Peter. Mrs. Jarratt was one of seven children, the
others being named: William Herbert, John Peter (who died
when thirteen years old), Richetta P., Thomas Everad, James
Edward and Francis Walter.

Mrs. Jarratt was educated in Saint Marys College at Burlington, New Jersey. At the age of eighteen she was married
to Mr. James Dunlop, a son of David and Anna Mercer (Minge)
Dunlop. Mr. Dunlop was born at Petersburg, and after completing his education in the Virginia Military Institute engaged
in the tobacco business at Owensboro, Kentucky, and in 1876
removed to Covington, Kentucky. In 1877 he returned to Petersburg, Virginia, and died there the same year. Mrs. Jarratt by
her first marriage has one daughter, Anna Mercer, a gifted
artist, who studied under Whistler in Paris. Mrs. Dunlop was
married to Walter Jefferson Jarratt, who was born at Petersburg, son of Thomas Jefferson Jarratt, a feed and produce
dealer in Petersburg, who served six years as mayor of that city.
Walter Jefferson Jarratt succeeded to the business of his father
and conducted it until his death in 1893. The Jarratt family was
in Virginia in Colonial times. Rev. Devereaux Jarratt came
from England and was rector of the Episcopal Church of Bath

Parish from 1762 to 1801. Tradition is that four of his brothers also came to Virginia.

Mrs. Jarratt had three children, Walter Jefferson, James Herbert and Margaret Buchanan. Her son Walter J. married Ruth Jones. James H. married Rebecca Michie, and their two children are James Herbert and Emily Norwood. Margaret B. is the wife of C. Langfitt and has a daughter, Margaret Jarratt.

Both Mr. and Mrs. Jarratt took an active part in St. Paul's Episcopal Church. Mr. Jarratt was vestryman and lay leader and superintendent of the Sunday School, and also a member of the St. Andrews Brotherhood.

THEODORE FRANKLIN KIDD. Inheriting the family traits of industry, economy and thrift that ever win success in worldly affairs, Theodore Franklin Kidd easily acquired when young a stable position among the noteworthy citizens of Petersburg, where he is now living retired from business cares and worries. He was born August 4, 1854, in Petersburg, coming on the paternal side of English ancestry. His father, Stith Jones Kidd, and his grandfather, James Kidd, were both born in Dinwiddie County, Virginia, on a plantation located in the near vicinity of Harpers Home.

James Kidd was a successful agriculturist, operating his well yielding plantation with slave labor. He was a man of magnificent physique, six feet and nine inches in height, well proportioned, and retained in a remarkable degree his mentality until his death at the venerable age of one hundred and four years.

Stith Jones Kidd learned the trade of a coach maker when young, that having been before the time of railroads and airplanes, when stage coaches were used for traveling from place to place, even long journeys being made in them. Quite successful in his business, he carried it on in Petersburg until accidentally killed when but sixty years of age. His wife, whose maiden name was Minnie H. Clatte, was born in Germany, and came with her father to America in 1850. Mr. Clatte was a fine musician, and for a number of years served in that capacity in the German Army. In a hard fought battle, when the German troops were on the losing side, he was commanded to sound a retreat. Explaining that he did not know how to do so, he played a funeral march. The German soldiers immediately rallied, charged and won the battle. The quick-witted musician for this action was subsequently decorated by the Kaiser. Upon retiring from the army he came to Virginia, in 1850, as above stated, and after living for a time in Richmond located in Petersburg, where he spent his remaining years. Mrs. Stith Jones Kidd died at her home in Petersburg at the age of four score and four years. To her and her husband ten children were born, and all were given good educational advantages.

A boy of seven years when the outbreak of the Civil war occurred, Theodore Franklin Kidd well remembers many incidents connected with the conflict. Plantations were devastated, live stock taken, contents of the family smoke houses seized, and people of wealth were stripped of their riches. For several years thereafter oxen were used in place of horses and mules, produce often being brought to Petersburg by an ox in shafts. The people, however, with true Virginian spirit began the reconstruction, not only of city and state, but of the entire South, and many of the events connected with it are still vivid in the mind of Mr. Kidd.

Until nineteen years of age Theodore Franklin Kidd performed any kind of labor he could secure. Ambitious to establish himself in a permanent position, he served an apprenticeship at the plumber's trade, which he conducted most successfully until compelled by an unfortunate accident to relinquish that work. On recovering his health and strength Mr. Kidd was for several years prosperously engaged in the real estate business, but is now living retired from active pursuits, devoting his time and attention to his family and friends, and thoroughly enjoying his well earned leisure.

In 1884, at the age of thirty years, Mr. Kidd married Lucy J. Alley, who was born in Prince George County, Virginia, a daughter of Abram and Cornelia Ann Alley. Mrs. Kidd died January 17, 1926. Seven children were born of the union of Mr. and Mrs. Kidd, as follows: Robert H.; Flora L., wife of Linwood A. Andrews, has five children; Blanche T., wife of Edison P. Phillips, has two children; Bessie, wife of W. Gray Andrews, has five children; Leonard W.; Willard C.; and Grace A., the wife of Rev. J. Ernest Gibson, pastor of Monumental Baptist Church at Petersburg, Virginia.

Mr. Kidd has always taken an intelligent interest in public affairs, more especially in local matters. Both as an alderman and as a member of the City Council, in which he served continuously for a period of thirty years, he was a strong advocate of all measures conducive to the advancement of the city's highest interests and prosperity. Mr. Kidd from his youth up was very active in the work of the Wesley Methodist Episcopal Church, South, was chairman of the Board of Stewards for many years, and a heavy contributor toward the support of the church. He was largely instrumental in the erection of the new church building. He was a strong advocate of prohibition and contributed largely to the cause in his home city.

GEORGE WRIGHT was a Virginian who gave all the years from early manhood to the close of his life in railroading, and was honored for length of service and efficiency throughout the Chesapeake and Ohio System. At the time of his death he was the oldest conductor of that great transportation system, with its headquarters at Richmond.

Captain Wright, as he was always known, was born in Essex County, Virginia, June 6, 1852, and died at Richmond April 13, 1923, at the age of seventy-two. His father was a physician, and enjoyed an extensive practice in Essex County, where he lived and worked until his death at the age of forty-five. The mother of Captain Wright was Mary Anne Jones, a descendant of Peter Jones, who came to Virginia in 1620.

George Wright was one of ten children, and he grew up in Essex County, getting his education in local schools. He was quite young when his father died, and for several years he remained with his mother, assisting on the farm. It was in 1870 that he moved to Richmond and began his long consecutive service for the Chesapeake & Ohio Railroad. His first position was clerk in the maintenance department. Later he rose to conductor in the transportation department, and from 1901 to 1913 had the responsibilities of trainmaster. Ill health compelling him to give over some of these heavy responsibilities, he once more resumed his position as a conductor, having a run between Richmond and Newport News, and when death came to him he had completed fifty-two years as a railroad man. He was very popular in railway organizations, was a Royal Arch Mason and Shriner and a member of the Holy Comforter Episcopal Church at Richmond. His wife belongs to the Tabernacle Baptist Church.

Mr. Wright first married Lulie Stanard, of Goshen, Indiana, who died three years after their marriage, the mother of two sons, Robert, now deceased, and Beverly. Captain Wright on October 7, 1890, married Loulie Evans, of Middlesex County, where she was reared and educated, being a graduate of the Teachers College at Farmville. Mrs. Wright, who resides at 2408 Hanover Street in Richmond, is a daughter of Doctor and Mrs. J. Mason Evans. Her father graduated in medicine from the old Columbian University at Washington and spent many years in practice in Middlesex County. Her mother was Ellen Bagby, of King and Queen County, the Bagbys being a prominent Virginia family. Mrs. Wright was seventh in a family of nine children.

Mrs. Wright has two sons and one daughter. Her son, George Wright, Jr., was educated in the University of Virginia and married Lorraine Ruffin, of Richmond, of the well known Ruffin family. Her daughter, Laura M., is the wife of W. S. Street, assistant cashier of the Commerce and Trust Bank of Richmond, and has two children, named Walter, Jr., and Lou Evans. Richard Bagby Wright is a young business man of Richmond.

JOHN HARRISON LAMBERT is cashier of the Bank of Rocky Gap in Bland County. He was born and reared in that county, and his people have lived there since pioneer times.

Mr. Lambert is a son of Thomas S. and Clara G. (Helvey) Lambert. His father was a great-grandson of one of two brothers who settled at what is Lamberts Point near Norfolk, Virginia. Thomas S. Lambert was born and reared in Bland County, and followed farming and stock raising until his death on May 7, 1900. He is buried in the Lambert Cemetery at Round Bottom. His wife, Clara G. Helvey, was born on Kimberling Creek in Bland County, and has always been an active worker in the Methodist Episcopal Church, South. She lives at the old homestead at Round Bottom. She was the mother of three children: John H.; Ida E., who died April 23, 1907, at the age of seventeen years; and James M., a farmer and stock raiser at Round Bottom who married Linnie Bivens and has one child, Virgie C.

John Harrison Lambert was born at Round Bottom October 16, 1888, and supplemented his advantages in the public schools there by attending Emory and Henry College. He left college in 1913 and for several years his time and energies were fully taken up with farming and stock raising. During the World war he was classified and assigned limited military service as a ship carpenter for the New York Ship Building Corporation in the yards at Camden, New Jersey.

Mr. Lambert since 1924 has been cashier of the Bank of Rocky Gap. The bank was organized in 1922, with Mr. John M. Tuggle as president, and it is an organization that affords adequate banking facilities to a very prosperous farming and cattle raising section in Bland County. Mr. Lambert has been a director of the bank since its organization. He is also a director of the Valley Park Land Company of Elizabethton, Tennessee, handling an extensive development project in that locality.

EDWARD WILSON GARDNER

Mr. Lambert is a member of the Masonic fraternity. He served four years as supervisor of the Rocky Gap District, from January 1, 1923, to January 1, 1927. He is a Democrat in politics, a member of the Methodist Episcopal Church, South, and for several years was superintendent of the Sunday School.

Mr. Lambert married at Camden, New Jersey, September 9, 1925, Miss Edna Black, who was educated in public schools in Camden and attended the University of Pennsylvania and was a teacher up to the time of her marriage, her work having been done in the public schools at Camden. She is a member of the Methodist Church and is a daughter of Clinton and Emma (Peak) Black. Her father for many years was an engineer with the Pennsylvania Railroad, and died February 22, 1898, being buried at Camden. Her mother is still living, a resident of Collingswood, New Jersey.

EDWARD WILSON GARDNER was for many years identified with the mechanical department of the Southern Railway Company, lived at Richmond, and while this service constituted a valid claim for his consideration among representative Virginians of his generation, he is also remembered as a man of popularity among his fellow citizens and a valuable man in the community of Richmond.

He was born in Richmond October 28, 1864, and died in that city May 31, 1926, at the age of sixty-two years. He was the oldest of the ten children of Cornelius and Sarah Gardner, and as a boy attended schools in his native city. His apprenticeship as a machinist was served with the John Tolbert Machine Works in Richmond. From there he went with the Southern Railway Company and had successive promotions until he was made foreman of the machine department. He gave an uninterrupted service until 1917, when with America's entry into the World war he accepted a position where his experience and skill would be of greater value to the country, in connection with the Newport News Ship Building Works. He returned to Richmond in 1925, where he lived in retirement until his death. He completed a record of twenty-nine years with the Southern Railway, and that company gave him a medal as a token of twenty-five years of service.

He was an active Democrat and served for a time as a member of the Democratic committee. He was several times elected president of the Richmond Machinists Union. He belonged to the Masonic order and Independent Order of Odd Fellows, and was a member of the First Baptist Church.

Mr. Gardner married in August, 1892, Miss Ellen Bethel, of Richmond, daughter of Thomas C. and Ellen Bethel. She was the fifth of eleven children and was reared and educated in Richmond. Mrs. Gardner resides at Richmond, Virginia. Her father was in the service of the Confederate government during the Civil war.

Mr. and Mrs. Gardner had a family of six children: Sarah Lillian is a teller in the savings department of the State Planters Bank and Trust Company at Richmond. Thomas Carter, who married Adele Inge and has a son, Thomas Carter, Jr., is now in the printing business. During the war he was in France with the One Hundred and Forty-third Company, Signal Corps, in the First Division, and was gassed at the battle of Cantigny. Edward Wilson, Jr., is in the plumbing business, and by his marriage with Ruth Masenberg has a daughter, Ruth Virginia.

Albert Bethel Gardner is an interior decorator at Richmond. He married Katherine Brooks, of Richmond. The two youngest of the family are Francis Ellyson, who married Ruth Evelyn Darne, of Washington County, and John Stuart.

BENJAMIN WILLIAM BEACH, Danville business man, has found the royal road to success one of hard work and close application. He started life without money or superior education, but has long enjoyed a position of marked esteem among his associates. For a quarter of a century he has been identified with the Danville Ice Company, of which he is manager.

Mr. Beach was born in Franklin County, Virginia, May 6, 1869, son of Richard Robert and Sallie Ann (Dyer) Beach. His great-grandfather was one of three brothers who came from England in the 1700s, two of the brothers locating in Prince Edward County, Virginia, while the other went out West and was never heard from again. Mr. Beach's grandfather was William Branch Beach, who was born and reared in Prince Edward County, and after his marriage moved to Franklin County, where he was a farmer. Richard Robert Beach was born and reared in Franklin County, and served all through the four years of the Civil war in the regiment commanded by Colonel Kemper and in Pickett's division. He was wounded during the famous charge of that division at Gettysburg. After the war he was a farmer in Franklin and later in Montgomery County, and died in 1905. He is buried at Christiansburg. Richard Robert Beach married Sallie Ann (Dyer) Patrick, widow of John Hughes Patrick, who lost his life as a Confederate soldier at the battle of Antietam. She was born and reared in Henry County, Virginia, and after the war became the wife of Richard Robert Beach. She was an invalid several years before her death, in 1876. She was the mother of two children, a son, John H. Patrick, by her first marriage, and Benjamin W. Beach by her second husband. John H. Patrick was for many years in the wholesale commission business at Hickory, North Carolina, where he is living retired. He married Mattie Bailey, of Halifax County, Virginia, and they have three children, Grace, a teacher of music; Sam Bailey Patrick, a graduate of Columbia University, now practicing law at Hickory, North Carolina, and Jessie, wife of Edward Hodnett, professor of English in Columbia University.

Benjamin W. Beach was seven years of age when his mother died. His advantages were limited to the district schools in Franklin County and for several years he lived in the home of an aunt. He was fifteen when he came to Danville and went to work in the Brown & Stovall tobacco factory for three years. For six or seven years he was employed by T. B. Fitzgerald, a contractor and builder. After a course in the Danville Business College he became local agent for the Standard Oil Company in 1895, and represented that business at Danville for seven years. For two years he resumed work in the building trade and in 1904 came with the Danville Ice Company, at first as clerk and bookkeeper and since January, 1919, as manager of the business and plant.

Mr. Beach is one of the prominent members of the Masonic fraternity of Southern Virginia. He is an honorary member of Roman Eagle Lodge No. 122, A. F. and A. M., a member of Euclid Chapter No. 15, Royal Arch Masons, Dove Commandery No. 7, Knights Templar, and was grand master of

Virginia from February 26, 1926, to February 26, 1927. He is also affiliated with Acca Temple of the Mystic Shrine and the Junior Order United American Mechanics. Mr. Beach is a Democrat and for two terms was a member of the Danville City Council. He is on the board of Stewards of Calvary Methodist Episcopal Church, South.

He married at Pelham, North Carolina, October 10, 1901, Miss Pattie Moore, of Danville. She was educated in public schools at Richmond, attended high school and the State Normal School and was engaged in educational work for thirty-three years, before and after her marriage. Mrs. Beach is a member of the Methodist Episcopal Church, South, the Home and Missionary societies of the church, the Eastern Star chapter. Her parents were Reuben C. and Sallie (Harris) Moore, of Danville. Her father was a wheelwright and miller.

HON. ROBERT BOLLING WILLCOX. Possessing a wide and intelligent knowledge of the law and its precedents, Hon. Robert Bolling Willcox maintains a noteworthy position among the foremost attorneys of Petersburg, where he has won an exceedingly large and lucrative patronage. A native of Prince George County, Virginia, he was born at Flower de Hundred, which was likewise the birthplace of his father, Robert Bolling Willcox, Sr. He comes of honored Virginian stock, his paternal grandfather, John P. Willcox, having been a native of Petersburg, while his great-grandfather, John V. Willcox, was born and reared in Charles City County, Virginia, on the old home plantation.

John V. Willcox located in early life in Petersburg, Virginia, where he was for many years profitably engaged in raising tobacco and exporting it to countries across the sea. There his son, John P. Willcox, was born, but as a young man he moved to Flower de Hundred, where he operated a large plantation with the aid of his slaves, residing there until his death at a venerable age.

Born at Flower de Hundred October 6, 1847, Robert Bolling Willcox, Sr., received excellent educational advantages, and as a young man was graduated from the law department of the University of Virginia. Beginning the practice of his profession in Paducah, Kentucky, he remained there a few years, but preferring life in the Old Dominion State, he returned to Flower de Hundred, where he managed a large plantation during the remainder of his years. His wife, whose maiden name was Martha Theodora Dodson, was born in Petersburg, Virginia, a daughter of Capt. Daniel Dodson. During the Civil war Capt. Daniel Dodson commanded the Petersburg Riflemen, a body of thoroughly organized soldiers. He married Elizabeth Romaine Mason, who lived to the good old age of seventy-two years. Seven children were born into their household.

Hon. Robert Bolling Willcox, the special subject of this brief sketch, was prepared for college under private tutorship. Entering the law department of the University of Virginia in 1898, he was there graduated in 1901, and has since been actively engaged in the practice of his chosen profession, his decisions being almost invariably just and satisfactory to all concerned.

A Democrat in his political affiliations, Mr. Willcox cast his first presidential ballot in favor of William J. Bryan, who was of Virginia ancestry. Mr. Willcox takes an active interest in local and state affairs, and has served very acceptably as presi-

dent of the City Council. He was among the first to advocate
the commission form of government for Petersburg, and has
served as city attorney since its adoption in 1921.

Mr. Willcox married, November 3, 1915, Lucy Landon Harrison, who was born in Danville, Virginia, a daughter of James
and Mary (Davis) Harrison, and a direct descendant of Dr. John
Staige, of the University of Virginia. Mr. and Mrs. Willcox
have five children, namely: Robert Bolling, James Harrison,
Elizabeth Mason, Donald Skipwith and Lucy Landon. Mr. Willcox is a valued member of the Episcopal Church, and has served
as a vestryman therein.

WILLIAM GOODWIN COSBY. There are some men whose
careers are outlined by circumstances and many others who
overcome circumstances and shape their own lives. To the latter
class undoubtedly belonged the late William Goodwin Cosby, of
Richmond. Tens of thousands, starting life as he did dependent
upon his own resources, never emerged from the rut of mediocrity. From his parents, however, he inherited the best of
legacies, birth, health, industry and integrity. These, united to
thrift, temperance and native business shrewdness, were the
equipment with which he won his way to a prominent position
among his fellow citizens.

Mr. Cosby was born in Albemarle County, Virginia, November 12, 1851, and was a son of William Harris and Sarah Frances (Goodwin) Cosby. His father, a native of Virginia, was a
large landowner in Albemarle and Hanover counties. Though
the heir of three fortunes, at the close of the Civil war he was
left practically without property and a family of five children.
He married Sarah Frances Goodwin, a member of the distinguished family of that name, and a direct descendant of Col.
George Reade and Elizabeth Martian.

The eldest of the children, William Goodwin Cosby, acquired
a public school education in Albemarle County, and as a young
man took up his residence in Richmond, where he secured a
position with the Chesapeake & Ohio Railroad. While his salary
was small, he exercised thrift and economy, and established a
business of his own. All of the money he could earn, aside from
that which he needed for the bare necessities of life, was put
into this business, and as the years passed his equipment grew
and developed, while his patronage increased in proportion. He
never shirked his duties with the railroad, but his great energy
and industry enabled him to carry on his own enterprise in an
able and expeditious manner. He remained in the employ of
the Chesapeake & Ohio Railroad for twenty-five years, as one
of its valued and trusted men, but by 1900 his own business had
expanded to such a size that he found it necessary to resign. He
continued as president of his warehouse and storage company
until his death, at which time, through his able management,
intelligence and shrewdness, he had developed one of the largest
and most prosperous enterprises of its kind in the capital. Mr.
Cosby was one of Richmond's reliable business citizens, and at
all times took a keen and helpful part in movements which added
to the city's greatness. He was a man of deep religious faith
and feeling, was superintendent of the Overbrook Presbyterian
Church Sunday School for nineteen years, and for twenty-five
years was clerk of the session. In his death Richmond lost a
man who had led a useful and honorable life and contributed not
a little to its business and civic prestige.

Pattie E Harris

On October 20, 1880, Mr. Cosby was united in marriage with Miss Mary Archer Royall Briggs, who was born in Stafford County, Virginia, the fifth of eleven children born to James McDonald and Louise Ann (Smith) Briggs, a granddaughter of James McDonald Briggs, the elder, and a great-granddaughter of David Briggs, a native of Scotland, who immigrated to the United States in young manhood and settled on land in Stafford County, Virginia, where the family have resided for five generations, still owning the original property. Mrs. Cosby, who died on June 5, 1929, received her education at West Middlesex, Pennsylvania, and was one of the highly respected women of Richmond, where she had been active for many years in the work of the Presbyterian Church and the Woman's Club. Mr. and Mrs. Cosby became the parents of three children: Edith Marshall Kieth, the wife of John Brown Wintersmith, a leading manufacturing chemist of Louisville, Kentucky, who has two children, Edith Cosby and John Brown; Robert Cullen, an enterprising and successful business man of Richmond, who succeeded his father as president of the storage company and has a number of other connections; and William Randolph, who attended Washington and Lee University, took the degree of Bachelor of Laws at Tallahassee, Florida, married Lorraine Johnson, of Chicago, Illinois, and is now a broker for Halsey, Stuart & Company, Chicago, at Decatur, Illinois.

MISS PATTIE ELIZABETH HARRIS. Talented and cultured, with an inherent love for good literature, which necessarily includes the daily newspapers, Miss Pattie E. Harris keeps well informed on the local, county, state, national and foreign affairs of the day, and expresses her opinions thereon most clearly and intelligently. A daughter of James Harris, she was born on October 31, 1852, in Southampton County, Virginia, of early Colonial ancestry.

James Harris, a life long resident of Southampton County, was born in 1809, and died in 1855, while yet in manhood's prime. His wife, whose maiden name was Mary Elizabeth Ryland, was born in Greensville County, Virginia, September 14, 1822, the descendant of a family of prominence in both public and private affairs. Her father, Edward Ryland, was a native of Brunswick County, Virginia, a son of Iverson Ryland, who was born and reared in England.

Iverson Ryland immigrated to America when young, settling in Brunswick County, Virginia, where he bought much land, which he cultivated with slave labor. He married a Miss Dorch, and they reared a fine family of boys and girls.

Edward Ryland, the maternal grandfather of Miss Harris, purchased a tract of land in Greensville County, Virginia, and was there engaged in agricultural pursuits the remainder of his life. His wife, whose name before her marriage was Martha Patsy Williamson, was born in Greensville County, a daughter of Col. Person Williamson, and granddaughter of Rev. Joseph Williamson, an Episcopalian minister, who was born in Scotland, and spent the last years of his life in Sussex County, Virginia.

Col. Person Williamson, the great-grandfather of Miss Harris, on the maternal side, who owned and operated a plantation in Sussex County, married Mary Mason, a daughter of Col. David Mason, and a granddaughter of George Mason, widely known as the author of the "Bill of Rights," which consisted of ten important amendments to the Constitution. During the

Revolutionary war Col. David Mason had command of the Fifteenth Virginia Regiment, which was on the firing line in several important engagements. He married a Miss Turner.

Mrs. Mary Elizabeth (Ryland) Harris, the mother of Miss Harris, was left a widow when young, with three children to care for. She was exceedingly faithful to the duties falling upon her, administering wisely to their physical needs, and carefully attending to their mental training. She survived her husband many long years, passing to the life beyond in November, 1898. They were the parents of three children, James Edward, Pattie Elizabeth and Mary Jane. In 1900 they moved to Petersburg, and there in 1903 James Edward's death occurred, and in 1925 his sister Mary answered death's summons. Thus left without parents, sister or brother, Miss Pattie E. Harris is busily employed in looking after her private affairs, bravely facing the trials and troubles that come to every one, young or old, rich or poor, in this land of freedom and promise.

JOHN WARWICK RUST, attorney and counsellor at law at Fairfax, has had a very extensive law practice, and also numerous business interests for his supervision, and has been an active participant in the public affairs of his community.

He was born in Warren County, Virginia, November 8, 1881, and is a descendant of William Rust, an English cavalier who settled in Westmoreland County, Virginia, in 1650. His wife, Anne Gray, was a daughter of Francis Gray, who came from England in 1634, living for a time in Maryland and moving to Westmoreland County, Virginia, in 1647. For generation after generation the Rust family lived in Westmoreland and adjoining counties. John W. Rust is a descendant of Samuel Rust, son of William, and Matthew, son of Samuel. Matthew was the father of Benedict Rust, who was born October 25, 1743, and died September 18, 1829. There is a family tradition that he was a Revolutionary soldier. There were many other names of the Rust family who participated in the war for independence, and the Rusts have done their part in practically every war in which this country has been engaged. Benedict Rust about the close of the Revolution established his home in Frederick County. He married Jane Middleton, and two of their sons, John and Matthew, were soldiers in the War of 1812. The record of John is: Member of Capt. Daniel Matthews' Company of Riflemen of the McDowell's Flying Camp of Virginia Militia to September 28, 1813; private in Captain Daniel Matthews' Company of Infantry of the same regiment, attached to the Fourth Militia from September 29, 1813, to January 10, 1814.

John Rust was born February 8, 1769, and died April 17, 1851. He owned a beautiful manor house on the Shenandoah River in Warren County, and for many years was judge of the County Court of Warren, and also senior justice of the peace. He married Elizabeth Marshall, daughter of William Marshall and member of the noted Marshall family of Virginia and Maryland.

Their son, Charles Buckner Carroll Rust, was born December 26, 1816, and died December 17, 1904. He married, September 12, 1839, Mary Ann Ashby, who was born October 19, 1817, and died April 18, 1885. Her grandfather, Benjamin Ashby, was a lieutenant in the Revolutionary war and the Ashbys have been noted as military heroes since early Colonial

times, one member of the family having been the distinguished Gen. Turner Ashby, of the Confederate Army.

Capt. John Robert Rust, son of Charles Buckner Carroll Rust, was born June 14, 1840, and died June 2, 1920. He left Piedmont College at the beginning of the war, joined the command of his cousin, Gen. Turner Ashby, as a private, enlisting April 18, 1861, the day after Virginia seceded. He became captain of Company I, Twelfth Virginia Regiment of Cavalry, and was in active service except for forty-nine days of imprisonment at Fort McHenry. He had six horses shot while under him in battle, was wounded twice, and as a member of Ashby's and Jackson's cavalry was in almost continuous action and service. He had seven first cousins in the war, four of them killed in battle, another cousin being Gen. Albert B. Rust. Capt. John Robert Rust made his home in his later years at Haymarket, Prince William County. He married, December 22, 1873, Nannie Antrim McKay, daughter of Joshua and Esther Ann (Haycock) McKay. Her ancestor, Robert McKay, was one of the grantees with Joist Hite of a great tract of land in Warren County in 1732, and built the first house in the Valley of Virginia, at Cedarville, Warren County.

John Warwick Rust, youngest of the four children of Capt. John Robert Rust, was reared in Warren County, attended Eastern College at Front Royal, studied law at Fairfax and was licensed to practice at Richmond in June, 1907. Besides responding to the demands upon his time and talents in a general law practice he has served as attorney for the Federal Land Bank at Baltimore, has supervised large land and real estate holdings of his own, has been vice president of the Vienna National Bank at Vienna, Virginia, and served as mayor of Fairfax. During the war he was county director of the National War Savings Committee. He has been a commander of the local camp of Sons of Confederate Veterans, is a member of the Presbyterian Church and a **Democrat**.

He married, September 27, 1911, Miss Anne Hooe, of Longwood, Fauquier County. She is a descendant of Rice Hooe, who was among the first settlers of Virginia and one of the early burgesses of the colony. His grandson, Rice Hooe, married Anne Howson, daughter of Robert Howson. Mrs. Rust is a daughter of Howson and Henrietta (Daniell) Hooe. Her father was a Confederate soldier, and the Howson and Hooes among her ancestors furnished many names in the military and civic affairs of the colony and state of Virginia. The children born to Mr. and Mrs. Rust are: Katharine Warwick, Eleanor McLean, John Howson and Anne Hooe.

WILLIAM HENRY PAINTER, mayor of Radford, has made an enviable record both as a business man and citizen. He has been well known in several communities of Southwestern Virginia, and his chief business activities since locating at Radford have been as a building contractor and real estate operator.

Mr. Painter was born in Wythe County, Virginia, September 21, 1869, son of William M. and Sallie (Hatcher) Painter. His great-grandfather Painter was killed by Indians in the Valley of Virginia in early pioneer times. His grandfather, Abraham Painter, was a farmer and stock raiser in Wythe County, and both he and his wife are buried at Ivanhoe. William M. Painter was born in Wythe County, was educated in private schools and was in Confederate service during the Civil war, being detailed for work in the lead mines. After the war he followed farming and general merchandising, and when he died in 1915 was one of the oldest merchants in Wythe County. His wife, Sallie Hatcher, was born and reared in Rockbridge County, Virginia, was educated in private schools and was a Methodist, while her husband was a Presbyterian. She died in December, 1915. They had a family of five children: Walter T., deceased; D. M. Painter, also deceased; Lula M., wife of S. S. Simmerman, of Wytheville; Minnie, wife of W. E. Miller, of Herndon, Virginia; and William H.

William H. Painter attended public schools in Wythe County and after completing his education in Roanoke College returned home and became associated with his father in the store at Ivanhoe and later became a member of the firm W. M. Painter & Son. After five years he sold out his interest and for three years was engaged in buying and selling farms in Greenbrier County, West Virginia, and for a time was also a real estate operator in the country around Washington, D. C. He returned to Ivanhoe to take the management of the store there, remaining another five years, and from there came to Radford, where he has been a contractor and builder, operating largely with his own property and capital.

The community of Radford has given him repeated evidences of its esteem for his leadership. For eight years he was a member of the City Council, and while living in Wythe County served on the Board of Education about fifteen years. For one year he was president of the Radford Chamber of Commerce and in 1928 was elected mayor of the city. He has been a director of banks and other public enterprises, although in recent years he has given over many of his connections with business affairs. In 1928 Mr. Painter erected a beautiful home on the hills above Radford, at Sixth and Harvey streets, a house corresponding to its beautiful location in architecture. This home represented many of the artistic ideals and the plans for convenience and comfort made by his good wife, who unfortunately did not live to see the home completed. Mr. Painter was formerly active in the Kiwanis Club, he is a Democrat and a trustee of the Methodist Episcopal Church, South.

He married at Ivanhoe, Virginia, in October, 1896, Miss Mattie L. Mitchell. After attending public schools she was educated in Sullins College at Bristol. She was identified with the work of the Methodist Episcopal Church and was a member of the Woman's Club of Radford. Mrs. Painter died August 8, 1928, and is buried in the West View Cemetery at Radford. Her parents were Rev. W. D. and Mary Rebecca (Burkey) Mitchell. Her father for half a century was a minister of the Methodist Episcopal Church, South, and widely known all over the Holston Conference. He and his wife spent their declining years at Radford and are buried in the West View Cemetery there. Mr. and Mrs. Painter were the parents of five children, two of whom died young. The living daughters are Ruth, Mary and Lois. Ruth was educated at Ivanhoe, in a private girls school at Wytheville, and was married to Ernest Bullard, of Radford, who died leaving two children, William P. and Barbara. Mrs. Bullard subsequently married Blackman Garner, of Dover, North Carolina, where they reside, and by this marriage there are two children, Janice Blackman and Jean Carolyn. The daughter Mary was educated at Radford, graduating from the high school there in 1916 and also attended the National Business College at

JOHN FREDERICK BLACK

Roanoke. Lois Painter graduated from the Radford High School in 1920, spent two years in Martha Washington College, one year in Randolph-Macon Woman's College and in 1924 graduated from Emory and Henry College. She taught three and a half years in the public schools of Virginia and North Carolina, and in January, 1928, became the wife of Mr. James E. Dooley, of Monita, Virginia. Mr. Dooley attended high school at Monita and Roanoke College, and his business is road construction work in North Carolina. Mr. and Mrs. Dooley have one son, James Beverly.

JOHN FREDERICK BLACK was a building contractor long and familiarly known in Richmond, where his individual skill and the skill of the organization which he built up and directed were impressed on many of the finer public buildings, as well as homes.

Mr. Black was born at Petersburg, Virginia, October 19, 1859, and was a small child when his parents moved to Richmond, where he lived practically all his life and where he died January 27, 1917. His widow now resides at 3300 Park Avenue. His father was Maj. B. J. Black, a prominent Virginia architect who made the designs and supervised the construction of a great many buildings in Richmond and elsewhere over the state. He was colonel of Virginia troops in the Civil war. Major Black married Lettie Hawkins. Their children were: Molly, who married Joe Myers; Katie; John Frederick, the oldest of three sons; Willie; Agnes, who married William Beattie; Nellie, whose first husband was John Murphy and the second Harry Welch; Annie, and Wilson.

John Frederick Black attended school at Richmond, and from school began learning the carpenter's trade. He had a very thorough training in woodworking and other branches of building mechanics, and was well equipped when he entered the contracting business. The work he did as a contractor from that time until his death could not be enumerated in detail. In the construction of the Sacred Heart Cathedral he made the form for many of the fine architectural figures, and he did all the special finishing work on the building. A number of the fine homes on Monument Avenue were put up by him, and he also erected several office buildings in the business quarter.

Mr. Black was a Democrat and a member of the Knights of the Maccabees. The family were members of St. Benedict Catholic Parish and Mrs. Black is a member of the Catholic Woman's Club of Richmond.

Mr. Black was twice married. By his first marriage he had one daughter, Mary, who finished her education in the Sacred Heart Academy and is now the wife of Joseph Amrhein. Mr. Amrhein for a number of years was with the First National Bank of Richmond and is now a state bank examiner. Mr. and Mrs. Amrhein have three children, Mary Catherine, Joe, Jr., and John.

On April 3, 1890, at Richmond, John Frederick Black married Kate O'Brien, daughter of Thomas and Mary Ann O'Brien. Her father was for over forty years employed in the locomotive works at Richmond, now a branch of the American Locomotive Works. Mrs. Black was one of a family of eight children and was the oldest of the five that grew up. Her sister Ellen T. married J. H. Duggan, of Richmond; Mamie married Tom Carroll, of South Richmond; Margaret became the wife of R. T. Collins, of St. Petersburg, Florida; and Miss Agnes is a Government employe.

Mrs. Black was educated in St. Joseph's Academy at Richmond. The following children were born to her marriage: Joseph F. married Sarah Burnett and had four children, Joseph, John F., Sarah and Mary; Bernard, the second son is married; Madeline, deceased, was the wife of L. S. Jewett and left two children, Jack and Ann; Katherine is the wife of James Wootton, of Detroit; Margaret is the fifth in age; John A. is an employe of the Chesapeake & Ohio Railroad; Thomas O'Brien is an architect; and Wilson is in school. These children were all educated in the Sacred Heart Academy except Wilson and Margaret, who attended Saint Benedict Academy.

EDWARD FRANKLIN COBB, who for many years was in the service of the Chesapeake & Ohio Railway, was a member of the Cobb family which settled in Virginia in the eighteenth century. The Cobbs were English, and the record of the family in England runs back into earliest recorded history.

Edward Franklin Cobb was born in Caroline County, Virginia, April 6, 1869, and died at Richmond March 25, 1919. His father, Montgomery Terrell Cobb, was a farmer and contractor in Caroline County, and served in the Confederate army. He married Margaret Faulkner, of Spotsylvania County. Their family of children consisted of the following: John L., a conductor with the Chesapeake & Ohio Railway; Mary, deceased; Edward Franklin; Virginia, deceased; George M., a Chesapeake & Ohio Railway conductor; Jesse Thomas, a farmer in

Edward Franklin Cobb attended schools in Caroline County, worked with his father on the home farm, and at the age of twenty-two moved to Richmond and went to work for the Chesapeake & Ohio Railroad. He was then apprenticed one year, then was transferred to the transportation department, and altogether spent twenty-six years in the railway service, being a conductor for twelve years. He was a loyal and efficient employe, and had a widely extended acquaintance among railroad men over the state.

He was a Democrat, a member of the Knights of Pythias, a Baptist, and belonged to the Brotherhood of Railway Trainmen. His wife is a member of the auxiliary of that organization, belongs to the Travel Club, and is a member of the Woman's Beneficial Association and the Eastern Star.

Mr. Cobb married at Washington, D. C., October 18, 1899, Miss Eva A. Terrell. Mrs. Cobb, whose home is at 2908 A. Park Avenue, Richmond, is a descendant of the Terrell family which has had many distinguished members in Virginia history, running back for two centuries or more. Her parents were John T. and Ella A. (Cobb) Terrell. John T. Terrell was a planter, lumber mill operator, and for a number of years served as deputy county tax collector. He and his wife had six children: Mrs. Eva A. Cobb; Aubin Cobb Terrell, who died while a student at Richmond University; Mrs. Louise Terrell Campbell, of Caroline County, mother of four children, named Durward C., who married Beatrice Chenault, Aurelett, now Mrs. Crawford Ginn, of Delaware, Preston Terrell and Leon; John T. Terrell, Jr., an engineer with the Chesapeake & Ohio Railway, has one daughter, Grace; Conway Elle Humphries lives in Caroline County; William L. Terrell married Maude Long, and their children are

Marion, Kedith, Ravena, Childress, Doris, Cora Lee, Conway Ella, Maude and John Thomas.

Mrs. Cobb is the mother of three children: Russell Terrell Cobb, who graduated Bachelor of Science from Richmond University; Aubin Terrell Cobb; and Beatrice Cobb, who is a graduate of the John Marshall High School. Both sons are members of the Masonic fraternity, and the daughter and mother belong to the Eastern Star.

NEAL BUNTS. A resident of Pulaski since 1908, Neal Bunts has been connected during this entire period with what is now a part of the General Chemical Company, of the plant of which he has been general superintendent since 1916. Mr. Bunts has followed the same line of industry all of his life, but of more recent years has extended his activities and abilities to various other concerns and is an official and director of a number of successful enterprises. He is likewise prominent and active in civic affairs, and for a number of years has been one of most energetic members of the City Council.

Mr. Bunts was born May 16, 1877, in Wythe County, Virginia and is a son of John M. and Lucinda (Carnal) Bunts. The Bunts family is of German descent, and the paternal grandfather of Mr. Bunts was a sea captain, being master of a steamship traveling between the United States and Germany. He had settled his family in old Virginia, and his death occurred at sea on one of his many voyages. John M. Bunts, the father of Neal Bunts, was born and reared in Wythe County, Virginia, where he received his education in a private school. Following his graduation he embarked upon a career as an educator, and was thus engaged at the time of the outbreak of the war between the states, when he espoused the cause of the South and enlisted in the Confederate army. During the four years that followed he took part in many of the major engagements of that great struggle, including the great battle of Gettysburg, and toward the close of the conflict was captured and spent some time in a Federal war prison. At the close of the war he returned to the pursuits of peace, resuming his work as an educator, and during the painful period of reconstruction did much to alleviate the worries and discomforts of his troubled community. He became widely known for his work as an educator, and was also a man of the strictest honor and integrity, serving with distinguished ability as a justice of the peace for a period of twenty-eight years. In his death, which occurred about 1902, his community lost a valued citizen, and he was laid to rest in the old family cemetery in Wythe County. Mr. Bunts married Miss Lucinda E. Carnal, who was born in North Carolina, and was a child when brought by her parents to Virginia, where she received her education in public schools in Wythe County. She and her husband were always active in the work of the Methodist Episcopal Church, South. She died in 1916, and was laid to rest at the side of her husband. Seven children were born to Mr. and Mrs. Bunts: Robert, Jr., deceased; Neal, of this review; M. L., of Saltville, Virginia; Rev. W. M., of Bristol, this state; J. E.. of the Pulaski Foundry at Pulaski; R. S., also of Pulaski; and Margaret, who died in 1922.

Neal Bunts attended public and private schools in Wythe County, and afterward became identified with the foundry department of the New River Mineral Company at Ivanhoe, Virginia, where he remained four years. He was then connected with the Mathieson Alkali Works, of Saltville for about five years as foundry superintendent, subsequently going to Pittsburgh, Pennsylvania, with the Westinghouse Foundry and Machine Company, where he was assistant foreman for three years. Mr. Bunts went then to the Pacific Coast and joined the Union Iron Works of San Francisco as foreman of the foundry department, but after one year returned to Virginia in 1904 and again was employed by the Mathieson Alkali Works, in charge of the foundry. He remained at Saltville for four years and in 1908 located at Pulaski, where with his brother, Robert Bunts, Jr., he organized the Pulaski Foundry and Machine Company, of which his brother was manager and Neal Bunts, assistant manager and treasurer. The business was operated under this firm name until 1916, when it was sold to the General Chemical Company of New York, and following this sale Robert Bunts, Jr., with others, organized the Pulaski Foundry Manufacturing Corporation of Pulaski, but he died in 1925, although the company still continues in operation. Since the Pulaski Foundry and Machine Company was sold in 1916 Neal Bunts has continued with the General Chemical Company of New York in the capacity of general superintendent, for the duties of which office he is admirably equipped by nature, training and experience. Mr. Bunts is also interested in a number of other enterprises, being a director in the Pulaski Trust Company, president and a director of the Pulaski Building and Loan Association, a director in the Blue Grass Hardware Company, and a stockholder in numerous other business and financial enterprises. A Democrat in his political views, he has long been interested in public affairs, and has served capably in the capacity of councilman. He is a thirty-second degree Mason and member of Kazim Temple, A. A. O. N. M. S., and the Benevolent and Protective Order of Elks, and for years was active in the Knights of Pythias and the Independent Order of of Odd Fellows. He is a charter member of the Pulaski Rotary Club and also a member of the Pulaski Country Club. Mr. Bunts belongs to the vestry of Christ Episcopal Church, of which he is junior warden.

At Saltville, August 29, 1905, Mr. Bunts married Miss Lillie S. Rodefer, of that place, who was educated in the public schools of Abingdon and Saltville, in Martha Washington College and Emory and Henry College. For a few years prior to her marriage she was engaged in teaching school at Saltville, and is an active member of the Woman's Club, the Episcopal Church Ladies' Guild and the Garden Club, of which she is secretary. She is a daughter of J. B. Rodefer, of Saltville, who was for many years connected with the Mathieson Alkali Works, and died in 1912, being buried in the Radford (Virginia) Cemetery. His widow still survives him as a resident of Pulaski.

RAYMOND LIPSCOMB SMITH had to his credit a veteran's service as a railroad man, giving practically all of his lifetime after his education was completed to the Chesapeake & Ohio System.

He was a native Virginian, born in 1869, and died at Richmond October 17, 1926. His father, George Smith, was one of the early employes of the Chesapeake & Ohio Railway. George Smith married a member of the well known Lipscomb family of Virginia, and Raymond L. was the second of their four children.

The late Mr. Smith had a private school education and then went to work in the transportation department of the Chesa-

WILLIAM JORDAN WINSTON

peake & Ohio. After various promotions he was made an engineer on the James River Division, and was forty years in the service, being at the time of his death one of the oldest men in that department, and as a token of respect for his faithfulness and his abilities the company draped his locomotive in mourning. In later years he was called upon for important duties as an inspector, and was a specialist in all matters connected with the efficient operation of the large type locomotive introduced by the Chesapeake & Ohio in recent years. He was a member of the Brotherhood of Locomotive Engineers and a member of the Episcopal Church.

Mr. Smith married, August 17, 1907, Mrs. Louise (Humphries) Barnes. Mrs. Smith, who survives him and resides at 22 South Boulevard in Richmond, by a previous marriage had a daughter, Louella G. Barnes Smith, who is a registered nurse and has done work for the health board in connection with the public schools of Richmond. Mrs. Smith's father, Thomas P. Humphries, came from Liverpool, England, to Virginia about 1889. Her mother, Fannie E. Baker, was a native of Hamburg, Germany. Mrs. Smith was the oldest of four living children of her parents. Her sister Gilmer is the wife of Nicholas Holt, who is connected with the Duke family of Durham, North Carolina. Elizabeth is the widow of C. H. Rowland, of Norfolk, Virginia. Her brother, John T. Humphries, volunteered at the outbreak of the World war, was assigned to Company K of the Twenty-ninth Division, Maryland Regiment, becoming a sergeant, and he married Marie A. Bushman of Baltimore, Maryland.

WILLIAM JORDAN WINSTON. The Winston family was established in Virginia in Colonial times, and through the successive generations members of the family have appeared worthily identified with substantial work, and have made honorable records as patriots and citizens.

The late William Jordan Winston, for many years well known in the building trades at Richmond, was born in Henrico County October 12, 1869, and died in the City of Richmond in November, 1918. His great-grandfather was a physician, served in the War of the Revolution, and was a hard working, kindly and devoted member of his profession in his rural district. The grandfather was William Jordan, a Methodist minister. William Patrick Winston, the father, was a planter in Henrico County, and married Louise Binford, of the old Colonial Binford family.

William Jordan Winston was the oldest of seven children and was educated in public schools at Richmond. As a young man he served his apprenticeship as a carpenter, and he found the best means of expressing himself and his talents through this trade and spent many years in work as a master carpenter in Richmond. He was a Democrat, a member of the Baptist Church, and belonged to the Junior Order United American Mechanics. His wife is a member of the Daughters of the American Revolution.

Mr. Winston married in April, 1903, Miss Mamie Florence Tiller, of Richmond, who resides at 2106 Stuart Avenue. She is a descendant of the Tiller family that came from England to Virginia before the Revolutionary war. Her parents were George W. and India Tiller, and her father for many years was an employe of the City of Richmond. Mrs. Winston was the fourth in a family of seven children and was reared and educated at Richmond. Her father served in the Confederate army and was wounded in one battle.

Mr. and Mrs. Winston had a family of five children, and the four now living are William Alton, Miss Mamie Louise, Margaret Lucile, wife of John O. Schaich, and they have a son, William Winston Schaich, and Miss Dorothy Evelin.

WILLIAM DONBAR EVANS. Foremost among the men of prominence in his profession in Middlesex County stands William Dunbar Evans, ex-member of the Virginia State Legislature, formerly commonwealth's attorney, and for thirty years a recognized leader at the bar at Saluda, Virginia.

Mr. Evans comes of old Virginia stock, the family ancestral lines tracing back to early Colonial settlement and notable achievements. He was born in Middlesex County, Virginia, March 29, 1875, son of Judge Andrew Browne and Alice (Dew) Evans, both of whom were born in King and Queen County, Virginia. Prior to the war between the states Judge Evans was already eminent at the bar. He served in the office of commonwealth's attorney, and later was elected a member of the Virginia Legislature. After the war period, on completing a term as circuit judge of Middlesex County, he devoted himself to his private law practice at Church View, Virginia, until his death, which occurred in April, 1912. The mother of William D. Evans was the daughter of John M. Dew, of King and Queen County, Virginia, and niece of Thomas R. Dew, early president of William and Mary College at Williamsburg, Virginia. She passed away in February, 1907. They were lifelong members of the Baptist Church.

William Dunbar Evans was reared in a home atmosphere that did much to urge and encourage ambition toward a worthwhile life. He attended local schools during boyhood and then completed a literary course in Bowling Green Academy in Caroline County and in Richmond College. Upon deciding to enter his father's profession, he took a preliminary course in law at the University of Virginia, and then entered Richmond College of Law, now Richmond University, from which institution he was graduated in the class of 1896, with his degree of LL. B.

In the above year Mr. Evans established himself in law practice at Saluda, and at the same time centered his permanent citizenship interests here, which have since, on many occasions, proved of paramount importance in promoting the welfare of the county. In the passing years he not only has built up a substantial business and an enviable local professional reputation, but is widely known and esteemed over a large territory, practicing extensively in the courts of Middlesex, Essex, Gloucester, Mathews and King and Queen counties. In addition to his professional activity and high standing Mr. Evans for years has been interested and influential in county and state Democratic politics, and at times has been his party's choice for responsible public offices. For eight years he served with the utmost efficiency as commonwealth's attorney of Middlesex County, and during his term as a member of the Virginia State Legislature, 1908-1910, he was honorably identified with important legislation.

Mr. Evans married, December 7, 1905, Miss Virginia McCandlish, daughter of Robert and Nannie M. (Eubank) McCandlish, and they have three children: Virginia Montague, born February 19, 1908; William Dunbar, Jr., born November 20,

1912; and Robert McCandlish, born July 21, 1916. All have been given educational advantages, opportunities to develop special talents, and a refined home environment that assures happiness and content. Mrs. Evans is an educated, accomplished lady, an active member of "Old Christ Church," Episcopal, near Saluda, and intelligently interested in public affairs. She belongs to the Daughters of the Confederacy, and to various social organizations.

For many years Mr. Evans has been attorney for the Bank of Middlesex, of which he is one of the Board of Directors. In addition to his pleasantly located private residence at Saluda he has valuable farm interests in Middlesex County. He has long been a member of advanced bodies in Masonry, and formerly, when he had more leisure at command, was identified with several other fraternities, and still preserves an interest in his old Greek letter college society, the Phi Kappa Sigma. He was reared in the Baptist Church.

JUDGE BENJAMIN WILSON COLEMAN is a native Virginian who has attained high distinction outside his home state. His career as a lawyer and jurist has identified him with the far West, and he is now chief justice of the Supreme Court of the State of Nevada.

Judge Coleman was born at Ballsville in Powhatan County, Virginia, July 1, 1869. His first Virginia ancestor was Richard Coleman, who came from England during the seventeenth century and located in the Northern Neck of Virginia. The parents of Judge Coleman were John and Arabella (Smith) Coleman.

Benjamin Wilson Coleman finished his law course and received his Bachelor of Laws degree from Richmond College, now the University of Richmond, in 1892, and soon afterward went west. He was admitted to the Colorado bar in 1893, and for three years practiced at Denver. From 1897 to 1906 his home was at Cripple Creek, then the throbbing center of the dent of Nevada since 1906, and first located at Ely. Since 1911 he has been on the bench, at first as judge of the District Court in the Ninth Nevada District from 1911 to 1915, and since 1915 mining activities of the West. Judge Coleman has been a resi- on the Supreme bench. He was an associate justice from January, 1915, to 1919, and since the latter year has been chief justice.

Many of the opinions he has written are expressed not only with his experience as a western lawyer, but his broad legal scholarship. His work as a jurist has attracted attention outside his home state, and one interesting illustration of this resulted in Judge Coleman going to Chicago to lecture at the summer session of the law school of Northwestern University in 1925. This invitation proceeded from Col. John H. Wigmore, dean of the Northwestern University Law School, who had become interested in some of the decisions rendered by Judge Coleman. Judge Coleman has been a regular attendant at the annual meetings of the American Law Institute and is a member of the American Bar Association and has recently been elected to membership in Pi Gamma Mu, national honor society, of which Dean William A. Hamilton, of William and Mary College of Williamsburg, Virginia, is secretary. Judge Coleman is a past sovereign of Joan of Arc Conclave, Red Cross of Constantine, of which society George W. Warvelle, LL. D., the learned legal author of Chicago, is the grand recorder. He is also a life member of the

Association of Virginia Antiquities. He was honored with the post of grand master of the Masonic Grand Lodge of Nevada in 1915. He is a Knight Templar Mason and Shriner and a member of the Sagebrush Club of Carson City.

Judge Coleman married, June 6, 1906, Miss Martha L. Attleton, of Boston, Massachusetts. They have four children, Elizabeth, Virginia, Margaret and John Attleton.

CHARLES STUART HABLISTON was a banker and insurance man, and in a comparatively brief life span earned a high place among his Richmond associates, and was a type of business man and citizen whose example might well be emulated by future generations.

Mr. Habliston was born at Richmond, May 29, 1874, and died in that city March 12, 1912. He was reared in a home of modest wealth and sound culture and had the excellent advantages of the McGuire Academy for Boys, where he completed his education. In 1894 he entered the banking business with his cousin, William H. Habliston, in the National Bank of Virginia, and remained with that institution until 1910. He gave up his bank work on account of ill health, and from that time until his death looked after a growing insurance business. He was a member of the Bankers Association, was a Democrat, member of Grace Trinity Church, and had membership in all the leading social clubs of Richmond.

His father was Frederick H. Habliston, a Pennsylvanian, who came to Richmond shortly after the close of the Civil war and was for many years in the furniture business there. Frederick H. Habliston married Kate Barron, and there were three children: Sadie married Allen Lyon, now deceased, a lumber merchant of Richmond; Frederick married Mattie Turner, of New Kent County, Virginia, and they have a daughter, Sadie, who is now Mrs. Charles Shields; and Charles S.

Charles Stuart Habliston married at Richmond, March 16, 1904, Miss Emily Terrell, who survives him and resides at 1118 Grove Avenue. She was reared and educated in Hanover County, Virginia, attending private schools and finishing her work in the Woman's College at Waynesboro. In 1895 she graduated as a nurse from Virginia Hospital. Mrs. Habliston is a member of Grace Holy Trinity Church.

Her grandparents were Dr. Nicholas and Maria (Doswell) Terrell, whose two children were Dr. Charles James and Maj. Lewis Frank Terrell. Major Terrell was educated in the University of Virginia, was a lawyer, and during the Civil war raised an artillery company, was made lieutenant, afterwards promoted to captain, and eventually commissioned a major.

Dr. Charles James Terrell, father of Mrs. Habliston, was also a Confederate soldier. He was born on a large plantation in Hanover County, Virginia, 1834, was educated in the University of Virginia, graduated from Jefferson Medical College at Philadelphia, and at the age of twenty-seven located in Hanover County, where he carried on an extensive practice until 1887. He died in 1891. At the outbreak of the war he organized the Ashland Artillery, was a lieutenant for two years and then served as a surgeon until the end of the war. He was active in the United Confederate Veterans and at one time held the rank of brigadier-general. Doctor Terrell married Betty Trevillion Anderson, of Hanover County. They were the parents of eight children: Lewis Nicholas, now deceased, married

Florence V. Dandridge and had two children, Lewis Frank and
Bessie Dandridge; Dr. Edmond Anderson Terrell married Lulu
Atkinson, who died leaving three children, Edmond Anderson,
William Amonett and Louise, and he afterward married her
sister, Eva Atkinson, and had one daughter, Marjory Terrell;
Maria Doswell Terrell married William H. Walker and was the
mother of a son, Terrell H.; Charles James Terrell is deceased;
Alice Lee is the wife of Andrew Lewis, her four sons being
George F., Charles T., Allen Leslie and Terrell; Frank is de-
ceased; Mrs. Habliston was the seventh child; Elizabeth Walker
married Rev. Thomas Green Faulkner, and had two sons,
Thomas Green and Donald Terrell.

BERTRAND GORDON BENTON. It has been the fortune of Bertrand G. Benton during an active and varied career to have been
identified with a number of lines of activity and to have demonstrated his versatility by making a success of each of his operations. Not satisfied with gaining prosperity along one line of
enterprise, he has extended his operations to include several
vocations, but of more recent years has applied himself principally to a real estate and general brokerage business at Clarendon, operating under the name of the B. G. Benton Realty Company. This concern has grown to large proportions, and one
of its latest developments is the charming subdivision known as
Waverly Hills, adjoining Clarendon, where the concern is building and developing, and establishing one of the most pleasant
residential districts of the community.

Mr. Benton was born in Loudoun County, Virginia, December 19, 1883, and is a son of William H. and Nannie B. (Gordon)
Benton. His father was born in Loudoun County, where he was
reared to agricultural pursuits, and during his young manhood
and for some years thereafter followed the vocation of tilling
the soil in Loudoun and Clarke counties, this state. Subsequently he turned his attention to contracting and building, and
for about fifteen years the family home was located at Charles
Town, West Virginia, but eventually he returned to Virginia,
where his death occurred in July, 1926. Mrs. Benton, who was
born in Clarke County, survives her husband and is one of the
highly esteemed residents of Hyattsville, Maryland.

Bertrand G. Benton was a child when taken to Charles Town,
West Virginia, where he was reared and received his education
in public schools. Upon his graduation from high school as a
member of the class of 1906 he secured a position with the Page
Fence Company of Adrian, Michigan, as a traveling salesman in
the territory which included Maryland, Virginia and the District
of Columbia. He was successful in his salesmanship and at the
end of three years had accumulated sufficient means to buy a
grocery store at Washington, D. C., of which he continued to be
the proprietor for two years. Disposing of his holdings, he
turned his attention to farming in Loudoun County, where he
still has farm interests, these being carried on by tenants. Subsequently Mr. Benton again engaged in the grocery business,
this time at Pleasant Valley, adjoining his farm, and this he
carried on for four years. In 1921 he established his family at
Clarendon and embarked in the real estate business at Washington, D. C., in partnership with Dave E. Berry, but at the end
of one year this business was dissolved and Mr. Benton became
sales manager for Ruby Lee Minar, a position which he retained
two years. His next connection was as manager for the Lyon

Park Realty Corporation, with which he remained one year, and then, with R. P. Hutchison, organized the Lyon Park Realty Company, the name of which was changed to its present style, the B. G. Benton Realty Company, in October, 1927. Mr. R. P. Hutchison died in October, 1927, and Mr. S. F. Hutchison is now a member of the firm. This firm, with headquarters in the Jones Building at Clarendon, owns Waverly Hills subdivision adjoining Clarendon, where they are building and selling homes, and also carry on a successful brokerage business. In addition to his realty business Mr. Benton still operates his farm of 175 acres, and has a modern dairy, with up-to-date machinery and a large patronage. Fraternally Mr. Benton is affiliated with the Masonic fraternity. He holds membership in the Chamber of Commerce and the Business Men's Club and has an excellent reputation in business circles as a man of integrity and ability. Politically he is a Democrat, and his religious faith is that of the Methodist Episcopal Church.

In October, 1908, Mr. Benton was united in marriage with Miss Bessie Hutchison, of Fairfax, Virginia, daughter of Joshua and Mattie (Mankin) Hutchison, natives of Fairfax County. Mr. Hutchison has spent his entire life in Fairfax County, where he is now living in comfortable retirement after a long, active, useful and honorable life passed in agricultural pursuits. Although he is now eighty years of age he is in remarkable health, and is one of the greatly respected men of his community. He enlisted in the Confederate army during the war between the states, in which he saw much active service. Mrs. Benton is active in the work of the Methodist Episcopal Church at Clarendon, and the pleasant family home, 505 Oak Street, is the scene of frequent social activities.

JOHN LLEWELLYN TUCKER, who is head of the largest tobacco warehousing organization in this country, is a native Virginian, and has been in the tobacco business practically all his life. His father for many years was a successful figure in the tobacco industry of Southern Virginia.

Mr. Tucker was born in Lunenburg County, Virginia, August 29, 1880, and is descended from a long line of Tucker ancestors. This family has been in the state since the early years of the 1600s. The earliest historic figure of the name was William Tucker, who came to Virginia in 1610, was one of the subscribers of the Charter of 1612, and sat in the first House of Burgesses, in 1619. In subsequent generations there were other Tuckers who were elected burgesses and were otherwise prominent in Colonial affairs. From tidewater Virginia George Tucker, an ancestor of John Llewellyn Tucker, moved to Lunenburg County as one of the first settlers. He was the father of Llewellyn Tucker and grandfather of Henry Tucker, who was the grandfather of John Llewellyn Tucker.

Mr. Tucker's father was the late Henry Williamson Tucker oldest son of Henry Tucker and Selina Skipwith Burwell, who was born and reared in Mecklenburg County, was educated in private schools and business college at Richmond, and was in business as a merchant and farmer until 1891, when he moved from Brunswick County, where he then lived, to Danville and became associated with the leaf tobacco warehouse business, and was after that a prominent factor in the tobacco industry of South Virginia until his death. He passed away December 11, 1914, and is buried in Green Hill Cemetery at

Danville. For upwards of a quarter of a century he was one
of the best known members of the tobacco interests in this part
of the state. His wife was Louisa Scott Nelson, a daughter of
Dr. Robert Carter Nelson, of Mecklenburg County, Virginia, a
direct descendant of "Secretary" Thomas Nelson, Colonial secretary for Virginia and also for many terms secretary of the
House of Burgesses; also a direct descendant of Robert
("King") Carter, of Corotoman, from whom he derived his
name. Mrs. Tucker's mother was Mary Scott Watkins, a daughter of Samuel Venable Watkins, of Petersburg, and a granddaughter of William Morton Watkins, whose ancestral home,
"Do-Well," is still standing in Charlotte County, Virginia, and
is still occupied by direct descendants. Mrs. Tucker was educated in private schools at Petersburg, Virginia, and was always
active in church and social life. She died October 27, 1915, and
is buried beside her husband in Green Hill Cemetery at Danville.

Henry Williamson Tucker and Louisa Scott Nelson, his wife,
were the parents of six children. One, a girl, died in infancy.
Their oldest son, Robert Henry Tucker, was born in Lunenburg
County, September 27, 1875, is professor of business administration at Washington and Lee University, and one of the ablest
educators in the state. In 1918 he married Miss Evelyn Page
Edmunds. He is chairman of the tax committee of the State
Chamber of Commerce, and his work along lines of political
economy and government has attracted much attention. The
next child, Mary Louise Nelson Tucker, is the wife of Harry C.
Ficklen, of Danville, at the present time (1928-30) representing
the city of Danville in the State Legislature. The fourth child
is John Llewellyn Tucker, the subject of this sketch. The
daughter Page Estelle, who died in 1912, was married in 1907
to Frank B. McFall, of Anderson, South Carolina, and is survived by one child, Henry Tucker McFall, a 1929 graduate of
Virginia Military Institute and now engaged in business in
Washington, D. C.

Their sixth and youngest child, Miss Annie Ursula Tucker,
was a teacher in the public schools of Danville for a number of
years, and recently engaged in missionary work under the
auspices of the Episcopal Church for the western diocese of Virginia.

John Llewellyn Tucker as a boy attended public school in
Brunswick County, also at Danville, and finished his education
in William and Mary College. After his college career he went
west and for fifteen years was a traveling salesman over an
extensive territory. On returning to Danville he became associated with his father in the warehouse business, and has been
a prominent factor as a tobacconist since that time. He succeeded his father in business and since 1925 has been president
and general manager of the Danville Warehouse Company.
This company, operating four large tobacco warehouses, has the
distinction of being the largest tobacco warehousing concern
anywhere.

Mr. Tucker is a director of the Chamber of Commerce, is a
past president of the Tuscarora Club, for several years was
active in Rotary Club work, is a Democrat and a former vestryman in the Episcopal Church.

He married at Louisville, Kentucky, December 26, 1918, Miss
Florence McCallum, of that city, where she was reared and educated, graduating from the University of Louisville. Before
her marriage she taught in public schools in Fredericksburg and

Danville, Virginia. Mrs. Tucker has found many duties in the Episcopal Church work and the guilds. She is a member of the Shakespeare Club. Her father, Harry McCallum, was active in business in Louisville, Kentucky, until his death in July, 1929. Her mother, Minnie (Smith) McCallum, died some years ago. Both are buried in Cave Hill Cemetery at Louisville.

John Llewellyn Tucker and his wife, Florence McCallum Tucker, have four children: Louisa Nelson, Margaret McCallum, Nancy Burwell and Harry McCallum Tucker.

OTWAY GILES BAILEY, JR., division superintendent of schools of Cumberland County, has had several variations of experience since boyhood, having for a time been identified with mercantile pursuits, and then came the World war, in which he answered the call to the colors, and the greater part of the time since the war has been spent in educational work.

Mr. Bailey was born at Pedlar Mills, Amherst County, Virginia, January 20, 1895, son of Otway Giles and Ellen B. (Preston) Bailey. His father was born in Amherst and his mother in Washington County, Virginia. His father was a graduate of the Virginia Military Institute and spent many years in the profession of civil engineering. In 1910 he was made collector of internal revenue at Lynchburg, served four years, and now, at the age of seventy-six, lives retired at Waugh, Virginia. In 1875 he was elected and served four years as superintendent of schools of Amherst County. His wife died March 3, 1923, at the age of sixty-seven.

Otway Giles Bailey, Jr., was reared in Amherst County, attended the elementary schools of Amherst and the secondary schools of Lynchburg, after which he was a student for two years in the Virginia Christian College, at Lynchburg, now known as Lynchburg College. After his college career he was employed for two years in a wholesale dry goods house at Lynchburg.

He enlisted in 1917 for service in the navy, and for a term of four years. He was made a petty officer, and part of the time was in the Medical Corps, having taken a course in Philadelphia in a school of pharmacy and serving as pharmacist mate. He was released from service May 19, 1919, and after returning home pursued a course in the Virginia Polytechnic Institute, where he was graduated with the Bachelor of Science degree in 1923. He has also attended several summer sessions at the University of Virginia. Mr. Bailey with this preparation became agricultural instructor in the Cumberland High School, and on June 20, 1924, was made division superintendent of schools for the county, an office which he has filled with credit to the present time.

He married, September 5, 1923, Miss Ella DeFord, of Norfolk, Virginia, daughter of Willoughby C. and Emma (Halstead) DeFord, natives of Norfolk County. Her father is a retired lumber man living at 3014 McLemore Street in Norfolk. Mr. and Mrs. Bailey have two children: Otway Giles III, born September 5, 1924, and Ellen Olivia, born October 10, 1926.

Mr. Bailey is a member of the Masonic fraternity, belongs to the Virginia Education Association and the National Education Association, the American Legion, is a Democrat, and teaches a class of men in the Presbyterian Sunday School. He is also a member of the Jefferson Graveyard Association, made up of the descendants of Thomas Jefferson.

Loretta Alice Adrienne Jones Pyle

AUGUSTUS JAMES PYLE. The name Pyle has had many years of honorable connection with the business and civic life of Richmond. Augustus James Pyle, Sr., a native of Richmond, where he was reared and educated, became an extensive land owner in Virginia. He married Mary Courtney. There were two children by that marriage, Sarah Frances and Augustus James, Jr. After the death of Mr. Pyle, Mrs. Pyle married Mr. Robinson and they had one son, Jefferson Davis Robinson, who is now prominent at Toledo, Ohio, being a partner and manager of the Libby Glass Works of that city. He married Mamie Hahn, of Toledo, and has two children, Joseph and Jefferson. The daughter Sarah, now deceased, was the wife of Joseph B. McKinney, and had eight children.

Augustus James Pyle, Jr., was also reared and educated in Richmond, and after leaving school at the age of seventeen entered the Confederate army. After the war he became identified with the *Religious Herald* and finally gave up his connection with that Richmond publication to engage in the dyeing and cleaning business, which he followed until his death.

He married Loretta Alice Adrienne Jones, a daughter of Charles Edmond and Martha Anne (Smith) Jones, and granddaughter of William Jones, also a native of Virginia. Mrs. Pyle since the death of her husband has continued to reside at Richmond and owns a business of her own at 213 East Grace Street. Mrs. Pyle is a descendant of the famous Terrell family of Virginia, a family that has been here since early Colonial times and whose descendants have been people of distinction in many other states. The Terrell family history has been fully recorded, and the connections run back into medieval times in France and England, where they were inter-married with royal lines, and many of them were people of rank, able soldiers and statesmen. The Terrells had their coat-of-arms and other insignia of their high rank. The parents of Mrs. Pyle had the following children: James Buckner Jones, who became a circuit judge in Missouri, married Kate Lupton; Mrs. Loretta Pyle; Martha Susan married Benjamin Crenshaw and they had a family of twelve children; Charles Henry and Emma Lee Jones are both deceased; Cortez Valesco; and Edna Terrell is now Mrs. John B. MacDowall and has five children, named Loretta, Mary Elizabeth, John, Martha and Douglas.

Mrs. Pyle is the mother of four children. Her daughter Martha Augusta is the widow of Sydney Putnam Owens, a native of Virginia, who for many years was in the service of the R. G. Dun Company, later conducted a business in women's ready-to-wear garments and conducted that until his death. Mr. and Mrs. Owens had two children, Dr. William Irving, a graduate of the Medical College of Virginia, who completed his training in the Lenox Hill Hospital at New York and now practicing at Pulaski, Virginia, married Gertrude Emberson, daughter of Dr. W. S. Emberson, of New Rochelle, New York, and has one son, William Emberson; and Sydney Willard Owens, who graduated from Columbia University, New York, married Ruth Pulliam. He is connected with the American Audit Company of Richmond. Wade Hampton Pyle, the oldest son of Mrs. Pyle, married a Miss Slaughter, of Richmond, and subsequently Miss Laura Crenshaw, of Albemarle County, having one child by his first wife, Robert Augustus, who married Ruth Farr, and is in business at Richmond. Robert E. Lee Pyle, a business man of Washington, D. C., married Mrs. Mae Kinney, and Ashby Barnes

Pyle, a Richmond business man, married Miss Nannie Pittman, of Richmond.

Mrs. Pyle had two grandsons in the World war. William Irving Owens was first lieutenant in the Fifteenth Machine Gun Battalion and saw active service in the Meuse-Argonne sector and the St. Mihiel. He later served in the Army of Occupation after the armistice was signed. Sydney Willard was an ensign in the Naval Aviation Service and had the hnor of being in the convoy of plains escorting the *George Washington* with President Wilson a passenger on each of his two visits to France. Both grandsons received diplomas from the Virginia Military Institute upon their return from the war.

Mrs. Pyle is a member of the Baptist Church and takes a prominent part in the missionary circle of the Grace Baptist Church. She is the oldest member of the Richmond Board for Needy Confederate Women.

JOHN THOMAS WEST, who made a long and honorable service record in the United States navy, was a resident of Portsmouth, and was born in that city November 6, 1852. He died at Norfolk June 14, 1917.

His father, John Thomas West, Sr., was a farmer and merchant. He entered the Confederate army and in the early part of the war was captured and held a prisoner until the final surrender. His first marriage was with Eliza Ann Weatherley, and John Thomas West was the only child by this marriage.

John Thomas West attended school at Portsmouth, had several years of clerical experience, and learned the trade of machinist in the Norfolk Navy Yard. He was twenty-five years of age when he entered the Government service as a machinist's mate, and was in the navy a quarter of a century, until he was put on the retired list in 1903. During the last fourteen years he was a warrant officer. During his first enlistment he went to the African coast on the U. S. S. *Concord,* and was also in Chinese waters before the Spanish-American war. He was on the battleship *Texas* in the war with Spain, and participated in the great running encounter with the Spanish fleet off Santiago, which was the outstanding naval battle of the war. Later he was on the *Puritan* and the *Ampherite.* He was awarded a medal for his part in the naval campaign of 1898, and in 1889 was given a medal for his service on the U. S. S. *Kearsarge.*

On July 15, 1896, he and Miss Mary Mallory Dye were married by Rev. Robert Gatewood in St. Paul's Episcopal Church at Berkeley, Virginia. Mrs. West is a daughter of James Dye, of Hampton, Virginia, a brick contractor, who also studied law. He entered the Confederate army early in the war, and was killed in action at Sharpsburg, Maryland, in September, 1862, while serving as captain of cavalry under General McGruder. Mrs. West's mother was Jean Sinclair Armistead, member of the distinguished Armistead family of Virginia. Mrs. West is a member of the Episcopal Church and the United Daughters of the Confederacy. The late Mr. West served as a vestryman in St. Paul's Church at Berkeley. He was a Democrat, a member of the Masonic fraternity and Knights of Pythias.

Mr. and Mrs. West had two children: Phillip Bevington West and Jean Sinclair Weatherley West, who graduated from the Virginia Teachers College at Farmville in 1925, and who now resides in Norfolk.

CHARLES WADE CRUSH, the present commonwealth's attorney of Montgomery County, is a World war veteran, and has had an experience in business, in his profession and as a soldier that has taken him a great deal about the world.

However, his present home is the progressive town of Southwest Virginia where he was born, April 14, 1893, and his people have been in Southwest Virginia for several generations. His grandfather, James E. Crush, was born near Fincastle, Virginia, and during the Civil war served as a member of Capt. John C. Wade's Company G in the Fourth Virginia Regiment, his company being known as the Montgomery Fencibles. After the war he was sheriff, jailer and deputy for a number of years, and prior to his death in 1908 had been a clerk in the treasury department at Washington. He is buried at Christiansburg. Charles H. Crush, father of the commonwealth's attorney, was born and reared in Montgomery County, attended public school, was a merchant in West Virginia, and prior to that had lived in Texas and Arkansas for a time. He was deputy sheriff at Dallas, Texas, in the crude and primitive times of that city. After returning to Christiansburg he resumed a business career and was a merchant at Coopers, West Virginia, for two years. He died shortly after his return to Christiansburg, in July, 1893. His wife, Mary Wade, was born and reared at Christiansburg, attended public schools and the Montgomery Female College, and she acted as deputy clerk under her father before her marriage, and after the death of her husband carried on a mercantile business with a great deal of skill and energy at Christiansburg from 1895 to 1915. She is now living retired and is an active worker in the Presbyterian Church. She is a daughter of Capt. John C. and Jane (Edie) Wade. Capt. John C. Wade was the captain of Company G of the Fourth Virginia Regiment of Volunteers, and after the war was agent for the railroad, and held the office of county clerk until a short time before his death. Captain Wade was a son of William Wade, who for years represented his county in the Lower House of the Virginia Legislature. Mrs. Mary Crush is also a granddaughter of Dr. Joseph S. Edie, a pioneer of Christiansburg and one of the first physicians to practice in that community. Doctor Edie married Elizabeth Randolph White, a cousin of the famous John Randolph of Roanoke.

Charles Wade Crush was the only child of his parents. He attended public school at Christiansburg, Washington and Lee University, and in January, 1915, was admitted to the bar. He carried on a law practice at Christiansburg and Roanoke until November, 1917, when he joined the colors, going for training to Camp Lee, Virginia. On May 26, 1918, he was sent overseas in Company A of the Three Hundred and Fourteenth Machine Gun Battalion, Eightieth Division. This was known as the Suicide Battalion, and he held the rank of corporal. He was in service in the Artois Sector, at St. Mihiel and the Meuse-Argonne, and his Victor medal shows four bars, indicating his participation in four major engagements. He returned to the United States June 7, 1919, and received his honorable discharge June 19, 1919, at Camp Lee.

After his release from military service Mr. Crush was for some months in the advertising business at Oklahoma City and then moved to Garland, Dallas County, Texas, where he practiced law and handled real estate. He also attended the University of Texas, and was admitted to the bar of that state. He was secretary of the Garland City Council during the two years he was located there.

In November, 1921, he returned to Christiansburg and was assistant postmaster until the spring of 1923, when he made the successful race for the office of commonwealth's attorney. By reelection he holds that office at the present time. Mr. Crush is also a second lieutenant with the Two Hundred and Forty-sixth Coast Artillery Corps, Virginia National Guard. He was invited to attend the staff of former Gov. E. Lee Trinkle at the inauguration of President Coolidge, and was with Governor Byrd at the Hoover inauguration in 1929.

Mr. Crush is vice president and trustee of the Cohee Country Club, is a Knight Templar Mason, being affiliated with McDaniel Lodge No. 86, A. F. and A. M., Kazim Temple of the Mystic Shrine, is treasurer of John Gardner Post of the Veterans of Foreign Wars, and member of Montgomery County Post No. 59, American Legion, of which he is vice commander. He is a member of the Modern Woodmen of America, the Patriotic Order Sons of America, the University Club of the Virginia Polytechnic Institute and the University Club of Richmond. He also belongs to the B. P. O. Elks, is a Democrat and a Presbyterian.

Mr. Crush married at Christiansburg, May 1, 1924, Miss Eliza Clay Allen, formerly of White Gate, Bland County. She attended school in Bland County and the Montgomery County High School at Christiansburg, and also had a business college course. For several years before her marriage she was in stenographic and clerical work for the Phoenix Furniture Corporation at Christiansburg. She is a Presbyterian, member of the United Daughters of the Confederacy and Daughters of the American Revolution. Her parents are J. C. and Florence (Richardson) Allen. The Allens are an old family of Southwest Virginia. Her father formerly lived in Bland County and is now retired at Christiansburg. He carried on farming and stock raising on a large scale in Bland County, and was also in the lumber business with the Ritter Lumber Company until retiring in 1928. Her mother died several years ago and is buried in Bland County. Mr. and Mrs. Crush have one daughter, Jane Allen Crush.

STEPHEN L. FARRAR, clerk of the Circuit Court of Amelia County, is a lawyer by profession, and his work has continued the traditional association of his family name with the bench and bar and public affairs of Amelia County through a long period of years.

He was born at Mohican, Amelia County, December 13, 1862, son of Judge F. R. and Nannie (Austin) Farrar, his father a native of Prince Edward County and his mother of Cumberland County. His father was a captain in the Confederate army, was liberally educated, having attended Hampden-Sidney College, and was a student of law at the University of Virginia and also attended Princeton University. He was an able lawyer, and served as judge of the County Court of Amelia County for twenty-seven years, practicing law at the same time. He was also widely known as a teacher and lecturer, and was called to many distant localities for special addresses. He died in August, 1898, at the age of seventy-one, while his wife passed away in 1870, at the age of forty-five.

The son Stephen L. Farrar was reared and educated in Amelia County, and had steadily before him from boyhood the life and ideals of his honest father. He attended private schools, the Worsham Academy, took his law course at the University of Virginia and was admitted to the bar in 1883. Judge Farrar has had a professional and public career of forty-five years. He practiced law at Amelia Court House, and when his father died succeeded him as county judge, holding the office seven years. In 1906 he was appointed circuit clerk to fill an unexpired term, and has been continued in that office by regular election for twenty-three years. No other man at the courthouse has enjoyed such honors, responsibilities and marks of esteem as Judge Farrar.

He married in November, 1908, Miss Clay Holland, daughter of Rev. J. L. T. and Emma (Walton) Holland, her father a native of Fluvanna County, Virginia, and her mother of Prince Edward County. Her father gave his active life to the ministry of the Christian Church, and was a Confederate soldier. He died in 1897. Judge and Mrs. Farrar have three children: Stephen L., Jr., born August 30, 1909, now deputy clerk of the Circuit Court of Amelia County; Clay H., born in October, 1911, a student in Intermont College at Bristol, Tennessee; and Lilly Virginia, born in October, 1915. Judge Farrar is a member and a past master of Amelia Lodge No. 101, A. F. and A. M., is a Democrat, is lay leader in the Methodist Episcopal Church and teaches a Bible class in Sunday School.

JOSEPH ANTHONY PETERS during a residence at Richmond of more than forty years gained a wide acquaintance in the city and over the state, and for a quarter of a century was prominent in the insurance business.

He was born in Bedford County, Virginia, in December, 1859, and died at his home in Richmond November 22, 1927. He was the second of nine children born to Robert Henry and Ann Elizabeth Peters. His father was a tobacco grower in Bedford County. The surviving sisters and brothers of the late Mr. Peters were: E. E. Peters, of Washington, D. C.; Mrs. A. F. Crenshaw and Mrs. Lynwood Peters, of Saint Louis, Missouri; H. D. Peters, of Keysville, Virginia; Mr. John C. Williams, of Dillwyn, Virginia; Mrs. W. O. Saunders and R. L. Peters, of Richmond.

Mr. Peters was reared on his father's farm in Bedford County, was educated in private schools, and for several years had employment with an uncle who was a leading building contractor in Prince George County. In 1886 he located at Richmond, for several years was with a grocery house, and left that to take up insurance work. He was in the active service of the Metropolitan Life Insurance Company a quarter of a century, finally being retired on the pension roll of that corporation in 1923. During the World war he had spent much of his time doing work under the auspices of the Y. M. C. A. in the great munition plant in Hopewell, Virginia. Mr. Peters during the last three years of his life also had employment with the First and Merchants National Bank of Richmond. He was a member of the Junior Order United American Mechanics and the Second Presbyterian Church.

He married, October 25, 1887, Miss Missouri Pearman, who was educated at Charles City, Virginia, where her father was a planter. She was next to the youngest in a family of eight daughters, her parents being William H. and

Elizabeth (Gill) Pearman. Mrs. Peters continues to reside at 3100 Stuart Avenue in Richmond. Mr. and Mrs. Peters had six children: William Malcolm, connected with the freight department of the Chesapeake & Ohio Railroad, married Gertrude Brothers, and has two children, named Margaret Lois and Grace Ann; Leroy Edward, assistant auditor and paymaster for the Packard Automobile Company at the factory at Detroit, married May Tolbert, of Pennsylvania, and has an adopted daughter, Ilene; Joseph Anthony, Jr., a business man of Kansas City, Missouri, married Cordia Wigle; Linwood McCray; Robert Eugene, with the Chesapeake & Ohio Railway; and Miss Idella Ann. The son Joseph Anthony, Jr., was a sergeant with the One Hundred and Fifty-fourth Infantry during the World war and spent eleven months on the battle front in France, where he was gassed.

ALFRED WASHINGTON DRINKARD, JR., director of the Agricultural Experiment Station at the Virginia Polytechnic Institute, has been an important contributor to the advancement of horticulture and agriculture in Virginia, has served on numerous boards and commissions, and is an alumnus of the Virginia Polytechnic Institute, his Doctor of Philosophy degree coming from Cornell University.

He is a member of one of the old families of Virginia and was born in Appomatox County, January 10, 1883. He is a descendant of John Drinkard, a planter and slave owner of Halifax County, who in the years immediately following the close of the Revolutionary war purchased upwards of 1,000 acres of land in Halifax County. This land he developed into a great plantation, worked by his numerous slaves, and the plantation provided a home and opportunity for his family of ten children. A son of John Drinkard was Archibald Drinkard, who served as a soldier in the Revolution and was a farmer and planter in Appomattox County. He married Judith Pendleton about 1818. Their son, James Drinkard, the grandfather of Dr. Alfred W., was a soldier in the Confederate army and devoted his life after the war to a farm in Campbell County, Virginia. He and his wife are buried in the Drinkard family cemetery eight miles from Lynchburg.

Charles M. Drinkard, the father of Doctor Drinkard, was born and reared in Campbell County, attended private schools, was a farmer and stock raiser in Appomattox County, and for eight years served as county supervisor. He died December 2, 1925. His wife, Mary Ann Martin, was a daughter of Capt. John Wellington and Amanda Harriet (Neighbors) Martin. Captain Martin was an officer in the Confederate army and a farmer in Campbell County. Mary Ann Martin was educated in a private school conducted by Major Evans, who is still living at the age of more than ninety years. Mary Ann Drinkard is now seventy-six years of age and lives in Appomattox. She was the mother of eleven children: Lucy, wife of C. W. Beasley, of Williamson, West Virginia; Lawrence M., who occupies the old homestead in Appomattox County; Dr. Alfred Washington; Hattie Aleen, wife of D. E. Turnes, of Appomattox; Lula Belle, wife of W. J. LeGrand of Appomattox; Charles Milton, Jr., who was drowned at the age of two years; Sallie Wellington, wife of D. R. Green, of Raleigh, North Carolina; Miss Mary Estelle, a high school teacher at Roanoke; Judith Lobelia, deceased, the wife of M. P. McNeely, of Monroe, North Carolina;

Mattie Cathleen, wife of Owen Carson, of Appomattox County; and Miss Nettie Florene, of Appomattox.

Alfred Washington Drinkard attended public schools in Appomattox County and in 1902 entered Virginia Polytechnic Institute, where he was graduated Bachelor of Science in 1906. He remained as a graduate student, taking his Master of Science degree in 1908. From 1910 until 1912 he continued studying in Cornell University at Ithaca, New York, and was awarded his Doctor's degree in 1913.

In the same year he returned to the Virginia Polytechnic Institute as associate horticulturist in the Agricultural Experiment Station, and since 1916 has been director of the experiment station. He also has a farm of his own in Appomattox County. Doctor Drinkard is a member of the honorary fraternity Phi Kappa Phi, is a Sigma Xi, fellow of the American Association for the Advancement of Science, member of the American Society for Horticultural Science, and was director of the Virginia State Horticultural Society for the years 1917-1918-1919-1920-1922-1923. He is a member of the Farmers Union, the Farm Bureau and the Grange, and was president of the Virginia Polytechnic Institute Science Club in 1919-20.

Doctor Drinkard is affiliated with Hunters Lodge No. 156, A. F. and A. M., Royal Arch Chapter No. 65 at Blacksburg, Knights Templar Commandery No. 32, and Kazim Temple of the Mystic Shrine at Roanoke. He also belongs to the Independent Order of Odd Fellows and Improved Order of Red Men, and in politics is a Democrat.

In 1924 Gov. E. Lee Trinkle appointed him a member of the Virginia Water Power and Development Commission and he was reappointed by Governor Byrd in 1926, serving until this commission was merged with the State Conservation and Development Commission. Doctor Drinkard was president of the Blacksburg Board of Trade 1916-1919. He is a deacon and chairman of the finance committee in the Baptist Church.

FRANK B. BEAZLEY is an attorney at law, formerly engaged in practice at Richmond, now at Bowling Green, and he divides his time between his law offices and his farm in Caroline County, where he has gained something out of the ordinary distinction as a pure bred cattle and poultry man.

Mr. Beazley was born at Sparta, Caroline County, September 3, 1897, son of William F. and Emma (Alsop) Beazley, who were also natives of Caroline County. His mother resides with her son on the home farm. The father died August 11, 1925. Mr. Beazley through his mother is descended from an old family which runs back in English history to the time of King Henry III. The Beazleys were also an old English family, and among other well known names in the early generations was a dean of Oxford University. The first Beazleys in America settled on Beazley's Island in North Carolina.

Frank B. Beazley grew up on the home farm in Caroline County, graduated from the Sparta High School in 1916, and he took the course of the liberal arts department at Richmond College, now the University of Richmond. He graduated in law at Washington and Lee University in 1923. He passed the bar examination in June, 1923, and in the same year began practice at Richmond, forming a partnership with his brother, J. Henry Beazley. The firm was Beazley & Beazley for three years, and after they dissolved partnership Mr. Beazley continued an individual practice in the city until 1927, when he opened his law office at Bowling Green and has concentrated his attention on his law practice.

The farm which he operates comprises four hundred acres and is situated ten miles southeast of Bowling Green. He makes his home on the farm and specializes in pure bred Jersey cattle and pure bred Barred Plymouth Rock chickens.

Mr. Beazley married, September 25, 1927, Miss Kate Rucker, daughter of D. Henry and Lulu (Harrison) Rucker. She is a great-granddaughter of President Henry H. Harrison. Her father was born in Fauquier County, Virginia, and her mother at Richmond. Her father is a professor in the William Fox School at Richmond.

During the World war Mr. Beazley was a member of the Students Army Training Corps at Richmond. He is a member of the Delta Theta Phi legal fraternity, and Theta Chi, social fraternity, the Caroline County and Richmond Bar Association, and was affiliated with the American Legion at Richmond. He is eligible to membership in the Sons of the American Revolution, is a Democrat in politics, a member of the Caroline County Democratic Committee, and a member of the Baptist Church. Mrs. Beazley is a member of the Richmond Woman's Club and the Country Club of Virginia. Mr. Beazley's brothers and sisters all graduated from college with degrees. His brother William Oswald died October 20, 1918. His brother J. Henry is still practicing law at Richmond. Lura Beazley married Warren Wright, a resident of Alexandria, Virginia, and West Palm Beach, Florida. Blanche E. Beazley married John Rhodes and lives in Baltimore.

THOMAS NATHANIEL WHITE was a Confederate soldier, and after the war for many years was prominent in the business life of Weldon, North Carolina.

Descended from the Masons and the Trotters of Brunswick County, Virginia, he was born at Danville, Virginia, in 1841, died at Richmond, Virginia, in February, 1894, and was buried at Weldon, North Carolina. His father, George White, from Tyrone County, Ireland, married Anne Mason, a daughter of Col. Nathaniel Mason, in 1830. The four children of this marriage were: Mary, who married Claiborne Sturdivant; Anne, who married Dr. Thomas Yandell Green Wynn; Capt. George D., who married Della Pope; and Thomas N., who married Laura Parker.

Thomas was educated in private schools and in Red Oak Academy in Brunswick County. At nineteen he entered the Confederate army, and served bravely in the cavalry under his brother, Capt. George D. White, of Company A, Third Virginia Regiment, Stuart's Brigade, until the end of the war.

After the war he located at Weldon, North Carolina, where he was engaged in the mercantile business with his brother. He developed one of the largest general merchandise stores in the state, and handled a great deal of raw cotton. In 1891 he moved to Richmond, Virginia. He was a Democrat in his political affiliations and a member of the Episcopal Church.

On October 25, 1871, Thomas Nathaniel White married Laura A. Parker, who is a descendant of the Bishop family, which was established in North Carolina in Colonial times. She finished her education at Warrenton College under the Greensboro College faculty, the latter school having been burned by the

Union army. Her father, Richard Bishop Parker, was a very able and scholarly man, an educator, editor and newspaper man, and served as a magistrate and was a special member of Halifax County Court. He was identified with the Methodist Episcopal Church. The mother of Mrs. White was Sarah Ann Priscilla Sledge.

Born of the union of Thomas N. and Laura A. White were six children. Thomas N., Jr., died in infancy. Anne Mason married Blake W. Corson, of Cumberland County, Virginia, a civil engineer. They have three children, named Blake W., Jr., Judith Parker and Georgia White. Richard Trotter White is an inventor. David Meade White is an attorney practicing at the Richmond bar. He married Bessie Turner, who is descended from the Eppeses and the Randolphs of Virginia. They have one son, David Meade, Jr. Thomas Obed White is in the coal business at Richmond. George Bonner White is an attorney, also practicing at the Richmond bar. He married Martha Fourqurean, a descendant of William Byrd I, the founder of Richmond.

VERNON MEREDITH GEDDY is a native son and grew up in the classic environs of the old Town of Williamsburg, and has made a notable record there during the past ten years as a member of the bar, commonwealth attorney and judge.

Judge Geddy, who has his offices in the Peninsula Bank and Trust Company Building, was born at Williamsburg November 11, 1897, son of Thomas Henley and Mattie (Piggott) Geddy, and grandson of Capt. George E. Geddy. His grandfather organized a company of militia in James City County and became its captain, and during his service was captured and during the last two years of the war between the states was held a prisoner. Thomas Henley Geddy was born in James City County and for several years was a merchant at Toano. In July, 1893, he was elected County and Circuit Court clerk of James City County, being the first Democrat chosen to that office since reconstruction. He gave thirty-five years and the most loyal and efficient service to that office, remaining by election and reelections until his death, which occurred May 9, 1928, at the age of seventy-one. His widow still resides at Williamsburg and is a member of the Daughters of the Confederacy.

Vernon M. Geddy attended William and Mary Academy with the class of 1913 and graduated A. B. from William and Mary College in 1917. He also attended the University of Chicago and for one year taught in the Woodberry Forest School for Boys in Orange County. In the spring of 1918 he enlisted, was trained at Fortress Monroe, and was discharged November 22, 1918, eleven days after the armistice, with the rank of second lieutenant. During 1919 Mr. Geddy was director of athletics at the College of William and Mary. He took his law course at the University of Virginia and passed the bar examination in June, 1920. Since that date he has been a busy attorney at Williamsburg. He was appointed and served as judge of the Juvenile and Domestic Relations Court in 1923. From January, 1924, to December 31, 1927, he was commonwealth attorney of James City County. In January, 1928, he was again appointed judge of the Juvenile and Domestic Relations Court.

Judge Geddy married, October 24, 1923, Carrie Cole Lane, daughter of Col. L. W. and Lizzie (Jordan) Lane, her father a native of James City County and her mother of Smithfield. Her father for several years has been treasurer of William and Mary College. Mr. and Mrs. Geddy have one son, Vernon Meredith, Jr., born April 12, 1926.

Judge Geddy is also a member of the Williamsburg City Council. He is a director of the Peninsula Bank & Trust Company, member of the Virginia State and American Bar Associations, belongs to the Masonic fraternity, the American Legion, the Kappa Sigma, is secretary of the Rotary Club, member of the Williamsburg Cotillion Club. His home is on Scotland Street at Williamsburg. He is active in one of the historic churches of Virginia, Bruton Parish Church, Episcopal, and is a trustee of the church and superintendent of its Sunday School.

JULIUS DREHER WILLIS, M. D. An unobtrusive man has been for years one of the forceful figures in the medical profession of Roanoke. Early training fitted him for a busy life, and he knows but little of idle waste. He firmly believes that expression of sympathy for the misfortunes of others is right and proper, and he also believes that a practical demonstration of that sympathy calls for material assistance at a time when it is needed. This phase of his character manifests itself in the many charitable acts which he performs.

Doctor Willis was born in Hylton, now Willis, Virginia, August 10, 1886, a son of George Augustus and Venie Anna (Brumbaugh) Willis, both of whom are natives of Virginia, and now residing in Bel Air, Maryland. For a number of years his father served as superintendent of public instruction in Floyd County, Virginia. He was also engaged in merchandising and farming. A man of education, educated at Roanoke College, he has always been a leader among his associates. Five children were born to him and his wife: Eula, who is married to John M. Bell, who operates a telephone company and lives at Chester, South Carolina; Doctor Willis, who was the second in order of birth; Peter Archer, who is a tobacco buyer for Liggett & Myers Tobacco Company, and resides in Reidsville, North Carolina; George Armand, who is a dental surgeon at Havre de Grace, Maryland; and Lena F., who married J. S. McDonald, a farmer of Rocks, Maryland. The parents belong to the Lutheran Church, in which they are active, and the father is a Democrat.

Doctor Willis attended both the public and private schools of his native county and Roanoke College, and he took his professional training at the Medical College of Virginia, Richmond, from which he was graduated in 1909, with the degree of Doctor of Medicine. He interned in the Johnson-Willis Hospital of Richmond, and has the distinction of being the first man to serve the hospital in that capacity. He was also supply interne in the Roosevelt Hospital, New York City, for six months. From 1912 to 1918 he was internist to the Lewis-Gale Hospital, Roanoke, and since that time has been internist to the Shenandoah Hospital. He is also a member of the staff of the Roanoke Hospital. Doctor Willis belongs to Pi Mu, medical Greek letter fraternity, the Shenandoah Club, the Country Club, the Roanoke County Medical Society, the Southwest Virginia Medical Society, the Virginia State Medical Society, the Southern Medical Association, the American Medical Association, and is a fellow of the American College of Physicians. His practice is confined to internal medicine, in which branch he is a recognized expert. During the World war he served as a first lieutenant in the Medical Corps of the United States army.

In 1915 Doctor Willis married Miss Mary Butler Evans, a native of South Carolina, but educated in the public schools of Roanoke and National Park Seminary, Washington, D. C. Doctor and Mrs. Willis have two children: Margaret Evans Willis and Jean Dreher Willis. Doctor Willis is a Lutheran and his wife is an Episcopalian.

SYLVESTER A. RATCLIFFE. Perhaps no public official in Wise County commands more confidence and respect or enjoys greater personal esteem than Sylvester A. Ratcliffe, postmaster at Norton, Virginia. This important office he has so efficiently filled for the past seven years that irrespective of partisan political sentiment his administration has met with universal public approval.

Postmaster Ratcliffe belongs to an old Virginia family that has branches in different sections of the state, and for many years identified with its agricultural and business development as well as public affairs. He was born at Shacks Mill, Buchanan County, Virginia, May 9, 1871, son of Capt. M. S. and Lucinda (Ratcliffe) Ratcliffe, the latter of whom was born in Tazewell County, Virginia, where her father, Shade Ratcliffe, was an extensive planter before the war between the states.

Capt. M. S. Ratcliffe, father of Postmaster Ratcliffe, was born and reared in Russell County, Virginia, and acquired his title as an officer in the Confederate army during the Civil war. A planter previously, he afterward became interested in politics and was elected a member of the Virginia Legislature, on the Republican ticket, and so great was his personal popularity that but one vote was registered against him in the entire county.

Sylvester A. Ratcliffe's boyhood was spent in Tazewell County, where he received his early schooling, which was supplemented by two years in Abingdon Academy at Abingdon, Virginia, and one year in Milligan College at Milligan, Tennessee. He then embarked in the mercantile business at Richlands, Virginia, his mother's old home, where he continued for about eight years, when he removed to Saint Paul in Wise County, where he remained in the mercantile line for almost two years. He came then to Norton to enter the employ of the Norton Hardware Company, and remained with that business house for thirteen years, retiring then to accept a position as salesman with the big packing firm of Swift & Company, where he continued for four years.

In the meanwhile Mr. Ratcliffe's marked business efficiency and fidelity to the interests with which he was concerned did by no means go unnoticed, and the appreciative word of comment, trustworthy, was often heard, and on many occasions tenders of favorable business opportunities came to him. His circle of friends grew with the passing years, and the time came when in his stalwart qualities they saw just the qualifications that are so essential in public life but not always found there, and then followed the movement that brought about his appointment on November 1, 1921, as acting postmaster of Norton. This was followed on April 10, 1922, by his appointment as postmaster of this city, which was endorsed by all of his fellow citizens practically, for whatever fault his Democratic neighbors might have found with President Harding's appointments, Republicans and Democrats were united in approving of this one, and the same public sentiment prevailed when on April 8, 1926, he was reappointed by President Coolidge, it being a tribute to the man

irrespective of party. His fellow citizens realize that however
strong his personal political convictions may be, and he has
always been an outspoken Republican, he considers himself as
an official, at the service of the entire public, and faithfully,
tirelessly and unselfishly performs his duties, maintaining a
high degree of efficiency and courtesy in every departme nt, and
carefully guarding the public revenues.

Mr. Ratcliffe married on September 29, 1892, Miss Helen
McGuire, of Cedar Bluff, Virginia, who was educated at Martha
Washington College, Abingdon, Virginia. Her family is an old
and substantial one of Tazewell County, and her father, the late
J. Marion McGuire, was for many years a prominent merchant
and woolen manufacturer there. During the war between the
states he served in the Sixteenth Cavalry, Brackenridge having
been his general, Ferguson his colonel, W. L. Graham his lieutenant-colonel and Jonathan Hawkins his captain. Mr. and
Mrs. Ratcliffe's family include two daughters and one son:
Irene, who, like her mother, enjoyed superior educational ad-
vantages at Martha Washington College and later at Millersburg
College, is the wife of E. M. Patton, civil engineer at Norton,
and they have two children, Billie Lois and Anna Lowery. Virgil
Allen, who was educated at Emory and Henry College, filled a
position as auditor in the Treasury Department at Washington,
D. C., for six years, served in a similar capacity at Miami,
Florida, and is now back in Washington. He married Miss
Mattie Effinger, of Blacksburg, and they have one son, Virgil
Allen, Jr. Marion is a student in the Norton High School.

Virgil Allen Ratcliffe, only son of Postmaster Ratcliffe, is an
overseas veteran of the World war. He enlisted in the navy at
an early date and was a member of that courageous body of
American Marines that by their bravery and sacrifice won victory on the French battlefields, in the memorable offensives at
Belleau Woods, Argonne Forest and St. Mihiel. Although Mr.
Ratcliffe survived through his two years of war zone and battle
exposure, it was only because of a strong constitution and his
sturdy Virginia spirit, for after being gassed at Belleau Woods
and confined for two months in a hospital at Paris, he returned
to his command only to receive the five wounds at St. Mihiel that
kept him in a Bordeaux hospital long after he should have had
his face happily turned toward home.

Postmaster Ratcliffe is a Knight Templar Mason and belongs
to the Blue Lodge at Norton. Both he and wife are active members of the Methodist Episcopal Church, South, and the entire
family gives earnest attention to those sterling community interests that promote social welfare.

ROBERT EMORY BLACKWELL has a distinction due not only to
the length but to the importance of his service as an educator,
having for over half a century been identified with one of the
chief institutions for the higher education of men in Virginia,
the Randolph-Macon College.

Doctor Blackwell was born in Warrenton, Virginia, November 14, 1854, son of Rev. Dr. John Davenport and Julia Anna
(Butts) Blackwell. He is an alumnus of Randolph-Macon College, where he took the A. M. degree in 1874. He has studied
abroad, having attended the University of Leipsic during
1875-76. In recognition of his scholastic attainments and services as an educator several institutions have conferred upon him
the Doctor of Laws degree, including Washington and Lee Uni-

Oscar C. B. Wev.   Bosquet. Neill. Wev

Mrs Nellie Bosquet - Wev

versity. Doctor Blackwell in 1876 became a professor in the faculty of Randolph-Macon College. He was vice president and acting president from 1900 to 1902, and since 1902 has filled the office of president. He is author of several text books, is a member of the Modern Language Association of America, and is a Phi Beta Kappa.

Doctor Blackwell has long been a prominent figure in the Methodist Episcopal Church, South, and represented the church in the joint commission working for unification of the northern and southern branches of the church. He has also served as state chairman of the Virginia Inter-Racial Commission from its organization in 1919, and for twelve years has been a member of the General Educational Board of the church. Doctor Blackwell married, August 28, 1877, Theela Epia Duncan, of Ashland, Virginia. They have one daughter, Epie Duncan, who married J. F. Messick.

OSCAR NEILL WEV was a Virginian, had a brief and heroic career, and was with the United States Navy for fourteen years.

He was born at Lynchburg, Virginia, August 18, 1877, and died November 18, 1907. His parents were Walter and Elizabeth (Neill) Wev. His mother was born in Virginia. Oscar Neill Wev attended public schools at Lynchburg, and as a youth enlisted for service in the United States Navy. He was with that branch of the American military establishment fourteen years, and was raised to the grade of chief petty officer. A high mark in his career while afloat came while on the cruiser *Olympia*, the flagship of Admiral Dewey, in the great naval battle in Manila Bay in May, 1898. Later he was transferred to the navy yard at Norfolk, Virginia, and met his death by accident at Bremerton Navy Yard, Washington.

At Washington, D. C., January 9, 1902, he married Miss Nellie Bosquet, a native Virginian, who now resides at Richmond at 1639 West Grace Street. She was reared and educated in Virginia. Her father, Michael Bosquet, came from Bordeau, France, to America, and was a merchant at Richmond for many years. He married Kate Baughn, of Louisa, Virginia, and of an old Virginia family. The children in the Bosquet family were: F. M., deceased; Mrs. Nellie Wev; Bessie, Mable and Felix, all deceased; and Katherine. Michael Bosquet served under Napoleon III in the Franco-Prussian war of 1870-71. Mrs. Wev's mother was a descendant of Dr. Thomas Triplett and Rev. Thomas Neill.

The two sons of Mrs. Wev are Basquet Neill and Oscar C. B. These boys are the great-grandson of Dr. Thomas Triplett, who was a surgeon in the United States Navy under Commodore Decatur when that great American made war against the Barbary pirates, and he distinguished himself for heroism at Tunis and Algiers. Mrs. Wev's sons are also great-grandsons of Rev. Doctor Thomas Neill, of Cooperstown, New York, who was president of Dickinson College of that state, and also president of the Presbyterian Board of Publications, and was minister and pastor of a large Presbyterian Church in Philadelphia in 1865.

Mrs. Wev's son Bosquet Neill was educated at Richmond, is a graduate of the United States Naval Academy at Annapolis, and is now an ensign in the navy. He married Miss Elizabeth Robinson, of Baltimore. The other son, Oscar, spent two years in the University of Virginia. He joined the U. S. Army to obtain an appointment to the U. S. Military Academy at West

Point as a candidate-at-large. He passed the entrance examination, but was barred from entrance to West Point due to age limitation. He is now a cadet at the United States Coast Guard Academy at New London, Connecticut.

LEVIN NOCK DAVIS is practicing law, performing the duties of commissioner of accounts, and representing other business interests at his home town of Accomac, and on the 6th of August, 1929, in the Democratic primaries, was nominated to the House of Delegates from Accomac County. Mr. Davis was born on the Eastern Shore of Virginia, and has exhibited a high degree of sagacity and fidelity in all the relationships of a very busy and useful career.

He was born in Accomac County, October 3, 1887, son of George Edward and Maggie (Nock) Davis, who were also born in that section of the Eastern Shore. His father was a carpenter and wheelwright by trade, and followed those occupations all his life, together with farming. He died December 1, 1911, and the mother died in Baltimore, Maryland, March 15, 1929.

Levin Nock Davis was reared and educated in Accomac County, graduating from the high school at Painter in 1906, and then attended a business college at Baltimore, and in June, 1917, took his law degree from the University of Maryland. He was admitted to the Maryland bar in July, 1917, and remained in Baltimore until April, 1918.

Then came his military experience during the World war. By appointment of secretary of war he was made an army field clerk, stationed at the Port of Embarkation at Hoboken, New Jersey, and later at Camp Merritt, New Jersey. He was with the colors about a year, getting his honorable discharge April 19, 1919. He then remained in the Government service at Washington as a claim examiner, and from October, 1921, to October, 1923, was district manager in charge of the Norfolk office of the United States Veterans Bureau.

Mr. Davis resigned this position to resume the practice of law in his home county of Accomac. He has a large volume of business both as a counselor and trial attorney, is filling the office of commissioner of accounts for Accomac County and is local representative for the Fidelity & Deposit Company of Baltimore and the United States Fidelity and Guaranty Company. For a year and a half he was auditor and adjuster for the Fidelity & Deposit Company at Baltimore.

Mr. Davis married, April 24, 1918, Miss Lela Ames, daughter of the late John S. and Lottie (Downing) Ames. Her parents were born in Accomac County, where her father spent his life as a farmer. He died in November, 1926, and her mother now resides with Mr. and Mrs. Davis. The latter have two children: Eleanor Ames, born November 8, 1920, and Levin Franklin, born March 10, 1923.

Mr. Davis is adjutant of the Accomac Post of the American Legion. He owns some farming properties on the Eastern Shore. He is a member of the Accomac County, Maryland State and Virginia State Bar Associations, is affiliated with Ocean Lodge No. 116, A. F. and A. M., the Royal Arch Chapter at Onancock, Virginia, is a Democrat, is charge lay leader and trustee of the Drummondtown Methodist Episcopal Church and president of the Men's Bible Class. While at Baltimore he was for two years superintendent of the Sunday School. Mrs. Davis is a member of the Accomac Woman's Club.

S. VERNON STRICKLER, whose people were among the earliest settlers of the Valley of Virginia, is a doctor of dental surgery who first practiced in the Valley, and since 1916 has been a prominent representative of his profession at Charlottesville.

He was born in Rockingham County, Virginia, July 10, 1884, son of B. F. and Susan Virginia (Cline) Strickler. His grandfather, Benjamin Strickler, was born in Shenandoah County, and his maternal grandfather, David Cline, in Rockingham County. B. F. Strickler was born in Shenandoah County, spent his active life as a farmer, and was a Confederate soldier in the Civil war. On account of wounds he was out of service for some time, but returned and was one of the troops under Lee at the final surrender at Appomattox. After the war he became a Republican in politics, and both he and his wife were members of the Church of the Brethren. On his paternal side Doctor Strickler is a direct descendant of the Massanutton family of Stricklers, Massanutton being the first settlement in the Valley of Virginia, near Luray, Virginia.

S. Vernon Strickler was the youngest in a family of seven boys. He attended public schools and the West Central Academy, the Bridgewater College at Bridgewater, Virginia, and in 1910 took the degree of Doctor of Dental Surgery at the University of Maryland at Baltimore. Doctor Strickler practiced for six years at Shenandoah and in 1916 removed to Charlottesville, where he performed the general service of a capable dentist. He is a member of the Charlottesville, Shenandoah Valley, Virginia State and American Dental societies.

Doctor Strickler married in 1914 Miss Beatrice Frances Elliott, who was born in Rockingham County and attended high school at Shenandoah. Her father, Benjamin M. Elliott, was in the railroad service for many years. Doctor and Mrs. Strickler have one son, Elliott LeRoy, born in 1916, now attending school at Charlottesville. Doctor Strickler is a deacon in the First Baptist Church, member of the Independent Order of Odd Fellows, and the Young Men's Business Club.

GILBERT RAYMOND REPASS, clerk of courts of Bland County, followed his father in that office, and the office has not been out of the family since the beginning of the present century.

Mr. Repass was born in Bland County April 12, 1893, son of R. C. and Julia E. (Kitts) Repass, and a descendant of Rev. Stephen Repass, who came to America from Germany and was one of the early German settlers in Western Virginia. His grandfather, Elias Repass, was from an early date identified with Bland County, where he was a farmer, stock raiser and merchant. Both he and his wife are buried at Ceres in Bland County.

The late R. C. Repass was born in Wythe County, Virginia, had a private school education, and was a man of sound knowledge and varied accomplishments. For a number of years he held the office of county surveyor. For six years he was deputy county clerk and served twenty-eight years as clerk of the courts. During the last year of his life he was elected without opposition for another term. He died February 19, 1928. His widow is still living at Bland, and she was reared in Bland County. She is an active member of the Methodist Episcopal Church, South. There were six children: Gilbert R.; Bessie, wife of M. Muncey, of Bland; Robert G., of Bland; Stella, wife of J. M. Honeycutt, of Charlotte, North Carolina; Catherine C., a teacher in the public schools of Richmond; and James C., of Bland.

Gilbert Raymond Repass was educated in public schools, including the Bland High School, attended the National Business College at Roanoke until 1913, in which year he went to work under his father in the office of the clerk of courts. He helped his father four years, then spent three years in farming and stock raising, and for seven years was a rural mail carrier. In February, 1928, he was appointed to fill out the unexpired term of his father, and has brought to the office the same care and systematic attention which distinguished the administration of the elder Repass in handling the records of the county. He is a member of the Masonic fraternity and the Eastern Star, is a Republican and a member of the Methodist Episcopal Church, South.

He married at Bland, May 6, 1916, Miss Hazel Bruce, of Bland County. She was educated in the county and in Sullins College, and is an active worker in the Methodist Episcopal Church, South, and the Eastern Star. She is a daughter of Rev. J. E. and Edna (Harris) Bruce. Her father gave the greater part of his life to his duties as a minister of the Gospel in the Holston Conference of the Methodist Episcopal Church, South. He died in 1915 and is buried in Bland County. Mrs. Repass' mother, who now lives in the Repass home at Bland, is a sister of former Governor Nathaniel Harris, of Georgia, who was born in Tennessee, member of an old and distinguished family of that name. Mr. and Mrs. Repass have two children, David Edward and Edna Elizabeth, both attending school at Bland.

DR. HEATH A. DALTON, physician and surgeon, now practicing at Bland, was born and reared in Southwest Virginia, and his people have lived in Carroll and adjacent counties since about the time of the Revolution.

The founder of the family was the great-grandfather, John Dalton, who came with three brothers to America. Two of these brothers settled in North Carolina and another in Eastern Virginia. One brother sought a home in the western wilderness, in what is now Carroll County. He settled down on a farm, cleared some land and like many other pioneers supplied much of his meat from wild game. He and his wife are buried at Hillsville. His son, Martin Dalton, owned 3,200 acres of land in Carroll County, and was one of its outstanding citizens. He represented the county in the Legislature for two terms in the early '80s. He died in 1893 and is buried at Hillsville.

The parents of Doctor Dalton were James and Hannah (Gardner) Dalton. His father was born and reared at Hillsville, attended private schools and was a soldier in the Confederate army, seeing active service at Saltville and as far east as Lynchburg the last year of the war. He was active as a farmer and stock raiser until he retired, and he died February 12, 1929, aged eighty-three years. He is buried at Hillsville. His wife was born and reared at Hillsville, attended school there, and she was an active member of the Primitive Baptist Church. She died in 1908. There were nine children: Tabitha, now Mrs. G. G. Montgomery, of Hillsville; Laura, who died in 1926, at the age of fifty-five; Ada, who died in 1918, at the age of forty-six; Dr. Martin L., a practicing physician at Floyd, Virginia; Miss Alice, of Hillsville; Lulu, who died in 1915, the wife of T. L. Cox;

J. Blair Fitts M. D.

Berta, now Mrs. Walter Stillwell, of Wytheville; Dr. James B., of Richmond; and Dr. Heath A.

Dr. Heath A. Dalton was born at Hillsville, April 21, 1889, attended public schools, including the Hillsville High School, and continued his education in the Virginia Polytechnic Institute. He was graduated from the Medical College of Virginia in the class of 1914, having his interne experience in The Retreat for the Sick at Richmond. Doctor Dalton in 1914 opened an office at Galax, and was in practice there until 1928, when he removed to Bland and established his office in the Newberry Building. He has a large professional business, and is a man who enjoys friendships not only in Bland County but over Carroll and Grayson counties and other sections of Virginia. He has an interest in his father's farming properties at Hillsville. He is a member of the Medical Society of Virginia, the Carroll and Grayson Counties Medical Society and is affiliated with Old Town Lodge No. 72, A. F. and A. M., Kazim Temple of the Mystic Shrine at Roanoke, is a Democrat and a Presbyterian.

He married at Washington, D. C., September 27, 1913, Miss Hattie Burnette, of Willis, Virginia. She was educated in public schools, in Sullins College at Bristol, Tennessee, and Marion College in Virginia. She is a Presbyterian. Her parents were Abram and Lina (Cox) Burnette. Her father was a farmer and cattle buyer in Floyd County, owning a large amount of land and being regarded as one of the wealthy and influential residents of that community. He died in 1907 and her mother in 1899. Doctor and Mrs. Dalton have two children, Heath A., Jr., and Harold C., both attending school at Bland.

JOHN BLAIR FITTS, M. D., is well fortified for the special branch of his profession to which he gives his major attention, that of orthopedic surgery, and is established in the successful practice of his profession in the City of Richmond, with office headquarters at 917 West Franklin Street.

Doctor Fitts was born at Blacksburg, Montgomery County, Virginia, in 1890, and is a son of James H. and Mary (Blair) Fitts. James H. Fitts, whose death occurred in 1893, was a representative of an old and honored Southern family, and the family name has appeared as one of special prominence in the history of North Carolina and also that of Alabama. James H. Fitts was graduated from the United States Naval Academy, Annapolis, and thereafter gave several years of service as an officer in the United States Navy. He gained distinction also in educational work, he having been for some time a member of the faculty of the Virginia Polytechnic Institute at Blacksburg, and having subsequently established a school of his own at Hopkinsville, Kentucky. His death occurred when his son John B., of this review, was a child of about three years. Doctor Fitts was named in honor of his maternal grandfather, John Blair, and the annals of Virginia show that the Blair family has here been one of prominence and influence for many generations, especially in professional and public life.

The public schools of Richmond afforded Doctor Fitts the major part of his preliminary education, and thereafter he continued his studies in historic old Hampden-Sidney College. In the Medical College at Richmond he was graduated as a member of the class of 1914, and after this received his degree of Doctor of Medicine he engaged in the general practice of his profession in Richmond. He eventually turned his attenion to orthopedic surgery as a specialty, and in this interesting field of practice he has since gained marked success and prestige. The Doctor was pursuing a post-graduate course in orthopedic surgery in leading institution in the City of Boston, Massachusetts, at the time the nation became formally involved in the World war, and soon thereafter he volunteered for service in the Medical Corps of the United States Army. After receiving preliminary training at Camp Greenleaf, Fort Oglethorpe, Georgia, he was assigned with his unit to overseas service. For several months he was stationed at Base Hospital No. 114 in France, and there gave special service in orthopedic surgery. He remained overseas for some time after the armistice brought the war to a close, returned to the United States in March, 1919, and after receiving his honorable discharge resumed his professional activities in Richmond as a specialist in orthopedic surgery. He is a popular member of the Richmond Academy of Medicine, and has membership also in the Virginia State Medical Society and the American Medical Association and is a fellow of the American College of Surgeons. He continues his deep interest in the national military organization, and in the Virginia National Guard he is surgeon of the First Regiment Infantry, with the rank of major. In March, 1919, he married Miss Marion Mantius, of Fairhaven, Massachusetts. The following children were born to the union: Marietta Moylan, John Blair, Jr., Ruth Morton and James Henry.

WYTHE G. WADDLE, whose home is near Ceres in Bland County, has had an experience covering six decades in farming and the live stock business in this section of Virginia, and he probably ranks as the oldest active trader in live stock in this part of the state. He has bought and sold cattle all over the southwestern counties, and is familiar with the market and other conditions in the live stock industry since nearly the close of the Civil war.

Mr. Waddle was born near Bland Court House August 16, 1848, son of James and Nancy (Steel) Waddle. His grandfather, James Waddle, came from Ireland and was an early settler on Walker's Creek, near Bland Court House, and he and his wife are buried in the old family cemetery there. Mr. Waddle's father, James Waddle, was born and reared in Bland County, had his education in private schools, was a farmer and stock man, and died in 1854. His wife, Nancy Steel, was born and reared on a farm adjoining the Waddle farm on Walker's Creek. She was a very devout Methodist. Her death occurred in February, 1880. These parents had nine children: Elcain, Rosana, Cosby, Pemelia, Charlotte, Newton, Kate, James and Wythe G. Three of the sons, Elcain, Newton and James, were soldiers in the Civil war.

Wythe G. Waddle attended private schools in Bland County, but had little education after the Civil war broke out. No one has a better knowledge of live stock than this veteran grower, shipper and trader, and it has been his constant occupation and business since he was twenty-one years of age. Mr. Waddle is still active on his farm near Ceres. His farm is improved with one of the most attractive country homes in that vicinity. He is a Democrat and for two years was commissioner of revenue for Bland County. He is a member of the Presbyterian Church.

He married at Clear Fork in Bland County, August 29, 1894, Miss Bettie Stowers, of Bland County, where she was educated.

She is an active member of the Methodist Episcopal Church, South, and is a daughter of Russell and Arminta (Robinette) Stowers. Her father was a well-to-do farmer and stock man of Bland County, and both her parents are buried in the family cemetery in Bland County. Mr. and Mrs. Waddle had five children. William Wayne, the oldest, now living in Kentucky, married Nellie Davis, of Bland County, and of their five children four are living. Rosalee became the wife of Walter Mergler, of Carmel County, Virginia, and has two children, William W. and Clara E. Gilbert C. Waddle is married and lives in Detroit, Michigan. Gobel Waddle, connected with the Firestone Rubber Company at Akron and now city policeman, married Golda Smith, of Smyth County, Virginia. Charles Waddle, the youngest child, associated with his father on the farm and stock ranch near Ceres, married Alees Wilson, of Bland County.

KENNETH HOWE FARRIER is one of the younger group of agricultural leaders in Southwestern Virginia, being manager of the Farmers Exchange at Pembroke, and is a graduate of the Virginia Polytechnic Institute at Blacksburg.

He is a son of Robert Henry Farrier, county superintendent of schools of Giles County. Robert Henry Farrier was born in Craig County, Virginia, son of Jacob and Harriet (Pence) Farrier. Both the Pences and Farriers represent the older families and older traditions of Virginia. Jacob Farrier was born in Craig County, was a soldier in the Confederate army and afterwards a merchant and farmer. He finally moved to the vicinity of Newport in Giles County, and lived there until his death in 1889. He is buried in Clover Hollow Cemetery. His widow survived him until 1914. Robert Henry Farrier was educated in the public schools of Craig County, in Roanoke College at Salem, and began teaching as a young man. His work has brought him active relations with the schools of Giles County for many years, and since 1912 he has been county superintendent of schools. He lives on his farm near Newport, owning a beautiful place there, where he specializes in orcharding. He is active in the Virginia Education Association and is a loyal minister of the Methodist Episcopal Church, South. Robert Henry Farrier married Minnie Howe Porterfield, who was born near Newport on a farm, attended a girls' school at Princeton, West Virginia, and has always taken an active part in church and missionary work. One of her daughters, Helen Mae, is now a missionary in the Congo of Africa. In all there were eight children, two of whom died in infancy. Kenneth Howe is the oldest; Paul Henry lives at Winchester, Kentucky; Nancy Lou is the wife of W. M. Phipps, of Hopewell, Virginia; Harriet Pence died when twelve years old; Helen Mae is the missionary previously mentioned; and Robert Henry, Jr., lives at Newport.

Kenneth Howe Farrier attended grade and high schools at Newport, had two years in Roanoke College, and two years in the Virginia Polytechnic Institute, where he completed a special course in agriculture in 1912. After leaving the institute he was for two years engaged in work with the Bureau of Forestry and Plant Life in Virginia, for two years engaged in farming and orcharding and was in the rural mail service, following which he gave his full time and energies to his farm and orchards until 1926, in which year he joined the Farmers Exchange of Giles County as manager of the Pembroke store. He is also interested in the home farm and orchard, his youngest brother, Robert Henry, now having active control there.

Mr. Farrier is a member of Newport Lodge No. 261, A. F. and A. M. He is a Democrat, a Methodist, and a man who is keenly interested in the development of a wholesome community program.

He married at Grundy, Virginia, September 19, 1917, Miss Josephine Hamilton, who was educated in public schools in Wise County, is a graduate of the Cincinnati Conservatory of Music, and before her marriage taught music in high schools in Giles County, and has continued keen interest in musical affairs, doing some teaching and also taking her part in musical organizations. She is a member of the United Daughters of the Confederacy. Mrs. Farrier is a daughter of Harve and Mary Caroline (Smyth) Hamilton. She is a descendant of that branch of the old Smyth family of Virginia which gave its name to Smyth County. Her father was one of the leading attorneys of South-western Virginia, practicing for many years at Mendota in Wise County, where he died in 1914. Her mother passed away in 1916, and both are buried at Mendota.

Mr. and Mrs. Farrier are the parents of two children, Graham Hamilton and Kenneth Howe, Jr., the former a pupil in the public schools at Newport.

ELMER E. CONNER, principal of the Pembroke schools, is a native of Southwestern Virginia, and one of the prominent younger leaders in the educational affairs of the state.

He was born at Simpsons in Floyd County February 11, 1897, son of George B. and Wilmoth Jane (Martin) Conner. His great-grandfather was one of three brothers who came to America from Ireland. The original spelling of the name was O'Conner. Mr. Conner's grandfather, Nathan Conner, was born and reared in Floyd County, combined farming with school teaching, and died about 1877. George B. Conner was born and reared in Floyd County, was educated in public schools, and has spent his active life as a farmer and stock raiser. He resides on his farm near Simpsons. He has been twice married. His first wife was Ellen Iddings, and the children of that marriage were: Annie, Waller, Elbert L., Guy, and a daughter Mary who died in infancy. His second wife, Wilmoth Jane Martin, was born and reared in Floyd County, and she and her family are members of the Baptist Church. Her parents were John W. and Cynthia (Martin) Martin, farmers and stock raisers. Her father died in 1899 and her mother still lives at the old Martin home in Floyd County. George B. Conner and his second wife had a family of ten children: Elmer E., Mamie, Willard A., Ernest R., Bessie, Clarence M., Carl N., Claude S., Vergie and Posie.

Elmer E. Conner attended public schools in Floyd County, the high school at Floyd Court House, after which he was a student for one year in William and Mary Academy, and followed that with the four years classical course in the College of William and Mary, from which he was graduated in 1921 with the Bachelor of Science degree. Since then he has had one year of post-graduate work in the George Peabody Normal College at Nashville, Tennessee. Mr. Conner taught for one year as principal of the high school at Chick, Virginia, for three years was principal of the high school at Denby and one year at Peters-town. He took charge of the Pembroke schools in 1924, being

principal of the high school and also has supervision over the grade school. Mr. Conner is a member of Warwick Lodge No. 336, A. F. and A. M., belongs to the County Teachers and State Education Associations, is a Democrat in politics and has always been active in the Baptist Church, interesting himself in the Sunday School work.

He married at Talcott, West Virginia, August 29, 1925, Miss Jenia Johnson McGhee, of Peterstown, West Virginia. She attended public schools in Giles County and high school at Homer City, Pennsylvania, and for several years before her marriage was assistant cashier of the Bank of Peterstown. For several years she was a steward of the Methodist Episcopal Church, South, and teaches a class in the Sunday School. She has membership in the Parent-Teachers Association and is deeply interested in the professional and community work of Mr. Conner. She is a daughter of L. J. and Roberta Pendelton (French) McGhee, of Penvir, Virginia, where her father is still carrying on his work as a farmer and stock raiser. Mr. and Mrs. Conner have one son, Wayne Johnson Conner.

Since Mr. Conner took charge of the schools at Pembroke a great advance has been made in the educational program and in the material equipment for the schools. The new Pembroke High School Building of brick and stone was completed in 1926. There is a large auditorium, with thirteen class rooms and library, and nearby is the grade school building, a stucco and concrete structure affording seven class rooms and library. The total enrollment of scholars in the grade and high schools is 453, and the staff of teachers under the direction of Mr. Conner are fifteen. Mr. Conner enlisted for service in the World war September 5, 1918, and was in training at Camp Lee, later was transferred to General Hospital No. 41 on Staten Island, ranking as a private of the first class. He spent nine months at Camp Lee and seven months on Staten Island, and was honorably discharged December 13, 1919.

ALEXANDER CAMERON was a Virginia tobacco manufacturer, and his name is one that held a high importance in the old days of individual management in the tobacco industry, when the master and the worker were on close terms of relationship, and when the owner of the factory came into daily contact with not only the personnel of the operating force, but with the producers of the leaf.

He was born at Grantown, Scotland, in November, 1832, and was a small child when his parents came to America. His father died in Scotland, and subsequently the widowed mother moved to Virginia and located in Petersburg, Virginia.

Alexander Cameron had most of his educational advantages in public schools in Petersburg. He was only thirteen when he came up from Petersburg to Richmond to go to work in a tobacco firm. He learned the business from the ground up, and came to know every process of tobacco manufacture. When the Civil war came on his business as a shipper was utilized for the direct benefit of the Confederate government, and he did a great deal of blockade running through the Federal fleet. Mr. Cameron in 1866 entered the tobacco business for himself under his individual name, and for many years that name was known in both the domestic and foreign tobacco markets. Like many others, the business he developed as Alexander Cameron eventually was consolidated. It was in 1906 that he sold his industry to the British Australian Company, and at that time he retired, being then seventy-four years of age. He died at Richmond in 1915.

Mr. Cameron was a member of the Presbyterian Church. For many years he was known as Colonel Cameron because of his service on the staff of a Virginia governor. He was a member of the Westmoreland Club and the Tobacco Association. As a prominent American business man he and his wife while touring abroad were presented at the Court of St. James before Queen Victoria.

Colonel Cameron married in 1868 Miss Mary Haxall, of Richmond. Her father, Richard Barton Haxall, came to Richmond from Petersburg, where his father, Phillip, had lived, and engaged in the flour mill business. He was one of the early leaders in the flour mill industry at Richmond, building up one of the largest milling plants in the state, and from these mills flour was shipped to all parts of the world, especially to South America. The mills were known as the Haxall Mills. Richard Barton Haxall was one of the bondsmen of Jefferson Davis after the Civil war.

Colonel and Mrs. Cameron had eleven children, and the eight now living are: Mary Haxall, Alexander, Barton Haxall, Elizabeth Grant, Janet Gordon, Flora MacDonald, James Blackwood and Ewan Donald.

JOHN W. MILLER is a member of the firm Miller Brothers, merchants at Newport, carrying on a business that was established many years ago by their father and has been under their direction for over a quarter of a century.

John W. Miller was born at Newport June 25, 1871, son of Adam P. and Martha Ann (Reynolds) Miller. His grandfather was John Miller, of Midway, Craig County, Virginia, a farmer. Adam P. Miller was born in Craig County, attended private schools, and after his marriage moved to Newport, buying a farm near that town, and also carried on merchandising. In 1892 he founded the firm of A. P. Miller & Sons, general merchants, and was active in the business until his death on March 13, 1900. His wife, Martha Ann Reynolds, was born and reared at Midway in Craig County, was also educated in private schools, and she and her husband were members of the Methodist Episcopal Church, South. She died in July, 1920. They were the parents of eight children: Laura V., deceased, was the wife of A. H. Price, of Newport; Anna M. is the wife of L. D. Snapp, of Burkes Garden, Virginia; Mason J. and John W. comprise the firm of Miller Brothers; Sallie is the wife of C. P. Logan, of Blacksburg; Dr. W. P. Miller, who married Frances Easley, of Pearisburg, Virginia, practiced medicine for many years at Newport, where he died in September, 1910; J. D. Miller is a farmer and stock raiser at Newport; and Dr. Frank B., who married Maud C. Prichett, of Newport, Virginia, was a dentist, and died in Pearisburg in September, 1928.

John W. Miller grew up at Newport, attended public schools there, and after leaving school had two years of experience clerking in a store at Blacksburg, Virginia, for the firm of Black & Payne. For two years he was with Johnson & Moseby of Christiansburg, and then returned to Newport to take his place as a member of his father's mercantile firm. In 1902 he and his brother took over the business as Miller Brothers. Theirs is one of the largest stores in this section of Giles County. They are

also partners in the ownership of some farming land. Mr. Miller
is a director of the Sinking Creek Valley Bank. He is a member
of Newport Lodge No. 261, A. F. and A. M., is a Democrat and
a member of the Methodist Episcopal Church, South, and on its
Board of Stewards.

He married near Norton, Virginia, June 19, 1919, Mrs. Bettie Irene (Fowlkes) Roberts. She was educated in high school
at Roanoke and taught school before her marriage. Two children were born to their marriage, one dying in infancy, and the
other is John Williams Miller, Jr., born April 6, 1923.

LEITCH L. MILLER is a member of a well known and prominent family of the Newport section of Giles County, and has
been a leading merchant of that community for over twenty
years.

Mr. Miller was born at Newport August 25, 1879, son of
John C. and Lizzie (Vermillion) Miller, and grandson of John B.
and Susan (Sibold) Miller. His grandfather moved from Roanoke County to Giles County, and was a farmer and stock
raiser near Newport. He and his wife are buried in the old
family cemetery at Clover Hollow near Newport. John C. Miller
was born and reared in Giles County, attended private schools,
and spent his active life as a farmer and stock man. He died
November 27, 1916, and is also buried in the Clover Hollow
Cemetery. His widow, Lizzie (Vermillion) Miller, lived to the
age of seventy-two years, making her home at Roanoke, and
she died April 6, 1929. She was born in Washington County,
daughter of Capt. John Vermillion, a Confederate soldier and
officer who lost his life at the battle of Gettysburg. Mrs. Miller
finished her education in Martha Washington College at Abingdon. She is a member of the Lutheran Church. Of her ten children one died in infancy, and the others are: Leitch L.; Kate,
wife of E. T. Cook, of Idaho; Rose, wife of I. A. Dillard, of
Roanoke; Paul M., of Idaho; George, of Salem, Virginia; Fannie, wife of L. M. Dunham, of Roanoke; John K., who entered
the World war, went overseas, was wounded at Chateau Thierry
and died in France in December, 1918, his body still resting on
French soil; Trigg Miller, of Roanoke; and Bertha Sue, who
married N. C. Dillard and died in April, 1920.

Leitch L. Miller had the advantages of the public schools of
Giles County, and after completing a course in the Roanoke Business College took up farming and the lumber business. These
were the lines he followed until 1908, when he started a general
store at Newport, and has built that up to be one of the chief
trading centers of the county. He carries a large stock of
goods, meeting all the requirements and demands of the territory which he serves.

Mr. Miller has been deputy treasurer of Giles County since
1924. He is affiliated with Newport Lodge No. 261, A. F. and
A. M., is a Democrat and a Lutheran.

He married at Newport in January, 1902, Miss Belle Puckett,
of Newport, where she was educated in the public schools. She
is a member of the Lutheran Church. Her parents were P. R.
and Elizabeth (Barnett) Puckett, of Montgomery County. Her
father was a merchant. He was born December 29, 1847, and
died January 10, 1911, while her mother was born July 30, 1846,
and died March 30, 1914. Mr. and Mrs. Miller have a family of
three children. Mary Elizabeth, born February 26, 1903, was
educated at Newport and in Martha Washington College at

Abingdon, and is now the wife of V. E. Deering, an employe of the Norfolk and Western Railway Company, living at Roanoke. Margaret C., born August 20, 1904, was educated in the Radford State Teachers College and is now teaching in the public schools of Glenlyn, Virginia. Annabel Miller, born July 13, 1909, attended public schools in Newport, spent two years in Virginia Intermont College at Bristol, and is now attending the State Teachers College at Harrisonburg.

HARVEY B. SHELTON is easily identified in Giles County as the head of the H. B. Shelton Company, one of the oldest and largest mercantile organizations at Pearisburg. He has been in business since early manhood, and his business career has steadily reflected his personal integrity and a public spirit that has been characteristic of the family in Southwest Virginia.

Mr. Shelton was born at White Gate, Virginia, February 21, 1862, son of Langston C. and Elizabeth (Bane) Shelton. The Sheltons are English and settled in Virginia in Colonial times. His grandfather, William Shelton, was a soldier of the American Revolution, and the daughters of Harvey B. Shelton are members of the Daughters of the American Revolution. William Shelton was a private in Capt. William Sanford's Company, Second Virginia Regiment, commanded by Col. Alexander Spotswood.

Langston C. Shelton was born in Pittsylvania County, Virginia, in 1810, was educated in private schools, taught school in early life, and was a soldier in the Confederate army, his oldest son, William J. Shelton, being with him in the war. They were through the four years of fighting, were soldiers in Stonewall Jackson's Brigade, and took part in the battle of Cloyd's Mountain as well as many other engagements. After the war Langston C. Shelton lived on a farm and also followed the business of Brick mason and building contractor, putting up a number of the brick houses at Pulaski and in other towns of Southwest Virginia. He died in 1882 and is buried at White Gate.

Langston C. Shelton married, January 21, 1841, Elizabeth Bane, member of another notable family in the Valley of Virginia. She was born October 11, 1820, daughter of Jesse and Anna (Carr) Bane. Jesse Bane was born November 23, 1791, and his wife, October 24, 1796, and they were married October 24, 1819, their daughter Elizabeth Havens being the oldest of ten children. Jesse Bane was a son of James and Elizabeth (Havens) Bane, and James was a son of James Bane, who settled in the Virginia Valley about 1748 and married in 1754 Rebecca McDonald, a granddaughter of Bryan and Mary (Combs) McDonald. There is a large relationship of the Bane family in Southwestern Virginia.

Elizabeth (Bane) Shelton was born at White Gate, was educated in private schools, was a member of the Baptist Church and died in 1889. She was the mother of nine children: Ann, who married George Surface; William J., who married Jennie Surface; Eliza Jane, who married Sam Williams; Adolphus; Mary, who died in early life; Sallie, who married John Johnston; Mrs. Emma Broyles; Hattie, who married Joe Surface; and Harvey Bane.

Harvey Bane Shelton attended private schools and White Gate Academy, and in the fall of 1889 moved to Bluefield, West Virginia, where for nineteen years he was in the mercantile business. In 1907 he located at Pearisburg and for twenty-one years

MRS. WM. E. BARRETT

JAMES ALBERT ROBERTSON   MRS. MARY L. BRAY

FRANCES LIGHTFOOT BARRETT   DOROTHY LEE BARRETT

FOUR GENERATIONS

has been a business man of that community. For two years he
was associated in partnership with Will Strader and about 1916
the H. B. Shelton Company was incorporated with Mr. Shelton
as president, A. D. Gerberich, secretary and treasurer, and
John H. Givens, vice president. The company owns a large and
well stocked department store. Mr. Shelton for a number of
years has also been active in the lumber business.

He owns one of the beautiful homes of Pearisburg, located
on the hill above the town. He is a Knight Templar Mason,
formerly was active in the B. P. O. Elks, is a Democrat, and
while living at Bluefield was treasurer of the Baptist Church.
He married at Bane in Giles County, July 3, 1889, Miss Sallie
Ann Strader, who was educated in the old Pearisburg Academy
and taught for two years in the public schools before her marriage. She is a member of the Methodist Church and the
United Daughters of the Confederacy. Her parents were Josiah
and Barbara (Johnston) Strader. Her father was a farmer
and cattle raiser. The Strader family came into Southwest Virginia from North Carolina. Mr. and Mrs. Shelton had seven
children: Harriett, died aged eight years; Frederick, died when
one year old; Elizabeth Havens is the wife of Dr. L. D. Whitaker, of Farmville, Virginia, and has two children, Lloyd Durham
and Harvey Shelton; Mary Barbara married F. N. Chisholm,
of San Francisco, California, and their two children are Rachael
Barbara and Patricia Ann; Sallie Catherine is the wife of
Martin Williams, Jr., of Washington, D. C., and has a son,
Martin Shelton; Eva Frances is Mrs. D. H. Matson, of Miami,
Florida, and they have a daughter, Sallie Ann; Miss Willie Mae,
the youngest child, is a graduate of the Pearisburg High School
and also attended the Farmville State Teachers College.

ROBERT T. BRAY during an all too brief lifetime was a distinguished teacher of engineering, and in later years was a resident of Danville as a merchant.

He was born in Virginia November 6, 1861, and lacked two
months of being forty years of age when he died September 6,
1901. He was a small child when his parents, John Bray and
wife, died. His father was a native of Halifax County. Robert
T. Bray attended the old Agricultural and Mechanical College
at Blacksburg, now the Virginia Polytechnic Institute. He graduated in mechanical engineering and then for several years
remained at the college as an instructor on the subject. The
college sent him for post-graduate work to the Stevens Institute
in New York, and after completing several courses he returned
to Blacksburg and resumed his teaching for two years. He
then accepted a call to the Texas Agricultural and Mechanical
College at College Station, where he held the chair of mechanical
engineering two years. Mr. Bray then gave up teaching and
returning to Danville, Virginia, was in the mercantile business
until his death. He was a Democrat and a member of the Blacksburg Christian Church. He also belonged to the Masonic fraternity. His wife is a Methodist.

Mr. Bray married, September 5, 1894, Miss Mary L. Robertson. She was born and educated in Halifax County, attending
the College for Women at Greensburg. Her father, James
Albert Robertson, was a farmer in Halifax County and one of
the best known and most respected citizens of that locality because of his public service. He was for thirty years a school
trustee in the county, serving without pay, and for twenty years

was a county magistrate. He married Frances Lightfoot Mason, a native of Halifax County, whose father was a large land owner and planter before the war. James A. Robertson and wife had five children: Mary, now Mrs. Bray; Sue J., a graduate of the Averett School for Girls, who has been a teacher in Halifax County for thirty years; Lucy; Sally, now Mrs. Sally F. Thompson; and Caleb J. Caleb J. Robertson was educated in Halifax and became one of the foremost business men of Danville. At the age of twenty-one he became a general merchant at Christie, later was a bank director and president of the Farmers Mutual Insurance Company of Danville and held the office of magistrate. He never married, and at his death his sisters were called upon to act as executors of his large estate.

Mrs. Bray since the death of her husband has established her home in Richmond, residing at 2203 West Grace Street. She is the mother of one daughter, Evelyn Lightfoot. Evelyn married William Evans Barrett, a business man at Richmond, and has two children, Frances Lightfoot and Dorothy Lee.

CHARLES WILLIAM SHANNON. The history of the Shannon family in Giles County, where Charles William Shannon, one of its representatives, a prominent farmer and stock raiser at Poplar Hill, began before the War of the Revolution.

The Shannons came originally from Ireland. They were settlers during the early Colonial period in Amherst County, Virginia. The founder of the family in the New River Valley was Samuel Shannon, who moved his family over the Alleghanies in 1774 and located at what is now Poplar Hill. This was then part of Fincastle County, now Giles County. After a residence there of ten years and after the marriage of his oldest son, Thomas, Samuel Shannon in the spring of 1784 moved with the other members of his family to the new colony known as Nashville, Tennessee.

Thomas Shannon, the representative of the family who remained at the old Poplar Hill locality, married Agnes Crowe. The property acquired more than a century and a half ago is still in the possession of the descendants of Thomas Shannon and wife. He became a man of much prominence during and after the Revolutionary period. He was magistrate and sheriff of Giles County, also represented his district in the State Legislature. In the month of February, 1781, the British army started its last advance northward through the Carolinas toward Virginia. Col. William Preston, military commandant of the Montgomery troops, with Joseph Cloyd, his major, called out the local forces to go to the aid of the Americans under General Greene. Thomas Shannon became captain of the New River company, with Alexander Mars, lieutenant, and other members of the company were Thomas Farley, Isaac Cole, Mathew French, John French, Joseph Hare, Edward Hale, the Clays and others. Captain Shannon and his company joined the battalion at the New River Lead Mines about the middle of February, and on the eighteenth day of the same month the command under Colonel Preston and Major Cloyd, 350 strong, marched to the Haw River section of North Carolina, and being in a strange country and not advised of the positions of the opposing armies they camped between the American and British forces. On the next day ensued a sharp skirmish between Preston's battalion and Tarleton's British cavalry, and on March 6th occurred a similar engagement at Wetzel's Mills between Pickens command, including Preston's forces, and the British advance. General Pickens retreated toward Guilford Court House, and the troops commanded by Preston were located on the American left wing in the great battle of Guilford Court House, which ended the British invasion of the Carolinas and marked the beginning of the withdrawal and loss of most of the British posts in the South, and before the end of the year the surrender of Cornwallis himself and the virtual conclusion of the war. After Guilford Court House the Virginia troops under Preston inflicted severe damage on Colonel Tarleton's men. Captain Shannon lived to be ninety years of age. His son Thomas married Julia Allen, and their children were Thomas, Joseph, James R., William R., Nancy, who married John Henderson Bane, Eliza, who married James B. Miller, and Samuel B., who lived for many years at the old homestead. The second Thomas Shannon served as a magistrate in his county and also as a member of the County Court for many years, and several times was elected to the Virginia Legislature. At the beginning of the War of 1861 he was said to have been the wealthiest man in Giles County. His sons proved brave and faithful soldiers of the Confederacy. He was the grandfather of Charles William Shannon.

Charles William Shannon was born at Poplar Hill in Giles County February 9, 1869, son of William Reed and Lucy (Bush) Shannon. William Reed Shannon was also born at Poplar Hill, was educated in private schools, and was a soldier of the Confederacy, acting as courier and dispatch bearer. After the war he followed farming and stock raising, and died in November, 1904, being buried at Poplar Hill. His wife, Lucy Bush, was born in Franklin County, Virginia, and died in November, 1916. Both are Presbyterians. Their three children were T. B. Shannon, of Roanoke, C. W. Shannon, and Juliet Allen, who is the wife of F. C. Whaling, living in Harford County, Maryland.

Charles William Shannon attended private schools, and from the time he finished his studies his time and energies have been taken up with farming and stock raising. He has about 700 acres of blue grass land, including part of the property acquired by his ancestor before the Revolutionary war. He and his family enjoy the beauties and comforts of a country home near Poplar Hill. Mr. Shannon is a director of the Peoples Bank of Giles County and is a member of the school advisory board. He was formerly active in the Independent Order of Odd Fellows, is a Democrat, a deacon in the Presbyterian Church and a worker in the Sunday School.

He married at Washington, D. C., October 21, 1916, Miss Roberta Frances Weaver, of Poplar Hill. She was educated in private schools and the Tazewell Seminary for Girls at Tazewell Court House. She is a Presbyterian. Her parents were Z. T. and Harriet Arminta (McDonald) Weaver, her father for many years a farmer and stock raiser and for eight years sergeant at arms of the Virginia State Senate. He served in the Confederate army with General Mosby's troops during the last three years of the war. He died September 1, 1926, and Mrs. Shannon's mother, in August, 1904. Mr. and Mrs. Shannon have no children of their own, but they took into their home E. Richard Sibley at the age of seven years, who had recently lost his mother, and this adopted boy was given the advantages of the high school at Eggleston and has come to the promise of a most useful career.

REV. CHARLES ALBERT BROWN has been an ordained minister of the Methodist Episcopal Church, South, for a great many years, but the outstanding service of his life has been as an educator. A number of educational institutions, both public and denominational, in Southwestern Virginia and in West Virginia have had the benefit of his active guidance and control.

Since retiring from the main work of his life Mr. Brown has lived at Narrows in Giles County. He was born in Monroe County, West Virginia, January 31, 1858, son of Lewis and Malinda (Shiers) Brown. His grandfather, Anderson Brown, was a pioneer of Monroe County, where he combined farming with hunting. Lewis Brown was born and reared in Monroe County, and served four years in the Confederate army in the Civil war, and after the war was a farmer and stock man until his death on May 5, 1919, when eighty-seven years of age. His wife, Malinda Shiers, was born and reared in Monroe County, and was a very devout Methodist. She died September 17, 1903. Of their twelve children one died in infancy, and the others were: Rev. H. A. Brown, who for many years was a minister of the Methodist Episcopal Church, South, died in 1927; Minerva C., deceased; Rev. Charles A.; Madora J.; Floyd J., deceased; Lewis Allen, deceased; Flora A.; Robert L., deceased; Minnie B.; Hugh. B.; John E., deceased.

Charles Albert Brown grew up in Monroe, Mercer and Giles counties, had the advantages of public and private schools, and in 1890 was graduated from Emory and Henry College. He soon afterward was ordained to the ministry and entered the Holston Conference of the Methodist Church. He has also been a member of the Baltimore Conference, and has carried on work as a minister locally in the different communities where he has been a teacher. For three years he taught in public schools and for six years was principal of the Hillsboro Female Academy in West Virginia, for three years was principal of the Alleghany Collegiate Institute, was associate principal of Randolph-Macon Academy at Front Royal two years, for five years was principal of the Princeton Collegiate Institute, four years principal of the Jonesville Collegiate Institute of Lee County, Virginia, and five years principal of the high school at Narrows, Virginia. Mr. Brown retired from the work of teaching in 1914, and since then has given his attention to his property at Narrows and answers calls for preaching in different pulpits. He has been an encouraging presence in many educational gatherings. Mr. Brown owns a beautiful home located on the hill overlooking Narrows and has a small farm near the town. For several years he was a member of the Town Council, is a Democrat and is a deacon in the local Methodist Church.

Rev. Mr. Brown married at Hillsboro, West Virginia, August 6, 1890, Miss Lillian M. Overholt, of Hillsboro, daughter of William H. and Mary (McNeal) Overholt. Her father was a merchant, lumberman and farmer at Hillsboro, and died there in 1927. His wife passed away in 1912, and both are buried in Princeton. Mrs. Brown attended public schools in West Virginia and the Valley Female College of Winchester, Virginia, and was constant in her response to service in the Methodist Episcopal Church, South. Mrs. Brown died July 21, 1928, and is buried in Fairview Cemetery in Narrows. She was the mother of two children, Edna Gertrude and William H. Edna Gertrude Brown attended private and public schools, Sullins

E. A. Ligon

College, the New York Musical Institute, and has been very successful as a music teacher, having a private studio at Roanoke.

The son, William H. Brown, was liberally educated, is a graduate of Emory and Henry College, and in 1917 joined the colors, being in training with the Artillery Corps, later was transferred to the Medical Corps, went overseas with Colonel McGuire's command, with a commission as second lieutenant, and while in France served with the heavy artillery until the armistice. He received his honorable discharge late in the fall of 1918, and then continued his graduate studies at the University of Virginia until he won his Bachelor of Philosophy degree. He was an instructor in West Virginia University and in Lafayette College of Pennsylvania, and is now professor of economics in the University of Southern California at Los Angeles.

COL. ELVIN SETH LIGON is president and owner of Blackstone, a Military School for Boys, an institution that has given training to hundreds of youths not only from Virginia but from many other states, and has a well earned prestige among the boys' preparatory schools of the South.

Its owner, Colonel Ligon, is a native Virginian, born in Appomattox County June 4, 1878, son of Willis H. and Nannie M. (Cunningham) Ligon. His father was born in Appomattox County and his mother in Prince Edward County. His father was a farmer, merchant, for thirty years county supervisor and for two terms a member of the State Legislature and in many ways an outstanding citizen of his county. He died February 4, 1925, at the age of seventy-five and the widowed mother now resides in Pamplin, Virginia.

Elvin S. Ligon was reared and received his early education in Appomattox County. For one year he attended an academy at Chase City and in 1898 was graduated with the A. B. degree from the University of Richmond and took the M. A. degree at the same school in 1899. He took post-graduate work at the University of Chicago in 1902. He has been a teacher and engaged in educational administration for over a quarter of a century. He spent one year at Dothan, Alabama, one year at Halifax, Virginia, one year at Blakely, Georgia, for five years was principal of the Newport News Academy, Virginia, was a member of the faculty of instruction at the University of Richmond two years and three years head master with the Fork Union Military Academy.

Colonel Ligon purchased the Blackstone Military Academy in 1912. He continued under the old name until in recent years he has changed the name to Blackstone, a Military School for Boys, affording a general academic, commercial and preparatory curriculum, combined with the wholesale discipline of militry regulations. The school has a wonderful plant, including twenty-one acres of ground. There is a faculty of twelve instructors and the regular enrollment is 125 boys.

Colonel Ligon married August 18, 1907, Miss Virginia Dickey, daughter of Dr. John R. and Sarah E. (James) Dickey. Her parents were born in Grayson County, Virginia, and her father was a manufacturing druggist at Bristol, Virginia. He died October 12, 1923, and her mother on June 12, 1892. Colonel and Mrs. Ligon have three children: William Arthur, born August 18, 1908, is a member of the class of 1930 in the University

of Richmond; Elvin Seth, Jr., born January 9, 1911, is a student
at the University of Richmond, and in July, 1930, enters West
Point Military Academy as a cadet; and John Dickey, born
January 29, 1913, is attending the Blackstone School.

Colonel Ligon is a member and at one time was treasurer
of the Co-operative Teachers Association, is a member of Southern Association of Schools and Colleges, of the Association of
Military Schools and Colleges of the United States. He is a
Mason, member of the Independent Order of Odd Fellows and
Owls, the Blackstone Golf Club and the University Club of
Richmond. Colonel Ligon is a Democrat. He is a deacon in the
Baptist Church at Blackstone and assistant superintendent of
the Sunday School, teaching the Men's Bible Class. Mrs. Ligon
is a member of the Daughters of the American Revolution and
the United Daughters of the Confederacy.

HON. PERCY M. MOIR. One of the most forceful citizens of
Roanoke, Hon. Percy M. Moir has always used his fine legal
talents in the furtherance of what he has conceived to be for the
best interests of his country, merging the two characters of
citizen and lawyer into a high personal combination which,
despite differences of intellectual opinion, has been generally
recognized as an example well worthy of emulation. Honors of
a high class have been bestowed upon him, and he has discharged
the responsibilities connected with them with dignified capability. His record as a district judge and as a justice of the
Supreme Court of Virginia alone entitles him to the lasting
gratitude of the people of this state, but he has accomplished
even more, for he served the Government in the Philippines, and
he has made valuable contributions to agriculture, to legal literature, and to the advancement of his home city.

Judge Moir was born in Stuart, Patrick County, Virginia,
February 24, 1870, a son of William W. and Caroline Virginia
(Martin) Moir, both of whom were born in Virginia, and are
now deceased. For forty years the father served as deputy
county clerk of Patrick County, and during the war between
the states he served as superintendent of iron mines. In political
faith he was a Democrat. While both he and his wife belonged
to the Methodist Episcopal Church, South, only she was active
in church work. Of the nine children born to the parents seven
are living, and Judge Moir was the seventh child in order of
birth. The paternal grandparents were Alex A. and Mary Moir,
he being a native of Scotland who was brought to Virginia in
childhood by his parents. The maternal grandfather was a
native of Virginia, so that on both sides of the house Judge Moir
has the distinction of coming from families long established in
the Old Dominion.

Judge Moir was educated in the Virginia Polytechnic Institute and Washington and Lee University, and was admitted to
the bar in 1892, and from then until 1898, was engaged in a
general practice of his profession in Roanoke. With the declaration of war with Spain he enlisted in the Second Virginia Infantry, and remained in the army for nine months, when he was
honorably discharged. He was then appointed to the Census
Bureau, Washington, under civil service, and was sent to the
Philippines, where for two years he served as treasurer of the
Cavite Province. In all he was in the Census Bureau for nineteen years, during that period serving as district attorney for
three and one-half years. From 1906 to 1918 he was judge of

the District Court, and from 1918 to 1920 he was on the Supreme bench of Virginia, but resigned to resume private practice in Roanoke.

In March, 1902, Judge Moir married Miss Maude Kirtland, born in Saint Louis, Missouri, who died in 1925, leaving no children. Judge Moir is a Scottish-Rite Mason, and belongs to the Shenandoah Club. He owns a valuable farm near Roanoke and resides on it, but manitains his office in the MacBain Building, Roanoke. Always a strong Democrat, he was the alternate delegate from the Philippines to the national convention of his party, and he was a delegate to the one held in New York City in 1924. As a lawyer Judge Moir has few equals, his sound judgment, his profound knowledge of the law, and his wide experience making him well fitted to handle the most intricate cases, and his practice is a large and very important one, his clients coming to him from a wide territory. The people of Roanoke are very proud of him, and feel that his selection of the city as a permanent place of residence confers an honor upon the community and his fellow citizens.

HON. NICHOLAS P. OGLESBY. The name of Oglesby is a well known one in Wythe County, and is associated with much of its history, both past and present, and those bearing it have always displayed those homely traits of character, rugged honesty, faithful industry and thoughtful economy which make for good citizenship, combined with business ability and in some cases statesmanship as well. One of those who bore the name with dignity and added to its distinction was the late Hon. Nicholas P. Oglesby, born in Wythe County, Virginia, September 12, 1837, a son of N. P. and Jane C. (Sayers) Oglesby, and grandson of John Thompson Sayers, of Revolutionary war fame.

On June 19, 1867, Nicholas P. Oglesby married Miss Sallie A. Crockett, a daughter of Thomas S. and Rachael L. (Cecil) Crockett, also of Wythe County, and they had eight children: John T., who was born April 4, 1868; Samuel C., who was born April 1, 1870; Jennie L., who was born September 13, 1872; N. P., who was born September 2, 1874; Mary S., who was born April 16, 1876; Albert C., who was born February 25, 1878; Frank S., who was born July 14, 1880; and William B., who was born September 12, 1883.

It is interesting to note that Nicholas P. Oglesby's maternal grandfather, already mentioned, John Thompson Sayers, during his service in the American Revolution was wounded in the lungs at the battle of Guilford Court House, it was thought fatally, but owing to his most remarkable constitution he recovered and lived to reach the age of sixty years. His brother, Robert Sayers, held a colonel's commission in the same great war, and was several times elected to represent his county in the State Legislature. Col. Robert Sayers was a man of great business ability, and owned the Anchor and Hope estate in Wythe County, and a large estate in Burkes Garden, Tazewell County, Virginia. The father of these two brothers, William Sayers, the great-grandfather of Hon. Nicholas P. Oglesby, was one of the early and very prominent settlers of Wythe County.

Hon. Nicholas P. Oglesby enlisted for service in the Southern army during the war between the states, and was with the Army of Northern Virginia. He participated in the battles of Spotsylvania Court House, the Wilderness and those about Richmond, including that of Mine Run. After the close of the war he

resumed his peaceful occupations, and in 1877 and 1878 represented Wythe County in the State Legislature. He owned one
of the largest blue grass farms, the old ancestral homestead,
where for many years he was active in the raising of Shorthorn
cattle. While a member of the Legislature he was greatly interested in legislative work in behalf of the public school system
of Virginia, and was prominent in framing the bill for the
system. On his homestead is the old John Thompson Sayers
orchard farm, from which the Old Dominion Nurseries obtained
their first grafts of the Virginia Beauty apple. These nurseries
were first known as the Franklin-Davis Nursery. While the
now famous Virginia Beauty apple is indigenous to Grayson
County, it was introduced to the public under its present name
from the Sayers orchard.

The death of Hon. Nicholas P. Oglesby occurred on his estate,
Elmwood, in Fort Chiswill District, February 15, 1892, and he
is buried in the old Sayers family cemetery, now known as the
Oglesby Cemetery. His widow survives him, although now
eighty years old, residing near Max Meadows, with her son,
William Bowen Oglesby, and her daughter, Mary S. Oglesby.
They are interested in cattle and sheep raising upon an extensive
scale. To complete the military service of the Oglesby family
it must be added that Dr. Nicholas P. Oglesby, son of Hon.
Nicholas P. Oglesby, now deceased, served in the Spanish-
American war; and that Nicholas E. Oglesby and Richard B.
Simmerman, grandsons of Hon. Nicholas P. Oglesby, served in
the World war, the former in the Chemical Warfare Corps and
the latter with the Third Division, A. E. F., in which he volunteered, was sent to France and participated in the Chateau
Thierry offensive and that of Argonne Forest.

The Oglesby family has in its possession the original grants
for the land on which they live, and a receipt from Daniel Boone
to Major Quirk for surveying the place for Maj. Thomas Quirk,
dated June 11, 1785. Another valuable family document in the
Oglesby collection is a plat of the place drawn by Ezekiel Calhoun, grandfather of John C. Calhoun, which bears the date of
"April ye 2nd., 1754;" autographs of John Montgomery and
Col. Joseph Crockett witnessing a deed of one Will Rogers to
William Sayers of that period; and another paper, dated October
8, 1771, issued during a court held for Botetourt County.

That some of the talents of the older Oglesbys have been
transmitted to the rising generation is shown in the following
poem written by Miss Jenny Lou Oglesby, granddaughter of
Hon. Nicholas P. Oglesby:

"THE CALL OF THE ALLEGHANIES."

"Come ye West to the Alleghanies,
    Where the towering mountains rise,
    Like the billows of the ocean,
    Towering upward toward the skies.
    Where the earth comes nearest Heaven;
    And God's handiwork is seen
    In the crimson pall of sunset
    O'er the valleys cool and green.
    Where the crystal river surges
    Westward, westward to the sea,
    Foaming at the reefs and rapids,
    Or moving deep and silently.

HENRY GIBSON HOUSTON

> Stand ye in the purple shadows
> Of the lofty mountain peaks,
> In the stillness learn the language
> That the God of Wisdom speaks.
> Here the thoughts of men are lifted
> By the stable mountain range,
> What'er skies may bend above them,
> They, the mountains, never change.
> But like truth are ever standing,
> Though oft hid in mist or clouds,
> They emerge in radiant sunshine
> From the false, deceiving shrouds.
> Enter ye this Hall of learning,
> Where ideals are great and pure,
> Modeled after majestic mountains
> Full of beauty and power secure.
> Here learn the worth that is in life,
> Of things that are not bought or sold.
> Join ye not in selfish yearnings,
> Nor struggle after tarnished gold.
> But come, oh come ye to that Virginia
> Where the light and shadows meet,
> Mingled with the laughing waters
> At the Alleghanies' feet."

HENRY GIBSON HOUSTON was a physician and surgeon, exceptionally gifted, and whose career as a man of medicine came to a close long before he had attained the prominence and success his talents and industry would have enabled him to realize.

He was born in Rockbridge County, Virginia, July 29, 1855, and died at Richmond, March 16, 1884. He was a descendant of Scotch ancestors, the Houstons having come from Scotland and settled in Virginia in the Colonial period. For a number of generations Rockbridge County has been the home of the Houstons of Virginia. The father of Doctor Houston was a cousin to Gen. Sam Houston, the Tennessee governor, whose greatest fame, however, was gained as leader of the Texas army in the war for independence from Mexico. Doctor Houston was a son of Dr. Mathew Hale Houston, who throughout the war between the states was in the service of the Confederate army as a surgeon, and who practiced his profession at Wheeling, West Virginia, and at Richmond. He lived in Richmond after the war, but his home was at Ashland when he died. Mathew Hale Houston was twice married, and the mother of Henry Gibson Houston was Eleanora Gibson. By this union eight children were born, Henry Gibson Houston being the oldest son. Of the first marriage, Rev. William Houston and Rev. Mathew Hale Houston were born. Harry Houston, a cousin, is present commissioner of fisheries of Virginia, appointed by Governor Byrd.

Henry Gibson Houston attended private schools and graduated in medicine from the University of Maryland in 1880. In the same year he engaged in practice at Richmond, and continued the work until his death. He was a member of the Virginia State and American Medical Associations. He was at one time editor of the *Atlantic Journal of Medicine*.

He married at Richmond in June, 1882, Miss Josephine Dooley, who attended the St. Joseph School in Richmond and finished her education in the Mount de Chantal Academy of Wheeling, West Virginia. Mrs. Houston is a daughter of John and Sarah Dooley, who came from Limerick, Ireland, and settled in Alexandria, Virginia, in 1833, and at Richmond in 1836. John Dooley was a hat manufacturer, and during the Civil war served in the Confederate army with the rank of captain and later as major. Mrs. Houston's brother, Major James H. Dooley, was at one time a member of the Virginia Legislature, and has been prominent in Richmond financial circles. Mrs. Houston was the youngest of nine children. She has one daughter, Eleanora Clare Houston, and their home in Richmond is at 416 West Franklin Street. Miss Houston is a very capable artist, and is finance chairman of the League of Women Voters, of which both she and her mother are members. They belong to the Catholic Woman's Club. Doctor and Mrs. Houston and their daughter, Miss Eleanora, were members of the St. Peters Catholic Church, which was the first cathedral at Richmond.

CLAUDE W. HOPPER, regional director of the National Relief Organization, with jurisdiction comprising the Southern States, maintains his executive headquarters in the fine old capital city of Virginia, and in his official capacity he has achieved a noteworthy service in providing consistent relief and care for those suffering from their service in foreign wars. In the World war he was in active overseas service for some time. He now has the rank of captain in the Virginia National Guard, and he is serving as aide-de-camp on the military staff of Governor Byrd.

Captain Hopper was born at Evansville, Indiana, in the year 1892, and was still a mere boy when his parents died, he having soon become almost entirely on his own resources and his sincerity of purpose having been shown in the advancement he has since won through his own ability and efforts. His father, the late William F. Hopper, was born in Virginia, and was a resident of the city of Evansville, Indiana, at the time of his death.

As a boy, after the death of his parents, Captain Hopper made his way to Missouri, and the public schools of that state afforded him the greater part of his youthful education. Later he was for two years a student in Ouachita College in the State of Arkansas, he having subsequently become superintendent of a large lumber mill at Helena, that state. In that state also he initiated his military career, as a private in the Arkansas National Guard. In the summer of 1916 his command enlisted for service on the Mexican border and became a part of the One Hundred and Fifty-third United States Infantry, attached to the Thirty-ninth Division. He was mustered out a few days prior to the nation's formal entrance into the World war, and with his regiment was forthwith called back to active service, he having at this juncture won commission as second lieutenant. His regiment was stationed in turn at Camp Pike, Camp Gordon and Camp Beauregard, and he served as an instructor in the Officers' Training School at Camp Gordon. From Camp Beauregard, Louisiana, in the summer of 1917, Captain Hopper was sent to Paris, France, in an important secretarial capacity, and he remained overseas during a period of five months, he having thereafter served as an instructor at Camp Gordon, Georgia, as previously noted, and having there been advanced to the office of captain of his company. He received his honorable discharge March 31, 1919, and it was shortly before this that he was tendered a position with the National Relief

Organization for foreign war sufferers. He was made an organizer in this connection and later was made regional director for the Southern States, the position of which he has since continued the loyal and efficient incumbent. In 1921 the National Relief Organization honored him with membership in the commission sent into the Near East for the purpose of studying conditions and making thereafter a report to the United States Congress. On this assignment he visited every country in the near Orient, including those in both Europe and Asia.

In the national campaign of 1924 Captain Hopper was acting director of the Democratic national finance campaign in Virginia, with headquarters in Richmond, and at the conclusion of that campaign Hon. John W. Davis, the Democratic standard-bearer, stated that the conducting of the Democratic finance campaign in Virginia surpassed in efficiency that of any similar organization in all the states. In the Democratic primaries of Virginia in 1927 Captain Hopper appeared as candidate for nomination to the position of representative of the Richmond district in the House of Delegates of the State Legislature, he having been at this time assistant secretary of the Democratic State Central Committee and a member of the City Democratic Committee of Richmond.

Captain Hopper has completed the circle of York and Scottish Rites in the Masonic fraternity, has received in the latter the thirty-second degree, and he is also a Noble of the Mystic Shrine. On the fair old city of Richmond he and his wife have membership in Ginter Park Methodist Episcopal Church, South.

Since the close of the World war Captain Hopper has maintained his residence in Richmond, and here was solemnized his marriage with Miss Lucy Terrell, a sister of Rev. G. Tyler Terrell, who is here pastor of Immanuel Baptist Church. Captain and Mrs. Hopper are popular factors in representative social activities in their home city.

ALEXANDER BEAR, M. D., was a native Virginian, saw service in the Confederate cause, but after the war went west and for many years was an honored and respected citizen as well as an indispensable professional man in Nebraska. When he retired from the work of his profession he returned to Virginia and established his home in Richmond, where he lived until his death and where his widow and children still reside. Mrs. Bear's home is at 2032 Monument Avenue.

Dr. Alexander Bear was born in Fauquier County, Virginia, February 4, 1841, and died at Richmond in April, 1924, at the age of eighty-three. His father, Emanuel Bear, was born in Germany and settled in Virginia when a young man. He married Caroline Bachrach, also a native of Germany, who had come to Richmond when a child. Alexander Bear grew up in Fauquier County, attended schools there and completed his medical education in the Maryland Medical College at Baltimore. He was only nineteen years of age when he was granted his medical diploma. About a year later the war broke out between the states and he enlisted in Smith Blues Regiment at Marion, Smith County, Virginia. In the early part of the war he was assigned duty as a surgeon in the field, but for the last two years had charge of the Marion Hospital for wounded soldiers at Marion, Virginia. He was promoted to official rank. After the war he practiced for a time in Virginia and then went to Nebraska, living for a time at Fremont and West Point. In

1872 he located at Norfolk, Nebraska, then a small village, and for thirty-seven years his time and talents were in demand by an increasing patronage, and he not only gave the community the best of his professional service, but in many ways was closely identified with its material growth and civic upbuilding. Norfolk when he left there in 1909 was one of the important cities of Central Nebraska.

Doctor Bear in 1909 returned to Richmond, and during the last fifteen years of his life lived in quiet retirement, enjoying many friendships in his native state. While in Nebraska he served as mayor of Norfolk, as president of the school board, was elected and served in the Nebraska State Senate, and was a member of the United States Pension Board. He was a director and vice president of the Norfolk National Bank. He was always a staunch Democrat in politics, and was a member of the Masonic and Elks fraternities.

Doctor Bear married, September 12, 1887, Miss Amelia Levy, a native of Virginia, who was reared and educated in Richmond. Her father, Leopold Levy, was born in Germany and when a young man came to America and settled at Amelia Court House, Virginia. He was a merchant in that city, and at the outbreak of the Civil war enlisted in Stonewall Jackson's Brigade. He was captured and after a term in prison was exchanged and rejoined his command. After the war he located at Richmond and eventually became one of the city's leading commission merchants. Leopold Levy married Rosena Hutzler, who was born at Richmond, member of an old family of that city. The Levy children were: Joseph L., of Richmond, who married Lenora Straus and has three children; Edwin L., Florence and J. Leo; Isaac Levy, of Baltimore, who married Emma Bachrach, and after her death married again, having one son by his first wife, named Irving; and Mrs. Amelia Bear.

Doctor and Mrs. Bear have had three children, one of whom is deceased. The daughter, Robinette, is the wife of Leo Greentree, a business man of Richmond, and has two children, named Jeanette Virginia and Meyer. Alexander L. Bear, the son, is in business at Richmond.

JOHN W. DANIEL left college to learn the printing trade in the plant of the *Northampton Times* at Cape Charles. His father owned the paper at the time, and John W. Daniel has been actively identified with that newspaper and business for ten years, is manager of the Times Publishing Company, and he has been instrumental in making the *Times* a paper of substantial circulation and influence throughout Northampton County.

He was born in Williamsburg, Virginia, February 5, 1894, son of John T. and Henrietta (Barlow) Daniel, his father a native of Middlesex County and his mother of Williamsburg. John T. Daniel is an attorney by profession, has practiced law and been identified with business and civic affairs at Cape Charles for many years, and is now the editor of the *Northampton Times*.

John W. Daniel was reared and educated in Cape Charles, graduated from high school in 1911, and for two years attended Randolph-Macon College at Ashland. He acquired his knowledge of printing and the newspaper business by an apprenticeship in the mechanical department and the business office of the *Northampton Times*, and worked there steadily until 1917, when

W. E. Hogg

he enlisted in the navy. He was on shore duty at Washington, D. C., until January 6, 1919, when he was released from active duty, but was kept on the reserve list until the full four-year time of his enlistment had expired.

Since the war he has had the business management of the Times Publishing Company. The company has a plant well equipped for commercial printing. The *Northampton Times* now enjoys a circulation of 2,500 copies.

Mr. Daniel married, June 24, 1918, Martha Fleet, daughter of Rev. Alexander and Josephine (Jeffries) Fleet, the former a native of King and Queen County and the latter of Essex County. Her father, who was a Baptist minister, died in 1911, and her mother in 1923. Mr. and Mrs. Daniel have one child, Rawley Fleet, born August 1, 1919.

Mr. Daniel and his father are also engaged in the fire insurance business at Cape Charles. He is a member of the Masonic fraternity, Junior Order United American Mechanics, the Sigma Phi Epsilon college fraternity, Cape Charles Rotary Club, Northampton Country Club. He is a member of the Sons of Confederate Veterans, the American Legion, is a Democrat, is active in the Baptist Church, and for many years served as secretary of the Sunday school.

WILLIAM EDWARD HOGG, commonwealth's attorney for York County, has in his career exemplified the qualities and talents that have long distinguished the Hogg family in Virginia.

Mr. Hogg is a descendant of George Hogg, who with six brothers came to America from Scotland in 1650. George Hogg in 1686 located in York County, Virginia, and that has been the home of one branch of this well known family for more than two hundred years. William Edward Hogg was born in York County March 3, 1890, son of William Henry and Frances Elizabeth (Winder) Hogg. Both his grandfathers, Samuel Hogg and Edward Thomas Winder, were Confederate soldiers in the Civil war. His great-great-grandfather, John Hogg, acquired in 1814 land in York County, a part of which has been continuously occupied by some of his descendants, a part of said land being devised to Lewis Hogg, father of Samuel Hogg, and on a part of which is now the home of William Henry and Frances Elizabeth Hogg. John Hogg was a son of Richard Hogg, who as a lieutenant of Marines was present at the surrender of Cornwallis at Yorktown at the close of the Revolutionary war. William Henry Hogg has spent his active life as a farmer and fisherman, and the old homestead where he resides is five miles from Yorktown. He and his wife were both born in 1867.

William Edward Hogg grew up and received his education in York County, completing a high school course under his cousin and had business training in the seminary at West Point, Virginia, and in the Smithdeal Business College at Richmond, where he graduated in June, 1905. For three years he studied law by correspondence with the Sprague Correspondence School of Law at Detroit, and he also attended the law department of Washington and Lee University. He was admitted to the bar in June, 1915, beginning practice at Hampton, and since January 1, 1920, has had his law offices at Yorktown, where he now has his home. While getting started in his profession he supplemented his income by work at the carpenter's trade and for

seven years before entering the law department of Washington
and Lee University assisted his father in the fishing business.

Mr. Hogg was elected commonwealth's attorney of York
County in 1919 and has twice been reelected to that office. At
the present time he is engaged in compiling a digest, to be called
the Virginia Criminal Annotations, a brief, condensed statement of facts with quotations from the opinions beginning with
the latest decisions and working backward. It is a unique legal
hand-book, and will comprise about eleven hundred pages.

Mr. Hogg married, May 12, 1917, Gertrude Virginia, only
daughter of J. J. and Sarah Elizabeth (Sparrer) Ironmonger,
natives of York County. Her father is a farmer living at Sea-
ford. Mr. and Mrs. Hogg have one daughter, Mildred Virginia.
Mrs. Hogg also has a son, Charles James, by a former marriage.
Mr. Hogg is affiliated with the Improved Order of Red Men,
is a Democrat, for several years a steward in the Methodist
Episcopal Church, South, and a substitute teacher in the Sunday School.

THOMAS E. SIMMERMAN, JR., cashier and executive officer
of the Bank of Max Meadows, is a native of Wythe County, and
represents one of the younger generations of a family that has
been identified with the agricultural and stock raising industry
in this Blue Grass region of Southwest Virginia for a number
of generations.

Mr. Simmerman was born in Wythe County, May 18, 1896,
son of Thomas E. and Mary (Hanson) Simmerman. His grandfather was Thomas H. Simmerman, who in turn was a son of
Thomas Q. Simmerman. Thomas E. Simmerman, Sr., was born
and reared in Wythe County, was educated in public schools, in
Hampden-Sydney College, and in the Eastman Business College
at Poughkeepsie, New York. He devoted his active life to farming and stock raising, was also a dealer in cattle, was a director
in the Bank of Max Meadows and the Farmers Bank of Southwest Virginia at Wytheville, and was otherwise a man of influence and distinction in his community, serving one term as
supervisor of the Wytheville district. He died in 1926. His
wife, Mary Hanson, was born and reared in Wythe County, and
was likewise descended from an old family of Virginia. She
was a member of Stewart Chapter, Daughters of the American
Revolution. She and her husband were active members of the
Presbyterian Church, in which he served as an elder. She died
in November, 1926, and both are buried at Wytheville. They
were the parents of eight children: Thomas E., Jr.; Miss Sidney
Major, a resident of Wytheville, a graduate of the Mary Baldwin
Seminary of Staunton, Virginia, and now a teacher at Winston-
Salem, North Carolina; Elbert L., who died in October, 1917, at
the age of seventeen; William H., assistant cashier of the
Farmers Bank of Southwest Virginia at Wytheville, who fin-
ished his education in Hampden-Sydney College; George B., a
farmer on the old homestead; Henry P., a farmer and cattle
man; Mary H., attending the Virginia State Normal School for
Women at Farmville; and Ellen Virginia, a student at Villa
Maria Convent at Wytheville.

Thomas E. Simmerman, Jr., attended public schools and finished his education in Hampden-Sydney College with the class
of 1920. In the meantime, in May, 1917, he joined the colors,
spent nine months in training at Fortress Monroe, attended the
Third Officers' Training School at Camp Lee, Virginia, for three

months, and was commissioned a second lieutenant in the Thirty-second Field Artillery. Following that he had four months of intensive training in the School of Fire at Fort Sill, Oklahoma, and was then transferred to Camp Meade, Maryland, and with the Eleventh Brigade, Thirty-second Artillery, was in readiness to go overseas when the armistice was signed. He received his honorable discharge at Camp Meade December 15, 1918.

For about a year after the war Mr. Simmerman was in the, garage business. In 1920, on the organization of the Bank of Max Meadows, he took the post of cashier, and has had the chief responsibilities of managing that institution, of which he is also a director. He owns a fine Blue Grass farm near Max Meadows, specializing in the raising of beef cattle, and he keeps himself in close touch with the spirit and the enterprise of the community.

Mr. Simmerman is a Royal Arch Mason, member of the Independent Order of Odd Fellows, the Pi Kappa Alpha fraternity, is a Democrat, is deacon and treasurer of the Presbyterian Church at Max Meadows and also one of the church trustees.

He married at Max Meadows, June 8, 1923, Miss Miriam Robinson, daughter of John W. and Nannie (Counselman) Robinson. Her father for many years has been a leading farmer and cattle man in Wythe County. The Robinsons have been in Southwest Virginia since very early times. Mrs. Simmerman finished her education in Sullins College at Bristol, Tennessee. She is a member of the Methodist Episcopal Church, South. They have four children, Thomas E. III, John Robinson, Nancy and Graham Hanson.

NEWTON FLOYD BURGE, JR., is associated with one of the prominent industrial organizations of the little city of Galax, on the line between Carroll and Grayson counties. Galax has become noted as a wholesale and jobbing center and also as a manufacturing center for the hard wood resources of this section of Virginia. Mr. Burge is assistant secretary and treasurer of the Vaughan-Bassett Furniture Company, which is one of the large furniture manufacturing enterprises of this section of the state.

Mr. Burge was born at Martinsburg, Virginia, June 26, 1892, son of Newton F. and Mary Jane (Hundley) Burge. His father, now living retired at Martinsville at the age of seventy-four, was born in Henry County, Virginia, in 1854, was educated in private schools, and spent many years in the mercantile business at Martinsville, retiring in 1925, after he had passed the age of three score and ten. His wife was a daughter of Capt. Hiram B. Hundley, who was born near Martinsville in 1817 and died in 1905, at the age of eighty-eight. He represented a prominent family of that section, and though too old for active duty as a soldier he served as a recruiting and training officer near Danville, with the rank of captain, in the Confederate army. Newton F. Burge, Sr., and wife had a family of six daughters and two sons: Ada, wife of J. F. Floyd, of Martinsville; Etta, wife of F. R. Brown, of Galax; Nannie, Mrs. L. H. Shumate, of Johnson City, Tennessee; William B., in the wholesale bakery business at Martinsville; Hepsie, wife of B. C. Vaughan, of Galax; Fannie, who died at the age of four years; Newton F.; and Jessie, wife of D. V. Carter, of Clinton, North Carolina.

Newton F. Burge, Jr., attended the grade and high schools at Martinsville and in 1912 graduated from the Fork Union

Military School. With this educational training he entered the mercantile business, and applied all his efforts during the next five years to his business affairs. In 1917 he enrolled in the National Guard in Virginia, and on June 28, 1917, was mustered in at Danville, Virginia. He was assigned duty with the Coast Artillery Corps and spent two years at Fortress Monroe. He was promoted to sergeant September 1, 1917, to plotter December 2, 1918, and to first-class gunner March 20, 1918. He received his honorable discharge December 3, 1918.

After leaving the army he took a course in the Eastman-Gaines Business College at Poughkeepsie, New York, and was an accountant for the Banner Grocery Company, a wholesale business at Martinsville, for one year. He then removed to Galax, taking charge of the books and as general office manager for the Vaughan-Bassett Furniture Company, and since 1925 has been assistant secretary and treasurer of that business.

Mr. Burge is a Scottish Rite Mason, member of Kazim Temple of the Mystic Shrine at Roanoke, is a member of the Knights of Pythias, Galax Country Club, and the Baptist Church.

He married at Bristol, Tennessee, September 5, 1924, Miss Maye Roberts, of Old Town, Grayson County, Virginia, daughter of T. F. and Florence (Cox) Roberts. Her father was a farmer and stock man. Mrs. Burge was reared a Methodist, but she and her husband are now active in the Baptist Church at Galax. She graduated from the Galax High School and the State Normal at Radford, and was a teacher in the Galax Grammar School during 1922-23.

MRS. CHARLES DAVENPORT, who died January 26, 1928, was one of the distinguished women of her generation in Richmond. Her husband, Charles Davenport, was a well known Richmond merchant, and her own people contributed some of the greatest names to the medical profession in Virginia.

Her father was Dr. James Brown McCaw, who was born at Richmond, July 12, 1823. Her ancestor, James Drew McCaw, was a nephew of Dr. James McClurg. Doctor McClurg, son of an English army surgeon, was born in 1747, graduated from William and Mary College in 1762, and took his degree in medicine at Edinburgh, Scotland. He lived for some years at Williamsburg, and after the close of the Revolution located at Richmond. Doctor McClurg was chosen a delegate to the Constitutional Convention when Patrick Henry declined that honor, but the Doctor was not present when the Federal Constitution was finally voted upon, and did not sign the document. James Drew McCaw grew up in the home of his uncle, Doctor McClurg, was sent by him to the University of Edinburgh, where he graduated in 1792, and on returning he located at Richmond. In 1799 he was pronounced "one of the greatest men of his profession in America." Dr. James Drew McCaw was the hero of the famous theater fire of 1811 in Richmond, when he stood at a window in the theater and passed the frantic women and children one by one to a negro slave standing just below. This slave subsequently for his bravery was given his freedom.

William R. McCaw, father of Dr. James Brown McCaw, was also a physician, and married Anne Ludwell Brown, whose father, James Brown, Jr., was state auditor of Virginia forty years.

James Brown McCaw graduated in 1844 in medicine from the University of New York. During the war between the

Edward Butts Kilby Ph G. M.D.

states he was chief surgeon of Chimborazo Hospital, the largest of all the hospitals on the Southern side, where it was estimated 75,000 patients were treated during the war. He was a professor and dean in the Medical College of Virginia and editor of the *Virginia Medical Journal*. Dr. James Brown McCaw married Delia Patteson, whose father, Dr. William A. Patteson, was also a prominent Richmond physician. Two of their sons, brothers of the late Mrs. Davenport, were eminent in the field of medicine and surgery, David and Walter Drew. Walter Drew McCaw, who was born at Richmond in 1863, was commissioned an assistant surgeon of the United States Army in 1884, and on March 5, 1919, was given the rank of brigadier-general as assistant surgeon general of the United States Army. He was with the volunteers during the Spanish-American war, and was chief surgeon of the American Expeditionary Forces from October, 1918, to July 15, 1919, and was awarded the distinguished service medal by the United States, besides honors from all the allied governments.

Ellen McCaw Davenport was seventy-four years of age when she died at her home, 1637 Monument Avenue, in Richmond. Throughout her life she was a part of the cultured society of Virginia, and had many activities in Richmond, being a member of the Colonial Dames of America, the Daughters of the Revolution, the Musicians Club, and was a charter member and former president of the Woman's Club. She was a member of St. Paul's Episcopal Church.

Her husband, Charles Davenport, was also a native of Richmond, where he spent his life engaged in the mercantile business. Mr. and Mrs. Charles Davenport had two daughters: Delia, now Mrs. Richard Watkins Carrington, of Richmond; and Ellen, wife of Dr. Henry Wiseman Cook, of Minneapolis, Minnesota.

EDWARD BUTTS KILBY, PH. G., M. D. James City County is noted for the skill, learning and high character of the men who make up its medical practitioners, and the profession here numbers some whose attainments are far beyond the ordinary. Among them one whose career is typical of modern advancement, his being a broad field of medical service, is Dr. Edward B. Kilby, physician and surgeon of Toano. He was born in Nansemond County, Virginia, February 28, 1890, a son of Walter G. and Susannah (Parr) Kilby, natives of the same county as their son. Walter G. Kilby was a general contractor of Newport News, Virginia, and a man of considerable consequence.

Doctor Kilby grew up in Newport News, and was graduated from its academy in 1907. He then entered the Medical College of Virginia, Richmond, from which he was graduated in pharmacy in 1909, and in medicine from the same school in 1915. For the following two years he was attached to Marine Hospital, Detroit, Michigan, where he gained a very valuable experience, and when he left that institution he established himself in practice in Southampton County, Virginia, and remained there for five years, or until January 6, 1923, when he came to Toano, James City County, and here he has since remained with enviable success.

On January 25, 1917, Doctor Kilby married Miss Jean Campbell Moody, a daughter of Rosser L. and Bertha (Robinson) Moody, natives of Petersburg, Virginia. Mrs. Moody died in 1920, and Mr. Moody is also deceased. For a good many years he was a druggist of South Richmond. Doctor and Mrs. Kilby have two children: Edward Butts, Junior, who was born August 23, 1918; and Patricia Jean, who was born March 16, 1921. The Doctor is a member of the Virginia State Medical Society, the Southern Medical Society and the Walter Reed Medical Society. A strong believer in fraternities, he belongs to a number of them, is a Mason, and also holds membership in Samis Grotto, Richmond; a member of the Junior Order United American Mechanics, and others. For several years he has been local surgeon for the Chesapeake & Ohio Railroad. Doctor Kilby votes the Democratic ticket, but aside from exercising his right of suffrage he takes but little part in politics. The Baptist Church is his religious home. The personal impression given by Doctor Kilby is quieting and satisfying, inspiring confidence and commanding respect.

J. EDWARD WILLIAMS. Self help has accomplished about all of the great things in the world, and the door of opportunity has generally been opened by the men who have found success awaiting them within. In every city every year there are young men who cherish ambitions in one direction or the other, but how few ever reach the top of the ladder. It requires a brave heart to fight one's way through discouragements, temptations and momentary failures, but that many have succeeded is proven by the long list of names honored in the business world through life and recalled with respect and admiration after their work in life is over. These remarks are particularly applicable to the late J. Edward Williams, who was for many years prominently identified with Government service, whose loss to his department, to his city, let alone to his family and friends, is irreparable.

J. Edward Williams was born in Northwest, Norfolk County, Virginia, November 11, 1867, and died in Newport News, Virginia, in December, 1920. When he was but a little child he had the misfortune to lose his mother, and his father died when he was eleven years old. His uncle, who was his guardian, also died when the youth was but sixteen years of age. At this time Edward was a student of the Gatewood School of Norfolk, Virginia. From then until his death J. Edward Williams was self-supporting. His first position was with the Crawford Furniture Company, which he served for five years, after which he came to Newport News and entered the furniture business for himself, conducting it for four years, during that period building up a large and valuable trade, but owing to a disastrous fire he was obliged to close his store, and then entered the customs department of the Federal Government at the port of Newport News. Two years later he was appointed first immigration officer of the Hampton Roads District. At the time of his death he was inspector in charge of the district embracing the ports of Hampton Roads, Wilmington, North Carolina, and Charleston, South Carolina.

In January, 1894, Mr. Williams married, in Portsmouth, Virginia, Miss Hattie Weaver, of Portsmouth, Virginia, a daughter of Joseph F. Weaver, a pharmacist, a member of the harbor commission and of the City Council. J. F. Weaver married Harriet Morgan, and they became the parents of five children that are now living, and several who are deceased. Of these children Mrs. Williams is the second, the others being: J. F. Weaver, Jr., city engineer of Portsmouth, a brother and two sisters. Mr. and Mrs. Williams had three children born to their

marriage: Geraldine, who is deceased; Dorothy, who is also
deceased; and Gray, who is a practicing attorney of New York
City, married Eleanor Fishburne, a daughter of Judge John W.
Fishburne, of Charlottesville, Virginia. Mr. Williams was a
past exalted ruler of the local lodge of the Benevolent and Protective Order of Elks, and was its secretary at the time of his
death. In political faith he was a Democrat, and at all times
he was faithful to party precedents. Trinity Methodist Episcopal Church, South, was his religious home, but Mrs. Williams
is a Presbyterian. During 1895 and 1896 Mr. Williams was
on the Board of Supervisors of Warwick County, and during
1897 and 1898 he was captain of the Huntington Rifle Club of
Newport News.

The Williams family came from Wales and England, and its
representatives came to the United States not long after the
organization of the present government, settling in Virginia.
The Weaver family was established in Virginia in a period ante-
dating the American Revolution, in which great struggle it was
represented by patriots bearing the name, one of whom was associated with the campaign in the vicinity of Hampton Roads.

Although some years have passed since the death of Captain
Williams, he is remembered as a man who lent his influence to
every good and worthy cause as a citizen, and every enterprise
with which he was connected benefited because of his association
with it. In the conduct of the affairs of his office he was recognized as a just man, honorable, incorruptible and capable, and
he had a wide acquaintance with men of moment throughout
the state and in the national capital.

WARD MARTIN, M. D. To win the unqualified trust and confidence of his fellowmen is something to live for, and this has
been honorably achieved by one of Tazewell County's well known
physicians, Dr. Ward Martin, chiropractic practitioner at Bluefield, Virginia. Doctor Martin well illustrates the general character of that body of noblemen who for ages have devoted themselves, often with great unselfishness, to the healing art, a guard
constantly on the defense line protecting humanity from its
subtle disease foes. It may follow different paths and favor
different systems, but the object is ever the same.

Doctor Martin belongs to an old Virginia family, of Scotch
extraction, that has many notable representatives in this and
adjacent Southern states. He was born on the old family homestead in Floyd County, Virginia, May 28, 1895, son of J. A. and
Amelia (Moore) Martin, and grandson of William Martin and
Noah Moore, all natives of Virginia. Before the war between
the states both grandfathers were extensive planters in Floyd
County, Grandfather Moore also owning slaves and serving
many years as a justice of the peace. Grandfather Martin
served hrough the above war as a soldier in the Confederate
army. The father of Doctor Martin followed agricultural pursuits all his life, was somewhat active in local politics as a
Republican, and both he and wife were members of the Lutheran
Church. His death occurred in 1915, but the mother of Doctor
Martin survives and makes her home at Wythesville, Virginia,
where she is well known and esteemed.

Ward Martin received his early educational training in the
public schools of his native county, after which he entered the
high school at Christiansburg, in Montgomery County, from
which he was creditably graduated. Ready then to make him-

self useful and independent, he accepted a clerkship in a local shoe store, but six months later, seeking wider opportunity, he went to Chicago, Illinois, where he soon found a position in the great business house of Montgomery Ward & Company, where, although he had practically no previous business training, he gave entire satisfaction in the department to which he was assigned, and one year later went on the road as a traveling salesman.

In the meanwhile Doctor Martin had lost his father, and when the United States entered the World war he hastened back to Virginia and attempted to enlist for service in the navy, but was not accepted on account of being under the prescribed weight. Not discouraged, however, he went on to Washington, but when he sought to enlist in the aviation service he met with the same refusal on the same ground. Intensely loyal and determined to be of use to his country, he then proceeded to Newport News and went to work in the Government Navy Yard there, and continued to work there until the close of the war.

Perhaps in his close association with this vast army of workers germinated that beneficent urge of helpfulness that inspires every true physician, for Mr. Martin could not help but be impressed by the many injuries suffered by his fellow workers in the way of sprains, wrenches and even spine dislocations, that were regarded as only temporary, but nevertheless in many cases were disfiguring for life if not fatal. He suddenly found himself interested as never before, and the more he observed and the closer he investigated, the greater became his interest in that medical system known as chiropractic, as especially adapted to this class of disability.

The proven virtues of this great system, described by one of its eminent expounders as "a philosophy, science and art of things natural" are as old as Doctor Martin himself, for it was in 1895 that the marvelous discovery was made that many of the diseases from which men suffer can be completely cured by proper adjustments of the spine. As soon as he was relieved from duty at Newport News Mr. Martin enrolled as a student in the Eastern College of Chiropractic at Newark, New Jersey, from which he was graduated in 1924, and after a course in dissecting in Bellevue Hospital, New York, he was ready to enter into practice. In the meanwhile the science of thirty years ago is no longer new, but is accepted and practiced in all parts of the world, Doctor Martin being but one of 8,000 chiropractic physicians in the United States alone. Before locating at Bluefield he practiced for a few months at Narrows, in Giles County, and is now the only chiropractor registered in Tazewell County. His professional success has been marked and he can number grateful patients in both large and small communities all through Southwest Virginia and even beyond.

On August 2, 1924, Doctor Martin married Miss Thelma Cook, daughter of Earl H. and Daisy Cook, of Wythesville, Virginia, members of one of the old established families of that section. Mrs. Martin is a graduate of the Wythesville High School, and both she and the Doctor are members of the Methodist Episcopal Church, South, at Bluefield, in which she is a teacher in the Sunday school. Not only as a man of science but as a good citizen, Doctor Martin endeavors to promote the social welfare and civic progress of Bluefield, belongs to the Chamber of Commerce, and is a member of the Masonic fraternity and of the Chiropractors Association.

MELVILLE LYLE MORRISON   ELIZABETH MAUDE (ATKINS) MORRISON

MELVILLE LYLE MORRISON. From the earliest settlement of Virginia the great and fertile plantations have been a source of wealth, and their owners have occupied positions of prominence in whatever community they were located. Prior to the war between the state these estates were, in many instances, princely, and the leading men and women of the country were made welcome with a lavish hospitality never before, or since, equaled. In spite of changes these plantations are still very valuable assets, and Southern hospitality lives, although, necessarily, upon a less expansive scale. One of the men of the Old Dominion, now deceased, who for many years gave his life to the supervision of the lordly Mount Vernon plantation in King William County, Melville L. Morrison was typical of the best element of the South, a thorough gentleman of the old school, and a man who numbered his warm personal friends by the hundreds. He was born on that same plantation July 27, 1874, and died there in June, 1917.

Mr. Morrison was a son of George B. and Sarah Thornton Black Morrison, the former of whom, also a Virginia gentleman, descended from Scotch forebears, but of a family established in Virginia during its Colonial epoch, owned and operated, with slave labor, the Mount Vernon estate. With the declaration of war between the North and the South he cast his lot with the Confederacy, and continued to serve as a cavalryman until peace was declared. Returning home, he bravely took up the problems of the Reconstruction period and brought his plantation back to something of its former value. Seven children were born to him and his wife, of whom Melville L. Morrison was the sixth in order of birth.

Following the completion of his educational training in several excellent private schools of King William County Melville L. Morrison assisted his father in the management of Mount Vernon, which property has been in the family for five generations. In 1898, in response to President McKinley's call for troops, he went to Newport News, Virginia, where he was assigned to service in the shipyards in an official capacity, and continued there during the Spanish-American war, and for several months following the declaration of peace, being in the service for one year. Honorably discharged, he returned to Mount Vernon, and buying the interests of the other heirs, gave himself up to the management of the estate, and continued to reside there until claimed by death while still in the very prime of life.

On December 17, 1901, Mr. Morrison married Miss Elizabeth Maude Atkins, a daughter of Alvey V. and Myrtle (Guthridge) Atkins, and a member of a family established in Virginia after the close of the American Revolution, and of English origin. Mrs. Morrison is proud of her family and its long connection with the history of the state. Her father was a planter, contractor and road supervisor of King William County, where she was born and reared. Like her husband she was educated in private schools, and is a lady of unusual mentality and charm. She is the eldest of the three children born to her parents.

Three children were born to Mr. and Mrs. Morrison: Theresa Elizabeth, who was educated in the schools of King William County and Richmond College, is now assistant cashier of the Home Benefit Insurance Company; Grace Evelyn, who is the wife of James L. Prince, of Richmond; and Ryland Maxey, who is a student in High School in King William County. After

the death of Mr. Morrison the family moved to Richmond, and
Mrs. Morrison maintains her home at 617 Bancroft Street. She
and her children are earnest members of the Methodist Episcopal
Church, South, of which Mr. Morrison was long a member, and
to which he always gave an active and generous support.
Although some years have passed since his death Mr. Morrison
still lives in the hearts of his family and friends and his memory
is cherished with tender faithfulness.

HARRY D. McWHIRT is a native Virginian, and has become
well known in the business and civic affairs of the Milford
community of Caroline County. He is cashier of the Milford
State Bank and one of the stockholders and directors of that
prosperous institution.

Mr. McWhirt was born in Spotsylvania County, Virginia,
October 31, 1886, son of Julian D. and Annie F. (Hicks)
McWhirt, his father a native of Spotsylvania and his mother of
Caroline County. Julian D. McWhirt, a farmer and merchant,
died in July, 1925, and his wife passed away in August, 1911.

Harry D. McWhirt was reared and educated in Spotsylvania
County, attended private school at Fredericksburg, and in the
way of preparation for a commercial career had several years
of employment as a clerk in his father's store. Mr. McWhirt
for about one year was a clerk in the Metropolitan Hotel at
Washington and then took up the life insurance business. For
two years he was located at Ashland, Virginia, and he also held
the office of postmaster of Spotsylvania and for four years was
commissioner of revenue of that county.

Since 1915 his home has been at Milford, in Caroline County,
and he became cashier of the Milford State Bank three years
after it was organized in 1912. The Milford State Bank has
capital of $22,500, surplus of $16,000, and average deposits of
$175,000. The president of the bank is Dr. E. C. Cobb, and
Walter Wilson is the vice president.

Mr. McWhirt married in December, 1911, Bertha E. Mussey.
Her parents, F. C. and Ellen (Reed) Mussey, came from England, and her father settled in Virginia and is still operating a
farm in Spotsylvania County. Mr. and Mrs. McWhirt have
three children: Arthur D., born in 1914; Harry Marvin, born
in 1916; and Walter Reed, born in 1921. Mr. McWhirt is a
past master of the Masonic Lodge, member of the Modern Woodmen of America, is an independent voter and takes an active
part with his family in the Baptist Church at Milford, being
church treasurer and a teacher in the Sunday school.

THOMAS LETCHER STONE was a prominent figure in the commercial life of Richmond for many years. He was a native
Virginian, and his people on both sides have been in the state
for many generations.

He was born in the City of Richmond, May 24, 1859, and
died there November 11, 1922. He was the fifth of the seven
children of Ellis Ware and Lucy Jane (Nunn) Stone. The Nunn
family lived in King and Queen County. Thomas Letcher Stone
was educated at Richmond, and his first business experience
was as an employe of the T. P. Campbell Lumber Company. A
few years later he went with Robert F. William & Company,
and acquired an interest in that business. The enterprise with
which his name and work were most intimately associated, how-

ever, was the Southern Biscuit Company of Richmond. He became its general manager in 1900, and during the next twenty-two years built up a remarkable business for the house, continuing active therein until his death.

Mr. Stone was a Democrat, a Baptist, and was affiliated with the Masonic fraternity and Royal Arcanum.

He married, June 13, 1881, Miss Roberta A. Smith. of Richmond, only child of Robert J. and Cornelia A. Smith. Her father served during the last year of the Civil war in Company R of the First Virginia Regiment, and was in Pickett's Division. Mrs. Stone, who resides at 1021 West Main Street, in Richmond, is the mother of two sons. Robert Ware Stone, who graduated from the Virginia Polytechnic Institute, married Adela Brooks, of Chesterfield, and has four children, named Dorothy, Margaret, Joseph and May Frances. John L. Stone, the younger son, an employe of the City of Richmond, married Blanche Puryear, and they also have four children, J. Letcher, Thomas William, Herbert Milton and Eugenia Mariam.

TYLER McCALL FRAZIER, of Wythesville, district chairman of the Democratic party of the Ninth Virginia District, is a member of an old and prominent family of Southwest Virginia.

He was born at Graham, April 30, 1900, son of Dr. Henry B. and Florence (McCall) Frazier. His grandfather, Rev. Taylor Frazier, is in point of service the oldest member of the Holston Conference of the Methodist Episcopal Church, South. He is now eighty-eight years of age and a resident of Chilhowie, Virginia. He is also one of the two surviving chaplains of the Confederate army. Dr. Henry B. Frazier was born and reared at Graham, attended public schools and Emory and Henry College, and was educated for the profession of medicine in Vanderbilt University and the University of Maryland. For several years he practiced at Bramwell, West Virginia, and for over thirty years has been a leading physician and surgeon at Graham. He has interested himself in the life of that community, is a past master of Harman Lodge No. 222, A. F. and A. M., and a member of the Mystic Shrine. His wife, Florence McCall. was born and reared in Tazewell County, Virginia, attended public and private schools and Martha Washington College. She and Doctor Frazier have five children: Tyler McCall; Henry B., attorney at Bluefield, West Virginia; Virginia, a public school teacher; Lucian, twin of Virginia, who died at the age of eleven years; and Louise, a student in the Graham High School.

Tyler McCall Frazier was educated in the public schools of Graham, in Roanoke College, and graduated in 1922 from the University of Virginia. For a young man he has had unusual opportunities for political experience and service. After leaving the university he became private secretary to Congressman George B. Peery, of the Ninth Virginia District, and was with Mr. Peery at Washington until February 1, 1928, when he was made chairman of the Ninth District Democratic Committee, and is also a member of the State Democratic Central Committee. He is the youngest man ever made a district chairman in Virginia, and is also the youngest member of the State Central Committee.

Mr. Frazier is a Royal Arch Mason, member of the B. P. O. Elks and the American Legion. He enrolled for service in August, 1918, and was on special duty at Roanoke and Salem until honorably discharged in December, 1918. He is a member of the Methodist Episcopal Church, South.

Mr. Frazier married in Washington, D. C., April 1, 1922, Miss Lillian Bowman, of Charlottesville, Virginia, where she was reared and educated, attending public schools and St. Anne's School for Girls. She is a daughter of Louis M. and Lillian (Childs) Bowman, of Charlottesville, and her father for many years has been a wholesale dealer in marble, granite and bronzes, now making his home at Washington, D. C.

JULIAN NEWTON HARRIS. At New Kent, judicial center of the county of the same name, Mr. Harris is to be found busily engaged in his official duties at the courthouse, where there is ample demand for his time and attention, in that he is serving not only as county clerk but also as the New Kent County clerk of the Circuit Court.

Mr. Harris was born at New Kent, January 9, 1905, and is a son of Thomas Newton Harris and Mamie Perkins (Robertson) Harris, of whom more specific mention will be found in later paragraphs of this review. It is interesting to observe in connection with the service of Julian N. Harris as county clerk of his native county that his father had served in this office during the long period of twenty-seven years, while his grandfather, the late John N. Harris, held the office about twenty-seven years, so that the record of the Harris family in this particular office has now covered a period of about 125 years.

After having duly profited by the advantages of the public schools of New Kent Julian N. Harris continued his studies in the high school in the city of Richmond until he was graduated therein as a member of the class of 1920. At the age of eleven years he began to assist his father in the office of county clerk, and he gained such proficiency that at the age of sixteen years he was made deputy county clerk of New Kent County. In June, 1924, he was appointed deputy clerk of Cumberland County, and in March of the following year he became deputy clerk of Prince Edward County. Of this latter position he continued the incumbent until the death of his father in November, 1927, when he was appointed the latter's successor as county clerk of New Kent County, he having subsequently been reappointed for the full term of eight years. In this important office he is well upholding the prestige and honors of the family name, as is he also in all other relations of life. Mr. Harris, fortified by his experience as county clerk and clerk of the Circuit Court, is giving close attention to the study of law, and the year 1929 will record his examination for admission to the bar of his native state.

Mr. Harris is a stalwart in the local ranks of the Democratic party, his religious faith is that of the Baptist Church, he is affiliated with the Independent Order of Odd Fellows, and he is a popular and appreciative member of the Holtz Creek Fishing and Hunting Club. His name still appears on the roster of eligible young bachelors in his native county.

Thomas Newton Harris, father of the subject of this review, was one of the most honored citizens of New Kent County at the time of his death, November 11, 1927, when he was forty-eight years of age. His widow still resides at New Kent.

Thomas N. Harris had become deputy county clerk in 1896, and in 1900 became clerk as successor to his father, John N. Harris. The wife of John N. Harris was Octavia Dandridge

Magdalena Woodson

Christian, whose father and grandfather, Bartholomew D.
Christian and John D. Christian, respectively, had consecutively
served as county clerk for many years, and the office prior to
that had been held by members of the Dandridge family, including Bartholomew Dandridge, father of Mrs. John D. Christian,
and William Clayton, father of Mrs. Bartholomew Dandridge.
Thus this office has been practically in one family since the
period of the Revolutionary war.

JOSEPH FRANCIS WOODSON for over forty years was identified
with Richmond's industrial affairs, his career having been one
of substantial usefulness and service, and bringing him a wide
acquaintance and friendship.

He was born in Richmond January 3, 1855, and died in that
city in April, 1918. He was the only son of the three children
of Alexander R. and Mary Virginia (Foulkes) Woodson. His
father located at Pittsburgh, Pennsylvania, and in 1856 permanently settled at Richmond, where for many years he was in
business as a contractor.

Joseph Francis Woodson was educated in schools at Richmond and as a young man took employment in the Palmer Har-
sock Company. He was with that firm twenty years, until it
went out of business, being cashier when he retired. The remainder of his active business career was spent with the great
Tredegan Iron Works and the Portner Brewing Company of
Richmond.

Mr. Woodson was a Democrat, and he and his wife were
members of the Episcopal Church. He married in September,
1880, Miss Magdalena Keller, who was reared and educated in
Richmond. She was one of ten children of Charles and Magdalena Keller. Her father was a manufacturer of cabinet work in
Richmond. The Keller family came originally from Frankfort
on the Rhine in Germany.

Mrs. Woodson, who resides at 2106 Lakeview Avenue, was the
mother of four children, and the two now living are: Josephine
Pearl, wife of Robert R. Danforth, of Richmond, and mother of
two sons, named Nicholas Allen and Robert R., Jr., and Robert
A. Woodson, who is connected with the Chesapeake & Potomac
Telephone Company.

SYDNA L. JOHNSON is a Virginia newspaper man, publisher
and owner of the *Free State News* at Kenbridge, in Lunenburg
County.

Mr. Johnson, who was initiated into the mysteries of the
printing art at a very early age, was born in Brunswick County,
Virginia, December 3, 1887, son of N. E. and Madora E. (Bennett) Johnson, who were also natives of Brunswick County. His
father was in the Confederate army for a short time, and after
the war followed farming until his death in 1907. The mother
passed away in 1915.

Sydna L. Johnson was reared and educated in Brunswick
County, and served a thorough apprenticeship in the printing
trade and in the work of a newspaper office. He has come in
contact with the printing and business departments of a number
of newspapers. Mr. Johnson has been associated with the *Free
State News* at Kenbridge since 1912, at first as an employe, and
in 1917 he bought the paper.

His personal time and attention have been given to the *News*
ever since except for eighteen months while he was with the

colors during the World war. He was overseas and also with
the Army of Occupation in Germany. He received his honorable
discharge in May, 1919, and at once resumed the active management of the *Free State News*. This paper has a circulation of
1,200 copies, and the plant also handles a large volume of job
business.

Mr. Johnson married, November 12, 1919, Miss Lucy May
Andrews, daughter of J. E. and Betty (Smith) Andrews, natives
of Mecklenburg County, where her father is a well-to-do farmer.
Mr. and Mrs. Johnson have two children: Jack Clayton, born
December 12, 1924, and Ann Harris, born September 12, 1926.
Mr. Johnson is town clerk of Kenbridge, is a member of the
Masonic fraternity and the Knights of Pythias, is a Democrat
and a Baptist.

HON. VINCENT L. SEXTON. A member of the Virginia bar
for more than thirty-five years, Hon. Vincent L. Sexton, senior
member of the firm of Sexton & Sexton of Bluefield, is the representative of large and important interests, and during his long
and distinguished career has been the recipient of a number of
honors, admittedly earning the right to be accorded a position
of leadership among the talented and thoroughly reliable
attorneys of the county of Tazewell.

Mr. Sexton was born in Smyth County, Virginia, September
1, 1868, and is a son of Thomas K. and Freelove Elizabeth
(Thomas) Sexton. He traces his ancestry back to his great-
great-great-great-great-great-grandfather, James Sexton, of
Limerick, Ireland, who moved to Great Britain and there
resided during the rest of his life. The son of James Sexton was
George Sexton, Sr., who was born in Great Britain and came
to this country in 1662, being related to Thomas Sexton, a well
known figure in the early life of Boston, Massachusetts. George
Sexton, Sr., purchased land on the Warranoke River at Westfield, Connecticut, from Thomas Cowper, and the deed, dated
June 10, 1663, is recorded on p. 33, vol. 1, of the records of
deeds at Springfield, Massachusetts. Mr. Sexton, who is called
George Sexton, Sr., of Windsor in the *History of the Colonies
of Connecticut*, first went to Westfield, Connecticut, but did not
take up his abode there until 1668. His time was divided between Windsor, Hartford and Boston, and it is thought that his
business was that of a trader. He held the office of "public
viewer," shown by the records February 5, 1677, and again
March 5, 1678-79, and December 9, 1686, was chosen by Select-
man Thomas Noble to appraise the buildings of the town. He
was a good citizen and highly educated man, and died intestate in
1690, his fourth son, Joseph Sexton, being appointed administrator of his estate. The records show that his wife, Catherine,
was connected with the church in 1690.

George Sexton, Jr., son of George Sexton, Sr., and great-
great-great-great-grandfather of Hon. Vincent L. Sexton, was
born in England in 1656, and was about six years of age when
brought to America by his parents. His wife, Hannah, was
born at Westfield, Connecticut, September 19, 1658. He moved
with his father to Huntington, Long Island, and signed a quit-
claim deed to his father's estate January 25, 1689. It is evident
that he either returned to England or was lost at sea, as he was
never heard from afterward. The great-great-great-grandfather of Vincent L. Sexton, Charles Sexton, was born September 9, 1680, at Westfield, Connecticut, subsequently moved to

Huntington, Long Island, and later to Hopewell, New Jersey, where he became the owner of a very large estate and died in 1752. In his will, made in 1751, he mentions his wife, Sarah, but her last name is unknown. Their son, Joseph Sexton, the great-great-grandfather of Vincent L. Sexton, was born at Huntington, Long Island, January 4, 1730, and February 4, 1754, married Phebe Campbell, a daughter of Thomas Campbell, of Long Island. She was born May 5, 1734, and died in Wythe County, Virginia, February 14, 1830.

The first of the Sexton family to move to Virginia was Thomas Campbell Sexton. He was born June 8, 1764, in New Jersey, in which state he married Charity Current, and then settled in Smyth County, Virginia, where he became a successful planter and reared a family of nine children. Among these was Aaron Sexton, who was born in that county April 3, 1793, spent his life as a planter, and died October 16, 1851. On January 11, 1816, he married Margaret Ann Feely, of Frederick County, Virginia, who was born in July, 1795, but the date of whose death has been lost. Thomas K. Sexton, the father of Vincent L. Sexton, was born in Frederick County, Virginia, April 11, 1821, and during his career was engaged in general merchandising and agricultural operations in Frederick and Smyth counties, in the latter of which he died November 21, 1891. He was a Democrat in his political convictions, was fraternally affiliated with the Independent Order of Odd Fellows, and his religious connection was with the Presbyterian Church, in which he was a member of the Board of Elders. On December 15, 1847, Mr. Sexton married Freelove Elizabeth Thomas, who was born about 1829, and died in January, 1874.

Vincent L. Sexton attended public schools, following which he became a student in Emory and Henry College. His educational career was interrupted at this time by the final illness of his father, and he returned to his home, where he remained in charge of the elder man's estate until about two years prior to the latter's death. Going then to Marion, he took up the study of law in the office of Capt. Preston Sheffy, and in 1892 attended the University of Virginia, where he studied under Hon. John B. Minor, professor of law at the university. In 1893 he was admitted to practice after examination before Hon. John A. Kelly, judge of the Circuit Court at Marion, and Hon. Robert A. Richardson of the Supreme Court of Virginia, and in the same year took up his residence at Tazewell, where he remained until 1901. The following two years were passed at Pocahontas, and he then sent his family back to Tazewell, although continuing to maintain his office at Pocahontas until 1918. In 1907 he took his nephew into partnership, and in 1907 moved his family to Graham, this state. Three years later he opened an office at Bluefield, West Virginia, although continuing his office at Pocahontas. This latter was changed to Bluefield in 1918, and here he has since been in charge. For a time his nephew, Mr. Roberts, was in charge of the office at Bluefield, West Virginia, but in 1926 the partnership was dissolved, and Mr. Sexton took in his son, Vincent L. Sexton, Jr., the firm since having been located at Bluefield, Virginia, engaged in the general practice of law as Sexton & Sexton.

As one of the strong and capable lawyers of the state Mr. Sexton has been identified with much important litigation and is attorney for the Graham Land and Improvement Company, of which he is also a member of the Board of Directors; the

Graham Manufacturing Company; and the Bluefield (West Virginia) Office Building Company, of which he is also vice president and a member of the Board of Directors. Since becoming a member of the Virginia State Bar Association, in 1903, he has been a member of many important committees, and belongs also to the American Bar Association, the Sigma Alpha Epsilon and the Virginia Omicron at the University of Virginia. He has been a member of the Independent Order of Odd Fellows since 1895. An active Democrat in his political affiliation, he served as chairman of the County Central Committee for several years, in 1897 was elected mayor of Tazewell and in 1910 was elected mayor of Graham (now Bluefield). With his family he belongs to the Presbyterian Church.

On April 23, 1895, Mr. Sexton was united in marriage with Miss Leola Alderson, of Tazewell, a member of one of the oldest and most distinguished families of Virginia, and a daughter of Col. Henry C. and Mary (Chapman) Alderson, the former of whom is deceased. Mrs. Sexton, who was educated in the public schools of Tazewell and under private instructors, has always been active in the work of the Presbyterian Church. To Mr. and Mrs. Sexton there have been born seven children. Henry, the eldest, is a graduate of the high school at Bluefield. In July, 1918, he enlisted in the Marine Corps at Washington, D. C., and was sent overseas as a corporal in the Eleventh Regiment, U. S. M. C., with which he saw service in France and was with the Army of Occupation in Germany. Upon his return to the United States he married Miss Margaret Lammers, of Bramwell, West Virginia, and then studied law at the University of Richmond, graduated and was admitted to practice. For about one year he was located at Bluefield, Virginia, and then moved to Bluefield, West Virginia, where he has since been engaged successfully in the practice of his profession. Thomas Kennedy Sexton, the second son, graduated from high school, and volunteered for service at the age of eighteen years in the same company as his brother, Henry A. Sexton. They enlisted about five days apart and were assigned to different regiments, but their father was able to get them into the same command through the aid of U. S. Senator Swanson of Virginia, and the brothers, both athletes, played on the army football team while in France. While there Thomas K. Sexton enjoyed a course of study at Berne University, and upon his return entered the University of Virginia, after his graduation from which he married Miss Nellie Estes, of Roanoke, Virginia, and they now reside at Cornice, West Virginia, where Mr. Sexton has a position with the Pocahontas Coal Company. Vincent L. Sexton, Jr., third son and child, is a graduate of the Graham High School and took his law degree at the University of Virginia and William and Mary College. He was admitted to practice July 1, 1925, and now is junior member of the firm of Sexton & Sexton, with his father, at Bluefield, Virginia. Miss Mamie Loise, eldest daughter and fourth child, is a graduate of the high school at Graham and the State Normal School at Farmville, Virginia, and is now engaged in teaching school at Rocky Mount, North Carolina. Miss Nancy Elizabeth Sexton is a graduate of Graham High School and a member of the senior class at William and Mary College; and William Chapman Sexton and Freelove Katheryn Sexton are members, respectively, of the junior and sophomore classes in high school.

WILLIAM CHARLES SMITH

WILLIAM CHARLES SMITH. From a period before the Civil war until recent years one of the most important industries of the city of Richmond was the carriage manufacturing establishment carried on by members of the Smith family.

One of the active men in this business was the late William C. Smith, who was born at Richmond in 1841 and died in that city in January, 1917. He was one of the four children of W. C. and Mary (Scott) Smith. His father was a carriage manufacturer, founder and proprietor for many years of the W. C. Smith Carriage Manufacturing Company, and was also one of the prominent citizens of Richmond in his time.

William C. Smith, Jr., was educated in private schools at Richmond before the war, and as a young man became associated with his father's manufacturing business. After the death of his father he carried it on individually and subsequently established a similar business of his own.

He married, October 12, 1866, Maria Louisa Locknane, of Richmond, where she was reared and educated. Her parents were John Marshall and Margaret (McNivin) Locknane, her father a planter. She had one brother, John Marshall Locknane, who became a well known Richmond contractor.

Mrs. Smith, who resides at 2515 Fifth Avenue in Richmond, is the mother of two children. Her son, Howard Marshall, was educated in Richmond and graduated from the University of Maryland. He married Edith Damon, of Connecticut, and has two children, Miss Norma Elizabeth and Miss Edith Marshall. Mrs. Smith's daughter, Lelia Scott, is the wife of Horace G. Buchanan, a Richmond attorney. Mr. and Mrs. Buchanan have two sons: Horace G. II, who married Miss Michaux Frances and has two sons, Horace G. III and William Michaux; and William Tazwell, who is now commonwealth attorney of Goochland County, Virginia, secretary of the First Baptist Church and affiliated with the Masonic fraternity and Knights of Pythias.

BENJAMIN THOMAS FISHER grew up on the Eastern Shore, learned the printing trade when a boy, and since 1912 has been editor and publisher of the *Eastern Shore Herald* at Eastville.

He was born at Locustville, in Accomac County, May 15, 1879, son of James A. and Sue E. (Addison) Fisher, both natives of Northampton County. His father was a lieutenant in the Confederate army. He owned and operated a farm in Accomac County, and for many years was in the lighthouse service in both Accomac and Northampton counties, and held the office of commissioner of revenue for Northampton County and also served as sheriff of the same county. He died April 2, 1892, and his wife in March, 1924.

Benjamin Thomas Fisher was reared and educated in Northampton County, attended public and private schools, and left school to learn the printing trade. He had a journeyman's experience on a number of newspapers prior to 1912, when he acquired the *Eastern Shore Herald*. The *Herald* is a member of the Virginia Press Association, and approximately 2,500 copies of every issue are distributed throughout Northampton and adjacent counties. Mr. Fisher also does a large amount of commercial printing.

He married, in June, 1910, Miss Ruth A. Tyler, daughter of John S. Tyler, who was born in Accomac County and was a Confederate soldier, and after the war was in business as a merchant, and at one time was candidate for governor of Virginia on the Prohibition ticket. He died in 1924. Mr. and Mrs. Fisher have four children: Ann Walston, Mary Rose, James Tyler and Nora.

Mr. Fisher is a citizen who has been alive to his responsibilities in the community. He takes an active part in the Democratic party, is owner of some farming interests, and for some time served as commissioner of wrecks. He is a Baptist, and Mrs. Fisher is a member of the United Daughters of the Confederacy.

JAMES HENRY FITTS, who died July 24, 1893, was a well known Virginian. He served as a lieutenant in the United States Navy, and after resigning from the navy he spent a number of years as member of the faculty of the Virginia Polytechnic Institute at Blacksburg.

Mr. Fitts married, June 7, 1883, Mary Mayo Blair, who survives him and resides in Richmond, at 3216 Hawthorne Avenue. She is now the widow of Samuel H. Hawes. By her marriage with Lieutenant Fitts there are two children.

The son, John Blair Fitts, was educated in Richmond schools, graduated from Hampden-Sidney College, the Medical College of Virginia, the Boston Children's Hospital and the Massachusetts General Hospital. He is an orthopedic surgeon of high attainments. He was a first lieutenant in France for twenty-two months during the World war. Doctor Fitts married Marion E. Manthius, of Massachusetts, and has four children, Maryetta, John Blair Jr., Ruth Morton and James Henry V.

The second son, Francis Moylan Fitts, was educated in Hampden-Sidney College, the Richmond School of Medicine, spent some time in the Roosevelt Hospital at New York, and in 1916 enlisted in a French Ambulance Corps. In 1917, on returning home, he joined the Regular Army with the rank of first lieutenant in the Medical Corps and subsequently was promoted to major and remained in the service until 1922. He was sent to Poland on typhus relief and for a time was with the Army of Occupation at Coblentz, Germany. He married, April 11, 1922, at Nancy, France, Marie Janet Crousier.

JOHN H. COLE commonwealth's attorney of Sussex County, is a member of the law firm Cocke & Cole at Stony Creek. His partner is his uncle, William B. Cocke, former state senator and member of a family that has been prominent in the legal profession in Virginia for several generations.

John H. Cole was born at Norfolk, Virginia, August 25, 1895, son of Frank W. and Sue (Cocke) Cole, his father a native of Greenville County and his mother of Sussex County. Both the Cocke and Cole families came to Virginia about 1732. His grandfather, John Cole, operated the first hotel at Petersburg, Virginia, known as the old Jarratt Hotel. This hotel occupied part of the site of the present Atlantic Coast Line Railway Station. John Cole also conducted a stage coach line between Petersburg and Richmond. Frank W. Cole was in the insurance business at Richmond for a number of years, he died in November, 1917, and his wife passed away in December, 1907. She was a daughter of Judge Charles L. Cocke, of Sussex County.

John H. Cole was reared and educated in Sussex County, graduating from high school in 1914. In order to support himself while preparing for the law he learned stenography and was employed in an office at Richmond while atending night classes in law. He also studied at the University of Virginia and also had instruction in law from his grandfather, Judge Cocke, and his uncle, Senator William Cocke. Mr. Cole was admitted to the bar in December, 1920, and since that date has been in practice at Stony Creek. The firm has a very extensive practice in all the courts.

Mr. Cole was elected commonwealth's attorney for Sussex County August 2, 1927. For several years he was judge of the Juvenile and Domestic Relations Court of Sussex and Surry counties and for several years was recorder and treasurer for the town of Stony Creek. During the World war period he was deputy clerk of court in Surry County. He enlisted for service during the war but was rejected on account of weight and heighth.

Mr. Cole married, October 9, 1925, Miss Louise T. Clements, daughter of Rev. P. H. and Cora (Coffee) Clements, both natives of Amherst County, Virginia. Her father is a minister of the Methodist Episcopal Church, South, and has completed a four year pastorate at Stony Creek Church. Mr. and Mrs. Cole have one daughter, Harriett Louise, born November 12, 1926. Mr. Cole is worshipful master of Edwards Lodge No. 308, A. F. and A. M., at Stony Creek and a member of the Modern Woodmen of America, is a Democrat in politics and belongs to the Episcopal Church.

JAMES NOAH GREEAR, physician and surgeon at Saint Paul, has been in that community of Wise County nearly all his life. His diploma as a doctor of medicine was not merely a key to unlock the door of material prosperity, but did unlock a door of great service to his fellow men, and the riches and honors of service have been more important than material rewards with this good and kindly doctor, who at the age of sixty-nine is still constant and diligent in his chosen work. He is going and coming night and day in the performance of his duties throughout the country around Saint Paul.

Doctor Greear was born near Coeburn, Wise County, February 27, 1859, and is a descendant of William Greear, an Englishman who settled in Loudoun County, Virginia, in Colonial times. He was named for his grandfather, Noah Greear, a native of Grayson County, Virginia, a farmer in that county and in Scott County. Doctor Greear's father, Francis B. Greear, was born in Grayson County, June 22, 1819, and as a youth came under the influence of a famous educator, James Hagan. He himself became a teacher, working in private schools in Scott and Grayson counties until 1851, and then took up farming. For many years he lived in the Coeburn community, dividing his time between his farm and a school. During the Civil war he was a Union Democrat, and afterwards became a Republican. For many years he held the office of magistrate. Francis B. Greear died February 21, 1908. He married, in 1851, Miss Sarah Mullens, who died in 1852, and in 1854 he married Priscilla Stallard. She was born in Scott County in 1828, and died March 31, 1905.

James Noah Greear was one of a family of eight children. He grew up on the homestead farm near Coeburn, attended private and public schools, graduated from the Abingdon District High School in 1880 and pursued his medical studies at the University of Virginia. He was graduated with the class of 1883, and during 1884-85 continued his training in the New York Polyclinic School of Medicine, to which he later returned as a student in 1890-91. Doctor Greear first practiced at Bickley Mills, later known as Castlewood, from 1892 to 1895 had his home at Toms Creek in Wise County, and since 1895 has been at Saint Paul. He has conducted a general practice, and in point of continuous service is now one of the oldest physicians in this section of Virginia. He is a member of the Medical Society of Virginia.

Doctor Greear is a Democrat, has been a trustee of the Methodist Episcopal Church, and is affiliated with the Masonic fraternity. He married, June 17, 1886, Miss Bessie E. Earnest, daughter of Isaac and Victoria (Burts) Earnest. She was educated in Martha Washington College at Abingdon and the Asheville Female College at Asheville, North Carolina. Doctor and Mrs. Greear had ten children, and two of the sons were with the colors at the time of the World war. Gertrude Gerster, the oldest child, married Howard Martin, a civil engineer. Dora Cabell married N. D. Spinedon, an electrical engineer. Ashby Virginia became the wife of Clifford McCall, a cotton buyer. Frances Norvell married Berkeley S. Gillespie, a civil engineer and road contractor. James Noah, Jr., the oldest son, graduated from the University of Virginia School of Medicine in 1920, during the World war was in the Medical Reserve Corps while a student at the university, and has specialized in eye, ear, nose and throat practice. Helen Louise, the sixth child, died at the age of two years and one month. Frederick Bonham volunteered in April, 1918, was in training with the Tank Corps, went to France in August, 1918, and received his honorable discharge in May, 1919. He took the law course at the University of Virginia. The younger children are: Lynn Earnest, Burton Mayre and Mary Elizabeth.

HON. RICHARD MASON MCCARTY, commissioner of revenue of Fauquier County, had an honorable business record behind him when he was elected to his present office which showed earnest effort, useful endeavor and constructive accomplishment. A man of stainless character, upright and able, he is well fitted to handle the problems of his present position, and the interests of his constituents are in safe hands. He was born in Loudoun County, Virginia, February 19, 1879, a son of Richard C. and Martha (Megeath) McCarty, both of whom were born in Loudoun County. During the war between the states the father served in Company K, Sixth Virginia Cavalry, and when peace was declared he returned home and patiently took up the burdens of the reconstruction period, and was engaged in farming the remainder of his useful and honorable life, dying in Fauquier County, to which section he had moved in 1881, the date of his death being April, 1921. The mother died many years before him, passing away in 1897.

Given the advantages offered by the local schools of Fauquier County and the Cleveland High School, a private institution where he spent two years, Richard Mason McCarty is well educated, and has added to this early training by close observation and contact with men of affairs. Until he was of age he remained on the farm with his parents, but after he reached his majority he went to Delaplane, Virginia, and for seven years was bookkeeper for Delaplane Brothers, and when he left their employ he remained in the place for seventeen years more,

Mary H. Powell.

engaged in the mercantile business. In 1920 he came to Warrenton, and for seven years thereafter successfully conducted a flourishing automobile business, but when he was elected in November, 1927, commissioner of revenue for Fauquier County, for a term of four years, he disposed of those interests so as to devote all of his time to the duties of his office.

On October 20, 1917, Mr. McCarty married Miss Katherine McCarty, a daughter of Dennis and Katherine (Blackmore) McCarty, natives of Fauquier County. Dennis McCarty was a life long farmer of Farquier County until his retirement, since which time he has lived at Delaplane. His wife died in 1917. Mr. and Mrs. McCarty of this review have one child, Katherine, who was born March 19, 1919. While at Delaplane Mr. McCarty served on the school board, having been elected to it on the Democratic ticket, and he was a regular candidate of his party when he was elected to his present office. He belongs to Ashby Lodge No. 232, A. F. and A. M., Markham, Virginia; Fauquier Chapter No. 25, R. A. M.; Piedmont Commandery No. 26, K. T., the last two connections being maintained at The Plains, Virginia; and Acca Temple, A. A. O. N. M. S., Richmond. Through his father's gallant service in the cavalry he holds membership in the Sons of Confederate Veterans. In religious faith he is an Episcopalian. The McCarty residence in Warrenton is one of the most desirable homes of the city, and here Mr. and Mrs. McCarty entertain their many friends with true Southern hospitality.

EDWARD WARREN POWELL was a successful business man of Richmond who began taking an active part in the commercial affairs of the city about the close of the war and reconstruction era, and gave the city its business leadership during the last quarter of the past century.

He was born in Henrico County, February 23, 1851, and died at Richmond, November 5, 1901, a son of George Warren and Mary (Allen) Powell.

The late Mr. Powell attended school in Henrico County, and his first training in commercial lines was in the grocery business. He was identified with the grocery business more or less actively the greater part of his life, and also for many years was interested in the ice, wood and coal business. He became prosperous, but did not give all his time exclusively to trade. He was much interested in local politics as a Democrat and served three terms as county supervisor. Mr. Powell was for forty-three years a member of the Grace Street Baptist Church at Richmond. He was a charter member of the Chosen Friends, and belonged to the Knights of Honor.

His first wife was Woody C. Walton, and by that union there were eight children. On February 10, 1886, he married Mary Hood Joynes, of Richmond, where she was educated in the Miss Griffin's School. Mrs. Powell, who survives him and resides at 2016 West Main Street, is a daughter of John L. and Catherine S. (Floyd) Joynes. Her father, John L. Joynes, served four years in General Lee's army during the war between the states, and died in 1871. For many years he was in business as a grocer. Mrs. Powell's uncle, Joseph Walker Floyd, was a South Carolina planter, and during the war lost his right arm in action. After the war he became a lieutenant governor of South Carolina and lived at Liberty Hill, South Carolina. J. Walker Floyd married Hattie Pittis and had five children. Mrs. Powell is a sister of William Henry Joynes, chief of the fire department of Richmond, and another brother is Joseph Berry Floyd Joynes, a merchant at Newport News. Mrs. Powell has six children: Bessie L. is the wife of G. F. Burton, of Richmond, and has two children, named G. F., Jr., and Mary Elizabeth; the second daughter is Miss Ruby B.; Margarette F. married Robert C. Toler, and has a son, Robert Warren; Louis Ayres Powell, connected with the Western Union Telegraph Company, is married and has two sons, Louis A., Jr., and Joseph Mann; Violet E. Powell married Arthur E. Christian, and their children are Arthur E., Jr., and Nell Winfry; Grace Elizabeth, the youngest of the family, is the wife of Terry V. Snow.

CORA STANWOOD DARDEN. Darden's Preparatory School in Portsmouth has for its principal a woman who has given her life to educational work—Cora Stanwood Darden. Mrs. Darden has had remarkable success in preparing youth for higher institutions of learning.

Her father, Robert Stanwood, a beloved and honored citizen of Portsmouth, was the grandson of Deacon Samuel Stanwood, of Brunswick, Maine.

Samuel Stanwood, the son of Deacon Samuel Stanwood and father of Robert Stanwood, was a navigator and captain of merchant vessels which sailed to all parts of the world.

Sophie Anne Edwards, the mother of Robert Stanwood, was the daughter of Oney Edwards, of Portsmouth.

Ephraim Stanwood, a great-great-uncle, of Brunswick, Maine, was a veteran of the War of 1812.

Mrs. Darden's mother, Martha Vaughan, was the daughter of Jack Vaughan and Martha Lee, of Nansemond County. The Vaughans were among the early Colonial settlers. Martha Lee was the daughter of Henry Lee and Betsy Pipkin, of Gates County, North Carolina. Henry Lee was a soldier of the Revolutionary war.

The twelve sons and daughters of this family grew to be men and women of outstanding ability.

No descendant of more real worth came from the Lee family than the granddaughter, Martha Vaughan Stanwood, who lived to honor her family until her eighty-fifth year. A woman of magnificent spirit and courage! A real heritage to her descendants is the life of this splendid woman.

Samuel James Stanwood, the only surviving son of Robert and Martha Vaughan Stanwood, is a veteran of the Spanish-American war.

Mrs. Darden was educated in Mrs. Jenkins' Classical School in Portsmouth. She has taken extension work from Harvard University, Wake Forest College, William and Mary College and the University of Virginia. She taught in the public schools of Nansemond and Norfolk counties, Virginia, and Hertford County, North Carolina. Later she taught mathematics in the following schools: Franklin Seminary, Virginia; Martin College, Tennessee; Logan College, Kentucky; Grenada College, Mississippi.

Paul Fisher Darden and Cora Lee Stanwood were married at the home of her brother-in-law and sister, Mr. and Mrs. Richard Beaman, in Nansemond County June 28, 1905.

The Dardens came in Colonial times and settled in the forks of the Nottoway and Blackwater rivers, now a part of Southampton County.

Paul Fisher Darden, who was born near Murfreesboro, North Carolina, in 1865, was a great-grandson of Jacob Darden, one of the pioneer Baptist preachers of Virginia. Jacob Darden represented his people as a member of the Virginia Assembly and was the founder of two Baptist Churches—prosperous churches today—the Meherrin and the Murfreesboro churches.

Paul Darden was the grandson of William Darden and Jane Jenkins and the son of George Darden and Missouri Eley, of Hertford County, North Carolina. George Darden was a Confederate veteran.

Paul Darden was educated at Coal Spring Academy, Hertford County. He worked for the Camp Manufacturing Company for many years. He received his training in civil engineering in North Carolina State College. As an engineer his work for the Camp Manufacturing Company continued throughout his life. He served as city engineer of Suffolk and county engineer of Southampton.

During the World war Paul Darden served his country loyally by the work he performed daily in the Norfolk Navy Yard. He died in San Angelo, Texas, in December, 1920.

After her marriage Mrs. Darden retired from formal educational work but later she began individual instruction in mathematics and English.

During the World war Mrs. Darden instructed two hundred young men in mathematics—these men, who represented twenty-three states, were enlisted in the United States Navy. Because of the skill shown in training these men Mrs. Darden received the highest commendation from the secretary of the navy.

Mrs. Darden has splendid success in training young men for the annual entrance examinations to the United States Naval Academy at Annapolis, Maryland.

Mrs. Darden is a member of the City School Board, the Business and Professional Woman's Club, League of Women Voters, Housewives League, National Education Association, League of Administrative Women in Education, Park View W. C. T. U. and Court Street Baptist Church.

A. BERKELEY CARRINGTON, an outstanding representative of the great tobacco interests centered at Danville, is a descendant of the distinguished Carrington family, which in various branches and through the services of individuals has exerted a continuous influence in the affairs of the state since early Colonial times.

He was born in Farmville, Virginia, January 27, 1862, son of Rev. A. B. and Fannie (Venable) Carrington, and grandson of Paul S. Carrington, all native Virginians. His father was educated at Washington College; served four years as chaplain in Gen. Stonewall Jackson's Corps; gave almost a lifetime to the service of the Presbyterian Church; and died in 1912, at the age of seventy-seven.

A. Berkeley Carrington lived in Charlotte County Virginia, from his infancy until he was sixteen years of age, obtaining a public school education.

In 1878, at the age of sixteen, he came to Danville to live with his uncle, the late Paul C. Venable, who was engaged in the tobacco business at that time. He has made a notable success in business through his industry and persevering attention to a rising scale of responsibilities. Since 1890 he has been with Dibrell Brothers, Inc., and president of that corporation since

1915.　This is one of the largest of Virginia's great tobacco companies.　Colonel Carrington is president of the Tobacco Association of the United States.

He is a director of the First National Bank of Danville, is a former president of the Chamber of Commerce and of the City Council of Danville, is a member of the Board of Trustees of Hampden-Sidney College, is a York and Scottish Rite Mason and Shriner, and was president of the Masonic Building Corporation when the Masonic Temple was erected at Danville.　He is a Presbyterian.

He married, in 1891, Mary Taylor, daughter of Albert G. and Eliza (Burks) Taylor.　They have three children, A. Berkeley Jr., Charles Venable and Mary Taylor.　Colonel Carrington held the rank of colonel on the staff of Governor Montague.

HARRY BURNS TRUNDLE, general manager of the *Danville Register and Bee,* has been a newspaper man practically all his life and has had thirty years of active connection with the daily press of Danville.

He was born in Frederick County, Maryland, December 26, 1875, and is descended from a family that came to America from England during the 1700s, settling on the eastern shore of Maryland, but chiefly at Carroll's Manor, in Frederick County, Maryland.　Mr. Trundle's great-grandmother was Mary Burns, a niece of the Scotch poet, Robert Burns.　Mr. Trundle is a son of Joseph H. and Emily Baker (Thomas) Trundle.　His father was reared and educated in Frederick County, was a soldier of the Confederacy with the Thirty-fifth Virginia Cavalry and Col. Elijah B. White of Loudoun County, and participated in battles in the Valley of Virginia, at Gettysburg and elsewhere during the last three years of the war.　After the war he became a Maryland farmer and subsequently was in the passenger service of the Baltimore & Ohio Railway Company until he retired.　He died in August, 1925, and his widow is now seventy-six and resides at Frederick.　He was born and reared in that county, attended private schools and has been a lifelong member of the Episcopal Church.　Her parents were Charles Edward and Elizabeth (Dutrow) Thomas.　Harry Burns Trundle was the second in a family of three children.　Her sister Emily Maud is the widow of John Wood, Jr., who was an attorney at Frederick, Maryland.　The other sister, Miss Bertha Thomas Trundle, lives in Frederick.

Harry Burns Trundle was educated in public and private schools at Frederick, and immediately after leaving school took up newspaper work, spending several years with the *Frederick Daily News.*　In 1899, when he was twenty-four years of age, he joined the office of the *Daily Bee* at Danville, then published by Col. Al Fairbrother.　In May, 1900, the late R. A. James acquired the *Bee,* having previously acquired the *Register,* and since that date Mr. Trundle has been associated with these two publications, and for many years has been general manager. The only intervals to his service with these papers, the only daily publications in Danville, was one year while he was in the advertising business at Atlanta, Georgia, and six months while he was publishing the *Journal* at Manassas, Virginia.

Mr. Trundle is a director of the Danville Chamber of Commerce, is a director of the Mutual Building & Loan Association and is a past exalted ruler of the Danville Lodge of Elks and a member of the Grand Lodge.　For several years he was also

much interested in the work of the Kiwanis Club. In Masonry he is affiliated with Marotock Lodge No. 210, A. F. and A. M., and Euclid Chapter of Royal Arch Masons. He is a director from the Fifth Congressional District to the Virginia Press Association and is a member of the Southern Newspaper Publishers Association. Mr. Trundle is a Democrat, and for a number of years was a member of the vestry of the Episcopal Church and a teacher in Sunday school.

He married at Danville, September 19, 1900, Miss Eloise Redd Arrington. She attended public school at Danville and Chatham Episcopal Institute. She has an active part in church work, is a member of the Virginia Society of Colonial Dames and the Daughters of the American Revolution and is former historian of the local chapter of the United Daughters of the Confederacy. Her father, Christopher Arrington, was a merchant in Danville, where he died at a comparatively early age. Her mother, Ann Marshall (Dillard) Arrington, resides at Danville. Mr. and Mrs. Trundle had four children: Wilson Burns, Dillard Arrington (who died in infancy), Joseph White and Ann Dillard Trundle. Wilson Burns Trundle was educated at Danville and in 1923 graduated from the United States Naval Academy at Annapolis, was commissioned a lieutenant in the Marine Corps and later was attached to the Aviation Corps. In January, 1929, he resigned to become chief pilot of the United States Air Transport at Washington. Joseph White Trundle attended private and public schools at Danville, and is now taking the pre-law course at the University of Virginia. The only daughter is a senior in the George Washington High School at Danville.

Mr. Trundle was elected president of the Virginia Press Association at the forty-first annual convention held at Danville July 18-20, 1929.

THOMAS OVERTON MOSS is one of the representative younger members of the bar of Richmond, the fair old capital city of his native state, has the rank of lieutenant commander of the Reserve Corps of the United States Navy, was in overseas service in the World war, and is now an aide-de-camp on the military staff of the governor of Virginia.

Mr. Moss was born in Hanover County, Virginia, in 1893, and in this state likewise were born his parents, Thomas O. and Nina (Wood) Moss. After having completed higher academic studies in Hampden-Sidney College, Mr. Moss became a student in the law department of Richmond College, in which he was graduated as a member of the Virginia bar. After receiving his degree of Bachelor of Laws he was engaged in the practice of his profession in Richmond until the nation entered the World war, in the spring of 1917. He forthwith volunteered for service in the United States Navy, in which he rose from the rank of seaman to that of ensign and finally won promotion to a junior lieutenancy. He was in active service on the French coast, and after remaining overseas nine months he was assigned to the United States Naval Academy as a student. After the close of the war he received his honorable discharge and was made a reserve officer of the United States Navy, in which he now has the rank of lieutenant commander, he having been the youngest officer of this rank in the reserve body of the navy at the time he was advanced to the office. By appointment by Governor Byrd he is now a member of the military staff of

Virginia's chief executive. After receiving his honorable discharge Mr. Moss resumed his law practice in Richmond, and his ability and personal popularity have enabled him to build up a very substantial and representative law business in the capital city.

Mr. Moss has received the thirty-second degree of the Scottish Rite of the Masonic fraternity, besides being a Noble of the Mystic Shrine, and he is a popular member of the University Club in his home city, besides which he is a member of the Virginia State Board of Accountancy. He married Miss Virginia Johnson, of Halifax County, this state, and they reside at 205 South Boulevard. The law office of Mr. Moss is maintained in the building of the State-Planters Bank.

REV. WILLIAM JACKSON MORTON, D. D., has for twenty-seven years been pastor of the church at Alexandria in which George Washington worshiped, and which for this and many other associations has become one of the patriotic shrines in the district around Washington. Doctor Morton is admirably qualified for this pastorate, a man of thorough learning, a zealous church man, and descended from and related to some of the oldest and most distinguished families of Northern Virginia.

He was born at "Soldier's Rest," in Orange County, Virginia, May 8, 1867, only son of Dr. Charles Bruce and Caroline May (Dickenson) Morton. His grandfather, Dr. George Morton, was one of four brothers, all of whom achieved more than ordinary distinction, William Morton serving for many years in the Virginia Legislature, Jackson Morton, one of the outstanding men of Florida in the territorial and statehood periods, representing Florida in the United States Senate, and Jeremiah Morton represented Virginia in Congress and was a member of the Secession Convention of Virginia. Dr. George Morton graduated from William and Mary College, from the University of Pennsylvania School of Medicine in 1823, and practiced his profession in Orange County, where he married Elizabeth Williams, whose ancestry included the Bruces of Orange.

Their son, Dr. Charles Bruce Morton, was born in Orange County September 3, 1835, and is now in his ninety-third year. He was educated at the University of Virginia, graduated from the Jefferson Medical College of Philadelphia in March, 1860, and during the war was senior surgeon of Kemper's Brigade, Pickett's Division. He practiced his profession for many years after the war, and then retired to his farm, "Nottingham Farm," near Fredericksburg, where he resides today.

Dr. Charles Bruce Morton married, in 1866, Caroline May Dickenson. She was born May 19, 1840, daughter of William I. and Jane Richard (Buckner) Dickenson, granddaughter of James and Sallie Dickenson, and through her mother a descendant of John Buckner, whose descendants have been distinguished in the history of the Colony and State of Virginia and in several southern and western states.

William Jackson Morton was prepared for college by private tutors, attended Richmond College in 1882-84, for two years assisted his father on the farm, and then entered the Theological Seminary of Virginia, near Alexandria, graduating in 1891. He was ordained a deacon June 26, 1891, and to the priesthood June 24, 1892. For nine months he was rector of St. George's Chapel at North Danville, was assistant rector of St. James at Richmond from June, 1892, to February, 1894, was rector of Epiphany Church at Knoxville, Tennessee, until October 1, 1896, rector of South Farnham Parish in Essex County, Virginia, 1896-1900, and rector of Emanuel Church at Harrisonburg until 1902. Doctor Morton accepted the call to the historic Christ Church at Alexandria in 1902, and to the service of his parish and its people he has given the best years of his life.

Outside of his home parish he has acted as a trustee of Stuart Hall at Staunton, trustee of the Protestant Episcopal Education Society of Virginia, trustee of the Diocesan Missionary Society, chaplain of the National George Washington Memorial Association. He has been chaplain of Alexandria-Washington Lodge No. 22, A. F. and A. M., and Mount Vernon Chapter, Royal Arch Masons. He is a member of the Sons of the Revolution, is a Phi Delta Theta and a Democrat.

He married, April 11, 1893, Dorothea Ashby Moncure, daughter of Powhatan and Dorothea (Ashby) Moncure, of Stafford County, Virginia, and a niece of Gen. Turner Ashby, a famous Confederate cavalryman who was killed June 6, 1862, and whose brother, Col. Richard Ashby, also gave up his life for the Southern cause. Mrs. Morton is a descendant of Capt. Thomas Ashby, who settled in Fauquier County in the early seventeen hundreds.

Doctor and Mrs. Morton had five children. Charles Bruce Morton, born January 10, 1900, is now assistant professor of surgery in the University of Virginia. William Jackson Morton, Jr., born September 2, 1902, graduated from West Point Military Academy in 1923, is now first lieutenant of the Field Artillery and assigned duty as an instructor in the military academy at West Point. Powhatan Moncure, born December 10, 1903, graduated from West Point Military Academy in June, 1928. The two daughters are Dorothea Ashby, born November 22, 1905, and Caroline Fitzhugh, born April 11, 1910. Dorothea attended Stuart Hall at Staunton and is now the wife of John Armistead Deming, of Baltimore, a Baltimore realtor. Mr. and Mrs. Deming were married December 3, 1927. Caroline Fitzhugh was educated in Saint Catherine's School at Richmond.

HENRY S. GROGAN. It is no mere idle, flippant curiosity that prompts men to wish to learn the private as well as the public lives of their fellows. It is true, rather, that such anxiety tends to prove universal brotherhood, and the interest in biography is not confined to men of any particular vocation or caste. The roll of those whose lot it is to play a conspicuous part in the dramas of national or civic life is comparatively short. Yet communities are made up of individuals, and the aggregate of achievements, no less than the sum total of human happiness, is made up of the deeds of those men and women whose primary aim through life is faithfully to perform the duty nearest at hand. Individual influence upon human affairs will be considered potent or insignificant according to the standpoint from which it is viewed. The lives of some men are so intimately connected with important affairs that a faithful narrative of their acts might furnish the recital of much that is valuable in the history of their country during a particular period, and in this connection there is herewith set forth the salient points in the career of Henry S. Grogan, a native Virginian, who left the estate of his birth to achieve prominence and success in the real estate business in Washington, D. C.

Henry S. Grogan was born on his father's farm, located near Emory, in Washington County, Virginia, July 23, 1891, and is a son of Isaac Clifton and Rhoda Ellen (Rhoton) Grogan, the former of whom died in September, 1926, and the latter in 1916. The parents were born in Scott County, Virginia, and both were descended from first families of the Old Dominion. Isaac Clifton Grogan was a farmer by natural vocation and a skilled tiller of the soil, but was a man of versatile talents and for some years followed the business of building contractor, erecting a number of fine homes in Washington County. He was a member of the Baptist Church, as was his worthy wife, and both were active workers in the church, lived their faith daily and had the love and esteem of those who knew and appreciated their many sterling qualities of heart and mind. They were the parents of the following children: Effie, educated in Emory High School and Schoemaker College, Gate City, Virginia, who married John G. Montgomery, one of the wealthy planters of Washington County, and resides on a beautiful country estate near Meadow View, Virginia; Abner, a trusted employe of the Norfolk & Western Railway, who makes his home at Bluefield, West Virginia; Lake G., educated in Emory and Henry College and Martha Washington College, who married Branch Worsham, a wealthy hardware merchant of Bluefield, West Virginia; Henry S., of this review; Maurice E., who was in the World war and saw eighteen months of overseas service and is now a prominent optician of Tampa, Florida; Gael, a trusted employe of the Washington Street Railroad Company, who makes his home in Washington, D. C.; and Miss Lollie M., educated in Emory and Henry College and Martha Washington College, who has been in the employ of the United States Government at Washington for several years.

Henry S. Grogan was reared in the midst of agricultural surroundings and under the influence of people of breeding, and those who know him will unite in bearing testimony that he never has departed from the gentleness, the simplicity of life and character and the truthful habits which were inculcated in the earliest lessons of his home. As in the case of so many farmers' sons, his boyhood was divided between attendance at the district school and working on the home farm in summer, but subsequently he was sent to Emory and Henry College at Emory, Virginia, and then, expressing a desire for a business career, supplemented his education by attendance at the National Business College. After his graduation from the latter institution he was for two years connected with the Shenandoah Hotel of Roanoke, Virginia, and then accepted a call to the Jefferson Hotel at Richmond, where he served as bookkeeper and auditor for about eighteen months. He was then asked to become connected with the Raleigh Hotel, Washington, D. C., in the capacity of bookkeeper, and his next step upward was to the assistant managership of the Lafayette Hotel, Washington. About one year later he severed this connection to go to the Congress Hotel as auditor and bookkeeper for three years, and then left the hotel business to become an accountant for the United States Shipping Fleet Corporation, with which he was identified for two and one-half years.

Mr. Grogan at this time decided to enter upon an independent career of his own, and accordingly embarked in the real estate business at Washington, first as general manager of the Apartment and Room-Seekers' Aid. Subsequently he established

Tazewell T Hubard

the Grogan Realty Company, of which he is now the sole proprietor. He has since built up an extensive business and has a large clientage among the wealthy and prominent residents of Washington, where he maintains offices at 201 McGill Building. Without being its slave, Mr. Grogan has been diligent in business, which has prospered under his hand. One of his most marked characteristics has been his detestation of whatever is base or ignoble. He has an intuitive perception of character and will have nothing to do with those whom he regards as deficient in integrity. Mr. Grogan is an enthusiastic citizen who has studied his community and its resources and has unbounded faith in its future. Throughout his career he has been highly reputed for honesty, integrity and ability,—virtues which, however homely, bring a higher reward than wealth or civic honor. Mr. Grogan is alert to the welfare of his home town of Falls Church, Virginia, where he owns a beautiful home and stands high in the esteem of his fellow citizens, and is also the owner of considerable property at the capital. Fraternally he is affiliated with the Loyal Order of Moose and the Junior Order United American Mechanics. Mr. Grogan is a Christian Scientist.

On July 16, 1916, Mr. Grogan was united in marriage with Miss Anne Catherine Swetnam, of Burke, Fairfax County, Virginia, a daughter of Charles and Jennie Swetnam, the former a well known merchant of Fairfax and a first cousin of Daniel Willard, the family being an old and distinguished one. Mrs. Grogan was educated in the Alexandria High School and the State Normal School at Farmville, Virginia, is a member of the Daughters of the American Revolution and the Order of the Eastern Star, and a leader in club and social circles of Washington and Falls Church. Mr. and Mrs. Grogan are the parents of two children: Charles Henry, born July 3, 1918; and Edward Berry Swetnam, born July 30, 1925.

TAZEWELL TAYLOR HUBARD was an attorney and public official, lived most of his life at Norfolk, and enjoyed a reputation for fine social qualities and a cultured mind, as well as abilities in his profession.

He was born at Norfolk, October 20, 1867, and died in that city February 15, 1918. He was a son of Rev. James R. and Sallie (Taylor) Hubard. His grandfather, James R. Hubard, Sr., was a prominent early lawyer of Norfolk. Rev. James R. Hubard was a minister of the Episcopal Church. The Hubards were of French-Huguenot stock, and on coming to Virginia first settled in Gloucester County. His grandfather on the maternal side, Tazewell Taylor, was also a noted lawyer of Norfolk, Virginia.

Tazewell Taylor Hubard was educated in private schools, in the Shenandoah Academy at Winchester, graduated in 1887 from the Virginia Military Institute, and then remained at the institute two years as an instructor in French language and as a tactical officer. In 1890 he graduated from the law department of the University of Virginia, after which he returned to Norfolk and throughout his professional career was associated with his brother, James Leighton Hubard. This was a firm which handled a large volume of general practice, but Mr. Hubard also gave a great deal of his time to his duties as commissioner of accounts for the city of Norfolk.

Mr. Hubard while in college became a member of the Kappa Alpha fraternity and for twenty years served as its grand historian. He was elected a Knight of its Council of Honor in 1893, and in 1915 the Richmond Convention of the fraternity elected him Chief Alumnus, but he was unable to accept the honor. He was a staunch Democrat, and he and his family were members of the Episcopal Church. He was on the staff for a numbers of years of the Norfolk Blues.

Mr. Hubard married at Norfolk, November 12, 1895, Miss Elizabeth Mallory Cannon, who was born in Norfolk, daughter of Dr. Douglas C. and Elizabeth Mallory (King) Cannon. Her ancestors, the Cannons, were of French Huguenot stock. Her mother was a descendant of the Boutwell and Curle families, early and prominent settlers around Hampton, Virginia. Mrs. Hubard's father served as a first lieutenant in the Signal Corps in the Confederate army, after the war took up the study of medicine, was graduated at the University of Virginia with the degree of Doctor of Medicine and Master of Arts and was the youngest graduate in the M. A. degree up to the time he graduated. He spent two years at Bellevue Hospital in New York, and then practiced for many years at Norfolk. Mrs. Hubard was the fifth in a family of twelve children. She was educated in the Leachwood Female Seminary and in the Philip West Academy. Mrs. Hubard, whose home is at 17 Pelham Place in Norfolk, has two sons. The older, Tazewell Taylor, Jr., was educated in the Norfolk Academy, the Episcopal High School at Alexandria, graduated in the electrical engineer course from the Virginia Military Institute in 1922, and is now associated with the Chesapeake & Potomac Telephone Company. The second son, James Douglas, is a student in the Episcopal High School at Alexandria.

ELIJAH MONROE WEBB was a Prince George County farmer, and while a soldier in the Confederate army married Sarah Jane Shands, who with her mother was a refugee at Petersburg.

The home of the Shands family is the historic "Hickory Hill" homestead in Dinwiddie County. Sarah Jane Shands' father, grandfather and great-grandfather all bore the name William. Her great-grandparents, William and Priscilla Shands, were the first of the family in Virginia, settling in Sussex County. Her grandfather, William, married Lucy Oliver, daughter of William Oliver. Her father, William Shands, married Sarah Bee Rives, of the distinguished Rives family connections in Virginia, and their five children were named Aurelias Rives, Elverton Adolphus, William Briggs, Cordelia Oliver and Sarah Jane Cureton, who became the wife of Elijah Monroe Webb. Mr. and Mrs. Webb have five children: Annie and Willie, both of whom died in infancy; Sarah Isabelle, Julia Amanda, wife of B. Thomas Meacham, and Mary C.

Mrs. Webb's grandfather, William Shands, was a farmer, and at one time represented Prince George County in the General Assembly. He owned a large farm in Prince George County and on it erected a house which was destroyed during the Civil war. This farm, "Hickory Hill," comprised a hundred-fifty acres of land. Near the center is the simple white cottage which was erected after the war and in which Mrs. Webb lived for many years and where her daughters, Miss Belle and Miss Mary, now spend their summers. Hickory Hill farm adjoins Fort Stedman, scene of one of the great battles in connection with the siege of Petersburg during 1864-65. To the rear of the cottage is a famous spring, marking the site of the encampment of the 209th Regiment of Pennsylvania Volunteers during the siege of Petersburg. It is further memorable for the fact that nearby President Lincoln sat on his horse watching the progress of General Grant's army in the battle of Fort Stedman.

Mrs. Webb was living in the old house there when the siege of Petersburg started, but in time the place became untenantable and the family had to seek refuge in Petersburg, where her mother and one of the other daughters died. After the war, when the family went back to Hickory Hill, the barren land was left, and many years were required in replanting and making possible the beauty which now adorns the spot.

Mrs. Webb outlived her husband many years. During the World war she saw Camp Lee constructed around her property, and part of her land was rented to the Government for use as a Veterinary Training School. Her home was a favorite rendezvous for soldiers from the cantonment, and Mrs. Webb was fond of relating Civil war scenes to these youthful soldiers, some of whom were descendants of the veterans of the Civil war. While the Eightieth Division was at Camp Lee she kept open house for officers and enlisted men, and almost daily she could be seen on the porch of her little home surrounded by men from the camp as she described the fighting she had witnessed fifty years before. A young corporal of the Eightieth Division erected a rustic bridge across the ravine in which the spring is located in order that the present day military establishment might be linked up with the older history. Mrs. Webb during her lifetime gave permission to a commision of veterans of the Civil war to make improvements for the spring as a memorial to the members of the 209th Pennsylvania who had died during the siege of Petersburg. Concrete steps were erected down to the level of the spring, and the spring itself was incased in concrete. A bronze plate on the slab covering the spring contains the following inscription: "Spring used by the 209th Pennsylvania Regiment during the Siege of Petersburg, 1864-65. Erected by M. A. Embick, F. H. Barker, Seward Jones." Both Captain Barker and Colonel Embick fought in the Civil war, and the father of Seward Jones was killed in the battle of Fort Stedman. During the World war a loving cup was presented to the spring by Captain Boher, son of a Confederate veteran and an officer in the Medical Corps of the United States Army.

Hickory Hill is now owned by Mrs. Webb's three daughters, Miss Belle Webb, who is principal of the Rives School in Dinwiddie County; Miss Mary Webb, a talented musician, and Mrs. Thomas Meacham.

CALEB W. WILLIAMS was born in the City of Norfolk, Virginia, July 17, 1849, and in this city his death occurred May 15, 1917, about two years after he had retired from active business, with rank as the oldest and most influential contractor in brick construction work in his native community. He made his life count in large and effective achievement, was unassumingly loyal and progressive as a citizen and business man, and his kindliness and human helpfulness brought to him the fullest measure of popular confidence and esteem.

Mr. Williams was the youngest of the three children of Caleb and Lydia (Connor) Williams, and his brother, John James, was killed at the battle of the Wilderness while serving as a gallant young soldier of the Confederacy in the Civil war. Caleb Williams, father of the subject of this memoir, was born in

Princess Anne County, Virginia, where he was reared to adult age, and he was for many years in Government service in Virginia, after which he engaged in the wheelwright business in Norfolk, where he and his wife passed the closing years of their lives.

As a boy and youth Caleb W. Williams attended private school in Norfolk, and thereafter he profited by the advantages of the old Norfolk Academy. He was a young man when, after learning the trade of brick mason, he engaged independently in the contracting business along this line. He continued to center his activities in Norfolk until 1873, when he went to Philadelphia as a contractor on buildings there erected for the great Centennial Exposition, and he in due course resumed his contracting business in Norfolk, where he continued his successful and important operations nearly forty years thereafter—until his retirement in 1915, as the dean of brick contractors in this section of the state. He was concerned in the erection of many of the leading business blocks of Norfolk, and was the brick contractor in the construction of many of the finest residences in the Ghent district and other sections of the city.

Mr. Williams had no desire for political activity or public office, but was a loyal supporter of the cause of the Democratic party, and his civic progressiveness was never known to fail. In a quiet way he was instant in works of charity and benevolence, and he was a zealous member of the First Methodist Episcopal Church, South, as is also his widow. Mr. Williams served three terms as president of the Bricklayers Association of Norfolk, and he was affiliated with the Independent Order of Odd Fellows, the Improved Order of Red Men and the Junior Order United American Mechanics.

October 27, 1881, recorded the marriage of Mr. Williams and Miss Emily Katharine Douglas, who was born at Elizabeth City, North Carolina, the third of the six children of Smith Cox and Sophia (Seeley) Douglas. Mr. Douglas was a skilled ship carpenter, and served as a foreman in the Joseph Lawrence shipyards at Elizabeth City, North Carolina. Prior to this he had owned and operated the steamboats Eagle and John C. Calhoun, which were in active commission in advancing Confederate interests in the Civil war, both having been sunk in Roanoke harbor to block the entrance of enemy vessels into the river and thence attacking Elizabeth City. A. B. Seeley, maternal uncle of Mrs. Williams, was three times wounded while in service as a soldier of the Confederacy. The Seeley family was founded in the eastern part of North Carolina within a short time after the close of the war of the Revolution.

Since the death of her husband Mrs. Williams has continued her residence in Norfolk, where her attractive home is at 703 West Princess Anne Road. Of the children of Mr. and Mrs. Williams the eldest is Annie Seeley, who is the wife of John Dod Ward, a retired business man of Norfolk. Mr. and Mrs. Ward have two children: Margaret, who is the wife of Eugene Scott and who has one child, Margaret Ward Scott; and John Frederick, who is active in business in Norfolk. Caleb W. Williams, Jr., is the successor of his father in the brick contracting business in Norfolk. He married Miss Nellie Minor, of Niagara Falls, New York, and they have six children: Marion M., Caleb W. III and John Randolph (twins), Carroll, Beverly and Jane. John A., next younger of the children of the subject of this memoir, likewise resides in his native city. Hazel G. remains

with her widowed mother and is a popular figure in educational
service in her native city. Grace May likewise remains with her
mother, and is in the employ of the Pender Company. Helen,
youngest of the children, is the wife of Livingston Trump, who
resides at Crewe, Nottaway County, and is in the employ of
the United States Government.

CLAUDE JENKINS IVES. The entire absence of competition
in his line of activity at Clarendon does not explain the success
of Claude J. Ives, who since August, 1911, has been the proprietor of a well established and perfectly equipped funeral directing and undertaking business. Mr. Ives was only a lad when
he started out to make his own way in life, and what he has
accomplished in the way of success has been gained entirely
through his own initiative, resource and natural ability. From
small beginnings he has built up a solid business structure and
a secure reputation, and few men of his community are more
greatly entitled to the esteem in which they are held.

Mr. Ives was born at Falls Church, Virginia, December 19,
1874, and is a son of Albert H. and Theodora (Jenkins) Ives.
His father, a native of the State of Connecticut, left his New
England home in youth and came to Prince William County,
Virginia, and later to Fairfax County, where he met and married
a native of that state. In his youth Mr. Ives had learned the
old established trade of wagon-making, and following his marriage he set himself up in business at Falls Church, where he
carried on a wagon-making factory until the time of his death
in June, 1920. Mrs. Ives passed away at the same place in
1887.

Claude J. Ives was reared at Falls Church, where he attended
the public schools, and was only sixteen years of age when he
graduated from high school. Shortly thereafter he secured
employment in the undertaking establishment of John R. Wright
at Washington, D. C., and remained with him for eight years,
during which time he learned the business in all its details.
During this period he attended the Prof. F. A. Sullivan's College of Embalming at Washington, D. C. He then resigned and
went to Sunbury, Pennsylvania, in the capacity of manager of
the E. S. Weimer Funeral Home, where he worked at the same
line of business for eight years, and eventually established himself in the furniture and undertaking business at Sunbury, where
he conducted a successful establishment for five years. During
the time he was located at Sunbury he had attended the Massachusetts College of Embalming, from which he was graduated
in 1899. During this course he was one of the instructors at
the College, under Professor Dodge. In August, 1911, Mr. Ives'
wife's health failed and her physician advised her to seek a
different climate. Accordingly the family came to Clarendon,
where Mr. Ives established himself in the hardware and undertaking business, but at the end of five years disposed of the
former business in order to give his entire time to his activities
as a funeral director and mortician. He now has a beautiful
funeral home, office and chapel, situated at the corner of Wilson
Boulevard and Spruce Street, and as the only undertaker at
Clarendon has every modern facility for the proper and dignified
care of the dead. He is a man of infinite judgment and has
made himself a friend in countless homes which have been
visited by the grim reaper. Mr. Ives is a past vice president and
one of the directors of the Arlington Hall Association of Arling-

ton, the Chamber of Commerce, the Monarch Club, the Masons, the Independent Order of Odd Fellows and the Junior Order United American Mechanics. He maintains an independent stand in politics, and although a good citizen of public spirit, has had no desire for the honors of office. He is a Presbyterian in his religious faith, while Mrs. Ives belongs to the Methodist Episcopal Church.

In January, 1898, Mr. Ives was united in marriage with Miss Annie Elizabeth Pearson, daughter of John S. and Virginia Catherine (Sanders) Pearson. Her father, who was a substantial agriculturist of Fairfax County, this state, served in the capacity of member of the Board of County Supervisors for twenty-five or thirty years, and wielded much influence in his community, where his death occurred in 1919, Mrs. Pearson passing away August 21, 1925. Four children have been born to Mr. and Mrs. Ives: Amy Gertrude, born in 1900, who is now the wife of W. H. Jordan, a resident of Clarendon; William, who died when two weeks old; Claude Pearson, born in 1904, who was in the employ of the local telephone company at Clarendon and is now associated with his father in business; and Gladys Elizabeth, born in 1915, who is attending high school.

HORATIO C. WOODHOUSE, who had a highly successful career and became one of the outstanding citizens of Norfolk, achieving prominence and distinction in a brief lifetime of less than forty-eight years, was born in Princess Anne County, Virginia, September 23, 1879, and died at Norfolk, April 8, 1926.

Nine generations of the Woodhouse family have lived in Princess Anne County, and for over two centuries consecutively his ancestors were vestrymen in Eastern Shore Chapel. That famous church edifice, still standing, was erected in 1754. One of his ancestors was Henry Woodhouse, a governor of the Bermudas. His great-great-grandfather, Jonathan Woodhouse, fought in the Revolutionary war. His father, Jonathan Woodhouse, who served as a member of the Constitutional Convention of Virginia in 1901, has for many years been a prominent business man of Norfolk. Jonathan Woodhouse married Clara Cornick, and of their six children H. Cornick was the oldest.

The late Mr. Woodhouse at the age of fourteen was sent to the Delaplane School in Fauquier County. Later he graduated from Randolph-Macon College. When he was a young man of twenty years he went out to Cripple Creek, Colorado, with his cousin, Harry Shepherd, and had two years of experience in that then most famous mining district of the West. After returning to Virginia he was secretary and treasurer of the Princess Anne Telephone Company, spent a few years in the Norfolk office of Swift & Company, meat packers, then was with the Hardy Wholesale Merchandise Company and for about five years was associated with his father in the electrical business.

Mr. Woodhouse in 1909, with his father and his brother John, established the Woodhouse Electrical Company on Commercial Place. Two years later they removed to a new three-story building on Bank Street. During the war boom this building was sold and a large and more ornate structure was then built on Court Street. Mr. Woodhouse was secretary, treasurer and active head of this successful business, which since his death has been continued by his father, Jonathan, and his brother, Thomas L. Woodhouse. Mrs. Woodhouse still retains an interest in the business.

Mr. Woodhouse was a member of the Electrical Club, the Chamber of Commerce, the Old Colony Club, the Rotary Club, and as a Mason was affiliated with Ruth Lodge No. 89 of Norfolk. He was a Democrat and a member of St. Andrews Episcopal Church. He had a great many friends, who admired him for his business success and his personal integrity.

He married, April 19, 1910, Miss Virginia May Macon. She was educated in the old Norfolk High School. Mrs. Woodhouse is a member of the Norfolk Society of Arts and St. Andrews Episcopal Church. Her father, James Barbour Macon, was for thirty-five years in the railway and steamship business of the Norfolk & Western Railroad and the Old Dominion Steamship Company. He married May Fanny Malbon, whose father, David Malbon, was a large plantation holder in Princess Anne County. Mrs. Woodhouse's grandfather was Edgar Barbour Macon, a quartermaster in the 64th Virginia Regiment in the Civil war. She is a descendant of the famous Macon family, including one of North Carolina's greatest statesmen in the Colonial period, Nathaniel Macon, also Gideon Macon of New Kent County, Virginia. Mrs. Woodhouse is a great-great-great-great-niece of James Madison, the fourth president of the United States. This comes through her descent from Rev. James Madison (1749-1812), who was president of William and Mary College and the first Episcopal bishop of Virginia. Bishop Madison was a son of John Madison.

Mrs. Woodhouse is the mother of four children: Horatio Cornick, Jr., Frances Macon, and Mary Conway and Barbara Know, twins. All are being given the advantages of a liberal education. They are all members of the Children of the American Revolution, and the three daughters are members of Hope Maury Chapter of the United Daughters of the Confederacy, of which Miss Frances is president. Mrs. Woodhouse resides at 709 W. Princess Anne Road in Norfolk.

GEORGE J. OLIVER, educator, at present division superintendent of schools of Northampton County, was born at Berryville, Clarke County, Virginia, April 26, 1898, the son of Dr. George H. and Kate (Cunningham) Oliver, and third of a family of four children.

His grandfather, Capt. William A. Oliver, of Essex County, was a physician, having received his training in medicine at the Jefferson Medical College, Philadelphia. Captain Oliver married Ellen Douglas Jeffries, a daughter of a prominent family in Virginia. In the war between the states Captain Oliver was in command of the Essex County Cavalry, part of the Fifth Virginia Cavalry, and was killed in the fighting around Amelia Courthouse during the third year of the war.

Mr. Oliver's father, Dr. George Hansford Oliver, was born in Essex County, and was educated for the profession of dentistry at the Baltimore College of Dental Surgery. He practised his profession for forty years, until he entered the ministry, an ambition with him of long standing. At the age of sixty-two he entered the Baptist Theological Seminary at Louisville, Kentucky, and began the study of theology. He was later ordained a minister of the Baptist Church, and preached at Newsoms, Virginia, until his death on September 22, 1928, at the age of sixty-six. His wife, Kate Cunningham, was born in Frederick County, Maryland, of a family well known and of distinguished record in that state. Mrs. Oliver now resides at Irvington, Virginia.

George J. Oliver was reared and educated at Irvington, the family having moved to that place in May, 1904, when he was six years old. He at first attended private school, later entered the high school, and graduated in 1913, when fifteen years of age. For two years he worked in the local newspaper office and in 1916 entered Richmond College. At the conclusion of his second year in college he went to Penniman, near Williamsburg, and for about two months was employed in the munitions plants there as a government inspector. While there he was selected as one of ten students of Richmond College to enter the First Students Army Training Camp at Plattsburg Barracks, New York. He remained there until September, 1918, when he was commissioned second lieutenant of field artillery, being only nineteen years and ten months of age when thus commissioned, becoming thereby one of the youngest men ever to hold a commission in the army. He was sent to the Field Artillery Central Officers Training School at Camp Zachary Taylor, Louisville, Kentucky, and was held on duty there until December 19, 1918, when he was honorably discharged.

After returning to Virginia he became principal of the Stevensville High School in King and Queen County, finishing the remainder of the school year 1918-19 and remaining for another year. In 1920 he became principal of the high school at Capeville, remaining there until 1927, when he was made acting division superintendent of schools. In May, 1928, he was appointed division superintendent. His offices are at Cape Charles and his residence at Capeville. During the past eight years his efforts on behalf of the school of which he was principal and of the schools of Northampton County have met with unusual success.

He married, February 3, 1923, Miss Clara Ellen Bell, daughter of Theron P. and Nellie (Mapp) Bell, both natives of Northampton County. Her father, who resides at Machipongo, is one of the leading farmers and business men of the Eastern Shore. Mr. and Mrs. Oliver have one child, George J., Jr., born November 10, 1923. Mr. Oliver is a member of the Cape Charles Rotary Club, belongs to the Pi Kappa Alpha social fraternity, and to the Northampton Country Club. He has attended summer sessions of the University of Virginia, the University of Richmond and the College of William and Mary. He is a Democrat, a Baptist, and teaches a class of young women in the Baptist Sunday School. Mrs. Oliver is a member of the Mothers' Club of Frankton, Virginia, the Woman's Club of the Eastern Shore, and is president of the Hollins College Alumnae Association.

CARVER V. WILLIAMS is one of the younger members of the Virginia bar, and has made a promising beginning of his professional career at South Hill, where he first established his office.

Mr. Williams was born at Chase City, Virginia, November 5, 1901, son of H. T. and Mary (Savage) Williams. His parents are natives of North Carolina, his father born in Gates County and his mother in Hertford County. H. T. Williams has given his active life to the ministry of the Baptist Church and is now pastor of the church of that denomination at Chase City.

Carver V. Williams was reared and educated in Chase City, graduating from high school in 1920, and took his Bachelor of

Science degree at Wake Forest College in North Carolina in 1924. His law studies were pursued at the University of Virginia, and he was admitted to the bar in June, 1928, at once locating at South Hill.

Mr. Williams is unmarried. He is a member of the Virginia Bar Association, is a Democrat, a member of the Baptist Church and teaches a class in Sunday School.

THOMAS SOMERVILLE SOUTHGATE gave his name and enterprise to some of the most noteworthy of the commercial organizations of the city of Norfolk. In business he was always thoroughly constructive, in citizenship enlightened and broad minded, and there were few Virginians who did not know something of the activities associated with his name.

He was born at Richmond, February 7, 1868, and died September 27, 1928, when in his sixty-first year. He was a son of Capt. Thomas M. and Mary E. Southgate. His father, master of a steamer of the Old Dominion Line, took the boy at the age of four aboard ship, and that was his home for some five years. At the age of nine he entered the elementary schools, but three years later entered upon his business career as a messenger boy at twelve dollars a month. His important education came to him in the intervals of work and was perhaps the more valuable for that reason. He attended night school for five years. Ships, railways and manufacturing were phases of industry in which he was most keenly interested, and he made a study of those activities at every successive point of his contact with commercial affairs. He was first in the commission business, and on October 10, 1892, in a small office room with one desk and one chair started T. S. Southgate & Company, which at the time of his death, with its subsidiaries and allied corporations, constituted one of the largest industrial establishments of its kind in the country. As a result of the tireless energy of the promoter the Southgate business by 1898 had its own office building, and three years later was constructed the first unit of what are now the great Southgate Terminals, the original structure being a warehouse affording 24,000 square feet. These terminals today have 400,000 square feet of floor space, with frontage of 900 feet on water and over 1,000 feet on land, representing a total investment of over a million dollars and affording facilities for thirty-six firms.

In addition to being president of T. S. Southgate & Company the late Mr. Southgate from 1915 had been president of the Southgate Terminal Corporation, president of the Southgate Packing Company, president of the Southgate Export Coal Company, the Southgate Produce Company, Southgate Molasses Company, Southgate Import and Export Company. He was a member of the executive board of the Norfolk National Bank of Commerce & Trust, a director of the Industrial Finance Corporation of New York, a director of the Norfolk & Western Railway Company, and financially interested in a number of other enterprises.

Throughout his business career he was actuated by a strong faith in the potentialities of Norfolk and in Hampton Roads. The president of the Norfolk & Western Railway Company in deploring his death referred to his wide and complete experience and knowledge of transportation and maritime affairs, and called him a great constructive force in the progress and development of Hampton Roads. For a number of years he was vice president of the Norfolk Chamber of Commerce, for eight years was a member of the Norfolk Common Council, and president of that body four years of the time. He served as a member of the City Port Commission and was a member of the commission which revised the city charter and worked out the plan under which Norfolk is operating its government. He was a member and first vice president of the Southern Commercial Congress, and in 1913 was vice president of the American commission which went to Europe to study rural credits. A report of this commission was the basis for the present Farm Loan Bank System. Governor Byrd in a tribute referred to some of his public activities, particularly the work he did as a member of the commission on simplification of Virginia's government. He had, said Governor Byrd, "a thorough grasp of the relationship which the state should bear toward business, and vice versa. It was my privilege to rely upon him for advice and counsel in recommendations affecting the business and transportation interests of Virginia."

Mr. Southgate was from 1904 to 1907 one of the four men who built and operated the Jamestown Exposition. He served as director of the campaign in Norfolk for the purchase of the Shenandoah National Park. He was one of the prominent laymen of the Methodist Church, for nineteen years being lay leader of the Virginia Methodist Conference, was president of the Southern Methodist Laymen's Association, and from early manhood had been a consistent worker in his church. He was a platform speaker of ability and personality, and appeared many times before audiences in behalf of religious and civic enterprises. He was much interested in the cause of Christian Missions and education, and was state chairman for Virginia in the campaign of his church to raise $3,500,000 for missions and over a million dollars for Christian education.

Mr. Southgate married Miss Nettie D. Norsworthy, who survives him. The three children are Nettie Virginia, Mary Portlock and Herbert Somerville Southgate, all of Norfolk.

The Norsworthy family, of which Mrs. Southgate is a descendant, is, as the name indicates, derived from the stock of Norsemen who settled in England. Representatives of the family were in Virginia soon after the establishment of Jamestown. The pioneer, Tristram Norsworthy, settled in about 1610 across the river from Newport News, having a land grant to that section of marsh land and small islands known as "Ye Ragged Islands." Early records show the family to have been planters, chiefly tobacco growers. Many of their homes were in Nansemond and Isle of Wight counties, where county records frequently have been destroyed by fire, and fire and time have also reduced many of their homes to ashes. Tristram Norsworthy and his son, Major (afterwards colonel) George Norsworthy, were both members of the First and Second House of Burgesses from Upper Norfolk County. A later descendant was Tristram Norsworthy, captain and afterwards colonel in the Revolution. The old residence of the family burned many years ago. Early in the nineteenth century the foundation of the house and the well were several feet under water and some distance from the shore, showing the inroads the water had made on the southern bank of the river.

The Revolutionary soldier, Tristram Norsworthy, was the father of Joseph Norsworthy, born in 1777. Joseph Norsworthy built his home on land deeded him by his father. He deeded land

east of his own plantation to his son, Nathaniel W., who was
born in 1804. Nathaniel W. had a large family, but only three
sons and one daughter married. One son, Joseph Chapman,
Norsworthy, born in 1831, was a valiant soldier in the Confederate army. His children consisted of one son and two daughters, one of whom is Mrs. Nettie Norsworthy Southgate. The
lands of the Norsworthys passed entirely out of the family
about the time of the Civil war, when all of the sons moved to
Norfolk. In crossing from Isle of Wight County to Newport
News the road approaching the James River Bridge passes
within a hundred feet of the burying ground of the family of
Joseph Norsworthy, son of the Revolutionary ancestor, Tristram.

ROBERT CARSON GILMER, member of a family widely and
prominently connected in Southwest Virginia, is a resident of
Pembroke, where he is local agent for the Norfolk & Western
Railway Company and owns and conducts the Gilmer Hotel, one
of the most popular hotels in Giles County for commercial
travelers and tourists.

He was born at Abingdon, Virginia, September 23, 1885, son
of W. R. and Maggie C. (Cecil) Gilmer, and grandson of George
Gilmer, an early farmer and cattle raiser of Russell County, who
is buried in the cemetery near Hansonville in that county. W. R.
Gilmer was born in Hansonville, served as a soldier in the Confederate army, and was wounded in a skirmish near Richmond
about two hours before the surrender at Appomattox. He rode
a mule into Richmond, then got on a train for Abingdon, and
from there went to his home in Russell County, where he recovered from his wound and entered with courage and indomitable
energy into the tasks of farming under the new conditions after
the war. After his marriage he moved to Washington County,
and lived there the rest of his life. He was a justice of the peace
and road commissioner and road supervisor, and for several
years bail commissioner. He held the post of steward in the
Methodist Episcopal Church, South, and was accounted one of
the best loved citizens of his community. He died April 10,
1916, and is buried at Bristol. His wife, Maggie C. Cecil, was
born and reared in Pulaski County, attending public school
there and the Martha Washington College at Abingdon. She
was a member of the Methodist Episcopal Church, South. Her
death occurred November 1, 1928, and both she and her husband
are buried at Bristol. Her parents were Thomas and Priscilla
(Buckingham) Cecil. The Cecils have been in Virginia from
Colonial times. W. R. Gilmer and wife had five children: Howard C. Gilmer, a prominent attorney at Pulaski; Bessie G., wife
of Mr. Nicar, of Bristol; Margaret C., wife of G. H. Gilmer, who
is president of the Interstate Railway Company at Big Stone
Gap, Virginia; Robert Carson Gilmer; and A. Gray Gilmer, a
leading member of the bar of Oklahoma City.

Robert Carson Gilmer attended public schools and Abingdon
Academy, and from the time he left school down to the present
time has been with the Norfolk & Western Railway Company,
at first as a telegraph operator, in which capacity he worked
from October 4, 1903, until February 7, 1912. On February 7,
1912, he became station agent at Pembroke, and has given a
continuous and efficient service in that capacity for seventeen
years. It was in 1922 that he built the Gilmer Hotel.

Mr. Gilmer is a trustee and member of the Board of Stewards of the Methodist Episcopal Church, South. A Republican,

he was candidate for the Lower House of the Legislature from
Bland and Giles counties in 1925, being defeated by a margin of
215 votes by George T. Bird, of Bland County. Mr. Gilmer is
one of the able representatives of his party in this section of the
state. He is affiliated with Castle Rock Lodge No. 334 A. F. and
A. M., and is a member of the Order of Railway Telegraphers.

He married at Pembroke, September 19, 1905, Miss Virginia
Catherine Price, who was educated in the public schools of Giles
County. She is a member of the Ladies Aid Society and its
secretary in the Methodist Episcopal Church, South. Her parents were Henry D. and Nannie (Albert) Price, her father a
farmer and stock raiser near Pembroke, and both her parents
are members of the Christian Church. Mr. and Mrs. Gilmer
have two sons: Eugene Hoge, born in 1909, a member of the
class of 1929 in the Pembroke High School; and Robert C., Jr.,
born in 1913, a member of the class of 1930 in the Pembroke
High School.

WINSTON ONEIDA MARTIN. The late Winston Oneida Martin, of Richmond, a direct descendant of Alexander Hamilton,
set an example in his frugal, painstaking, useful career that the
rising generation would do well to follow, and it is well to give
a brief review of his life and character in these days of abun-
dance, free expenditure of money, and the too prevalent neglect
of the prosaic tasks of local government. Comparatively speak-
ing, he was a young man when he died, for he was born in Powhatan County, Virginia, September 24, 1887, and died in Richmond February 25, 1926, but he left behind him a record of self-
denial, self-control, thrift and practical idealism, and the warm
friendship of the man with whom he was associated in the
American Locomotive Works for so many years.

The private schools of his native county gave Winston Oneida
Martin his educational training, and when he had completed
his schooldays he went into a saw-mill for a year or two, leaving
that employment in Powhatan County for similar work in
Lunenburg, Virginia. In 1909 he came to Richmond and entered the locomotive works, rising during fifteen years to the
position of assistant manager of the locomotive tank department,
and he was holding it when death claimed him. A stalwart
Democrat, he supported his party, but never sought office himself, his work occupying him to the exclusion of outside matters.
He was a sincere member of the Baptist Church, but his family
are Methodists. In fraternal life he formed connections with
the Junior Order United American Mechanics and the Knights
of Pythias, and both organizations mourned his loss, as did all
who knew him.

In March, 1911, Mr. Martin married Matie Poulson, who
was educated in Wisconsin. She is a daughter of James and
Kristine (Jacobson) Poulson, and one in a family of five children. Mr. Poulson was born in Denmark, but came to the
United States and settled in Wisconsin in 1870, and there became a successful farmer and prominent citizen. He married
in Chicago, and his wife was also a native of Denmark. Two
children were born to Mr. and Mrs. Martin, Woodley Kristine,
a graduate of John Marshall High School and of Mrs. L. E.
Spencer's School of Music, and Blanche Oneida, a student in the
public schools of Richmond.

Mr. Martin belonged to the type of men who have built this
nation. In everything he did he lived up to American tradi-

tions. He was a plain-spoken, law-abiding, hard-working, upright man, with common sense and character. Practicing as he did the elementary virtues, it never occurred to him that success worthy the name could be achieved by speculation. As a faithful and devoted husband and watchful father he provided for the needs of his family through his own industry and frugality, and in such homes as his have been reared some of the finest people this country has produced. The nation cannot afford to forget such men as he or belittle their influence and the social and political atmosphere they created—an atmosphere of austere thinking, rational living and faithful performance of private duty.

WILLIAM PHILIP MATHEWS, M. D. From 1891 until his death the late Dr. William Philip Mathews was engaged in the practice of medicine and surgery at Richmond and in the more important work of medical education. His specialty was orthopedic surgery, and his knowledge and skill were such as to put him in the lead among his professional brethren, and to manifest the beneficent influence which professional acquirements, guided by high motives, have and exert upon the welfare of the community.

Doctor Mathews was born in Prince Edward County, Virginia, June 30, 1868, a son of Dr. Thomas Philip and Bettie Bolling (Marshall) Mathews, and a descendant of an ancient Virginia family who were among the first settlers of that county. His great-grandfather was Rev. Philip Mathews, a minister of the Baptist faith, who passed the entire ninety years of his life in that section, and his grandfather was Capt. William Mathews, a valiant officer of the War of 1812. Dr. Thomas Philip Mathews was born in Prince Edward County, August 21, 1835, and completed his medical education at Jefferson Medical College, Philadelphia, from which he was graduated with the degree of Doctor of Medicine as a member of the class of 1855. He immediately returned to the community of his birth and was engaged in practice there until the outbreak of the war between the states, when he promptly enlisted in the Confederate army and became captain of Company H, Fourteenth Regiment, Virginia Infantry, with which he served gallantly until the second battle of Manassas, in which he was severely wounded. When he recovered he was placed in charge of a hospital at Farmville, Prince Edward County, and subsequently became a surgeon under the great Gen. A. P. Hill, serving in that capacity until the close of the war. He then returned to his private practice, and in 1874 located at Richmond, where he became a leader in his profession and continued as such until his death January 12, 1905, interment being made in Hollywood Cemetery. On December 24, 1856, Doctor Mathews married Miss Bettie Bolling, daughter of Thomas R. Marshall, of Hampden-Sidney College, and they had the following children: John D., Thomas Gibson, Col. W. Kirk and Dr. William and five other children who are deceased.

After attending the public schools of Richmond, including high school, William Philip Mathews pursued a course at Richmond College, and then spent some time studying medicine under the able preceptorship of his distinguished father. In 1890 he graduated from the Medical College of Virginia with the degree of Doctor of Medicine and subsequently served his interneship at Charity Hospital, New York City. Returning to Richmond in 1891, from that time forward until his death, July 25, 1918, he was engaged in the practice of his profession, specializing in orthopedic surgery. He was professionally connected with the Medical College of Virginia for many years. In 1891 he was elected adjunct professor of surgery, in which capacity he served four years; in 1895 was elected professor of anatomy and in 1905 professor of orthopedic surgery. He served as president of the Board of Health at Manchester (Richmond) for one year, and was a director of the Manchester Light, Heat and Power Company. Doctor Mathews was a member of the Henrico County Medical Society, the Virginia State Medical Society, the American Medical Association and was a fellow of the American College of Surgeons. He was identified with every important movement which interested the medical and surgical faculty or concerned the public health. In spite of the onerous and never-ending duties of his profession, Doctor Mathews found the time and inclination to engage with great activity and usefulness in religious matters. He was one of the pillars of the Second Baptist Church of Richmond, president of the Inter-Denominational Sunday School Association for five years, president of the Baptist Sunday School Association, and a member for many years of the Board of Foreign Missions of the General Baptist Convention and chairman of the committee on appointments thereof, a position which had been held by his father for twenty-one years prior to the latter's death. Fraternally Doctor Mathews was a member and an honored past master of Meridian Lodge No. 284, A. F. and A. M.

On October 17, 1893, Doctor Mathews married at Cincinnati, Ohio, Miss Annie Sanborn Graham, who was born at Burning Springs, West Virginia, August 21, 1869, and is a daughter of David L. and Martha Jane (Watt) Graham, of Scotch and Irish parentage, formerly of the State of Pennsylvania. He enlisted and served as a soldier of the Union army during the war between the states. Four children were born to Doctor and Mrs. Mathews: Margaret Spencer, a graduate of the Woman's College, class of 1913, and the Richmond Normal School, class of 1917, who has been a teacher in the public schools of Richmond for eleven years, and is popular and distinguished as an educator; David Graham, of Richmond, who entered the United States Army for the World war as a member of the famous Richmond Blues, was later transferred to the Munitions Corps, saw active service in France and attained the rank of second lieutenant, and, returning to the United States, married, October 9, 1919, Miss Ada Long, of Richmond; Thomas Philip, Jr., who volunteered for service when the United States entered the World war, was first in training with the Ambulance Corps at Camp Lee and subsequently at Camp Meade, whence he went to Camp Worgert, England, where he finished training, saw active service on the battlefields of France, where he was wounded, was made a sergeant at the age of seventeen years, and, returning to the United States, married, October 17, 1922, Miss Elizabeth Bagby, and they have two children, Elizabeth Bagby and Thomas Philip III.; and William Watt, a graduate of John Marshall High School, who has a position in the offices of the Lorillard Tobacco Company of Richmond. Mrs. Mathews, who survives her husband and resides at 3115 Edgewood Avenue, is a graduate of Richmond Female Institute. She is active in the work of the Baptist Church and of the American Legion Auxiliary.

JAMES BASIL KEESLING was a newspaper man in Tennessee for a number of years, but eventually returned to his ancestral home in Southwest Virginia, where he has been a farmer and pure-bred stock breeder, and more recently has become identified as cashier with the Peoples Bank of Rural Retreat in Blythe County.

Mr. Keesling owns the Meadow Brook Farm, comprising part of a grant of land made to his ancestor, his great-grand-father, George Kisling, as the family name was spelled up to 1850. This George Kisling acquired an extensive area of land in the vicinity of Cedar Springs, Virginia, from William Bus-tard, who in turn had received it as a grant in 1785. The old grant was signed by Governor Patrick Henry, and James B. Keesling has in his possession the old document with the signa-ture of the great Virginia orator and statesman, and has all the other transfers that have been made since the time of his great-grandfather, George Kisling.

James Basil Keesling was born at Cedar Springs in Smyth County, Virginia, January 17, 1869, son of Emory Sullins and Emeline Francis (Dutton) Keesling. His father was born and reared in the same house, was educated in private schools, and entered the Confederate army and was a soldier during the last year of the war. He was a miller both before and after the war. Part of the old homestead comprises the Keesling Mill. Henry S. Keesling died April 29, 1916, and is buried in the old Asbury Church Cemetery near the old Asbury camp ground. His wife was born near Blue Spring, Virginia. Both were active mem-bers of the Methodist Episcopal Church, South. She died in 1907. Of the six children born to them two died in infancy, and the other four are: Peter P.; Clara Virginia, wife of J. W. Lantz; James B., of Cedar Springs, Virginia; and Minnie Sul-lins, wife of Leon C. Cornett, of Fresno, California.

James B. Keesling after public schools continued his educa-tion in Emory and Henry College, graduated from the Knoxville Business College in 1891, and for fifteen years gave his full time to newspaper work, the first three years with the *Knoxville Tribune*, and for about twelve years with the *Knoxville Sentinel*.

The death of his father caused him to return to Southwest-ern Virginia in order to take charge of Meadow Brook Farm, his fine property, comprising a great deal of blue grass land, an ideal spot for cattle raising. His home is one of the beauty spots of this section of Southwestern Virginia.

On July 1, 1927, Mr. Keesling became cashier of the Peoples Bank at Rural Retreat. He is also a director and stockholder of the same, and vice president and director of the Marion Handle Mills at Marion. He is a director of the Smyth County National Farm Loan Association and a member of the Smyth County School Board. He takes an active interest in public affairs, and none of his people have ever sought political office. He is a member of the Masonic fraternity and the Knights of Pythias, is a Democrat, and belongs to the Methodist Episcopal Church, South.

Mr. Keesling married at Moberly, Missouri, November 7, 1894, Miss Jessie Lee Briney, of Moberly. Her father, Rev. John Benton Briney, was one of the outstanding ministers, writers and debaters of the Christian Church, and died in 1927 at Cedar Springs, being buried in Cave Hill Cemetery in Louisville, Ken-tucky, beside his wife. Mrs. Keesling was educated at Memphis and at Louisville, and since early girlhood has been a leader in her church, being an accomplished singer and a choir worker. Mr. and Mrs. Keesling had two children, one son, Emory Basil, dying at the age of thirteen months. The daughter, Edith Holbert, was educated in public schools at Knoxville, in the Randolph-Macon Woman's College, and the Mary Baldwin Seminary. She is now the wife of Lee M. Cole, a resident of Marion, where he is president and manager of the Marion Handle Mills. Mr. and Mrs. Cole have a son, Lee Marion, Jr., attending public school.

NORMAN CLARENCE SMITH, commonwealth's attorney of Tazewell County, has achieved a great reputation in Southwestern Virginia as a brilliant lawyer, excelling in the resourcefulness which characterizes the successful man in criminal practice. He is a resident of Pocahontas, and has practiced there since the close of the World war, in which he took an honorable part.

He was born at Joliett, Schuylkill County, Pennsylvania, April 15, 1891. His grandfather, William Smith, a native of England, spent the greater part of his active life as a miner in Schuylkill County. He married in Pennsylvania Esther Bowles, also a native of England. George B. Smith, father of the Pocahontas attorney, was born at Tremont, Pennsylvania, December 23, 1869, and devoted many years to the mining industry, starting as a miner underground. In 1890 he located at Keystone, West Virginia, was superintendent of the Keystone Coal & Coke Company, and in 1912 became superintendent of the Big Vein Pocahontas Coal & Coke Company at Pocahontas, Virginia. He retired from active business in 1921. He was prominent in fraternal affairs, being a member of the various York Rite bodies of Masonry, the Beni Kedem Temple of the Mystic Shrine at Charleston, West Virginia, and was a member of the Knights of Pythias, and Independent Order of Odd Fellows. He was a Republican. George B. Smith married at Tremont, Pennsylvania, Elizabeth Roberts, who was born January 9, 1872. They had two sons, Norman Clarence and George Emmerson.

Norman Clarence Smith was educated in public schools at Tremont, Pennsylvania, and Keystone, West Virginia, graduating from high school at the latter place in 1906. In 1908 he graduated from Emory and Henry Academy and in 1912 took the A. B. degree at Emory and Henry College. Mr. Smith completed his law course at Columbia University, New York, in 1915, was admitted to the Virginia bar in June of that year, and for two years practiced at Grundy in Buchanan County, Virginia.

In August, 1917, he volunteered and attended the Second Officers Training Camp at Fort Myer, Virginia, where he was commissioned first lieutenant of infantry December 15, 1917. His first assignment of duty was with the Forty-eighth Infantry at Camp Hill, Newport News. On August 15, 1918, he was promoted to captain, became acting adjutant of the Fortieth Brigade, Twentieth Division, Camp Sevier, South Carolina, and was under orders to go overseas when the armistice was signed. He received his honorable discharge April 23, 1919.

On leaving the army Captain Smith established his law offices at Pocahontas.

Few men achieve more of the substantial honors of real accomplishment than Mr. Smith has attained in less than ten years. He has had a crowded program of general practice and

has been remarkably successful in the criminal cases he has handled. He has defended a number of men on trial for murder. He was attorney for and instrumental in securing the largest award ever given in a damage suit in Tazewell County. This was the case of Lumpkins versus the Norfolk and Western Railroad. The judgment was for $25,000.

Mr. Smith has served as attorney for the City of Pocahontas. He has been a leader in the Democratic party of the county since beginning practice, and his sterling merits as a lawyer and his character as a citizen, together with his convincing powers as a public speaker, have brought him a most exceptional distinction in being the first Democrat elected commonwealth's attorney in Tazewell County in forty years. Also he broke a custom in that no other attorney has been elected to this office who lived outside the county seat of Tazewell. In 1923 he was a candidate for the office and was defeated by 894 votes. In November, 1927, he was elected on the Democratic ticket by a margin of 353 votes. Mr. Smith is a member of the County Democratic Central Committee and has done much effective campaign work for the party in the Ninth Congressional District.

Mr. Smith is a lay leader of the Methodist Episcopal Church, South, at Pocahontas, and assistant district lay leader of the church for the Tazewell district. He teaches a class of boys in the Sunday School. He is junior warden of Pocahontas Lodge No. 240, A. F. and A. M., member of W. G. Bottimore Chapter No. 28, Royal Arch Masons, at Bluefield, Bluefield Commandery No. 22, Knights Templar, Kazim Temple of the Mystic Shrine at Roanoke, and a member of Pocahontas Lodge No. 60, Knights of Pythias.

He married at Crockett, Virginia, June 17, 1917, Miss Bessie Wampler, who was a graduate of Emory and Henry College and of Columbia University. She died January 31, 1919. Her parents were Lefrich P. and Tabitha (Fielder) Wampler. On June 16, 1922, Mr. Smith married Miss Lucille Hanna, daughter of William and Mollie (Bennett) Hanna. They have two children, Bess Lucille, born June 13, 1923, and Robert Norman, born December 10, 1925.

JUNIUS EDGAR WEST, lieutenant governor of the commonwealth of Virginia from 1922 to 1930, has for many years been a Suffolk business man, and was born at Waverly, Sussex County, July 12, 1866, son of Henry T. and Sue T. (Cox) West. His father was a Virginia planter and farmer.

Mr. West's first active contacts with his home state were as a teacher. He attended public schools, was a student in the Suffolk Collegiate Institute, the University of North Carolina, and studied law in Washington and Lee University and the University of Virginia. However, most of his business career has been devoted to insurance rather than the law. For nearly two years he was county superintendent of schools for Sussex County.

His home has been in the city of Suffolk since 1890, when he became a member of the firm of Harper West, general insurance, and since that time he has expended much time and effort in the development of proper commercial facilities, in the raising of the standards of education and in directing the attention of Virginia and the nation at large to the proper utilization of the great advantages and resources of Tidewater Virginia. He was at one time one of the owners of the *Suffolk Herald,* and since 1906 has been head of the general insurance firm of West & Withers.

His friends have referred to him as Colonel West, since he served as a member of the staff of Governor Swanson. He was elected to the House of Delegates in 1909, and after one term in the House served two and a half consecutive terms in the senate. Colonel West was author of the West Fee Bill, and author of the act providing for medical and dental inspection of school children, known as West Health Law. He was a patron of the State Purchasing Act, and he has been one of the constructive advocates of tax reform, health and educational legislation.

It was largely on the basis of his known constructive attitude in legislative and public affairs that he was chosen lieutenant governor in 1921. As presiding officer of the Senate he was distinguished by his parliamentary skill, and was always dignified and fair in directing the deliberations of the body. During 1928 he was looked upon as a leading candidate of the Democratic party for the office of governor, but withdrew his candidacy in 1929. Colonel West was at one time chairman of the Democratic committee of Nansemond County, has been a member of the State Central Committee and State Democratic Executive Committee, president of the Democratic clubs of Suffolk, and was a delegate to the National Democratic Convention of 1896. He has served as president of the Suffolk City Council.

He is a trustee of Elon College of North Carolina, was on the Board of Trustees of the State Teachers College at Farmville, and during the World war was chairman of the United War Work campaign in Suffolk and Nansemond counties and a four minute speaker. He is a past president of the Suffolk Rotary Club, is a Mason, a member of the Sons of the American Revolution and is also affiliated with the B. P. O. Elks. He is a prominent layman of the Christian Church, having served for many years as chairman of the mission board of the Eastern Virginia Conference and chairman of the mission board of the Southern Christian Convention, and has long taught a class of women in the Suffolk Christian Church Sunday School. Colonel West has been honored with the office of vice president of the Virginia Insurance Agents Association, and is a member of the Westmoreland Club of Richmond.

He married, February 17, 1903, Miss Ollie Beale, of Suffolk. They have one daughter, Margaret Beale West.

FRANCIS R. PAYNE is a member of a firm of brothers prominently identified with the business life of Newport in Giles County, and he has lived in that locality most of his life.

He was born at Newport December 7, 1895, son of R. Y. and Flora C. (Puckett) Payne, and grandson of John R. Payne and great-grandson of Charles Payne. Charles Payne was a pioneer of Southwest Virginia, a farmer and hunter in the early days of Giles County. The Payne family have been in Virginia since early Colonial times. R. Y. Payne was born and reared in Giles County, received advantages in private schools and spent his early years as a farmer. In 1908 he moved to the coal fields of West Virginia, but in 1929 returned to Newport, where he and his wife reside. He has always voted the Republican ticket, and is a member of the Masonic fraternity. His wife, Flora C. Puckett, was born in Giles County, grew up at Newport, where she attended public school, and for about twenty years held the office of postmaster there, serving until the advent of the Wilson administration. She is a member of the Methodist Episcopal Church, South. These parents had a family of seven children: W. C.

Andrew F. Horne M. D.

Payne, now in the lumber business at Welch, West Virginia, was in training at Camp Lee during the World war, getting his honorable discharge December 1, 1918; Francis R., of Newport; Harry W., of Widemouth, West Virginia; James M., of Newport; Helen, who died at the age of nine years; Miss Grace, a teacher in the public schools of Narrows, Virginia; and Miss Tootsie, who is attending the State Teachers College at Harrisonburg.

Francis R. Payne attended public schools in Newport, getting his high school work there. When he left school he went to Kayford, West Virginia, and for eight years clerked in stores in that vicinity, and for several years was postmaster of a West Virginia community. During the World war Mr. Payne joined the colors at Fort Hamilton, New York, where he was in training with the Motor Transport Corps until honorably discharged on December 15, 1919.

Mr. Payne in 1924 returned to Newport and has since been associated with his brother in the automobile and garage business. They operate the Newport Service Station, are distributing agents for the Standard Oil Company products, and handle the Chevrolet cars. Mr. Payne has always interested himself in community affairs and is very public spirited. He is affiliated with Newport Lodge No. 261, A. F. and A. M. He is a Republican and a member of the Board of Stewards of the Methodist Episcopal Church, South.

He married at Buchanan, Virginia, April 10, 1918, Miss Dora Ellen Kelly. She attended public schools in Pulaski and the Harrisonburg State Teachers College, and was a teacher for several years before her marriage, being thus engaged at Newport and also in Russell County and Smyth County. Mrs. Payne is active in the work of the Methodist Episcopal Church, South. She is a daughter of John P. and Mary (Groseclose) Kelly, of Marion. Her father is now living on a farm at White Gate, Virginia. Mr. and Mrs. Payne have two children, Frank R. and Mary Camelia, both attending the Newport public schools.

ANDREW F. HORNE, M. D. When in 1884 Dr. Andrew F. Horne located at Glade Springs he was newly graduated from a medical college, and was contented to take his place among the citizens of a growing community and to accept such opportunities for professional advancement that came his way. He was enterprising and ambitious, and his skill in diagnosis and successful treatment of several complicated cases of long standing almost immediately created a gratifying demand for his services, thus laying the foundation for what has been a career of exceptional breadth and usefulness. During the more than forty-four years that have followed he has risen to acknowledged leadership in his community, not alone along the lines and duties of his profession, but in every avenue of advancement. Today he is one of the most influential and best beloved citizens of his part of Washington County.

Doctor Horne was born in November, 1856, near Emory, Washington County, Virginia, and is a son of John E. and Mary Buchannon (Fullen) Horne, natives of Virginia, both of whom are now deceased. His father, who was of German descent, was a farmer in Washington County, where he passed his entire career, and was a man of influence and prominence, serving for many years as justice of the peace and member of the Board of County Supervisors. He and his worthy wife were devout members of the Methodist Episcopal Church, South, and did much for the betterment of their community.

The boyhood and youth of Andrew F. Horne were passed on his father's farm in Washington County, where he assisted the elder man in his operations while acquiring his primary education in the country schools. The finding of a groove in life in which one's heart and mind are emphatically enlisted assures success to nine out of ten of the toilers of the earth. The farm is the largest and most beneficent camping ground for the survey of life's possibilities, and it was among these fortunate if not congenial surroundings that Doctor Horne determined upon his humanitarian career. After completing his public school education he entered Emory and Henry College at Emory, where he obtained the degree of Master of Arts, following which he enrolled as a student in the medical department of the University of Virginia. This course was supplemented by attendance at the College of Physicians and Surgeons at Baltimore, Maryland, from which he was graduated with the degree of Doctor of Medicine as a member of the class of 1884.

In the same year Doctor Horne settled at Glade Springs, where he has since been located, and which community has watched with sincere interest his constantly growing fortune. He early won the confidence of the people by his skill in diagnosis and his successful treatment of disorders of all kinds, and he has always been a student who has recognized no end to the road of science and who forges ahead patiently and conscientiously. At an age when most men are content to retire upon their laurels he continues to go about his daily round of duties, just as he did in the early years when it was a necessity for him to work constantly to keep body and soul together. During the World war he offered his services to his country as a member of the Medical Corps and served as a volunteer in that body, and at present is acting in the capacity of health officer of Glade Springs. He belongs to the Southwest Virginia Medical Society, the Virginia Medical Society and the American Medical Association. He is a Democrat, and while not active in politics, is a man of great influence in his community and active in all of its affairs. He belongs to the Masonic Blue Lodge and to the Board of Stewards of the Methodist Episcopal Church, South.

Doctor Horne married Miss Laura M. Lincoln, of Marion, Virginia, daughter of the late Charles Lincoln, who was engaged in manufacturing at Marion until his death. She was educated at Marion Female College and is a consistent member of the Presbyterian Church. To Doctor and Mrs. Horne there have been born the following children: Charles Lincoln, educated at Emory and Henry College, and now engaged in the automobile and radio business at Glade Springs; Mary, a graduate of Sullins College, Bristol, Virginia, and now a teacher in the public schools of Sparta, North Carolina. Andrew, a graduate in electrical engineering of the Virginia Polytechnic Institute, who is identified with the Appalachia Power Company of Bluefield, West Virginia; H. A., a student at Emory and Henry College; Margaret, a graduate of Marion Female College, Marion, who took special courses in music at Martha Washington College, Abingdon, and the Chicago Conservatory of Music,, Chicago, Illinois, and is now teaching music in the schools of Sparta, North Carolina; and John, who attended the Glade Springs High School and is a graduate of the Bliss Electrical College of Washington, D. C., class of 1929.

JOHN BAKER ROLLER is principal of the high school at Pearisburg, and is a director of vocational agricultural education for all the high schools of Giles County. Mr. Roller, who was with the Coast Artillery Corps during the World war, has had a very interesting experience and career as an educator.

His people have been Virginians for a number of generations, but he was himself born at Oxford, North Carolina, May 8, 1895, son of John B. and Sallie (Easley) Roller. The Rollers are of remote German ancestry, and some of them served as burgomasters of their home town in Prussia. The family came to America at an early date, and one of the relics in the family carefully preserved is a rolling pin made from the limb of the tree under which the Rollers camped the first day they were on American shores. In Germany the family had a coat of arms. John B. Roller was born and reared in Ohio and as a young man moved to Virginia where his father owned a large interest in the Mecklenburg Hotel. He attended a private school in Ohio and the Virginia Agricultural and Mechanical College, now the Virginia Polytechnic Institute. After his marriage he moved to Oxford, North Carolina, and engaged in the insurance business, establishing what is still known and operated as the J. B. Roller & Son Company. He was a man of prominence in that locality, a deacon in the Baptist Church, and at one time secretary and treasurer of the Taylor-Cannady Buggy Company and later the Oxford Buggy Company. He died in 1909 and is buried at Oxford. His wife, Sallie Easley, born and reared in Halifax County, Virginia, and educated at Hollins College, taught school for several years before her marriage, is a resident of Richmond with her only daughter, and for years has been active in the Baptist Church. The Easleys are a family readily identified with prominent connections in old Virginia, particularly in Halifax and other eastern counties. Among other descendants of the family is John W. Craddock, a prominent shoe manufacturer. John B. Roller and wife had five children. Frank, the youngest, died in infancy. Joseph Rose is an operator with the Western Union Telegraph Company, a resident of Ontario, Canada, and is married, but his only child died in infancy. Charles Easley Roller is in the tobacco sales and manufacturing business at Oxford, North Carolina, married Louie Mitchell, a widow with a son, John, by her first husband, and two children have been born to them, William and Charles, Jr. Miss Hallie Hall Roller, the only daughter, is connected with the Virginia Industrial Commission at Richmond.

John Baker Roller attended public schools at Oxford, North Carolina, the Cluster Springs Academy in Virginia, and in 1916 graduated with the Bachelor of Science degree from the Virginia Polytechnic Institute. In 1924 advance credits gave him the Master of Science degree. For one year after leaving the institute he taught in the Appomattox High School.

In June, 1917, he joined the colors, in the Regular Army, in training with the Coast Artillery Corps on Chesapeake Bay, and later was commissioned a provisional second lieutenant. He went overseas with the rank of first lieutenant in the Seventy-fifth Regiment, Coast Artillery Corps, in October, 1918, and was at St. Nazaire and was moving up with the artillery at the headquarters at Mailly Le Camp at the time of the armistice. He remained with the Army of Supply until June, 1919, and came back in charge of a company of casuals, discharging them at Camp Mills, New York, and then reported to Fort Scriven,

Georgia, where his resignation was accepted and he was honorably discharged with the rank of first lieutenant. He is now a captain in the Field Artillery Officers Reserve Corps.

Captain Roller after being relieved of military duty became teacher of agriculture and for three years was principal of the Apple Grove High School in Virginia. While he was there the efficiency of the school was improved to a point where the school was placed on the accredited list. Mr. Roller came to Pearisburg in 1923 as principal of the high school. He takes deserved pride in the fine physical plant and the personnel of the teaching and student body. The high school is a large two-story brick and concrete building with basement and six rooms, providing quarters for the agricultural class, while on the second floor is an auditorium with seating capacity of about six hundred. He has fourteen teachers under his supervision and about 350 students. The Pearisburg High School is held in high respect in this part of Virginia for the achievements of its athletic and other representative teams. It has won many trophies in competition, in basketball, baseball, and other sports. In 1925 the basketball team won the championship of District E, and in the state contest at the University of Virginia stood fourth in its class. In 1924, 25 and 26 the school won the county silver cup for best literary and athletic work. In 1927 a new cup was provided by the county, and it is now held by the Pearisburg High School, which has won one leg on that cup, three years of winning being necessary for permanent possession. Near the high school building is the elementary school, a brick Colonial building, with accommodations for seven grades and three rooms for domestic science department. The eight teachers there are under the grade supervisor, Miss Annie Brotherton. Captain Roller, in charge of the instruction in vocational agriculture for the county, has supervision of departments in the high schools at Newport, Eggleston and White Gate, his assistant in this work being W. L. Hargis, one of the teachers in the Pearisburg High School.

Captain Roller owns his home at Pearisburg and is interested in the Pearisburg Hatchery. He is a member of the Pi Gamma Mu fraternity, is a Royal Arch Mason, member of the Chamber of Commerce, a Democrat, and is active in the Baptist Church, being superintendent of the Sunday School and a leader in the Baptist Young People's Union.

He married at Fort Moultrie, South Carolina, September 10, 1918, Miss Margaret Bolling Atkinson, of McKinney, Virginia, where she attended public schools. She graduated in 1916 from the Randolph-Macon Woman's College at Lynchburg and taught for several years, being assistant principal of the high school at Waverly, Virginia. She is a Presbyterian and a member of the Alpha Omicron Pi sorority. Her parents were John Pryor and Sallie (Jones) Atkinson. Her father was a farmer in Dinwiddie County and died in 1909. Her mother, who still occupies the old homestead near McKinney, has had much to do with community affairs there. She is a sister of Dr. J. Bolling Jones, a prominent physician and surgeon of Petersburg, Virginia. Her father was a Presbyterian minister, and the Jones family has had many representatives in educational work. They deeded the land and were instrumental in the foundation of the Sunnyside High School, an accredited high school near McKinney. Captain and Mrs. Roller have three children: John Baker, Jr., and Sallie Jones, both attending public schools at Pearisburg, and Roger Pryor.

Capt. William B. Peters M.D.

WILLIAM B. PETERS, M. D. One of the widely known medical
men of Wise County, who has long contributed, both professionally and personally, to the prestige of Southwest Virginia, is Dr.
William B. Peters, prominent citizen of Appalachia, Virginia,
eminent surgeon, health officer for fifteen years, house surgeon
of the Appalachia Masonic Hospital, a veteran officer of the
World war, and a past post commander of the American Legion.

   Dr. William B. Peters belongs to an old Virginia family of
German descent that many years ago was established here by
one Jacob P. Peters, who settled first in Shenandoah County but
later removed to Scott County, where he is recorded as a large
planter and citizen of local importance. Doctor Peters generations later, in 1882 was born in Scott County, Virginia, son of
Rev. William B. and Elizabeth (Templeton) Peters, and grandson of William Peters and W. F. Templeton, all natives of Scott
County. The Templetons were of English ancestry and, like the
Peters came early to Virginia, and both grandfathers were extensive planters before the war between the states. In this war
two uncles of Doctor Peters, Joseph and Abel Peters, were soldiers in the Confederate army. His father, however, was a man
of peace, a minister of the Methodist Episcopal Church, filling
many important charges during his eminently useful life.

   William B. Peters' early schooldays were passed in Scott
County, Virginia, and at Bristol, Tennessee. He then entered
Shoemaker College at Gate City, Virginia, where he completed
the prescribed course and in 1904 was graduated with the degree
of A. B. His medical education followed as an alert and ambitious student in the Central University of Kentucky at Louisville, from which institution he was graduated in 1907 with the
degree of M. D. Subsequently he took an exhaustive course on
surgery, a branch of his profession in which he has become distinguished, in the New York City Post-Graduate School, and
throughout his professional life has continued to take advantage
of opportunities for further study in many other leading medical
centers.

   Upon entering medical practice Doctor Peters selected Appalachia, Virginia, as his home and field of professional effort, and
has never found reason to change his first favorable impressions,
while the hearty welcome he then received would, today, be of
still greater emphasis, as his fellow citizens now recognize his
worth and accord him universal confidence and esteem. He early
began to show an interest in civic matters, and through this spirit of general helpfulness became so well and favorably known
that general approval was expressed when President Taft appointed him to the office of postmaster. He served with complete
efficiency for one year and then retired, as by that time his practice was demanding all of his attention, particularly as he had
been appointed health officer, in which office he has continued
ever since.

   Like many another medical man, Doctor Peters at the beginning of the World war found himself so heavily engaged professionally in work at home that he could not feel free to set aside
his work, but later, when the Government's call became urgent
for experienced medical aid, he hesitated no longer but enlisted
in December, 1917, for either home or foreign service, in the
United States Medical Corps. For five weeks he was under military training at Fort Oglethorpe, Georgia, and for eight weeks
at the Mitchell Aviation Field, New York, and then was assigned

to Manhattan Camp as camp surgeon, where he remained until
the close of the war. That his professional services were faithful and appreciated is indicated by his promotion in rank from
a lieutenancy to a captaincy, the signing of the armistice taking
place before his recommendation for major had passed through
the necessary official channels. He was honorably discharged in
December, 1918.

As house surgeon of the Appalachia Masonic Hospital Doctor
Peters fills a most responsible position, being practically at the
head of this thoroughly equipped institution. It was established
in 1906, has fourteen beds and also conducts a training school for
nurses, its maintenance being provided for by the Masonic fraternity, Doctor Peters himself being a Knight Templar and a
Shriner. He is physician for the Louisville & Nashville Railroad, and examiner for all the leading life insurance companies,
a pleasing natural personality, inspiring trust and confidence in
young and old, always having been a professional asset.

Doctor Peters married in 1911 Miss Georgia Harmon, who
was born in North Carolina, where her father, Rev. George Harmon, was a prominent minister in the Baptist Church. She was
mainly educated at Bristol, Tennessee, is a member and a past
worthy matron of the Eastern Star, and president of the Ladies
Auxilliary to the American Legion. Doctor and Mrs. Peters have
four sons: Carl, Herbert, William B., Jr., and George, aged respectively, fifteen, thirteen, six and one year. The family home
is very pleasantly located with congenial friends all about them,
and they are members of the Episcopal Church.

Doctor Peters is a member of the Wise County Medical Society and its secretary in 1917; the Clinch Valley Medical Society; the Virginia State Medical Society; and the American Medical Association. He still preserves membership in his old college
Greek letter fraternity, the Phi Chi, belongs to the American Legion at Appalachia Post, of which he is a past commander, and
additionally is Legion state executive for the Ninth District of
Virginia. He has always given encouragement to substantial local enterprises, frequently has consented to lecture before civic
bodies, and is on the directing board of the Appalachia Hotel
Corporation.

WILLIAM LEONARD HARGIS, professor of agriculture in three
of the high schools of Giles County, is a representative of the
enthusiastic twentieth century generation of Virginians. He is
member of an old well known Russell County family.

He was born at Lebanon in Russell County, November 4,
1903, son of George J. and Henrietta (Buckles) Hargis, and
grandson of Leonard Hargis, also of Russell County, George
Hargis was born and reared in Russell County, attended public
schools and Lebanon Academy, and has made his life work
farming and stock raising. He owns a fine blue grass farm near
Lebanon and was one of the first men in that section to use
improved methods and pure bred livestock. His present hobby is
pure bred Hampshire sheep and he has some of the finest speci-
mens of that strain in Southwest Virginia. He is treasurer of
his Masonic Lodge at Lebanon and has been clerk of the Camp
of the Modern Woodmen since its organization. His wife, Henrietta Buckles, is a daughter of Rev. William and Sallie (Pile)
Buckles. Her father was an early Baptist minister in Southwestern Virginia. Henrietta Buckles was born and reared at
Lebanon, attended the Lebanon Academy and taught in public

schools for several years before her marriage. She and her husband are members of the Baptist Church. They had four children: Miss Nannie B., who was educated in the Lebanon High School, in Carson and Newman College, and lives at Lebanon; William Leonard; Miss Margaret Buckles, a graduate of the Lebanon High School, attended the Radford State Normal College and is now a teacher at Wise Court House, Virginia; and Miss Henrietta, in the third year of the Lebanon High School.

William Leonard Hargis after graduating from the Lebanon High School in 1922 entered Virginia Polytechnic Institute, where he completed his work in the class of 1926. His early training as well as his college work gave him decided qualifications for his duties as agricultural instructor for the three high schools at White Gate, Eggleston and Newport in Giles County. His home is at Pearisburg, from which point he supervises the work in connection with the high schools.

Mr. Hargis is also associated as a partner with his father in the cattle and sheep business at Lebanon. He is a member of the Masonic fraternity, a Democrat, a Missionary Baptist, and has taken much part in both church and Sunday School work. Mr. Hargis is well known in college and university athletic circles, having been the undefeated state champion and the champion of the South Atlantic and Southern Intercollegiate group in 1926, and was placed on the All Southern wrestling team. He was also a member of the Virginia Polytechnic football team in 1926.

JOHN L. CRIST. The history of chemistry, taken as a whole, is a decidedly interesting one. The Egyptians, of all nations of antiquity, appear to have had the greatest amount of chemical knowledge, although the Chinese were very early acquainted with the processes of dyeing and the preparation of metallic alloys. From the Egyptians the Greeks and Romans derived what chemical knowledge they possessed, but added little or nothing; and at the migration of the northern tribes and the overthrow of the Roman Empire a stop was put for a time to the advancement of all science in Europe. The first germs of the real science of chemistry appear about the end of the seventeenth and beginning of the eighteenth century, and after this chemistry has been continuous and rapid in its advancement. One of the most important branches of chemistry is that which has to do with the manufacture of dyestuffs, in which connection mention is made of the Beaver Chemical Corporation of Damascus, the only concern of its kind in the southern states. This has been developed to large proportions under the direct supervision and management of John L. Crist, a practical chemist and capable business man, who is also an important factor in the civic life of his adopted community.

Mr. Crist was born at Vesuvius, Rockbridge County, Virginia, August 30, 1890, and is a son of William McClung and Nancy (Bryan) Crist. His paternal great-grandfather was a native of Holland, who immigrated to the American colonies and settled in Virginia, where the family has since made its home and has contributed many of its members to leading positions in business, agricultural, political, military and civil life. John F. Crist, the grandfather of John L. Crist, was born in Virginia, where he passed his entire life as a planter. William McClung Crist was born in the Old Dominion, and spent the greater part of his life at Vesuvius, where he followed planting and died in

1904. He enlisted in the Confederate army at the outbreak of the war between the states, and was assigned to the artillery division, with which he served valiantly. He received several minor wounds before being completely disabled at the battle of Petersburg by the loss of one of his legs, and thus throughout the remainder of his life was handicapped in his various operations, although always a man of industry and good judgment. He was a member of the Independent Order of Odd Fellows and was devout in his adherence to the faith of the Methodist Episcopal Church, South. His widow still survives him. Both great-grandfather Bryan and wife, who was a Campbell, came to America from Scotland and located in Augusta County Virginia, where was born their son, Elisha Bryan, an iron manufacturer, who was one of the first to open iron furnaces in Augusta County. He was a man who was widely and favorably known in his community for his high character, integrity and good citizenship.

John L. Crist acquired his early education in the country schools of Rockbridge County, Virginia, and then pursued a course at the high school at Woodstock, and graduated in chemistry with the degree of Bachelor of Science from Washington and Lee University as a member of the class of 1912. For three years thereafter he served as chemist at the plant of the Matheison Alkali Works at Saltsville, leaving this concern to become identified for six months with the Hooker Electro Chemical Company of Niagara Falls, New York. His next position was with the Federal Dye Stuff and Chemical Company of Kingsport, Tennessee, in the capacity of chemical engineer in charge of the chlorine department, and retained this important post during the entire period of the World war in the manufacture of war supplies and munitions. Late in the fall of 1918 Mr. Crist was called to Damascus, Virginia, where he supervised the building the plant of the Beaver Chemical Corporation for the manufacture of dyes, the only concern of its kind in any of the southern states. This has been carefully developed, step by step, new additions being constantly made, until it is now an enterprise of large and important proportions and one that adds considerably to the manufacturing prestige of the state. Mr. Crist is also president of a new corporation which has recently been formed under the corporate name of the Calcium Sulphide Corporation, which is now engaged in the manufacture and distribution of a new fungicide for the control of fungus diseases on apples, peaches and kindred fruits, as well as fungus appearing on many plants and flowers. This is an enterprise which appears to have much promise of filling a needed place in the industry of the commonwealth. Mr. Crist is a wide-awake and properly progressive young man who is thoroughly up to the minute in his knowledge of his specialty. He is a member of the American Institute of Chemical Engineers, The American Association of Textile Colorists and Chemists, and enjoys a broad and well-merited reputation in his difficult, complicated and interested calling. In his political convictions Mr. Crist is a stanch and unwavering Democrat, but has had no time in his busy career to devote to office seeking. He is president of the Citizens Club of Damascus, an organization of business men that has the same status as the Chambers of Commerce in most cities, and his religious connection is with the Episcopal Church.

In 1914 Mr. Crist was united in marriage with Miss Bess Rector, of Saltsville, Virginia, daughter of Leland W. and Linda

(Branson) Rector, both of whom are now deceased, Mr. Rector having passed his life as a planter in Washington County. Mrs. Crist was educated at the grammar and high schools of Saltville, Smyth County, and is an active member of the United Daughters of the Confederacy, the Community League and the Episcopal Church. To Mr. and Mrs. Crist there has come one son, John L., Jr., who was born at Damascus, May 20, 1923.

GARY LAUGHON. During a long, active and useful career Gary Laughon has been identified with a number of lines of business activity, in all of which he has met with success. A man of high character and strict integrity, he has the full confidence of those who have been associated with him in any line of endeavor, and it has been his fortune to have surrounded himself with many close and sincere friends. At present he is devoting his attention principally to the Pulaski Motor Car Company, of which he is half owner.

Mr. Laughon was born May 26, 1863, in Bedford County, Virginia, and is a son of Joshua and Elizabeth (White) Laughon, and a member of a family of Scotch-Irish origin which was founded in Virginia by the grandfather of Mr. Laughon, a Scotchman, who came to America in young manhood and became a pioneer agriculturist of Bedford County. Joshua Laughon was born in Bedford County, where he was reared and educated in a private school and prepared for the vocation of teaching, which he took up in young manhood. He was thus engaged at the outbreak of the war between the states, when he enlisted in General Watts' command, which was attached to the Army of Northern Virginia, commanded by Gen. Robert E. Lee, and rose to a captaincy. During the four years of his service he participated in a number of major engagements, and at all times showed himself a brave and faithful soldier. At the close of hostilities he returned to the duties of peace and carried on agricultural pursuits during the remainder of his life, his death, hastened by the hardships and privations of army life, occurring in 1877, and he was buried in the old family cemetery in Bedford County. Mr. Laughon married Miss Elizabeth White, who was born and reared in Bedford County, where she received a private school education. She and her husband were members of the Methodist Episcopal Church, South, in the faith of which she died and she was buried in the old family cemetery. There were seven children in the family: One who died in infancy; Alonzo, Walter and Lavenia, who are deceased; Oscar, of Pulaski, president of the Laughon Lumber Company, a review of whose career will be found elsewhere in this work; Gary, of this review; Beauregard, who is engaged in the sand and gravel business at Pulaski, with offices over the Pulaski Trust Company; and Joshua, who is deceased.

Gary Laughon attended one of the many private schools that flourished in the vicinity of his boyhood home, and his first employment was with the firm of Jones, Watts, Brothers & Company, as a clerk, at a salary of twenty dollars per month. He remained with this concern for six years and then came to Pulaski, where he joined his brothers, Oscar and Beauregard, in the hardware business, first in a store near the old depot and then in the first store built north of Peak Creek, in Pulaski. This partnership continued for about four years, at the end of which time Gary Laughon sold his interests to his brothers and embarked in the cattle business and farming, and continued in that line for twenty years. In 1908 he returned to Pulaski and embarked in the coal and stone business, with which he was identified for about fourteen years, or until 1923. In the meantime his eldest son, Fred J. Laughon, had engaged in the automobile business, as the Pulaski Motor Car Company, in partnership with H. W. Steger. When Mr. Laughon's son died he took over the latter's interest in the business and is now conducting it with Mr. Steger, who acts as manager. Mr. Laughon is a member of the Board of Directors of the Peoples National Bank, a director of the Pulaski Trust Company and president of the City Improvement Company, and is also the owner of much valuable city property. He is a thirty-second degree Mason and belongs to Marion Chapter, R. A. M., Acca Temple, A. A. O. N. M. S., the Benevolent and Protective Order of Elks, and the Rotary Club. He is a Democrat in his political convictions, and his religious faith is that of the Methodist Church.

On May 27, 1886, in Pulaski County, Mr. Laughon was united in marriage with Miss Mollie Hage Jordan, of that county, who was educated in public schools and at Martha Washington College, and is active in church and social life, although more a home maker and home lover. She is a daughter of William T. and Letitia (Simmerman) Jordan, the former of whom for many years was a prominent farmer and cattle man of Pulaski County. Mr. Jordan died in 1890 and his wife, in 1908, and both were laid to rest in the Thorn Spring Cemetery. Both the Jordan and Simmerman families are prominent in Virginia, and Mrs. Laughon is a granddaughter on the maternal side of John P. M. Simmerman, of Wythe County. To Mr. and Mrs. Laughon there have been born six children: Fred J., deceased; Willie J.; Lettie, who died at the age of three and one-half years; Mary Elizabeth, Gary, Jr., and Lavenia.

Fred J. Laughon received his education at the Virginia Military Institute and Emory and Henry College, following which he returned to Pulaski and embarked in the electrical business, having a general repair and supply shop at Pulaski for some time. Recognizing the future of the automobile business, he formed a partnership with H. W. Steger in organizing the automobile and garage business, which was conducted as the Pulaski Motor Car Company. Under the able management of the partners the company soon outgrew its original quarters and moved to the present establishment near the center of Pulaski's business district, but later it was found necessary to add several additions to the structure, which made it finally a two-story brick building, 175 by 110 feet. The company handles Ford and Lincoln automobiles and Fordson trucks, as well as all accessories, and its large repair shop, capable of handling any order, is said to be one of the best in the state. Fred J. Laughon was identified with this business until his demise July 16, 1923, when he was buried in the Pulaski Cemetery. Willie J. Laughon, who now resides with her father at Pulaski, is the widow of the late H. W. Thaxton, of Bedford County, who was engaged in the real estate business until his death in 1918. Mary Elizabeth Laughon married M. E. Bowman, of Pulaski, treasurer and auditor of the Pulaski Iron Company, and formerly of Roanoke, this state, and has two children, M. Edwin and Mary Elizabeth. Gary Laughon, Jr., a graduate of the public schools, is engaged in the junk bus-

Sam N. Hurst

iness at Pulaski. He married Miss Lois Caldwell, of Pulaski County, and they are the parents of one child, Peggy.

SAM N. HURST, of Appalachia, Wise County, is one of the most versatile and gifted men among his contemporaries. In an active career of a little more than thirty years he has been teach-. er, preacher, lawyer, author and publisher, and in his career he has lived up well to his motto of living not for himself alone, but for his brother, his country and his God.

Mr. Hurst was born in Pulaski County, Virginia, February 16, 1867, one of a large family of children born to Allen and Nancy (Cook) Hurst. Allen Hurst was born in Pulaski County March 2, 1825, son of Thomas and Jemima (Breeding) Hurst, Thomas Hurst being a son of John Hurst, who was a son of Absalom Hurst, the pioneer of the family in Pulaski County, Virginia. In all the generations the Hursts were pioneers, and pioneering was the lot of Allen Hurst, who after his marriage went with his young wife and took up a tract of raw land, cutting down trees and building a log cabin home, and while he was in the Confederate army his wife proved herself a heroine by remaining at home and looking after her children and at times taking the youngsters to the field with her, where they would lie on a blanket-pallet while she herself followed the plow to earn a living for her family.

Sam N. Hurst has shown much of the spirit and disposition of the pioneer, possessing an intellectuality of a wide range and willing to venture into new ways and methods of serving humanity. He had a very limited education in the rural community where he grew up, and was fourteen years old before he began his real education. He attended Snowville Academy in 1883-84, the Virginia Polytechnic Institute in 1884-85, won a Peabody scholarship which enabled him to attend the University of Nashville during 1885-87, concluding with his graduation and a diploma qualifying him for teaching. In the meantime he had studied law privately, took a summer course under John B. Minor at the University of Virginia in 1888, and was admitted to the bar April 24, 1889. He taught in Snowville Academy, held a chair in a college at Terrell, Texas, and also taught in the Wytheville Male Academy in Virginia, and did some teaching in Tennessee and Kentucky. Soon after beginning the practice of law he discovered the necessity for a magistrate's guide, and that was responsible for the first of his many law books, now comprising nine works, twenty-five volumes, all well known to the legal profession throughout Virginia. Some of the better known are: Hurst's J. P. Guide and Manual, Hurst's Digest of Virginia Decisions, Hurst's Pocket Code of Virginia, Hurst's Annotated Virginia Constitution, Hurst's Encyclopedia of Virginia Law. His law books have been endorsed and have received many high commendations from lawyers, judges of the Supreme Court, governors and attorney-generals. Mr. Hurst printed and published his books, and as a publisher was also his own advertising and sales manager. Mr. Hurst recently published his first novel, "The Mountains Redeemed," a story of life and love in Southwest Virginia, a work which is receiving strong reviews by the press of the country, and is specially sponsored by Southwestern Virginia, Inc.

From the outset of his career as a lawyer Mr. Hurst was also deeply interested in religious teaching and preaching. He joined the Primitive Baptist Church in 1889, and in 1903 was ordained to the full work of the Gospel ministry. In June, 1909, he and his wife united with the First Baptist Church of Roanoke, and in that year he gave up the law for the ministry. After being ordained in the Baptist ministry he spent a year at Louisville in the Southern Baptist Seminary and for fifteen years gave most of his time to the work of the ministry, serving many pastorates and circuits. On leaving his last regular charge as a minister he located at Appalachia, where he has built up a very favorable reputation and connections in the law. While in the ministry he withdrew from the Baptist Church and became a minister of the Virginia Conference of the Methodist Episcopal Church, South. He withdrew from the itinerant ministry November 15, 1926, and returned to the law.

Mr. Hurst through all the years has continued his literary work. One of his notable productions was "Biographical Sketches of all Supreme Court Judges of Virginia from 1779-1896," and "Lincoln from the Standpoint of the Southern Lawyer."

Mr. Hurst married, February 18, 1890, Anna Louise Evans, whom he lost July 23, 1893, leaving one daughter, Virginia L., born August 13, 1892. On March 6, 1895, Mr. Hurst married Ida May Hopson, daughter of J. W. and Nancy D. (Ward) Hopson, her father having been a prominent Kentucky attorney. Her father's mother was a Newberry of the Virginia Newberrys, while her mother's mother was a Clay of the Kentucky Clays. The children born to Mr. and Mrs. Hurst were: Erskine, born July 12, 1897; Elsie and Ressie, twins, born January 31, 1899; Aubrey, born August 13, 1901; Evangeline, born June 15, 1903; Vivian, born June 15, 1905; Evelyn, born August 26, 1907; Samuel N., Jr., born February 8, 1912; and Alliene, born September 2, 1918.

RUDOLPH B. FELTHAUS. For about fifteen years the late Rudolph B. Felthaus was engaged in the building and contracting business at Richmond, and this period, comparatively short as it was, served to gain him a recognized position among the leaders of his calling and to establish for him a reputation of being a material contributor to the development and architectural beautification of his native city. While his activities were cut short by death when he was still in the prime of life, he had led an active and useful career, and the many beautiful residences and other structures that grew under his skillful direction still stand as monuments to his ability and substantial workmanship.

Mr. Felthaus was born in Richmond, March 3, 1867, and was a son of William and Anna (Wotte) Felthaus, natives of Steinwild, Germany. His parents were married in their native land and soon thereafter immigrated to the United States and settled in Virginia, whence William Felthaus enlisted in the Confederate army during the war between the states. At the close of that struggle he took up his residence in Richmond, where he passed the remainder of his life as a merchant tailor. He and his worthy wife were the parents of seven children, of whom Rudolph B. was the third in order of birth.

Rudolph B. Felthaus had the advantages of an excellent educational training, attending the Richmond public schools, the Mechanics Institute of Richmond and Belmont College of Belmont, North Carolina. Following his graduation as a young man he entered the employ of the Montroy Manufacturing Com-

Larry J. Hammack

pany, but after a few years turned his attention to the contracting and building business, with which he was identified until his death, February 9, 1909. Mr. Felthaus, as before noted, made a name and reputation in his field of activity and had the esteem and sincere admiration of his business associates, who appreciated his high character and sterling integrity no less than his skill and mastery of his business affairs. During his career in addition to remodeling beautiful St. Mary's Church he contracted for and built more than one hundred of Richmond's finest homes. He was one of the city's most public spirited citizens, and at all times could be depended upon to contribute to worthy enterprises and movements. Fraternally he was affiliated with the Benevolent and Protective Order of Elks, and also was a member of St. Mary's Social Club.

On June 5, 1894, Mr. Felthaus married Miss Elizabeth Ryan, who was educated in private schools at Richmond, and is a daughter of James and Helen M. (Finigin) Ryan, and a granddaughter of Thomas Ryan, a professor at Carlow, Ireland. James Bryan was born at Carlow, Ireland, whence he came in young manhood to the United States, prior to the war of secession, and settled at Richmond, where he carried on merchandising for many years. His wife was born in Dublin, Ireland, and they were the parents of twelve children, of whom Elizabeth was the seventh in order of birth. Mrs. Felthaus, whose mother was an educator for some years, is a woman of education and refinement and an active member of St. Mary's Church. She resides in an attractive home at 1614 Pope Avenue. Of the five children born to Mr. and Mrs. Felthaus three lived to maturity: Helen, who was private secretary to one of the officials of the Richmond, Frdericksburg & Potomac Railroad for ten years, now a social worker for the betterment of the poor of Richmond in a quiet and unostentatious way, and a member of the Society of Profession of Faith; William John, who was educated at private schools and the Junior Polytechnic Institute at Blacksburg, Virginia, enlisted in the World war as a member of the famous Richmond Blues, saw active service with the Twenty-ninth Division in France for one year, and is now a member of the American Legion and successfully engaged in the automobile business at Richmond; and Elizabeth, the wife of Ernest L. Martin, who is identified with the American National Bank of Richmond.

LORENZA JOHN HAMMACK is senior member of the Lawrenceville law firm of Hammack & Harrison. He is one of the strong and resourceful members of the bar in Southern Virginia, has to his credit a service record in the World war and is a member of one of the old families of Brunswick County.

He was born in that county February 16, 1895, son of P. T. and Alice E. (Palmer) Hammack. His father was born in Brunswick County and his mother in Northampton County, North Carolina. P. T. Hammack spent all his active life as a merchant at Gasburg, Brunswick County, where he died in September, 1923.

Lorenza J. Hammack after the common schools spent three years in college at Lynchburg, Virginia, and had his law work at Washington and Lee University. He was graduated with the LL. B. degree in June, 1917.

He at once located at Lawrenceville, and so far as the distractions of the war permitted made some attempt to build up a practice. Then in January, 1918, he himself joined the colors, becoming a chief yeoman in the navy, and spent most of his time in transport duty. He made six round trips to France before getting his honorable discharge in April, 1918.

After being relieved of service in the navy he returned to Lawrenceville and started anew to build up a law practice. In his profession he has enjoyed wonderful success and in June, 1928, he took into partnership Mr. A. S. Harrison, Jr., in order to handle more expeditiously the large volume of law work of the firm.

Mr. Hammack married in August, 1921, Miss Mary Heath Raney, daughter of L. H. and Bessie (Watkins) Raney, natives of Brunswick County. Her father is a real estate operator and banker at Lawrenceville. Mr. and Mrs. Hammack have two children, Lorenza John, Jr., born October 3, 1922, and Elizabeth Lewis, born January 6, 1924.

Mr. Hammack in addition to his law practice has farming interests and is a member of the House of Delegates of the Virginia Legislature, representing Brunswick County. He is a member of the Virginia Bar Association, the Masonic fraternity, Lions Club, American Legion, Knights of Pythias, Delta Theta Phi legal fraternity. He is a Democrat and a member of the Methodist Episcopal Church, South.

PAUL VINTON DALTON is a native of Southwestern Virginia, comes of a family of merchants and business men, and at the age of thirty has become president and general manager of the Dalton Grocery Company at Galax.

He was born near Hillsville in Carroll County, Virginia, September 27, 1897. His great-grandfather, Tom Dalton, came from England and settled in Southwestern Virginia. The grandfather, Jonathan Dalton, was born in 1839, and spent all his active career as a merchant at Dugspur in Carroll County, where he died in 1926, at the age of eighty-seven. He was a Confederate soldier in the Fourteenth Virginia Regiment of Cavalry, his name being one of those recorded on the Confederate Monument at Hillsville. Jonathan Dalton married Anis McGrady, who came from Wales with her parents. Gordon Dalton, father of Paul Vinton Dalton, was born at Dugspur, September 10, 1871, attended public school there, and as a young man engaged in retail merchandising. He was a retail merchant until 1917, at which time he established a wholesale business at Sylvatus, Virginia. He closed this out in 1924 and resumed business as a wholesale merchant at Radford, where he now resides. Gordon Dalton married Lucy A. Hurst, daughter of G. M. and Jane (Branscome) Hurst. Her father spent a number of years in educational work, teaching about twenty terms of school. He is now living retired at Dugspur. Jane Branscome was a daughter of Burts Branscome, who owned several thousand acres of land and many slaves in Carroll County. Gordon Dalton and wife had a large family of children: Minnie M., wife of Harley Dalton, of East Radford; Claudie H., now Mrs. D. C. Jennings, of Sylvatus; Paul Vinton; Violet, wife of Ed Jennings, of Foster Falls, Virginia; Pansy F., wife of Ray Richardson, of East Radford; Miss Averill, born in 1911, at home; Darrell Willard, born in 1916, attending school at East Radford; Phyllis, who died at the age of two years, Clyne, who died when two years old, and another who died in infancy, all of whom are buried in the McPeak Cemetery at Dugspur.

R. A. Sievels.

Paul Vinton Dalton was educated in public schools and as a boy learned the retail business with his father. He spent three years in the store at Dugspur, was with his father in the whole-sale grocery business at Sylvatus until 1924, and in that year moved to Galax and established the Dalton Grocery Company, with capital of $100,000. He has built up this business until it now supplies a large part of the retail trade in Southwestern Virginia.

Mr. Dalton is a member of the United Commercial Travelers, is affiliated with Fulton Lodge of Masons at Hillsville, Modern Woodmen of America, Galax Country Club, and is a Democrat.

He married at Laurel Fork, April 23, 1917, Miss Lula A. Jett, daughter of Burro Monroe and Lurenda (Short) Jett. Her father was a merchant at Hillsville and formerly lived at Willis in Floyd County. Mrs. Dalton attended public school at Hills-ville. She is a member of the Presbyterian Church and the Dora Green Chapter of the Eastern Star at Hillsville. Mr. and Mrs. Dalton have two children, Cecil Vinton, born May 23, 1918, and Paul Lynton, born April 10, 1923. The older child is in school at Galax.

RICHARD ALVIN SIEWERS for about a quarter of a century before his death, which occurred June 18, 1909, was one of the outstanding building contractors of the city of Richmond, and through his business contributed in a large measure to the constructive progress of the city in its most bustling modern period.

Born on January 3, 1859, at Hoexter, in the province of Westphalia, Germany, Richard A. Siewers was the third of five children of Adolph and Elizabeth Siewers. His father was an educator, most of whose career was engaged in the duties of superintendent of a college in his home province.

After passing through the elementary schools Richard A. Siewers received a liberal education in the Arts and Crafts College in his native city, where he graduated with high honors, being proficient especially in structural designing. Subsequently he chose the latter for his life's work, combining with it the practical work of a builder.

A few years after the death of his parents he came to America and settled in Richmond, Virginia, in 1880. For a time he was employed as an architect in the offices of the Chesapeake & Ohio Railroad. One of his characteristics was tremendous energy for work, and in those early years he employed his night time in studying English and otherwise perfecting himself for the career of an American citizen and business man. Constant application and careful thrift soon enabled him to take up the contracting business in association with Henry Miller, under the firm name of Siewers & Miller. When, some time afterward, he acquired the interest of his partner, he continued the business, including the mill and lumber department, under the firm name of R. A. Siewers until his death.

Some of the notable buildings in Richmond and vicinity which stand today as good examples of the substantial work of the Siewers contracting firm are the Shenandoah Apartments, the Bishop's Residence and the Rectory of the Sacred Heart Cathedral, the Knights of Columbus Home, the Jewish Club, the Merchants Cold Storage Plant, and a great number of fine residences besides.

The late Mr. Siewers was chief fire inspector for the German American Loan Association, and held an honorary membership in both the Police Association and Fire Association. He was a Democrat, a member of the Knights of Columbus, and, with his wife and children, belonged to the congregation of the Sacred Heart Cathedral.

Mr. Siewers on February 19, 1885, married Miss Sabina Ruppert, the youngest of the four children of John E. and Barbara Ruppert. She was educated in St. Benedict's Academy at Richmond. Her father was a linen manufacturer in Germany, and died shortly after settling in Virginia in 1860. Mrs. Siewers' grandfather was a flour miller in Hessen, Germany, and at one time was burgomaster of that town.

Mrs. Siewers has her home in Richmond, at 609 West Cary Street, the residence designed and built by her late husband. Of her family of children one is dead. The oldest son, John Christian, is now manager of the R. A. Siewers Planing Mill and Lumber Yard, and is affiliated with the Knights of Columbus. Rose Elizabeth Siewers married George J. Hulcher, a Richmond druggist, and they have three children, George, Jr., Rose Elizabeth and Sabina Siewers. Emil Richard Siewers, the second son, is assistant manager of the R. A. Siewers Mill and Lumber Company, and is a director of the German-American Loan Association. The Misses Sabina Josephine and Cecilia Ida are unmarried and live with their mother. Helen Julia is the wife of James E. Foster, chief clerk in the Richmond offices of the Chesapeake & Ohio Railway, and with their three children, named Helen Siewers, Anne Cecilia and Jean Marie, live in Richmond. Frederick W. Siewers, youngest of the three sons who carry on the business founded by their father, is office manager of the R. A. Siewers Mill and Lumber Company.

JOHN FRANKLIN CALFFE represented one of the old families of the Drapers Valley community, where representatives of the Calfee family still reside, owning land and other property in that historic section and keeps up a keen interest in all civic affairs.

John Franklin Calfee was born at Drapers Valley, April 8, 1850, son of James Davis and Nancy (Sayers) Calfee. His father was born and reared in the Draper Valley section, attended a private school and was a farmer and stock raiser until his death in 1883. He is buried in the Reed Island Cemetery. He was a son of John Franklin Calfee, the pioneer of the Calfee family in Drapers Valley, and who took up and developed land at Reed Island.

John Franklin Calfee attended a private school in Wythe County and had the distinction of teaching the first public school in the Fort Chiswell District. He married Elizabeth Sayers, a daughter of John G. and Rachael Sayers, of Drapers Valley. After his marriage he engaged in merchandising, at first as a hardware merchant and later as a dealer in boots and shoes at Pulaski, where he remained for many years. He died November 14, 1901, and is buried at Pine, Virginia, where he had served as postmaster until his death. His widow survived him and passed away September 28, 1917, and is buried beside him.

These parents had a large family of children, a brief record of them being as follows: Mary Blanche, deceased, who married Walter Crockett, mayor of Dublin, Virginia, mentioned elsewhere in this publication; Susan Jane, wife of J. H. Koger; Miss

Cynthia Helen, of Drapers Valley; Sallie, wife of James Bayless; Rachael Grayson, who died in infancy; Nancy Hamilton, wife of W. T. Laprod, a professor at Duke University, Durham, North Carolina; Ruby Frances, widow of A. C. Oglesby, of Drapers Valley, and mother of four children; Anna Elizabeth, of Drapers Valley; Ellen Tapscott, of Drapers Valley; John Franklin, who is secretary with the Brown-Williamson Tobacco Company at Winston Salem, North Carolina.

WILLIAM BANE SNIDOW, of Pearisburg, has probably gained as many of the substantial elements of professional success as any of his contemporaries at the bar of Southwestern Virginia. Mr. Snidow has won an enviable record for himself, and has contributed to the distinctions of one of the oldest families in this part of the state.

He was born at White Gate in Giles County, Virginia, March 2, 1877, and is a descendant of Christian Snidow, who was one of the colonists who came from the Palatinate of Germany and settled in Pennsylvania in 1727. The family lived for a number of years in Lancaster County. His son, John Snidow, moved from Lancaster County in 1765 to the Valley of Virginia. John Snidow was the father of Col. Christian Snidow, a lieutenant in the Revolutionary forces, and who was a native of Lancaster County. Col. Christian Snidow was the father of John Snidow, whose son, James Harvey Snidow, was grandfather of the Pearisburg attorney. James Harvey Snidow was a Confederate soldier in the early years of the war, was at the battle of New Market, and in the latter part of the war was engaged in the performance of civil duties as official of the County Court. He was a farmer, land and slave owner, and died in 1883. John D. Snidow, father of William Bane, was born November 17, 1847, and was a youthful Confederate soldier in the final year of the war, being a member of French's Battery, Stark's Battalion. William B. Snidow, his son, has in his possession his father's parole signed by Captain Stark. John D. Snidow served for many years in the office of sheriff of Giles County, was a farmer by occupation, and died September 29, 1927. He and his wife are buried at White Gate. His wife, Jane Bane, was a daughter of Capt. William Bane, granddaughter of Col. James Bane, whose father and grandfather also bore the name James. The Banes were early established in the Valley of Virginia, near Staunton. The first James Bane married Rebecca McDonald, a granddaughter of Brian McDonald, who was massacred at Glencoe, Scotland, in 1680, and who was a lineal descendant of Donald Bane, who succeeded his brother Malcolm III as King of Scotland in the eleventh century. Mrs. (Bane) Snidow was educated in a private academy at White Gate under Professor James M. Humphreys. She was a devout Presbyterian. She died August 9, 1884. There were three children. The son James H. Snidow enlisted in the Spanish-American war in the Third Virginia Volunteers, and after it was disbanded joined the Fourth Virginia Regiment. He spent a winter in Cuba, and after the disbanding of the Fourth Regiment joined the Third United States Regular Infantry, was sent to the Philippines, detailed for special service as an aid to Captain Nichols in Company L of the Third Infantry. After his discharge he returned to the United States, became a messenger for the Southern Express Company, and was killed in a railroad wreck at Williamson, West Virginia, November 9, 1902. The only daughter of the family, Janie, is the wife of Wharton O'Keefe, an employe of the Norfolk & Western Railroad at Bluefield, West Virginia.

William Bane Snidow was educated in private schools at White Gate, attended the College of William and Mary, and studied law at the University of Virginia. He was admitted to the Virginia bar in July, 1901, and has had more than a quarter of a century for working out an unusually successful professional career. He has offices in the Law Building at Pearisburg. Mr. Snidow in 1903 was elected commonwealth's attorney of Giles County, serving four years. In 1911 he was again elected commonwealth's attorney and reelected in 1915. During 1916 a case arose involving a contest over taxes on the Union Tanning Company, which Mr. Snidow for several years had represented as counsel. There being a conflict between his private clientage and his official duties he resigned as commonwealth's attorney and handled the tanning company's litigation through the Court of Appeals, a case recorded in 123 Va. 610. For his work in that case he received a fee of five thousand dollars, up to that time the largest fee ever paid an attorney by any client in Giles County. About the same time Mr. Snidow was retained by the Byrnes heirs to recover certain lands in Bland County, these lands having become very valuable because of the deposits of manganese ore, a metal that was indispensable during the World war. In that case he was associated with Senator Roland E. Chase, of Dickenson County. They won the case, and again he received a fee of five thousand dollars.

Mr. Snidow in 1919 was elected a member of the Virginia General Assembly, serving one term. By appointment of Judge Fulton Kegley he was examiner of records from 1909 to 1916. Probably the most famous of all the cases in which Attorney Snidow has participated was that originally known as Johnson versus Day, involving the construction of the will of John Howard Wilburn. Mr. Snidow represented the illegitimate child of Ada Wilburn, the only daughter of the testator, John Howard Wilburn. The case will be found in the Supreme Court Report, 145 Va. 721, where it is entitled Snidow versus Day. Mr. Snidow secured a decision favorable to his client, who was awarded all the Wilburn property. The court fixed the fee of eight thousand dollars for the services of Mr. Snidow in this instance.

Mr. Snidow is deeply versed in the law and for many years has been an enthusiastic student. His law library comprises about three thousand volumes, and he also has a library of equal size of general and historical work. He is a member of the Virginia and American Bar Associations, belongs to the Sons of the American Revolution, is a Knight Templar Mason, and a Republican in politics.

He married at Barboursville, Orange County, Virginia, February 28, 1905, Miss Sadie Patton Slaughter, daughter of Dr. Alfred E. and Eugenia (Taylor) Slaughter. Her great-grandfather, Capt. Phillip Slaughter, was a captain of the Culpeper minute men in the Revolution. Her grandfather, Dr. Thomas Towles Slaughter, married Jane Chapman, daughter of Reynolds Chapman, who married the daughter of Gen. William Madison, brother of President James Madison. Mrs. Snidow was educated in Randolph-Macon Woman's College at Lynchburg and taught for several years before her marriage. She is a member of the Episcopal Church. Four children were born to the marriage of Mr. and Mrs. Snidow: William Bane, Jr., was educated in the College of William and Mary, is a Kappa

Alpha, and is now at Brooks Field, San Antonio, Texas, studying
aviation; Eugene Tilghman graduated from Stuart Hall at
Staunton in 1925, later attending Randolph-Macon Woman's
College; John Temple is in his second year at the College of
William and Mary, and is a member of the Kappa Alpha; and
Carroll is attending the Pearisburg High School.

LEVIN JAMES HOUSTON, JR., city manager of the City of
Fredericksburg, has many qualifications for the technical and
administrative duties in connection with that office. He is a
prominent consulting engineer, and has done a vast amount of
work in the field of civil engineering, in connection with railroad
building and maintenance, and has been employed on many projects involving problems of municipal and sanitary engineering.

Mr. Houston was born at Stockton, Worcester County, Maryland, October 22, 1881. Both his paternal and maternal ancestors
have lived in Worcester County, Maryland, for eight generations.
His parents were Levin J. and Sarah (Mezick) Houston. His
father during the Civil war was captain of a Flag of Truce
steamer engaged in the exchange of prisoners between the North
and South. After the war he was in business as a merchant at
Stockton, also operated a mill, oyster plant and two farms. He
was born in 1841 and died in November, 1906. His wife was
born in 1846, and is still living at Stockton.

Levin J. Houston, Jr., was reared and educated in the town
where he was born in Maryland, and had a liberal education.
He graduated with the Bachelor of Arts degree from the Maryland Agricultural College of the University of Maryland at College Park with the class of 1898. He continued his technical
training in Cornell University of New York, where he took the
degree in civil engineering in 1901.

On leaving Cornell Mr. Houston went with the Canadian
Pacific Railway, beginning as transit man. Within a few months
he was assigned to experimental work in connection with utilizing the momentum stored in a train in ascending grades, and
subsequently published in the transactions of the Society of Civil
Engineers of Cornell a thesis on the subject "Momentum Grades
on Railroads," and this publication has ever since been used for
textbook purposes at Cornell. During the next two years he had
charge of new construction work and the maintenance of way
from Lake Superior to Winnipeg. He next became division engineer of the Chesapeake & Ohio Railway on the old Kentucky
Division, with headquarters at Ashland, Kentucky, for one year.
Leaving that and going to Baltimore, he was one of the construction engineers for the city's sewerage commission six years,
and during the next year was assistant city engineer and assistant chief engineer of the paving commission.

Mr. Houston since 1913 has had an extensive private practice in engineering, largely of a consulting nature. In 1916, in
addition to this practice, he was made chief engineer of the Potomac Ship Building Company at Quantico, Virginia, and in 1917
was made assistant manager as well as engineer. In October,
1918, he accepted his present post as city manager of Fredericksburg, and has been the engineering and administrative
authority in practical charge of all the city's business during the
past eleven years. Mr. Houston in 1927 was honored with election as president of the League of Virginia Municipalities. In
addition to the heavy routine of his work as city manager Mr.
Houston prepared the interesting pamphlet on "Historical Fred-

ericksburg," and he also prepared the map of the city showing the location of its many points of historical interest.

He married, December 17, 1903, Miss Mary Wilmer of Baltimore, who was born in that city February 12, 1884, daughter of Lemuel and Henrietta (Robertson) Wilmer. Her parents were born in Charles County, Maryland, and her father for many years was a Government official in Baltimore. He died in 1884, and her mother is now eighty-nine years of age, residing with her daughter, Mrs. Houston. Mr. and Mrs. Houston have three children: Levin James III, born January 30, 1905, who graduated from the Virginia Military Institute, remained as an instructor there one year, and is now an art student in New York. The second son, Lemuel Wilmer, born February 14, 1909, also attended Virginia Military Institute and is now engaged in newspaper work at Fredericksburg. The youngest child is Mary Wilmer, born December 3, 1911, and now a student attending Westhampton College, of the University of Richmond at Richmond, Virginia.

Mr. Houston is a Royal Arch Mason, member of the B. P. O. Elks, the Mansfield Hall Country Club, is a Democrat and member of the Episcopal Church. He is a vestryman in Trinity Church. He is eligible to membership in the Sons of the American Revolution, and his wife has qualifications for being enrolled as a daughter of the American Revolution. While at the university of Maryland he was manager of the baseball team. Mr. Houston was a member of the Gamma Alpha fraternity and president of his Chapter, and was president of the Maryland Club at Cornell University.

GEORGE A. ALLEN, the chairman of the Bland County Democratic Committee, is one of the popular native sons of that section of Virginia, is a member of families that have lived there for several generations, and his own career has been devoted to the livestock and farming industry.

He was born at Ceres, Virginia, February 19, 1893, son of W. B. and Maggie T. (Hudson) Allen. His grandfather was William Allen, son of the Scotch founder of this branch of the family in Southwestern Virginia. William Allen was born at Poplar Hill in Giles County and spent all his life there. W. B. Allen was a farmer and dealer in livestock, and for a number of years held the office of commissioner of revenue in Bland County. He was a member of the Masonic fraternity. He died in 1926 and his wife, on March 8, 1901, and both are buried in the Ceres Cemetery. His wife was a teacher before her marriage. W. B. Allen and wife had five children: William, a farmer on the old homestead at Ceres; George A.; Rev. James L., a minister of the Methodist Episcopal Church, South, at Ceres; A. B. Allen, of White Gates, Virginia; and Elizabeth, a teacher in the public schools at Rocky Gap.

George A. Allen attended public schools in Bland County, completed a course in the National Business College at Roanoke in 1916, and immediately thereafterwards joined his father in the cattle business. In October, 1917, he answered the call to the colors, going into training at Camp Lee for three months, was then transferred to the Veterinary Corp of Camp Greene, North Carolina, and remained until after the armistice. He was honorably discharged at Camp Greene, February 7, 1919.

Mr. Allen after the war followed farming and the business of livestock dealer at White Gates, Virginia, until February, 1923, when he returned to Bland County and bought a large

JAMES HAYES, I

blue grass farm of over 800 acres, using this for general farming and cattle raising.

Mr. Allen was elected county chairman of the Democratic party in Bland County in February, 1928, and very systematically organized the county for the campaign of that year. He is a member of the American Legion and the Methodist Church. At Bland, Virginia, June 25, 1919, he married Miss Ethel Newberry, who was educated in public schools in Bland County, in Sullins College, and is a member of the Methodist Episcopal Church. Her parents were L. M., Sr., and Louise (Bird) Newberry. Mr. and Mrs. Allen have three children, Donald, George A., Jr., and Edwin, Donald being a student in public schools.

JAMES HAYES was a business man whose career was identified with Fredericksburg, and he represented a family that has been in Virginia for several generations. He was born at Richmond, and died there in 1908.

His grandfather, a wealthy planter and business man of the state, also named James Hayes, was born in England in 1760 and died October 6, 1804, at the age of forty-four. This James Hayes married Mrs. Ann Bent Hardiman, the daughter of a well-to-do Scotchman, William Black, who had owned the Falls Plantation or Aberdeen, as it was sometimes called, just below Manchester. The date of that marriage is not known, as the family register was destroyed by the British during the Revolutionary war. James Hayes succeeded to the ownership of that property, and he is also remembered as having been publisher of the *Virginia Gazette*. He figured in an episode interesting to recall as showing the general dread of the recurring epidemics of smallpox a century or more ago. Such an epidemic broke out in 1793-94, and James Hayes moved his family into Richmond, but attempted to visit his Falls River Plantation every day. In doing so he violated the quarantine and the residents and his neighbors near the plantation objected to his visits, and for a time he was confined at the Chesterfield courthouse, and he and his friends gathered a large number of armed men about them with a view to resisting forcibly the quarantine, but eventually the matter was peaceably settled.

William Black, of Scotland, lived at Falls Plantation, which he called Aberdeen, opposite Richmond, Virginia. He married Ann Dent, of Maryland. Their daughter, Ann Dent Hardiman (widow), married James Hayes, of England. James Hayes, born in 1760, died October 6, 1804. Ann Dent Hardiman Hayes, his wife, died November 13, 1831. Their son, Dr. John Hayes, died October 22, 1834. Delia Hayes, daughter of James Hayes, died August 2, 1842. Dr. John Hayes married Ann Sommerville Knox, of Fredericksburg, Virginia. They left two sons and two daughters, James Hayes, Mary Ann Hayes, Sarah Stuart Hayes and John Hayes. Delia Hayes married Herbert A. Claiborne. They left several sons and one daughter.

Ann Dent Hayes married Alexander McRae, lieutenant governor of Virginia and prosecuting attorney in the Aaron Burr trial. He studied law with Chief Justice John Marshall and was the devoted friend of President James Monroe. Their children were Amanda Pamela, James Hayes, Alexander, Richard and Ann Dent. The sons never married. Amanda married John J. Werth. Their children were: John James Rhodes, Henry Hobard and Ann Dent. James Rhodes married Mary Herndon Maury, daughter of Commodore Mathew Fontaine

Maury. Ann Dent married James Dunlop. They left James N., Ann Dent, Margaret Carlisle, Richard Alexander II, Amanda Pamela and Frank Deane.

A son of this wealthy planter and publisher was Dr. John Hayes, who became a prominent physician. Doctor Hayes married Anne Somerville Knox, of Fredericksburg, Virginia, daughter of Mary McBryde Rieley. The Knox family are direct descendants of the Earl of Ranfurly, Ireland. Dr. John Hayes was the father of the late James Hayes, of Fredericksburg. Doctor Hayes, with his grandmother Hayes, his grandfather Black, his sisters and a twin brother of Delia Claiborne, are buried at Falls Plantation. Dr. John Hayes died of Asiatic cholera October 22, 1834.

James Hayes spent all his active business career in the wholesale grain trade. He married at Richmond in June, 1861, Miss Elizabeth Travers Green, member of the distinguished Green family of Virginia. Mrs. Hayes died May 18, 1929, and is buried in the Green section, Hollywood Cemetery, Richmond, Virginia.

Elizabeth Travers Green was a descendant of William Green, who served as a soldier to King William of Orange. His son, Robert Green, born in 1695, came to Virginia when about twenty-two years old with his maternal uncle, William Duff, a Quaker, and settled in King George County. They were associated as partners with Joist Rite and Robert McKay in the settlement of those wonderfully rich tracts of land in what is now known as Shenandoah Valley. Lord Fairfax claimed these lands by nominal grant, and this was the origin of a famous lawsuit which was contested before the courts for many years and which was finally settled in 1786 in favor of the Joist Rite claimants. George Washington was the surveyor who ran the lines for Lord Fairfax.

Col. John Williams Green, of Green Wood, Culpeper County, fourth of the seven sons of Robert Green and his wife, Eleanor Dunn Green, was a soldier of the Revolution, participating in the battles of Brandywine, Monmouth and Guilford Court House. He was a member of George Washington's staff and a friend of General La Fayette, whom he entertained at Green Wood in 1825. He married Sussana Blackwell, daughter of William Blackwell. They were the parents of William Green, who married Lucy Clayton Williams. A son of this marriage was John Williams Green, born November 9, 1781, and who died in 1834. He was a soldier in the War of 1812, having risen to the rank of colonel. He equipped a company in Fredericksburg and carried them to Norfolk at his own expense. He served as a chancellor of the commonwealth, member of the Legislature and as judge of the Supreme Court of Appeals. Judge Green married in 1805 Mary Browne, a greatniece of Mary Washington and a direct descendant of Sir Walter Raleigh, and the oldest of their four sons was William Green. By a second marriage he was the father of Thomas Claiborne Green, who also had a long career as a judge and president of the Court of Appeals.

William Green, son of Judge John Williams Green, was born at Fredericksburg November 10, 1806, and finished his law studies under his father. He practiced law in Culpeper, Rappahannock, Orange and Louisa counties, and in 1855 moved to Richmond, there better to look after his extensive business in the courts of the state. He lived out his life there, dying July 27, 1880, and is buried in Hollywood Cemetery. He became pro-

ELIZABETH TRAVERS GREEN HAYES

fessor of law in Richmond College in 1870, and he was vice president of Virginia Historical Society and for a long time chairman of its executive board. During the Civil war he was in the treasury department of the Confederate states, and after the war became judge of the tribunal known as the Court of Conciliation.

William Green married, April 6, 1837, Columbia Elizabeth Slaughter, daughter of Samuel and Virginia (Stanard) Slaughter, of Western View, the latter a daughter of William and Eliza (Carter) Stanard. Betty Washington Lewis, while visiting Elizabeth Carter, her daughter, wife of Charles Carter, owner of Western View, died there in 1797 and is buried there. Slaughter, Stanard and Carter are all names of distinguished families of Virginia. William Green by this marriage had two children, one being Elizabeth Travers Green Hayes and the other, John Williams Green, a gallant soldier of the Confederacy who was killed while gallantly leading his charge at the battle of Liberty Mills in Madison County, Virginia, September 22, 1863.

Mr. and Mrs. James Hayes had a family of eleven children: John Green Hayes, a tobacco merchant, married Mildred Boyd and has a son, John Green Hayes, Jr.; William Green Hayes is a state department employe at Richmond; Etta is the widow of John Hyatt Wight, who was vice president of the Fidelity Trust Company of Baltimore, and her home is in Richmond, at 817 Floyd Avenue; Anne Somerville married Ewing Eaches, a stock and bond broker at Louisville, Kentucky, and had two children, Katherine Ewing, wife of Robert Coleman Walker, a Philadelphia attorney, and mother of two sons, Robert Coleman, Jr., and James Ewing Walker, and Miss Elizabeth Travers Green Eaches; Columbia Stanard is the widow of William James Walker; Miss Elizabeth Travers Hayes was the fifth child; Mary Stuart married Axel Gustave Mathiason, a chemist and experimental engineer; Virginia Carter married Frank Wheatley McCullough, of Norfolk, and has two children, Virginia Carter and Alan; and Lucy Green is the wife of Thomas Stokes, of Elk Hill, Virginia.

REV. H. GUTHRIE ALLEN was a soldier overseas during the World war, is a native son of Virginia, a graduate of old Hampden Sydney College, and after the war he took up study for the ministry, and his present assignment is as pastor of the Presbyterian congregation at Max Meadows.

Rev. Mr. Allen was born in Prince Edward County, Virginia, January 6, 1892, son of Frank E. and Mary Belle (Anderson) Allen, grandson of Joseph Allen, and great-grandson of Sims Allen. His paternal line goes back to James Allen of Hanover, as follows: Rev. H. Guthrie Allen; Frank E. Allen; Joseph Watson Allen; Sims Allen; John Allen, sergeant in Virginia Continentals in the Revolutionary war, and died in 1816; James Allen, Sr., Cumberland and Prince Edward Counties; James Allen, of Hanover County, Virginia. The maternal-paternal ancestry line includes: Rev. H. Guthrie Allen, Mary (Anderson) Allen, Charles T. Anderson, Francis Anderson, Thomas Anderson, who died before 1806, and James Anderson who died before 1782. Sims Allen was a farmer in Prince Edward County and married a niece of the famous South Carolina statesman, John C. Calhoun. The Allen family has lived in Virginia since early Colonial times. Joseph Allen was a Confederate soldier, and after the war lived out his life on his plantation in Prince Edward County. He married Letitia McDearmon, and both are buried in the Douglass Church Cemetery. Frank E. Allen was born and reared in Prince Edward County, attended public schools there, and up to the age of thirty-two followed business as a contractor for the building of bridges with the Chesapeake & Ohio Railroad and the Yadkin Valley Railroad. Since giving up contracting work he has been a farmer, and he and his wife now reside at Darlington Heights. His wife was born and reared in Prince Edward County, was educated in school there, and both she and her husband are members of the Presbyterian Church. Her parents were Charles T. and Mary Etta (Guthrie) Anderson, well-to-do Prince Edward County farmers. Charles T. Anderson was a son of Frank Anderson, grandson of Thomas Anderson and great-grandson of James Anderson, of Cumberland County, Virginia. Frank E. Allen and wife had five children; H. Guthrie; Charles, who died in infancy; Miss Mary Margaret, who is a graduate of the Farmville State Teachers College with the class of 1920, now teaching in the public schools at Max Meadows; Francis Anderson, who died at the age of nineteen, while a student at Hampden Sydney College; and Marietta Letitia, who was educated in public schools and the Farmville Teachers College, taught a year or two, then took up the work of the Presbyterian Assembly School at Richmond, in preparation for home missionary work, for about two years, and is now the wife of J. W. Elliott, a farmer and postal employe at Darlington Heights.

H. Guthrie Allen was educated in public schools in Prince Edward County, graduated from the Cluster Springs Academy in 1913, and took his A. B. degree at Hampden-Sydney College in 1917.

In December, 1917, he joined the colors, receiving his first training at Fort Thomas, Kentucky, then at Camp Hancock, Georgia, until April, 1918, was at Camp Greene, at Charlotte, North Carolina, until July, 1918, when he went overseas with Company Eighteen of the Fourth Regiment, Motor Mechanics, in the Aviation Corps. He landed at LeHavre, France, was at St. Jean De Monts until Christmas, 1918, and then at St. Nazaire, France, and from March, 1919, to August was a student with the American Expeditionary Forces at Cambridge University in England. He enlisted as a private, was promoted to sergeant, and was a second lieutenant when honorably discharged at Camp Meade, Maryland, in September, 1919.

Mr. Allen after his return from overseas spent three years in the Union Theological Seminary at Richmond, graduating in 1922 with the Bachelor of Divinity degree. In June of that year he was ordained in the Presbyterian ministry and at once accepted the call to the pastorates at Max Meadows in Wythe County, and has enjoyed a most profitable relationship with this community, having a loyal congregation, accepting the opportunities for disinterested service to the people of his church, and for four years of this time he has also combined the duties of the ministry with the principalship of the Max Meadows High School.

Rev. Mr. Allen is a member of Theta Chi fraternity of Hamden Sydney College, is a member of the Max Meadows Business Men's Club, is a Democrat and a member of the Abingdon Presbytery.

He married at Charlotte Court House, Virginia, June 28, 1922, Miss Carrie Anderson, daughter of Frank and Mary (Carson) Anderson, residents of Charlotte Court House. Mrs. Allen

A. Pendleton Strother

was educated in public schools, in the Williamsburg Institute and the State Teachers College at Farmville, and taught for about two years before her marriage. She was a very devout Presbyterian. Mrs. Allen died November 19, 1927, and is buried in the Douglas Church Cemetery in Prince Edward County.

ALBERT PENDLETON STROTHER. With thirty-five counties under his supervision as division chief of the Internal Revenue Department, Albert Pendleton Strother, of Roanoke, is one of the very important figures in governmental work in Virginia, and is handling the affairs of his office with great capability. For years prior to his appointment to his present office he had proved his worth as a business man and good citizen, and his selection met with the approval of his district. Mr. Strother was born in Giles County, Virginia, in 1873, a son of Philip and Nannie (Pendleton) Strother, natives of Virginia, he born in Culpeper County and she in Giles County, both of whom are deceased, having passed away at a ripe old age. The father was a distinguished lawyer, educated in Columbia College, Washington, District of Columbia. During the latter part of his life he was engaged in practice in West Virginia, where he had as his clients some of the largest coal operators of that state. Seven children were born to the parents, those living being: Hon. James French Strother, who served in the National Congress from the Fifth Congressional District of West Virginia, and resides in Welch, that state; Mrs. Joseph G. Barnes, who resides in Tazewell County, Virginia, where her husband is engaged in farming and merchandising; Elizabeth R., who lives in Pearisburg, Giles County, Virginia; Albert Pendleton, whose name heads this review; Mrs. Ira C. Hale, who resides in Giles County, Virginia, where her husband has business interests; and Lucy, who married G. L. Morris, of Botetourt County, Virginia, a farmer and cattleman. The father was an Episcopalian and a Republican. During the war between the states he served in the Confederate army as a lieutenant, and was very seriously injured in the battle of Spotsylvania, May 12, 1864. His father, James F. Strothers, was also a lawyer, and served in the Virginia Legislature for many years, and for twelve years was speaker of the House. Subsequently he was a member of the National Congress for two terms. The paternal great-grandfather, George French Strother, was still another member of the family to go to Washington, he having been a member of the National Congress in 1817, but resigned the office to go to Saint Louis, Missouri, in the interests of the Federal Government.

Albert Pendleton Strother attended the public schools in Tazewell County and Tazewell College at Williamsburg, Virginia. He began his life career as a farmer, and continued in that occupation for twenty years, and then relinquished it to become assistant cashier of the sergeant-at-arms of the House of Representatives for three years. On July 9, 1921, Mr. Strother came to Roanoke to assume his present duties, and has remained here ever since, becoming one of the city's highly valued residents.

In 1903 Mr. Strother married Miss Alice Williams, who was born in Giles County, Virginia, a sister of John W. Williams, clerk of the House of Delegates. Mr. and Mrs. Strother have two children: Philip William, who was educated in the schools of Washington, D. C., and is now living at Washington, D. C.;

and James William, who attended the Roanoke and Washington, D. C., public schools, the Greenbrier Military School at Lewisburg, West Virginia, Virginia Military Institute and William and Mary College, and is in the employ of the Virginia Railroad Company. Mr. Strother is an Episcopalian, while his wife is a Methodist. He is a Republican, and very active in party affairs. From 1908 to 1912 he served as a member of the Virginia Senate; was an elector-at-large on the ticket with William Howard Taft, and is regarded as one of the very astute politicians of this part of the state. In spite of the fact that since he assumed control of his division the business has increased many times over, his administration has been marked by the promptness and accuracy of its operation, and he is regarded as the very best man that could be found for the place in question.

RANDOLPH MARSHALL GRAVES. A progressive young business man and a native son of the busy and beautiful city of Bristol, Virginia, is found in Randolph Marshall Graves, realtor, mine manager, veteran of the World war, and officer in the United States Reserve Corps. Lieutenant Graves is a worthy representative of old and distinguished Virginia families that for generations have been identified with the history and substantial development of this state.

Randolph Marshall Graves was born at Bristol, Washington County, Virginia, August 30, 1897, son of Herbert Elgin and Patsy (Cochran) Graves, and has one sister and one brother: Susie Katherine, who is the wife of Ralph W. Ealand, a mine operator at Santa Barbara, California; and Benjamin Conway, who is assistant superintendent of the High Rock Knitting Company at Bristol.

The late Herbert Elgin Graves was born in 1858 in Halifax County, Virginia, and came to Bristol in 1878, where his death occurred on September 17, 1924. He had been a very active business man here, having large real estate and mine interests during all this interval with the exception of five years when he was in the cattle trade in Liverpool, London and Paris as business representative of his step-father, Col. James Byers, an extensive dealer at that time. His father, Capt. Henry Vinson Graves, grandfather of Randolph Marshall Graves, was a noted civil engineer at Richmond, Virginia, and connected with railroad construction prior to the Civil war, during which period he served with distinction as an officer in the Confederate army. The founder of the Graves family in Virginia was born in England and when he came to the United States was accompanied by two brothers, one of whom settled in Connecticut and the other in Louisiana. In political sentiment the late Herbert Elgin Graves was a Republican, and he was a faithful member of the Presbyterian Church. His marriage with Miss Patsy Cochran brought the Graves family into kinship with another prominent old Virginia connection, the Cochrans, of Scotch-Irish extraction, having come to the American colonies in Colonial days and many later proving heroic qualities as patriot soldiers in the Revolutionary war. The maternal grandfather of Randolph Marshall Graves, Col. James Cochran, was born at Staunton, Virginia, and became eminent in the law and influential in Republican politics in the state. For many years he published a newspaper at Culpeper and also served as postmaster, was

very active in Masonic affairs and liberal in his support of the Presbyterian Church.

Randolph Marshall Graves, with his sister and brother, was afforded exceptional educational advantages. After completing his course in the Virginia High School at Bristol Mr. Graves entered Bingham Military School at Mebane, Accomac County, North Carolina, then moved on to Riverside Military Academy at Gainesville, Georgia, and then became a student in the University of Virginia. His military school training, without his knowledge, partly prepared him for a later period of his life, for in 1917 he enlisted for real soldiering, and with a contingent from Bristol was sent to Fortress Monroe to be prepared for overseas service in the World war, but before the unit to which he was attached was called to activity the need for further transportation of troops to a foreign land was over, and he received his honorable discharge November 21, 1918.

Upon his return to Bristol Mr. Graves became interested in the real estate business, in which his father had so long and successfully been engaged, and has continued in this line ever since, and under his wise and intelligent methods and management large and desirably situated sections of land have been developed and highly improved recently, including such choice residential additions to Bristol as Lee Heights and Highland Park. Since the death of his father the latter's extensive mining properties have been under his control, a heavy business responsibility. These Feldstar mines are of great value, providing the mineral clay the kaolin, that is the essential element in the making of fine pottery, an industry of large importance here and elsewhere.

Earnest and hard-working, every civic interest of Bristol is dear to him as his native city, and he not only commands the confidence of his fellow citizen but also their esteem. He is a member of the Presbyterian Church and belongs to the Bristol lodge of Elks and to the Country Club.

HARRY EUGENE OULD. One of the largest and most prosperous mercantile establishments in Giles County is the W. T. Ould Store at Glenlyn, now under the active management of Harry Eugene Ould, who became associated with the business at an early age and was well qualified to carry on the active responsibilities after the death of his father, the late Walter T. Ould.

Walter T. Ould was a highly regarded citizen of Giles County and a most capable business man. He was born in Campbell County, Virginia, November 22, 1860, son of John Thomas Ould, a native of the same county, and grandson of John Thomas Ould, who came from Ireland. Walter T. Ould was reared and educated in Campbell County, and as a young man learned the trade of shoemaker. He followed that occupation until 1888. It was in that year, forty years ago, that he moved to Glenlyn and started a store carrying a general stock of merchandise. He kept the business steadily growing and increasing its scope of service throughout the rest of his life. He was also deeply interested in the welfare of his community and was mayor of Glenlyn at the time of his death, which occurred April 16, 1927. He was buried in the Fairview Cemetery at Narrows.

Walter T. Ould married Lula Tiller, who was born and reared in Mercer County and was educated in public schools there. She is a member of the Methodist Episcopal Church,

South, and is affiliated with the Union Church at Glenlyn. Of her five children one died in infancy. The daughter Etta Carrene is Mrs. George C. Moore, of Parkersburg, West Virginia, and has a daughter, Madeline Carrene. Harry Eugene Ould is the second in age. Eula Earline is Mrs. Emory Johnson, of Pearisburg, Virginia, and has a son, Thomas Eugene. Miss Blanche Evelyn Ould is a graduate of the Pearisburg High School and is at home.

Harry Eugene Ould was born at Glenlyn, attended public schools there and at the age of fourteen was helping his father in the store. The business is still conducted as the W. T. Ould Estate, of which he is the active administrator. He is unmarried and is a member of the Knights Templar Masons and Kazim Temple of the Mystic Shrine at Roanoke. He is a Democrat, a Methodist and a member of Southwestern Virginia, Incorporated.

REV. CLYDE JONES WALSH. The clergy of today face problems more serious than have come before those of their profession for many years. The latitude of the post-war period and distractions of modern life, the tendency of the age toward a disregard of the principles of the older generation, all are grave matters for anyone to handle, and especially for the men whose lives are devoted to religious work. That all are not influenced by the above mentioned conditions is fortunately true, but there are enough of them to create a serious state of affairs, and one that requires the continued efforts of these "Men of God," if a betterment is to be looked for in the near future. One of these men who is accomplishing much in the good cause is Rev. Clyde Jones Walsh, pastor of the Presbyterian Church of Dublin, Pulaski County, and a vital force in his community.

Reverend Walsh was born in Charlotte, North Carolina, January 17, 1888, a son of Thomas D. and Rose (Williamson) Walsh. Thomas D. Walsh was born and reared in Charlotte, and attended several excellent private schools of that city. Later he entered Andersonville College, and was graduated therefrom. With the outbreak of war between the states he enlisted in the Southern army, and served as a brave soldier until peace was declared. After the close of the war he went on the road as a traveling salesman, and continued in that line of work until his death in 1908. He is buried in the cemetery in Charlotte. His father was Rev. Tracy D. Walsh, one of the pioneer Methodist ministers of Charlotte and that section of North Carolina, and for many years served as president of Andersonville College. The family came to Charlotte, North Carolina, from South Carolina and became prominent in its affairs.

Mrs. Rose (Williamson) Walsh was born and reared at Pineville, North Carolina, and she was educated in its private schools and those of Statesville, and the Statesville Female College. Her father, Dr. Eldred Williamson, was a practicing physician of Pineville, North Carolina, for many years. Mrs. Walsh is a zealous member of the Presbyterian Church, and she still resides in Charlotte. Six children were born to her and her husband who lived, and two who died in infancy. Those living are: Edna, Walter, Tom, Robert, Reverend Walsh and Rose.

Reverend Walsh first attended the public schools of Charlotte and later Charlotte Military Institute, and was graduated therefrom in 1907. For the subsequent eleven years he was in the hotel business, but during all of that period he cherished the

hope of entering the ministry, and in 1916 entered Union Theological Seminary and was graduated therefrom in 1919. Following his graduation he was assigned as pastor of the Presbyterian Church at Elon, Amherst County, Virginia, and remained there for six years, during which time he accomplished some very effective work, and when he left his people were loath to let him go. In October, 1925, he came to Dublin, Virginia, as pastor of the Dublin group of Presbyterian Churches, which includes the church at Dublin, the one at New Dublin and the one at Belspring. Here he has a splendid field for work, and he is putting into it strength, talent, zeal and consecrated work, with results that are most encouraging. He is a Master Mason, belonging to Henry Clay Lodge, Dublin, Virginia; and he is a member of the local lodges of the Modern Woodmen and Independent Order of Odd Fellows. In 1928 he served as vice president of the Business Men's Club of Dublin. He is now attached to the Appalachian Synod of the Presbyterian Church. In political faith he is a Democrat.

On October 1, 1919, Reverend Walsh married in Greensboro, North Carolina, Miss Alma Louise Henley, of that city, who had the misfortune to lose her mother in early childhood, and she was reared by Judge T. J. Shaw, of Greensboro. Mrs. Walsh attended the public schools of her native city and Greensboro College, and is a well educated highly cultured lady, very active in all church work. Reverend and Mrs. Walsh have one son, Clyde Jones Walsh, Junior. While he is a scholarly man, deeply imbued with the doctrines of his church, he is broad-minded enough to realize that all work for the betterment of humanity is of value, and so does not neglect his civic responsibilities, but assumes them and discharges them intelligently and effectively. It is men like Reverend Walsh who are checking the tide of irreligious thoughtlessness and positive crime, and bringing home to parents the grave necessity for stricter living and religious observance on their part so that they may in this way influence for good the children growing up about them.

SIDNEY WARNER IRONMONGER, chief of police of the City of Norfolk, is a World war veteran and is a member of one of the old and interesting families of Virginia.

The Ironmongers came from England and settled in Virginia in Colonial times. A brother of Mr. Ironmonger's grandfather was said to have been the youngest drummer boy in the Confederate army. The grandfather owned and occupied a farm in Norfolk County located eight miles from the courthouse.

Chief Ironmonger's father was Sidney Bailey Ironmonger, who was born in Norfolk County, inherited part of his father's estate and spent a number of years as a farmer, but is now living retired at Norfolk. He married Katherine Elizabeth Warner, who was born in Baltimore, daughter of Andrew E. and Barbara Warner. They reared three children, Sidney Warner, Edith Elizabeth and Charles Grayson.

Sidney Warner Ironmonger was born at Norfolk, attended the Patrick Henry School and the Maury High School, the Davis Wagner Business College, and for some years was an accountant in the offices of the Virginia Electric Power Company.

Mr. Ironmonger as a young man joined Battery B of the Norfolk Light Artillery Blues and in 1916 went with his battery to the Mexican border. In 1917 he was trained with the National Guard, and in July, 1918, went overseas. He was sent to the

front and later put on detached duty and saw many different
points in France and also in England. He returned to the
United States with his command, and received his honorable
discharge at Newport News May 25, 1919.

Soon after leaving the military service of the Government
he was appointed deputy United States marshal. He was in
the marshal's office until January 26, 1924, when he was
appointed chief of police of the City of Norfolk. Mr. Ironmonger is commander of Old Dominion Post No. 67 of the
American Legion at Norfolk, Virginia. He is active in the
Masonic fraternity, being affiliated with Atlantic Lodge No. 2,
A. F. and A. M., John Walter Chapter No. 68, Royal Arch
Masons, Grice Commandery No. 16, Knights Templar, and
Khedive Temple of the Mystic Shrine. He and his wife are
members of the Methodist Episcopal Church, South.

He married, May 18, 1918, Ruth Mae George, who was born
in Scranton, Pennsylvania, daughter of William and Eliza
George. They have two children, Sidney Warner, Jr., born
August 15, 1920, and Nancy Elizabeth, born March 26, 1927.

J. PAUL CAMPBELL.   The art of embalming, or preserving
the human body after death, which is one of the chief functions
of the modern mortician, was probably invented by the Egyptians. The custom seems to have originated in the idea that the
preservation of the body was necessary for the return of the
soul to the human form, and is as old as 4000 B. C. Chaussier's
discovery, in 1800, of the preservative power of corrosive sub-
limate introduced new means of embalming, and the discovery
of the action of a mixture of equal parts of acetate and chloride
of alumina, in 1834, by Gannal, and of arsenic by Tranchini,
pyroxilic spirits by Babington and Rees in 1839, and of the
antiseptic nature of chloride of zinc, added much to the sum
total of the knowledge of the art of embalming. Later developments have made this one of the most difficult of the callings,
and the modern undertaker must undergo a long and careful
training before he can consider himself as fully qualified to practice. One of the men who has kept himself fully abreast of all
the developments in this difficult and important vocation is J.
Paul Campbell, a substantial business man and respected citizen of Abingdon.

Mr. Campbell was born at Lebanon, Virginia, June 16, 1897,
and is a son of T. W. and Laura (Carpenter) Campbell, natives
of that place, but at present residents of Abingdon. The Campbell family has been prominent in Virginia for many years,
and the grandfather of Mr. Campbell, Wesley J. Carpenter, was
likewise a Virginian and served as a soldier of the Confederacy
during the war between the states. T. W. Campbell was engaged in the furniture business at Lebanon for many years, but
when his son's business grew to large proportions at Abingdon
he disposed of his Lebanon business and moved to Abingdon,
where he has since acted as his son's assistant.

J. Paul Campbell attended the public schools of Bristol, and
after his graduation from high school embarked in the undertaking business as manager for the firm of Sterchi Brothers.
Subsequently he came to Abingdon as manager of the same
concern's establishment at this point, and at the end of about
four and one-half years he and a Mr. Huff purchased the Sterchi
Brothers' two houses at Bristol and Abingdon, continuing them
under the style of Huff & Campbell. In 1925 Mr. Campbell

Thos. G. Hardy, M.D.

bought his partner's interest, disposed of the Bristol establishment, and has since been sole proprietor of the establishment at Abingdon, which is one of the most complete in Southwestern Virginia, located opposite the court house. Mr. Campbell maintains a beautiful chapel, and his business is motorized throughout, no detail being overlooked for the proper and dignified care of the dead. He is a graduate of the Cincinnati College of Embalming, class of 1920, is very progressive in his views, and is a member of the Southern Funeral Directors Association, the Virginia Funeral Directors Association and the National Funeral Directors Association, and attends all meetings and conventions of these bodies. Fraternally he is a member of the Independent Order of Odd Fellows, in which he is a past grand three times, and is also an active member of the Civitan Club.

In 1915 Mr. Campbell was united in marriage with Miss Margaret Musgrove, of Bristol, Virginia, daughter of Sam and Emma Musgrove, both of whom are now living at Clayton, North Carolina, where Mr. Musgrove is engaged in the livestock business. Mrs. Campbell was educated at Pineville, Kentucky, and is an active member of the Methodist Episcopal Church, South. She is a graduate embalmer, and is of great assistance to her husband in his business activities. To Mr. and Mrs. Campbell there have been born two children: Samuel, aged eleven years; and June, aged nine years.

THOMAS GRIFFIN HARDY, M. D., is a native of Lunenburg County, and since graduating in medicine has found his opportunities for useful service in his profession at Farmville, where he is busy with a surgical and obstetrical practice, and is also associated with the splendid South Side Community Hospital there.

Doctor Hardy was born in Lunenburg County December 19, 1889, son of Louis Atkins and Sallie (Matthews) Hardy. His family has been in Virginia since 1750. His grandfather, Griffin O. Hardy, was a farmer in Lunenburg County, and died there in 1898, at the age of seventy-seven. Griffin Hardy married Lucy Bridgeforth, who died in 1905. Louis Atkins Hardy was a lawyer by profession, also followed farming, and took a keen interest in politics, though never seeking public office. He was a delegate to the Constitutional Convention of Virginia in 1901. He died in 1915, and is survived by his widow and four of eight children.

Doctor Hardy was liberally educated, and graduated from the Medical College of Virginia in 1914. After one year of hospital training he began practice at Farmville. He is president of the Prince Edward County Medical Society, is vice president of the Virginia State Medical Society and councillor of the Fourth District of the Medical Council of Virginia.

Doctor Hardy held the rank of captain in the Medical Reserve Corps during the World war. He was sent overseas and attached to the British Army Medical Corps, and was at the front both in France and Belgium. He returned to the United States February 11, 1919.

Doctor Hardy is visiting surgeon to the South Side Community Hospital at Farmville. This hospital was opened November 9, 1927. Erected at a cost of $200,000, one-third of the cost being furnished by the Commonwealth Fund of New York City, it has been pronounced one of the best equipped institutions for its size in the United States. It provides adequate hospital care partly on a free and partly on a paid basis. In addition to this service it has a well developed educational branch as a health center in Southern Virginia, and is the first of valuable health and sanitary propaganda. The head of the institution is Dr. J. L. Jarman. The hospital has equipment of fifty beds.

Doctor Hardy is a member of the Kappa Sigma social fraternity and Phi Chi medical fraternity, and belongs to the Methodist Episcopal Church, South. He married, July 28, 1917, Miss Elizabeth Parker Jarman, of Farmville. Her father is Dr. J. L. Jarman, president of the State Teachers College of Farmville. Her mother is Mrs. Mary H. (Wiley) Jarman. Doctor and Mrs. Hardy have four children: Elizabeth Jarman, born December 10, 1919; Helen Wiley, born October 19, 1922; Sarah Matthews, born October 5, 1923; and Thomas Griffin, Jr., born February 25, 1927.

Roy W. Sexton is president and manager of a manufacturing business at Wytheville, and is one of the native sons of that section of the state, where the Sextons have lived for several generations.

Mr. Sexton was born at Wytheville, August 10, 1880, son of George Stuart and Elizabeth (Williams) Sexton and a grandson of John Sexton and great-grandson of Joseph Sexton. Joseph Sexton was born in Ireland and was brought by his parents to America, his father dying on the way, while the widowed mother continued with her children to Wythe County, Virginia, where members of the family have lived ever since. George Stuart Sexton was born and reared in Wythe County, attended private schools and gave his active life to the lumber business. For a number of terms he was mayor of Wytheville. He died in 1925. His wife, Elizabeth Williams, was a daughter of Thomas Williams and granddaughter of Thomas Williams. She was born and reared in Wythe County, attended private schools, and both she and her husband were active members of the Presbyterian Church. She died in 1904. In the family were five children: Annie, wife of Thomas Ford, of Morton, Virginia; J. Garland, of Wytheville; Roy W.; Charles Stuart, with the Westinghouse Electric Company at Pittsburgh, Pennsylvania; and George N., of Wytheville.

Roy W. Sexton had private school training at Wytheville and attended the Virginia Military Institute, entering the class of 1900, and has been one of the most loyal alumni of the school, being now a member of its Board of Visitors. After completing his education he traveled for several years. In 1909 he established at Wytheville The Initial Company, Inc., manufacturing dry goods specialties, and has developed it to a very valuable business, occupying a plant with floor space of 7,500 square feet. The output of the company is sold and distributed all over the world. Mr. Sexton is president and manager of this business. He is a life member of the B. P. O. Elks and is active in the Presbyterian Church, having served as superintendent of its Sunday School.

He married at Abingdon, Virginia, December 12, 1905, Miss Katherine Kahle, who was educated in Martha Washington College with the class of 1902, and taught for several years before her marriage. She is a Presbyterian and a member of the United Daughters of the Confederacy. Her parents were Rev. E. F. and Eva (Gillette) Kahle, her father a native of

Virginia and her mother of Texas. Her father spent his active
life as a minister of the Methodist Episcopal Church, South.
Mr. and Mrs. Sexton have had six children: Fletcher died
when three years old. Elizabeth Gillette, who was educated in
public schools in Wythe County, in the Mary Lyons School at
Swarthmore, Pennsylvania, and the Chatham Episcopal Institute at Chatham, Virginia, in Sweetbrier College of Virginia,
in May, 1929, married Richard la Cour, of Flushing, Long Island,
New York. Roy W., Jr., who attended school at Wytheville,
the Swarthmore Preparatory School, the Virginia Episcopal
School at Lynchburg and the Virginia Military Institute, since
1927 has been connected with the American Telephone and Tele-
graph Company at New York City. This son married Francis
Clark, of Lynchburg, and has a daughter, Anne Clark. G.
Stewart was educated in public schools in Wytheville and the
Swarthmore Preparatory College, and is now with the American
Telephone and Telegraph Company at New York. Patricia
Alson and Katherine McLean are the two youngest children.

ARTHUR KYLE DAVIS is eminent among the present generation of Virginians for his work in the field of higher education
and also as a literary and historical scholar. In the educational
life of the state it has been well said that no one has exerted an
influence finer in quality and purpose, an influence deriving
from a character of quiet strength, sanity and disinterestedness.
As president of Southern College at Petersburg, a non-sectarian
junior college for women, Mr. Davis is carrying on an institution that was founded by his father and is still operating under
the charter granted by Virginia when Virginia was one of the
states of the Confederate States of America.

His family record includes many honored Virginia names.
Arthur Kyle Davis was born at Petersburg, Virginia, July 16,
1867, son of Williams Thomas and Carolina Virginia (Robinson)
Davis. The Davis family came from Wales to Colonial Virginia.
His paternal grandfather, Rev. William Edward Davis, was born
in Gloucester County, Virginia, where he spent the greater part
of his life as a planter and as a clergyman of the Methodist
Episcopal Church. He died in Petersburg and was buried in old
Blandford Cemetery in the family square, where the obelisk
marking his grave was chipped by a Federal shell during the
siege of Petersburg.

Williams Thomas Davis was born in Gloucester County in
1816. He graduated from Randolph-Macon College, then located
at Boydton, Virginia, with the degree of Master of Arts. For
five years he was head of the preparatory department of Randolph-Macon College, then became professor of mathematics and
Latin in the Petersburg Female College, and was president of
that college until 1863. He then founded and became president
of the Southern Female College, an office he filled until his death
in 1888. The activities of Williams Thomas Davis were not
confined to the school room. He was a member of the City
Council many years, active in all civic affairs. In the Washington Street Methodist Episcopal Church he was a member of the
Board of Stewards and teacher of the Men's Bible Class, and
represented his church in the sessions of the Virginia annual
conference and was prominent in the conference boards of education, of Sunday schools, of home and foreign missions. He
was a delegate from Virginia to the Baltimore Centennial Con-

ference of Methodism in 1884, when he read a special paper on "The Mission of Methodism to the People," recognized as one of the ablest papers read before that body and later published in the Centennial Conference volume.

Williams Thomas Davis was opposed to secession until Virginia was called on for its quota of troops to force South Carolina back into the Union. Thereupon he became an advocate of secession, and he and his three sons and two sons-in-law all volunteered for service in the Confederate army. As an educator he was exempt by reason of both age and occupation, but when Petersburg was suddenly besieged on June 9, 1864, he, as one of the 125 Home Guards, halted 1,300 Federal cavalry until reinforcements could be sent up by General Lee, thus helping to preserve the Confederacy for ten months longer. Locally the battle of the 9th of June, when many of the old men and boys belonging to the leading families of the city were killed or wounded, and when the ten months' siege of Petersburg practically began, has become so identified with the sentiments and recollections of its people that it is annually observed as a special memorial day.

The first wife of Williams Thomas Davis was Elizabeth Tayloe Corbin Beale, sister of Gen. Richard Beale, of Westmoreland County. She died and was buried at Petersburg, leaving six children. The oldest son, William Hoomes Davis, a college graduate and a member of the Petersburg Riflemen, Twelfth Virginia Infantry, Mahone's Brigade, A. P. Hill's Division, in the Army of Northern Virginia, was in active service from the beginning of the war, and became captain of infantry, A. N. V. Shortly after the battle of Chancellorsville he died of typhoid fever. The oldest daughter, Mattie, married William Arthur Shepard, of Boston, Massachusetts, a graduate of Harvard University, who came to Virginia as professor of chemistry in the Southern Female College and there met his future wife. Later he was for many years professor of chemistry in Randolph-Macon College at Ashland, where he died in the 1890s. Alice married Maj. Olive Branch Morgan, a veteran of the war between the states, who afterwards became manager of the bag department of the Virginia Carolina Chemical Company of Richmond.

Richard Beale Davis, the second son, graduated from Randolph-Macon College and the University of Virginia, and served throughout the entire Civil war in the Petersburg Riflemen, Twelfth Virginia Infantry, Mahone's Brigade, A. P. Hill's Division. With that company he participated in many of the chief battles, and was wounded twice in the Battle of the Crater. After the war he practiced law at Petersburg until his death, about 1900, being associated as a law partner about fifteen years of the latter part of his life with his youngest half-brother, Charles Hall Davis. He served repeatedly in the Legislature, was one of the committee appointed to recommend changes in the Code in order to make it conform to the Constitution of 1902, and for many years was assistant attorney general of the state.

Joseph Claiborne Davis, the third son, who continued in active business at Portsmouth until advanced years, entered the Confederate army at the age of fourteen, was wounded twice, was captured and carried to Governor's Island, and was released

only on the termination of hostilities. He was a member of the
Richmond Howitzers, an organization still in existence.

The daughter Emma became the wife of T. H. H. Young,
who just after the Civil war started a manufacturing plant at
Petersburg. That being unsuccessful, he subsequently went into
the timber business, and in later life moved to North Carolina,
becoming a traveling salesman.

The second wife of Williams Thomas Davis was Carolina
Virginia Robinson, daughter of Clark Robinson, owner of an
extensive plantation on the Roanoke River, North Carolina, on
which plantation she was born. Her mother was Anne Johnson,
a descendant of John Johnson, who came to this country as a
political refugee, and thereby forfeited his claim to the Annan-
dale estates. He built a home on Tanner's Creek, then outside
of Norfolk, but since embraced within the city's limits, where
its avenue of magnolia trees and the family burying ground
give it notable prominence. The old homestead is still occupied
by descendants of John Johnson. Carolina Virginia Robinson
Davis died in Petersburg in 1912, leaving the following children:
Sannie Robinson, who became the wife of Clarence Preston
Ehrman, a retired capitalist of Lynchburg. A second daughter,
Carolina Robinson, died at Petersburg of typhoid fever at the
age of twenty. Arthur Kyle Davis was the oldest son of the
second marriage. Williams Thomas Davis, the second son, was
for many years special attorney for the Atlantic Coast Line Railroad at Charleston, South Carolina, Savannah, Georgia, and
Wilmington, North Carolina. Charles Hall Davis, the youngest
member of the family, has practiced law at Petersburg since
he came to the bar in 1893, at the age of twenty-one.

Arthur Kyle Davis was educated during his childhood by his
father, who had the gift of teaching and who recognized the
necessity for thoroughness. As a boy he attended McCabe's
University School in Petersburg—a school conspicuous for its
Honor System and for its insistence upon a thorough knowledge
of Latin and Greek. Leaving McCabe's School, Mr. Davis went
to Randolph-Macon College, Ashland, Virginia, in which his
father had many years before been head of the preparatory
department for five years. From Randolph-Macon College he
graduated with the degrees of Bachelor of Arts and Master of
Arts in the class of 1886, at the age of nineteen. For two years
thereafter he taught in the Southern Female College under the
direction of his father, and in the summer of 1888 went to the
University of Virginia to take the summer law course under
Prof. John B. Minor, with the idea of entering the legal profession. But the death of his father during that summer ended
these plans, and in the fall of 1888 he was elected president of
the Southern Female College, at the age of twenty-one, and has
held this position ever since.

Doctor Davis had a prominent part in the Junior College
movement in Virginia. The college at Petersburg was one of a
number of institutions, chartered as colleges but without the
equipment and resources to measure up to the strict standards
of modern educational classifications, and Doctor Davis shared
fully in the ideas of prominent educational leaders all over the
country that such institutions should be denominated Junior
colleges, performing the service of a school giving the first two
years of a standard college course. In line with this idea Mr.
Davis changed the name to the Southern College, Junior, of

Petersburg. The college affords a thorough preparatory and
two years' standard college course, also finishing courses in
music, art, expression, home economics and other subjects.

Doctor Davis was twice honored with election as president
of the Virginia Association of Colleges and Schools for Girls, has
been president of the Virginia Association of Junior Colleges,
is a member of the American Historical Association, Archæo-
logical Institute of America, Southern Association of Colleges
and Schools, Virginia Classical Association, Southern Socio-
logical Congress, is a member of the Sons of Confederate
Veterans, Kappa Alpha, Westmoreland Club of Richmond, University Club of Richmond, Country Club of Petersburg.

He was founder and for two years lecturer of the Shakespeare Club of Petersburg and is a member of the Authors Club
of London. For many years he has been well known in literary
circles in Virginia. He has written verse, but is best known
as an historian. A small book which he wrote a number of years
ago has been printed and reprinted, and is one of the most read-
able of concise histories of historic Virginia communities. Its
title is "Three Centuries of an Old Virginia Town," telling the
story of Petersburg. He is also author of "Education in Virginia," "Virginia and the Methodist," "Virginia's War History,"
and has been editor of quarterly supplements, calendars and
reports in the *Virginia Historical Magazine.*

During the World war he made an address in which he out-
lines a plan for preserving Virginia's war history. The Virginia War History Commission was created in 1918, and it
seemed natural that Mr. Davis should be selected to direct the
effort, and accordingly in January, 1919, was appointed by the
governor as chairman of the commission. In that capacity he
brought together a body of distinguished scholars and others
prominent in state and locality to carry out his plan for preserving the war history of Virginia, and gave almost unlimited
time and effort to this patriotic work, a service which, needless
to say, carries with it no compensation in monetary terms.
Doctor Davis is a member of the Phi Beta Kappa and was
awarded the honorary degree of Doctor of Letters by Hampden
Sydney College in recognition of his decade of work as chairman
of the War History Commission of Virginia and as editor of
the *Seven Source Volumes of Virginia War History,* including
*Virginia's Distinguished Service in the World War, Virginia
War Letters, Diaries and Editorials, Virginia War History and
Newspaper Clippings, Virginia War Agencies, Selective Draft
and Volunteers, Virginia Military Organization in the World
War, Virginia Committees in War Times* (first and second
series). Doctor Davis is vice president of the National Association of State War Historians, and read a paper recounting some
phases of his work at a meeting of the American Historical
Association at Cleveland, Ohio. This paper was later published
by the association in its quarterly.

Doctor Davis married, November 12, 1890, Lucy Pryor McIlwaine, daughter of Robert B. and Lucy (Pryor) McIlwaine,
her mother being the only sister of Gen. Roger A. Pryor, who
for many years was a judge in New York City and who attained
an enviable position at the bar of that city. Mrs. Davis graduated from St. Paul's School at Petersburg and for six years was
state historian of the Daughters of the American Revolution
of Virginia, and later became state registrar. She is a member

of the Colonial Dames, formerly one of its Board of Governors, belongs to the United Daughters of the Confederacy and has been state historian of the Woman's Auxiliary of the American Legion of Virginia. Doctor and Mrs. Davis have three children, Lucy McIlwaine, Caroline Robinson and Arthur Kyle, Jr. The daughter Lucy M. married Ralph Harvey Jones, of Cleveland, Ohio, and has one daughter, Lucy McIlwaine Jones. Caroline Robinson is the wife of Dr. Wright Clarkson, X-ray specialist of Petersburg, and they have a son, Julian Wright Clarkson.

Arthur Kyle Davis, Jr., was born in 1895, attended the Tome School for boys in Maryland, graduated with the Bachelor of Arts and Master of Arts degrees from the University of Virginia, was a Rhodes scholar from Virginia to Oxford, and was awarded the degree Litt. B. by Balliol College, and later took the Doctor of Philosophy degree at the University of Virginia. He then became an associate professor of English at the University of Virginia. He is author of a volume, *Virginia Ballads,* issued by the Harvard Press. During 1929, with leave of absence from the University of Virginia, he was Sterling Research Fellow in English at Yale University, where he prepared for publication his forthcoming volume on *Poets and Politics of the Victorian Era.*

WILLIAM WADLEY APPLER. During the comparatively short career of the late William Wadley Appler, who died when less than thirty-eight years of age, September 9, 1919, his activities had invaded varied fields of enterprise, including railroading, insurance and cigar manufacturing, in all of which he showed the possession of marked ability, adaptability and great energy. A resident of Richmond for some years, he had become recognized as one of the rising young men of the community, but at the time of his sudden death was located at Norfolk, where he had intended entering business.

Mr. Appler was born at Columbus, Georgia, October 6, 1881, a son of David Weaver and Emma Rebecca (Thornton) Appler, the latter being a descendant of the great American statesman, Henry Clay. The Appler family is of English origin and the American ancestor came to this country just after the close of the War of the Revolution, settling at Baltimore, Maryland. David Weaver Appler was born in Virginia, and during the war between the states was employed as a train dispatcher in this state. At the close of the war he went to Georgia, and for fifty-four years served as freight agent for the Central Railroad of Georgia, his home being at Columbus. He and his wife were the parents of three children.

William Wadley Appler received his education in the public schools of Atlanta, Georgia, and in young manhood became cashier and later traveling passenger agent for five years of the Mexican National Railroad. Subsequently he went to Chicago, Illinois, where he was chief clerk for the Sun Insurance Company, and also was identified with his brother in the insurance agency business. In September, 1914, Mr. Appler came to Richmond, Virginia, where he became connected with the Straus Cigar Company, but severed his connections therewith in 1919 and went to Norfolk, where he intended embarking in business on his own account. Not long after his arrival in that city he was taken ill and died. He was a young man of much promise and ability and his death caused universal mourning among countless friends in all of the communities in which he had resided. He was a member of the Presbyterian Church.

On March 20, 1904, Mr. Appler was united in marriage with Miss Emily J. Oberweiser, who was educated in Wisconsin and was a daughter of Pauline and Michael Oberweiser. Mr. Oberweiser was a leading contractor and builder of his day, as well as an architect, and erected the first bridge across the Chicago River at Chicago. Later he located at Richmond, where he continued to hold a place among the leaders of his profession until his death. Five children were born to Mr. and Mrs. Appler: Florence Estelle, who was educated at a college at Bristol, Tennessee, and is now employed in a secretarial capacity with one of the large concerns of Richmond; Misses Marjorie Elizabeth and Ruth Emily, who reside with their mother; and David Weaver and William Howard, who are still attending school. Mrs. Appler, who resides at 2808 Fendall Avenue, is one of the highly esteemed ladies of Richmond and has been active in the work of the Presbyterian Church.

HENRY JACKSON RIPPON. The late Henry Jackson Rippon was a resident of Richmond from 1889 until 1909, during which time he formed as large an acquaintance and made as many friends as any other man in the city. Although he died at the early age of forty-five years, his career had been a decidedly successful one, and he was particularly well known to the traveling public, having been for almost all of his residence at Richmond clerk of the Jefferson Hotel. A man of warm impulses and open-handed generosity, his presence was welcomed in any circle, and while he passed away in January, 1909, there are still many who mourn his death.

Mr. Rippon belonged to a family which had its origin in France and found settlement on the east coast of Virginia during the early Colonial period of this country's history. His father was Thomas Rippon, a sea captain, who traveled on many waters, and his mother was Elizabeth, there being eight children in the family, of whom Henry Jackson was the youngest. The public schools of Brambleton, Norfolk County, furnished Mr. Rippon with his educational training, he having been born at that place October 10, 1864. In his boyhood he went to Norfolk, where he was employed by several firms in various capacities, and then embarked in the cafe business at Tenth and Broad streets, Richmond, although he also had five years of experience as a clerk in the Murphy Hotel. After two years in the cafe business he was offered the position of clerk in the Jefferson Hotel, which had just been completed and was ready to open, and he accordingly sold his cafe business to accept the post. He was the first clerk of that establishment, and was holding this position when it was destroyed by fire. During its rebuilding he was manager of the Virginia Club for two years, and then returned to the Jefferson Hotel to resume his old position, which he held until a few days before his early death. As before noted, Mr. Rippon was a man of many friendships. He was possessed of strict integrity and probity and had the confidence and esteem of all with whom he was connected. He was a member of the Sacred Heart Cathedral, and in his political views was a Democrat. While he was very public spirited and took an honest pride in his adopted city, he never cared for the honors of public life.

On October 7, 1892, Mr. Rippon was united in marriage with Miss Katherine Nowlan, who was educated at St. Joseph's Academy, Richmond, and was a daughter of James and Marguerite (Redmond) Nowlan, both families having originated in Ireland. James Nowlan was engaged in the manufacture and blasting of stone at Richmond for many years, and furnished the majority of the cut stone for the city hall, the postoffice and many other public, business and financial structures. During the war between the states he served as a cavalryman in a Virginia regiment of the Confederate army, and at one time was taken prisoner by Northern troops, but made his escape and returned to his regiment. Of the children born to Mr. and Mrs. Rippon, four grew to maturity: Ethel Elizabeth, who is now deceased; Eileen, the wife of Jackie E. Creery, who is connected with the Chesapeake & Ohio Railroad; Grace, deceased, who was the wife of J. Leo O'Brien, and left one child, Jack, Jr.; and Nelda, the wife of Lawrence J. DelPaka, who has two children, Lawrence, Jr., and Charles. All of the daughters of Mr. and Mrs. Rippon received their education at Sacred Heart School. Mrs. Rippon survives her husband and resides at 1407 Claremont Avenue, where she has a wide acquaintance and is held in high esteem.

CHARLES Q. COUNTS. Perhaps the Virginia bar offers no more interesting example of personal effort abundantly rewarded than is revealed in the encouraging life story of Charles Q. Counts, attorney at law at Coeburn, Virginia, an honored citizen and distinguished lawyer, who for many years has been both commissioner of accounts and commissioner in chancery for Wise County. In our great country it is not unusual to discover self-made men in all walks of life, but not so often is found one who, entirely through his own efforts, has reached high place in a professional field in which great qualifications are essential and competition is strong.

Charles Q. Counts was born on his father's plantation in Scott County, Virginia, in October, 1862, son of Noah W. and Harriett (Quillin) Counts, and grandson of James Counts and Elisha Quillin. The mother of Commissioner Counts spent her entire life in Scott County, but her father, Elisha Quillin, in his later years moved to Tennessee. He was a musician and a well known singing master in his day. The father of Commissioner Counts was born in Russell County, Virginia, where his father, a native of Eastern Virginia, had settled early, but died on his own estate in Scott County. They were all Virginia people of sturdy character and religious lives, and it is impossible not to believe that such upbringing had influence in moulding the character of their children.

Educational opportunities in Scott County were not as they are today when Charles Quillin Counts began to go to school in boyhood, and he easily recalls the little old log schoolhouse nearby in which he received his primary instruction. Later he was able to attend Holston Institute in Tennessee for a few months, where he applied himself closely to his studies and made such headway that he was accepted as a teacher in the country schools, first in Scott County and afterward in Tennessee. Although, perhaps, not generally known, but during this teaching period Mr. Counts could have undoubtedly won the medal, had any been offered, for being the most industrious and ambitious of the students, for he had undertaken the responsibility of preparing himself for the law, alone and unaided, this undertaking requiring prodigious mental and physical effort under the circumstances.

Later in life courage and determination have been his winning factors in many a legal contest, and Mr. Counts made them his close companions through the long struggle, and when, at last, he presented himself before the State Examining Board he found it all had been well worth while, for he was one of the twenty accepted petitioners of a class of forty-two. He had located at Wise in 1894, and after being admitted to the bar in 1898, maintained his law office in the courthouse there for ten years. He removed then to Coeburn, of which city he has been a resident ever since.

In 1899 Mr. Counts was made commissioner of accounts for Wise County, and in 1900 was appointed commissioner in chancery, and during this long period has had some very important and difficult cases in chancery, in all of which the wisdom shown by his findings have been confirmed by the County Court. His general practice has been eminently successful, and he enjoys an established reputation of being one of the ablest legists in Southwestern Virginia and a citizen deserving both professionally and personally the high esteem in which he is held. In political sentiment he is a Democrat and to some extent is active in county and city public matters, and for a number of years was a member of the Coeburn School Board, interest in schools and educational matters generally having been urgent since his youth.

Mr. Counts' first marriage took place October 9, 1895, to Miss Harriet Carico, daughter of Joseph M. Carico, of a family of prominence in Wise County. Mrs. Counts died March 12, 1902, the devoted mother of three children: Inez, who was educated at Sullins College, Bristol, Virginia, and is talented in music, teaching the same before her marriage in Scott and Wise counties, Virginia, and at Bluefield, West Virginia, is the wife of T. E. Jenkins, of Elizabethtown, Tennessee, and they have a daughter, Dorothy Ann; Ada, who died when two years old; and Joseph Bruce, who is an employe of the Virginia State Highway Department. Mr. Counts married, on October 5, 1902, Miss Lula Bruce, of Big Stone Gap, Virginia, daughter of Hoge Bruce. Like the former Mrs. Counts, she was a sincere member of the Methodist Episcopal Church, South, and served as district secretary of the Big Stone Gap Woman's Missionary Society. Prior to her marriage she was highly esteemed as a school teacher in Wise County. She passed away on January 27, 1923, survived by all but two of her eleven children: Lenette, who was educated in the Coeburn High School and Hiawassee College, Tennessee, is the wife of Pearson Clark, of Coeburn, and they have one daughter, Virginia Lee; Robert Carl, who completed his education at Emory and Henry College, is now a traveling salesman in Georgia and Florida for large business houses; Bernice, who is a graduate of the Coeburn High School, fills the office of assistant postmaster at Wilder, in Russell County, Virginia; Ruth, who on completing her high school education entered a hospital at Louisville, Kentucky, for training as a nurse; Glenn, Louise and Gean, all of whom are in school at Coeburn; Christie and Christine, twins, who died in infancy; and Ralph and Charles Q., Jr., who are at home. Mr. Counts' third marriage

took place October 25, 1925, to Mrs. Nellie G. (Richmond) Carico, widow of James Carico, and daughter of David and Jane Richmond, a lady of education and social prominence, a member of the local lodge of Rebekahs, and very active in the work of the Methodist Episcopal Church, South.

No record of Commissioner Counts' life of worth-while achievement would be complete without dwelling on his continuous devotion to the interests of the great religious body, the faith of which was instilled in childhood. For the greater part of thirty years he has served as steward and church trustee; formerly was district lay leader for the Big Stone Gap District; for thirteen successive years has attended the annual church conferences and was a member of the General Conference which met at Oklahoma City in 1914; for many years has been a member of either the Finance, Commissions or Sunday School Conference Board, of which general board he is now vice president. He has always been foremost in promoting the many charitable movements of this great Christian organization, and his sound, practical advice concerning church policy in relation to many modern public questions has been acceptable and acted upon. He is a member of the Wise County Bar Association, and belongs to the Kiwanis Club and the fraternal order of Modern Woodmen of America.

WALTER CLEVELAND CAUDILL is a physician and surgeon who has gained distinction and rank in his profession and has made his skill a source of comfort and indispensable service to hundreds of people and families in Giles and adjacent counties. He is president of St. Elizabeth's Hospital at Pearisburg and is also vice president of Elizabeth's Hospital at Elizabethton, Tennessee.

Doctor Caudill was born in Ashe County, North Carolina, June 9, 1888, and represents some of the sturdy and sterling people of the mountain country of Western North Carolina. His parents were Tyrell R. and Caroline (Fender) Caudill, and his grandfather, Jesse Caudill, was a prominent land owner, planter and stock man in Alleghany County, North Carolina, where he died and is buried. Jesse Caudill was twice married, and had eleven children by each wife, twenty-two in all. Tyrell R. Caudill was born and reared in Western North Carolina, attended private schools, was a farmer and stock man, and widely known for his strength of character and sound judgment. He held the office of justice of the peace for over twenty years, and in all that time never had one of his decisions reversed by a higher court. He died in 1919 and is buried at Whitehead, North Carolina. His wife, Caroline Fender, was born and reared in Alleghany County, North Carolina, attended private schools, and is still living at the old homestead at Whitehead. For many years she has been a member of the Primitive Baptist Church. She was the mother of thirteen children. Two of them died in infancy and one at the age of nineteen. Those to grow up were: Rev. Shade G. Caudill, an elder in the Baptist Church, Mrs. Nannie C. Waddell, Mrs. Mattie C. Greene, Mrs. Candace Edwards, Mrs. Florence C. Edwards, Oscar Caudill, Dr. Walter C., Dr. E. L. Caudill, Muncy Edwin Caudill and Mrs. Blanche Edwards.

Walter Cleveland Caudill was educated in public schools in Alleghany County, North Carolina, attended the Appalachian

Training School at Boone, that state, and the Elk Creek Training School at Elk Creek, Virginia. He completed his professional preparation at the Medical College of Virginia, graduating M. D. in 1913, and was an interne in the Lewis Gale Hospital at Roanoke and in St. Elizabeth's Hospital in Richmond. Doctor Caudill in 1914 located at Pearisburg, and soon established a promising general practice in medicine and surgery. He opened his office in the Law Building. His work as a local physician came to a temporary interruption when in 1917 he enlisted for service in the Army Medical Corps, and in September, 1917, was assigned immediate service at Newport News, and on December 1, 1917, left for France with the Three Hundred and Second Stevedore Regiment. On arriving in France he was detached and put in Camp Hospital No. 2 near Bordeaux. On October 1, 1918, he was again transferred, to the Twenty-third Engineers, and accompanied that famous regiment to the Verdun Sector, and was in the drive through the Argonne Forest to Stenay. After the armistice he was sent home and received his honorable discharge at Camp Lee, Virginia, with the rank of captain, in July, 1919. He was in the service nearly two years, going in with the rank of first lieutenant.

After the war he resumed his work at Pearisburg, and he and his brother, Dr. Estill L. Caudill, founded St. Elizabeth's Hospital, a twenty-bed general hospital with excellent equipment and well planned for service to the growing community. In January, 1928, his brother, Dr. E. L. Caudill, moved to Elizabethton, Tennessee, and subsequently he and his brother Walter and Dr. J. O. Woods, of Elizabethton, formed a partnership and founded St. Elizabeth's Hospital there. They put up a building costing $60,000, of brick and stone construction and of Colonial architecture, a very handsome and attractive building and affording the facilities of a high class hospital. There are fifty-five rooms. Dr. W. C. Caudill is a third owner of this hospital and serves as vice president. He is a director in the First National Bank of Pearisburg and is a member of the County, State, Tri-State, Southern and American Medical Associations.

Doctor Caudill during 1928 was chairman of the Giles County Democratic Committee. He is a member of the Primitive Baptist Church, the American Legion, is a member of the Masonic fraternity and Kazim Temple of the Mystic Shrine at Roanoke.

He married at Bluefield, West Virginia, June 30, 1920, Miss Mary Ring Cornett, of Bluefield. She was reared in Grayson County, Virginia, attended public schools there and the Elk Creek Training School, and graduated in 1911 from the State Teachers College at Farmville, Virginia. She taught in grade and high schools for several years before her marriage, and has always taken part in the working organizations of the Methodist Episcopal Church. She is a daughter of F. A. and Hester (Ring) Cornett, of Grayson County, Virginia, who later moved to Bluefield. Her father was a farmer and stock man, owning a farm four miles from Bluefield, toward Princeton, and after selling that lived at Graham, Virginia, and finally at Pearisburg, Virginia, where he died in September, 1927, and her mother died in June of the same year. Both are buried in Elk Creek Cemetery in Grayson County. Doctor and Mrs. Caudill had two sons, Carrel Mayo and Walter C., Jr. The latter died at the age of five months and the older is attending school at Pearisburg.

PROF. ZELMA TALMAGE KYLE. Looking backward through
the records of many generations, the family name of Kyle is
found a familiar and respected one in Southwest Virginia, at
all times representing a substantial group in which thrift and
industry prevail, and education and morality encouraged. A
prominent member of this old Virginia family who is now
claimed by Tazewell County is Prof. Zelma T. Kyle, superintending principal of the schools of Bluefield, Virginia, a man of
marked personality, great executive ability and widely and
favorably known.

The Kyle family is of Irish extraction and was founded in
America by two brothers, both of whom settled in the South,
one in Georgia and the other in Tennessee, and of the latter,
his great-great-grandfather, Professor Kyle is a direct descendant. He was born at Woodlawn, in Carroll County, Virginia, in
1892, son of Henry F. and Sallie Jane (Walker) Kyle, both of
whom still reside at Woodlawn, his father owning a valuable
farm in Carroll County. He was born in Carroll County, son of
James Madison Kyle, a prominent farmer and Democratic politician in Botetourt County, and died in 1901, a brother of Judge
William Kyle, who served many years on the county bench. The
great-grandfather of Professor Kyle, James Kyle, was born after
his parents moved from Tennessee to Virginia. He lived and
died on his estate in Botetourt County, near Fincastle. Both he
and his sons were active members of the Methodist Episcopal
Church, South, conscientious men in both public and private life.

Henry F. Kyle, father of Professor Kyle, is a leading citizen
of Carroll County, where he has served on the election board
and the school board, a trustworthy man in every capacity. In
his religious belief he is a Quaker, a member of the Friends
Church at Woodlawn, and one of its Board of Overseers. The
mother of Professor Kyle was also born in Carroll County, Virginia, daughter of John Walker, and great-granddaughter of
John Walker, who was born in Ireland. He founded the Walker
family in Kentucky, and the maternal grandfather of Professor
Kyle was born in Boone County. About the time of the war
between the states he came to Carroll County, Virginia, where
he engaged in farming until he was accidentally killed by a
falling tree. In politics he was a Republican, and in religious
faith was identified with the Primitive Baptist body, in which
he was a deacon and moderator and frequently served as a local
preacher.

Zelma Talmage Kyle can easily call to memory the one-room
log schoolhouse near his father's farm in which he received his
early educational training, but, to one like himself, eager to
learn, his surroundings were more or less immaterial, as he
had an earnest and competent teacher who soon prepared him
for the Woodlawn High School, from which he was creditably
graduated in 1911. He then entered William and Mary College
for a preparatory course, after which he taught school for a
time and then returned to William and Mary College, from
which he was graduated in 1917, as president of his class, with
the degree of A. B. Since then he has attended Peabody Normal
College, Nashville, Tennessee, preparing for his A. M. degree.

Upon his graduation from William and Mary College Professor Kyle became principal of the Woodlawn High School, and
during the two years he continued there gave evidence of the
progressive spirit that has since assisted him in the accomplish-

ment of so much for higher education in the communities with which he has been identified. While at Woodlawn he established there the first Smith Hughes Agricultural School in Virginia, which was the first to receive an appropriation from the Federal funds. On retiring from the Woodlawn High School he went to Appalachia, Virginia, as principal of its city schools, and during the six years he remained there brought about remarkable changes. He found one eleven-room school building and about 500 pupils in attendance. When he left one building had been erected at a cost of $75,000; a new high school building, costing $750,000; an athletic field secured for $15,000; and had further obtained a bond issue of another $150,000 for the schools.

Professor Kyle then accepted the call to Bluefield, Virginia, as supervising school principal. He has here four buildings under his direction: The Graham High School, with twenty teachers; the Logan Street School, with five teachers; the West Graham School, with one teacher; and the colored school, with five teachers. Since taking charge he has caused a fine gymnasium to be built and many large and desirable improvement propositions are being considered. His heart is in his work, and seemingly no details can weary him or obstacles discourage him.

At Woodlawn, Virginia, on February 15, 1919, Professor Kyle married Miss Mary Elizabeth Kenny, of that city, daughter of John A. and Florence (Beamer) Kenny. The late John A. Kenny was a prominent and substantial citizen of Carroll County, a farmer and lumber dealer. He was a justice of the peace and active in Democratic politics, served many years on important county boards, and in the Methodist Episcopal Church, South, at Woodlawn, was a steward, church treasurer and superintendent of the Sunday school. Mr. Kenny was born in Carroll County, son of William Kenny, a native of Grayson County, Virginia, but later a farmer in Carroll County, and a grandson of William Kenny, who was born in Ireland. The mother of Mrs. Kyle was born in Carroll County, and still resides at Woodlawn. Her father, Harden Beamer, was born in Carroll County, of Tennessee parentage and Irish extraction. He was a very prominent man in Carroll County, a member of the school board for twenty years and deputy county treasurer. He was engaged in farming all his life, was a Democrat in politics, and a faithful member and liberal supporter of the Methodist Episcopal Church, South.

Mrs. Kyle, an educated, accomplished lady, who is fully in sympathy with her husband in his aim to further educational opportunities and advantages in the public schools, was graduated from the Woodlawn High School in 1916, attended Leesburg College for two years, and was graduated from Radford State Teachers College in 1925. She received her teacher's diploma in 1923 from this college and then took a course in the Peabody Normal School at Nashville, Tennessee. For two years she was an instructor in the Appalachia High School, and for the past three years has been teacher of home economics in the Bluefield schools. She is a member of the State Teachers Association and of the American Home Economics Association, is active in the Methodist Episcopal Church, South, and belongs to the Eastern Star.

A man of Professor Kyle's sterling character, inspiring energy and agreeable personality finds confidence and esteem

awaiting him in many important lines of community life. He is active as a member of the Bluefield Chamber of Commerce and is interested in all worthwhile public movements here. A Democrat in politics, he has frequently attended state conventions of his party as a delegate and is considered a wise and safe party adviser. He is a Chapter Mason and was senior warden of the Masonic Lodge at Appalachia, is worthy patron in the Order of the Eastern Star, and belongs to the State Teachers Association and the National Education Association, as well as to the old fraternal organizations in which he took a deep interest while in William and Mary College. He frequently lectures on educational subjects. Like his father, he is a member of the Friends Church, never having departed from the simple faith in which he was reared.

WILLIAM GEORGE WARING with the exception of one year since he left college has been engaged in banking. He is cashier of the Farmers and Mechanics Bank of West Point, one of the prosperous and successful banking institutions of King William County. The bank operates on capital and surplus of over fifty thousand dollars and has total resources of over $350,000.

Mr. Waring was born in King William County, April 11, 1894, son of Thomas Bromley and Elmira Gertrude (Hill) Waring. His father was born at Liberty Hall in King William County, and his mother was born in the house where history states George Washington and his bride first met at Poplar Grove, in New Kent County. Thomas B. Waring served as a Confederate soldier, running away from home at the age of sixteen to join the army. In one battle he was shot from his saddle. After the war he engaged in farming in King William County, was also a county official, and died in January, 1900, as the result of being thrown from his horse. His widow survived him until February 16, 1914. They had a family of nine children, and after the death of the father the oldest son, Robert Payne Waring, assumed the responsibility of rearing the younger children, and performed that duty with a high degree of credit for a young man.

William George Waring was reared and educated in King William County, attended college at Lynchburg three years, and after leaving college spent a year with Lane Brothers, contractors, while this firm was engaged in the construction of the disposal plant at Baltimore, Maryland. Mr. Waring in 1915 became bookkeeper in the State Bank of West Point and in 1920 was chosen cashier. He was in charge of the executive details of the bank until January 31, 1927, when it was sold to the Farmers and Mechanics Bank, and he became cashier in the latter institution.

Mr. Waring married April 26, 1924, Jessie Carter Lewis, daughter of Herbert Iverson and Mattie (Parks) Lewis. Her mother is living at West Point. She was born at Norfolk, Virginia. Herbert R. Lewis, a native of King William County, was a distinguished member of the bar at West Point and held the office of commonwealth attorney of the county forty-three and a half years, until his death on May 5, 1928. Mr. and Mrs. Waring have three children, Betty Carter, Burnet Lewis and Robert Lawrence. Mr. Waring is affiliated with the Knights of Pythias, Junior Order United American Mechanics, Kiwanis Club, Cypress Park Club, is a Democrat and a member of the Episcopal Church.

HON. JOSEPH GRAHAM, ex-sheriff of Pulaski County, and a farmer upon an extensive scale, is one of the best examples of the modern farmer the county possesses. His home farm is a model one, and his experiments are watched with great interest by his neighbors. In his office of sheriff he gave to Pulaski a clean administration, entirely free from graft or sinister influences, and succeeded in driving out and keeping out of his domain those who would not conform to the laws, both Federal and local.

Mr. Graham was born in Pulaski County, Virginia, December 9, 1870, a son of Dr. Joseph D. and Mary (Currin) Graham, the former of whom was born and reared in Pulaski County. He first attended the private schools of this locality, and later took his medical training in a college of Baltimore, Maryland. Enlisting at the outbreak of the war between the states, he served with the Pulaski Guards, Fifty-fourth Virginia Infantry, and was a brave soldier of the Confederacy. During his service he participated in a number of the major engagements, and was wounded in action in the battle of Gettysburg. After the close of the war he was engaged in the practice of his profession, and was an active practitioner at the time of his death, May 1, 1896. He was one of the old-time physicians, traveling over long distances, in all kinds of weather, giving of his skill, his time and his sympathy without thought of remuneration, and was long held to be the "beloved physician." His remains are interred in Oglesby Cemetery, Pulaski County. His father was Joseph Graham, a native of Wythe County, Virginia, a farmer by occupation, a calling he followed all his life. Both he and his wife are deceased, and they lie side by side in the Oglesby Cemetery. Robert Graham, father of Joseph Graham, and great-grandfather of former Sheriff Graham, was born in Scotland and came to this country at an early day, settling in Wythe County, where he was a farmer and stockman, and he and his wife are also buried in Oglesby Cemetery. During the years that have followed the settlement in Virginia of Robert Graham those bearing the name have taken a prominent part in the history of the state and have been law-abiding, self-respecting men and women worthy of the confidence and esteem they have always inspired.

Mrs. Mary (Currin) Graham, mother of Joseph Graham, was born February 7, 1844, in Montgomery County, Virginia, but early in life was taken to Newburn, Virginia, by her parents, Lynch A. and Elizabeth (Haller) Currin. Mr. Currin was county clerk during the war between the states. Mrs. Graham was educated in Mrs. McGavock's School for Young Ladies, Wytheville, Virginia. She was a devout member of the Presbyterian Church, and until her death July 17, 1929, at the age of eighty-five years, she made her home with Mr. Graham and a married daughter, Mrs. Painter, of Draper, Virginia. There were five children born to her and her husband: C. S. Graham, a farmer, who is now deceased; Elizabeth, who married A. S. Painter, lives at Draper; Joseph Graham, who is the third in order of birth; C. F. Graham, who died when one year old; and Willie Sue, who married B. T. Gilmer, a rural mail carrier of Draper.

Growing up in Pulaski County, Joseph Graham attended public schools and a private school, and when old enough began farming. From then on until the present he has been engaged in farming and stock raising, owning the old Graham homestead of 200 acres of fine bluegrass land. Part of the house is over 100 years old, and is in splendid condition, so well was it built in the beginning. Upright, honorable, knowing the people of Pulaski County as he does, Mr. Graham was honored by his fellow citizens by election to the office of sheriff in 1906, and he continued in it from May of that year to December 31, 1915. He is an active Democrat, and one of the local leaders of his party. Fraternally he is a Royal Arch Mason, and he belongs to the Benevolent and Protective Order of Elks and the Modern Woodmen of America. He is a Presbyterian, and is serving the local church as deacon.

On November 11, 1889, Mr. Graham first married at Bristol, Tennessee, Miss Berta L. Graham, of Draper, Virginia, a daughter of Thompson and Ellen (Grills) Graham, first of Mercer County, West Virginia, but later of Draper. Seven children were born to this marriage: Mary Ellen; Lucy Jane, who is the wife of A. F. Clark; Joseph Thompson; Virginia Berta, who died at the age of twenty-one years; Elizabeth, who is the wife of John T. Sayre, of Roanoke, Virginia; Nell M., who is the wife of O. H. Buchanan, of Tazewell, Virginia; and Gertrude, who lives at home.

On April 3, 1916, Mr. Graham married in Draper's Valley Miss Janie H. Draper, of Draper's Valley. An extensive account of the Draper family is given elsewhere in this work. Mrs. Graham was educated in a private school, Montgomery Hall, Christiansburg, Virginia. While she is a member of the Episcopal Church, she is active in the work of the Presbyterian Church of Draper's Valley. Sheriff and Mrs. Graham have had two children born to them: Joseph, Jr., and Jane Draper, both of whom are attending the Draper's Valley public school.

CHESTER CLAUDE SHELBURNE, county superintendent of schools of Montgomery County, has been prominently identified with educational work in Virginia for a number of years and has won a very favorable reputation as a school man.

He was born at Riner, Virginia, May 14, 1891, son of William J. and Milinda J. (Altizer) Shelburne. The Shelburne family came to America from Wales in Colonial times, first settling in Lunenburg County. Mr. Shelburne's grandfather, John Thomas Shelburne, was a Confederate soldier all through the four years of the war and afterwards followed farming and stock raising. He and his wife are buried in the Shelburne family cemetery. William J. Shelburne was born and reared in Montgomery County, and is a farmer and stock raiser. His wife. Milinda J. Altizer, was born and reared in Floyd County. She is a member of the Christian Church. Of their three children one died in infancy. Mr. Shelburne has a sister, Juanita, wife of W. B. Whitt, a farmer and stock man at East Radford.

Chester Claude Shelburne attended public schools in Montgomery County, and in the intervals of teaching and other work continued his higher education through Milligan College in Tennessee, Daleville College, and in 1927 graduated Bachelor of Science from the University of Virginia. While he owns a farm and is engaged in farming and stock raising in Montgomery County, his chief hobby for many years has been teaching and educational work.

An interruption to his career as an educator came when he joined the colors on September 21, 1917, for service in the World war. He was in training at Camp Lee until May, 1918, and went overseas with Company H of the 317th Infantry in the Eightieth Division. He was on duty in the Artois Sector, in the St. Mihiel and Meuse Argonne campaigns, and after returning home following the armistice received his honorable discharge at Camp Lee June 13, 1919. After the armistice he was assigned duty for three months as an inspector in a post school at Planay, France, and he also had the opportunity of attending the University of Beaune in France for one term.

Mr. Shelburne was principal of the Showsville High School in Montgomery County for nine years and was principal of the high school at Blacksburg during 1927-29. On March 9, 1929, he was elected superintendent of schools for Montgomery County. He is well qualified for the responsibilities of this office, his teaching experience having given him a thorough familiarity with school conditions in the county.

Mr. Shelburne is a member of the State Education Association, the Lions Club, the Phi Delta Kappa and Pi Gamma Mu fraternities, the American Legion and Veterans of Foreign Wars.

MOSES P. LAWRENCE is an electrical engineer with a wide experience in public utility management, and is now superintendent of the Electric Power Plant at Glenlyn, in Giles County. He comes of an old Virginia family but is a native of North Carolina, born at Tarboro, February 12, 1882, son of Louis H. and Carrie C. (Knight) Lawrence. His great-grandfather, Rev. Joshua Lawrence, was the son of a colonel in the Revolutionary war, and at that time the Lawrence family lived in Virginia. The grandfather of Mr. Lawrence also bore the name of Joshua, and lived at Tarboro, North Carolina. Louis H. Lawrence was born at Tarboro, attended Oxford College, in North Carolina, and served four years in the Confederate army, in Company C, Thirty-third North Carolina Regiment. After the war he was a farmer and cotton planter until 1908, and is now retired at the age of eighty-seven, living with his son in Glenlyn. His wife, Carrie C. Knight, is a daughter of John C. and Martha (Cromwell) Knight, and her grandfather, Elisha Cromwell, was a colonel in the Revolutionary war. Mrs. Carrie C. Lawrence died November 20, 1920. Of her eleven children, two died in infancy. Those now living are Bessie, Joshua, Carrie, Moses P., Cleveland, Harvey, Rosa and Douglas.

Moses P. Lawrence was educated in North Carolina public schools, and was on his father's farm until the age of sixteen. In 1898 he went with the Norfolk & Ocean View Railway Company, spending two years with that electric line and then four years was located at Norfolk for the same company. For one year he was connected with the Trenton & New Brunswick Railway Company at Princeton, New Jersey, and the same interests sent him out to Erie, Pennsylvania, for one year as power house engineer. In 1904 he was located at Hampton, Virginia, in the service of the Newport News and Old Point Railway & Electric Company, remaining there until 1907, and was then transferred to the new plant of the company at Norfolk. From 1909 to 1918 he was chief engineer of the power house at Chattanooga, Tennessee, for the Tennessee Power Company.

Mr. Lawrence has been plant superintendent at Glenlyn for the Appalachian Power Company since April, 1918. He is a director of the First National Bank of Narrows and is a stock-

C. C. Simmons

holder in a number of business corporations in this part of Southwest Virginia. He is a Knight Templar Mason and Shriner, member of the American Society of Mechanical Engineers, is a Democrat and an Episcopalian.

He married at Chattanooga, Tennessee, January 17, 1912, Miss Ella Risley, who was reared and educated at Cincinnati, Ohio. She is a daughter of Henry Risley, who was prominent in business and politics in Chattanooga, and at the time of his death was sheriff of Hamilton County, Tennessee. Her mother is still living at Chattanooga.

CREED COLUMBUS SEMONES, commissioner of revenue of Carroll County, has given nearly all his active years to public service in his home county or to the banking business.

Mr. Semones was born at Hillsville, Virginia, in 1872, son of Louis Pleasant and Martha (Pendleton) Semones. This family has been in Southwest Virginia for several generations. His father was born near Hillsville January 1, 1839, was educated in private schools and saw four years of service in the Confederate army. He was in Pickett's famous division at the battle of Gettysburg. After the war he returned to Hillsville, and became a stock raiser and farmer on his father's land, and later bought part of the Semones estate, where he lived until his death in February, 1926. The Semones family came originally from Ireland. His wife, Martha Pendleton, was a daughter of John Pendleton, who was born in Patrick County, Virginia, where his father settled on coming from England. Martha Pendleton was born in Patrick County, near Meadows of Dan Post Office, in 1843, and was educated in private schools, and was a member of the Baptist Church.

Louis P. and Martha (Pendleton) Semones had a family of eight sons, the eldest, John, dying at the age of three years. The second, Joel Wilson, born in 1869, now a retired teacher living at Hillsville, married Mary Farris, and they have four children: Harney Forest, an attorney at Indianapolis, Indiana, married Miss Blankenship, of Carroll County; Mrs. Rosa Hoskin lives at War, West Virginia; Mrs. Eppie Brewster is also a resident of War; and Claude, unmarried, is a civil engineer living in Wyoming. Noah Burton Semones, the fourth child, born in 1875, whose home is three miles from Hillsville, married Elva Bolen and has two sons, Ray, born in 1907, and Buster, born in 1905. Wiley Albert Semones, born in 1878, a teacher in the Hillsville High School, married Ida Beamer, and their sons are Marlie, born in 1906, and Carlos, born in 1910. Armstead Ellis Semones, born in 1881, a resident on the old homestead, married Ada Horton. George E. Semones, born in 1884, a merchant three miles southeast of Hillsville, is the seventh son in the family. The youngest, Norman Ernest, died when three years old.

Creed Columbus Semones was educated in public schools, and life has brought him a sound training in business, farming and public administration. In 1903 he was elected county treasurer of Carroll County, and served in that office eight years, retiring in 1912. Following that he was cashier of the Farmers Bank of Hillsville until 1917. For several years he was in business as a brick manufacturer at Galax, Virginia, selling his interest in the business in 1926 to B. C. Lineberry. He then resumed his residence at Hillsville and in 1927 was elected commissioner of revenue for a term of four years, ending in 1932. Mr.

Semones is a member of the Masonic fraternity at Hillsville and is a Baptist.

He married in February, 1897, Miss Hattie C. Webb. Her father was L. F. Webb, sheriff of Carroll County, one of the county officials who were killed in the well remembered Hillsville tragedy in 1912. The second wife of Mr. Semones was Miss Lillian Reeves. Her father, Horton Reeves, moved from Alleghany County, North Carolina, to Llano, Texas, where he was a merchant. Miss Lillian Reeves met Mr. Semones while visiting in Carroll County, Virginia. To Mr. Semones first marriage were born six children. Ila, born December 5, 1900, graduated from the Hillsville High School in 1920, and in 1925 completed the work of the State Teachers College at Radford. She taught at Red Bank in Patrick County, Virginia, in 1920, at Shelton, North Carolina, in 1921, at Brim, North Carolina, 1922-23, in the Mills school of Patrick County in 1924, at Amelia Court House in 1925-27. She was married, April 6, 1922, at Hillsville, to Mr. Edgar T. Anderson, and since their marriage they have carried on their educational work together. Mr. Anderson is a graduate of the Red Bank High School and also attended the State Teachers College at Radford. He is a son of Robert Marion and Eva Frances (Thompson) Anderson, of Patrick County.

Mr. Semones second child, Lewis Raymond, born April 21, 1903, graduated from the Hillsville High School in 1919 and from the dental department of the Medical College of Richmond in 1924, and is now practicing at East Radford, Virginia. He is a member of Fulton Lodge No. 93 of Masons at Hillsville. Howard Everett Semones, born in July, 1905, is a graduate of the Hillsville High School, and for the past six years has been employed as a machinist in Illinois. Norman Ernest Semones, born February 4, 1907, is a graduate of the high school at Galax, and now deputy commissioner of revenue, Carroll County, Virginia. Lena, born July 1, 1909, graduated from the Galax High School, and is the wife of Ernest Kirby, who is employed in the office of the Vaughn Furniture Company, Galax. Mrs. Kirby is now taking the nurses training course at Galax Hospital. Hallie, the youngest child, born August 21, 1911, is a graduate of the Galax High School and is in training in the Jackson Memorial Hospital at Lexington, Virginia. She is the wife of James C. Hutton, of Lexington, who is in the oil business.

BENTLEY HITE, one of the active younger members of the bar at Christiansburg, is a descendant of that historic character Joise Hite, who left Pennsylvania and went down into the Valley of Virginia about 1732, squatting on lands that were claimed by Lord Fairfax, and it was largely to protect these claims against the sturdy settlers led by George Hite that George Washington went out to the West as a land surveyor.

Bentley Hite was born in Montgomery County, Virginia, December 26, 1900, a son of W. B. and Martha Jane (Scott) Hite, and a grandson of William Ballard Preston Hite, who moved from the Valley of Virginia to Montgomery County about 1832, settling at Price's Fork. He was overseer of the Ballard Plantation there and a farmer and stock raiser for many years. W. B. Hite was born and reared at Price's Fork, near Blacksburg, attended public schools, and has given his life to the farm and stock ranch. His wife was born and reared at Charlottesville. She is a Methodist, while he is a member of the Christian

Church.   There were five children, the daughter Bessie dying at the age of eight years.   The others are: Shirley, a Radford business man, married Lena Talbert and has two children, Shirley, Jr., and Margaret; Guy, a farmer in Pulaski County, married Stella Hedge and has three children, Merle, Gwendolyn and an infant; Maggie is Mrs. R. D. Weeks, wife of a merchant at Snowville, Virginia, and has three children, Earlynn, Raymond and Billy Van; and Bentley.

Bentley Rite attended public schools in Montgomery County, had his high school course in Milligan Academy at Milligan College, Tennessee, was graduated with the A. B. degree from Roanoke College in 1923, and pursued his law studies in the University of Virginia.   He was graduated in 1928, was admitted to the bar that year, and soon afterward opened his law office in the First National Bank Building of Christiansburg and has come into very favorable recognition and a successful business as a lawyer.

Mr. Hite is unmarried.   He was a member of the Students Army Training Corps while at Milligan College during the war. He is a member of the firm Hite & Weeks, general merchants at Snowville.   Mr. Hite is affiliated with Snowville Lodge No. 159, A. F. and A. M.   After graduating from Roanoke College he was principal of the high school at Bowling Green, Virginia, for the year 1923-24, and principal of the high school at Willis in 1924-25.   He is a Republican and a member of the Christian Church.

ANDREW JACKSON WHITE was for a quarter of a century a prominent business man of Richmond.   He was a native Virginian, was a boy soldier of the Confederacy, and lived a life in keeping with the high standards of citizenship of the Old Dominion.

Mr. White was born in Lunenburg County, Virginia, March 12, 1847, and died at Richmond, January 25, 1912, at the age of sixty-five.   His parents were Cephas Allen and Mary (Winn) White, the former of Lunenburg County and the latter of Mecklenburg.   Their children were: Ann; Richard, who was killed in battle in the Confederate army; Mary, Alice, Andrew Jackson and Fanny.

Andrew Jackson White had the advantages offered by the schools of Lunenburg County.   He was only fourteen when the war broke out, and before it was ended he was in the ranks doing what he could as a soldier of the Confederacy.   After the war he assisted his father, who was a brick contractor, and among other work he helped build the Lunenburg County courthouse.   Following that he moved to Richmond and from 1886 until his death was engaged in business as a brick contractor. In that capacity he and his organization had a reputation among the best for finished work, and there are some buildings in Richmond today which exemplify his skill, some of them being the Jefferson Hotel, the brick work on the Chamber of Commerce Building and the Richmond City Hall.

Mr. White was a member of the Independent Order of Odd Fellows, Knights of Pythias and Junior Order United American Mechanics.   He was a Baptist and a Democrat.

He married, November 19, 1876, Miss Josephine Cornelia Marable.   She was reared and educated in Lunenburg County, where her people were among the first settlers.   Mrs. White attended the first public school in Lunenburg County, a school that was opened March 6, 1871.   Her father, Champion Marable,

was a saddler by trade and in later years was a traveling salesman for saddlery and harness. Her mother, Cornelia Ann Kee-
ton, of Lunenburg County, had four children: Isabella, John,
Martha Lucretia and Cornelia. Champion Marable was a Confederate soldier throughout the four years of the war, and in
one battle was severely wounded.

Mrs. White, whose home is at 3311 Grove Avenue, at Rich-
mond, had a family of six children, and she also has several
grandchildren. Her oldest child, Eldon Sanders, died in 1923.
Andrew Eugene is a traveling salesman. The third is Miss
Isabella, and the fourth, Lumlie Lee. Josephine is the wife of
George R. Langston, of Richmond, and has a daughter, Frances
Josephine. Cephas Alexander White married Abdiel Linebeek,
of North Carolina, and their three children are Isabelle May,
Louise and Nancy.

STUART C. COTTRELL is superintendent of public schools for
Goochland County, an office he has held for the past seven years,
and in that time has accomplished some important results in
the advancement of the county's facilities and standards of
public education.

Mr. Cottrell was born at Cardwell, in Goochland County,
August 21, 1890, and is a descendant of Richard Cottrell, who
arrived in Goochland County in 1697 and acquired a large tract
of land on both sides of the James River. The successive generations of the family have continued to live in that community for
over two centuries. Mr. Cottrell's grandfather, John W. Cottrell, was a Confederate soldier and developed and operated one
of the early gold mines in Goochland County. Mr. Cottrell's
father, S. H. Cottrell, has given his life to the farming industry.
He married Harriet Bowles, who was born in Goochland County
and died in November, 1910.

Stuart C. Cottrell was well educated in schools in Virginia,
and has carried on advanced work in intervals of his teaching,
having taken an extension course with William and Mary College
at Williamsburg, and during the summer of 1928 was in the
School of Business Administration at Columbia University, New
York. He began teaching in 1913, and was principal of schools
at Carrollton in Isle of Wight County. He served fourteen
months with the colors during the World war and was wounded
in battle while overseas. Before returning home he took a
special course in Bordeaux University. He was honorably discharged in August, 1919.

He has been county superintendent of schools since September 19, 1922. At that time the county had only one high school,
with a total enrollment of only thirty-five students, while there
are now three high schools for white pupils and one training
school for colored, and the enrollment in the high schools are
three hundred white students and fifty colored. The enrollment
of scholars in the public schools of the entire county is 2,900.

Mr. Cottrell married Miss Edna Kent, daughter of George
Henry and Florence (Wood) Kent, natives of Fluvanna County.
Her father is a druggist at Kent Store, Virginia. Mr. and Mrs.
Cottrell reside in the Crozier community, Lee Post Office. They
have one son, Stuart Guy, born March 28, 1921.

Mr. Cottrell is affiliated with the Masonic fraternity, in which
he has attained the thirty-second degree of the Scottish Rite,
with the Independent Order of Odd Fellows, Woodmen of the

World, American Legion, is a member of the Virginia State Education Association and the National Education Association, and is a director of the Goochland Chamber of Commerce. At his home he has thirty acres of fine land and uses this country estate to specialize in purebred Plymouth Rock chickens. He is a stockholder in the Morris Plan Bank. Mrs. Cottrell is a member. of the United Daughters of the Confederacy and of the local Woman's Club and the Community Welfare Association. She was a teacher before her marriage. Mr. Cottrell was appointed by Governor Trinkle delegate from Goochland County to the National Literary Council at Washington, D. C., where Governor Byrd appointed him a delegate to the National Institute of Public Affairs.

SETH G. HOBART holds the office of district forester for Southwestern Virginia, his jurisdiction covering seventeen counties.

Mr. Hobart is well qualified for his official duties. He was born at Friendship, New York, June 8, 1892, son of Manley W. and Mary E. (Guilford) Hobart. The Hobart family came from England about 1640, settling in New England and afterwards moving to New York. His father, Manley Hobart, was born and reared at Friendship, New York, was a farmer and dairyman and for a number of years supervisor of his township. He is now living retired at Friendship. His wife, Mary E. Guilford, represented the Guilford family that came from England and settled in Massachusetts about 1660. Mary E. Guilford was born in Belfast Township, New York, and both she and her husband attended the old Friendship Academy and both of them taught school before their marriage. They have been devout Baptists. Seth G. Hobart is one of three children. His sister, Miss Lotta Hobart, is supervisor of English in the Olean High School, New York, and his other sister, Ruth E., is the wife of Clarence R. Martin, of Detroit, Michigan.

Seth G. Hobart was educated in Friendship High School, graduated from the University of Michigan in 1916, and for several months was employed by the Conservation Commission of New York State. In December, 1916, he became an employe of the Gaulay Coal Land Company at Rupert, West Virginia, and remained with that corporation for ten years, until March 31, 1926. At that date he was appointed district forester for Southwest Virginia. His duties at first were in the department of the State Geological Commission. In November, 1926, that commission was taken over by the State Conservation and Development Commission, and since then Mr. Hobart has been responsible to this department of state government. In the seventeen counties comprising his district about 500 chief or local forest wardens report to him.

Mr. Hobart is a Mason, is independent in politics, is a member of the Society of American Foresters and is a Baptist. He married at Cuba, New York, August 1, 1917, Miss Hazel B. Keller, who was educated in the public schools of Friendship and in Alfred University of New York. She taught school before her marriage, is active in church, in the Daughters of the American Revolution and the Eastern Star Chapter. She is a daughter of M. Cicero and Nellie (Blossom) Keller. Her father for many years was active as a farmer and stock raiser at Cuba, New York. Her mother died in April, 1917. Mr. and Mrs. Hobart have four children: Seth G., Jr.; Keith Keller, Helen Blossom and William Lansing. Mr. Hobart has his home at Bristol, Virginia, and his two older children are attending the public school of that city.

JUNIUS BOOKER MOSBY was one of "Mosby's Men" in the Confederate army, being a youthful follower of his great kinsman, Gen. John S. Mosby, and after the close of the war he rose to distinction and success in the mercantile field at Richmond, being founder of what is today the great department store of J. B. Mosby Company.

He was born in Powhatan County, Virginia, October 18, 1843, and died at Richmond September 20, 1915. The Mosby family originated in England, and is widely dispersed in Virginia, the early Colonial records of four or more counties showing settlements by them. The founder of this branch of the family was Junius Booker Mosby, who came to America in 1538 and became a man of great landed possessions. One other member of the family was Edward Mosby, who in 1655 was a member of the vestry of the Westover Parish of the Episcopal Church.

Junius Booker Mosby was a son of Benjamin and Rachael Nevirah (Cardozo) Mosby, being their only child. The Cardozos were a prominent family of planters in Powhatan County. Benjamin Mosby was also a soldier under General Mosby during the war.

Junius Booker Mosby attended private schools in Powhatan County and was seventeen and a half years old when the war broke out. A large part of "Mosby's Men" were recruited in Powhatan County, and he enlisted in Company E of the Fourth Virginia Regiment. He had four years of arduous service, participating in some of the notable exploits of Mosby's Men. After the war he returned to Richmond, began his career as a bookkeeper, later bought an interest in the firm of his employer, and through many years remained steadfast in close and successful application to his work, eventually retiring from business in 1913 and leaving a house which continues to this modern time as one of the great department stores of the city, known as the J. B. Mosby Company. He was also a director of the American National Bank, the First National Bank and the Virginia Trust Company.

He married, November 11, 1897, Mrs. Louise (Burwell) Cardozo. She was the daughter of John Lewis Burwell and Ann Washington Womack (named for her grandmother, Ann Washington Stith), and through her mother is connected with the Washington family, from which descended George Washington. Mrs. Burwell, mother of Mrs. Mosby, was the daughter of Louisa Stith and John Pernell Womack, Louisa Stith's sister, Arianna, was the aunt of George Washington through her marriage with Warner Washington, brother of Augustine, who was the father of George Washington, the first president of the United States. Mrs. Mosby's father was John Lewis Burwell, son of Peyton Randolph Burwell, of Mecklenburg County, and Jane Sewell, of Gloucester County.

Mrs. Mosby by her first marriage had two children, Lewis Burwell Cardozo and Randolph Burwell Cardozo. Lewis Burwell died at the age of seventeen years. The surviving son, Randolph Burwell Cardozo, now in the railway supply business, under the name Fleming and Cardozo, at Richmond, married

Constance Gooding, of London, England, whom he met while overseas during the World war. Mr. and Mrs. Cardozo have four children, Mosby Gooding, Randolph Burwell, Jr., Lewis Burwell and Thomas Clow Gooding Cardozo. Mrs. Mosby resides at 1800 West Grace Street, Richmond.

MACK EVANS. No profession or calling has ever presented such opportunities for the really capable man as that of the law, and from its ranks have come the ablest men of the country. However, it has always been impossible for any man to rise to distinction in the law without a thorough preparation, and the study and thought thus required naturally develop the brain and character and make it possible to solve the many problems which arise in the lives of all. Coeburn is proud of the fact it has assisted in swelling the long list of Virginia's distinguished lawyers, and especially so of Mack Evans, whose reputation as a criminal and civil lawyer far outruns local boundaries. He is a man of delightful personality, pleasing address, and he is not only learned, but acutely capable, an able speaker and advocate, and his practice is fast assuming very large proportions.

Mack Evans was born in McDowell County, West Virginia, February 27, 1887, a son of E. M. and Elizabeth (Puckett) Evans. The family was established in Virginia by the great-grandfather of Mack Evans, a native of Wales, and for many years a very extensive planter and prominent citizen of the Old Dominion. His son, Hiram Evans, was the grandfather of Mack Evans, and he was a veteran of the Confederate army, having served with great valor during the war between the states. For years he was an active Democrat, holding local offices and wielding considerable influence. He, too, was a planter, and went to Welch, Virginia, where he was a pioneer. E. M. Evans is a noted minister of the Primitive Baptist faith, now living at Honaker, Virginia, and has been very active in his denomination in West Virginia and Southwest Virginia. In former years he was extensively engaged in coal mining as an operator in West Virginia and Southwest Virginia, but more recently has leased his mines and is now giving all of his attention to his ministerial duties. A loyal Republican, he is one of the leaders of the party in his district, and could, probably, have any office within the gift of the people did he care to accept nomination. The maternal grandfather of Mack Evans was Malichi Puckett, and he lived in McDowell County, West Virginia, where he was a planter and an active Republican. During the war between the states he served in the Union army, and because of injuries received in the service received a pension from the Government until his death.

Mack Evans attended the public schools of McDowell County, and there proved himself an apt and ambitious student. Later he entered Concord State Normal School, Athens, West Virginia, from which institution he went to Valparaiso University, Indiana, and was graduated therefrom with the degree of Bachelor of Arts, and subsequently took the degree of Bachelor of Laws from the same university. In 1916 he was admitted to practice at the bar of Indiana, and in the Federal Courts of Indiana that same year, and later in the Supreme Court. From 1916 to 1917 he was engaged in practice in Hammond, Indiana. With this country's entry into the World war he returned to the South and took charge of his father's mines so as to speed up coal pro-

duction, and continued to serve in that capacity until the close
of the war. He was then admitted to practice in the courts of
Virginia, located in Coeburn, and here he has attained to the
prominence already noted. He is a member of the Wise County
Bar Association. One of the leaders of the Republican party
in Wise County, he has served Coeburn as mayor since June,
1926, and the city has prospered under his able administration.
His fraternal connections are those which he maintains with
the Blue Lodge in Masonry and the Improved Order of Redmen.
The Methodist Episcopal Church, South, holds his membership.

On November 2, 1917, Mr. Evans married Miss Vera Dilley,
of Hebron, Indiana, a daughter of John M. and Cotolia Dilley,
both of whom survive and are living in Hebron, Indiana, being
farming people. The family, however, is of Virginian stock,
and Mrs. Evans is a direct descendant of the forebears of Governor Dinwiddie. She was educated in Valparaiso University,
is a member of the Eastern Star, to which her husband also
belongs, and is a social leader, club worker, and a valued member
of the Methodist Episcopal Church, South. Doctor and Mrs.
Evans have one of the finest sons in the county, John Mack
Evans, who was awarded the gold medal prize by the Wise
County Fair Association. He was born November 2, 1926, on
the anniversary of his parents' wedding day. Mr. Evans is an
ardent student and owns a very valuable law library, and is
recognized as an authority on all matters pertaining to his
profession and also to county and state history. It would be
difficult, perhaps, to find a man more generally respected or honored than he, or one who is more representative of the highest
ideals of his honorable profession.

FAYETTA HENRY LAIGHTON, who died in New York City
Easter Monday, April 1, 1929, gave the best years of her life
to the noble work of education in her home City of Petersburg,
Virginia. Her life work did not lack appreciation. To quote
from one of the resolutions drawn up by her school workers, "she
showed great wisdom, heartfelt interest and devotion to those
in her care; holding the position of principal of D. M. Brown
School, she proved her right to lead others of her profession and
won their devotion and respect thereby; she, the faithful citizen,
served her city, state and nation with great distinction and
honor."

Her grandfather, John Laighton, was a life long resident of
Portsmouth, New Hampshire. He took an active part in civic
affairs, serving as mayor of that city several terms, his ability
and integrity having been recognized and appreciated. Miss
Laighton's father, Octave Laighton, was born and reared in
Portsmouth, New Hampshire, remaining there until 1849. Suc-
cumbing in that year to a severe attack of the gold fever, he
went in a sailing vessel by way of Cape Horn to San Francisco,
the Golden Gateway to the mines. His quest proving unsuccessful, he returned east by the overland route, crossing mountains,
rivers and plains, almost in daily sight of countless buffalo and
other wild animals and occasionally coming close to bands of
hostile Indians. After weeks of travel he arrived at Fulton,
Illinois, then a place of considerable importance, and, locating
there, he took up newspaper work, publishing the *Fulton
Advertiser* until 1859. Returning then to Dinwiddie County,
Virginia, he located on a farm one mile from Petersburg. At

the outbreak of the Civil war he was exempt from military duty on account of ill health and partial blindness. He lived through the conflict, passing to the life beyond in 1866.

Octave Laighton married Lucy Dorothea Henry, of very distinguished Virginia ancestry. She was born in Charlotte County, a daughter of Edward Winston Henry and a granddaughter of the famous Patrick Henry, the inspiring orator of the Revolution and twice governor of Virginia. Patrick Henry married Dorothea Dandridge, while his son, Edward Winston Henry, married Jane Yuille. After the death of her husband Mrs. Octave Laighton moved to Petersburg, where she lived until her death in 1899. She was the mother of two children: Fayetta Henry Laighton and Alberta Winston Laighton. The younger daughter at the age of seventeen began teaching in one of Petersburg's primary schools, later becoming assistant principal in the high school. She is now living retired at Quaker Hill, Dutchess County, New York.

Fayetta Henry Laighton was born in Dinwiddie County, on a farm about a mile from Petersburg. After graduating from the Petersburg High School she began her career on November 11, 1886 as special teacher of reading. She held this position until September, 1889, when she became a grade teacher in the East Ward School (later D. M. Brown School). She continued as grade teacher until the summer of 1893 when she was appointed principal, which position she held until her death in 1929.

She was a member of the Virginia State Educational Association and the National Education Association, and in her religious affiliations was a member of the Episcopal Church.

After being taken ill on October, 1928, she gave up her school work and went to New York City for medical treatment and to be near her sister in her winter home. In appreciation of the great loss her absence meant to the school the superintendent, Mr. Henry G. Ellis, wrote: "Miss Laighton's work and personality have made an indelible impression on the school system of Petersburg and on the entire city. It has been a genuine pleasure to me, personally and professionally, to be associated with her in recent years and to be helped in my own life and work by her devotion to the cause of education, by her original and incisive thinking, and her rich personality."

Her funeral service with the ritual of the Episcopal Church was held in Old Blandford Church on the afternoon of a lovely Virginia spring day of the Easter season. The members of the choir were men and women former pupils of the D. M. Brown School, the organist was one of Miss Laighton's teachers, a close associate of many years. The church was filled with her friends and many others flowed out into the sunlit paths leading to the church. Among them were many children, present D. M. Brown school pupils, also parents of the children whom she had taught in more than forty years of educational service. She was buried in the family plot in Blandford cemetery as a mockingbird sang its evening song from a nearby cedar tree. "Never have I witnessed in my long life here," said one of her friends, "such an outpouring of respectful admiration, sincere grief and spontaneous affection on the part of so large a group of all sorts and conditions of people as are here today."

This brief sketch may properly be concluded with some other quotations from the resolutions passed by the Teachers' Club and the Parent-Teachers Association.

"We are truly thankful for the example of her life and for the privilege of a knowledge of and association with her. Firm in her friendships, possessing a masterful mind and memory stored with gems of a lifetime of application, a keen discrimination in matters of justice and honor, and occupying a position in which these qualities were daily manifested, it is doubtful whether any individual has made a more profound impression upon the present generation of this community. Truly in her was fulfilled the prophecy of the poet: 'Those about her

From her shall read the perfect ways of honour.' "

"Miss Laighton without thought of self gave all of her splendid powers of heart and intellect to the upbuilding of the school whose welfare she sought so zealously; and under whose guidance and magnetic and forceful personality the highest ideals of life and conduct were impressed upon all who came within the sphere of her influence; the memory of her noble character will remain graven upon the hearts of those to whom was given the privilege of serving under her leadership, and who will ever be mindful of her unfailing consideration and kindly assistance at all times. We, the Faculty of the D. M. Brown School, deeply regret the death of Miss Laighton, who 'yet speaketh' through her example of an unselfish life of service, as a principal whose devotion to duty was unsurpassed, whose ideals were an incentive to the attainment of all that was noble and good; and as a friend whose love it was a benediction to serve."

"Nothing is here for tears, nothing to wail
Or knock the breast, no weakness, no contempt
—Nothing but well and fair,
And what may quiet us in a death as noble."

HUGH GOODWIN BONHAM, general manager of the Pulaski Foundry & Machine Manufacturing Corporation, is a native of Virginia, received his technical education at Blacksburg, and since early manhood has been identified with his profession as a mechanical engineer.

He was born at Chilhowie, Virginia, October 28, 1884, son of A. F. and Lina (Goodwin) Bonham. His grandfather, Joseph Bonham, and his great-grandfather, Hezekiah Bonham, lived in Smyth County, in Southwest Virginia, and both of them were wagon and gun smiths. Mr. Hugh Bonham at his home has an old rifle made by his great-grandfather. Both these ancestors are buried in the Baptist Church Cemetery at Sinklers Bottom, in Smyth County. A. F. Bonham was born and reared at Chilhowie, attended private schools, and for a number of years did work as a surveyor and civil engineer. He is still living on his farm near Chilhowie at the age of eighty years. His wife, Lina Goodwin, was born and reared in Louisa County, attended private schools and for a year or two after the Civil war was a teacher. She was a regular attendant at the services of the Baptist Church. She died October 26, 1927, and is buried at Chilhowie. There were five children: Mary, of Chilhowie; Hugh G.; Nicie, wife of John Snavely, of Chilhowie; Joseph, of Chilhowie, an employe of the State Road Commission; and Daisy, wife of Dr. O. G. McConnell, a physician at Blair, West Virginia.

Hugh G. Bonham attended public schools in Chilhowie and was a member of the class of 1908 at the Virginia Polytechnic Institute. During the following year he was employed in the

testing department of the General Electric Company, and then located at Pulaski, where he spent nine years as a mechanical engineer with the Virginia Iron, Coal & Coke Company. Since 1918 he has been with the Pulaski Foundry & Machine Manufacturing Corporation, at first as mechanical engineer and since 1928 as general manager of the plant and business.

Mr. Bonham for a number of years has been active in the B. P. O. Elks. He is a member of the Rotary Club and a Democrat. At Philadelphia, Pennsylvania, May 12, 1917, he married Miss Alice Blocksidge, of Pulaski. She was educated in a private school and takes part in the various organizations of the Episcopal Church, and is a member of the Garden Club. She is a daughter of Benjamin and Elizabeth (Simkiss) Blocksidge, who came to America from Walverhampton, England, about 1880, locating at Pulaski, where her father for over forty years was auditor for the Pulaski Iron Company. Her parents still reside at Pulaski. Mr. and Mrs. Bonham have one daughter, Elizabeth, attending the Pulaski public schools.

ROBERT AUGUSTUS McINTYRE. The subject of this sketch is the oldest son of Colonel Robert Charles McIntyre, and Martha Louisa (Murdoch) McIntyre, his wife, of South Carolina. He was born February 5, 1862, at Albany, Georgia, while his parents were visiting in that city. Robert Charles McIntyre was a son of Captain Archibald McIntyre, of Marion, South Carolina, of Clan McIntyre, from Argyleshire, Scotland, a Clan distinguished in letters and in war. The Arms of the family bear testimony to their achievements in the Crusades; the greatest of Gaelic poets was Duncan Ban MacIntyre. His mother was of the Clan MacLachlan, descended from Conn of The Hundred Battles Nine Hundred, A. D.

Captain McIntyre married Sophia Eliza Howard, a daughter of Colonel Richard Howard, of the Effingham Branch of the Howard family, and lineal descendant of Thomas Howard, Duke of Norfolk, victor of Flodden Field. Colonel Howard owned a large estate and many slaves in West Marion, where he lived the life of an English Gentleman, had his private race track, and ran his thoroughbreds at Charleston, in the "good old days." This representative couple of the old aristocracy, had nine children, five sons in the Confederate Army, four of whom were severely wounded, and the fifth killed, at Sharpsburg.

The McIntyres for generations have placed the highest value on education, and each of these children received the best educational advantages. Robert Charles, father of Robert Augustus, was a graduate of Mt. Zion (Military) College, and of South Carolina College under Dr. Thornwell; a lawyer by education and profession, a well known literatus and classical scholar, and an eloquent speaker.

Robert Charles McIntyre married Martha Louisa Murdoch, daughter of Alexander Murdoch, a son of John Murdoch of Beauty Spot, and his wife, Janet MacGreggor. John Murdoch was scion of the Murdochs descended from Muredach, King of Scotland in 733. Janet MacGreggor was of the famous MacGreggor Clan.

Alexander Murdoch, father of Mrs. Robert Charles McIntyre, married Martha Louisa Wayne, a daughter of Major Francis A. Wayne, son of William Wayne, who was a grandson of Captain Anthony Wayne, distinguished as a captain of Dragoons under William of Orange at the battle of The Boyne. Captain Anthony Wayne was the grandfather of William Wayne and General Anthony Wayne of Revolutionary fame. General Wayne was William's Guardian, and carried his ward to South Carolina during the Revolution, where he remained after the Revolution, and married Elizabeth Trezevant, a great granddaughter of Daniel Trezevant, one of the first Huguenots that settled in Charleston, South Carolina, 1689, after the Revocation of The Edict of Nantes, Mrs. McIntyre's father and mother having died when she was twelve years old, General William Evans, her uncle, acted as her guardian, and directed her education. She entered Wesleyan Female College, Macon, Georgia, at thirteen years of age, where she was known as the "Little Giant," and afterwards finished her education at LaGrange College, La-Grange, Georgia. She was a great reader, and had a quick, retentive memory. She was an accomplished writer, and her letters were models of epistolary composition. She was her son's first teacher and directed his earlier education.

Robert Augustus McIntyre, the subject of this sketch, through his father and mother, received an excellent education independently of the opportunities that were given him in the schools of the day. It was his father's influence that inspired in him a life-long love for classic learning. It was contact with his father and mother that directed him to high aspirations and purposes in life, and stimulated his ambition.

When young Robert McIntyre was entered as a cadet in Bethel Classical and Military Academy, near Warrenton, Virginia, where many young Southerners were educated, the superintendent paid him the compliment of informing him that he was the best prepared student that had ever entered the Academy from the South.

Having finished his academic studies and his full course in law, he was admitted to the practice of his profession before the County Court of Fauquier, in the State of Virginia; but shortly afterwards returned to Bennettsville, South Carolina, and was licensed to practice his profession in that state, by the Supreme Court sitting in Columbia, in 1883. He was successful in practice from the start; but having received an offer of a position in the faculty of Bethel Classical and Military Academy, of which his father-in-law, Major Albert G. Smith was superintendent and founder, he accepted and continued to hold the position until the death of Major Smith, when he was advanced to the position of superintendent. While connected with the academy he was at the head of the department engaged in the preparation of students for the law course at the University of Virginia, which he conducted with unusual success. While a member of the faculty, Major McIntyre wrote a text book on Bookkeeping, on English Grammar and on English Composition. He also contributed to the press and wrote other works on different subjects. He was a very hard student and seized every opportunity to extend his knowledge by original research in letters, and in the sciences.

His interest in education has never ceased. He was for several years chairman of the School Board of Center District, has been a member of the State Board of Teachers Colleges of Virginia for almost two terms, having been first appointed by Governor Trinkle, and re-appointed by Governor Byrd. He is in demand as a speaker at commencement exercises, and takes a lively interest in the local public schools.

Having retired from the position of superintendent of Bethel Military Academy, he opened an office and resumed the practice of his profession in Warrenton, Virginia, in June, 1902. Since that time he has given his life to the profession to which his parents had dedicated him upon the day of his birth. He had practiced but a few months before he had many clients and had earned a place among the leading members of an able bar. Few important cases are heard in the local courts, either criminal or civil that McIntyre's name does not appear as counsel on one side or the other. His practice has grown and spread, until few lawyers in the Eighth Congressional District are better or more favorably known. He is counsel for the Peoples National Bank, The International Harvester Company, Virginia Public Service Company, Standard Oil Company, The United States Fidelity and Guaranty Company.

He has been a member of the State Bar Association and held official position in it, from the second year of its organization. He has been a member of the American Bar Association for many years, he is vice president of the local Bar Association, practices in the Federal Courts, and is a member of the Bar of the Supreme Court of the United States. A vacancy having occurred on the Circuit Bench in his county in 1929, he received the unanimous endorsement of the bar for the judgeship, but declined to consider the honor.

He is a member of the University Club of Richmond, of the Country Club of Warrenton, is a Royal Arch Mason, a member of the Patriotic Order Sons of America, lieutenant commander of the Sons of Confederate Veterans, an active supporter of the Warrenton Horse Show, having presided at its organization thirty years ago, has been an active director in the Chamber of Commerce, a director in the Peoples National Bank, and is a Vestryman of St. James Episcopal Church of Warrenton, Virginia.

During the World war, Major McIntyre was chairman of The Legal Advisory Board, chairman of the United War Work Campaign, chairman of The Four Minute Men, speaker on the Propaganda Committee of the Red Cross, and his name is recorded in the history of Virginia's part in the World war as one of the *ten most distinguished men for service* from Fauquier County.

In public life of his county and state, he has taken an active part since he was twenty-one years of age. He was generally endorsed for the Constitutional Convention of 1902, but declined in favor of an old Confederate soldier. He was elected a member of the State Democratic Committee from the Eighth Congressional District, and served for twelve years, during which time he performed a number of most important duties. He was chairman of the Special Committee named to investigate the Second Congressional District Primary, in the controversy between Maynard and Young, which led to cleaning up conditions in the politics of Norfolk City. He was named chairman of a committee to prepare a Primary Law for the State of Virginia, and secure its adoption. He did all of the work, no other member of the committee having appeared, and the present Primary Law of the State is the result of his service. He has been one of the speakers in every Presidential Campaign for the past twenty-five years, for the Democratic Party. When the historic and supreme effort of the people of Virginia swept the Commonwealth into the dry column, McIntyre was chairman and led the fight in the Eighth District, including the ten counties of Northern Virginia, and the City of Alexandria. He

was a candidate for the nomination as member of the House
of Delegates before the Democratic Primary of August 6, 1929,
and was nominated by an overwhelming majority; while the
Republicans offer no opposition to his election in November.

He has been one of the most active advocates and supporters
of road improvement in his county, and has given of his means
freely. He was attorney for the first Bond Issue in Center District, contributed largely to the building of the Bethel Road,
which was the first example of hard surface road construction
in Fauquier; represented all of the counties from the Potomac
River to the City of Winchester, in securing the adoption by
the Legislative Committee, of the "project" then unnamed, but
now known as the Lee-Jackson Memorial Highway, from the
Key Bridge to Winchester. For his services before the Legislative Committee in assisting to locate the "project" from Raleigh,
North Carolina, to Frederick, Maryland, he was rewarded by
having the same routed through Fauquier County, and was
elected it's first vice president. He opposed the Fifty Million
Dollar Bond Issue when that question was before the people,
and advocated the Pay As You Go Plan. Few men in Northern
Virginia have taken a livelier interest in a rational road building and improvement policy, than the subject of this sketch.

Major Robert Augustus McIntyre, married Elizabeth Blackwell, daughter and only child of Major Albert G. Smith, a son
of Col. William R. Smith of Alton, and member of the distinguished Smith family of Fauquier. Major Smith was
founder of Bethel Classical and Military Academy, and enjoyed
the well earned reputation of being one of the greatest educators of his day. He was especially distinguished for his gal-
lantry in the Charge of Pickett's Division at Gettysburg, where
he went through the enemy's lines, recovered the colors of his
Regiment, and succeeded in escaping untouched. Mrs. McIntyre's Mother, was Elizabeth Carter Blackwell, a daughter of
Mr. James Blackwell of The Meadows, and a lineal descendant
of Robert Carter, generally known as "King" Carter. Five
children were born of this union: Albert Galatin, who died in
childhood, Louisa Murdoch, Elizabeth Carter, Robert Charles,
and Agnes Conway.

Major McIntyre has been from early manhood, one of the
most prominent and successful business men in his county. He
owned and managed Bethel Military Academy with patronage
from twenty-two states and foreign countries, and the Fauquier White Sulphur Springs, which brought more foreign capital into the county than any other enterprises in it. He is one
of the large land owners of his section, among which holdings
are the Bethel Academy property, "Springfield," and "Argyle,"
his home place near Warrenton.

HOMER KING BOWEN, executive secretary of the Southwestern
Virginia, Incorporated, with headquarters at Wytheville, comes
of a family highly connected in this part of the state, and the
Bowens were among the first families of Virginia.

Mr. Bowen was born at Pembroke, in Giles County, November 15, 1897, son of A. M. and Sarah Etta (Scott) Bowen. His
father was born in Alleghany County, Virginia, was educated in
public schools, studied law, and practiced that profession for a
number of years in Alleghany and Giles County. The last ten
or fifteen years of his life were devoted to farming and stock
raising. He died February 28, 1928, and is buried in the Hoge

Chapel Cemetery in Giles County. His wife, Sarah Etta Scott, was born and reared in Scott County, Virginia. She is a member of the Christian Church, and her husband also joined that church, though reared a Methodist. There were eight children in the family: R. J. Bowen, of Bluefield, West Virginia; P. C. Bowen, of Christiansburg, Virginia; Alonzo Pembroke; M. M. Bowen, of Columbus, Ohio; L. B. Bowen, of Narrows, Virginia; Hallie Payne, wife of R. L. Carico, of Patoaka, West Virginia; Homer King; and J. Porter Bowen, of Rock, West Virginia.

Homer King Bowen attended public schools in Giles County, and for several years he used the equipment of a liberal education in the profession of teaching. He was graduated Bachelor of Arts from Roanoke College in 1919, and did post-graduate work in Columbia University of New York and in the George Peabody Normal College at Nashville, Tennessee, where he received the Master of Arts degree in 1923. For five years he was with a private school for boys, the Gallatin Institute, near Nashville. Mr. Bowen spent two years as an instructor in the Augusta Military Academy at Fort Defiance, Virginia, and one year in the Woodbury Forest School.

In July, 1927, he located at Wytheville as executive secretary of the Southwestern Virginia, Incorporated. Under this title is carried on a notable work of publicity and in other lines for a regional Chamber of Commerce, representing nineteen counties in Southwest Virginia. Mr. Bowen and one of his brothers operate the home farm, and he is also owner of the Haynes Motor Company at Winchester, Tennessee.

He is a member of the Masonic fraternity, Knights of Pythias, Modern Woodmen of America, Rotary Club, is an independent Republican, and is active in the Christian Church, teaching a class in the Sunday school. Mr. Bowen married at Lynchburg, Virginia, September 3, 1927, Miss Beatrice Margaret Watts, of Sweet Briar College, Virginia, a graduate of that splendid woman's college with the class of 1925. She is a daughter of Robert W. Watts, for many years a leading contractor at Sweet Briar, where he and his wife still reside.

FREDERICK ALBERT WHITTAKER, who represents a family with residence in Giles County for four generations, lives at Eggleston, and has a varied and important connection with the civic and business affairs of that locality.

He was born at Staffordsville, Virginia, March 22, 1888. His grandfather, Jim Whittaker, was also born and reared in Giles County, and was a private soldier in the Confederate army. He and other members of his family are buried in Rye Hollow Cemetery. David Lewis Whittaker, father of Frederick Albert, was born and reared at Staffordsville, attended private schools, and spent his active life as a farmer, cattle raiser and dealer. He was a member of the Masonic fraternity and the Christian Church. He died in March, 1928. He married Margaret Jane Albert, whose father, Riley Albert, was a Confederate soldier, a farmer and stock raiser in the Rye Hollow community. The farm where she was born and reared is now owned by her son, Frederick A. She attended public schools, and for many years has been a faithful member of the Christian Church. She was born July 4, 1856, and still lives at the old home. Of her eleven children, one, Charles, died in infancy; Cora, deceased, was the wife of Robert Meadows; Elliot lives at Trigg, Virginia; Vert is the wife of A. J. Munsey, of Staffordsville; Bent lives at Staffordsville; Ada is at home; Clayton S. is a merchant at Eggleston; Frederick Albert is the next in age; Tracy is a farmer and cattle raiser at the old home place at Staffordsville; Blanche is the wife of Ophus Agee, of New River; and Clara is the wife of Reece Ross, of Lynchburg.

Frederick Albert Whittaker attended public schools in Giles County, and since leaving school his business has been farming, cattle raising and trading cattle, at first associated with his father and now independently. He is also a director in the Peoples Bank of Giles, is a stockholder in the Eggleston Motor Company, in the State National Bank of Roanoke and in the Shenandoah Life Insurance Company. For some time he served as deputy agent of the Internal Revenue Bureau. He is a Republican, member of the Christian Church and a Master Mason.

Mr. Whittaker married at Eggleston, July 14, 1915, Miss Annie Laurie Walker, of Eggleston. They were married in the Baptist Church by Rev. H. E. Bailey, a Lutheran minister. Mrs. Whittaker is a daughter of John F. and Maggie (Jones) Walker. Her father was a Confederate soldier, and after the war a farmer and cattle man. More details concerning the Walker family are published on other pages. Mr. and Mrs. Whittaker have three children, Frederick Albert Jr., Wilmet Walker and Margaret Virginia, all attending public school at Eggleston.

J. HORACE LUSTER is a Blacksburg business man, and has achieved a successful career in that community, where his name is associated with business success and the public spirited activities of a citizen of fine integrity and reliability.

Mr. Luster was born in Montgomery County, Virginia, September 26, 1891. His grandfather, Edwin B. Luster, was the son of an early Baptist minister in Virginia. Edwin B. Luster spent the greater part of his life as a merchant at Fincastle, Virginia, where he died in 1910. James O. Luster, father of the Blacksburg business man, was born and reared in Botetourt County, attended school there and for many years conducted a hardware business at Fincastle. After selling his interests there he moved to Blacksburg and became interested with his son in a hardware business in that city. He and his wife reside in Blacksburg, and are active members of the Baptist Church. James O. Luster married Bettie Ross, who was born and reared in Botetourt County, and attended school there. She is a daughter of John and Mary Alexander Ross, the former from Scotland and the latter from Union, West Virginia. J. Horace Luster was one of four children, two of whom died in infancy. His sister, Miss Kathleen, was educated in the Virginia Intermont College and the Peabody Conservatory at Baltimore, and is a very talented vocalist, well known in concert work and in church choirs at Richmond.

J. Horace Luster attended public schools at Fincastle, the West Virginia Wesleyan College, and on leaving school he went to work for his uncle, A. W. Luster, a hardware merchant at Blacksburg. He has remained there through the years, and after the death of his uncle he took over the hardware store and has given his chief attention to this business. He is also a director in the National Bank of Blacksburg and a director and stockholder in a number of other commercial enterprises in that

part of the state. Mr. Luster is a former president of the Blacksburg Rotary Club, is a Democrat and a Methodist.

He married at Blacksburg, December 6, 1916, Miss Mary
Louise Black, who was educated in Hollins College. She was an
adopted daughter of Alexander Black, the well known Blacks-
burg banker and business man. She died November 24, 1918,
and is buried in the Blacksburg Cemetery. On July 21, 1928,
Mr. Luster married at Blacksburg Mrs. Mary (Powell) Burr.
Her father, William Powell, was a leading attorney of Emporia,
Virginia. Mrs. Luster by her first husband, Charles Gilbert
Burr, has two children, Charles Gilbert, Jr., and Sue Macklan
Burr. Mrs. Luster is a church worker, being identified with the
Methodist Episcopal Church, South, and is a member of the
United Daughters of the Confederacy and Daughters of the
American Revolution.

HON. JOHN C. SMITH. A member of the bar of Southwestern
Virginia for thirty-three years, during his long and active career
at Clintwood Hon. John C. Smith has been engaged in work of
the highest professional character, and through the exercise of
native and acquired talent, comprehensive knowledge of legal
lore and great industry has gained and held a position of leadership among his contemporaries. He has likewise been a leading figure in public and political affairs, and on various occasions
has been the recipient of high honors at the hands of his appreciative fellow citizens in Dickenson County.

Mr. Smith was born November 12, 1870, at Nora, Dickenson
County, Virginia, and is a son of Elexius and Margaret (Counts)
Smith. The Smith family is of English descent and settled early
in Russell County, Virginia, where was born the grandfather
of John C. Smith, George W. Smith. He was a lifelong planter
and stockman, a man of high character and of influence in his
community, an unswerving Democrat and a faithful member of
the Primitive Baptist Church. Elexius Smith was born in Russell County, and was still a youth when he enlisted in the Confederate army for service during the war between the states.
Following that struggle he settled in Dickenson County, where
he passed the rest of his life as a planter. He and his worthy
wife were members of the Primitive Baptist Church. The maternal grandfather of John C. Smith, William Counts, was born
in what was then Wise County, but is now a part of Dickenson
County, where he passed his life to the ripe old age of ninety-
five years as a planter and a pioneer grower of orchids for
the market.

The public schools of Dickenson County furnished John C.
Smith with his early educational training, and like many of the
lawyers who have risen to success in this part of the state entered
upon his career as a school teacher. For four years he instructed
the young, including a term as principal of the institution known
as Clintwood College, and then pursued a course at the Pike
County Academy at Dorton, Kentucky. In 1895 he graduated
from the Northern Indiana Normal School at Valparaiso, Indiana, with the degree of Bachelor of Laws, and located immediately at Clintwood to engage in the practice of his profession.
For the first two years he was a member of the law firm of
Evans & Smith, but since then has practiced alone and has a
large and lucrative general practice, with offices on Main Street.
Mr. Smith is a Republican in his political views, and served for

twenty years as a member of the State Republican Executive Committee, representing the Ninth Congressional District, of which district he was supervisor of the census in 1910. In 1898 he was elected commonwealth's attorney for a four year term, being the first Republican ever elected to that office in the county. He was sent back to that office in 1914 and again in 1918, and established a splendid record for efficiency and conscientious attention to duty. During the World war he was chairman of the War Savings Stamp committee of Dickenson County, and put over the county's quota.

Mr. Smith married Miss Lillie Jane Compton, of Scott County, Virginia, a daughter of Berry and Susan Compton, the former a farmer and stockman and of an old and distinguished Virginia family. She completed her education in Shoemaker College, Gate City, Virginia, and taught school in Scott and Dickenson counties for a number of years prior to her marriage. She is a popular member of the Order of the Eastern Star and an active worker in the activities of the Missionary Baptist Church. To Mr. and Mrs. Smith have been born the following children: Stella Richmond, educated in Clintwood High School, Virginia Intermont College at Bristol and Hollins College, who took a course in music at Hood College, Maryland, married Lawrence T. Long, now deceased, a mine inspector for the United States Coal and Coke Company of Gary, West Virginia, with headquarters at Dante, Virginia, and has one child, Lucile Tierney; Mamie Fulton, who died in infancy; and Lucile Marrison, her twin, who lived to be fourteen years of age. This was the first pair of twins to be born in Dickenson County.

ISAAC H. LOONEY, purchasing agent and commissary manager of the Virginia Hardwood Lumber Company at Bastian, is representative of one of the old families of Southwestern Virginia.

His great-grandfather, Joseph Looney, at a very early time, accompanied by his brother, moved out of Botetourt County, where the Looneys had lived for a long time, and settled in Buchanan County, in Northwestern Virginia, when that district was well out on the frontier. It was in Buchanan County, near Grundy, that Isaac H. Looney was born September 25, 1898. He is a son of Rev. Birdine and Rosa C. (Boyd) Looney. His father was born and reared in the same county, and is a farmer and local minister of the Methodist Episcopal Church, South, still carrying on the work of his farm and church at Leemaster, Virginia. His wife, Rosa C. Boyd, was a daughter of Rev. Isaac Newton and Nancy Boyd, her father having been one of the early Methodist ministers in Southwestern Virginia. She was reared and educated in Buchanan County, and all her life has been a devoted worker in the Methodist Church. The six children of these parents were: Isaac H., Nancy Rosa, Elihu Holland, Leah, Carl and Webster.

Isaac H. Looney was educated in public schools in Buchanan County, attending high school, and when he left school his first work was with I. C. Boyd & Company, a mercantile firm. He clerked in their establishment until 1918, and then for a few months was at home. In 1917 he resumed his service with I. C. Boyd & Company at Putnam, but since 1920 has been with the Virginia Hardwood Lumber Company as manager of the commissary, at first at South Clinchfield and in 1927 the company moved its band mill operations to Bastian in Bland County, where Mr. Looney is located as manager of the commissary and as purchasing agent. He is a stockholder in the Pocahontas Fire Creek Coal Company.

Mr. Looney is one of the public spirited men of his community and is active in the Masonic fraternity. He took his first degree in Masonry at Honaker, Virginia, and is a member of the Scottish Rite body and Kazim Temple of the Mystic Shrine at Roanoke. Mr. Looney is a Democrat, is a member of the Board of Stewards of the Methodist Episcopal Church, South, and teaches a class of young people in the Sunday School.

He married in Tazewell County, Virginia, June 15, 1921, Miss Lucille Edith Boyd. She was educated in public schools in Russell County and in the class of 1918 in the Stonewall Jackson College at Abingdon, Virginia, and also attended a business college in Kentucky. For about a year before her marriage she was bookkeeper with the I. C. Boyd Mercantile Company, where Mr. Looney was also employed. She is a member of the Methodist Episcopal Church, South. Mr. and Mrs. Looney have one son, William Boyd Looney, now in public school at Bastian.

Mrs. Looney is a daughter of C. W. and Vina (Phillips) Boyd. Her mother died a number of years ago at Richland, Virginia. C. W. Boyd has for many years been one of the outstanding lumber operators in Southwestern Virginia. About 1920 he organized the Virginia Hardwood Lumber Company, and is the active head of that business, with main offices at Tazewell. This company has operated mills in a number of hardwood districts, formerly at Fort Blackmore, then at South Clinchfield, and since 1927 at Bastian, where the company owns 34,000 acres of timber land. The business is one that employs about 300 people and the daily cut is 70,000 feet.

PAUL L. COMER is one of the organizers and is cashier of the Farmers & Merchants Bank of Rich Creek, Giles County. He is a very able and popular business man and citizen, and is well known through his connections on both sides of the state line in West Virginia as well as in Virginia.

He was born at Wikel, West Virginia, August 17, 1903, son of J. A. and Minnie (Mann) Comer. His great-great-grandfather, Frederick Comer, was one of three brothers who came from France to America, and he settled in what is now West Virginia in pioneer times. J. A. Comer was born in 1868, and has spent his active life in Monroe County, West Virginia. He has been a farmer and for many years in the lumber business, and still occupies his homestead at Wikel. He is a member of the Independent Order of Odd Fellows. His wife, Minnie Mann, was born and reared in West Virginia, and, like her husband, had the advantages of public schools, and both are members of the Baptist Church. She is a member of the Rebekahs. They were the parents of six sons: Carl A., a lumberman and truck farmer at Wikel; Samuel H., who died at the age of fifteen; Paul L.; Howard E., in the automobile business at Lindside, Monroe County, West Virginia; Thurman H. and Eugene E., both attending high school at Greenville.

Paul L. Comer was educated in public schools at Wikel. For four years he was a teacher in West Virginia, and he received one of the first life certificates granted by the State Educational Department of West Virginia. After giving up teaching he entered the National Business College at Roanoke, and completed the work required for a diploma in the shortest time of any graduate, this being largely due to his exceptional proficiency in mathematics. After graduating he was bookkeeper for the American National Bank at Roanoke for a time.

Mr. Comer in 1924 was associated with J. S. Taylor in the organization of the Farmers & Merchants Bank of Rich Creek, Mr. Taylor becoming the first cashier and Mr. Comer, bookkeeper and assistant cashier. Since January 1, 1926, Mr. Comer has performed the duties of cashier of this bank. He is also secretary, treasurer and promoter of the Rich Creek-Peterstown Power Company, which buys and sells electric current in the Rich Creek and Peterstown community. He is a half owner of the Comer Chevrolet Company at Lindside, West Virginia.

Mr. Comer is an independent Republican, a Baptist, and is affiliated with Camp No. 10004, Modern Woodmen of America. He married at Peterstown, West Virginia, May 27, 1925, Miss Thelma Dickson, who is a graduate of the Peterstown High School and taught in Monroe County before her marriage. She is a member of the Methodist Episcopal Church. Her parents are R. L. and Juda (Dillon) Dickson, who live on a farm near Lindside. Her father is a farmer and for four years was sheriff of Monroe County and is now one of the county commissioners. Mr. and Mrs. Comer have one daughter, Betty Grey.

WILLIAM H. NEWBERRY, former commissioner of revenue of Bland County, is a nephew of Senator Samuel H. Newberry, one of the four members of the Virginia State Senate whose services in reconstruction times were of such importance that they have been always referred to as "the Big Four."

Mr. William H. Newberry was born in Bland County, October 26, 1889. This Newberry family has had many prominent members not only in Virginia but in other states. His great-grandfather, Samuel Newberry, was one of the early settlers of Bland County. His grandfather's name was Allen T. Newberry. William H. Newberry is a son of Dunn B. and Jane (Harmon) Newberry. Dunn B. Newberry was the youngest son of the distinguished Senator Samuel H. Newberry. Dunn B. Newberry was born January 9, 1842, in Bland County, was educated in private schools, was a Confederate soldier in Company F of the Forty-fifth Virginia Regiment, and saw active service in twenty-three battles and skirmishes, including the fight at Cloyd's Mountain and also the great battle of Sharpsburg. After the war he followed farming and stock raising, and died April 13, 1918, being buried in the Newberry Cemetery near Bland. His wife, Jane Harmon, represented another family that has lived from earliest times in Bland County. She was educated in private schools, and was an active member of the Methodist Episcopal Church, South. She died in 1890.

William H. Newberry was the only child of his parents. His educational opportunities were provided by public schools, and when he left school he had experience in the mercantile business as clerk with the firm of Newberry Brothers.

On September 4, 1917, he joined the colors and was in training at Camp Lee, Virginia, until taken ill with pneumonia, and was in the hospital for some time, being disabled for further active service, and received his honorable discharge on July 18, 1918. Mr. Newberry in 1919 was elected commissioner of revenue for Bland County and served two full terms, until January 1, 1928. Since leaving public office he has been an automobile salesman with the Central Garage Company of Bland.

Mr. Newberry is affiliated with Lodge No. 206, A. F. and A. M., Wythe Chapter No. 51, Royal Arch Masons, Lynn Commandery No. 9, Knights Templar, Kazim Temple of the Mystic Shrine at Roanoke, and is a member of the American Legion Post and the Methodist Episcopal Church, South.

He married at Bland, July 3, 1920, Miss Bertha Thompson, of Point Pleasant, Virginia, where she was reared and educated and also attended the Sidney Lanier School at Baltimore. She was in service during the World war as a yeomanette in the navy. Mrs. Newberry is a member of the Presbyterian Church and the Eastern Star. Her parents were M. H. and Mollie (Ashworth) Thompson, of Point Pleasant, Virginia, where her father is still active in business as a merchant, farmer, miller and lumberman. Up to 1928 he had served fourteen years as democratic chairman of Bland County. Mrs. Newberry's mother died in 1922. The two daughters of Mr. and Mrs. Newberry are Mary Catherine and Harriet Ellen, both attending public school at Bland.

JAMES WILLIAM BANE, farmer, stock raiser and banker at White Gate, is one of the sterling representatives of the Bane family which traces its descent from Donald McBane, one time King of Scotland. The family coat-of-arms is a shield, one-quarter having the figure of a lamb, another a glove, and the lower quarters contain a sword and ship of commerce. The motto is "Touch not a cat—but a glove."

The pioneer of the family in Southwest Virginia was James Bane, who married Betty Haven. James Bane settled at Walkers Creek, Virginia, in 1793, and acquired a large amount of land around what is now White Gate, extending up and down the valley for several miles. The father of James W. Bane was Lieut. James Edward Bane, who was born and reared at White Gate, attended private schools, and was a first lieutenant in Company I of the Thirty-sixth Virginia in General McCausland's Brigade during the war between the states. After the war he followed farming and stock raising, and died December 17, 1886, at the age of fifty-seven. His wife, Mary Olive Miller, was born and reared at White Gate, attended Walker Creek Academy there, and she was a Presbyterian, while her husband was a Missionary Baptist. She died January 7, 1916, at the age of eighty-two, and both are buried in the Bane family cemetery at White Gate. She was a daughter of Tobias and Betsy (Bane) Miller. Her father settled at White Gate in 1827 and was a son of Jacob Miller, who came from Germany and moved from Franklin County to Montgomery County, settling in the portion subsequently made into Giles County. James Edward Bane and wife had a family of nine children, and those to grow up were: Rev. Tobias Miller, of Pulaski, Virginia; Laura Elizabeth, who died in 1890, at the age of twenty-seven, wife of C. T. Moore, now of Bristol, Tennessee, and left a daughter, Barbara B. Moore, who is the wife of William T. Allen, of Ceres, Bland County, Virginia; Miss Annie W. Bane, of White Gate; James W.; Mary Jane, who is the wife of Rev. G. H. Broyles, a Baptist minister at Roanoke, and they were the parents of nine children, Bessie dying at eleven months and Olive dying at the age of sixteen and Lacy, at the age of fifteen, while the others are Annie May, Wilma, James Bane, Paul, Frank and Gordon; Miss Nannie, of White Gate, who lives with her sister Annie.

James William Bane was educated in public schools at White Gate, and his father's death made him the head of the family and threw upon him unusual responsibilities, so that since an early age he has been in the full swing of a busy career, engaged in farming and cattle raising at the old homestead. The place he occupies is property bought by his father in 1876 and on which the family have made their home since 1877. The mother of James W. Bane built a beautiful home there. His farm comprises 377 acres, blue grass land, much of it under cultivation. Mr. Bane is also a director and vice president of the Peoples Bank of Gile County and in 1925 served as land assessor. He is a Democrat, a deacon in the Missionary Baptist Church, and for a number of years superintendent of the Sunday School.

He married at Tazewell, Virginia, December 26, 1906, Miss Bessie Rose Davidson, who attended the grade and high schools at Tazewell and was born near Rocky Gap in Bland County. She taught two years in that county before her marriage. She is a Methodist. Mrs. Bane is a member of some of the older families in Southwest Virginia. Her parents were John A. and Mattie (Harmon) Davidson. Her father was a farmer and stock raiser in Bland County and for one term represented the county in the State Legislature. He died in 1896. His father was James Davidson, a farmer and cattle man of Bland County. The Davidson family in its various members in this part of Virginia and West Virginia have a common ancestor, John Goolman Davidson, who was born in Dublin, Ireland, was a cooper by trade, and came to America about 1755, settling at Beverly Manor, Augusta County, Virginia. Subsequently he moved with his family to the famous Drapers Meadows settlement and in 1780 to the head of Beaver Pond Creek, in what is now Mercer County, West Virginia. During the same year he was joined by Richard Bailey, and they erected a block house or fort below the head of Beaver Pond Springs. A portion of the present city of Bluefield comprises lands originally settled by John Goolman Davidson, and one of his great-grandsons was the late Hon. A. C. Davidson of Mercer County.

Mr. and Mrs. Bane had five children: James Edward, born October 2, 1907, is a graduate of the White Gate High School, spent two years in Washington and Lee University, taught during 1927-28 in the Boys Latin School at Baltimore, and is now finishing his education in the Columbia University Teachers College at New York; John D. Bane, born February 28, 1909, graduated from the White Gate High School in 1927, and is associated with his father on the farm; Eugene M., born January 18th, 1911, is a member of the class of 1929 in the White Gate High School; Mary Harmon, born June 21, 1917, is in grade school; and William Doak was born January 19, 1923.

THEODORE WILLIS KNOTE, founder and head of the School of Business Administration at the Virginia Polytechnic Institute at Blacksburg, is a native of Ohio, but is member of an old Virginia Colonial family in the paternal line.

The Knote family settled in Virginia in the vicinity of Richmond about 1732. Mr. Knote's father, John William Monroe Knote, was born in Virginia and in 1859 went from there to what is now Wheeling, West Virginia, and later to the State of Ohio, and for many years was a merchant at Springfield, where he died February 19, 1918, and is buried. John William Monroe Knote married Lillian McBride, who was born in Logan County, Ohio, and attended private schools in Springfield, and during the year before her marriage taught in a private seminary at

Springfield. She was always active in the Presbyterian Church, being the daughter of a Presbyterian minister, Rev. Jacob Copenhaver McBride. John W. M. Knote and wife had three children: Alice Rosetta, wife of W. K. Shilling; John McBride, deceased; and Theodore Willis, who was born at Springfield, Ohio, November 22, 1885.

Theodore Willis Knote was educated in private schools at Springfield and in 1906 graduated from Wittenburg College, Springfield, Ohio, with the A. B. degree. For a number of years after leaving college, Mr. Knote was engaged in commercial work at New York, and for three years his business required his residence abroad in Europe. He has traveled extensively. in this country, in Europe, and also in the Orient.

In 1920 Mr. Knote completed a course in the College of Business of the University of New York, receiving the degree M. R. S., and at that time he accepted the invitation to come to Blacksburg, Virginia, and establish the Department of Business Administration at the Virginia Polytechnic Institute. Since it was established he has been head of the department.

Mr. Knote is a member of the Beta Theta Pi, Pyramid Lodge of the Masonic fraternity at New York City, Mecca Temple of the Mystic Shrine at New York, Roanoke Consistory at Roanoke, Virginia, the Cohee Country Club at Blacksburg, Virginia, and the Beta Theta Pi Club of New York City. He is a member of the American Management Association, the National Economic League, and the American Association of University Professors. Mr. Knote is an independent Democrat, a member of the Lutheran Church, and is unmarried.

JAMES MERRITT THOMAS has had a very constructive part in the wholesale commercial activities of Danville for many years. He has been a factor in the growth of two very prosperous organizations of the city, one of which is the J. M. Thomas Company, of which he is president and owner.

Mr. Thomas was born in Halifax County, Virginia, August 22, 1873. His ancestors have been in Virginia for many generations. His father, W. H. Thomas, was born in the eastern part of the state, was educated in some of the private schools and served all through the four years of struggle between the North and South. He was wounded in the battle of Gettysburg and participated in many of the great battles of the war. When the war was over he returned to his farm and followed planting and agriculture in Halifax County until his death in 1904. He is buried in the home cemetery at Cluster Springs. His wife, Patty Merritt, was born and reared near Cluster Springs, was educated in private schools and was interested in the Methodist Episcopal Church, South. She died in 1889. There were six children: James M.; J. D. Thomas, of North Carolina; Fannie, widow of C. L. Loftus; Miss Maud, of Cluster Springs; Mary, wife of Robert Loftus; and J. D. Thomas, who died at the age of forty-four.

James Merritt Thomas was educated in public schools in Halifax County, also attended the Danville Business College under Professor Cook, and with this education and with his natural abilities followed a career that has been one of eminent usefulness. For one year he was a clerk in the establishment of E. S. Arnett, of Danville, following which he spent five years with Booth Brothers, general merchants. Mr. Thomas has been identified with the wholesale business since 1901. He became associated with Mr. James R. Tate in the wholesale grocery business, in what is known as the Tate & Thomas Company, and he is still president of this corporation. Since 1923, however, he has given his chief attention to dry goods. In that year he established a wholesale dry goods house under the name of J. M. Thomas & Company, specializing in a line of dry goods and notions, and represented by six traveling salesmen. Both firms are well established in the wholesale trade and do a splendid business over half a dozen or more counties in Virginia and North Carolina. Mr. Thomas is sole owner and manager of the dry goods house.

He is a business man with well developed public spirit and a willingness to do his part. He is a trustee of Averitt College, for several years was a director of the Y. M. C. A., and is a former director of the Chamber of Commerce. He is a thirty-second degree Scottish Rite Mason and Shriner, and has membership in Roman Eagle Lodge No. 122, A. F. and A. M., Euclid Chapter, Royal Arch Masons, Dove Commandery, Knights Templar and Acca Temple of the Mystic Shrine. He is a member of the Rotary Club and for several years has been especially interested in the promulgation of the splendid principles of Rotary. He is a member of the Danville Golf Club, votes for the Democrats and for about twenty-five years was a deacon of the First Baptist Church.

Mr. Thomas married at Danville, September 21, 1904, Miss Florence Swain, of Danville. She was educated in public schools there, is a member of the Baptist Church and the Daughters of the American Revolution. Her parents were E. L. and Ada (Norburn) Swain. Her father for many years was a tobacconist in Danville, and served for a time as president of the City Council and was also a member of the school board. He died about 1919 and is buried in Green Hill Cemetery. Mrs. Swain makes her home with Mr. and Mrs. Thomas.

GUY G. JOHNSON, proprietor of the Alleghany Hotel of East Radford, was on the road as a traveling salesman for a number of years, and his associations with the traveling public has given him unusual qualifications for his present work. Mr. Johnson is a member of one of the old families of Southwest Virginia.

He was born at East Radford, February 8, 1891, son of Albert Sidney and Illa James (Stone) Johnson and grandson of Dr. Elijah Johnson. His grandfather lived in Campbell and Tazewell counties, practiced medicine during and after the Civil war, and spent his later years in Montgomery County. He married Elizabeth Holland, and both are buried in the Fairview Cemetery at Radford. Elizabeth Holland had seven brothers in the Confederate army under General Lee, and three of them were killed in Pickett's famous charge at the battle of Gettysburg.

Albert Sidney Johnson was born in Tazewell County in 1865, and was ten years of age when his parents moved to Montgomery County. He was educated in public schools in both counties, and for a number of years was a commercial salesman and for the past fifteen years has conducted a real estate business at Radford. He is also financially interested in the Alleghany Hotel and other Radford property. His wife, Illa James Stone, was born at Green Bay, Virginia, attended public schools there and Holland College. She is a member of the Baptist Church, the United Daughters of the Confederacy and the Daughters of the American Revolution. Her parents were Dr. James L. and Mattie (Wooten) Stone.

Her father moved from Radford to Roanoke about 1880, being one of the early physicians in that town, and practiced medicine and surgery there until his death in 1908. His wife died in 1912. Albert Sidney Johnson and wife had a family of seven children: Frank Taylor, a merchant at Radford; Miss Maud E.; Agnes M., wife of R. S. Hopkins, of Radford; Guy G.; Albert Sidney, a member of the bar at Radford; William Thomas, who was with the colors during the World war, was gassed during the Argonne offensive and after returning to America developed tuberculosis and died in the Mount Alto Hospital at Washington in 1922 and is buried at Radford; and James E. Johnson, a student of medicine in the Medical College at Richmond.

Guy G. Johnson was educated in public schools at Radford, attended Roanoke College at Salem and on leaving college in 1912 became a commercial representative in the Virginia and West Virginia territories for John E. Hurst & Company of Baltimore. He was on the road for this house seven years and for six years was with Richardson Brothers & Fickling of New York, commission agents. Mr. Johnson in 1925 leased the Alleghany Hotel at East Radford, and has made that hotel a good business and an institution known far and wide to the traveling public. Mr. Johnson is a member of the Phi Kappa Phi fraternity, is a Democrat and is of Methodist affiliations.

He married at Stewart, Virginia, October 20, 1920, Miss Caroline Virginia Moir, who was educated in public schools in Patrick County, Virginia, and the Radford State Teachers College, and taught a year in Patrick County before her marriage. She is a member of the Methodist Episcopal Church, South, and the Radford Music Club. Her parents were Harry M. and Blanche (Chilton) Moir, of Patrick County, her mother being a member of the noted family of Chiltons of Lynchburg. Her father is a farmer and stock raiser, and for twenty years has been treasurer of Patrick County. Mr. and Mrs. Johnson have one daughter, Jane Moir Johnson.

JAMES M. LEA, pharmacist, has been a factor in the commercial life of Danville for many years, and is a director and manager for the Park Place Mercantile Company of that city.

Mr. Lea was born in Caswell County, North Carolina, July 12, 1878. One of the communities of Caswell County is Leasburg, named for one of the early members of the Lea family. John Greenleaf Lea come from England during the 1700s and secured a land grant of land in North Carolina comprising the site of the present town of Leasburg. James M. Lea is a son of Thomas L. and Sallie (King) Lea and a grandson of Thomas L. Lea, who for many years was sheriff of Caswell County and otherwise prominent in that locality. Thomas L. Lea, Jr., was born and reared in Caswell County, attended private schools, and during the Civil war, after completing his military training in what is now Virginia Polytechnic Institute at Blacksburg, entered the ranks and became captain of Company G in the 71st North Carolina Infantry, participating in several major engagements and was with the coast defenses in North Carolina. After the war he followed farming in Caswell County until his death. He was a member of the Baptist Church. He died in 1904. His wife, Sallie King Lea, was born and reared in Halifax County, Virginia, and was reared by her aunt and uncle, Mr. and Mrs. Sidney S. Lea, in Caswell County, North Carolina. Her parents died when she was an infant. She attended public school, the Yancyville School for Girls, Roanoke Female College, and Averett College, of which her uncle, Sidney Lea, was a trustee. She died in 1914 and is buried in Green Hill Cemetery at Danville. These parents had twelve children, three of whom died in infancy and all the others are still living: Sidney S., a tobacconist of Danville; James M.; Hunter Y., a Danville tobacconist; Alice N., wife of Irley Stokes, of Kentridge; Susie K., wife of Dr. William I. Pritchard, of Petersburg, Virginia; Fay Belle, Mrs. Fred Norton, of East Orange, New Jersey; Thomas L., a tobacconist at Louisville who has charge of the Dark Belt Tobacco Market for the Export Leaf Tobacco Company; Walter Clark, superintendent of the Durham branch of the American Tobacco Company at Durham, North Carolina; and Inza, wife of L. C. Manson, of Kansas City, Missouri.

James M. Lea grew up in Caswell County, attended public schools there, and finished his literary education in Wake Forest College, North Carolina. In 1898, when he was twenty years of age, he came to Danville, and for three years was employed as clerk in the drug store of Thomas G. Moore. In 1902 he graduated in pharmacy from the University College of Medicine at Richmond, being an honor member of the Rho Chi fraternity. The four years following were spent as pharmacist in the drug store of Paul Massey at Roanoke, and in 1908 he returned to Danville and for twenty years has been associated with the business known as Park Place Mercantile Company, Inc., as manager of the Park Place Pharmacy and one of the partners and in the corporation, which operates four stores, the pharmacy, a market and grocery and the Schoolfield Furniture Company. Mr. Lea is also a director of the American National Bank of Danville.

He is affiliated with Roman Eagle Lodge No. 122, A. F. and A. M., Euclid Chapter, Royal Arch Masons, Dove Commandery, Knights Templar, is a thirty-second degree Scottish Rite Mason and Potentate's representative for Danville in the Mystic Shrine. He also is past exalted ruler of Danville Lodge, B. P. O. Elks, is president of the Kiwanis Club, a member of the Danville Golf Club, and Tuscarora Club. He is one of the very popular and progressive men in the metropolitan community of Danville. In politics he supports the Democratic ticket, and is a member of the First Baptist Church.

THOMAS WASHINGTON HUNTER. The time and place of the career of Thomas Washington Hunter was the quarter of century after the Civil war and the locality made famous by the concluding scene of that war, Appomattox County.

He was born there in January, 1856, and died April 15, 1893. He attended school in Appomattox County, took up teaching as a profession, but at the time of his marriage his father presented him with a farm as a wedding gift, and from that time until his death he was occupied with his duties as an agriculturist. Outside of his home and farm his chief interest was in the Reddy Springs Baptist Church in Appomattox County, and he was not only clerk of the church but superintendent of the Sunday School.

He married, December 8, 1883, Isabella D. Coleman, of Appomattox County, where she was reared and educated. Her father, Capt. William G. Coleman, served four years in the Confederate army and was wounded in the battle of Petersburg. After the war he was a merchant, lumberman and farmer. Captain Coleman married Mary D. W. Abbott, and Mrs. Hunter was one of nine children.

Mrs. Hunter now resides in Richmond, at 2317 Rosewood Avenue. She is the mother of four children. Her daughter Miss Mary W., attended school in Appomattox County, the Normal School at Charlottesville, and is now an assistant secretary in a Richmond business house. Miss Mabrie, who was educated in the same schools as her sister, is assistant secretary with another Richmond firm. Miss S. Ethel was educated with opportunities similar to those of her sisters; John Washington, the only son, is in business at Richmond, and by his marriage to Louise Sowel has a son, John Washington, Jr.

ANDREW JOHNSTON FRANCIS, representative of Giles and Bland counties in the Virginia House of Delegates, is a resident of White Gate. He is a man of college training, and has made a success of his business as a farmer and stock raiser, being a recognized leader in one of the most progressive agricultural communities in Southwest Virginia.

He was born at White Gate June 9, 1873, son of Miles A. and Cynthia M. (Bane) Francis. The Francis family came to America from Ireland in 1768, settling near Norfolk, and the family was represented in the American forces in the War of 1812. Miles A. Francis was born and reared at Christiansburg, Virginia, educated in private schools and the Christiansburg Academy, and in the Civil war served as color sergeant of Company F, Eleventh Virginia Infantry, Kemper's Brigade, Longstreet's Division, until seriously wounded in the battle of Seven Pines. After a long stay in a hospital at Richmond he was made captain of Company K, Twenty-second Virginia Cavalry, and later was promoted to colonel but the war ended before he received his commission. Captain Francis after the war located at White Gate, where he bought a farm and married, and engaged in farming and cattle raising until his death on March 6, 1915. He is buried in White Gate Cemetery. His wife, Cynthia M. Bane, was born at Pearisburg, was educated in private schools and the White Gate Academy under Rev. J. M. Humphries. She is now eighty years of age, living with her son, Andrew J. One of her great interests all her life has been the Presbyterian Church. She is a daughter of Henderson and Nancy (Shannon) Bane. Her father was a prominent and wealthy farmer and stock raiser. He is a descendant of Donald Bane, a son of Malcolm Bane, one of the early kings of Scotland. Miles A. Francis and wife had four children: Nannie Shannon, wife of Dan P. McMullen, of Cheboygan, Michigan; Andrew J.; T. B., a farmer at White Gate; and Julia Adair, wife of Rev. Benjamin K. Hay, a minister of the Reformed Church at Woodstock, Virginia.

Andrew Johnston Francis was reared at White Gate, attending private schools and the White Gate Academy, and finished his education in Roanoke College. While in college he was captain of the football team during 1895-98. In the thirty years since he finished his college education Mr. Francis has given his chief time to cattle raising and is owner of blue grass farms in the vicinity of White Gate. At the age of twenty-two he performed the duties of tax collector under Jesse Woodrum. He is director and vice president of the Bank of Mechanicsburg. Mr. Francis was elected to the Virginia House of Delegates in 1927, and is the nominee of his party to succeed himself in the Virginia Legislature, session of 1930. He is a Master Mason, a Democrat, an elder in the Presbyterian Church, and has been teacher or superintendent of the Sunday School for many years.

He married at Poplar Hill, Virginia, March 1, 1904, Miss Jeanie Shannon, of Poplar Hill. She attended private schools at Pearisburg and taught school there and at Bluefield, West Virginia, and Jessamine Institute in Nicholasville, Kentucky. She is a Presbyterian. Her parents were Samuel B. and Nancy (King) Shannon, both members of prominent families of Giles County. Mr. and Mrs. Francis have five children: Mary Fairfax, was educated at Stonewall Jackson College, and in Columbia University, is the wife of Charles Tate Graham, farmer and cattle man at Grahams Forge, and has one son, Charles Tate, Jr.; Samuel M. Francis is a member of the class of 1930 at the University of Virginia; Jean Shannon is in the class of 1929 at Randolph-Macon Woman's College, Lynchburg; Andrew J., Jr., is a member of the class of 1929 in the White Gate High School and will pursue the electrical engineering course in the Virginia Military Institute; and David Woodrum is a student in the grade school at White Gate.

PLUMER WISEMAN, an engineer and contractor, has been a very useful and influential figure in the life of his native City of Danville for many years.

He was born at Danville September 8, 1881, son of Henry A. and Willie A. (Yager) Wiseman and grandson of John and Mary A. (Downs) Wiseman. His great-grandfather came from England and his great-grandmother from Ireland. John Wiseman was born and reared at Baltimore, Maryland, and spent his active career as a planter in Pittsylvania County, Virginia. Henry A. Wiseman was born and reared at Danville, attended private schools and an academy, and during the Civil war was a soldier in Longstreet's Division and later with the Medical Corps. He served under Captain Wooding, the venerable mayor of Danville. Henry A. Wiseman after the war became a pharmacist and druggist, and for a number of years held the office of city treasurer. He was one of the highly honored and influential men of the city, where he died in 1902. His wife, Willie A. Yager, was born and reared in Orange County, Virginia, and attended Roanoke College for Girls at Danville. She has been a lifelong Presbyterian and is now eighty-three years of age. Her great-great-grandfather, Isaac Davis, was a colonel in the Revolutionary war. Henry A. Wiseman and wife had a family of four children: Mary W., wife of H. E. Kendall, of Shelby, North Carolina; Dr. H. A. Wiseman, a physician and surgeon at Danville; Plumer Wiseman, and Willie A., wife of Lee B. Weathers, of Shelby, North Carolina.

Plumer Wiseman grew up at Danville, attended public schools, graduated from the Danville Military Institute in 1899 and completed his engineering course in Purdue University at Lafayette, Indiana, in 1907. For the past twenty-two years he has been engaged in engineering and contracting work, and since 1912 has had his permanent business headquarters at Danville. He has been employed as engineer in designing a number of industrial and municipal undertakings. He is treasurer of the Masonic Building Corporation and in charge of the management. He is a director of the First National Bank, a director of the Hughes Memorial School and a director of the Memorial Hospital and Jefferson Avenue Improvement Company. He is also a director of the Mechanics Loan & Savings Company, the Perpetual Building & Loan Association and the Danville Military Institute.

Mr. Wiseman has always enjoyed social contact with his fellow men and is a member of a number of organizations that express the fraternal spirit and give him opportunity for effective influence as a citizen. He was a Sigma Alpha Epsilon in college, and in Masonry is senior warden of Roman Eagle Lodge No. 122, A. F. and A. M., member of Euclid Chapter, Royal Arch Masons, Dove Commandery, Knights Templar, Danville Lodge of Perfection, Dalcho Consistory of the Scottish Rite at Richmond and Acca Temple of the Mystic Shrine. He is a past president of the Danville Rotary Club, is a past senior councellor of the United Commercial Travelers of America, is an independent voter and is a deacon of the First Presbyterian Church, and for a number of years was treasurer of his church.

Mr. Wiseman married at Danville, October 19, 1910, Miss Nora Mosely, of Danville. She finished her education in Randolph-Macon Institute at Danville and is a leader in the Presbyterian Church and Woman's Club. Her parents were Beverly E. and Florence L. (Millner) Mosely. Her father was a leading tobacconist. Her mother is still living in Danville. The Moselys were a prominent Virginia family, whose original seat was in Buckingham County. Mr. and Mrs. Wiseman had a family of four children, one of whom, Nora M., died in infancy. The three sons are: Edward, who graduated from the Danville Military Institute in 1929 and is now a student in Davidson College at Davidson, North Carolina; William Plumer, a student in Danville Military Institute; and Robert Whitelaw, attending public school.

ROBY CALVIN THOMPSON. Among the forceful and progressive young lawyers of Washington County who are making their influence felt in the interests of better citizenship, Roby Calvin Thompson is deserving of more than passing mention. The energetic city attorney of Abingdon has been engaged in the practice of his profession since 1922, and during the short space of less than seven years has built up a large and lucrative practice, specializing to some extent in corporation law. Although still a young man in years, he is one of the leaders of the Republican party in Washington County, and in 1924 made a strong bid for the office of mayor of Abingdon.

Mr. Thompson was born in Washington County, Virginia, March 30, 1898, and is a son of John Harvey and Minnie Gertrude (Moore) Thompson, both of whom are now living at Saltville, this state, where John H. Thompson is master mechanic for the United States Gypsum Company. He is a member of the Independent Order of Odd Fellows, the Knights of Pythias and the Improved Order of Red Men, and with his family belongs to the Methodist Episcopal Church, South. He and Mrs. Thompson have had the following children: Roby Calvin, of this review; Thomas Moore, a machinist in the employ of the United States Gypsum Company at Saltville; William P., who is engaged in merchandising at that place; Lena Gertrude, the wife of Lee Gillenwater, an electrician employed at the Mathieson Alkali Works at Saltville; and John Harvey, Jr., who is attending high school at Saltville. The paternal grandfather of Roby Calvin Thompson, Calvin Thompson, was born in North Carolina, whence he came as a young man to Virginia and spent the remainder of his life as a planter in Washington County. The maternal grandfather of Mr. Thompson, James Moore, was born in Washington County, and passed his life as a carpenter and building contractor.

The country schools of Washington County furnished John Calvin Thompson with his early educational training, following which he attended the Glade Springs High School and the Saltville High School, and graduated from the latter as a member of the class of 1917. On July 5 of that year he entered the service of the United States Navy, during the World war, and was stationed at Newport News until September, when he was sent to the University of Virginia Officers Training School and eventually commissioned a seaman of the second class in the United States Naval Reserves. In the meantime he had continued his education in the University of Virginia, where he received his degree of Bachelor of Arts in 1920, and in June, 1922, when twenty-four years of age, received the degree of Bachelor of Laws from the same institution.

At the time of his graduation Mr. Thompson commenced the practice of his profession at Abingdon, in partnership with Hon. H. H. Honaker, which connection was mutually severed one year later, since which time Mr. Thompson has carried on an independent practice of a civil and corporation character, his offices being opposite the courthouse. He has formed a number of important connections, and is attorney for the Beaver Chemical Corporation of Damascus, Virginia; attorney and secretary of the Smithfort Extract Company of Damascus, of which he is also a member of the Board of Directors; attorney for the Dearbow Hassinger Corporation; associate counsel for the Hassinger Lumber Company of Kilmarnock, Virginia; and attorney for the Clinchburg (Virginia) Bank. He is accounted a lawyer of ability and sound learning, and is a member of the Washington County Bar Association and the Virginia State Bar Association, and of the Delta Theta Phi legal fraternity. A Republican in his political convictions, Mr. Thompson is one of the leaders of his party, secretary of the County Central Committee and a speaker of note, force and eloquence during political campaigns. At present he is serving as city attorney of Abingdon, an office in which he has established an excellent record, and in 1924 was the Republican candidate for the mayoralty.

Mr. Thompson is senior warden of Abingdon Lodge, A. F. and A. M., and belongs to the Independent Order of Odd Fellows. He is adjutant of Washington County Post No. 12, American Legion, and a member of the Abingdon Chamber of Commerce, in the work of which he has taken an active and helpful part. Having joined the Methodist Episcopal Church, South, in his youth, he is now a steward, and has served as secretary of the board. He was a charter member of the Civitan Club of Abingdon, and in 1924 was delegate to the National Civitan Convention held at Miami, Florida. His interests have touched many sides of life, and for two years he was scoutmaster of Troop No. 1 of Abingdon, Boy Scouts of America. Mr. Thompson is unmarried.

JUNIUS PARKER FISHBURN is one of the prominent younger
men in the citizenship of Virginia, at the age of thirty-four
engrossed in a broad range of business and public responsibilities.

A son of Junius Blair and Grace (Parker) Fishburn, he was
born at Roanoke September 30, 1895. He was graduated from
the Mercersburg Academy of Pennsylvania in 1914, took his
Bachelor's of Arts degree at Princeton University in 1919 and
the Master of Arts degree from Columbia University in 1923.
He left college at the time of the World war and in 1917 was
chief petty officer and later ensign with the United States Naval
Reserve. and was commissioned an ensign in the United States
Navy in 1918.

Mr. Fishburn's chief interest in a business way has been in
the newspaper field. In 1919 he became vice president and since
1923 has been president of the Times-World Corporation, publishers of the *Roanoke Times* and the *Roanoke World-News*, of
which he has been active editor since 1920. He is also a director
of the Federal Reserve Bank of Richmond, a director of the
Virginia Bridge & Iron Company and the Old Dominion Fire
Insurance Company, all of Roanoke.

Mr. Fishburn in 1924 became president of the Virginia Historic Highway Association. From 1926 to 1929 he was president of the Virginia State Chamber of Commerce. He is a
member of the State Conservation and Development Commission,
Roanoke Chamber of Commerce, and is a member of the board
of regents of Mercersburg Academy. He was president of the
Rotary Club of Roanoke in 1929, and among other affiliations
belongs to such organizations as the American Newspaper Publishers Association, American Society of Newspaper Editors,
Southern Newspaper Publishers Association, American Historical Association, American Economics Association, American
Association of Political Science, the Roanoke Country and Shenandoah Club of Roanoke, the Commonwealth and Country of Virginia Clubs of Richmond, the University and Press Clubs of
Washington, and the Princeton Club of New York and Philadelphia. He is a Democrat and a Presbyterian.

Mr. Fishburn married January 14, 1926, Katherine Rodes
Nelson of Roanoke.

ANDY S. LAWSON, Sheriff of Grayson County, is a public
official whose service has won repeated commendation from the
people of that county. Mr. Lawson has distinguished himself by
his promptness and fidelity to duty at all times. He has lived
in Grayson County practically all his life, and for many years
has been a farmer and farm owner there.

He was born in Grayson County in 1870, son of Dotson and
Agnes (Shaffer) Lawson. His grandfather, James Lawson, was
a minister of the Primitive Baptist Church, preaching in North
Carolina for many years. His last years were spent as an invalid
in the home of his son Dotson, near Baywood. Dotson Lawson
was born at Danbury, North Carolina, in 1830, was educated in
private schools, and during the Civil war was in the service of
the Confederate government, detailed on duty at a forge in Virginia. He married in Wythe County, Virginia, and then settled
on a farm near Baywood, Grayson County, where he engaged
in farming and stock raising until his death in 1884 at the age
of fifty-four. His wife, Agnes Shaffer, was born in Wythe County, near Wytheville, attended private schools, and was a daughter

of James Shaffer of Wythe County. Dotson Lawson and wife
had seven children. James Alexander, born in August, 1860, a
farmer and stock man in Colorado, owns a ranch of about a
thousand acres near Telluride; he married Marjorie Ison of
Grayson County, Virginia, who died, and later he married Miss
Hattie Adams of Delta, Colorado, and has a son, Edward, born in
1916. Julia Ann Lawson, born in 1861, is the widow of Wilburn
Wilson and resides near Baywood, and has one son, Jacob, born
in 1902. Joseph Dotson Lawson, born in 1864, a farmer and
stock raiser near Wytheville, married Florence Shaffer, who
died in 1900, and later he married Minerva Blair of Wytheville;
the children of his first marriage are: Edith, wife of John
Poston, near Wytheville; Mrs. Bertha Blair, near Wytheville;
Jacob, of Wythe County; and Charles, in the laundry business in
Tennessee. The children of his second marriage are: Blair, a
student at Emory and Henry College; James, in high school;
Annie, a teacher in Wythe County; and Sam and Nellie, attending public school. Martha Florence Lawson, born in 1867, is the
widow of Robert Cox and a resident of Alleghany County, North
Carolina. John William Lawson, born in 1874, living near Baywood, Grayson County, married Fannie Robinson and has three
children, Ray, attending high school, Kate and Nellie. Sophrania
Lawson, the youngest of the children, is the wife of Alexander
Austin, of Independence, Virginia, and has a son, Glen, born in
1907, now living at Akron, Ohio, and a daughter, Vera, born in
1917, a pupil in the public school at Independence.

Andy S. Lawson was educated in public schools near Baywood and for seven years lived with his brother on the ranch in
Colorado, near Telluride. After returning to Virginia he acquired a farm at Baywood in Wythe County, and later bought
a second farm in the same locality. His present place of residence is a county estate a mile southwest of Galax.

Mr. Lawson's first public service was in the office of justice
of the peace. He was elected in 1904 and served eight years. In
1912 he was chosen county commissioner of revenue and filled
that office eight years, until 1920. This was followed by his
election as sheriff, and he has been the incumbent of that important office for two terms.

Mr. Lawson is a Republican in politics. He is a Royal Arch
Mason and member of the Baptist Church. He married in 1900,
Miss Mattie Higgins, of Baywood. Three children were born to
them: Myrtle Ollie, born in 1904, is a graduate of high school
and attended the State Normal College at Radford, is the wife
of T. W. Williams of Galax, and is a teacher in the high school
there. Earl Higgins Lawson, born in 1906, graduated from the
Galax High School, attended a business college, and is now an
employee of the county of Grayson. Andy Jacob Lawson, born
in 1907, graduated from the Galax High School in 1928, and is a
student of medicine at the University of Virginia. The mother
of these children died in 1923 and is buried at Baywood. Subsequently Sheriff Lawson married Miss Effie McGee, daughter of
Richard and Martha (Mabe) McGee, of Galax.

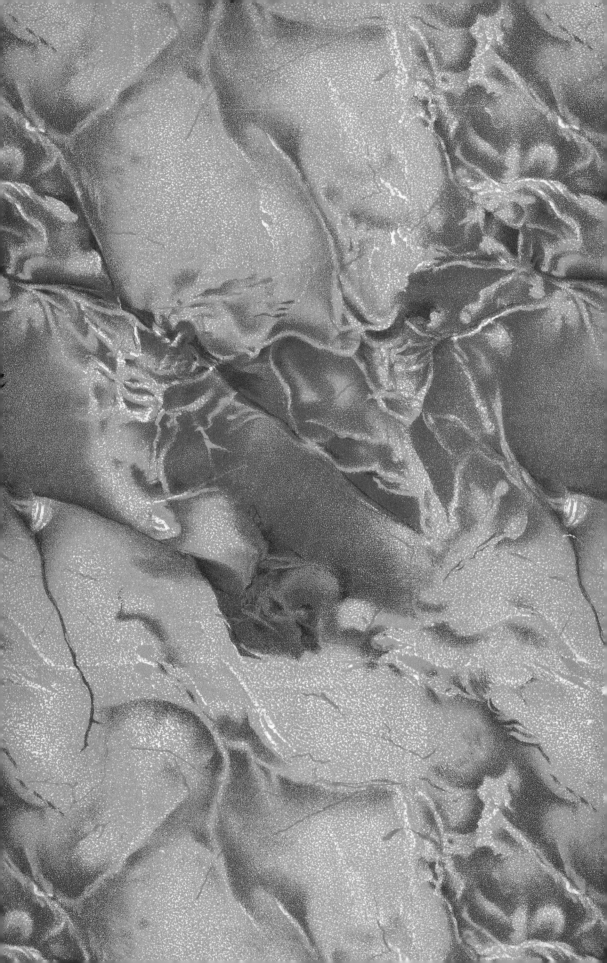